Lecture Notes in Computer Science 825

Edited by G. Goos and J. Hartmanis

Advisory Board: W. Brauer   D. Gries   J. Stoer

Joseph L. Mundy   Andrew Zisserman
David Forsyth (Eds.)

Applications of Invariance in Computer Vision

Second Joint European – US Workshop
Ponta Delgada, Azores, Portugal
October 9-14, 1993
Proceedings

Springer-Verlag

Berlin Heidelberg New York
London Paris Tokyo
Hong Kong Barcelona
Budapest

Series Editors

Gerhard Goos
Universität Karlsruhe
Postfach 69 80
Vincenz-Priessnitz-Straße 1
D-76131 Karlsruhe, Germany

Juris Hartmanis
Cornell University
Department of Computer Science
4130 Upson Hall
Ithaca, NY 14853, USA

Volume Editors

Joseph L. Mundy
The General Electric Corporate Research and Development Laboratory
P. O. Box 8, Schenectady, NY 12309, USA

Andrew Zisserman
Department of Engineering Science, University of Oxford
Parks Road, Oxford OX1 3PJ, United Kingdom

David Forsyth
University of Iowa, Department of Computer Science
Iowa City, Iowa 52242, USA

CR Subject Classification (1991): I.3-5, I.2.9-10

ISBN 3-540-58240-1 Springer-Verlag Berlin Heidelberg New York
ISBN 0-387-58240-1 Springer-Verlag New York Berlin Heidelberg

CIP data applied for

© Springer-Verlag Berlin Heidelberg 1994
Printed in Germany

Typesetting: Camera-ready by author
SPIN: 10472584   45/3140-543210 - Printed on acid-free paper

Preface

This book is the proceedings of the Second Joint European–US Workshop on "Applications of Invariance in Computer Vision", held in Ponta Delgada, Azores during October 1993.

The First Workshop, held in Reykjavik, Iceland 1991, and subsequent proceedings, demonstrated the fruitfulness of using projective geometry and geometric invariance in computer vision. At that time, some areas, such as projective geometry and the classical theory of algebraic invariance, were well understood, while other issues such as invariants of 3D structures and recognition using invariants were only just emerging. Consequently, study and implementation initially focused on the planar case, since many invariants for the projective plane were known. Invariants then were primarily for sets of points, lines and conics in the plane, and their derivation largely based on geometric constructions. Ideas on 3D curved objects were sketchy and there was a lack of statistical analysis, except for a few empirical studies.

Now, a host of single view invariants for non-algebraic curves and 3D smooth surfaces are available. A sophisticated algebraic structure has developed, complementing geometric constructions, for modelling and partitioning camera projections, and the projective relationships among sets of cameras. New areas and applications, particularly the use of uncalibrated stereo in robotic navigation and surveillance, have proven feasible. These significant advances since the Reykjavik Workshop are extensively documented in this volume.

We are extremely grateful for workshop funding for European participants provided by ESPRIT (Working Group 76096) administered originally by Michel Bosco and subsequently Jakub Wejchert. European research in invariance is supported primarily by ESPRIT Project 6448 'VIVA', coordinated by Luc Van Gool. US participants were supported by NSF grant no. IRI 93-11050, with substantial ARPA participation in the award.

We particularly acknowledge Jennet Batten for her efficient and thoughtful organization of both the Azores Workshop and the assembly of the manuscripts into the final form for this book. Jennet provided the necessary gentle pressure which causes authors to yield their manuscripts to press. Richard Offer and Andrew Wildenberg solved our Latex problems.

May 1994

Joseph L. Mundy
Andrew Zisserman
David Forsyth

Contents

Introduction and Chapter Summary 3
  Joseph L. Mundy, Andrew Zisserman and David Forsyth

Foundations

Cartan's Moving Frame Method and Its Application to the Geometry and
Evolution of Curves in the Euclidean, Affine and Projective Planes.............. 11
  Olivier Faugeras

Representation of Three-Dimensional Object Structure as Cross-Ratios of
Determinants of Stereo Image Points.. 47
  Eamon Barrett, Gregory Gheen and Paul Payton

A Case Against Epipolar Geometry 69
  Andrew Zisserman and Stephen J. Maybank

Repeated Structures: Image Correspondence Constraints and 3D Structure
Recovery... 89
  Joseph L. Mundy and Andrew Zisserman

How to Use the Cross Ratio to Compute Projective Invariants from Two
Images... 107
  Patrick Gros

On Geometric and Algebraic Aspects of 3D Affine and Projective Structures
from Perspective 2D Views.. 127
  Amnon Shashua

The Double Algebra: An Effective Tool for Computing Invariants in Computer
Vision 145
  Stefan Carlsson

Matching Perspective Views of Parallel Plane Structures...................... 165
  Luc Van Gool, Theo Moons, Marc Van Diest and Eric Pauwels

Invariants for Recovering Shape from Shading 185
  Isaac Weiss

Fundamental Difficulties with Projective Normalization of Planar Curves........ 199
  Kalle Åström

Invariant Size Functions... 215
  Alessandro Verri and Claudio Uras

Recovery

Euclidean Reconstruction from Uncalibrated Views............................ 237
   Richard I. Hartley

Accurate Projective Reconstruction 257
   Roger Mohr, Boubakeur Boufama and Pascal Brand

Applications of Motion Field of Curves.. 277
   Theo Papadopoulo and Olivier Faugeras

Affine Reconstruction from Perspective Image Pairs Obtained by a
Translating Camera... 297
   Theo Moons, Luc Van Gool, Marc Van Diest and Eric Pauwels

Using Invariance and Quasi-Invariance for the Segmentation and
Recovery of Curved Objects.. 317
   Mourad Zerroug and Ramakant Nevatia

Representations of 3D Objects that Incorporate Surface Markings............... 341
   David Forsyth and Charlie Rothwell

Model-based Invariant Functions and Their Use for Recognition................ 359
   Daphna Weinshall

Recognition

Integration of Multiple Feature Groups and Multiple Views into a 3D
Object Recognition System... 381
   Jianchang Mao, Anil K. Jain and Patrick J. Flynn

Hierarchical Object Description Using Invariants 397
   Charles A. Rothwell

Generalizing Invariants for 3-D to 2-D Matching.............................. 415
   David W. Jacobs

Recognition by Combinations of Model Views: Alignment and
Invariance 435
   Ronen Basri

Statistics

Classification Based on the Cross Ratio.. 453
    Stephen J. Maybank

Correspondence of Coplanar Features Through P^2-Invariant
Representations.. 473
    Peter Meer, Sudhir Ramakrishna and Reiner Lenz

Integrating Algebraic Curves and Surfaces, Algebraic Invariants and
Bayesian Methods for 2D and 3D Object Recognition........................... 493
    Daniel Keren, Jayashree Subrahmonia and David B. Cooper

Introduction

Introduction and Chapter Summary

Joseph L. Mundy, Andrew Zisserman and David Forsyth

Geometry is the most successful and ubiquitous tool in computer vision. The analysis of the geometric relationships inherent in the perspective camera image projection of objects in 3D space dominates current literature in object recognition and scene analysis. Geometric reasoning underpins the many working systems that have been developed for tasks ranging from visual inspection and virtual reality modelling to active visual tasks such as grasp and free space path planning.

The study of geometric invariance, the subject of this book, has arisen from the desire to identify geometric properties of objects which do not depend on internal perspective image camera calibration parameters or upon the viewpoint from which the image is acquired. Such considerations are deeply rooted in the study of projective geometry, since the effects of 2D and 3D projective transformations of space encompass the effects of perspective projection. Indeed, projective geometry was initially developed to provide an effective mathematical framework for the analysis of perspective.

Multiple View Invariants

If cameras are uncalibrated then, in the absence of other information, it has been shown [4, 7] that structure can only be recovered up to a projective ambiguity from an image pair. That is, the recovered structure will differ from the true (Euclidean) structure by an unknown 3D projective transformation. However, if additional *constraints* are available this projective ambiguity can be reduced to affine or scaled Euclidean (similarity).

One type of constraint is that the same camera, with fixed intrinsic parameters, is used to acquire multiple views of a static 3D structure. In this case, the camera can be calibrated from points matched over three or more views under general motion, without requiring a calibration object. This approach, pioneered by Faugeras *et al.* [5], is termed "self-calibration". The original method involved solving a set of polynomial equations. More recent methods are linear for special circumstances, for example pure rotation [8], or starting from affine structure [12]. After calibration, structure ambiguity is reduced to similarity, i.e. a scaled Euclidean transformation. Hartley (*this volume*) presents a new algorithm for scaled Euclidean reconstruction which extends to an arbitrary number of views and provides an implementation with good theoretical and experimental numerical stability.

Another possibility is to constrain the motion of camera position and orientation between views (the extrinsic parameters). Moons *et al.* (*this volume*) demonstrate that if camera motion is pure translation, i.e. no rotation and fixed intrinsic parameters, then structure is recovered up to an affine ambiguity. Mundy and Zisserman (*this volume*) develop a framework for specifying the ambiguity resulting from various types of imaging constraints and catalogue a number of examples with an emphasis on repeated 3D structures seen from a single view.

An additional form of constraint is introduced by holding one of the multiple images fixed. Shashua (*this volume*) shows that the 3D stereo reconstructions of an object from an arbitrary set of pairs of perspective views are *relatively* affine. The notion of relative transformation means that all of the structures derived from the set are within an affine transformation of each other, but any single structure is within a full projective transformation of the actual Euclidean structure.

Inherent in the analysis of multiple views is the notion of epipolar geometry which relates corresponding image points across views. The projection of a 3D point in one view determines an epipolar line in any other view, on which the corresponding projected point lies. In Mundy and Zisserman (*this volume*), it is shown that under certain restrictions on the transformation between views an *auto-epipolar* geometry results where the image points of repeated structures all lie on the same epipolar line. This auto-epipolar condition leads to efficient correspondence grouping. Epipolar geometry is widely used in 3D reconstruction, e.g. Barrett [14], Faugeras [4] and Hartley *et al.* [7]. Zisserman and Maybank (*this volume*) show that epipolar geometry can become degenerate under critical viewing conditions and due to isotropies inherent in the 3D object geometry. They describe approaches to 3D reconstruction and the computation of invariants which do not suffer from such degeneracies.

On the theoretical side, Carlsson (*this volume*) shows that the machinery of bracket algebra can be applied to the analysis of multiple views. He shows that the resultant framework can be used to derive classical multiple view invariants. Similarly, Barrett (*this volume*) uses techniques of algebraic elimination to derive multiple view invariants. These efforts raise the possibility that new invariants can be discovered analytically, an approach which has had limited success in the past. The paper by Weiss (*this volume*) suggests that methods taken from the invariants of physical laws may provide a framework for discovering new invariants.

Single View Invariants

Much debate focused on a theorem, proven by a number of authors [2, 3, 13], which states that invariants can not be measured for a 3D set of points in general position from a single view. The theorem has frequently been misinterpreted to mean that *no* invariants can be formed for three dimensional objects from a single image. For the theorem to hold, however, the points must be completely unconstrained (like a cloud of gnats). If a 3D structure is *constrained*, then invariants are available. Examples include: objects with bilateral symmetry and polyhedra [15]; surfaces of revolution [6]; straight homogeneous generalised cylinders [Zerroug & Nevatia (*this volume*)]; extruded surfaces [Forsyth & Roth-well (*this volume*)].

A union of single and multiple view invariants is provided by repeated structures [11]. A single view of a repeated structure is equivalent to multiple views of one instance of the structure, superimposed. For example, a view of two identical objects related by a translation is equivalent to a stereo pair of images of one object, with the cameras related by a pure translation. This idea allows any multiple view result to be reinterpreted in the single view domain.

The paper by Van Gool *et al.* (*this volume*) explores the idea of constraining the pose of the camera with respect to the object. Such constraints are expected to provide more invariants with lower complexity geometric computation than for unconstrained views. For example, in aerial photography, it is often possible to identify the horizon, which imposes a constraint on camera viewpoint. This constraint is exploited by Van Gool to construct affine invariants from a perspective view of plane figures.

Recognition

A major application area of single view invariants is as index functions in model based recognition systems. The advantage is that, unlike such methods as "pose clustering" or "alignment", with indexing using invariants a recognition hypothesis can be generated without first computing object pose.

Previous work on invariant representations for recognition typically used flat lists of invariant values computed on isolated portions or simple sequences of the object boundary. Rothwell (*this volume*) shows that invariant geometric relations can be used to build a more structured description corresponding to a part-whole hierarchy. The paper by Subrahmonia *et al.* (*this volume*) demonstrates that high order algebraic curve approximations to planar shapes can be used to derive shape invariants, using a new approach based on a subspace of the algebraic coefficients. The subspace is selected using Bayesian learning over the recognition task.

Mao *et al.* (*this volume*) illustrate the importance of describing objects in terms of *salient* features. This concept was originated by Flynn in his recognition system for 3D range data. By Flynn's definition, saliency is an invariant property which is also effective in discriminating among object classes. For example, a right angle corner is invariant under similarity transformations, but is not salient for classes of man-made objects which typically have all right angles. Weinshall (*this volume*) derives affine invariants which can be acquired from a small number of views of a specific object. For perspective imaging, the affine approximation holds only over a region of the viewsphere, i.e. a *quasi-invariant* [1]. Weinshall demonstrates that the extent of this region is essentially independent of viewpoint, a surprising result.

One goal of the Workshop was to expose and debate different viewpoints on the use of invariants in recognition. In the paper by Jacobs (*this volume*) the problem of the non-existence of invariants for general 3D point sets is confronted by the development of indexing subspaces. He shows that while there are no single viewpoint invariants, there do exist subspaces for affine object representation under parallel projection. Different objects define mostly disjoint subspaces and recognition proceeds by table lookup. Basri presents another alternative which uses the general model based vision approach of *alignment* [9]. He shows that general 3D point sets can be represented by a set of 2D views. The appearance of any new 2D view can be computed by a linear combination of the coordinates of corresponding points in the model views. Such an image-based construction is used to align the features of the model images in any new image of the object. Basri also demonstrates how image-based measurements over the model views can be used to construct model specific invariant indexing functions.

Statistical Analysis

This is an area which was originally sparse, with only empirical stability results. Through the work of Gros, Maybank, Meer and their co-workers (all *this volume*) there is now a much sounder theoretical basis for understanding invariant performance measures, such as stability and controlling discrimination thresholds for classification. However, Astrom (*this volume*) raises a cautionary note on invariant stability if proper care is not taken in the precision of their measurement and if some restriction is not placed on the application of extreme projective transformations.

Such worries are already partially addressed by the meticulous attention paid to accuracy of camera modelling by Mohr *et al.* (*this volume*) and image smoothing by Sapiro & Tannenbaum [16] and Faugeras (*this volume*) with the aim of identical measurements in any view if image processing and projection commute. Papadopoulo and Faugeras (*this volume*) present an approach to accurate computation of curvature which is likely to be applicable to the extraction of invariants from arbitrary curves.

Future Prospects

As always, successful research and development opens up new research areas and opportunities. While invariant approaches have achieved a certain level of maturity, advances are expected along several lines of investigation.

First, for recognition and other modelling tasks, richer, more salient, object descriptions are required, which capture intra-object constraints. Sets of points or low-order algebraic features are too impoverished a representation of shape, containing the minimum description possible (e.g. position) but no connectivity, and lacking the richness of curves or surfaces. Invariant descriptions must be extended from primitive, rigid objects to composite non-rigid cases, such as articulated and deformable structures. The paper by Verri and Uras (*this volume*) gives some indication of developments along this line. It is expected that rapid progress will be made in understanding the invariants of large *classes* of curved

3D objects, and that the concept of repeated structures will extend and merge with ideas about symmetry and extrusion.

Next, there are two main threads of development concerning 3D structure, object-centred and view-centred. It is expected that these themes will be integrated and an understanding developed of which representation is best for a given computation, in terms of stability, accuracy and efficiency. For example, the work of Basri could be reinterpreted by using his model views to reconstruct a 3D representation of the object and then using conventional resectioning to *align* the 3D object model into the new image.

The stratification provided by the hierarchy of transformation groups: projective, affine, and equiform (similarity), has been very helpful in defining precisely the structure obtainable from a number of views [10, 12]. This stratification is also proving useful in eliciting quasi-invariants [1], which are generally invariant to a transformation lower in the hierarchy than that required. Quasi-invariants are often effective in feature grouping and correspondence analysis. Their study is likely to be very productive in the future.

Finally, there is also the sense that the relatively isolated results of many researchers on various aspects of invariant analysis should be integrated into a single environment for scene description and recognition. In this system context, the emerging statistical analyses will be invaluable to produce optimal decisions about the design of object descriptions, library indexing schemes, and geometric reconstruction. It is likely that the building of such an integrated system will uncover new requirements which will drive future research on geometric invariance.

References

1. Binford, T., Kapur D. and Mundy J.L., "The Relation between invariants and quasi-invariants", *Proc. 1st ACCV*, November, 1993.
2. Burns, J.B., Weiss, R.S. and Riseman, E.M. "The non-existence of general-case view-invariants," in [14].
3. Clemens, D.T. and Jacobs, D.W. "Model group indexing for recognition," *IEEE Trans. PAMI*, Vol. 13, No. 10, p.1007-1017, October 1991.
4. Faugeras, O., "What can be seen in three dimensions with an uncalibrated stereo rig?", *Proc. ECCV*, LNCS 588, Springer-Verlag, 1992.
5. Faugeras, O., Luong, Q.T., and Maybank, S.J., "Camera self-calibration: theory and experiments", *Proc. ECCV*, LNCS 588, Springer-Verlag, 1992.
6. Forsyth D.A., Mundy J.L., Zisserman A. and Rothwell C.A., "Recognising rotationally symmetric surfaces from their outlines", *Proc. ECCV*, LNCS 588, Springer-Verlag, 1992.
7. Hartley, R., Gupta, R. and Chang, T., "Stereo from uncalibrated cameras" *Proc. CVPR*, 1992.
8. Hartley, R., "Self-calibration of stationary cameras", *Proc. ECCV*, LNCS 800/801, Springer-Verlag, 1994.
9. Huttenlocher, D.P., and Ullman, S., "Recognizing solid objects by alignment with an image,", *IJCV*, 5(2), pp. 195-212, 1990.

10. Koenderink, J.J. and Van Doorn, A.J., "Affine structure from motion", *J. Opt. Soc. Am. A*, Vol. 8, No. 2, p.377-385, 1991.

11. Liu, J.S., Mundy, J.L. and Walker, E.L., "Recognizing arbitrary objects from multiple projections", *Proc. 1st ACCV*, 422-426, 1993.

12. Luong, Q.T. and Vieville, T., "Canonic representations for the geometries of multiple projective views," *Tech. Rep. ucb/csd-93-772*, Univ. of Cal., Berkeley, 1993.

13. Moses, Y. and Ullman, S. "Limitations of non model based recognition systems", *Proc. ECCV*, LNCS 588, Springer-Verlag, 1992.

14. Mundy, J. L. and Zisserman, A. (editors), *Geometric Invariance in Computer Vision*, MIT Press, Cambridge Ma, 1992.

15. Rothwell, C.A., Forsyth, D.A., Zisserman, A. and Mundy, J.L. "Extracting projective structure from single perspective views of 3D point sets", *Proc. ICCV*, 1993.

16. Sapiro, G. and Tannenbaum, A., "Affine invariant scale spaces", To appear *IJCV*, 1994.

Foundations

Cartan's Moving Frame Method and its Application to the Geometry and Evolution of Curves in the Euclidean, Affine and Projective Planes

Olivier Faugeras

INRIA Sophia-Antipolis, 2004 Route des Lucioles, B.P. 93, 06902 Sophia-Antipolis,
France

1   Introduction and Motivation

A renewed interest in the theory of invariants has emerged in the vision and robotics communities speared by the need to increase the capabilities of artificial systems to represent objects shapes and their robustness in performing recognition tasks. This has produced a large number of publications and a book [16]. It is not too surprising that the question of invariance is also at the heart of another problem central to computer vision, namely the problem of scale-space analysis. These two questions, namely invariant shape representation and scale-space are at he heart of the core of Koenderink and his coworkers [14, 13, 7].

This article addresses the question of describing the differential properties of shapes which are invariant to the action of a group. The shapes of interest are differentiable manifolds such as curves and surfaces but can also be differentiable sets of lines such as complexes or congruences. The groups of interest in computer vision are the euclidean, affine (or unimodular affine) and projective groups.

Among the methods that can be used to obtain such descriptions there is one that clearly emerges because of its simplicity, elegance, generality, and because it is quite amenable to computer implementation. This method is known as the Cartan's moving frame method and has been developed in the first decades of this century by Elie Cartan and his students [2, 3]. The method is widely used in mathematics and physics but has not yet attracted many researchers in computer vision with the notable exception of ter Haar Romeny and his coworkers [17].

In section 2 of this article we give a detailed description of the moving frame method which is completely general and can be used (and automated) in all practical cases. This description uses the tools of the modern exterior differential calculus which were being invented at the time Cartan was developing his moving frame method and is an extended version of what can be found in [2].

We then attempt to help the reader develop some intuition about how the method actually works by using it on three simple and useful examples: plane curves subject to the action of the euclidean, affine, and projective groups. To help even further the intuition we present geometric interpretations of the affine and projective arc lengths. We also relate projective and affine invariants to the more familiar euclidean ones. We found these relations quite useful in applications.

The question of scale-space is discussed in the context of curve evolution. This approach is closely related to the scale-space defined for grey-scale images [23] through for example the evolution of isophotes. But it is also closely related to the question of shape description as shown for example in the work of Kimia Tannenbaum and Zucker [12]. For the three groups of interest we show that the Cartan's method provides a natural framework in which to think about curve evolution as predicted by an *intrinsic* heat equation. One important idea which follows from the study of differential invariants is that the evolution of the curve is defined, up to a transformation of the group of interest, by the evolution of its arc length and of its curvature. The euclidean case had been covered by Gage and Hamilton [8, 9, 10] from the viewpoint of mathematicians and by Mackworth and Mokhtarian in computer vision [15]. The affine case has been worked out by Sapiro and Tannenbaum [19, 18, 21, 20] and by Alvarez, Guichard, Lions and Morel [1]. The projective case is new and we shed some light on it in this article.

One interesting fact is that the three scale-spaces are intimately connected in the sense that they can be thought of as forming a hierarchy. It is likely that this hierarchy can be used in several ways. In this article we develop only the application that consists in reducing the order of derivation that is required to compute the invariants. For example, we show that the affine scale-space reduces the order of derivation necessary to compute the affine curvature from four to three by trading space for scale. A similar property holds in the projective case.

2 Method of Moving Frames

The method of moving frames, due to Elie Cartan [2, 3], deals in a very simple way with problems of differential calculus on curves and surfaces in a context which is not necessarily the usual Euclidean one. In our opinion, the efficiency of the method lies in its potential for being automated, i.e., we can easily write it in an algorithmic form.

We will consider essentially *projective*, *affine* and *Euclidean* spaces which can be regarded as specialisations of each other. Groups of the same name are fundamental for understanding these spaces.

2.1 Background on projective frames

A projective frame in $\mathcal{P}^n$ is a set of $n + 2$ projective points such that no subset of $n + 1$ of these points belongs to the same hyperplane. We will designate them by $A_0, A_1, \cdots, A_{n+1}$. If we choose A_{n+1} such that

$$\mathbf{A}_{n+1} = \sum_{i=0}^{n} \mathbf{A}_i$$

then the representatives of points A_i, $i = 0, \cdots, n$ are defined up to global scale, i.e., if $\mathbf{A}_i$ is a representative of point A_i, then so is $\lambda \mathbf{A}_i$, for any $i = 0, \cdots, n$.

With this choice, the fact that no subset of $n + 1$ of these points belongs to the same hyperplane is equivalent to saying that the determinant of size $(n + 1) \times (n + 1)$ of representatives of the first $n + 1$ is different from 0

$$det(\mathbf{A}_0, \cdots, \mathbf{A}_n) \neq 0$$

The set of frames of the vector space R^{n+1} satisfying the previous condition is an open set U of $(R^{n+1})^{n+1}$, the complement of the closed set defined by

$$det(\mathbf{A}_0, \cdots, \mathbf{A}_n) = 0$$

We can normalize things in such a way that we have the important condition

$$det(\mathbf{A}_0, \cdots, \mathbf{A}_n) = 1 \qquad (1)$$

The mappings $A_i : U \to R^{n+1}$ will be considered as the differentiable mappings of the open set of $(R^{n+1})^{n+1}$ into R^{n+1}. For a given frame r, we note $\mathbf{A}_i(r)$ the value of that function at the point r of U, i.e. the representative of the i+first point of the frame r.

2.2 Cartan equations: projective case

We will consider a frame $r \in U$ depending on one or more parameters. Such a frame is called a *moving frame*.

The $n + 1$ functions $A_0, A_1, \cdots, A_n$ defined on the open set U naturally give us n differential forms of degree one. Therefore $dA_i(r) \in \mathcal{L}((R^{n+1})^{n+1}; R^{n+1})$, the set of linear mappings from $(R^{n+1})^{n+1}$ into R^{n+1}. One of the key points of the method of moving frames is to write the value of this linear mapping in the projective frame r

$$dA_i(r) = \sum_{j=0}^{n} \omega_{ij}(r) \mathbf{A}_j(r) \qquad (2)$$

Therefore the functions ω_{ij} are differential forms of degree one with values in $R..$. This relation is true for $i = 0, \cdots, n + 1$.

The differential forms ω_{ij} are not independent, they satisfy a number of equations, called the Cartan or Lie equations which we now derive.

By differentiating the condition (1) on the determinant of points A_i, we immediately obtain the following relation satisfied by the forms ω_{ij}

$$\sum_{i=0}^{n} \omega_{ii} = 0 \qquad (3)$$

This means that there are only $(n + 1)^2 - 1$ independent differential forms. This is precisely the dimension of the projective group of $\mathcal{P}^n$. By writing that the second differentials of forms dA_i are zero we obtain $n + 1$ additional relations which must be satisfied by the forms ω_{ij}. In effect, from well-known properties of exterior differentiation, these relations can be written

$$d(d\mathbf{A}_i) = \sum_{j=0}^{n}(d\mathbf{A}_j \wedge \omega_{ij} + d\omega_{ij}\mathbf{A}_j) = 0 \tag{4}$$

If we replace $d\mathbf{A}_j$ in this equation by that given in (2) , we obtain the following relations

$$0 = \sum_{j=0}^{n}(d\omega_{ij} - \sum_{k=0}^{n}\omega_{ik} \wedge \omega_{kj})\mathbf{A}_j \quad i = 0, \cdots, n$$

and since the points A_j form a projective frame, we deduce

$$d\omega_{ij} = \sum_{k=0}^{n}\omega_{ik} \wedge \omega_{kj} \tag{5}$$

These equations, called the structure or Cartan equations, are fundamental for the study of projective curves and surfaces.

2.3   Cartan equations: Affine and Euclidean cases

This is a specialization of the previous ideas to the affine and Euclidean cases. We will need coordinates and we denote by $x_0, \cdots, x_n$ the coordiantes of a point of $\mathcal{P}^n$. In the first case, we choose a particular hyperplane H of $\mathcal{P}^n$ to which we can give an affine space structure as the hyperplane at infinity of space $\mathcal{P}^n$. The affine transformations constitute the subgroup of the projective group that leaves H invariant. The points of H represent the directions of the affine space $\mathcal{A}^n$ thus constructed. If we choose for H the hyperplane of equation $x_n = 0$, then a point of $\mathcal{A}^n$ with coordinates $x_0, \cdots, x_{n-1}$ corresponds to the point of $\mathcal{P}^n$ with coordinates $x_0, \cdots, x_{n-1}, 1$ and a vector $\mathbf{v}$ of R^n corresponds to the point of H with coordinates $[\mathbf{v}^T, 0]^T$, to within a nonzero scalar.

   An affine frame consists of a point A, the origin of the frame, and n vectors of R^n written $e_i, i = 1, \cdots, n$. We suppose that these vectors are linearly independent, i.e.,

$$det(e_i) \neq 0 \tag{6}$$

An affine frame can thus be considered as a particular projective frame for which A_0 is in $\mathcal{P}^n \backslash H$ and the $A_i, i = 1, \cdots, n$ are in H. Condition (6) implies that the set of affine frames is an open set U of $R^{n(n+1)}$. A and e_i are thus differentiable functions $U \rightarrow R^n$. As in the projective case, we can consider an affine frame r which depends on one or more parameters. This frame is called *moving frame*. Using reasoning similar to the projective case allows us to write the differential forms $d\mathbf{A}, de_1, \cdots, de_n$ as linear combinations of vectors e_i

$$d\mathbf{A} = \sum_{i=1}^{n}\omega_i e_i$$

$$de_i = \sum_{i=1}^{n}\omega_{ij}e_j$$

In effect, we have the particular case $\mathbf{A}_0 = [\mathbf{A}^T, 1]^T$, $\mathbf{A}_i = [\mathbf{e}_i^T, 0]^T$, $i = 1, \cdots, n$, thus $d\mathbf{A}$ and $d\mathbf{e}_i$ only depend on $\mathbf{e}_i$, $i = 1, \cdots, n$.

Equations (5) are still valid

$$dw_i = \sum_{k=1}^{n} \omega_k \wedge \omega_{ki} \tag{7}$$

$$d\omega_{ij} = \sum_{k=1}^{n} \omega_{ik} \wedge \omega_{kj} \quad i, j = 1, \cdots, n \tag{8}$$

If we consider the subset of affine frames such that $det(\mathbf{e}_i) = det(\mathbf{A}_0, \cdots, \mathbf{A}_n) = 1$, we must add an equation similar to equation (3)

$$\sum_{i=1}^{n} \omega_{ii} = 0 \tag{9}$$

Corresponding to this restriction on frames is a restriction on the group of transformations of the space in which we are interested. Here we consider the unimodal subgroup of the affine group. This subgroup is defined as follows. The transformation M' of a point M of $\mathcal{A}^n$ by an affine tranformation is given by the relation

$$\mathbf{M}' = \mathbf{HM} + \mathbf{b}$$

where $\mathbf{H}$ is a matrix of size $n \times n$ such that $det(\mathbf{H}) \neq 0$, and $\mathbf{b}$ is a vector of size n. The unimodal subgroup is the one for which we have $det(\mathbf{H}) = 1$. The unimodular affine group depends upon $n^2 - 1 + 1$ parameters which, according to (9 is precisely the number of independent differential forms ω_i and ω_{ij}.

We consider the Euclidean case similarly by introducing Euclidean frames which are affine frames such that the matrix of the vectors $\mathbf{e}_i$ is orthogonal. We express it in the form

$$\mathbf{e}_i \cdot \mathbf{e}_j = \delta_{ij}$$

and by differentiating these relations, we obtain

$$\mathbf{e}_i \cdot d\mathbf{e}_j + d\mathbf{e}_i \cdot \mathbf{e}_j = 0$$

We deduce by replacing the differentials with respect to ω_{ij}

$$\omega_{ij} + \omega_{ji} = 0 \quad i, j = 1, \cdots, n$$

and thus we have in particular

$$\omega_{ii} = 0 \quad \forall i$$

The euclidean group depends upon $q = \frac{n^2 + n}{2}$ parameters which, according to our analysis, is precisely the number of independent differential forms ω_i and ω_{ij}.

2.4 Introduction to the method of moving frames

We will consider a set D of points operated on by a finite and continuous group G with q parameters. In practice, D will be a Euclidean, affine, or projective space and G will be one of the groups previously studied. In this section, we note $\omega_1, \cdots, \omega_q$ the differential forms attached to a general frame.

We will consider manifolds of dimension λ in D. In practice, we have $\lambda = 1$ or 2, i.e., we will study curves or surfaces. To a point A of manifold V_λ we attach two types of elements

Frames : an infinity of inclusive families of frames: frames of order $0, \cdots$, frames of order P.

Integers : μ_0, the number of invariants of order $0, \cdots, \mu_P - \mu_{P-1}$, the number of invariants of order P.

We then define *the contact element of order P* of the point A of V_λ as the family of frames of order P of this point and by the set of invariants of order $\leq P$ of this point. Note that the transformations of these frames into each other constitute a subgroup $\mathcal{G}_P$ of G, called the subgroup of order P of the contact element considered.

In other words, each contact element is characterized by a family of frames relative to which it occupies the same position, and by a system of numbers concerning its "form", the invariants. This notion of families of included frames is interesting for many reasons. One of them is that it will allow us to compare the Frenet frames obtained for groups of included transformations: the Frenet frame for the Euclidean group will be a particular frame of order three for the affine group. Similarly, the affine Frenet frame is a particular frame of order 3 for the projective group.

Let us take a contact element of order P; its most general frame of order P depends on ν_P parameters, which we call *secondary parameters of order P* and write $x_1, \cdots, x_{\nu_P}$. These parameters are different from the λ parameters, called *principal parameters*, on which depend the points of the manifold V_λ and which are written $t_1, \cdots, t_\lambda$. Note that the frames of a contact element correspond to constant values of principal parameters since the origin A of the frame is fixed. We can show that infinitesimal translations of this frame are characterized by the property that $q - \nu_P$ linear combinations of the ω_i components disappear. More precisely, infinitesimal translations of the most general frame of order $P-1$, attached to the contact element being considered, eliminate $q - \nu_{P-1}$ independent linear combinations of $\omega_1, \cdots, \omega_q$. In effect, for a frame of order $P - 1$, the forms $\omega_1, \cdots, \omega_q$ depend on $\lambda + \nu_{P-1}$ parameters and we can write

$$\omega_i = \sum_{j=1}^{\lambda} a_{ij} dt_j + \sum_{k=1}^{\nu_{P-1}} b_{ik} dx_k$$

where a_{ij} and b_{ik} are functions of $t_1, \cdots, t_\lambda, x_1, \cdots, x_{\nu_{P-1}}$. By eliminating the ν_{P-1} forms dx_k from among the q forms ω_i, we obtain $q - \nu_{P-1}$ linear combinations of the q forms ω_i which are expressed as linear combinations of the λ forms

dt_j and which disappear when the principal parameters are constant, that is for a frame belonging to a contact element of order $P - 1$, or in fact, to a contact element of any order higher than $P - 1$.

The infinitesimal translation of a frame of order P eliminates these $q - \nu_{P-1}$ linear combinations and $\nu_{P-1} - \nu_P$ others that we will call *principal components of order P*. We note them $\pi_\alpha, \alpha = q - \nu_{P-1} + 1, q - \nu_P$.

Let us now consider the most general contact element of order 0, i.e., any point A of D and vertex frames of this point. Reasoning similar to the above shows that the principal parameter differentials are linear combinations of λ forms suitably chosen among the principal components of order 0. We assume in the following, to simplify without loss of generality, that these λ forms are the first λ principal components of order 0, of which there are $q - \nu_0$, i.e., $\pi_1, \cdots, \pi_\lambda$.

A frame which varies while always remaining of order P depends on the λ principal parameters of V_λ and on ν_P secondary parameters of order P. By definition, its principal components of orders $\leq P$ are independent of the differentials of the secondary parameters; these are thus linear combinations of $\pi_1, \cdots, \pi_\lambda$. Therefore, we have the following proposition

Proposition 1. *The principal components of orders $< P$ of the frames of order P of V_λ are linear combinations of $\pi_1, \cdots, \pi_\lambda$ with coefficients in terms of invariants of order $\leq P$.*

Since the invariants are functions of the principal parameters only, we can also state the following proposition

Proposition 2. *The differentials of invariants of orders $< P$ are linear combinations of $\pi_1, \cdots, \pi_\lambda$ with coefficients which are functions of the invariants of orders $\leq P$. The differentials of the invariants of order P and the principal components of order P of the frames of order P are thus linear combinations of $\pi_1, \cdots, \pi_\lambda$ with coefficients in terms of the invariants of order $\leq P$*

$$dk_\alpha = \sum_{i=1}^{\lambda} b_{\alpha i} \pi_i \quad \mu_{P-1} < \alpha \leq \mu_P \tag{10}$$

$$\pi_\alpha = \sum_{i=1}^{\lambda} b'_{\alpha i} \pi_i \quad q - \nu_{P-1} < \alpha \leq q - \nu_P \tag{11}$$

The coefficients $b_{\alpha i}$ and $b'_{\alpha i}$ are functions of the invariants of order $\leq P$ and of the secondary parameters of order P. They are called *coefficients of order P*. The fundamental idea of the method of moving frames is to study how the group $\mathcal{G}_P$ affects coefficients of order P.

Let $\pi_i, i = 1, \cdots, q - \nu_P$ be the $q - \nu_P$ principal components of order P which are linear combinations of q forms ω_i

$$\pi_i = \sum_{j=1}^{q} a_{ij} \omega_j \quad i = 1, \cdots, q - \nu_P \tag{12}$$

The coefficients a_{ij} are either constants or functions of invariants or order $\leq P$. Let us compute the exterior differentials of the π_i

$$d\pi_i = \sum_{j=1}^{q} da_{ij} \wedge \omega_j + \sum_{j=1}^{q} a_{ij} d\omega_j \tag{13}$$

Differentials of a_{ij} can be written in the form

$$da_{ij} = \sum_{m=1}^{\mu_P} D_{ijm} dk_m \tag{14}$$

and we know the structure equations of group G

$$d\omega_p = \sum_{s,t} c_{pst} \omega_s \wedge \omega_t$$

To simplify the developement we then suppose that the rank of the first square submatrix of size $q - \nu_P$ of the matrix $[a_{ij}]$ equals $q - \nu_P$ which allows us to compute $\omega_i, i = 1, \cdots, q - \nu_P$ with respect to π_i

$$\omega_i = \sum_{j=1}^{q-\nu_P} a'_{ij} \pi_j + \sum_{n=1}^{\nu_P} d_{in} \omega_{q-\nu_P+n} \quad i = 1, \cdots, q - \nu_P \tag{15}$$

If we now consider the differential system

$$\pi_1 = 0 \cdots \pi_{q-\nu_P} = 0$$

this system is completely integrable when the principal parameters are constant. Therefore, according to Frobenius's theorem, we have the following relations

$$d\pi_i \wedge \pi_1 \wedge \cdots \wedge \pi_{q-\nu_P} = 0 \quad i = 1, \cdots, q - \nu_P$$

By replacing $d\pi_i$ by its value (13) in this expression we obtain the relations

$$\sum_{j=1}^{q} da_{ij} \wedge \omega_j \wedge \pi_1 \wedge \cdots \wedge \pi_{q-\nu_P} +$$
$$\sum_{s,t} \left(\sum_{j=1}^{q} a_{ij} c_{jst} \right) \omega_s \wedge \omega_t \wedge \pi_1 \wedge \cdots \wedge \pi_{q-\nu_P} = 0$$
$$i = 1, \cdots, q - \nu_P$$

The first part of this relation including the terms in da_{ij} identically equals zero, by (14) and (10). The other part will contribute to eliminating all terms containing factors $\omega_s \wedge \omega_t$ with s and $t > q - \nu_p$. More precisely, let us rewrite the second part of the previous relation as

$$\sum_{s,t} A_{ist} \omega_s \wedge \omega_t \wedge \pi_1 \wedge \cdots \wedge \pi_{q-\nu_P} = 0$$

If we replace in this expression all values of ω_s and ω_t for values of the indexes s and t less than or equal to $q - \nu_P$ by the expressions (15) and group the terms together, we will end up with an expression like

$$\sum_{s,t>q-\nu_P, s<t} A'_{ist} \omega_s \wedge \omega_t \wedge \pi_1 \wedge \cdots \wedge \pi_{q-\nu_P} = 0$$

in which only the indexes s and t larger than $q - \nu_p$ are left. Since the differential forms which appear in this sum are linearly independent, it implies that all the coefficients A'_{ist} are equal to 0. But these coefficients are precisely those which appear in the second part of the expression for $d\pi_i$ in (13), hence the corresponding terms will disappear from this expression and there will remain only the terms for which the differential form $\omega_s \wedge \omega_t \wedge \pi_1 \wedge \cdots \wedge \pi_{q-\nu_p}$ is identically 0 i.e. those terms of the form $\pi_\alpha \wedge \omega_t \wedge \pi_1 \wedge \cdots \wedge \pi_{q-\nu_p}$, $\alpha = 1, \cdots, q - \nu_p$, $t > q - \nu_p$ and those of the form $\pi_\alpha \wedge \pi_\beta \wedge \pi_1 \wedge \cdots \wedge \pi_{q-\nu_p}$, $\alpha, \beta = 1, \cdots, q - \nu_p$. We can thus write

$$d\pi_i = \sum_{\alpha,\beta=1}^{q-\nu_p} C_{i\alpha\beta} \pi_\alpha \wedge \pi_\beta + \sum_{\alpha=1}^{q-\nu_p} \sum_{n=1}^{\nu_p} A_{in\alpha} \pi_\alpha \wedge \omega_{q-\nu_p+n} +$$
$$\sum_{m=1}^{\mu_p} \sum_{\alpha=1}^{q-\nu_p} D_{im\alpha} dk_m \wedge \pi_\alpha + \sum_{m=1}^{\mu_p} \sum_{n=1}^{\nu_p} B_{imn} dk_m \wedge \omega_{q-\nu_p+n} \qquad (16)$$
$$i = 1, \cdots, q - \nu_p$$

We now reach the climax of the plot. Let us take the exterior differentials of equations (10) and (11)

$$0 = \sum_{i=1}^{\lambda} db_{\alpha i} \wedge \pi_i + \sum_{i=1}^{\lambda} b_{\alpha i} \wedge d\pi_i \quad \mu_{P-1} < \alpha \le \mu_P \qquad (17)$$

$$d\pi_\alpha = \sum_{i=1}^{\lambda} db'_{\alpha i} \wedge \pi_i + \sum_{i=1}^{\lambda} b'_{\alpha i} \wedge d\pi_i \quad q - \nu_{P-1} < \alpha \le q - \nu_P \qquad (18)$$

and make two substitutions.

The first substitution consists of replacing the $\nu_P - \nu_{P-1}$ principal components π_α of order P in the equations (16) by their values given by (11), thus depending on coefficients of order P which we represent as the vector $\mathbf{b}'$ of size $\lambda(\nu_P - \nu_{P-1})$, the $q - \nu_{P-1}$ principal components of order $< P$ by their values with respect to $\pi_1, \cdots, \pi_\lambda$ and coefficients of order $< P$. Similarly, let us replace in these equations the differentials of the $\mu_P - \mu_{P-1}$ invariants of order P by their values taken from (10), that is with respect to coefficients of order P which we represent as the vector $\mathbf{b}$ of size $\lambda(\mu_P - \mu_{P-1})$, and the μ_{P-1} differentials of invariants of order $< P$ by their expressions with respect to $\pi_1, \cdots, \pi_\lambda$ and coefficients of order $< P$. We thus obtain

$$d\pi_i = \sum_{\alpha,\beta=1}^{\lambda} E'_{i\alpha\beta}(\mathbf{b}, \mathbf{b}') \pi_\alpha \wedge \pi_\beta + \sum_{\alpha=1}^{\lambda} \sum_{n=1}^{\nu_P} A'_{i\alpha n}(\mathbf{b}') \pi_\alpha \wedge \omega_{q-\nu_P+n} +$$
$$\sum_{\alpha=1}^{\lambda} \sum_{n=1}^{\nu_P} B'_{i\alpha n}(\mathbf{b}) \pi_\alpha \wedge \omega_{q-\nu_P+n}$$

or

$$d\pi_i = \sum_{\alpha,\beta=1}^{\lambda} E'_{i\alpha\beta}(\mathbf{b}, \mathbf{b}') \pi_\alpha \wedge \pi_\beta + \sum_{\alpha=1}^{\lambda} \sum_{n=1}^{\nu_P} F'_{i\alpha n}(\mathbf{b}, \mathbf{b}') \pi_\alpha \wedge \omega_{q-\nu_P+n} \quad i = 1, \cdots, q - \nu_P$$

The second substitution consists of replacing the $d\pi_i$ by their values in equations (17) and (18). We then obtain

$$\sum_{j=1}^{\lambda} \left(db_{\alpha j} - \sum_{n=1}^{\nu_P} f_{\alpha j n}(\mathbf{b}, \mathbf{b}') \omega_{q-\nu_P+n} + \sum_{h=1}^{\lambda} r_{\alpha h}(\mathbf{b}, \mathbf{b}') \pi_h \right) \wedge \pi_j = 0$$

$$\sum_{j=1}^{\lambda}(db'_{\alpha j} - \sum_{n=1}^{\nu_P} g_{\alpha j n}(\mathbf{b},\mathbf{b}')\omega_{q-\nu_P+n} + \sum_{h=1}^{\lambda} r'_{\alpha h}(\mathbf{b},\mathbf{b}')\pi_h) \wedge \pi_j = 0$$

From these relations we deduce that

$$db_{\alpha j} - \sum_{n=1}^{\nu_P} f_{\alpha j n}(\mathbf{b},\mathbf{b}')\omega_{q-\nu_P+n} + \sum_{h=1}^{\lambda} r_{\alpha h}(\mathbf{b},\mathbf{b}')\pi_h$$

and

$$db'_{\alpha j} - \sum_{n=1}^{\nu_P} g_{\alpha j n}(\mathbf{b},\mathbf{b}')\omega_{q-\nu_P+n} + \sum_{h=1}^{\lambda} r'_{\alpha h}(\mathbf{b},\mathbf{b}')\pi_h$$

are linear combinations of λ differential forms π_i. If we denote by $e_{q-\nu_P+n}$ the restriction of the differential form $\omega_{q-\nu_P+n}$ when the principal parameters are constant and the principal forms $\pi_1, \cdots, \pi_\lambda$ of order 0 disappear, we finally obtain differential equations yielding the action of the group $\mathcal{G}_P$ on coefficients of order P

$$db_{\alpha j} = \sum_{n=1}^{\nu_P} f_{\alpha j n}(\mathbf{b},\mathbf{b}')e_{q-\nu_P+n}$$

$$\tag{19}$$

$$db'_{\alpha j} = \sum_{n=1}^{\nu_P} g_{\alpha j n}(\mathbf{b},\mathbf{b}')e_{q-\nu_P+n}$$

Let us examine in more detail how this leads to an *algorithmic* method for computing the different classes of frames. At the beginning of step $P+1$, we assume known

1. The number of invariants of order 1, 2, $\cdots$, P;
2. The definition of frames of order 1, 2, $\cdots$, P;
3. The definition of principal components of orders $< P$ of frames of order P, their expressions in terms of $\pi_1, \cdots, \pi_\lambda$, and invariants of orders $\leq P$;
4. The expressions of differentials of invariants of orders $< P$ with respect to $\pi_1, \cdots, \pi_\lambda$ and invariants of orders $\leq P$;

We then obtain the information at order $P+1$ as follows

1. If necessary, we orientate the contact element of order P in order for the family of frames of order P to be continuous
2. We define the principal components of order P. To do so, we deduce, from the tables of secondary coefficients of orders P and $P-1$, a system of $\nu_{P-1} - \nu_P$ principal components of order P (equations (12)).
3. We compute their exterior derivatives (16).
4. Using formulas (10) and (11) we define coefficients of order P and compute infinitesimal transformations (19) of the group $\mathcal{G}_P$ taken as operating on these coefficients.

5. Considering the space W_P of these coefficients, we then determine orbits of points of W_P under the action of $\mathcal{G}_P$.

6. We then trace in W_P as simply as possible [1] a manifold w_P which intersects each orbit in one and only one point. Thus each point of W_P has one and only one homolog on w_P. Choosing a point of w_P amounts to choosing an orbit of W_P.

7. As frames of order $P+1$ we choose frames of order P to which corresponds a point of w_P. We choose as invariants of order $P+1$ parameters which allow us to distinguish the point of w_P. In the very important special case when $\mathcal{G}_P$ operates transitively on W_P, w_P is reduced to one point and there are no invariants of order $P+1$.

When point B is on w_P, equations (10) and (11) yield the expressions of differentials of invariants of order P and principal components of order P in terms of $\pi_1, \cdots, \pi_\alpha$ and the invariants of order $P+1$. $\mathcal{G}_{P+1}$ is the subgroup of $\mathcal{G}_P$ which leaves point B fixed. The table of secondary components of order $P+1$ is obtained from the table of order P by linking differential forms e_q with the relation (19) where we take $db_{\alpha j} = db'_{\alpha j} = 0$. These relations supply the principal components of order $P+1$ since it is precisely the linear combinations of forms ω_i which disappear for all frames of order $P+1$ with fixed origin.

We will show by the example of plane curves how the ideas developed above are applied in the case of the projective, affine and Euclidean geometry.

3 Curves in the Euclidean Plane

This well-known case will allow us to explain the method of moving frames. We consider Euclidean frames in the plane (A, e_1, e_2). From what we have seen above, the equations of the most general moving frame are written

$$dA = \omega_1 e_1 + \omega_2 e_2$$
$$de_1 = \omega_{12} e_2$$
$$de_2 = -\omega_{12} e_1$$

These frames thus depend on $q = 3$ parameters which is the number of parameters of the plane Euclidean group. Cartan's structure equations are very simple

$$d\omega_1 = -\omega_2 \wedge \omega_{12} \tag{20}$$
$$d\omega_2 = \omega_1 \wedge \omega_{12} \tag{21}$$
$$d\omega_{12} = 0 \tag{22}$$

We now consider a curve (c) of class C^2 which we will assume parametrized by t. We will consider the set of frames whose origin is at a point of the curve (c). This is a family of frames with two parameters, the parameter t, called the *principal* parameter, and the orientation θ of e_1 with respect to the horizontal, called the *secondary parameter*.

---

[1] This is all a matter of flair and insight!

3.1 Frames of order 0

A contact element of order 0 consists of a point A and all the euclidean frames having origin A. Frames of order 0 are characterized by the fact that point A is fixed. These frames depend on only one parameter θ, and we thus have, according to the notation of the previous section, $\nu_0 = 1$. Also according to that section, we must find that $q - \nu_0$ independent linear combinations of ω_1, ω_2 and ω_{12} disappear when we restrict them to this subclass of frames.

In effect, the three forms ω_1, ω_2 and ω_{12} are linear combinations of the forms dt and $d\theta$. They are thus not independent. If we eliminate $d\theta$ within these three forms, we will obtain two two linear combinations depending only on dt. A linear combination of these three forms containing only dt disappear for $dt = 0$, i.e., when varying the frame in the family with one parameter θ relative to point A. Let us find these two linear combinations.

Since frames of order 0 are characterized by the fact that the point A is fixed, we have $d\mathbf{A} = 0$. We will call secondary coefficients, denoted by e_1 and e_2, the differential forms induced by ω_1 and ω_2 on this subfamily of frames, (similarly, we denote by e_{ij}, the restriction to the subfamily of frames under consideration of the differential form ω_{ij}). The condition $d\mathbf{A} = 0$ implies that the secondary coefficients e_1 and e_2 equal zero. We have thus found our two linear combinations of the forms ω_1, ω_2 and ω_{12} which disappear along with dt: they are clearly ω_1 et ω_2 ! We call them principal components of order 0 and, according to the previous section, we denote them by $\pi_1 = \omega_1$ and $\pi_2 = \omega_2$. It is useful to visualize in table form, called the table of secondary components of order 0, the differential forms which disappear on the subfamily of frames being considered, and the relations between the others. We obtain

$$\begin{bmatrix} 0 & 0 \\ 0 & e_{12} \\ -e_{12} & 0 \end{bmatrix}$$

The principal components of frames of order 0 are

Order 0
ω_1, ω_2

3.2 Frames of order 1

According to the above section, we have two principal components of order 0 which are ω_1 and ω_2. In proposition 1 of the previous section, these principal components are linear combinations of π_1 which is equal to ω_1. We thus have $\omega_2 = a\omega_1$ and a is called the coeffecient of order 0.

We consider a frame which varies while always remaining of order 0 (its origin is fixed at a point of the curve). From the above, its principal components of order 0 are ω_1 and ω_2, which introduces a secondary coefficient a of order 0, such that

$$\omega_2 = a\omega_1$$

a is a function of the secondary parameter θ and of the principal parameter t. Let us compute the exterior differential of ω_2, using on the one hand the previous expression, and on the other hand the structure equations (8)

$$d\omega_2 = da \wedge \omega_1 + a\, d\omega_1 = \omega_1 \wedge \omega_{12}$$

Let us use the fact that $d\omega_1 = -\omega_2 \wedge \omega_{12} = -a\omega_1 \wedge \omega_{12}$. We obtain

$$\omega_1 \wedge (da + \omega_{12}(1 + a^2)) = 0$$

We thus have $da + \omega_{12}(1 + a^2) = \alpha\omega_1$, and since $\omega_1 = 0$ for frames of order 0, we finally obtain

$$da = -(a^2 + 1)e_{12}$$

The group $\mathcal{G}_0$ operates transitively on a and we can choose a subset such that $a = 0$ from the class of frames of order 0. These frames are called frames of order 1. They therefore satisfy the condition $\omega_2 = 0$. The vector e_1 is thus tangent to the curve. According to the previous equation, this implies $e_{12} = 0$. Frames of order 1 do not depend on any secondary parameter and we thus have $\nu_1 = 0$. From the previous section, an infinitesimal translation of the frame of order 1 zeros $q - \nu_0 = 2$ linear combinations of $\omega_1, \omega_2, \omega_{12}$ (ω_1 and ω_2) and $\nu_0 - \nu_1 = 1$ new one, which is consequently ω_{12}.

Thus the table of secondary components of order 1 is

$$\begin{bmatrix} 0 & 0 \\ 0 & 0 \\ 0 & 0 \end{bmatrix}$$

The principal components of frames of order 1 are

Order 0	Order 1
$\omega_1, \omega_2(= 0)$	ω_{12}

We find here again that the secondary coefficient of order 1, the ratio $\frac{\omega_{12}}{ds}$, is an invariant of order 2 which we identify as the curvature κ. We have the classical Frenet formulas

$$\frac{d\mathbf{A}}{ds} = \mathbf{e}_1$$

$$\frac{d\mathbf{e}_1}{ds} = \kappa\mathbf{e}_2 \tag{23}$$

$$\frac{d\mathbf{e}_2}{ds} = -\kappa\mathbf{e}_1$$

3.3 Application to the evolution of curves

We are now going to consider the case of a family of curves. In order to deal with this problem, we change our notation slightly and consider a closed embedded smooth curve (i.e. a curve with no self-intersections). We denote by p the principal parameter. The curve can be considered as a mapping $\mathbf{A} : S^1 \rightarrow R^2$ where S^1 is the unit circle. We now consider smooth embedded plane curves deforming in time. Let $\mathbf{A}(p,t) : S^1 \times R \rightarrow R^2$ be a family of such curves where p parametrizes the curve and t represents the time. Let s be the euclidean arc-length along a curve of the family, a function of p and t. We now propose to study the following evolution equation:

$$\mathbf{A}_t = \mathbf{A}_{ss} \tag{24}$$

in which the partial with respect to t is taken at p constant and the partials with respect to s are taken at t constant. This equation can be thought of as a heat equation (because of the formal similarity with the usual heat equation) which is *intrinsic* to the curve. It has been studied by Gage and Hamilton [8, 9, 10] who proved that a planar convex embedded curve converges to a round point when evolving according to (24) and Grayson [11] who proved that a planar embedded nonconvex curve converges first to a convex one and then to a round point.

Since a curve in the euclidean plane is defined up to a rigid transformation by its arclength and curvature, it is natural to establish how they evolve in time when the curve changes according to (24). The key is of course to use the Frenet equations (23).

We first derive a general result which we will use also in later sections. It is related to the fact that the operators of partial derivative with respect to t (at p constant) and with respect to s (at t constant) do not commute since s is a function of p and t. Let then g equal $\frac{ds}{dp}$, it is easy to show that the Lie bracket $[\frac{\partial}{\partial t}, \frac{\partial}{\partial s}]$ is equal to

$$[\frac{\partial}{\partial t}, \frac{\partial}{\partial s}] = \frac{\partial^2}{\partial t \partial s} - \frac{\partial^2}{\partial s \partial t} = -\frac{g_t}{g} \frac{\partial}{\partial s} \tag{25}$$

Applying this formula twice, we obtain the following expressions which we will find useful later:

$$\frac{\partial}{\partial t} \frac{\partial^2}{\partial s^2} = -[\frac{g_t}{g}]_s \frac{\partial}{\partial s} - 2\frac{g_t}{g} \frac{\partial^2}{\partial s^2} + \frac{\partial^2}{\partial s^2} \frac{\partial}{\partial t} \tag{26}$$

and

$$\frac{\partial}{\partial t} \frac{\partial^3}{\partial s^3} = -[\frac{g_t}{g}]_{s^2} \frac{\partial}{\partial s} - 3[\frac{g_t}{g}]_s \frac{\partial^2}{\partial s^2} - 3\frac{g_t}{g} \frac{\partial^3}{\partial s^3} + \frac{\partial^3}{\partial s^3} \frac{\partial}{\partial t} \tag{27}$$

Similarly, we will need the following expressions of the higher order derivatives of $\mathbf{A}$ with respect to the arclength s which we obtain from the Frenet formulae:

$$\mathbf{A}_{s^3} = -\kappa^2 \mathbf{e}_1 + \kappa_s \mathbf{e}_2 \tag{28}$$

$$\mathbf{A}_{s^4} = -3\kappa_s \kappa \mathbf{e}_1 + (\kappa_{ss} - \kappa^3) \mathbf{e}_2 \tag{29}$$

$$\mathbf{A}_{s^5} = (\kappa^4 - 3\kappa_s^2 - 4\kappa_{ss}\kappa)\mathbf{e}_1 + (\kappa_{s^3} - 6\kappa_s\kappa^2)\mathbf{e}_2 \tag{30}$$

Evolution of arc-length It is now easy to characterize the evolution of arc-length. We use the relation

$$\mathbf{e}_1 \cdot \mathbf{e}_1 = 1$$

which can be rewritten as

$$\mathbf{A}_s \cdot \mathbf{A}_s = 1$$

and take its derivative with respect to t:

$$\mathbf{A}_{ts} \cdot \mathbf{A}_s = 0$$

We then use equations (25) and (24) to rewrite

$$\mathbf{A}_{ts} = -\frac{g_t}{g}\mathbf{A}_s + \mathbf{A}_{s^3}$$

Using equation (28) we finally get

$$g_t = -\kappa^2 g \tag{31}$$

Evolution of curvature The principle of the method is to use a differential equation that is satisfied by each curve of the family. Using the Frenet equations and equation (28) we obtain

$$\kappa \mathbf{A}_{s^3} - \kappa_s \mathbf{A}_{s^2} + \kappa^3 \mathbf{A}_s = 0$$

We take the derivative of this equation with respect to t:

$$\kappa_t \mathbf{A}_{s^3} + \kappa \mathbf{A}_{ts^3} - \kappa_{ts} \mathbf{A}_{s^2} - \kappa_s \mathbf{A}_{ts^2} + 3\kappa_t \kappa^2 \mathbf{A}_s + \kappa^3 \mathbf{A}_{ts} = 0$$

We then use equations (25)-(27), the Frenet equations and equations (28)-(30) to obtain the equation

$$P(\kappa, \kappa_t, \kappa_s, \kappa_{s^2})\mathbf{e}_1 + Q(\kappa, \kappa_t, \kappa_s, \kappa_{s^2}, \kappa_{s^3}, \kappa_{ts})\mathbf{e}_2 = 0$$

This implies $P = Q = 0$. The first equation yields the sought for evolution equation:

$$\kappa_t = \kappa_{ss} + \kappa^3 \tag{32}$$

We then replace κ_{ts} by $-\frac{g_t}{g}\kappa_s + \kappa_{st}$ in Q thanks to equation (25), use equation (32) and find that Q is identically 0. Equation (32) is an example of a special kind of partial differential equation called a *reaction diffusion* equation. These equations have been studied quite extensively in mathematics (see for example [22]). In fact we have here a system of two coupled pde's (equations (31) and (32)) which must be studied as such.

4 Affine Unimodal Bidimensional Geometry

We will consider the affine frames of the plane (A, e_1, e_2). In section 2, the equations of the most general moving frame are written

$$dA = \omega_1 e_1 + \omega_2 e_2$$
$$de_1 = \omega_{11} e_1 + \omega_{12} e_2$$
$$de_2 = \omega_{21} e_1 - \omega_{11} e_2$$

Thus these frames depend on $q = 5$ parameters which is the number of parameters of the plane unimodular affine group.

4.1 Frames of order 0

A contact element of order 0 consists of a point A and all the affine frames of origin A. Frames of order 0 are characterized by the fact that the point A is fixed, thus $dA = 0$, which implies that the secondary coefficients e_1 and e_2 equal 0: $q - \nu_0 = 2$. Thus frames of order 0 depend on $\nu_0 = 3$ parameters. We have two principal components of order 0, $\pi_1 = \omega_1$ and $\pi_2 = \omega_2$. As mentioned above, it is convenient to set the differential of the principal parameter which defines the position of a point of the curve equal to the first principal component, i.e., to ω_1. The table of secondary components of order 0 is given by

$$\begin{bmatrix} 0 & 0 \\ e_{11} & e_{12} \\ e_{21} & -e_{11} \end{bmatrix}$$

The principal components of frames of order 0 are

Order 0
ω_1, ω_2

4.2 Frames of order 1

Given a frame which varies while always remaining of order 0 (its origin is fixed at one point of the curve). According to the above, its principal components of order 0 are linear combinations of π_1, which introduces a coefficient a of order 0, such that $\pi_2 = a\pi_1$, i.e.,

$$\omega_2 = a\omega_1$$

Let us compute the exterior differential of ω_2 using on the one hand the previous expression, and on the other hand the structure equations (8)

$$d\omega_2 = da \wedge \omega_1 + a d\omega_1$$

Using the facts that $d\omega_1 = \omega_1 \wedge \omega_{11} + \omega_2 \wedge \omega_{21} = \omega_1 \wedge (\omega_{11} + a\omega_{21})$ and $d\omega_2 = \omega_1 \wedge \omega_{12} + \omega_2 \wedge \omega_{22} = \omega_1 \wedge (\omega_{12} + a\omega_{22})$, we obtain

$$\omega_1 \wedge (da + \omega_{12} + a(\omega_{22} - \omega_{11}) - a^2 \omega_{21}) = 0$$

Therefore we have $da + \omega_{12} + a(\omega_{22} - \omega_{11}) - a^2\omega_{21} = \alpha\omega_1$, and as $\omega_1 = 0$ for frames of order 0, we obtain

$$da = -e_{12} - a(e_{22} - e_{11}) + a^2 e_{21}$$

The group $\mathcal{G}_0$ thus operates transitively on a. We can choose a subset such that $a = 0$ from the class of frames of order 0. These frames are called frames of order 1. They thus satisfy the condition $\omega_2 = 0$. The vector e_1 is therefore tangent to the curve. According to the equation shown above, this implies $e_{12} = 0$.

We thus have a principal component ω_{12} of order 1. Thus $\nu_0 - \nu_1 = 1$ and frames of order 1 depend on $\nu_1 = 2$ secondary parameters. The table of secondary components of order 1 is given by

$$\begin{bmatrix} 0 & 0 \\ e_{11} & 0 \\ e_{21} & -e_{11} \end{bmatrix}$$

The principal components of frames of order 1 are

Order 0	Order 1
$\omega_1, \omega_2(= 0)$	ω_{12}

4.3 Frames of order 2 and 3

The same method applied to frames varying while always remaining of order 1 (resp. of order 2) allow us to determine the principal components of frames of order 3.

Order 0	Order 1	Order 2	Order 3
$\omega_1, \omega_2(= 0)$	$\omega_{12}(= \omega_1)$	$\omega_{11}(= 0)$	ω_{21}

The form ω_1 satisfies $d\omega_1 = 0$ and is therefore exact. We let

$$\omega_1 = d\sigma$$

where σ is called the affine arc length parameter. We have an invariant of order 4, the ratio $\frac{\omega_{21}}{d\sigma}$, which is the affine curvature k. Frames of order 3 are Frenet frames and we have the following equations

$$\frac{d\mathbf{A}}{d\sigma} = \mathbf{e}_1$$

$$\frac{d\mathbf{e}_1}{d\sigma} = \mathbf{e}_2 \tag{33}$$

$$\frac{d\mathbf{e}_2}{d\sigma} = k\mathbf{e}_1$$

4.4 Analytic determination of arc length and affine curvature

Supposing the curve parametrized by any parameter t and using the Frenet formulas, we have

$$\frac{d\mathbf{A}}{dt} = \frac{d\mathbf{A}}{d\sigma}\frac{d\sigma}{dt} = \mathbf{e}_1\frac{d\sigma}{dt}$$

$$\frac{d^2\mathbf{A}}{dt^2} = \mathbf{e}_1\frac{d^2\sigma}{dt^2} + \mathbf{e}_2(\frac{d\sigma}{dt})^2$$

Taking the vector products and with $\mathbf{e}_1 \times \mathbf{e}_2 = 1$, we obtain

$$\frac{d\sigma}{dt} = (\frac{d\mathbf{A}}{dt} \times \frac{d^2\mathbf{A}}{dt^2})^{1/3} \tag{34}$$

This equation will allow us to compute the affine arc length parametrization from any parametization of the curve. Pushing the derivative further will enable us to compute the affine curvature. In effect

$$\frac{d^3\mathbf{A}}{dt^3} = (k(\frac{d\sigma}{dt})^3 + \frac{d^3\sigma}{dt^3})\mathbf{e}_1 + 3\frac{d\sigma}{dt}\frac{d^2\sigma}{dt^2}\mathbf{e}_2$$

Taking the vector product with $\frac{d^2\mathbf{A}}{dt^2}$ and extracting k yields

$$k = -\frac{\frac{d^3\sigma}{dt^3}}{(\frac{d\sigma}{dt})^3} + 3\frac{(\frac{d^2\sigma}{dt^2})^2}{(\frac{d\sigma}{dt})^4} - \frac{1}{(\frac{d\sigma}{dt})^5}\frac{d^2\mathbf{A}}{dt^2} \times \frac{d^3\mathbf{A}}{dt^3} \tag{35}$$

This expression is true for any parameter t. In the case where $t = s$, the Euclidean arc length, we have

$$\frac{d\mathbf{A}}{ds} = \mathbf{t} \qquad \frac{d^2\mathbf{A}}{ds^2} = \frac{\mathbf{n}}{R} \qquad \frac{d^3\mathbf{A}}{ds^3} = -\frac{\mathbf{t}}{R^2} - \frac{\frac{dR}{ds}}{R^2}\mathbf{n}$$

$$\frac{d\sigma}{ds} = R^{-\frac{1}{3}} \quad \frac{d^2\sigma}{ds^2} = -\frac{1}{3}\frac{dR}{ds}R^{-\frac{4}{3}} \quad \frac{d^3\sigma}{ds^3} = -\frac{1}{3}\frac{d^2R}{ds^2}R^{-\frac{4}{3}} + \frac{4}{9}(\frac{dR}{ds})^2R^{-\frac{7}{3}}$$

By replacing these terms with their values in equation (35), we obtain

$$k = -R^{-\frac{4}{3}} + \frac{1}{3}\frac{d^2R}{ds^2}R^{-\frac{1}{3}} - \frac{1}{9}(\frac{dR}{ds})^2R^{-\frac{4}{3}}$$

We recognize the common term $\frac{1}{2}\frac{d^2R^{\frac{2}{3}}}{ds^2}$ in the last two terms of the right-hand side, and we obtain this handsome formula

$$k = -R^{-\frac{4}{3}} + \frac{1}{2}\frac{d^2R^{\frac{2}{3}}}{ds^2} \tag{36}$$

Note that we have obtained the relation between the affine arc length parameter σ and the Euclidean arc length parameter s

$$\frac{d\sigma}{ds} = \kappa^{\frac{1}{3}} \tag{37}$$

where κ is the Euclidean curvature. This, naturally, also yields the Euclidean norm of the affine tangent e_1

$$\mathbf{e}_1 = \frac{d\mathbf{A}}{d\sigma} = \frac{d\mathbf{A}}{ds}\frac{ds}{d\sigma} = \mathbf{t}R^{\frac{1}{3}}$$

so that

$$|\mathbf{e}_1| = |R|^{\frac{1}{3}} = |\kappa|^{-\frac{1}{3}} \tag{38}$$

We can continue and compute the components of the affine normal e_2 in the basis $(\mathbf{t}, \mathbf{n})$

$$\mathbf{e}_2 = \frac{d\mathbf{e}_1}{d\sigma} = \frac{dR^{\frac{1}{3}}}{ds}\kappa^{-\frac{1}{3}}\mathbf{t} + \kappa^{\frac{1}{3}}\mathbf{n}$$

The component of the affine normal on the Euclidean normal is therefore equal to $\kappa^{\frac{1}{3}}$. This remark turned out to be of great importance in the affine "scale-space" analysis [19, 18, 20, 1].

4.5 Geometric interpretation

We take two points A and B, and two line directions d and d' represented by two vectors that we denote $\mathbf{A}'$ and $\mathbf{B}'$. These four elements determine a triangle ABA_{01}, where A_{01} is obtained as the intersection of the lines passing through A parallel to $\mathbf{A}'$ and through B parallel to $\mathbf{B}'$. It is easy to show that the area S of the triangle ABA_{01} is given by the following formula

$$S = \frac{1}{2}\frac{(\mathbf{A}' \times \mathbf{BA}) \cdot (\mathbf{BA} \times \mathbf{B}')}{\mathbf{A}' \times \mathbf{B}'} \tag{39}$$

The quadruple A, B, $\mathbf{A}'$ and $\mathbf{B}'$ also determines in a unique way a parabola passing through A and B, and tangent to $\langle A, A_{01}\rangle$ and $\langle B, A_{01}\rangle$. The equation of this parabola is written

$$\mathbf{A}(t) = \mathbf{A}_0 + t\mathbf{A}_0' + \frac{t^2}{2}\mathbf{A}_0'' \tag{40}$$

with

$$\mathbf{A}_0 = \mathbf{A}(t_0) = \mathbf{A}(0) = \mathbf{A} \quad \mathbf{A}_1 = \mathbf{A}(t_1) = \mathbf{B}$$
$$\frac{d\mathbf{A}}{dt}\big|_{t=t_0} \times \mathbf{A}' = 0 \quad \frac{d\mathbf{A}}{dt}\big|_{t=t_1} \times \mathbf{B}' = 0$$

Let us compute the area of the triangle ABA_{01} in terms of t_1. We use (39) to write

$$S(t_1) = \frac{1}{2}\frac{(\mathbf{A}_0' \times \mathbf{A}_0\mathbf{A}_1) \cdot (\mathbf{A}_0\mathbf{A}_1 \times \mathbf{A}_1')}{\mathbf{A}_0' \times \mathbf{A}_1'}$$

We replace $\mathbf{A}_0\mathbf{A}_1$ in the previous equation by $t_1\mathbf{A}_0' + \frac{t_1^2}{2}\mathbf{A}_0''$ and $\mathbf{A}_1'$ by $\mathbf{A}_0' + t_1\mathbf{A}_0''$, and we obtain

$$S(t_1) = \frac{1}{8}t_1^3\mathbf{A}_0' \times \mathbf{A}_0''$$

The area of the triangle defined by two points of the parabola at parameters t_1 and t_2 is thus given by the formula

$$S(t_1, t_2) = \frac{1}{8}(t_2 - t_1)^3 \mathbf{A}_0' \times \mathbf{A}_0''$$

From which we deduce the following addition law

$$S(t_0, t_1)^{\frac{1}{3}} + S(t_1, t_2)^{\frac{1}{3}} = S(t_0, t_2)^{\frac{1}{3}}$$

which was already known to Möbius (see figure 1).

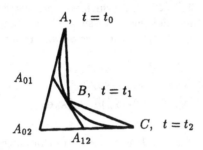

Fig. 1.   We   have   the   curious   relation
$Area(ABA_{01})^{\frac{1}{3}} + Area(BCA_{12})^{\frac{1}{3}} = Area(ACA_{02})^{\frac{1}{3}}$

Let us demonstrate that this law is nothing but the addition law of affine arc length along the parabola. In effect, according to the equation (34), we have

$$\frac{d\sigma}{dt} = (\frac{d\mathbf{A}}{dt} \times \frac{d^2\mathbf{A}}{dt^2})^{1/3}$$

so that, according to (40)

$$\frac{d\sigma}{dt} = (\mathbf{A}_0' \times \mathbf{A}_0'')^{\frac{1}{3}}$$

We can conclude that $\sigma(t) = 2S(t)^{\frac{1}{3}}$, which gives the addition formula.

4.6 Application to the evolution of curves

Similarly to the euclidean case (see section 3.3), we are now going to consider the case of a family of curves. We use the same notations as in this section and consider smooth embedded plane curves deforming in time. Let $\mathbf{A}(p, t)$: $S^1 \times R \to R^2$ be a family of such curves where p parametrizes the curve and t represents the time. Let σ be the affine arc length along a curve of the family, a function of p and t. We now propose to study the following evolution equation:

$$\mathbf{A}_t = \mathbf{A}_{\sigma\sigma} \tag{41}$$

in which the partial with respect to t is taken at p constant and the partials with respect to σ are taken at t constant. This equation, as (24), can be thought of as a heat equation (because of the formal similarity with the usual heat equation) which is *intrinsic* to the curve. It has been studied by Sapiro and Tannenbaum [19, 18, 21, 20] who proved that a planar convex embedded curve converges to an elliptic point when evolving according to (41) and that a planar embedded nonconvex curve converges first to a convex one and then to an elliptic point.

Since a curve in the affine plane is defined up to an affine transformation by its arc length and curvature, it is natural to establish how they evolve in time when the curve changes according to (41). The key is of course to use the Frenet equations (33).

We use the equations (25), (26), (27) which are unchanged in the affine framework. We will also need the following expressions of the higher order derivatives of $\mathbf{A}$ with respect to the arc length σ which we obtain from the Frenet formulae:

$$\mathbf{A}_{\sigma^3} = k\mathbf{e}_1 \tag{42}$$

$$\mathbf{A}_{\sigma^4} = k_\sigma \mathbf{e}_1 + k\mathbf{e}_2 \tag{43}$$

$$\mathbf{A}_{\sigma^5} = (k^2 + k_\sigma^2)\mathbf{e}_1 + 2\kappa_\sigma \mathbf{e}_2 \tag{44}$$

Evolution of affine arc length It is now easy to characterize the evolution of arc length. We let $g = \frac{d\sigma}{dp}$ and use the relation

$$\mathbf{e}_1 \wedge \mathbf{e}_2 = 1$$

which can be rewritten as

$$\mathbf{A}_\sigma \wedge \mathbf{A}_{\sigma\sigma} = 1$$

and take its derivative with respect to t:

$$\mathbf{A}_{t\sigma} \wedge \mathbf{A}_{\sigma\sigma} + \mathbf{A}_\sigma \wedge \mathbf{A}_{t\sigma\sigma} = 0$$

We then use equations (25) and (41) to rewrite

$$\mathbf{A}_{t\sigma} = -\frac{g_t}{g}\mathbf{A}_\sigma + \mathbf{A}_{\sigma^3}$$

Using equation (42) we obtain

$$\mathbf{A}_{t\sigma} \wedge \mathbf{A}_{\sigma\sigma} = (k - \frac{g_t}{g})\mathbf{A}_\sigma \wedge \mathbf{A}_{\sigma\sigma} = k - \frac{g_t}{g}$$

Similarly, using equations (26) and (43), we obtain

$$\mathbf{A}_\sigma \wedge \mathbf{A}_{t\sigma\sigma} = (k - 2\frac{g_t}{g})\mathbf{A}_\sigma \wedge \mathbf{A}_{\sigma\sigma} = k - 2\frac{g_t}{g}$$

and finally

$$g_t = -\frac{2}{3}kg \tag{45}$$

which is the affine analog of (31).

Evolution of affine curvature The principle of the method is to use a differential equation that is satisfied by each curve of the family. Using the Frenet equations and equation (42) we obtain

$$\mathbf{A}_{\sigma^3} - k\mathbf{A}_\sigma = 0$$

We take the derivative of this equation with respect to t:

$$\mathbf{A}_{t\sigma^3} - k_t\mathbf{A}_\sigma - k\mathbf{A}_{t\sigma} = 0$$

We then use equations (25)-(27), the Frenet equations, equations (42)-(45) to obtain the equation

$$(\frac{1}{3}k_{\sigma\sigma} - \frac{4}{3}k^2 - k_t)\mathbf{e}_1 = 0$$

This yields the sought-for evolution equation:

$$k_t = \frac{1}{3}k_{\sigma\sigma} - \frac{4}{3}k^2 \tag{46}$$

which is the affine analog of (32).

Evolution of euclidean curvature It is interesting to look at the temporal evolution of the *euclidean* curvature when the curve evolves according to (41). In order to do this, we use equation (38) which says:

$$\mathbf{A}_\sigma \cdot \mathbf{A}_\sigma = \kappa^{-\frac{2}{3}}$$

where κ is the euclidean curvature. If we take the derivative of this equation with respect to time, we obtain

$$\mathbf{A}_{t\sigma} \cdot \mathbf{A}_\sigma = -\frac{1}{3}\kappa_t\kappa^{-\frac{5}{3}}$$

From previous computation, we know that $\mathbf{A}_{t\sigma} = \frac{1}{3}k\mathbf{A}_\sigma$, where k is the affine curvature. Thus we obtain

$$\kappa_t = -k\kappa \tag{47}$$

This equation is interesting because it says that we can save one order of derivation by using the scale-space defined by the curve evolution (41). Indeed, according to equation (36), the affine curvature can be obtained from a second order derivative of the euclidean curvature with respect to euclidean arc-length. But, according to equation (47), we can obtain the affine curvature from a first order derivative of the euclidean curvature with respect to time.

5 Plane Projective Geometry

We will now consider projective frames in the plane (A, A_1, A_2). As in §2.2, the equations of the most general moving frame are

$$dA = \omega_{00}A + \omega_{01}A_1 + \omega_{02}A_2$$
$$dA_1 = \omega_{10}A + \omega_{11}A_1 + \omega_{12}A_2$$
$$dA_2 = \omega_{20}A + \omega_{21}A_1 + \omega_{22}A_2$$

with the relation

$$\omega_{00} + \omega_{11} + \omega_{22} = 0$$

The most general moving frame thus depends on $q = 8$ parameters, which is the number of parameters of the plane projective group.

The moving frame method can be applied in a straightforward fashion to this case and we do not give the details here. The interested reader is referred to [4]. We find that, in order to get to the Frenet frame, we have to consider frames of order up to 6.

The differential ω_{01} is exact. Let $\omega_{01} = d\sigma$ where σ is called the projective arc length parameter. The secondary coefficient $\frac{\omega_{10}}{\omega_{01}}$ of order 6 is an invariant of order 7. We write

$$\frac{\omega_{10}}{\omega_{01}} = \frac{\omega_{10}}{d\sigma} = -k$$

where k is the projective curvature. Frames of order 6 are the Frenet frames and we have the following equations

$$\frac{dA}{d\sigma} = A_1$$
$$\frac{dA_1}{d\sigma} = -kA + A_2 \tag{48}$$
$$\frac{dA_2}{d\sigma} = -A - kA_1$$

5.1 Geometric interpretation

We now give a useful geometric interpretation of the projective arclength. Let us consider two points A and B on a curve (c), the tangent T_A to (c) at A, the tangent T_B to (c) at B and the chord $\langle A, B \rangle$. We then consider the pencil of conics going through the points A and B and tangent there to T_A and T_B. The equation of each conic in this pencil can be written as

$$T_A T_B + \lambda \langle A, B \rangle^2$$

where λ varies between $-\infty$ and ∞. Indeed the degenerate conic (c_1) composed of the two lines T_A and T_B of equation $T_A T_B = 0$ and the degenerate conic (c_2) composed of the double line $\langle A, B \rangle$ of equation $\langle A, B \rangle^2 = 0$ both belong to the pencil, the first one being obtained for the value $\lambda_1 = 0$ of λ, the second for the value $\lambda_2 = \infty$. Among the conics of this pencil, there is one (c_A) with a contact of order 3 with the curve (c) at A and one, (c_B) with a contact of order 3 with the curve (c) at B. Let λ_A (resp. λ_B) the corresponding values of the projective parameter λ. We consider the cross-ratio of the four conics $((c_A), (c_B), (c_1), (c_2))$. It is a projective invariant equal to the ratio λ_A / λ_B. We relate it to the projective arc-length $\sigma_B - \sigma_A$ between the two points A and B on the curve (c).

Let us consider the Frenet frame (A, A_1, A_2) at A. We represent each each point M of the projective plane by its coordinates x, y in this coordinate system, i.e.:

$$M = A + xA_1 + yA_2$$

Finally, we choose A as the origin of arclength σ. Let $X(\sigma), Y(\sigma)$ be the coordinates of B and let us compute the equations of $T_A, T_B, \langle A, B \rangle$. Clearly, since $T_A \equiv \langle A, A_1 \rangle$, the equation of T_A is simply $y = 0$. Since $\mathbf{B} = \mathbf{A} + X\mathbf{A}_1 + Y\mathbf{A}_2$, we have $B_1 = X'\mathbf{A}_1 + Y'\mathbf{A}_2$ where $'$ indicates the derivative with respect to arclength. Since $T_B \equiv \langle B, B_1 \rangle$, the equation of T_B is $(X - x)Y' + (y - Y)X' = 0$. Finally, the equation of $\langle A, B \rangle$ is $yX - xY = 0$. The equation of our pencil of conics can thus be written as:

$$((X - x)Y' + (y - Y)X')y + \lambda(yX - xY)^2 = 0 \tag{49}$$

Let us now compute λ_A and λ_B. To find λ_A, we rewrite (49) as:

$$y = -\frac{\lambda}{XY' - X'Y - xY' + yX'}(yX - xY)^2 =$$
$$-\frac{\lambda}{XY' - X'Y}(yX - xY)^2 (1 - \frac{-xY' + yX'}{XY' - X'Y} + \cdots$$

expanding the square we find:

$$y = -\frac{\lambda Y^2}{XY' - X'Y}x^2 + \alpha xy + \beta y^2 + \text{terms of higher degree in } x \text{ and } y$$

Since the reduced equation of the curve (c) is $y = \frac{x^2}{2} + o(x^4)$ ([4]), the conic (c_A) of the pencil which has a contact of order 3 with (c) at A is defined by:

$$\lambda_A = \frac{X'Y - XY'}{2Y^2} \tag{50}$$

The Frenet frame at B is defined by B and B_1 which we have already discussed and B_2 whose coordinates in the Frenet frame at A are X'' and Y''. Thus the equation of the line $\langle B, B_2 \rangle$ is $(X - x)Y'' + (y - Y)X'' = 0$. We let $u = (X - x)Y'' + (y - Y)X''$ and $v = (X - x)Y' + (y - Y)X'$. The equation of (c) in the Frenet frame (B, B_1, B_2) can be written $v = \frac{u^2}{2} + o(u^4)$. A straightforward computation shows that x and y can be expressed as functions of u and v as follows:

$$x = X + \frac{vX'' - uX'}{Y''X' - Y'X''} \qquad y = Y + \frac{vY'' - uY'}{Y''X' - Y'X''}$$

This allows us to rewrite equation (49) as follows:

$$v(Y + \frac{vY'' - uY'}{Y''X' - Y'X''}) + \lambda(\frac{v(XY'' - X''Y) + u(X'Y - Y'X)}{Y''X' - Y'X''})^2$$

from where it follows that:

$$v = -\frac{\lambda}{Y(Y''X' - Y'X'')^2}(u^2(X'Y - XY')^2 + \alpha uv + \beta v^2)\frac{1}{1 + \frac{vY'' - uY'}{Y(Y''X' - Y'X'')}}$$

and therefore:

$$v = -\frac{\lambda(X'Y - XY')^2}{Y(Y''X' - Y'X'')^2}u^2 + \gamma uv + \delta v^2 + \text{terms of higher degree in } u \text{ and } v$$

Since the reduced equation of the curve (c) is $v = \frac{u^2}{2} + o(u^4)$, the conic (c_B) of the pencil which has a contact of order 3 with (c) at B is defined by:

$$\lambda_B = -\frac{Y(Y''X' - Y'X'')^2}{2(X'Y - XY')^2} \tag{51}$$

From this we write the ratio λ_A/λ_B:

$$\frac{\lambda_A}{\lambda_B} = \frac{(XY' - X'Y)^3}{Y^3(Y''X' - Y'X'')^2}$$

Considering the fact that we have $Y = \frac{X^2}{2} - \frac{X^5}{20} + o(X^7)$ (see for example [4]), we find that:

$$\log^{1/3}(\frac{\lambda_A}{\lambda_B}) = (\frac{11}{10})^{1/3}X + o(X^2)$$

Since $X = \sigma + O(\sigma^2)$ ([4]), we have obtained the following important result:

Proposition 3. *Let A and B be two points of a curve (c) and σ be the projective arc-length of the portion of the curve between A and B. If we consider the four conics $(c_1), (c_2), (c_A), (c_B)$ defined above and belonging to the pencil of conics tangent in A to the tangent to (c) at A and in B to the tangent to (c) at B, we can define their cross-ratio $\tau = \{(c_1), (c_2); (c_A), (c_B)\}$. We have the following property:*

$$\lim_{\sigma \to 0} \frac{\log^{1/3}\tau}{\sigma} = (\frac{11}{10})^{1/3}$$

This proposition gives a geometric interpretation of the projective arclength.

5.2 Analytic determination of the arc length parameter and projective curvature

We shall use a method which is somewhat different from the affine case, i.e., the method of differential equations. This gives a complementary insight, even if the moving frame theory is more geometrical. We thus consider a point A of a plane curve (c) parametrized by t with projective coordinates $x_0(t), x_1(t), x_2(t)$. We let $\mathbf{A} = [x_0(t), x_1(t), x_2(t)]^T$. The coordinates x_i of A all satisfy the same third order differential equation obtained by setting the determinant of order 4

$$\begin{vmatrix} \theta''' & \theta'' & \theta' & \theta \\ A''' & A'' & A' & A \end{vmatrix}$$

to 0 (take $\theta = x_i$, $i = 0, 1, 2$).

We write this equation in the following form

$$\theta''' + p\theta'' + q\theta' + r\theta = 0 \qquad (52)$$

by letting

$$p = -\frac{\left|\mathbf{A}''' \; \mathbf{A}' \; \mathbf{A}\right|}{\left|\mathbf{A}'' \; \mathbf{A}' \; \mathbf{A}\right|} \quad q = \frac{\left|\mathbf{A}''' \; \mathbf{A}'' \; \mathbf{A}\right|}{\left|\mathbf{A}'' \; \mathbf{A}' \; \mathbf{A}\right|} \quad r = -\frac{\left|\mathbf{A}''' \; \mathbf{A}'' \; \mathbf{A}'\right|}{\left|\mathbf{A}'' \; \mathbf{A}' \; \mathbf{A}\right|}$$

and excluding the points of inflexion for which

$$\left|\mathbf{A}'' \; \mathbf{A}' \; \mathbf{A}\right| = 0$$

Equation (52) defines a class of curves projectively equal to each other and to the curve (c), but it does not necessarily give all curves projectively equal to (c). In effect, if we change $\mathbf{A}$ into $\overline{\mathbf{A}} = \lambda(t)\mathbf{A}$, we obtain a new equation (52) which, from the same curve (c), also defines curves that are projectively equal to it. This also applies to the change of parameter $t \to \bar{t} = f(t)$. This indeterminacy allows us to simplify the equation (52). We look for two functions $\lambda(t)$ and $f(t)$ in order to eliminate the terms in θ' and θ'' in the equation. We shall see that there are infinitely many possible ways, as $\bar{t}$ is only defined up to homography.

Reducing the differential equation We thus want to convert the equation

$$\frac{d^3\mathbf{A}}{dt^3} + p\frac{d^2\mathbf{A}}{dt^2} + q\frac{d\mathbf{A}}{dt} + r\mathbf{A} = 0 \qquad (53)$$

to the form

$$\frac{d^3\overline{\mathbf{A}}}{d\bar{t}^3} + \bar{r}\overline{\mathbf{A}} = 0 \qquad (54)$$

by means of the transformations

$$\overline{\mathbf{A}} = \lambda(t)\mathbf{A}$$
$$\bar{t} = f(t)$$

In the following, we represent derivatives in t by superscripts. We easily compute the following expressions

$$\frac{d\overline{\mathbf{A}}}{d\bar{t}} = \frac{d\overline{\mathbf{A}}}{dt}\frac{dt}{d\bar{t}} = \frac{\lambda'}{f'}\mathbf{A} + \frac{\lambda}{f'}\mathbf{A}',$$

$$\frac{d^2\overline{\mathbf{A}}}{d\bar{t}^2} = (\frac{\lambda''}{f'^2} - \frac{\lambda'f''}{f'^3})\mathbf{A} + (\frac{2\lambda'}{f'^2} - \frac{\lambda f''}{f'^3})\mathbf{A}' + \frac{\lambda}{f'^2}\mathbf{A}'',$$

$$\frac{d^3\overline{\mathbf{A}}}{d\bar{t}^3} + \bar{r}\overline{\mathbf{A}} = (\frac{\lambda'''}{f'^3} - \frac{3\lambda''f''}{f'^4} - \frac{\lambda'f'''}{f'^4} + \frac{3\lambda'f''^2}{f'^5} + \bar{r}\lambda)\mathbf{A}$$

$$+ (\frac{3\lambda''}{f'^3} - \frac{6\lambda'f''}{f'^4} - \frac{\lambda f'''}{f'^4} + \frac{3\lambda f''^2}{f'^5})\mathbf{A}'$$

$$+ (\frac{3\lambda'}{f'^3} - \frac{3\lambda f''}{f'^4})\mathbf{A}'' + \frac{\lambda}{f'^3}\mathbf{A}'''.$$

Thus in order to determine $\bar{r}(t)$, $\lambda(t)$, $f(t)$ we obtain the system of three equations

$$\frac{3\lambda'}{\lambda} - \frac{3f''}{f'} = p$$

$$\frac{3\lambda''}{\lambda} - \frac{6\lambda'}{\lambda}\frac{f''}{f'} - \frac{f'''}{f'} + \frac{3f''^2}{f'^2} = q$$

$$\frac{\lambda'''}{\lambda} - \frac{3\lambda''}{\lambda}\frac{f''}{f'} - \frac{\lambda'}{\lambda}\frac{f'''}{f'} + \frac{3\lambda'}{\lambda}\frac{f''^2}{f'^2} + \bar{r}f'^3 = r$$

The first equation gives the ratio $\frac{\lambda'}{\lambda}$

$$\frac{\lambda'}{\lambda} - \frac{f''}{f'} = \frac{p}{3} \tag{55}$$

hence the ratio $\frac{\lambda''}{\lambda}$ by derivation. If we replace these two ratios by their expressions in the second equation after simplifying, we obtain

$$\frac{1}{2}\frac{f'''}{f'} - \frac{3}{4}\frac{f''^2}{f'^2} = -\frac{1}{12}p^2 - \frac{1}{4}p' + \frac{1}{4}q \tag{56}$$

The first member of this equation is the *Schwarzian* of $\bar{t}$ with respect to t. Once $\bar{t}$ is known we deduce λ by means of (55).

We easily see that $\bar{t}$ is defined only up to homography. In effect we have the following proposition

Proposition 4. *If we consider two functions $f(t)$ and $F(t)$ of the same variable t, then a necessary and sufficient condition for F and f to be related by a homographic relation with fixed coefficients*

$$F(t) = \frac{af(t) + b}{cf(t) + d}$$

is that the Schwarzians $\{F\}_t$ and $\{f\}_t$ are equal.

Proof. The proof involves eliminating the three unknown parameters defining the homographic transformation by successive derivations. We first obtain

$$F'(t) = \frac{(ad - bc)f'(t)}{(cf(t) + d)^2}$$

and the logarithmic derivative of both sides of this equation gives

$$\frac{F''(t)}{F'(t)} = \frac{f''(t)}{f'(t)} - \frac{2f'(t)}{f(t) + \frac{d}{c}}$$

A further derivation eliminates the constant $\frac{d}{c}$ giving the equation

$$\frac{F'''(t)}{F'(t)} - \frac{3}{2}\frac{F''^2(t)}{F'^2(t)} = \frac{f'''(t)}{f'(t)} - \frac{3}{2}\frac{f''^2(t)}{f'^2(t)}$$

i.e., as required

$$\{F\}_t = \{f\}_t$$

It follows that if we consider the cross-ratio of the four values of $\bar{t}$ corresponding to any four points of (c), this ratio does not depend on the particular choice of $\bar{t}$. This is an *invariant* for the four point system. We shall call it the four point *cross-ratio* on (c).

Projective arc length parameter If we take into account the expressions of $\bar{t}$ and of $\lambda(t)$ in the last equation of the previous system, this reduces to

$$\bar{r}f'^3 = r - \frac{1}{3}pq + \frac{2}{27}p^3 - \frac{1}{2}q' + \frac{1}{3}pp' + \frac{1}{6}p'' \equiv H(t) \tag{57}$$

which can also be written

$$\bar{r}d\bar{t}^3 = H dt^3$$

Thus whatever the choice of $\bar{t}$ as the solution of the Schwarz equation, the expression of $\bar{r}d\bar{t}^3$ always has the same value. We obtain the differential $d\sigma$ of the arc length parameter by letting

$$d\sigma^3 = \bar{r}d\bar{t}^3 = H dt^3$$

Thus we have

$$d\sigma = \bar{r}^{\frac{1}{3}}d\bar{t} = H^{\frac{1}{3}}dt \tag{58}$$

Since H involves derivatives of the fifth order, we find that the differential of the projective arc length parameter is an invariant of (c) of the fifth order.

Projective curvature Using σ to parametrize (c), equation (53) has no terms in $\frac{d^2\mathbf{A}}{d\sigma^2}$ and is written in the form

$$\frac{d^3\mathbf{A}}{d\sigma^3} + 2k\frac{d\mathbf{A}}{d\sigma} + h\mathbf{A} = 0$$

The quantities h and k are invariant by a projective transformation on (c), but they are not independent since, for any parameter t, we must have

$$d\sigma^3 = H dt^3$$

In particular, if we have $dt = d\sigma$, we have $H = 1$ which, taking into account equation (57) enables us to write

$$h - k' = 1$$

When parametrized by its projective arc length, the differential equation of the curve is written in the form

$$\frac{d^3\mathbf{A}}{d\sigma^3} + 2k\frac{d\mathbf{A}}{d\sigma} + (k' + 1)\mathbf{A} = 0 \tag{59}$$

This leaves only one invariant k in the equation, and it is the projective curvature introduced previously. As σ is the chosen parameter, we can compute the projective curvature, and

$$t = \sigma \ p = 0 \ q = 2k \ r = k' + 1$$

The Schwarzian $\{\bar{t}\}_\sigma$ of $\bar{t}$ with respect to σ is given by (equation (56))

$$\{\bar{t}\}_\sigma = \frac{1}{2}k$$

and we can deduce

$$k = 2\{\bar{t}\}_\sigma$$

To determine k we need the following theorem

Theorem 5. *Given two functions $x(t)$ and $y(t)$ of the same variable t, we have*

$$\{y\}_x dx^2 = [\{y\}_t - \{x\}_t]dt^2$$

Applying this theorem to $x(t) = \sigma(t)$ and $y(t) = \bar{t}(t)$, we obtain

$$\{\bar{t}\}_\sigma d\sigma^2 = [\{\bar{t}\}_t - \{\sigma\}_t]dt^2$$

hence, taking into account the expression of k, we have

$$k = 2\frac{\{\bar{t}\}_t - \{\sigma\}_t}{\frac{d\sigma}{dt}^2}$$

We know $\{\bar{t}\}_t$ and we need to compute $\{\sigma\}_t$. We have

$$\frac{d\sigma}{dt} = H^{\frac{1}{3}}$$

Deriving logarithmically

$$\frac{\sigma''}{\sigma'} = \frac{1}{3}\frac{H'}{H}$$

and a further derivative yields

$$\frac{\sigma'''}{\sigma'} - \frac{\sigma''^2}{\sigma'^2} = \frac{1}{3}\frac{H''}{H} - \frac{1}{3}\frac{H'^2}{H^2}$$

From these two relations we immediately deduce

$$\{\sigma\}_t = \frac{1}{2}\frac{\sigma'''}{\sigma'} - \frac{3}{4}\frac{\sigma''^2}{\sigma'^2} = \frac{1}{6}\frac{H''}{H} - \frac{7}{36}\frac{H'^2}{H^2}$$

Hence by replacement in the expression of k

$$k = H^{-\frac{2}{3}}[-\frac{1}{2}p' - \frac{1}{6}p^2 + \frac{1}{2}q - \frac{1}{3}\frac{H''}{H} + \frac{7}{18}\frac{H'^2}{H^2}] \tag{60}$$

Relation with unimodal affine geometry Let us suppose that the curve (c) is
parametrized by its affine arc length σ_a. The affine Frenet frame is a special case of the projective frame where the vectors e_1 and e_2 represent A_1
and A_2, two points of the line at infinity, whose projective coordinates are
$A_i = [e_i^T, 0]^T$, $i = 1, 2$. Also, the origin A_a of the frame defines a projective
point A_p with coordinates $A_p = [A_a^T, 1]^T$. According to the affine Frenet equations (33), the point $A(\sigma_a)$ satisfies the differential equation

$$\begin{vmatrix} \theta''' & \theta'' & \theta' & \theta \\ k_a e_1 & e_2 & e_1 & A_a \\ 0 & 0 & 0 & 1 \end{vmatrix} = 0$$

written in the form

$$\theta''' - k_a \theta' = 0$$

where k_a is the affine curvature. We thus have

$$p = 0 \quad q = -k_a \quad r = 0$$

The differential equation that gives the projective parameter $\bar{t}$ (equation (56))
is

$$\{\bar{t}\}_{\sigma_a} = -\frac{1}{4} k_a$$

As for the projective arc length σ_p (equation (57)), we have

$$H(\sigma_a) = \frac{1}{2} \frac{dk_a}{d\sigma_a}$$

By making this equation closer to the equation (60) we obtain the relation between the projective curvature k_p and the affine curvature

$$k_p = (\frac{k_a'}{2})^{-\frac{2}{3}} [-\frac{k_a}{2} - \frac{1}{3} \frac{k_a'''}{k_a'} + \frac{7}{18} (\frac{k_a''}{k_a'})^2] \tag{61}$$

where $'$ indicate a derivative in σ_a. We also obtain the relation between the
projective arc length and the affine arc length

$$\frac{d\sigma_p}{d\sigma_a} = (\frac{1}{2} \frac{dk_a}{d\sigma_a})^{\frac{1}{3}} \tag{62}$$

We can also consider the scale factor λ, a function of σ_p, which enables us
to transform from the affine point A_a to the normalized point of the projective
Frenet frame. We write that $A = \lambda A_a$ and we determine λ so that $|A \ A_1 \ A_2| = 1$. We then apply the affine and projective Frenet formulas

$$\begin{aligned} A_1 &= \lambda' A_a && +\lambda \frac{d\sigma_a}{d\sigma_p} e_1 \\ A_2 &= (\lambda'' + \lambda k) A_a &&+ (2\lambda' \frac{d\sigma_a}{d\sigma_p} + \lambda \frac{d^2\sigma_a}{d\sigma_p^2}) e_1 &&+ \lambda (\frac{d\sigma_a}{d\sigma_p})^2 k_a e_2 \end{aligned} \tag{63}$$

where $'$ indicates a derivative in σ_p and we find

$$\left| \mathbf{A} \; \mathbf{A}_1 \; \mathbf{A}_2 \right| = \lambda^3 (\frac{d\sigma_a}{d\sigma_p})^3 = 1$$

Hence, given the equation (62),

$$\lambda = (\frac{k'_a}{2})^{\frac{1}{3}} = \frac{d\sigma_p}{d\sigma_a} \tag{64}$$

where the $'$ indicates a derivative in σ_a.

5.3 Application to the evolution of curves

Similarly to the euclidean and affine cases (see sections 3.3 and 4.6), we are now going to consider the case of a family of curves. We use the same notations as in these sections and consider smooth embedded plane curves deforming in time. Let $\mathbf{A}(p, t) : \mathcal{S}^1 \times R \rightarrow \mathcal{P}^2$ be a family of such curves where p parametrizes the curve and t represents the time. Let σ be the projective arc-length along a curve of the family, a function of p and t. We now propose to study the following evolution equation:

$$\mathbf{A}_t = \mathbf{A}_{\sigma\sigma} \tag{65}$$

in which the partial with respect to t is taken at p constant and the partials with respect to σ are taken at t constant. This equation, as (24) and (41), can be thought of as a heat equation (because of the formal similarity with the usual heat equation) which is *intrinsic* to the curve. It has been studied by this author [5, 6].

Since a curve in the projective plane is defined up to an projective transformation by its arclength and curvature, it is natural to establish how they evolve in time when the curve changes according to (65). The key is of course to use the Frenet equations (48).

We use the equations (25), (26), (27) which are unchanged in the projective framework. We will also need the following expressions of the higher order derivatives of $\mathbf{A}$ with respect to the arc-length σ which we obtain from the Frenet formulae:

$$\mathbf{A}_{\sigma^3} = -2k\mathbf{A}_\sigma - (1 + k_\sigma)\mathbf{A} \tag{66}$$
$$\mathbf{A}_{\sigma^4} = (-k_{\sigma^2} + 2k^2)\mathbf{A} - (1 + 3k_\sigma)\mathbf{A}^{(1)} - 2k\mathbf{A}^{(2)} \tag{67}$$
$$\mathbf{A}_{\sigma^5} = (-k_{\sigma^3} + 7kk_\sigma + 3k)\mathbf{A} + 4(k^2 - k_{\sigma^2})\mathbf{A}^{(1)} - (1 + 5k_\sigma)\mathbf{A}^{(2)} \tag{68}$$

In these equations, we have written $\mathbf{A}^{(1)}$ and $\mathbf{A}^{(2)}$ instead of the usual $\mathbf{A}_1$ and $\mathbf{A}_2$ to avoid problems with partial derivatives.

Evolution of projective arc-length It is now easy to characterize the evolution of arc-length. We use the relation

$$\left| \mathbf{A}\ \mathbf{A}^{(1)}\ \mathbf{A}^{(2)} \right| = 1$$

and take its derivative with respect to t:

$$\left| \mathbf{A}\ \mathbf{A}^{(1)}\ \mathbf{A}^{(2)} \right|_t = \left| \mathbf{A}_t \mathbf{A}^{(1)} \mathbf{A}^{(2)} \right| + \left| \mathbf{A}\mathbf{A}_t^{(1)}\mathbf{A}^{(2)} \right| + \left| \mathbf{A}\mathbf{A}^{(1)}\mathbf{A}_t^{(2)} \right| = 0 \quad (69)$$

According to the equations (65) and (48) the first determinant is equal to $-k$. According to the equations (25), (66) and (48) we have

$$\mathbf{A}_t^{(1)} = \mathbf{A}_{t\sigma} = -\frac{g_t}{g}\mathbf{A}^{(1)} + \mathbf{A}_{\sigma^3} = -(\frac{g_t}{g} + 2k)\mathbf{A}^{(1)} - (1+k_\sigma)\mathbf{A}$$

and thus the second determinant of the right-hand side is equal to $-(\frac{g_t}{g} + 2k)$. Similarly, the second Frenet equation allows us to write

$$\mathbf{A}_t^{(2)} = \frac{\partial}{\partial t}(k\mathbf{A} + \mathbf{A}_{\sigma\sigma}) = k_t\mathbf{A} + k\mathbf{A}_{\sigma\sigma} + \mathbf{A}_{t\sigma\sigma}$$

Using equations (26) and (67), we can compute the coefficient of the term $\mathbf{A}^{(2)}$ in that expression which yields $-(2\frac{g_t}{g} + k)$ for the value of the third determinant in the right-hand side of equation (69). Adding these three values and equating them to zero, we obtain

$$\mathbf{A}_{t\sigma} \wedge \mathbf{A}_{\sigma\sigma} = (k - \frac{g_t}{g})\mathbf{A}_\sigma \wedge \mathbf{A}_{\sigma\sigma} = k - \frac{g_t}{g}$$

Similarly, using equations (26) and (43), we obtain

$$g_t = -\frac{4}{3}kg \quad (70)$$

which is the projective analog of (31) and (45).

Evolution of projective curvature The principle of the method is once again to use a differential equation that is satisfied by each curve of the family. We can write equation (66) as

$$\mathbf{A}_{\sigma^3} + 2k\mathbf{A}_\sigma = -(1+k_\sigma)\mathbf{A}$$

The two sides of this equation represent the same projective point., i.e. A. The projective point represented by the left-hand side follows the same curve, for a constant value of p, as the point A. This implies that the tangents must be the same, and therefore that the two vectors $\mathbf{A} \wedge \mathbf{A}_t$ and $\mathbf{A} \wedge \frac{\partial}{\partial t}(\mathbf{A}_{\sigma^3} + 2k\mathbf{A}_\sigma)$ are parallel. Using equations (65) and the Frenet equations, it is easy to show that

$$\mathbf{A} \wedge \mathbf{A}_t = \mathbf{A} \wedge \mathbf{A}^{(2)} \quad (71)$$

In order to compute $\frac{\partial}{\partial t}(\mathbf{A}_{\sigma^3} + 2k\mathbf{A}_\sigma)$ we use equations (25), (27) et (68) to obtain

$$\mathbf{A}\wedge\frac{\partial}{\partial t}(\mathbf{A}_{\sigma^3}+2k\mathbf{A}_\sigma) = (2k_t-4k_{\sigma^2}+4k\frac{g_t}{g}-[\frac{g_t}{g}]_{\sigma^2})\mathbf{A}\wedge\mathbf{A}^{(1)}-(1+5k_\sigma+3[\frac{g_t}{g}]_\sigma)\mathbf{A}\wedge\mathbf{A}^{(2)}$$

$$(72)$$

The condition that the two vectors are parallel is thus equivalent to the two equations

$$2k_t - 4k_{\sigma^2} + 4k\frac{g_t}{g} - [\frac{g_t}{g}]_{\sigma^2} = 0$$
$$1 + 5k_\sigma + 3[\frac{g_t}{g}]_\sigma = \alpha$$

where α is a function that is equal to $1 + k_\sigma$ according to the equation (70). Replacing in the first equation the value of $\frac{g_t}{g}$ and of its second order derivative with respect to σ computed from the second equation, we obtain the sought-for evolution equation:

$$k_t = \frac{4}{3}(k_{\sigma^2} + 2k^2)$$

$$(73)$$

which is the projective analog of (32) and (46).

Evolution of the affine arc-length and curvature We now relate the previous results to affine geometry for two reasons. The first reason is that the analog of equation (65) has been studied in the affine case and therefore it is interesting to compare the evolutions of the curve in the two cases. the second reason is that, in some sense, the affine results will shed some light on the projective ones.

Let then $E_i, i = 1, \cdots, 4$ be the standard projective basis of $\mathcal{P}^2$ which is represented by the standard basis of R^3 and the vector $[1, 1, 1]^T$. The set $\mathcal{P}^2\backslash\langle E_1, E_2\rangle$ i.e. the projective plane minus the "line at infinity" is isomorphic to the affine plane $\mathcal{A}^2$. This identification allows to define a family of curves embedded in $\mathcal{A}^2$ from a family of curves embedded in $\mathcal{P}^2$.

Let X, Y and Z be the coordinates of the vector $\mathbf{A}$ representing the projective point A belonging to one the curves in the family. Since we are interested in the part of the curve included in $\mathcal{A}^2$, we can assume that $Z \neq 0$. Let $\mathbf{a} = \frac{1}{Z}\mathbf{A}$ be the representative of the point A in $\mathcal{A}^2$. At each time instant t, we can assume that this point is parametrized by its projective arc-length σ_p. From section 4 we know that we can define an affine arc-length as

$$\frac{d\sigma_a}{d\sigma_p} = \mid \mathbf{E}_3, \mathbf{a}_{\sigma_p}, \mathbf{a}_{\sigma_p\sigma_p} \mid^{\frac{1}{3}}$$

if we stay away from the inflection points where $\mathbf{a}_{\sigma_p} \wedge \mathbf{a}_{\sigma_p\sigma_p} = 0$. We use the affine Frenet equations (33) in

$$\frac{d\mathbf{a}}{d\sigma_a} = \mathbf{e}_1$$

$$\frac{d\mathbf{e}_1}{d\sigma_a} = \mathbf{e}_2$$

$$\frac{d\mathbf{e}_2}{d\sigma_a} = k_a\mathbf{e}_1$$

We consider the vectors e_1 and e_2 as vectors of R^3 whose last coordinate is 0 to be compatible with our study of $\mathcal{P}^2$. The vectors e_1 and e_2 are related by

$$e_1 \wedge e_2 = \mathbf{E}_3 \tag{74}$$

We have also derived in a previous section the following relations between the affine and projective Frenet frames (equations (63))

$$\mathbf{A}^{(1)} = Z_{\sigma_p} \mathbf{a} + Z \frac{d\sigma_a}{d\sigma_p} e_1$$

$$\mathbf{A}^{(2)} = (Z_{\sigma_p \sigma_p} + Z k_p) \mathbf{a} + (2 Z_{\sigma_p} \frac{d\sigma_a}{d\sigma_p} + Z \frac{d^2 \sigma_a}{d\sigma_p^2}) e_1 + Z (\frac{d\sigma_a}{d\sigma_p})^2 e_2$$

and (equation (64))

$$Z = \frac{d\sigma_p}{d\sigma_a}$$

If we now consider for convenience the quantity

$$\Lambda = \frac{1}{2} \frac{dk_a}{d\sigma_a} \tag{75}$$

we can prove (see [5, 6] for details) the following two results

Proposition 6. *Let* $h = \frac{d\sigma_a}{dp}$, *the temporal evolution of the affine arc-length is*

$$h_t = -\frac{h}{3} (4k_p + \Lambda^{-\frac{2}{3}} (\frac{\Lambda_{\sigma_a \sigma_a}}{\Lambda} - (\frac{\Lambda_{\sigma_a}}{\Lambda})^2)) \tag{76}$$

and

Proposition 7. *The function* Λ *evolves according to the equation*

$$\Lambda_t = \Lambda^{\frac{1}{3}} [\frac{\Lambda_{\sigma_a \sigma_a}}{\Lambda} - (\frac{\Lambda_{\sigma_a}}{\Lambda})^2] = \Lambda^{\frac{1}{3}} [\log | \Lambda |]_{\sigma_a \sigma_a} \tag{77}$$

Moreover, if we perform the change of variable $V = \frac{1}{3} \log \Lambda^2$, V *evolves according to the equation*

$$V_t = e^{-V} V_{\sigma_a \sigma_a} \tag{78}$$

Looking back at equation (61) giving the relation between the projective and affine curvatures, we see that equation (77) allows to compute the ratio $\frac{k_a'''}{k_a'} = \frac{\Lambda_{\sigma_a \sigma_a}}{\Lambda}$ which involves a *third order* derivative of the affine curvature with respect to the affine arc length as a function of the second order derivatives of the affine curvature with respect to the affine arc length and the time parameter of the projective evolution equation (65). Thus, just as in the affine case we gain one order of derivation if we trade space (arc length) for time (scale).

6 Conclusion

This article is a general introduction to Cartan's moving frame method which is elegant, simple, and of an algorithmic nature. We have demonstrated how to use it systematically on three examples relevant to computer vision, curves in the euclidean, affine and projective planes, and derived the corresponding Frenet equations. We have then used these equations to show that the analysis of the deformation of plane curves according to an intrinsic heat equation could be done in a common framework, yielding very similar expressions for the evolution of the three curvature invariants.

References

1. Luis Alvarez, Frédéric Guichard, Pierre-Louis Lions, and Jean-Michel Morel. Axioms and Fundamental Equations of Image Processing. Technical Report 9231, CEREMADE, 1992.
2. Elie Cartan. *La Théorie des Groupes Finis et Continus et la Géométrie Différentielle traitée par la Méthode du Repère Mobile.* Jacques Gabay, 1992. Original edition, Gauthiers-Villars, 1937.
3. Elie Cartan. *Leçons sur la Théorie des Espaces à Connexion Projective.* Jacques Gabay, 1992. Original edition, Gauthiers-Villars, 1937.
4. O.D. Faugeras. Géométrie affine et projective en vision par ordinateur : I le cas des courbes. Technical report, INRIA, 1993. To appear.
5. Olivier Faugeras. On the evolution of simple curves of the real projective plane. *Comptes rendus de l'Académie des Sciences de Paris, Tome 317, Série I,* (6):565–570, September 1993. Also INRIA Technical report number 1998.
6. Olivier Faugeras. On the evolution of simple curves of the real projective plane. Technical Report 1998, INRIA, 1993.
7. L. M. J. Florack, B. M. ter Haar Romeny, J. J. Koenderink, and M. A. Viergever. Scale and the differential structure of images. *Image and Vision Computing,* 10:376–388, July/August 1992.
8. M. Gage. An isometric inequality with applications to curve shortening. *Duke Mathematical Journal,* 50:1225–1229, 1983.
9. M. Gage. Curve shortening makes convex curves circular. *Invent. Math.,* 76:357–364, 1984.
10. M. Gage and R.S. Hamilton. The heat equation shrinking convex plane curves. *J. of Differential Geometry,* 23:69–96, 1986.
11. M. Grayson. The heat equation shrinks embedded plane curves to round points. *J. of Differential Geometry,* 26:285–314, 1987.
12. Benjamin B. Kimia, Allen Tannenbaum, and Steven W. Zucker. On the Evolution of Curves via a Function of Curvature. I. The Classical Case. *Journal of Mathematical Analysis and Applications,* 163(2):438–458, 1992.
13. Jan J. Koenderink. *Solid Shape.* MIT Press, 1990.
14. J.J. Koenderink and A.J. van Doorn. Dynamic shape. *Biological Cybernetics,* 53:383–396, 1986.
15. A. Mackworth and F. Mokhtarian. Scale-Based description and recognition of planar curves and two-dimensional shapes. *IEEE Transactions on Pattern Analysis and Machine Intelligence,* 8(1), January 1986.

16. Joseph L. Mundy and Andrew Zimmerman, editors. *Geometric Invariance in Computer Vision*. MIT Press, 1992.
17. A.H. Salden, B.M. ter Haar Romeny, and M. Viergever. Affine and projective differential geometric invariants of space curves. In Baba Vemuri, editor, *Geometric Methods in Computer Vision II*, pages 60–74. SPIE, July 1993.
18. Guillermo Sapiro and Allen Tannenbaum. Affine shortening of Non-Convex Plane Curve. Technical Report EE PUB 845, Technion Israel Institute of Technology-Haifa, August 1992.
19. Guillermo Sapiro and Allen Tannenbaum. On Affine Plane Curve Evolution. Technical Report EE PUB 821, Technion Israel Institute of Technology-Haifa, February 1992.
20. Guillermo Sapiro and Allen Tannenbaum. Affine Invariant Scale Space. *The International Journal of Computer Vision*, 11(1):25–44, August 1993.
21. Guillermo Sapiro and Allen Tannenbaum. On Invariant Curve Evolution and Image Analysis. *Indiana University Journal of Mathematics*, 1993. To appear.
22. Joel Smoller. *Shock Waves and Reaction-diffusion Equations*. Springer-Verlag, New-York, 1983.
23. A.P. Witkin. Scale-space filtering. In *Proceedings of the International Joint Conference on Artificial Conference*, pages 1019–1021, 1983.

Representation of Three-Dimensional Object Structure as Cross-Ratios of Determinants of Stereo Image Points

Eamon Barrett   Gregory Gheen   Paul Payton

Lockheed Missiles and Space Company, 1111 Lockheed Way
Sunnyvale, California, USA 94089

Abstract. A uniform algebraic procedure is presented for deriving both epipolar geometry and three-dimensional object structure from general stereo imagery. The procedure assumes central-projection cameras of unknown interior and exterior orientations. The ability to determine corresponding points in the stereo images is assumed, but no prior knowledge of the scene is required. Epipolar geometry and the fundamental matrix are derived by algebraic elimination of the object-variables from the imaging equations. This provides a transfer procedure to any other perspective as long as 8 or more corresponding points can be identified in the new perspective. Next, invariant coordinates of the scene-points are derived by algebraic elimination of the camera-parameters from the imaging equations. Identical coordinates are obtained from any stereo images of non-occluding scene points as long as the same set of 5 corresponding points can be identified in both stereo pairs. The procedure extends methods utilizing the cross-ratios of determinants and cyclopean vectors, presented in earlier work. A technique for reconstructing the 3-dimensional object from the invariant coordinates is also given.

1. Introduction

Consider the scenario where the only information known about a general distribution of points in 3-space is obtained from a pair of stereo images and the knowledge that the images were formed by "central projection". No other information regarding the camera stations or the spatial locations of the object points is assumed. Invariant methods can provide answers to the following questions:

(1) How are the parameters of the camera stations related to each other? (relative orientation)
(2) What would the object points look like, in an image acquired by a third camera station? (transfer)
(3) What are the positions of the object points, relative to each other? (spatial structure, and scene reconstruction)

The first and second questions are addressed by a collection of results that involve "epipolar geometry." The third question has been addressed for 3-D objects by a collection of recent, and ingenious theorems [3,5,6,7,8] extending the epipolar methods so as to capture the relative positions of the object points. These theorems imply the following general observations:

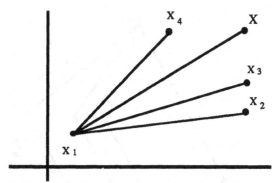

Fig. 1 $C_1(X)$ = cross ratio of the 4 rays joining X_1 to X_2, X_3, X_4 and X

If the object points are known to be coplanar, four "salient" points are selected as a basis for the remainder. To avoid singularities in the algorithm, it is important that no three salient points be colinear. One point is selected as an origin, and a pencil of three rays from this origin, X_1, to the other three points, $X_2X_3X_4$, is constructed. For any fifth "general" point, X, a fourth ray is constructed from X_1 through X. The cross-ratio of this "pencil" of four rays is computed, and becomes the first" invariant coordinate" $C_1(X)$ of the point, X. This is illustrated in Figure 1. A second invariant coordinate is constructed by using a different point, X_2, as origin, and the pencil of 4 rays joining X_2 to X_1, X_3, X_4, and X is constructed. The cross-ratio $C_2(X)$ becomes the second invariant coordinate of X.

These invariant coordinates $C_1(X)$, $C_2(X)$ can be derived from any single image of the distribution of coplanar object points. The characterization is entirely view-independent; once the different observers agree on the same basis-set X_1 ... X_4, their characterizations of any general point $[C_1(X), C_2(X)]$, will be identical. Any general curve, $F(C_1(X), C_2(X)) = 0$, will have the same characterization for all viewers, even though its appearance may vary from image to image due to perspective distortion.

New results emerging from invariance research enable us to extend this principle to three dimensional distributions of object points. Five "salient" object points are required, X_1 ... X_5. To avoid singularities in the algorithm it is important that no four salient points be coplanar. Two, e.g. X_1 and X_2, are selected, and the line passing from X_1 through X_2 becomes the "spine" of a pencil of three planes; $X_1X_2X_3$, $X_1X_2X_4$, $X_1X_2X_5$. For any general point X, a fourth plane in this pencil may be constructed, X_1X_2X. The cross-ratio of these four *planes* is the first invariant coordinate of X; $C_1(X)$. This is illustrated in Figure 2 The procedure is repeated for two other choices of the "spine" of the pencil...e.g. X_2X_3 and X_3X_1. The resulting set of cross-ratios of planes: $C_1(X)$, $C_2(X)$, $C_3(X)$ provides an invariant characterization, in terms of the basis set (X_1 ... X_5), of three planes in space "hinged" on the spines X_1X_2, X_2X_3 and X_3X_1. These three plane intersect at the general point X, except for points in the "plane of indeterminacy" containing all three "spines". Points in this plane can be determined by a different selection of "salient" points and spines.

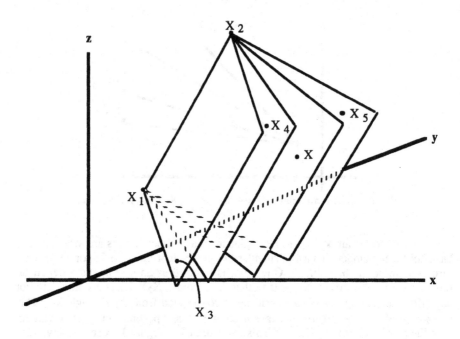

Fig. 2 $C_1(X)$ = cross-ratio of the 4 planes: $X_1X_2X_3$, $X_1X_2X_4$, $X_1X_2X_5$, X_1X_2X

The remarkable fact that these cross-ratios of planes in object space can be computed from functions of conjugate pairs of image points in stereo images is derivable by geometric procedures from the extensions of epipolar geometry referenced above.

In the following pages, a uniform algebraic procedure is presented for deriving both epipolar geometry and 3-dimensional object structure from stereo imagery. The procedure consists of two steps. First, the object-variables are algebraically eliminated from the imaging equations. This produces a "pure" relationship between image-points and camera parameters. The fundamental matrix, and epipolar geometry, are a consequence of this elimination.

In the second step, the camera-parameters are algebraically eliminated from the imaging equations. This produces a "pure" relationship between image points and object-points. The algebraic method extends the "ratio-of-determinants" technique described in earlier work [1]. From this pure relationship between object and image-points, 3-D invariant coordinates of the object points are formed as cross-ratios of planes in object-space, or equivalently cross-ratios of volumes of tetrahedra. Any general distribution of object points will have the same characterization for all viewers who "agree" on the same set of basis points (X_1 ... X_5), even though the appearance of the distribution of points may vary among the multiple images due to perspective distortion.

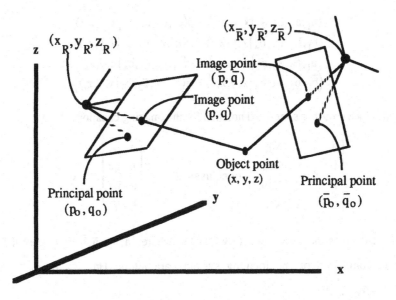

Fig. 3 Imaging System Configuration

2. Notation for the Camera Models

The two camera stations used to take a stereo pair of images are illustrated in Figure 3. The imaging equations may be written as:

$$p - p_o = F \frac{\langle m_{11}, m_{12}, m_{13} | x - x_R, y - y_R, z - z_R \rangle}{\langle m_{31}, m_{32}, m_{33} | x - x_R, y - y_R, z - z_R \rangle}$$

$$q - q_o = F \frac{\langle m_{21}, m_{22}, m_{23} | x - x_R, y - y_R, z - z_R \rangle}{\langle m_{31}, m_{32}, m_{33} | x - x_R, y - y_R, z - z_R \rangle}$$

$$\bar{p} - \bar{p}_o = \bar{F} \frac{\langle \bar{m}_{11}, \bar{m}_{12}, \bar{m}_{13} | x - x_{\bar{R}}, y - y_{\bar{R}}, z - z_{\bar{R}} \rangle}{\langle \bar{m}_{31}, \bar{m}_{32}, \bar{m}_{33} | x - x_{\bar{R}}, y - y_{\bar{R}}, z - z_{\bar{R}} \rangle} \tag{1}$$

$$\bar{q} - \bar{q}_o = \bar{F} \frac{\langle \bar{m}_{21}, \bar{m}_{22}, \bar{m}_{23} | x - x_{\bar{R}}, y - y_{\bar{R}}, z - z_{\bar{R}} \rangle}{\langle \bar{m}_{31}, \bar{m}_{32}, \bar{m}_{33} | x - x_{\bar{R}}, y - y_{\bar{R}}, z - z_{\bar{R}} \rangle}$$

where (p, q) are the coordinates in the image plane of the first camera and p_0 and q_0 is a translation of the image coordinate system from the optical axis, F is the focal length of the camera, the quantities m_{ij} are the elements of the rotation matrix that describes the orientation of the camera, and the vector (x_R, y_R, z_R) denotes the projection center of the first camera. Similar definitions for the "barred" quantities refer to the second camera station. Elementary algebraic manipulations allow us to re-write these equations as:

$$\langle a_1,a_2,a_3,a_4 \,|\, x,y,z,1\rangle = p\langle c_1,c_2,c_3,c_4 \,|\, x,y,z,1\rangle$$
$$\langle b_1,b_2,b_3,b_4 \,|\, x,y,z,1\rangle = q\langle c_1,c_2,c_3,c_4 \,|\, x,y,z,1\rangle$$
$$\langle \overline{a}_1,\overline{a}_2,\overline{a}_3,\overline{a}_4 \,|\, x,y,z,1\rangle = \overline{p}\langle \overline{c}_1,\overline{c}_2,\overline{c}_3,\overline{c}_4 \,|\, x,y,z,1\rangle$$
$$\langle \overline{b}_1,\overline{b}_2,\overline{b}_3,\overline{b}_4 \,|\, x,y,z,1\rangle = \overline{q}\langle \overline{c}_1,\overline{c}_2,\overline{c}_3,\overline{c}_4 \,|\, x,y,z,1\rangle \tag{2}$$

We introduce a further simplified notation for the imaging equations:

$$\begin{bmatrix} a \\ b \\ \overline{a} \\ \overline{b} \end{bmatrix} X = \begin{array}{c} \langle c|X\rangle p \\ \langle c|X\rangle q \\ \langle \overline{c}|X\rangle \overline{p} \\ \langle \overline{c}|X\rangle \overline{q} \end{array} \quad \text{or equivalently} \quad \begin{bmatrix} a-pc \\ b-qc \\ \overline{a}-\overline{p}\overline{c} \\ \overline{b}-\overline{q}\overline{c} \end{bmatrix} X = 0 \tag{3}$$

where X denotes the four-vector $(x,y,z,1)$ and where $\left(a,b,c,\overline{a},\overline{b},\overline{c}\right)$ represent four-vectors comprised of the imaging system parameters; $\left(m_{ij},X_R,p_0,q_0,F\right)$ and $\left(\overline{m}_{ij},X_{\overline{R}},\overline{p}_0,\overline{q}_0,\overline{F}\right)$.

Under certain conditions, the imaging equations (3) can be approximated by a set of linear equations. This leads to a simplification of the methods developed in this chapter. In order to realize this simplification, it is sufficient that the dimensions of the object under consideration be small in relationship to the range of the object from the imaging system. This is the case in many remote sensing applications. In addition, certain types of imaging systems (e.g., pushbroom sensors and SAR) are approximated by an orthogonal projection which is a special case of the affine transformation. Thus, a theory of image transfer and invariant coordinates for affine imaging is useful in a variety of applications [8].

To obtain a linear (or affine) relationship between the image coordinates (p, q) and the object position (x, y, z), a Taylor's expansion of (1) is performed at a point interest $X_o^t = \left[x_o, y_o, z_o\right]$. If the distance between X_o and an arbitrary point X is small, we obtain

$$p \cong p_o' + (x-x_o)\frac{\partial p}{\partial x}\Big|_{X=X_o} + (y-y_o)\frac{\partial p}{\partial y}\Big|_{X=X_o} + (z-z_o)\frac{\partial p}{\partial z}\Big|_{X=X_o}$$

$$q \cong q_o' + (x-x_o)\frac{\partial q}{\partial x}\Big|_{X=X_o} + (y-y_o)\frac{\partial q}{\partial y}\Big|_{X=X_o} + (z-z_o)\frac{\partial q}{\partial z}\Big|_{X=X_o} \tag{4}$$

with similar expressions for the barred quantities. The affine imaging equations can be written succinctly as

$$\langle a_1,a_2,a_3,a_4 | x,y,z,1 \rangle = p$$
$$\langle b_1,b_2,b_3,b_4 | x,y,z,1 \rangle = q$$
$$\langle \bar{a}_1,\bar{a}_2,\bar{a}_3,\bar{a}_4 | x,y,z,1 \rangle = \bar{p}$$
$$\langle \bar{b}_1,\bar{b}_2,\bar{b}_3,\bar{b}_4 | x,y,z,1 \rangle = \bar{q}$$

(5)

The four-vectors a, b, $\bar{a}$, and $\bar{b}$ can be written in terms of the camera parameters as

$$a_1 = \frac{\partial\, p}{\partial\, x}\bigg|_{X=X_o} = F \frac{\langle m_3 | X_o - X_R \rangle m_{11} - \langle m_1 | X_o - X_R \rangle m_{31}}{\langle m_3 | X_o - X_R \rangle^2}$$

$$a_2 = \frac{\partial\, p}{\partial\, y}\bigg|_{X=X_o} = F \frac{\langle m_3 | X_o - X_R \rangle m_{12} - \langle m_1 | X_o - X_R \rangle m_{32}}{\langle m_3 | X_o - X_R \rangle^2}$$

(6)

$$a_3 = \frac{\partial\, p}{\partial\, z}\bigg|_{X=X_o} = F \frac{\langle m_3 | X_o - X_R \rangle m_{13} - \langle m_1 | X_o - X_R \rangle m_{33}}{\langle m_3 | X_o - X_R \rangle^2}$$

$$a_4 = p_o' - a_1 x_o - a_2 y_o - a_3 z_o = F \frac{\langle m_1 | X_o - X_R \rangle}{\langle m_3 | X_o - X_R \rangle} - a_1 x_o - a_2 y_o - a_3 z_o$$

with similar expressions for the four-vectors b, $\bar{a}$, and $\bar{b}$. The imaging equations given in (5) are equivalent to those in (2) with c = [0, 0, 0, 1]. A detailed treatment of affine imaging is presented in [8].

3. Derivation of Transfer Vector and Fundamental Matrix from Image Measurements

The fundamental matrix can be derived from the observation that the imaging equations (3), i.e.

$$\begin{bmatrix} a - pc \\ b - qc \\ \bar{a} - \bar{p}c \\ \bar{b} - \bar{q}c \end{bmatrix} X = 0$$

(7)

implies that the coefficient determinant must vanish. Expanding this determinant, we have:

$$0 = \begin{vmatrix} a \\ b \\ \bar{a} \\ \bar{b} \end{vmatrix} - p \begin{vmatrix} c \\ b \\ \bar{a} \\ \bar{b} \end{vmatrix} - q \begin{vmatrix} a \\ c \\ \bar{a} \\ \bar{b} \end{vmatrix} - \bar{p} \begin{vmatrix} a \\ b \\ \bar{c} \\ \bar{b} \end{vmatrix} - \bar{q} \begin{vmatrix} a \\ b \\ \bar{a} \\ \bar{c} \end{vmatrix} + p\bar{p} \begin{vmatrix} c \\ b \\ \bar{c} \\ \bar{b} \end{vmatrix} + p\bar{q} \begin{vmatrix} c \\ b \\ \bar{a} \\ \bar{c} \end{vmatrix} + q\bar{p} \begin{vmatrix} a \\ c \\ \bar{c} \\ \bar{b} \end{vmatrix} + q\bar{q} \begin{vmatrix} a \\ c \\ \bar{a} \\ \bar{c} \end{vmatrix}$$

(8)

We refer to this nine-component vector of image-system parameters as the "transfer vector." If we denote the fundamental matrix (F) as (e_{ij}), and the fundamental equation of epipolar geometry as:

$$\begin{bmatrix} \bar{p} & \bar{q} & 1 \end{bmatrix} (e_{ij}) \begin{bmatrix} p \\ q \\ 1 \end{bmatrix} = 0 \tag{9}$$

then the transfer vector may be written in terms of the components of the fundamental matrix:

$$0 = e_{33} + p e_{31} + q e_{32} + \bar{p} e_{13} + \bar{q} e_{23} + p\bar{p} e_{11} + p\bar{q} e_{21} + q\bar{p} e_{12} + q\bar{q} e_{22} \tag{10}$$

The transfer vector, (and the fundamental matrix) have been determined, up to a multiplicative constant, by linear methods, once a minimum of eight conjugate image points are determined:

$$(p_i, q_i, \bar{p}_i, \bar{q}_i), \ i = 1 \dots 8 \tag{11}$$

This is accomplished simply by observing that if eight conjugate pairs are known, we can write the matrix-vector equation:

$$\begin{bmatrix} p_1\bar{p}_1 & p_1\bar{q}_1 & \cdots & \bar{p}_1 & \bar{q}_1 \\ p_2\bar{p}_2 & p_2\bar{q}_2 & \cdots & \bar{p}_2 & \bar{q}_2 \\ \vdots & \vdots & \cdots & \vdots & \vdots \\ p_7\bar{p}_7 & p_7\bar{q}_7 & \cdots & \bar{p}_7 & \bar{q}_7 \\ p_8\bar{p}_8 & p_8\bar{q}_8 & \cdots & \bar{p}_8 & \bar{q}_8 \end{bmatrix} \begin{bmatrix} e_{11} \\ e_{21} \\ \vdots \\ e_{13} \\ e_{23} \end{bmatrix} = -e_{33} \begin{bmatrix} 1 \\ 1 \\ \vdots \\ 1 \\ 1 \end{bmatrix} \tag{12}$$

Equation (12) can be solved for the (e_{ij}), (up to a multiplicative constant, e_{33}).

Alternative methods for estimating the coefficients (e_{ij}) from redundant measurements on conjugate image pairs and subsequently using the coefficients of (e_{ij}) to estimate epipolar points, epipolar lines, and to "transfer" point-pairs to new images, are now well-known. These methods are discussed in a variety of recent papers [2, 3, 4].

Under certain circumstances, only 4 conjugate pairs are required to determine the fundamental matrix. This occurs when $c = \bar{c}$. This restricted type of stereo image formation is referred to as "cyclopean imaging" and is treated in [1]. For cyclopean imaging, (10) simplifies to

$$e_{31} p + e_{32} q + e_{13} \bar{p} + e_{23} \bar{q} + e_{33} = 0, \tag{13}$$

because all the determinants in (8) that contain both c and $\bar{c}$ are singular. The affine approximation given in (5) is a special case of cyclopean imaging.

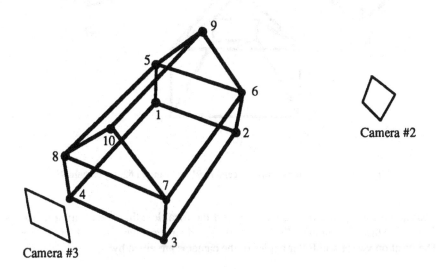

Fig. 4 Model of house with the three camera stations used in the simulations

The explicit representation of the fundamental matrix in terms of the parameters of interior and exterior orientation of the cameras tends to get lost in this derivation. The explicit representation of the fundamental matrix in terms of the camera parameters is derived in Chapter 23 of [5], and is repeated, for convenient reference, in the Appendix to the present chapter.

The transfer technique is illustrated with a simple example where the object consists of a line drawing of a house as shown in Figure 4. Here the house is shown along with the imaging planes of three cameras. The points of interest occur at the corners of the house and are given by the following set of three-dimensional Cartesian coordinates:

Point #1 - (5, 3, 0)	Point #2 - (5, -3, 0)
Point #3 - (-5, -3, 0)	Point #4 - (-5, 3, 0)
Point #5 - (5, 3, 3)	Point #6 - (5, -3, 3)
Point #7 - (-5, -3, 3)	Point #8 - (-5, 3, 3)
Point #9 - (5, 0, 6)	Point #10 - (-5, 0, 6)

The images from camera 1 and camera 2 are used to model the house with the transfer being performed to the perspective seen by camera 3. The camera parameters are: the

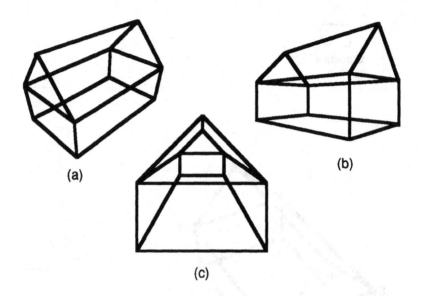

Fig. 5 Images of house from (a) camera #1, (b) camera #2, (c) camera #3.

position vector X_R, the rotation matrix, and the focal length. The rotation matrix is defined by the Euler angles $\Psi = (\theta_1, \phi, \theta_2)$. All cameras have a focal length $F = 1$. The position vector and Euler angles of the cameras are given by:

Camera #1	$X_R = (10, 10, 10)$	$\Psi = (45°, 130°, 90°)$
Camera #2	$X_R = (10, -10, 2)$	$\Psi = (-45°, 90°, 90°)$
Camera #3	$X_R = (-10, 0, 5)$	$\Psi = (180°, 90°, 90°)$

The images obtained by the three cameras are shown Figure 5a-c. To effect a transfer to camera 3 the fundamental matrix F13 derived from images 1 and 3 and the fundamental matrix F23 derived from images 2 and 3 are computed. The fundamental matrices can be obtained from the camera parameters if they are known or from the images only. Both approaches were tested and both produced the same fundamental matrices up to a constant. The values obtained for F13 and F23 are given by:

$$F13 = \begin{bmatrix} 1.22 & -5.70 & 1.46 \\ -4.71 & -0.95 & 2.73 \\ -2.67 & 0.95 & 1.00 \end{bmatrix} \quad \text{and} \quad F23 = \begin{bmatrix} 0.00 & 10.00 & 3.33 \\ 9.43 & 1.00 & -1.00 \\ -4.71 & 1.00 & 1.00 \end{bmatrix}.$$

The nullspace of the transpose of these two matrices (i.e., the eigen vector with zero eigenvalue) defines the epipolar points in the image produced by camera 3. These two epipolar points are shown in Figure 6a. The epipolar points indicate the projection centers of expansion of cameras 1 and 2 as seen by camera 3. Transfer is performed by substituting the values of (p, q) for each point in image #1 into equation

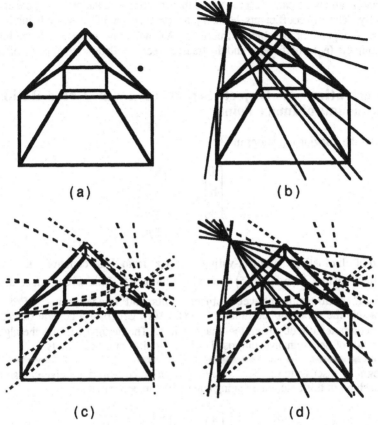

Fig. 6 Camera #3 images with (a) epipolar points, (b) transfer lines from F13, (c) transfer lines from F23, and (d) both sets of transfer lines.

(11) using the fundamental matrix F13. This defines a set of epipolar lines in image 3 as shown in Figure 6b. A similar procedure is implemented using the coordinates of the points in image 2 and the fundamental matrix F23. The resulting set of epipolar lines is shown in Figure 6c. If both sets of lines are plotted, the pair of lines corresponding to each object point intersect each other at its image point in camera 3. This is illustrated in Figure 6d. This example provides a graphical illustration of the image transfer technique.

In actuality, the coordinates values of the two unknowns $(\bar{p}, \bar{q})$ are obtained by solving two simultaneous equation generated by the two fundamental matrices F13 and F23 and the corresponding values (p, q) and $(\bar{p}, \bar{q})$ of the image points in Camera #1 and Camera #2 respectively.

In the preceding discussion, the (e_{ij}) coefficients were obtained by eliminating the object-vector, X, from the imaging equations. The (e_{ij}) coefficients therefore contain information about the camera stations and their relative orientation ... i.e., the epipolar geometry. The (e_{ij}) coefficients, however, are independent of the scene being imaged, and are independent of object structure. We will now introduce a method for exploiting the (e_{ij}) coefficients and the transfer vector to determine object structure as well.

4. Derivation of Object Structure from Cross-Ratios of Determinants of Image Points

Consider the imaging equations in (3):

$$
\begin{bmatrix} a \\ b \\ \bar{a} \\ \bar{b} \end{bmatrix} X = \begin{array}{c} \langle c|X\rangle p \\ \langle c|X\rangle q \\ \langle \bar{c}|X\rangle \bar{p} \\ \langle \bar{c}|X\rangle \bar{q} \end{array} \tag{14}
$$

Instead of eliminating the object-variables (x,y,z) from these equations, the camera-dependent vectors $(a,b,c,\bar{a},\bar{b},\bar{c})$ are to be eliminated. This will produce a pure " invariant" relationship between object-points and image points. From this relationship the invariant coordinates $(C_1(x), C_2(x), C_3(x))$ of a general object point can be computed directly from the image points. The method will use the algebraic cross-ratios of determinants comprised of image-points or object points.

We begin by discussing the case where the imaging equations are given by an affine relationship. In this case, the imaging equations can be written as:

$$
\begin{bmatrix} a \\ b \\ \bar{a} \\ \bar{b} \end{bmatrix} X = \begin{bmatrix} p \\ q \\ \bar{p} \\ \bar{q} \end{bmatrix}. \tag{15}
$$

This equation can be written for any four points X_i, X_j, X_k, X_l, as:

$$
\begin{bmatrix} a \\ b \\ \bar{a} \\ \bar{b} \end{bmatrix} \begin{pmatrix} X_i & X_j & X_k & X_l \end{pmatrix} = \begin{bmatrix} p_i & p_j & p_k & p_l \\ q_i & q_j & q_k & q_l \\ \bar{p}_i & \bar{p}_j & \bar{p}_k & \bar{p}_l \\ \bar{q}_i & \bar{q}_j & \bar{q}_k & \bar{q}_l \end{bmatrix} \tag{16}
$$

The simplex coordinates are now introduced to describe the object points. The motivation for this will become evident shortly. A simplex is the simplest geometric structure in a space of a given dimension. For example, the simplexes of a line are line segments, the simplexes of a plane are triangles, and the simplexes of 3-D space are tetrahedra. A simplex coordinate system is formed by choosing a basis simplex.

Here the 4 points (X_1, X_2, X_3, X_4) are selected as the corners of the basis tetrahedron. All other points of the object are described in relationship to these points. The simplex coordinates are given by the ratio of the volume of two tetrahedra. The denominator is always the volume of the basis tetrahedron. The numerator of the kth simplex coordinate is the volume of the tetrahedron formed by substituting X_i for the kth column of the basis tetrahedron. The simplex coordinates of an arbitrary point X_i are given by:

$$\zeta_1(X_i) = \frac{\begin{vmatrix} X_i & X_2 & X_3 & X_4 \end{vmatrix}}{\begin{vmatrix} X_1 & X_2 & X_3 & X_4 \end{vmatrix}}, \qquad \zeta_2(X_i) = \frac{\begin{vmatrix} X_1 & X_i & X_3 & X_4 \end{vmatrix}}{\begin{vmatrix} X_1 & X_2 & X_3 & X_4 \end{vmatrix}}$$

$$\zeta_3(X_i) = \frac{\begin{vmatrix} X_1 & X_2 & X_i & X_4 \end{vmatrix}}{\begin{vmatrix} X_1 & X_2 & X_3 & X_4 \end{vmatrix}}, \quad \text{and} \quad \zeta_4(X_i) = \frac{\begin{vmatrix} X_1 & X_2 & X_3 & X_i \end{vmatrix}}{\begin{vmatrix} X_1 & X_2 & X_3 & X_4 \end{vmatrix}}. \tag{17}$$

A useful property of simplex coordinates is their invariance to affine transformations. Since an affine relationship exists between the object and image point in (16) the simplex coordinates provide an invariant description of the image points. To prove this a ratio of determinants of equation (16) is formed. Substituting in the values $i = i$, $j = 2, k = 3, l = 4$ in the numerator, and $i = 1, j = 2, k = 3, l = 4$ in the denominator gives:

$$\frac{|A| \begin{vmatrix} X_i & X_2 & X_3 & X_4 \end{vmatrix}}{|A| \begin{vmatrix} X_1 & X_2 & X_3 & X_4 \end{vmatrix}} = \frac{\begin{vmatrix} R_i & R_2 & R_3 & R_4 \end{vmatrix}}{\begin{vmatrix} R_1 & R_2 & R_3 & R_4 \end{vmatrix}} \tag{18}$$

where $A = \begin{bmatrix} a \\ b \\ \overline{a} \\ \overline{b} \end{bmatrix}$, $X_i = \begin{bmatrix} x_i \\ y_i \\ z_i \\ 1 \end{bmatrix}$, and $R_i = \begin{bmatrix} p_i \\ q_i \\ \overline{p}_i \\ \overline{q}_i \end{bmatrix}$. In (18), the matrices containing the camera parameters cancel leaving a pure invariant relationship. The result is simply the first simplex coordinate for image point X_i i.e.,

$$\zeta_1(X_i) = \frac{\begin{vmatrix} X_i & X_2 & X_3 & X_4 \end{vmatrix}}{\begin{vmatrix} X_1 & X_2 & X_3 & X_4 \end{vmatrix}} = \frac{\begin{vmatrix} R_i & R_2 & R_3 & R_4 \end{vmatrix}}{\begin{vmatrix} R_1 & R_2 & R_3 & R_4 \end{vmatrix}}. \tag{19}$$

Similar expression can be written for the other simplex coordinates.

Equation (19) provides an invariant relationship between the object points and a stereo pair of image points for the case where the imaging equations are given by an affine relationship. A model of an object is formed by describing its points in terms of simplex coordinates. To verify that a stereo pair of images correspond to a specific object, its points are expressed in simplex coordinates according to the recipe given in (19). Once this is done a straight forward comparison is performed without any regard to camera parameters.

Next, consider the some what more general case where the stereo image formation is restricted to "cyclopean imaging" (i.e., equation (3) with $c = \bar{c}$). This restricted type of stereo imaging is described in reference 1. With this assumption the imaging equations (3) become

$$
\begin{bmatrix} a \\ b \\ \bar{a} \\ \bar{b} \end{bmatrix} X = \begin{bmatrix} p \\ q \\ \bar{p} \\ \bar{q} \end{bmatrix} \langle c|X \rangle \tag{20}
$$

If this equation is written for any four observations we obtain

$$
\begin{bmatrix} a \\ b \\ \bar{a} \\ \bar{b} \end{bmatrix} \begin{pmatrix} X_i & X_j & X_k & X_l \end{pmatrix} = \begin{bmatrix} p_i & p_j & p_k & p_l \\ q_i & q_j & q_k & q_l \\ \bar{p}_i & \bar{p}_j & \bar{p}_k & \bar{p}_l \\ \bar{q}_i & \bar{q}_j & \bar{q}_k & \bar{q}_l \end{bmatrix} \begin{bmatrix} \langle c|X_i \rangle & 0 & 0 & 0 \\ 0 & \langle c|X_j \rangle & 0 & 0 \\ 0 & 0 & \langle c|X_k \rangle & 0 \\ 0 & 0 & 0 & \langle c|X_l \rangle \end{bmatrix} \tag{21}
$$

A cross ratio of determinants is constructed from (21) for a general vector X with image points (p, q) and ($\bar{p}$, $\bar{q}$) in term of five fiducial points X_1, X_2, X_3, X_4 and X_5. with corresponding image points (p_j, q_j) and ($\bar{p}_j$, $\bar{q}_j$) where j = 1, 2...5. The cross ratio is given by

$$
\frac{|A|\,|X_1X_2X_3X_4|\,|A|\,|X_1X_2X_5X|}{|A|\,|X_1X_2X_3X_5|\,|A|\,|X_1X_2X_4X|} = \frac{\prod\limits_{i=1,2,3,4}\langle c|X_i \rangle\,|R_1R_2R_3R_4|\;\prod\limits_{i=1,2,5,X}\langle c|X_i \rangle\,|R_1R_2R_5R|}{\prod\limits_{i=1,2,3,5}\langle c|X_i \rangle\,|R_1R_2R_3R_5|\;\prod\limits_{i=1,2,4,X}\langle c|X_i \rangle\,|R_1R_2R_4R|} \tag{22}
$$

where $A = \begin{bmatrix} a \\ b \\ \bar{a} \\ \bar{b} \end{bmatrix}$, $X_i = \begin{bmatrix} x_i \\ y_i \\ z_i \\ 1 \end{bmatrix}$, and $R_i = \begin{bmatrix} p_i \\ q_i \\ \bar{p}_i \\ \bar{q}_i \end{bmatrix}$. All parameter dependent quantities

cancel from the numerator and denominator of the equation, leaving a "pure" invariant relation between the cross ratio of object tetrahedra and the cross ratio of determinant of image points:

$$
\frac{V_{1234}\,V_{125X}}{V_{1235}\,V_{124X}} = \frac{|R_1R_2R_3R_4|\,|R_1R_2R_5R|}{|R_1R_2R_3R_5|\,|R_1R_2R_4R|} \tag{23}
$$

(See reference 1 for a more complete discussion of this stereo invariant).

This derivation can be extended to the case $c \neq \bar{c}$ by the following method: First, assume that the four four-vectors a, b, $\bar{a}$, and $\bar{b}$ are linear independent. Therefore,

$$\begin{vmatrix} a \\ b \\ \overline{a} \\ \overline{b} \end{vmatrix} \neq 0 \qquad (24)$$

The vectors c and $\overline{c}$ can be represented as linear combinations of these four vectors, i.e.,

$$c = \alpha a + \beta b + \gamma \overline{a} + \delta \overline{b}$$
$$\overline{c} = \overline{\alpha} a + \overline{\beta} b + \overline{\gamma} \overline{a} + \overline{\delta} \overline{b} \qquad (25)$$

The values $\alpha, \beta, \dots \overline{\gamma}, \overline{\delta}$ can be determined from the fundamental matrix (e_{ij}), which we assume known (estimated in terms of measured conjugate pairs). This is accomplished by substituting the values of c and $\overline{c}$ in (25) into the transfer vector given in (8). Expanding the terms of the transfer vector, gives:

$$\begin{vmatrix} c \\ b \\ \overline{a} \\ \overline{b} \end{vmatrix} = \alpha \begin{vmatrix} a \\ b \\ \overline{a} \\ \overline{b} \end{vmatrix}, \quad \begin{vmatrix} a \\ c \\ \overline{a} \\ \overline{b} \end{vmatrix} = \beta \begin{vmatrix} a \\ b \\ \overline{a} \\ \overline{b} \end{vmatrix}, \quad \begin{vmatrix} a \\ b \\ \overline{c} \\ \overline{b} \end{vmatrix} = \overline{\gamma} \begin{vmatrix} a \\ b \\ \overline{a} \\ \overline{b} \end{vmatrix}, \quad \begin{vmatrix} a \\ b \\ \overline{a} \\ \overline{c} \end{vmatrix} = \overline{\delta} \begin{vmatrix} a \\ b \\ \overline{a} \\ \overline{b} \end{vmatrix},$$

$$\begin{vmatrix} c \\ b \\ \overline{c} \\ \overline{b} \end{vmatrix} = \begin{vmatrix} \alpha a + \gamma \overline{a} \\ b \\ \overline{\alpha} a + \overline{\gamma} \overline{a} \\ \overline{b} \end{vmatrix} = \alpha \overline{\gamma} \begin{vmatrix} a \\ b \\ \overline{a} \\ \overline{b} \end{vmatrix} + \gamma \overline{\alpha} \begin{vmatrix} \overline{a} \\ b \\ a \\ \overline{b} \end{vmatrix}, \quad \begin{vmatrix} c \\ b \\ \overline{a} \\ \overline{c} \end{vmatrix} = \begin{vmatrix} \alpha a + \delta \overline{b} \\ b \\ \overline{a} \\ \overline{\alpha} a + \overline{\delta} \overline{b} \end{vmatrix} = \alpha \overline{\delta} \begin{vmatrix} a \\ b \\ \overline{a} \\ \overline{b} \end{vmatrix} + \delta \overline{\alpha} \begin{vmatrix} \overline{b} \\ b \\ \overline{a} \\ a \end{vmatrix}, \qquad (26)$$

$$\begin{vmatrix} a \\ c \\ \overline{c} \\ \overline{b} \end{vmatrix} = \begin{vmatrix} a \\ \beta b + \gamma \overline{a} \\ \overline{\beta} b + \overline{\gamma} \overline{a} \\ \overline{b} \end{vmatrix} = \beta \overline{\gamma} \begin{vmatrix} a \\ b \\ \overline{a} \\ \overline{b} \end{vmatrix} + \overline{\beta} \gamma \begin{vmatrix} a \\ \overline{a} \\ b \\ \overline{b} \end{vmatrix}, \text{ and } \begin{vmatrix} a \\ c \\ \overline{a} \\ \overline{c} \end{vmatrix} = \begin{vmatrix} a \\ \beta b + \delta \overline{b} \\ \overline{a} \\ \overline{\beta} b + \overline{\delta} \overline{b} \end{vmatrix} = \beta \overline{\delta} \begin{vmatrix} a \\ b \\ \overline{a} \\ \overline{b} \end{vmatrix} + \delta \overline{\beta} \begin{vmatrix} a \\ \overline{b} \\ \overline{a} \\ b \end{vmatrix}$$

Therefore:

$$\alpha = \frac{-e_{31}}{e_{33}}, \quad \beta = \frac{-e_{32}}{e_{33}}, \quad \overline{\gamma} = \frac{-e_{13}}{e_{33}}, \quad \overline{\delta} = \frac{-e_{23}}{e_{33}},$$

$$e_{11} = (\alpha \overline{\gamma} - \gamma \overline{\alpha})e_{33}, \qquad e_{21} = (\alpha \overline{\delta} - \delta \overline{\alpha})e_{33}, \qquad (27)$$

$$e_{12} = (\beta \overline{\gamma} - \gamma \overline{\beta})e_{33}, \text{ and } e_{22} = (\beta \overline{\delta} - \delta \overline{\beta})e_{33}.$$

From (27) it can be seen that the α, β, $\overline{\gamma}$, and $\overline{\delta}$ are immediately determined in terms of measured quantities. The ratios

$$\frac{\overline{\alpha}}{\overline{\beta}} = \frac{\alpha\,\overline{\gamma} - e_{11}/e_{33}}{\beta\,\overline{\gamma} - e_{12}/e_{33}} \quad \text{and} \quad \frac{\gamma}{\delta} = \frac{\alpha\,\overline{\gamma} - e_{11}/e_{33}}{\alpha\,\overline{\delta} - e_{21}/e_{33}} \tag{28}$$

are likewise determined.

Returning to the imaging equation (3), and substituting in the expression in (25) for $\overline{c}$, produces

$$\begin{bmatrix} a \\ b \\ \overline{a} \\ \overline{b} \end{bmatrix} X = \begin{matrix} \langle c|X\rangle p \\ \langle c|X\rangle q \\ \langle \overline{\alpha}a + \overline{\beta}b + \overline{\gamma}\overline{a} + \overline{\delta}\overline{b}|X\rangle\overline{p} \\ \langle \overline{\alpha}a + \overline{\beta}b + \overline{\gamma}\overline{a} + \overline{\delta}\overline{b}|X\rangle\overline{q} \end{matrix}. \tag{29}$$

This expression simplifies to

$$\begin{bmatrix} a \\ b \\ \overline{a} \\ \overline{b} \end{bmatrix} X = \begin{matrix} \langle c|X\rangle p \\ \langle c|X\rangle q \\ \langle \overline{\alpha}a + \overline{\beta}b + \overline{\gamma}\overline{a} + \overline{\delta}\overline{b}|X\rangle\overline{p} \\ \langle \overline{\alpha}a + \overline{\beta}b + \overline{\gamma}\overline{a} + \overline{\delta}\overline{b}|X\rangle\overline{q} \end{matrix} \tag{30}$$

where the fact that $\langle a|x\rangle = p$ and $\langle b|x\rangle = q$ was used. Equation (30) can be rewritten as

$$\begin{bmatrix} 1 & 0 & 0 & 0 \\ 0 & 1 & 0 & 0 \\ 0 & 0 & 1-\overline{p}\overline{\gamma} & -\overline{p}\overline{\delta} \\ 0 & 0 & -\overline{q}\overline{\gamma} & 1-\overline{q}\overline{\delta} \end{bmatrix} \begin{bmatrix} a \\ b \\ \overline{a} \\ \overline{b} \end{bmatrix} X = \begin{bmatrix} p \\ q \\ \overline{\beta}\overline{p}\left(\frac{\overline{\alpha}}{\overline{\beta}}p+q\right) \\ \overline{\beta}\overline{q}\left(\frac{\overline{\alpha}}{\overline{\beta}}p+q\right) \end{bmatrix}\langle c|X\rangle. \tag{31}$$

Multiplying (31) through by the inverse of the left most matrix gives:

$$\begin{bmatrix} a \\ b \\ \overline{a} \\ \overline{b} \end{bmatrix} X = \begin{bmatrix} p \\ q \\ \overline{\beta}r \\ \overline{\beta}s \end{bmatrix}\langle c|X\rangle \tag{32}$$

where $r = \overline{p}\left[\frac{\overline{\alpha}}{\overline{\beta}}p+q\right]\Big/\left[1-\overline{p}\overline{\gamma}-\overline{q}\overline{\delta}\right]$ and $s = p\overline{q}\left[\frac{\overline{\alpha}}{\overline{\beta}}p+q\right]\Big/\left[1-\overline{p}\overline{\gamma}-\overline{q}\overline{\delta}\right]$. The parameters r and s are known functions of the elements of the fundamental matrix (e_{ij}).

Forming the cross ratio of determinants once again gives:

$$\frac{V_{1234}\ V_{125X}}{V_{1235}\ V_{124X}} = \frac{|R_1R_2R_3R_4|\ |R_1R_2R_5R|}{|R_1R_2R_3R_5|\ |R_1R_2R_4R|} \tag{33}$$

where $R^t = [p, q, r, s]$ is the "cyclopean" vector. Equation (33) is the desired result. The quantity:

$$\frac{V_{1234}\ V_{125X}}{V_{1235}\ V_{124X}} = C_1(X) \tag{34}$$

is an invariant projective coordinate for the point X in 3 space. Repeating the procedure with different combinations produce additional invariant coordinates, e.g.,

$$\frac{V_{1324}\ V_{135X}}{V_{1325}\ V_{134X}} = C_2(X) \text{ and } \frac{V_{2314}\ V_{235X}}{V_{2315}\ V_{234X}} = C_3(X) \tag{35}$$

These coordinates can be derived from the measurements on the reference images and determine the projective coordinates of any points X relative to the five fiducial points $X_1, .. X_5$. In addition, the three invariant coordinates listed in (34) and (35) are sufficient to uniquely describe any point in 3-space except for points that lie in the plane defined by the three points X_1, X_2, and X_3. This will be discussed in more detail in the following section.

The invariant projective coordinates of the 10 points of the house given in Figure 4 were calculated from the two different stereo pairs of images from cameras 1 and 3 and from cameras 2 and 3. The fiducial points were selected as X1, X2, X3, X6 and X8. The values of the cyclopean image vectors and the invariant coordinates are listed for the two different stereo pairs in Table 1. From this table it is evident that although the cyclopean vectors differ for the two different stereo pairs the invariant coordinates derived from the two different stereo pairs are identical. Thus, a perspective invariant description of the house is achieved.

5. Scene Reconstruction

Suppose that the representation for a collection of object points has been derived from a stereo image pair and recorded. This record may be a list of invariant co-ordinates; $(C_1(i), C_2(i), C_3(i))$, $i=1 ... N$. In these co-ordinates the five basis points are implicit. In some situations we may have instead a function: $F(C_1, C_2, C_3) = 0$, in which once again the five basis points are implicit.

We are asked to reconstruct a view of the object as it might appear if viewed from a specified perspective. "What would it look like?" A direct way to address this question is as follows. We embed the object into a 3-D cartesian co-ordinate system by assigning locations to the five basis points so that no four are coplanar. A convenient assignment is to the vertices of the unit cube as shown in Figure 7.

Point #	Cyclopean Vector Camera 1&3 (p, q, r, s)	Cyclopean Vector Camera 2&3 (p, q, r, s)	Invariant coordinates Camera 1&3 (C_1, C_2, C_3)	Invariant coordinates Camera 2&3 (C_1, C_2, C_3)
1	(-.11, .17, .12, -.20)	(.44, .16, .07, -.12)	(∞, 1.00, ∞)	(∞, 1.00, ∞)
2	(-.35, -.03, -.1, -.16)	(.17, .24, -.11, -.18)	(∞, ∞, 1.00)	(∞, ∞, 1.00)
3	(.07, -.23, -.07,-.12)	(-.36, .13, -.06,-.10)	(1.00, ∞, ∞)	(1.00, ∞, ∞)
4	(.31, -.13, .09, -.14)	(-.07, .10, .05, -.08)	(1.00, 1.00, 1.00)	(1.00, 1.00, 1.00)
5	(-.13, -.01, .14,-.10)	(.44, -.08, .07, -.05)	(∞, 0.00, -1.00)	(∞, 0.00, -1.00)
6	(-.40,-.20,-.11, -.07)	(.17,-.12, -.11, -.07)	(∞, ∞, ∞)	(∞, ∞, ∞)
7	(.07,-.37, -.08, -.05)	(-.36,-.06,-.06,-.04)	(0.00, ∞, -1.00)	(0.00, ∞, -1.00)
8	(.34, -.28, .10, -.06)	(-.07,-.05, .05, -.03)	(0.00, 0.00, 0.00)	(0.00, 0.00, 0.00)
9	(-.33, -.35, .00, .05)	(.33, -.38, .00, .03)	(∞, -3.0, -1.67)	(∞, -3.0, -1.67)
10	(.22, -.52, .00, .03)	(-.20, -.23, .00, .02)	(-1.00, -3.00, -.60)	(-1.00, -3.00, -.60)

Table 1 Cyclopean vectors and invariant coordinates for the points in Figure 4

For any general point with invariant co-ordinates $(C_1(i), C_2(i), C_3(i))$ we compute the corresponding cartesian co-ordinates (x_i, y_i, z_i) by solving a system of simultaneous linear equations, for example:

$$|X_1X_2X_3X_4||X_1X_2X_5X_i| = C_1(i)|X_1X_2X_3X_5||X_1X_2X_4X_i|$$
$$|X_1X_3X_2X_4||X_1X_3X_5X_i| = C_2(i)|X_1X_3X_2X_5||X_1X_3X_4X_i|$$
$$|X_1X_4X_2X_3||X_1X_4X_5X_i| = C_3(i)|X_1X_4X_2X_5||X_1X_4X_2X_i| \qquad (36)$$

(note that $X^t(i) = [x_i, y_i, z_i, 1,]$, a four-vector).

Once these calculations are completed, we create a view of the object points (x_i, y_i, z_i) by the standard method. We select a position and orientation for a camera, specify a focal length and principal point, and back-project the object points into the image plane.

Once these calculations are completed, we create a view of the object points (x_i, y_i, z_i) by the standard method. We select a position and orientation for a camera, specify a

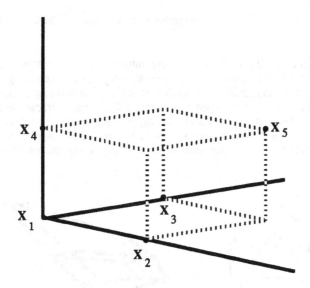

Fig. 7 Assignment of Basis Points to Vertices of Unit Cube

focal length and principal point, and back-project the object points into the image plane.

The assignment of the basis points to cartesian points depends on the user's judgment, and the appearance of the scene reconstructed by this method will vary according to this assignment. If "ground truth" on the 5 basis points can be determined, the reconstructed scene will (ideally) be identical with the "true" scene. A different assignment of basis points to scene positions will result in a variation or "projective morphing" of the reconstructed scene which is still consistent with the invariant coordinates. (An alternative treatment of morphing, as well as interesting applications to images of human faces, is presented in [3]). As observed in [6, 7], the invariant methods determine the scene up to an affine transformation of the basis points. These alternative reconstructions constitute a space of projectively equivalent scenes. The user can explore this space by varying the (x, y, z) assigments of the basis points.

These concepts were illustrated by reconstructing the model house depicted in Figures 4 and 5 In these simulations a redundant set of five invariant co-ordinates, rather than three, were used, to remedy the "plane of indeterminacy" phenomenon. The basis points used were X_1, X_2, X_3, X_6 and X_8. Space-coordinates (x, y, z) were assigned to these, and the remaining points $(X_4, X_5, X_7, X_9, X_{10})$ were reconstructed by the algorithm. Assignment of "true" co-ordinates to the basis resulted in exact reproduction of the remainder of the house ... a "sanity check" on the algorithm.

To illustrate "projective morphing," a sequence of affine transformation was applied to the basis points, and the reconstruction of the model house was completed using the "correct" invariant co-ordinates together with the "warped" basis. The results are shown in Figure 8.

In these simulations, the basis points were subjected to: (a) rotation through 45° around the vertical, (b) shearing along the x-axis, (c) variable rescaling along the z-axis, (d) simultaneous rotation, z-dependent re-scaling and shearing along the x-axis. According to the theory developed in sections 1-4, the reconstructed points will be displaced from their "true" positions by the affine transformation applied to the basis vectors. The reconstructed houses shown in Figure 8 (a-d) display the effects of rotation, shearing, and z-dependent rescaling, confirming the predictions of the theory.

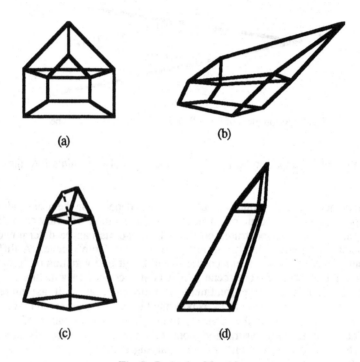

(a)

(b)

(c)

(d)

Fig. 8 Projective Morphing

Acknowledgements

This research was performed under a contract funded by the Advanced Research Projects Agency (ARPA) and monitored by the Air Force Office of Scientific Research (AFOSR). Computing facilities were provided by Lockheed's Research and Development Division, Palo Alto Research Laboratories, and Space Systems Division, Sunnyvale, California.

References

1. Barrett, Eamon B., Payton, Paul M., Haag, Nils N., Brill, Michael H.; General Methods for Determining Projective Invariants in Imagery; CVGIP Image Understanding, 53, (1991) 46-65.

2. Barrett, Eamon B., Brill, Michael H., Haag, Nils N., Payton, Paul M.; Invariant Linear Methods in Photogrammetry and Model-Matching; in *Geometric Invariance in Computer Vision*, J. L. Mundy and A Zisserman, editors, MIT Press, 1992.

3. Shashua, Amnon; Projective Structure from Two Uncalibrated Images: Structure from Motion and Recognition; AI Memo No 1363, MIT Artificial Intelligence Laboratory, Sept., 1992.

4. Luong, Quang-Tuan, Deriche, Rachid, Faugeras, Olivier D., Papadopoulo, Theodore; On determining the fundamental matrix: analysis of different methods and experimental results; INRIA Report de Recherche No. 1894, May 1993.

5. Mundy, J.L. and Zisserman, A. editors; *Geometric Invariance in Computer Vision*; JMIT Press, 1992.

6. Faugeras, Olivier, Robert, Luc, What can two images tell us about a third one? INRIA Report de Recherche No. 2018, Sept 1993.

7. Hartley, Richard, Gupta, Rajiv, Chang, Tom; Stereo from Uncalibrated Cameras; *Proc of CVPR 92*, Champaign, Illinois, pp 761-764, June 1992.

8. Shapiro, Larry S., Zisserman, Andrew P., Brady, Michael; Motion from point matches using affine epipolar geometry; Oxford University, Department of Engineering Science Report No. OUEL 1994/93, June 1993.

APPENDIX

Derivation of the Essential Matrix From Colinearity and Coplanarity Conditions

This derivation may be found in Chapter 23 of [5] and is repeated here for completeness.

$$[X - X_R] = \langle m_3 | X - X_R \rangle [M]^t [P] \begin{bmatrix} p \\ q \\ 1 \end{bmatrix}$$

(A-1)

$$[X - X_{\overline{R}}] = \langle \overline{m}_3 | X - X_{\overline{R}} \rangle [\overline{M}]^t [\overline{P}] \begin{bmatrix} \overline{p} \\ \overline{q} \\ 1 \end{bmatrix}$$

These are the colinearity conditions. The coplanarity condition asserts that the three points X, X_R, $X_{\overline{R}}$ lie in a plane:

$$[X - X_{\overline{R}}] \cdot [X_R - X_{\overline{R}}] \times [X - X_R] = 0$$

(A-2)

Next, we observe that for any two vectors f and g, their cross-product may be written as the product of a matrix with a vector:

$$\begin{bmatrix} f_1 \\ f_2 \\ f_3 \end{bmatrix} \times \begin{bmatrix} g_1 \\ g_2 \\ g_3 \end{bmatrix} = \begin{bmatrix} 0 & -f_3 & f_2 \\ f_3 & 0 & -f_1 \\ -f_2 & f_1 & 0 \end{bmatrix} \begin{bmatrix} g_1 \\ g_2 \\ g_3 \end{bmatrix}$$

(A-3)

Therefore:

$$[X_R - X_{\overline{R}}] \times [X - X_R] = \begin{bmatrix} 0 & -(z_R - z_{\overline{R}}) & (y_R - y_{\overline{R}}) \\ (z_R - z_{\overline{R}}) & 0 & -(x_R - x_{\overline{R}}) \\ -(y_R - y_{\overline{R}}) & (x_R - x_{\overline{R}}) & 0 \end{bmatrix} \begin{bmatrix} x - x_R \\ y - y_R \\ z - z_R \end{bmatrix}$$

(A-4)

Making the appropriate substitutions in the coplanarity relation, we see that:

$$0 = \langle \overline{m}_3 | X - X_{\overline{R}} \rangle [\overline{p} \quad \overline{q} \quad 1]$$

$$\left[(\overline{P})^T (\overline{M}) \begin{bmatrix} 0 & -(z_R - z_{\overline{R}}) & (y_R - y_{\overline{R}}) \\ (z_R - z_{\overline{R}}) & 0 & -(x_R - x_{\overline{R}}) \\ -(y_R - y_{\overline{R}}) & (x_R - x_{\overline{R}}) & 0 \end{bmatrix} (M)^T (P) \begin{bmatrix} p \\ q \\ 1 \end{bmatrix} \langle m_3 | X - X_R \rangle \right]$$

(A-5)

The scalar quantities $\langle \overline{m}_3 | X - X_{\overline{R}} \rangle$ and $\langle m_3 | X - X_R \rangle$ cancel from this homogeneous equation, which may be rewritten as;

$$[\overline{p} \quad \overline{q} \quad 1][F] \begin{bmatrix} p \\ q \\ 1 \end{bmatrix} = 0 \qquad\qquad (A\text{-}6)$$

Equation (A-5) provides an explicit representation of the fundamental matrix, [F], in terms of the camera parameters. This representation is valid up to a multiplicative constant; what we "really" have is a representation of ratios of elements of the fundamental matrix ... e.g. $[e_{11}/e_{33}, e_{12}/e_{33} ... e_{32}/e_{33}]$ ... in terms of combinations of the camera parameters.

A Case Against Epipolar Geometry

Andrew Zisserman and Stephen J. Maybank

Robotics Research Group,
Department of Engineering Science,
University of Oxford,
Parks Rd,
Oxford

Abstract. We discuss briefly a number of areas where epipolar geometry is currently central in carrying out visual tasks. In contrast we demonstrate configurations for which 3D projective invariants can be computed from perspective stereo pairs, but epipolar geometry (and full projective structure) cannot. We catalogue a number of these configurations which generally involve isotropies under the 3D projective group, and investigate the connection with camera calibration. Examples are given of the invariants recovered from real images. We also indicate other areas where a strong reliance on epipolar geometry should be avoided, in particular for image transfer.

1 Introduction

The theory of epipolar geometry is, without doubt, one of the major achievements in the applications of projective geometry to computer vision. The number of points required, ambiguities, geometric and algebraic properties are well established and understood [4, 10, 12, 16]. The essence of epipolar geometry is that it depends *only* on the relative location of the optical centers and image planes; there is no dependence on structure. The primary use of epipolar geometry is in providing a disambiguating constraint for correspondences between images planes i.e., that a point in one image constrains the corresponding point in another image to lie on a line. However, epipolar geometry is also the kernel in a number of other areas:

1. **Multiple view invariants**
   Invariants of a 3D configuration are computed from two perspective images of the configuration, based on the epipolar geometry between the views.
2. **Transfer**
   Typically, novel images of 3D structures are constructed from a stereo pair of images by intersecting epipolar lines [3, 7, 21] and Barrett (this volume).
3. **Camera self-calibration**
   Constraints from the fundamental matrix are exploited to determine intrinsic camera parameters [5, 13, 17].

In this paper we investigate whether epipolar geometry is necessary for these applications, and, furthermore, whether the use of epipolar geometry as the central tool is *detrimental*.

1.1 Two View Invariants

In general invariants of 3D configurations are computed in two stages: first, the fundamental matrix is computed from point matches between the two perspective images; second, invariants of the 3D configuration are computed either from the recovered 3D structure [6, 10] or from image measurements together with the epipolar geometry [9, 20] and (Gros and Shashua, both this volume). The computation of the fundamental matrix generally uses all available scene points, not exclusively points on the target 3D configuration.

Here we investigate invariants of 3D configurations, computed from two views, where only elements of the projected configuration are used. Section 2 describes a number of configurations for which there is an isotropy group. Section 3 uses these as examples in discussing epipolar geometry and multiple view invariants. For a number of these configurations it is not possible to determine the fundamental matrix, however invariants can be computed from two images. Section 4 establishes the relation with camera calibration for particular configurations.

1.2 Image Sequences and Structure

When more than two images are available, image point correspondence ambiguity can be reduced from an area around a line (using only a single fundamental matrix) to an area around a point. Two methods are routinely used to achieve this: in the first approach, 3D structure together with 3×4 projection matrices are computed (see [27], Mohr and Hartley, this volume), the imaged point is obtained by projecting the 3D point onto the target image; in the second approach, the imaged point in the target image is obtained by intersecting epipolar lines computed between image pairs (epipolar transfer). Section 5 describes the limitations of using epipolar geometry for image transfer.

Even in the two view case, using structure might improve the accuracy of fundamental matrix computation. Assuming that outliers have been removed [28], two possible least square minimisations are: first, to minimise distances between image points and putative epipolar lines [5]; or second, to compute structure for matched points, and minimise distances between measured imaged points and putative points predicted by projecting computed 3D structure with computed 3×4 projection matrices (see Hartley, this volume). In the latter case there is a tighter constraint (point to point). The former (point to line) is only affected by the distance of the measured point to the epipolar line, but not by its distance "along" the line. Similar considerations apply in the case of parallel projection [24].

1.3 Definitions and Notation

In the following, we assume a perspective camera, with unknown intrinsic parameters, and measure only projective properties in the image.

Epipolar Geometry and Camera Projection Matrix The geometric and algebraic properties of epipolar geometry and the fundamental matrix are well documented elsewhere [5, 10] so are not repeated here. Image points in a stereo pair, corresponding to a 3D point $\mathbf{X}$, are $\mathbf{x}$ and $\mathbf{x}'$, with $\mathbf{x} = \mathbf{PX}$ and $\mathbf{x}' = \mathbf{P'X}$, where $\mathbf{P}$ and $\mathbf{P}'$ are the 3×4 projection matrices for the 'left' and 'right' cameras. In general homogeneous vectors are used, and equality is up to a non-zero scale factor. The fundamental matrix is represented by $\mathbf{F}$. For corresponding point pairs, $\mathbf{x}'^{\mathsf{T}}\mathbf{Fx} = 0$.

3D Invariants These are invariants under a projective transformation of $\mathcal{P}^3$, i.e. a transformation $\mathbf{X}' = \mathbf{TX}$, where $\mathbf{X}$ and $\mathbf{X}'$ are homogeneous four-vectors and $\mathbf{T}$ is a 4×4 non-singular matrix. For six 3D points in general position there are three functionally independent scalar projective invariants:

$$I_1 = \frac{|\mathbf{I}_{3561}|\cdot|\mathbf{I}_{3542}|}{|\mathbf{I}_{3564}|\cdot|\mathbf{I}_{3512}|}, \qquad I_2 = \frac{|\mathbf{I}_{3562}|\cdot|\mathbf{I}_{3142}|}{|\mathbf{I}_{3512}|\cdot|\mathbf{I}_{3642}|}, \qquad I_3 = \frac{|\mathbf{I}_{3564}|\cdot|\mathbf{I}_{5612}|}{|\mathbf{I}_{3561}|\cdot|\mathbf{I}_{5642}|}, \qquad (1)$$

where $\mathbf{I}_{abcd} = [\mathbf{X}_a, \mathbf{X}_b, \mathbf{X}_c, \mathbf{X}_d]$ and $|.|$ is the determinant.

2 Isotropy Sub-Groups

An isotropy group is the set of elements of a transformation group which do not alter a configuration. For example, a line is unaffected by translation in the direction of the line, and a circle unaffected by rotation about its center. If there is an isotropy, then there may well be invariants which naive constraint-counting would not predict. A simple example is a configuration of two coplanar lines under a plane similarity transformation, where the angle between the lines is invariant. This configuration has four degrees of freedom (two for each line) and under the group of plane similarity transformations ($\dim G = 4$), naive counting predicts no scalar invariants. However, there is a one-dimensional isotropy group in this case (scaling of coordinates with origin the line intersection) which does not affect the configuration.

The number, n_I, of (functionally independent scalar) invariants under the action of a group G is given by [21]:

$$n_I = \dim S - \dim G + \dim Is \qquad (2)$$

where $\dim S$ is the "dimension" of the structure (the number of degrees of freedom), $\dim G$ the dimension of G, in the 3D projective case 15, and $\dim Is$ the dimension of the isotropy sub-group (if any) which leaves the structure unaffected under the action of G. A simple planar example is a configuration, S, of two lines and two points (not lying on the lines), under a plane projective transformation. S has eight degrees of freedom (because each point and each line has two degrees of freedom), $\dim G = 8$ for a plane projective transformation, and there is a one-dimensional isotropy sub-group of the projectivities which leaves the structure unchanged (given explicitly in [8]). There is one projective scalar invariant (from equation (2) $n_I = 8 - 8 + 1$) which can be expressed as:

$$I = \frac{(l_1^\top x_1)(l_2^\top x_2)}{(l_1^\top x_2)(l_2^\top x_1)} \tag{3}$$

where l_i, x_i are homogeneous line and point coordinates respectively. The 3D analogue of this configuration is two planes and two points (not lying on the planes), which has an invariant under 3D projective transformations. Other 3D examples are given in Table 1.

Structure (S)	dim S	dim Is	n_{I_3}
6 points general position	18	0	3
7 points general position (*)	21	0	6
5 points, 4 coplanar	14	1	0
6 points, 4 coplanar (*)	17	0	2
line and 4 coplanar points	15	2	2
2 lines and 4 coplanar points	19	0	4
four lines	16	1	2

Table 1. n_{I_3} is the number of functionally independent scalar invariants for 3D configurations under the action of the projective group. In all cases general position is assumed e.g. the line is not coplanar with any two points. (*) indicates that the epipolar geometry can be determined from two views of the structure. In the case of seven points, the fundamental matrix is determined up to a finite number of possibilities.

2.1 Configurations and Coordinates

In the following we describe a number of configurations for which there is an isotropy sub-group of the 3D projective group. All the examples are variations on a configuration containing four co-planar points. The configurations are defined in Table 2.

For the six point configuration (**VI**), we may arbitrarily choose coordinates for any five of the points (not containing all four of the coplanar points):

$$\mathbf{X}_1 = (1, 0, 0, 0)^\top$$
$$\mathbf{X}_2 = (0, 1, 0, 0)^\top$$
$$\mathbf{X}_3 = (0, 0, 1, 0)^\top$$
$$\mathbf{X}_5 = (0, 0, 0, 1)^\top$$
$$\mathbf{X}_6 = (1, 1, 1, 1)^\top$$

Type	Structure S		$DOFS$	dim Is	n_{I_3}
I	single line		15	2	2
II	single point		14	1	0
III	point on line		16	1	2
IV	two coplanar lines		18	1	4
V	two skew lines		19	0	4
VI	two points		17	0	2

Table 2. The structure S consists of four coplanar points together with other elements not on the plane. The table gives the number of degrees of freedom of S, the dimension of the isotropy group (if any), and the number of functionally independent scalar 3D projective invariants. In all cases general position is assumed. Identical results hold if the four coplanar points are replaced by four coplanar lines.

Any other coordinates of the five points can be transformed to these by a collineation of $\mathcal{P}^3$. The fourth point has coordinates:

$$\mathbf{X}_4 = (\alpha, \beta, \gamma, 0)^{\mathsf{T}}$$

The points are shown in Figure 1a.

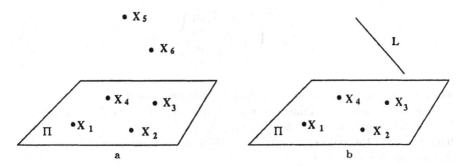

Fig. 1. The basic configurations consisting of four coplanar points and either (a) two points (configuration **VI**) or (b) a line (configuration **I**), not on the plane Π .

2.2 Four Coplanar Points and a Non-Coplanar Line

This is configuration **I** in Table 2. Coordinates are chosen in $\mathcal{P}^3$ such that the coplanar points $\mathbf{X}_1, .., \mathbf{X}_4$ have coordinates as above (configuration **VI**), and such that the line, **L**, is represented in homogeneous parametric form as

$$\mathbf{L} = \zeta(1, 1, 1, 1)^{\mathsf{T}} + \eta(0, 0, 0, 1)^{\mathsf{T}} \qquad (4)$$

See Figure 1b.

The isotropy sub-group is determined in two stages as follows. First, in order for Π to be a plane of fixed points it is necessary and sufficient that the 4×4 transformation matrix **T** satisfies

$$\mathbf{X}_i = \lambda \mathbf{T} \mathbf{X}_i, \qquad i \in \{1, .., 4\}$$

It is a simple matter to show that **T** must have the form

$$\mathbf{T} = \begin{pmatrix} \mu_1 & 0 & 0 & \mu_2 \\ 0 & \mu_1 & 0 & \mu_3 \\ 0 & 0 & \mu_1 & \mu_4 \\ 0 & 0 & 0 & \mu_5 \end{pmatrix} \qquad (5)$$

where $\mu_i, i \in \{1, .., 5\}$ parameterises the sub-group which has four DOF (only the ratio of the μ's is significant).

Second, we determine the sub-group which leaves **L** fixed. This can be carried out using Plückerian line coordinates [23], but here we use the parametric representation (4) above. Under the action of the isotropy group the points on the line need not be fixed, but the transformed points must still lie on **L**. The transformation of two points is sufficient to determine the transformed lines (three are required to determine the transformation of all the points on the line). By inspection $\mathbf{TX}_5$ and $\mathbf{TX}_6$ satisfy (4) iff $\mu_2 = \mu_3 = \mu_4$. Hence we arrive at

$$\mathbf{T}_2 = \begin{pmatrix} \mu_1 & 0 & 0 & \mu_2 \\ 0 & \mu_1 & 0 & \mu_2 \\ 0 & 0 & \mu_1 & \mu_2 \\ 0 & 0 & 0 & \mu_5 \end{pmatrix} \tag{6}$$

which is a two dimensional sub-group of the collineations of $\mathcal{P}^3$.

It is interesting to examine the transformation of $\mathcal{P}^3$ under the action of $\mathbf{T}_2$. The clearest way to see this is to determine the eigen-vectors of $\mathbf{T}_2$. These are the fixed points of the collineation. The first three are degenerate with eigen-value μ_1, and may be chosen as

$$\begin{aligned} \mathbf{E}_1 &= (1,0,0,0)^\mathsf{T} = \mathbf{X}_1 \\ \mathbf{E}_2 &= (0,1,0,0)^\mathsf{T} = \mathbf{X}_2 \\ \mathbf{E}_3 &= (0,0,1,0)^\mathsf{T} = \mathbf{X}_3 \end{aligned} \tag{7}$$

The fourth has eigen-value μ_5:

$$\mathbf{E}_4 = (\mu_2, \mu_2, \mu_2, \mu_5 - \mu_1)^\mathsf{T} \tag{8}$$

As expected any point on the plane $\mathbf{X} = \nu_1 \mathbf{X}_1 + \nu_2 \mathbf{X}_2 + \nu_3 \mathbf{X}_3$ is unchanged by $\mathbf{T}_2$ (since after the transformation all the basis vectors are multiplied by μ_1). The fourth eigen-vector is a fixed point on **L**. To see the effect of the isotropy group on points not on Π, consider any line **L** containing $\mathbf{E}_4$. This will intersect Π at some point, $\mathbf{X}_\Pi$ say, and any point, $\mathbf{X}$, on the line is given by $\mathbf{X} = \zeta \mathbf{E}_4 + \eta \mathbf{X}_\Pi$. After the transformation the point is $\mathbf{T}_2 \mathbf{X} = \mu_5 \zeta \mathbf{E}_4 + \mu_1 \eta \mathbf{X}_\Pi$ which still lies on **L** i.e. any line through $\mathbf{E}_4$ is a fixed line under the isotropy. Consequently, since every point in $\mathcal{P}^3$ lies on a line through $\mathbf{E}_4$, the action of $\mathbf{T}_2$ on $\mathcal{P}^3$ is to move points towards (or away from) $\mathbf{E}_4$, with only $\mathbf{E}_4$ and points on Π remaining unchanged. This eigen-vector structure is the key to understanding the isotropies in the next section.

2.3 Four Coplanar Points and a Non-Coplanar Point

This is configuration **II** in Table 2. Without loss of generality the non-coplanar point can be chosen to be $\mathbf{X}_5 = (0,0,0,1)^\mathsf{T}$. Then for an isotropy under collineation **T**

$$\mathbf{X}_i = \lambda \mathbf{TX}_i, \qquad i \in \{1, .., 5\}$$

As above, a plane of fixed points restricts T to the form (5). For $\mathbf{X}_5$ to be fixed under the isotropy

$$T_1 = \begin{pmatrix} \mu_1 & 0 & 0 & 0 \\ 0 & \mu_1 & 0 & 0 \\ 0 & 0 & \mu_1 & 0 \\ 0 & 0 & 0 & \mu_5 \end{pmatrix} \tag{9}$$

which is a one dimensional sub-group of the collineations of $\mathcal{P}^3$.

This form also follows immediately from the discussion of eigen-vectors in Section 2.2. The (ratio of) parameters $\{\mu_1, \mu_2, \mu_5\}$ determine the position of $\mathbf{E}_4$, the fixed point not on the plane. For $\mathbf{X}_5$ to be fixed we require

$$\mu_2 = 0$$
$$\mu_1 - \mu_5 \neq 0$$

which directly produces T_1 as in (9).

There are a number of variations on the five point structure for which there is again a one-dimensional isotropy group. Firstly (Table 2 **III**), any line through $\mathbf{X}_5$ will be a fixed line (*not* a line of fixed points). This is obvious because (9) is a sub-group of (6) which preserves $\mathbf{L}$, but also because any line containing $\mathbf{X}_5$ intersects Π, and consequently there are two fixed points on $\mathbf{L}$, so the line is fixed. Furthermore, a star of lines through $\mathbf{X}_5$ will be fixed by (6) (i.e. any number of lines). In particular, there is a one-dimensional isotropy group for a configuration of two coplanar lines, not on Π, together with four points on Π (Table 2 **IV**).

3 Multiple View Invariants and Epipolar Geometry

Here we contrast configurations **I**, **II**, and **VI** in terms of whether epipolar geometry and 3D projective invariants can be determined from two views.

3.1 Six Point Configuration, Four Coplanar

This is configuration **VI** in Table 2. It has been reported by a number of authors [1, 3, 19] that it is possible to recover epipolar geometry (and hence, subsequently, projective structure) and invariants for this configuration. Here we summarise the construction.

Epipolar Geometry See Figure 2. There are six corresponding points $\mathbf{x}_i, \mathbf{x}'_i, i \in \{1, .., 6\}$ in two views, with the first four $i \in \{1, .., 4\}$ the projection of coplanar world points.

1. Compute the plane projective transformation matrix T, such that $\mathbf{x}'_i = T\mathbf{x}_i, i \in \{1, .., 4\}$.
2. Determine the epipole, $\mathbf{p}'$, in the $\mathbf{x}'$ image as the intersection of the lines $(T\mathbf{x}_5) \times \mathbf{x}'_5$ and $(T\mathbf{x}_6) \times \mathbf{x}'_6$.

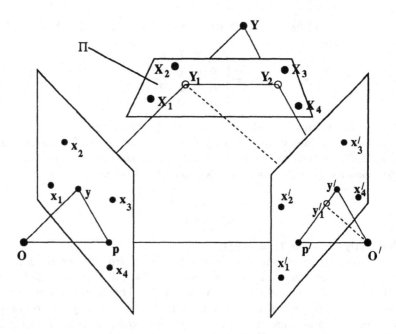

Fig. 2. Epipolar geometry. The points $X_1, \ldots, X_4$ are coplanar, with images x_i and x_i' in the first and second images respectively. The epipolar plane defined by the point Y and optical centers O and O' intersects the plane Π in the line $L(Y) = \langle Y_1, Y_2 \rangle$, where Y_1 and Y_2 are the intersections of Π with the lines $\langle Y, O \rangle$ and $\langle Y, O' \rangle$ respectively. The epipolar line may be constructed in the second image as follows: Determine the plane projective transformation such that $x_i' = Tx_i, i \in \{1, .., 4\}$. Use this transformation to transfer the point y to $y_1' = Ty$. This determines two points in the second image, y' and Ty, which are projections of points (Y and Y_1) on the line $\langle O, Y \rangle$. This defines the epipolar line of y in the second image. A second point, not on Π, will define its corresponding epipolar lines. The epipole lies on both lines, so is determined by their intersection. A similar construction gives epipolar lines and hence the epipole in the first image.

3. The epipolar line in the x' image of any other point x is given by $(Tx) \times p'$.
4. Hence $F = [p']_\times T$, where $[p']_\times$ is the skew matrix formed from the components of p'.

Projective Invariants This configuration has seventeen degrees of freedom (three for each point less one for the planarity constraint), and there is no isotropy group. From the counting argument in Section 2, the configuration has two projective invariants. The invariants can be computed using (1) for the 3D invariants of six points (one of the three invariants will be zero due to planarity of four points). Equivalently the invariants can be computed from the planar invariants of the four coplanar points together with the intersection of the line through X_5 and X_6 and the plane Π. See Figure 3.

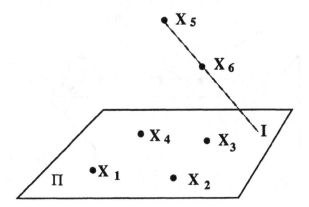

Fig. 3. The projective invariant of 6 points, 4 coplanar (points 1-4), can be computed by intersecting the line, **L**, through the non-planar points (5 and 6) with Π. There are then 5 coplanar points, for which two invariants to the plane projective group can be calculated.

1. The $\mathbf{x}'$ image of the point of intersection, $\mathbf{X}_I$, of the line $< \mathbf{X}_5, \mathbf{X}_6 >$ and the plane, is given by the intersection [22] of the lines $(\mathbf{Tx}_5) \times (\mathbf{Tx}_6)$ and $\mathbf{x}_5' \times \mathbf{x}_6'$.
2. Two plane projective invariants can be calculated from five points (in this case the four coplanar points and $\mathbf{x}_I'$) by

$$I_1 = \frac{|m_{431}||m_{I21}|}{|m_{421}||m_{I31}|} \qquad I_2 = \frac{|m_{421}||m_{I32}|}{|m_{432}||m_{I21}|} \qquad (10)$$

where m_{jkl} is the matrix $[\mathbf{x}_j' \mathbf{x}_k' \mathbf{x}_l']$ and $|m_{jkl}|$ its determinant.

3.2 Five Point Configuration, Four Coplanar

As shown in Section 2.3 there is a one dimensional isotropy group for configuration **II**. There are only fourteen degrees of freedom, and consequently (equation 2) no projective invariants. Furthermore, the epipolar geometry cannot be determined.

It is instructive to consider how the epipolar geometry is constrained by images of this configuration. It is clear from Figure 4 that in each image the epipole is constrained to lie on a line. To see this algebraically we again use the notation in Section 2 for the 3D points $\mathbf{X}_i, i \in \{1,..,5\}$. In this case we can, without loss of generality, choose $\mathbf{X}_4$ to have coordinates $\mathbf{X}_4 = (1,1,1,0)^\mathsf{T}$. We choose the projective coordinates of their images in both views to be:

$$\begin{aligned}
\mathbf{x}_1 = \mathbf{x}_1' &= (1,0,0)^\mathsf{T} \\
\mathbf{x}_2 = \mathbf{x}_2' &= (0,1,0)^\mathsf{T} \\
\mathbf{x}_3 = \mathbf{x}_3' &= (0,0,1)^\mathsf{T} \\
\mathbf{x}_4 = \mathbf{x}_4' &= (1,1,1)^\mathsf{T}
\end{aligned}$$

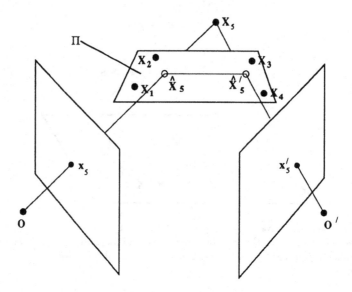

Fig. 4. As in Figure 2 the line $< \hat{\mathbf{X}}_5, \hat{\mathbf{X}}'_5 >$ is coplanar with the line joining the optical centers $< \mathbf{O}, \mathbf{O}' >$. Thus one point off the plane constrains the epipole to lie on a line in each image, namely the projection of $< \hat{\mathbf{X}}_5, \hat{\mathbf{X}}'_5 >$.

and $\mathbf{X}_5$ to project to $\mathbf{x}_5 = (a, b, c)^{\mathsf{T}}$ and $\mathbf{x}'_5 = (a', b', c')^{\mathsf{T}}$ in the left and right images respectively. With this notation coordinates for points on the plane, Π, are identical for both images (and given by the first three homogeneous 3D coordinates). The projection matrix can be shown to be:

$$\mathbf{P} = \begin{pmatrix} \rho\,0\,0\,a \\ 0\,\rho\,0\,b \\ 0\,0\,\rho\,c \end{pmatrix}. \tag{11}$$

Up to an overall scaling, this has one degree of freedom (since only the ratio of $\{a, b, c\}$ is significant). Solving for the optical center $\mathbf{C} = (C_1, C_2, C_3, C_4)^{\mathsf{T}}$ via $\mathbf{PC} = 0$ gives

$$\mathbf{C} = C_4 \begin{pmatrix} \frac{a}{\rho} \\ \frac{b}{\rho} \\ \frac{c}{\rho} \\ 1 \end{pmatrix} = \alpha \begin{pmatrix} a \\ b \\ c \\ 0 \end{pmatrix} + \beta \begin{pmatrix} 0 \\ 0 \\ 0 \\ 1 \end{pmatrix}$$

which, as expected, constrains $\mathbf{C}$ to lie on the line through $\mathbf{X}_5$ intersecting Π in the point $\hat{\mathbf{X}}_5 = (a, b, c, 0)^{\mathsf{T}}$. Corresponding results for the primed image are obtained by priming a, b, c etc. Consequently, both optical centers are constrained to lie on lines containing $\mathbf{X}_5$ (i.e. the lines are coplanar), and so the image of one optical center from the other (the epipole) is constrained to a line.

A complementary picture is obtained by considering the action of the isotropy group: Under the (one dimensional) isotropy group, $\mathbf{T}_1$, the configuration $\mathbf{X}_i, i \in$

$\{1, .., 5\}$ is unchanged, but the optical centers *are* moved - they travel along the line $< \hat{\mathbf{X}}_5, \mathbf{X}_5 >$ and $< \hat{\mathbf{X}}_5', \mathbf{X}_5 >$ respectively (i.e. the orbit is along the fixed lines as described in Section 2.2). Clearly, a projective transformation cannot alter projective invariants, and indeed the action of the isotropy group maintains the image projective coordinates.

3.3 Four Points and a Line Configuration, Four Points Coplanar

As shown in Section 2.2 there is a two dimensional isotropy group for configuration **I**. There are fifteen degrees of freedom, and consequently (equation 2) two projective invariants. These are determined in the same manner as the six point configuration **VI**.

Projective Invariants

1. Compute the plane projective transformation matrix $\mathbf{T}$, such that $\mathbf{x}_i' = \mathbf{T}\mathbf{x}_i, i \in \{1, .., 4\}$.
2. The $\mathbf{x}'$ image of the point of intersection, $\mathbf{x}_I'$, of the plane Π and line $\mathbf{L}$, is given by the line intersection $(\mathbf{T}^{-1}\mathbf{l}) \times \mathbf{l}'$, where $\mathbf{l}$ and $\mathbf{l}'$ are the images of $\mathbf{L}$ [22].
3. Two plane projective invariants can be calculated for the five points (in this case the four coplanar points and $\mathbf{x}_I'$) as in (10).

The epipolar geometry cannot be determined in this case. The epipole is not even constrained to a line. This is clear from the action of the isotropy group on the optical center, which moves $\mathbf{C}$ on a *surface* (as the isotropy group is two dimensional) whilst the structure, S, is unchanged. As this is a projective transformation both the image projective invariants, and the 3D projective invariants of S are unaltered. So there is a surface, the orbit of $\mathbf{C}$ under Is, over which $\mathbf{C}$ can move which has no effect on projective image measurements. Conversely, the image projective invariants are *only* affected by motions of $\mathbf{C}$ transverse to this surface. Consequently, image projective invariants can only place constraints on this transverse motion, so $\mathbf{C}$ is restricted to a one-parameter family of surfaces. From Section 2.2 it can be shown that this orbit (the surface) is a plane.

Counting constraints and unknowns indicates why 3D projective invariants can be recovered from two images in this case: There are four "unknowns" (two 3D invariants and the one degree of freedom of each optical center which affects the image i.e. can be measured) and four measurements (the two projective coordinates of the line in each image). Consequently, it is possible to solve for the 3D invariants in this case.

Experimental Results Invariants using (10) are measured from the images shown in Figure 6. Points are extracted as follows: A local implementation of Canny's edge detector is used to find edges to sub-pixel accuracy. These edge chains are linked, extrapolating over any small gaps. A piecewise linear graph is obtained by incremental straight line fitting. Edgels in the vicinity of tangent discontinuities ("corners") are excised before fitting as the edge operator localisation degrades with curvature. Vertices are obtained by extrapolating and intersecting the fitted lines. The results are given in Table 3 with the labelling indicated in Figure 5.

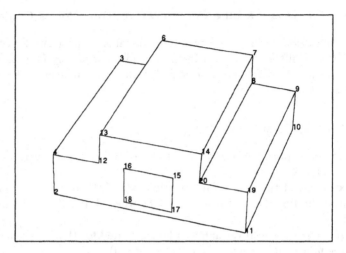

Fig. 5. Line drawing of the hole punch extracted from image A in Figure 6. Points 1 and 5 are occluded in this view.

Images	I_1	I_2
D,B	0.378	-1.117
B,A	0.371	-1.170
C,E	0.370	-1.150
F,A	0.333	-1.314

Table 3. Line and four coplanar point two view invariants extracted from several combinations of views using points 2,4,14,17 and the line between points 6 and 13.

3.4 Summary

We have demonstrated that multiple view invariants of 3D configurations can be recovered without epipolar calibration being necessary, and argued that if a configuration has a non trivial isotropy group under projective transformations of 3D, then it is not possible to recover epipolar geometry using projective measurements.

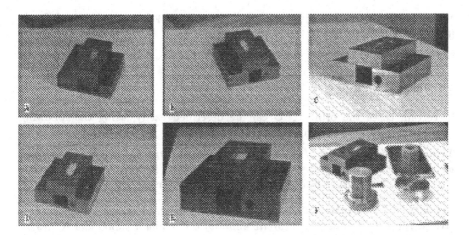

Fig. 6. Images of a hole punch captured with different lenses and viewpoints.

The discussion applies as well to analogues of these configuration, for example: four coplanar lines and two non-coplanar points, and five lines (four coplanar). If the configurations are enlarged by adding lines or points to the plane Π, there are no additional constraints on the optical center position or epipolar geometry, since Π is a plane of fixed points under the isotropy group. However, additional planar projective invariants will then be available.

4 Isotropy Sub-Groups and Camera Calibration

Suppose a configuration S for which a non-trivial isotropy $\mathbf{T}_s$ exists, is used to determine epipolar geometry. Under a projective transformation $\mathbf{T}$ of 3D all projective image measurements are unaffected. In particular under $\mathbf{T}_s$ the configuration S is unchanged. However, the optical centers are moved by $\mathbf{T}_s$ (e.g. for configuration **I** they move on a surface). Consequently, it is not possible to determine the optical centers, $\mathbf{C}$, since they can move on an orbit without affecting image measurements. To summarise:

Theorem *Suppose a configuration S is perspectively imaged onto one or more images. Then, if there exists an isotropy sub-group, $\mathbf{T}_s$, for S under the group of 3D projective transformations, the optical center(s) cannot be uniquely determined from projective image measurements.*

If $\mathbf{x} = \mathbf{P}\mathbf{X}$ and $\mathbf{X}' = \mathbf{T}\mathbf{X}$, then for image points to be preserved, $\mathbf{x} = \mathbf{P}\mathbf{T}^{-1}\mathbf{T}\mathbf{X} = \mathbf{P}'\mathbf{X}'$, where $\mathbf{P}' = \mathbf{P}\mathbf{T}^{-1}$. For the isotropy group and points on S,

$\mathbf{X}' = \mathbf{T}_s \mathbf{X} = \mathbf{X}$. Consequently, $\mathbf{x} = \mathbf{P}\mathbf{T}_s^{-1}\mathbf{X} = \mathbf{P}\mathbf{X}$, so $\mathbf{P}$ is not uniquely defined. If $\mathbf{C}$ is a solution for the opical center, then any point on the orbit $\mathbf{T}_s^{-1}\mathbf{C}$ is also a solution, since $\mathbf{P}(\mathbf{T}_s^{-1}\mathbf{C}) = \mathbf{P}\mathbf{C} = 0$.

4.1 Twisted Cubics

In certain cases the orbit $\mathbf{T}_s^{-1}\mathbf{C}$ can be described easily, using the following theorem stated by Buchanan [2].

Theorem *Let $\mathcal{R}$ be a set of reference points in real 3-space. Let $\mathbf{P}$ be a projection of maximal rank from 3-space onto 2-space with $K = \text{Ker}(\mathbf{P})$. Then there exists a projection $\mathbf{P}'$, distinct from $\mathbf{P}$, with $\mathbf{P}(R) = \mathbf{P}'(R)$ for all $R \in \mathcal{R}$ if and only if*

(a) $\mathcal{R} \cup \{K\}$ *is a subset of a possibly composite twisted cubic or*
(b) $\mathcal{R}$ *is a subset of the set theoretic union of a line and a plane, and K lies on the line.*

Note that the kernel $\text{Ker}(\mathbf{P})$ is the optical center of the camera. Buchanan lists the curves in case (a) as follows:

1. a proper (i.e. non singular) twisted cubic;
2. the union of a conic and a line which cuts the conic but which is not coplanar with the conic.
3. the union of two skew lines and a common transversal.

Properties of the Twisted Cubic Let c be a non-singular twisted cubic [23]. Then c is not contained in any plane of $\mathcal{P}^3$; it intersects a general plane at three distinct points. There is a unique c through six points in general position. The curve c is rational, and has a parameterisation of the form $t \mapsto \mathbf{T}(1, t, t^2, t^3)^\mathsf{T}$ where $\mathbf{T}$ is an invertible 4×4 matrix. It follows that there is a collineation of $\mathcal{P}^3$ that maps c to a standard twisted cubic $t \mapsto (1, t, t^2, t^3)^\mathsf{T}$. Thus any two proper twisted cubics are projectively equivalent.

4.2 The Twisted Cubic and Camera Calibration

The twisted cubic plays a key rôle in (extrinsic) camera calibration because of the following property. Let $\mathbf{A}$, $\mathbf{B}$ be two distinct points on the non-singular twisted cubic c, and $\mathbf{X}$ a variable point on c. The chords $< \mathbf{X}, \mathbf{A} >$, as $\mathbf{X}$ moves on c, form a subset of the star of lines $\text{st}(\mathbf{A})$, and similarly for $\mathbf{B}$. Then there is a unique collineation $\mathbf{U} : \text{st}(\mathbf{A}) \to \text{st}(\mathbf{B})$ such that $\mathbf{U}(< \mathbf{X}, \mathbf{A} >) =< \mathbf{X}, \mathbf{B} >$ for all $\mathbf{X}$ in c.

It is the existence of the collineation $\mathbf{U}$ that is the basis of the above theorem quoted from [2]. If the true optical center $\mathbf{C}$ and data points $\mathbf{X}_i$ used in the camera calibration all lie on a twisted cubic c then all points on c are candidates for the optical center of the camera. Each putative optical center yields a camera calibration compatible with the $\mathbf{X}_i$ and their projections $\mathbf{x}_i$ to the image. There is always a twisted cubic though six points in general position in space. Thus a unique camera calibration cannot be obtained from five or fewer data points.

We have seen that when there is an isotropy (for example as in configuration **II**) it is not possible to solve for the optical centers. Here we show that this ambiguity is a result of the points lying on a twisted cubic. Let Π be the plane containing the four points and let the optical center be a point **C** not contained in Π. Then there is a unique conic through the five points $\mathbf{X}_\Pi = (< \mathbf{C}, \mathbf{X}_5 > \cap \Pi)$ and $\mathbf{X}_i, i \in \{1, .., 4\}$. Consequently, the configuration **II** together with **C** is contained in the degenerate case (2) of a twisted cubic, and there is not a unique solution for **C**. Any point on the line is a candidate for the optical center. For configuration **VI**, there is no longer freedom to choose the line. In general, the configuration and the true optical center **C** do not lie on a twisted cubic. Consequently, it is possible to obtain a unique solution for **C**.

4.3 Critical Surfaces

The twisted cubic of Section 4.2 also appears in the theory of critical surfaces for reconstruction from two views of points [18]. Let ψ be a critical surface and let **O**, **C** be the optical centres from which the images of ψ are obtained. It is well known that ψ is in general a hyperboloid of one sheet and that it contains **O**, **C**. The reconstruction is ambiguous thus there is a second critical surface ϕ defining the same set of image correspondences as ψ. Let the optical centres for ϕ be **O**, **C**'. It can be shown that ψ and ϕ contain all three points **O**, **C**, **C**'.

Let **X** be a general point on ψ or ϕ. If the coordinates of **X** are known then it is possible to distinguish the true reconstruction from the false. For example, if **X** is on ψ but not on ϕ, then ψ is the true reconstruction and ϕ is false. There are certain exceptional points **X** which cannot be used to distinguish between the two reconstructions even when their coordinates are known. These points are contained in $\psi \cap \phi$.

The intersection $\psi \cap \phi$ is a space curve of degree four which splits into a line **L** and a twisted cubic c. The line **L** contains **O** whilst c contains **C** and **C**'. Let $\mathbf{x} \leftrightarrow \mathbf{x}'$ be a pair of corresponding image points such that $\mathbf{x}$ is the image of **L**. If the optical centre of the camera is at **C** then there is a point $\mathbf{X}_1$ on **L** projecting to $\mathbf{x}'$. Similarly, if the optical centre of the camera is at **C**' then there is a point $\mathbf{X}_2$ on **L** projecting to $\mathbf{x}'$. The points $\mathbf{X}_1$, $\mathbf{X}_2$ are in general different; this is possible because the entire line **L** projects to a single point $\mathbf{x}$ in the first image. The true reconstruction can be found once it is known which of the points $\mathbf{X}_1$, $\mathbf{X}_2$ gives rise to the correspondence $\mathbf{x} \leftrightarrow \mathbf{x}'$.

The true reconstruction cannot be distinguished from the false by giving the coordinates of the points on c. To see this, let $\mathbf{X}_1$ be a general point of c projecting to $\mathbf{x}$ when the camera is at **O** and to $\mathbf{x}'$ when the camera is at **C**. Let $\mathbf{X}_2$ be the point of ϕ projecting to $\mathbf{x}$ at **O** and to $\mathbf{x}'$ at **C**'. The line $< \mathbf{O}, \mathbf{X}_1 >$ cuts ϕ at a unique point, $\mathbf{X}_1$, distinct from **O**. It follows that $\mathbf{X}_1 = \mathbf{X}_2$. The images of c taken from **C** and **C**' are indistinguishable. In the case of calibrated cameras this means indistinguishable up to a rotation of the camera; for uncalibrated cameras this means indistinguishable up to a collineation of the image. Both cases are examples of the rôle of the twisted cubic in camera calibration, as described in Section 4.2.

5 Transfer

The process of rendering new images given only *image(s)* of the original structure is known as *transfer*. Typically, two images are provided, and a new view of a 3D structure is rendered based on a number of "reference" points. Epipolar geometry is often used to carry out this process (see Barrett [21] and [3, 7]). For example, in the affine case (parallel projection) only four points are required to determine epipolar geometry. Suppose four points are in correspondence between two acquisition images, and a third target image. This is sufficient to determine the epipolar geometry between each acquisition image and the target image. Any other point imaged in both acquisition images can then be transferred by intersecting epipolar lines, as shown in Figure 7.

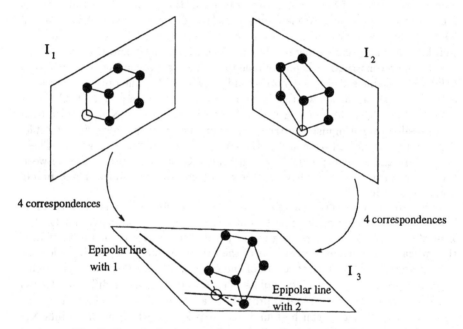

Fig. 7. Transfer by intersecting epipolar lines in the affine case.

Clearly, this process fails when epipolar lines are coincident, and becomes increasingly ill-conditioned as the lines become less "transverse". This occurs in the affine case when a camera rotates about a fixed object axis. In this case the epipolar lines in the target image are parallel.

In the projective case at least seven points are needed to determine epipolar geometry. Transfer fails for 3D points on the tri-focal plane (the plane containing all three optical centers). The epipolar lines for such points are coincident in the target image. The tri-focal plane intersects the target image in the line containing the epipoles of the two acquisition views. For points "close to" the trifocal plane, transfer will be very poorly conditioned. Examples of transfer using this method are shown in Barrett's paper in this volume. The worst situation is when the three optical centers are collinear, in which case transfer is not possible for any point by epipolar line intersection.

Ths problem is avoided if structure is used. For example, consider the affine case with four points again in correspondence between the three images. From the two acquisition images the 3D affine coordinates of all corresponding points can be determined. The projection matrix P from this 3D affine structure to the target image is also determined from four points, and is used to project the 3D structure onto the target image. In fact, the actual reconstruction of 3D structure is not required [25]. A similar argument applies in the projective case, where seven points are required in general.

Shashua [26] derives a trilinear function of image coordinates in three views, which can be used for transfer. Unlike epipolar transfer, this method does not fail when the optical centers are collinear.

6 Discussion

We have demonstrated that for a number of configurations, although it is possible to recover invariants in a stable fashion from two views, it is not possible to recover structure or epipolar geometry. This is important in terms of stability: As is well known for configurations "close to" critical surfaces [13, 18] numerical procedures for recovering structure are ill-conditioned. In the same way, one would expect ill-conditioning in configurations close to an isotropy (e.g. if a significant part of the point set used to determine the epipolar geometry is near planar).

It has also been shown that transfer from two views to a third can be ill-conditioned, and may fail, if epipolar geometry alone is used.

Epipolar geometry is also not necessary for self-calibration. Hartley [11] describes a self-calibration method for the case of a camera rotating about its optical center, but not translating. In this case there is no epipolar geometry. Luong and Viéville [14] and Hartley (this volume), show that intrinsic parameters can be determined from projection matrices computed from two or more views of structure known up to an affine ambiguity.

It remains to be seen whether other procedures, such as structure recovery, are more tractable and better conditioned if epipolar geometry is displaced from its central role.

Acknowledgements

A number of people contributed to the ideas in this paper, particularly: David Forsyth, Richard Hartley, Joe Mundy, Larry Shapiro, Phil Torr and Charlie

Rothwell. Thanks to Amnon Shashua for questioning the relation of isotropies to critical surfaces, which lead to the clarification of the relationship with twisted cubics. Sabine Demey [3] carried out the numerical experiments.

References

1. Beardsley, P., Sinclair, D., Zisserman, A., Ego-motion from six points, *Insight meeting, Catholic University Leuven*, Feb. 1992.
2. Buchanan, T., The twisted cubic and camera calibration. *Computer Vision, Graphics, and Image Processing*, 42, 130-132, 1988.
3. Demey, S., Zisserman, A., and Beardsley, P., Affine and projective structure from motion, *Proc. BMVC92, Springer-Verlag*, 1992
4. Faugeras, O.D. and Maybank, S.J., Motion from point matches: multiplicity of solutions, *IJCV-4*, 225-246, 1990.
5. Faugeras, O.D., Luong, Q.T., and Maybank, S.J., Camera self-calibration: theory and experiments, *Proc. ECCV-92*, Springer-Verlag, 321 – 334, 1992.
6. Faugeras, O.D., What can be seen in three dimensions with an uncalibrated stereo rig?, *Proc. ECCV-92*, Springer-Verlag, 563 – 578, 1992.
7. Faugeras, O.D. and Robert, L., What can two images tell us about a third one? *Proc. ECCV-94*, Springer-Verlag, 485-492, 1994.
8. Gros, P. and Quan, L., Présentation de la théorie des invariants sous une forme utilisable en vision par ordinateur, *TR*, LIFIA, 1991.
9. Hartley, R.I., Invariants of points seen in multiple images, *G.E. Internal Report 1992*, also to appear *PAMI*.
10. Hartley, R.I., Gupta, R. and Chang, T., Stereo from uncalibrated cameras, *Proc. of CVPR-92*, 1992.
11. Hartley, R.I., Self-calibration of stationary cameras. *Proc. ECCV-94*, 1994.
12. Longuet-Higgins, H.C., A computer algorithm for reconstructing a scene from two projections, *Nature, Vol.*, 293, 10, Sept. 1981.
13. Luong, Q.T., *Matrice Fondamentale et Autocalibration en Vision par Ordinateur.* PhD thesis, Université de Paris-Sud, France, 1992.
14. Luong, Q.T. and T. Viéville. Canonic representations for the geometries of multiple projective views. Tech. Report UCB/CSD-93-772, University of California, Berkeley, USA, 1993.
15. Maybank, S.J., The projective geometry of ambiguous surfaces, *Phil. Trans. Roy. Soc. Lond. Series A* Vol. 332, 1-47, 1990.
16. Maybank, S.J., Properties of essential matrices, *Int. J. Imaging Systems and Technology*, 2, 380–384, 1990.
17. Maybank, S.J. and Faugeras, O.D., A theory of self-calibration of a moving camera. *International Journal of Computer Vision*, 8:123–151, 1992.
18. Maybank, S.J., *Theory of Reconstruction from Image Motion.* Springer Series in Information Science vol 28. Springer-Verlag: Berlin, 1993.
19. Mohr, R., Projective geometry and computer vision, *Handbook of Pattern Recognition and Computer Vision*, Chen, Pau and Wang editors, 1992.
20. Mohr, R., Sparr, R. and Faugeras, O., Multiple image invariants, *Proc. ESPRIT Workshop on Invariants in Vision, Santa Margherita Ligure*, 1992.
21. Mundy, J. L. and Zisserman, A. (editors), *Geometric Invariance in Computer Vision*, MIT Press, Cambridge Ma, 1992.

22. Quan, L. and Mohr, R., Towards structure from motion for linear features through reference points, *Proc. IEEE Workshop on Visual Motion,* 1991.
23. Semple, J.G. & Kneebone, G.T., *Algebraic Projective Geometry.* Oxford: Clarendon Press, 1953 (reprinted 1979).
24. Shapiro, L.S., Zisserman, A. and Brady, J.M., Motion from point matches using affine epipolar geometry, *Proc. ECCV-94,* 1994.
25. Shapiro, L.S., *Affine analysis of image sequences,* PhD thesis, Oxford University, 1993.
26. Shashua, A., Trilinearity in visual recognition by alignment, *Proc. ECCV-94,* 1994.
27. Szeliski, R. and Kang, S.B., Recovering 3D shape and motion from image streams using non-linear least squares, *DEC Tech. Rep.,* 93/3, 1993.
28. Torr, P.H.S. and Murray, D.W., Stochastic motion clustering, *Proc. ECCV-94,* Springer-Verlag, 328-337, 1994.

Repeated Structures:
Image Correspondence Constraints and
3D Structure Recovery

Joseph L. Mundy[1] and Andrew Zisserman[2]

[1] The General Electric Corporate Research and Development Laboratory,
Schenectady, NY, USA.
[2] Robotics Research Group, Department of Engineering Science, Oxford University,
England

Abstract. Recently, a number of classes of 3D structures have been identified which permit structure recovery and 3D invariants to be measured from a single image of the structure. A large class with this property is the case of *repeated structures* where a structure (such as a pointset, curve or surface), and a transformed copy of the structure are both observed in a single perspective image. In general the 3D reconstruction is only possible up to a 3D projectivity of space, but smaller ambiguities are possible, depending on the nature of the 3D transformation between the repeated structures. An additional theme of the paper is the development of feature correspondence relations based on the epipolar geometry induced in the image by the repeated structure. In some cases, correspondence is based on projective homologies rather than a true epipolar geometry.

1 Introduction

The motivation for this paper arises from the case of repeated structures imaged by a single camera. An image of a repeated structure is equivalent to multiple views of the single structure. For example, an image of an object and a copy of the object translated to a new position is identical in projection properties to two images of the single object obtained by translating the camera.

Recent work [1, 3] has demonstrated that 3D structure can be recovered from a pair of uncalibrated cameras, up to a 3D projective ambiguity in general. Thus, stereo analysis can be applied to a single, uncalibrated camera view of repeated structure to recover 3D structure with the same projective ambiguity.

Repeated geometric configurations often occur in man-made structures and even some natural forms. Some examples are:

- An object repeated in a single scene by an Euclidean transformation, e.g. a row of development houses along a street.
- An object repeated with a more general transformation such as affine or projective, e.g., two ends of a wrench are related by an affine transformation.
- Various 3D spatial symmetries such as,
  - bi-lateral symmetry (e.g. a spoon)

- discrete axial symmetry (e.g. a hex bolt)
- rotational symmetry (e.g. a vase)

These structures impose an epipolar geometry on a single image which determines image correspondences between related points. That is, a point in a structure determines a line through the epipole, on which the corresponding point must lie. An example is given in Figure 1. This epipolar relationship reduces the complexity of determining feature correspondences. An epipolar structure is not always possible. For example, in the case of repetition by reflection, when the plane of symmetry passes through the camera center. However, a correspondence structure still exists, based on a specialized projective transformation, a planar homology which maps corresponding image features of the repeated structures.

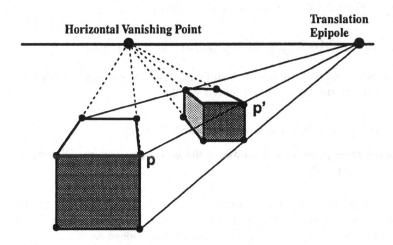

Fig. 1. Two identical structures separated by a horizontal 3D translation. For repetition by translation, corresponding points on the repeated structure generate lines which all converge to a single epipole. The case where corresponding points lie on the same epipolar line is called auto-epipolar.

The full 3D projective transformation is the most general ambiguity which arises from repeated structures viewed by an uncalibrated camera. Projective invariants can be constructed from a single image of repeated structures as for invariants of multiple views[9]. For example, six 3D points determine three independent projective invariants: five points determine an invariant projective coordinate frame so that the remaining point has three invariant coordinates in this five point basis. The ambiguity can be smaller if the camera calibration is partially known or if some restriction applies to the transformation which relates the repeated structures. When the coordinate frames of a stereo pair of identical uncalibrated cameras are related by translation alone, the resulting stereo reconstruction of space is ambiguous only up to a 3D affine transformation. This result was reported by Moons et al [7] and is elaborated elsewhere in this volume. The advantage of an affine reconstruction is that more invariants can be constructed from a given set of features[3].

In this paper we make the following contributions: First, a general process for determining 3D reconstruction ambiguity of various repeated structures is developed (Section 3). Second, a given repeated structure induces an epipolar or other correspondence relationship in the image which can be used to establish corresponding points from each copy of the repeated structure. The basic concepts of epipolar correspondence are introduced in Section 4. The overall approach is illustrated by a number of examples of repeated structure in Section 6. Finally, in some cases the repeated structure does not support a true epipolar structure, however a correspondence structure based on planar homology is still available. These results are discussed in Section 7.

2 Camera Models and Epipolar Geometry

The following analysis is based on techniques developed by Hartley for the study of the essential and fundamental matrix [3, 4].

2.1 Projective Cameras and Standard Forms

The perspective projection from 3D to the image plane, is modeled by a 3 × 4 projection matrix, P, so that

$$\mathbf{x} = \mathbf{P}\mathbf{X} \tag{1}$$

where homogeneous coordinates are used, $\mathbf{X} = (X, Y, Z, 1)^T$, $\mathbf{x} = (x, y, 1)^T$ and equality is up to a non-zero scale factor in the case of homogeneous vectors.

The general perspective camera, P, can be partitioned as

$$\mathbf{P} = [\mathbf{M} \mid -\mathbf{M}\mathbf{t}_0]$$

where M is an arbitrary 3×3 matrix and $\mathbf{t}_0$ is a 3-vector from the world coordinate origin to the center of projection.

We can put the camera in a *standard reference frame*, i.e., the principal ray along $\mathbf{Z}$ and $(\mathbf{u}, \mathbf{v})$ aligned along $(\mathbf{X}, \mathbf{Y})$, by a suitable 3D transformation of coordinates. That is,

$$\mathbf{P}_c = [\mathbf{I}|\mathbf{0}] = \mathbf{P}\mathbf{B} \tag{2}$$

where the 4 × 4 matrix B is

$$\mathbf{B} = \begin{bmatrix} \mathbf{M}^{-1} & \mathbf{t}_0 \\ \mathbf{0}^T & 1 \end{bmatrix}$$

---

[3] A projective transformation of 3D space has 15 degrees of freedom while an affine transformation has only 12. Therefore, an invariant coordinate frame can be constructed from four 3D points in the affine case, while five points are required for the projective case.

To be more specific about B, the camera matrix, M, differs from the standard frame by a rotation of the center of projection as well as an arbitrary change in internal calibration. That is,

$$M = KR$$

where the matrix, K is a 3 × 3 upper triangular matrix and R is a rotation matrix. If K = I, which is the case for a calibrated camera, then B is simply a 3D Euclidean transformation. For an uncalibrated camera an affine transformation of space is required to bring P to standard form[4]

For example, when the camera has square pixels, the matrix, K, is given by,

$$K = \begin{bmatrix} 1 & 0 & \frac{u_0}{f} \\ 0 & 1 & \frac{v_0}{f} \\ 0 & 0 & \frac{1}{f} \end{bmatrix}$$

where (u_0, v_0) is the principal point and f is the focal length. In this case P can be brought to the standard form with a 3D affine transformation,

$$B = \begin{bmatrix} L & t_0 \\ 0^T & 1 \end{bmatrix}$$

where $L = M^{-1}$, or

$$L = R^T \begin{bmatrix} 1 & 0 & -u_0 \\ 0 & 1 & -v_0 \\ 0 & 0 & f \end{bmatrix}$$

2.2 Epipolar Geometry

For two cameras, P_a and P_b,

$$x_a = P_a X \qquad\qquad x_b = P_b X$$

where x_a and x_b are corresponding points in the images formed by each camera. Corresponding points in the two images satisfy the epipolar constraint:

$$x_b^T F x_a = 0 \tag{3}$$

where F is a 3 × 3 matrix of maximum rank 2, called the fundamental matrix. The epipolar line in image b corresponding to x_a is $l_b = F x_a$, and in image a corresponding to x_b is $l_a = F^t x_b$, where l is the vector of homogeneous line coefficients.

---

[4] In Section 3.5 we discuss the possibility of *self-calibration* where the internal parameters of a camera can be determined from a set of initially uncalibrated views. If such calibration is possible, then the ambiguity can be less than affine.

For two cameras, $[\mathbf{I}|\mathbf{0}]$ and $[\mathbf{M}| - \mathbf{Mt}]$, the fundamental matrix is given by[3],

$$\mathbf{F} = \mathbf{M}^{-T} [\mathbf{t}]_\times = [\mathbf{Mt}]_\times \mathbf{M} \tag{4}$$

where the notation $[\mathbf{v}]_\times$, with $\mathbf{v} = (x, y, z)^T$, is the matrix

$$[\mathbf{v}]_\times = \begin{bmatrix} 0 & -z & y \\ z & 0 & -x \\ -y & x & 0 \end{bmatrix}$$

Given some other three-element vector, $\mathbf{w}$, the cross-product, $\mathbf{v} \times \mathbf{w}$, is

$$[\mathbf{v}]_\times \mathbf{w}$$

In the case of calibrated cameras, where $\mathbf{K} = \mathbf{I}$, the fundamental matrix is known as the essential matrix, and equation (4) becomes

$$\mathbf{E} = \mathbf{R} [\mathbf{t}]_\times = [\mathbf{Rt}]_\times \mathbf{R}$$

The epipole is defined as the point common to all epipolar lines, i.e., ϵ_b is defined by,

$$\epsilon_b^T \mathbf{l}_b = \epsilon_b^T \mathbf{F} \mathbf{x}_a = 0$$

for all $\mathbf{x}_a$. Thus, $\epsilon_b^T \mathbf{F} = \mathbf{0}^T$ or $\mathbf{F}^T \epsilon_b = 0$ and ϵ_b is the null space of $\mathbf{F}^T$. Similarly, $\mathbf{F}\epsilon_a = \mathbf{0}$.

2.3 3D Reconstruction

For two cameras, $[\mathbf{I}|\mathbf{0}]$ and $[\mathbf{M}| - \mathbf{Mt}]$, the the rays in 3D space defined by corresponding points, $\mathbf{x}_a$, and $\mathbf{x}_b$ are,

$$\mathbf{x}_a = \lambda_a \begin{bmatrix} u_a \\ v_a \\ 1 \end{bmatrix} = \begin{bmatrix} X \\ Y \\ Z \end{bmatrix}$$

$$\mathbf{x}_b = \lambda_b \begin{bmatrix} u_b \\ v_b \\ 1 \end{bmatrix} = \mathbf{M} \begin{bmatrix} X \\ Y \\ Z \end{bmatrix} - \mathbf{M} \begin{bmatrix} t_x \\ t_y \\ t_z \end{bmatrix}$$

Thus,

$$\lambda_a \begin{bmatrix} u_a \\ v_a \\ 1 \end{bmatrix} + \begin{bmatrix} t_x \\ t_y \\ t_z \end{bmatrix} = \lambda_b \mathbf{M}^{-1} \begin{bmatrix} u_b \\ v_b \\ 1 \end{bmatrix} \tag{5}$$

Solving for λ_a and λ_b determines $(X, Y, Z)^T$.

3 Ambiguity of 3D Reconstruction

We will first proceed as if there are two cameras observing a single copy of the repeated structure and then show how standard stereo reconstruction is related to repeated structures in a single view. The ambiguity is determined in four stages:

1. The constraints that apply to the two cameras (arising from the transformation on the repeated structure) are found.
2. The cameras are transformed such that P_a takes the standard form. This is not strictly necessary but considerably simplifies the subsequent analysis.
3. The most general transformation of 3D is determined which preserves the constraints on the cameras.
4. The resulting ambiguity in the reconstructed 3D structure is then computed.

The approach to ambiguity analysis is illustrated by considering a specific example.

3.1 Two Cameras Related by Translation

Suppose we have two cameras, P_a and P_b whose external 3D coordinate frames differ only by a translation, t. The 3×3 matrices, M_a, M_b are related by,

$$M_a = K_a R$$
$$M_b = K_b R$$

where K_a, K_b are upper triangular[5] and represent the internal calibration of each camera.

Applying the standard transformation to P_b,

$$P'_b = P_b B = \left[M_b M_a^{-1} \mid - M_b t \right]$$

But,

$$M_b M_a^{-1} = K_b R R^{-1} K_a^{-1} = K_0$$

where K_0 represents the difference in the internal calibration of P_a, P_b. The final form of the cameras is then:

$$P'_a = [I|0] \qquad (6)$$
$$P'_b = [K_0| - M_b t]$$

For identical cameras, $K_0 = I$ (since $K_a = K_b$). For the case of repeated structures, the cameras are always identical.

---

[5] Note that upper triangular matrices form a group under multiplication, e.g. $K_1 K_2 = K_3$ and $K_1^{-1} = K_4$, where K_i are upper triangular.

3.2 Ambiguity of the Camera Relation

The next step in analyzing the ambiguity of reconstruction is to determine what transformations can be applied to the cameras without affecting their relationship. Consider a general projective transformation, D, where

$$D = \begin{bmatrix} E & s \\ a^T & 1 \end{bmatrix}$$

In order to keep the standard form for the first camera,

$$[I|0]D = [I|0]$$

so $s = 0$, $E = I$. Applying the resulting matrix D to the second camera, we have the following constraint on the vector, a.

$$K_0 - t'a^T = K'_0$$

where $t' = M_b t$ and K'_0 is of the same form as K_0, i.e. the same constraints on the matrix elements. For example, a zero element of K_0 is also zero in K'_0. Such constraints hold since the cameras in the standard frame differ only in internal calibration which must be the same form as K_0. Considering identical cameras where $K_0 = I$ and expanding the matrices,

$$\begin{bmatrix} 1 & 0 & 0 \\ 0 & 1 & 0 \\ 0 & 0 & 1 \end{bmatrix} - \begin{bmatrix} t'_1 a_1 & t'_1 a_2 & t'_1 a_3 \\ t'_2 a_1 & t'_2 a_2 & t'_2 a_3 \\ t'_3 a_1 & t'_3 a_2 & t'_3 a_3 \end{bmatrix} = k \begin{bmatrix} 1 & 0 & 0 \\ 0 & 1 & 0 \\ 0 & 0 & 1 \end{bmatrix}$$

So it follows that $k = 1$ and

$$a_1 = a_2 = a_3 = 0$$

since t' is a general vector. Thus the transformation, D, is forced to be the identity.

In general, not all components of the vector a will be forced to zero. Examples where $a \neq 0$ will arise in analyzing other repeated structure classes in Section 6.

3.3 Reconstructing 3D Geometry

From equation (5) we obtain in this case:

$$\lambda_a \begin{bmatrix} u_a \\ v_a \\ 1 \end{bmatrix} + t' = \lambda_b K_0^{-1} \begin{bmatrix} u_b \\ v_b \\ 1 \end{bmatrix} \tag{7}$$

This vector equation is homogeneous in λ_a, λ_b, t', so we can scale all the 3D coordinates of space by a constant k without affecting the solution. In general, uniform scaling is the only new source of ambiguity arising from the reconstruction of 3D space. Uniform scaling can be represented as,

$$S = \begin{bmatrix} I & 0 \\ 0^T & s \end{bmatrix}$$

3.4 The Overall Ambiguity

The total ambiguity of reconstruction is found by multiplying the 3D transformation matrices encountered in producing the final reconstruction. For our example, the total transformation is $T = BDS$

$$T = \begin{bmatrix} M_a^{-1} & t_0 \\ 0^T & 1 \end{bmatrix} \begin{bmatrix} I & 0 \\ 0^T & 1 \end{bmatrix} \begin{bmatrix} I & 0 \\ 0^T & s \end{bmatrix}$$

Thus, for pure translation the overall reconstruction is 3D affine. To summarise, the overall reconstruction ambiguity is obtained by analyzing the following three stages of transformation.

1. Transform one of the cameras to the standard frame (using B). For uncalibrated cameras, this transformation introduces an affine transformation of space. A general affine transformation exhibits 12 degrees of freedom, but the transformation to the standard camera frame is often restricted to 10 parameters since the internal calibration involves only unknown focal length, aspect ratio, and principal point. This ten parameter transformation is the least ambiguity that can occur for cameras with unknown internal calibration.

2. Determine what projectivities of 3D space leave the standard form for the cameras unchanged. At this stage, a full projective transformation might be allowable. For example, when the two cameras are related by a general 3D rotation and translation, all elements of a are non-zero.

3. Determine the ambiguity of stereo reconstruction itself. The only ambiguity which can occur is an isotropic scaling of space (which is covered by an affine transformation).

Even though our main interest is in repeated structures which corresponds to identical cameras, other cases have been considered according to these steps to compare with the results of Moons *et al* (in this volume).

The overall ambiguity for two cameras under translation is summarized in Table 1.

Case	Relation Between Cameras	Resulting Ambiguity
1	Identical Calibrated Cameras	Isotropic Scaled Euclidean
2	Identical Uncalibrated Cameras	Affine
3	Different Focal Lengths	Affine
4	Same Principal Points, $\neq 0$, Same f's	Affine
5	Same Principal Points, $\neq 0$, Different f's	Projective
6	Different Principal Points, Same f's	Affine
7	Different Principal Points, Diff. f's	Projective

Table 1. Results for the ambiguity of 3D reconstruction for cameras related by translation only. Only cases 1, 2 and 4 apply to repeated structures under translation.

3.5 Camera Self-Calibration

Recent work on camera calibration from images taken of arbitrary scenes and arbitrary viewpoints bears some relation to the investigation of ambiguity of reconstruction for repeated structures[6]. Suppose a 3D structure, $\mathbf{X}$, is known up to an affine ambiguity. We define an image pair $\mathbf{x}_a = P_a\mathbf{X}$ and $\mathbf{x}_b = P_b\mathbf{X}$ and the plane at infinity $X_4 = 0$. For points on the plane at infinity, $\mathbf{X}^\infty = (X, Y, Z, 0)^\top$, $\mathbf{x}_a = M_a\mathbf{X}^\infty$, $\mathbf{x}_b = M_b\mathbf{X}^\infty$, and

$$\mathbf{x}_b = M_b M_a^{-1}\mathbf{x}_a = H_\infty\mathbf{x}_a \tag{8}$$

where H_∞ is the *infinite homography* [6] which maps image points from the first image to the second image for 3D points on π_∞, i.e. vanishing points are mapped to vanishing points. It can be shown [6] that under H_∞

$$C_b = H_\infty C_a H_\infty^\top \tag{9}$$

where $C_i = K_i K_i^\top$. C_i is the image in view i of the dual (i.e. the inverse) of the absolute conic. The image of the absolute conic, $(K_i K_i^\top)^{-1}$ is independent of the camera's position and orientation, and only depends on the camera's intrinsic parameters [2]. Equation (9) is the transformation of a conic under the linear transformation H_∞.

If camera intrinsic parameters are fixed between views, $C_a = C_b = C$ then

$$C = H_\infty C H_\infty^\top. \tag{10}$$

This is a linear equation for C. In general there is a one parameter family of solutions (as well as an overal scale), but this is reduced to a two fold ambiguity by assuming there is no skew between the image axes (a quadratic constraint on the elements of C). Once C is determined (up to scale), K can be obtained simply by a Choleski decomposition of $C = KK^\top$. Subsequently, the affine structure ambiguity can be reduced to only a scaled Euclidean ambiguity by the transformation

$$\begin{bmatrix} X \\ Y \\ Z \end{bmatrix}^S = K^{-1} \begin{bmatrix} X \\ Y \\ Z \end{bmatrix}^A \tag{11}$$

It can be shown [6] that

$$H_\infty = KRK^{-1} \tag{12}$$

where R is the rotation between images. If there is no rotation, equation (10) reduces to $C = C$ and there is no constraint on C. It appears that in all self-calibration methods (e.g. [2, 5] and Hartley (in this volume)) if there is no rotation between views then there is no self-calibration constraint on the intrinsic parameters. Thus the ambiguity of reconstruction remains at least affine.

---

[6] This material was recently added in response to the paper by Luong and Vieville [6] since it is appropriate to characterize their results in the ambiguity framework just presented. The notation used here differs from that in [6], where K is the image of the dual of the absolute conic.

4 Epipolar Correspondence Structure

An important aspect of 3D reconstruction from repeated structures is the determination of epipolar geometry. Epipolar geometry defines the image relationships between corresponding features on the repeated structure. These relationships are encapsulated in the fundamental matrix, F.

This is illustrated using again two identical cameras related by a translation. When the two camera frames are related by the translation vector, t, the fundamental matrix is,

$$F_t = [t]_\times = \begin{bmatrix} 0 & -t_z & t_y \\ t_z & 0 & -t_x \\ -t_y & t_x & 0 \end{bmatrix}$$

and $F_t^T = -F_t$, $\epsilon_a = \epsilon_b = \epsilon$. where

$$\epsilon = \begin{bmatrix} t_x \\ t_y \\ t_z \end{bmatrix}$$

so in image plane coordinates,

$$\epsilon_u = \frac{t_x}{t_z} \qquad \epsilon_v = \frac{t_y}{t_z}$$

Consequently, from the epipoles alone, t can only be recovered up to scale - this leads to an unknown scale in the stereo 3D reconstruction.

This case also illustrates a useful constraint which applies more generally: corresponding image points lie on the same epipolar line. That is,

$$l = F_t x_a = [t]_\times x_a$$

But, $[t]_\times x_a = t \times x_a$ and

$$x_a \cdot (t \times x_a) = x_a \cdot l = 0$$

so x_a also lies on l. This convenient epipolar correspondence geometry is called *auto-epipolar*. In subsequent discussion, we will focus on repeated structure classes which result in auto-epipolar feature correspondence.

5 Repeated Structures

Now we relate the procedures developed for two cameras observing a single structure, the usual stereo configuration, to the case of a single image of a repeated structure.

Suppose we have a structure, S, and a transformation which generates a *copy* of S, i.e. $S' = T_g(S)$, where $g \in G$, for some group G. S and S' are viewed in a single perspective image. This is equivalent to a stereo pair (with the *camera's* related by g^{-1}). As in the stereo case, there are three goals:

1. Determine the ambiguity of the reconstruction (and consequently the appropriate invariants).
2. Determine the correspondence geometry within the single image.
3. Develop an algorithm for carrying out the reconstruction and computing invariants based on the correspondence geometry.

In this general setting, it becomes clear that it is not necessary that we restrict ourselves to simple translations or rotations (Euclidean transformations) of S. Many 3D objects can be represented as repeated structures where G is an equiform or affine transformation. For example, a rod with two different diameter spheres at each end, can be defined as a translation followed by an equiform scaling. The case of extruded surfaces can be viewed as translation and scaling of the cross-sectional boundary curve.

Repeated structures can also be defined by other transformational symmetries between S and S'. A case we consider in detail below is bilateral symmetry where T_g is a mirror reflection about the symmetry plane. A similar transformation arises in the case of rotationally symmetric objects where the outline curve on the object surface can be considered as a bilateral symmetry structure where the plane of symmetry passes through the camera center of projection.

5.1 Ambiguity of Reconstruction

If the transformation which generates the copy is T_g, then an equivalent camera configuration is given by P_a and $P_a T_g^{-1}$. Without loss of generality, we take

$$P_a = K[I|0]$$

Suppose T_g^{-1} is an affine transformation. This can be represented as:

$$T_A = \begin{bmatrix} A & t' \\ 0^T & 1 \end{bmatrix}$$

Then P_b is given by

$$P_b = K[I|0] \begin{bmatrix} A & t' \\ 0^T & 1 \end{bmatrix}$$
$$= K[A|t']$$

To determine the ambiguity we follow the procedure in Section 3, and first put P_a into standard form giving:

$$P_a = [I|0] \tag{13}$$
$$P_b = K[AK^{-1}|t']$$
$$= KAK^{-1}[I| - (-KA^{-1}t')]$$

where P_b has the canonical form $M[I| - t]$. We describe a number of special cases of affine transformations in Section 6.

5.2 Epipolar Geometry

Using the second form from equation (4) the fundamental matrix for the equivalent camera pair given in equation (13) is

$$F = [Kt']_\times KAK^{-1}$$

Using the identity,

$$[Mt]_\times = M^{-T}[t]_\times M^{-1} \tag{14}$$

gives

$$F = K^{-T}[t']_\times AK^{-1}$$

We now return to the question of when is the epipolar geometry auto-epipolar? From Section 4 this is when the quadratic form $x^T Fx = 0$. In this case,

$$x^T Fx = (K^{-1}x)^T [t']_\times A(K^{-1}x)$$
$$= x'.[t']_\times Ax'$$

where $x' = K^{-1}x$, which is again a quadratic form. The quadratic form is zero if the matrix

$$[t']_\times A \tag{15}$$

is skew, which provides a simple test for auto-epipolar geometries.

6 Examples of Repeated Structure

6.1 Translation

The transformation between a point X in S and the corresponding point, X' in S' is given by,

$$X' = X + t$$

so that $A = I$ and $t' = t$. An example is shown in Figure 1.

The equivalent cameras in standard form are from equation (13)

$$P_a = [I|0]$$
$$P_b = [I|Kt]$$

This is the case examined in Sections 3 and now considered as a single image of a repeated structure. The overall ambiguity is affine.

The correspondence geometry is clearly auto-epipolar, since $[t]_\times$ is skew.

6.2   Translation and Rotation

Consider a structure and a copy of the structure which has been translated and then rotated and observed in a single view. In this example, the transformation between a point $\mathbf{X}$ in $\mathcal{S}$ and the corresponding point, $\mathbf{X}'$ in $\mathcal{S}'$ is given by,

$$\mathbf{X}' = \mathbf{R}\mathbf{X} + \mathbf{t}$$

where $\mathbf{R}$ is a rotation matrix. The equivalent cameras for this repeated structure are given by $\mathbf{A} = \mathbf{R}$ and $\mathbf{t}' = \mathbf{t}$:

$$P_a = [\mathbf{I}|\mathbf{0}] \tag{16}$$
$$P_b = [\mathbf{KRK}^{-1}|\mathbf{Kt}]$$

The reconstructed 3D geometry is ambiguous up to a projectivity of space which is shown as follows. The form of camera P_b should be preserved by $\mathbf{D}$ so,

$$\mathbf{KRK}^{-1} + \mathbf{a}^T(\mathbf{Kt}) = k\mathbf{K}'\mathbf{R}'\mathbf{K}'^{-1}$$

In this case, all components of $\mathbf{a}$ are, in general non-zero, since the projective transformation is indistinguishable from a difference in camera calibration. That is $\mathbf{a}$ can be accounted for by the difference between $\mathbf{K}$ and $\mathbf{K}'$.

   The epipolar correspondence structure with both translation and rotation is not as convenient as the case of pure translation as it is not auto-epipolar in general. This is clear from the skew test: equation (15) in this case is $[\mathbf{t}]_\times \mathbf{R}$ which is not skew in general.

6.3   Affine Repeated Structures

In this example, the transformation between a point $\mathbf{P}$ in $\mathcal{S}$ and the corresponding point, $\mathbf{P}'$ in $\mathcal{S}'$ is given by,

$$\mathbf{X}' = \mathbf{A}\mathbf{X} + \mathbf{t}$$

where $\mathbf{A}$ is an affine matrix. The equivalent cameras for this repeated structure are,

$$P_a = [\mathbf{I}|\mathbf{0}] \tag{17}$$
$$P_b = [\mathbf{KAK}^{-1}|\mathbf{Kt}] \tag{18}$$

Examples of the general affine copy transformation are shown in Figure 2. The ambiguity of reconstruction is in general projective, since the affine transformation of the copy is indistinguishable from the effects of $\mathbf{a}$. For example, consider the special case of scaling only in Z. In this case,

$$\mathbf{A}_s = \begin{bmatrix} 1 & 0 & 0 \\ 0 & 1 & 0 \\ 0 & 0 & s \end{bmatrix}$$

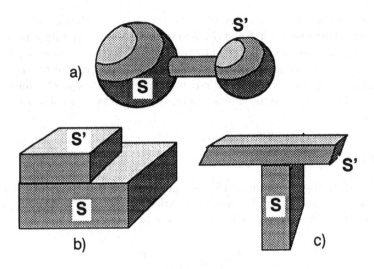

Fig. 2. Examples of repeated structures where the copy, S', is an affine transformation of S.

Expanding the matrices,

$$KA_sK^{-1} = \begin{bmatrix} 1 & 0 & k_{13}(s-1)/k_{33} \\ 0 & 1 & k_{23}(s-1)/k_{33} \\ 0 & 0 & s \end{bmatrix}$$

where

$$K = \begin{bmatrix} 1 & 0 & k_{13} \\ 0 & 1 & k_{23} \\ 0 & 0 & k_{33} \end{bmatrix}$$

In this case the requirement that P_b remain the same form under the transformation, D yields,

$$\begin{bmatrix} 1 & 0 & k_{13}(s-1)/k_{33} \\ 0 & 1 & k_{23}(s-1)/k_{33} \\ 0 & 0 & s \end{bmatrix} + \begin{bmatrix} t_1a_1 & t_1a_2 & t_1a_3 \\ t_2a_1 & t_2a_2 & t_2a_3 \\ t_3a_1 & t_3a_2 & t_3a_3 \end{bmatrix} = k \begin{bmatrix} 1 & 0 & k'_{13}(s'-1)/k'_{33} \\ 0 & 1 & k'_{23}(s'-1)/k'_{33} \\ 0 & 0 & s' \end{bmatrix}$$

It follows that a_3 is not constrained to be zero by this relation, and thus, for anisotropic scaling between S and S', the reconstruction ambiguity is projective.

The epipolar geometry is not auto-epipolar in general because $[t]_\times \mathbf{A}$ is not skew in general. However, if the affine transformation is restricted to an isotropic scaling ($\mathbf{A}_i = s\mathbf{I}$) then the epipolar structure has the auto-epipolar form, since $[t]_\times \mathbf{A}_i$ is skew. The case of simple scaling is shown by examples a and b in Figure 2.

6.4   Bilateral Symmetry

Rothwell *et al* [10] have studied the case of objects with a plane of symmetry, i.e., bilateral symmetry. In this case the relationship between a 3D point, $\mathbf{P}$ and its symmetric corresponding point, $\mathbf{P}'$ is given by,

$$\mathbf{P}' = \mathbf{T} \begin{bmatrix} \Sigma & 0 \\ 0^T & 1 \end{bmatrix} \mathbf{T}^{-1}\mathbf{P}$$

where

$$\Sigma = \begin{bmatrix} -1 & 0 & 0 \\ 0 & 1 & 0 \\ 0 & 0 & 1 \end{bmatrix}$$

and $\mathbf{T}$ is an Euclidean transformation. $\mathbf{T}$ is given by,

$$\mathbf{T} = \begin{bmatrix} \mathbf{R} & \mathbf{t} \\ 0^T & 1 \end{bmatrix}$$

where $\mathbf{R}$ is a 3D rotation matrix and $\mathbf{t}$ is a 3D translation. The coordinate system for bi-lateral symmetry is shown in Figure 3.

The composite reflection transformation is

$$\mathbf{A} = \mathbf{R}\Sigma\mathbf{R}^T$$
$$\mathbf{t}' = -\mathbf{R}\Sigma\mathbf{R}^T\mathbf{t} + \mathbf{t} = \mathbf{R}(\mathbf{I} - \Sigma)\mathbf{R}^T\mathbf{t} = \mathbf{R}\Gamma\mathbf{R}^T\mathbf{t}$$

where

$$\Gamma = (\mathbf{I} - \Sigma) = \begin{bmatrix} 2 & 0 & 0 \\ 0 & 0 & 0 \\ 0 & 0 & 0 \end{bmatrix}$$

It can be shown that the ambiguity of reconstruction is projective. Note that when the plane of symmetry passes through the center of projection, $\mathbf{t} = 0$, and 3D structure cannot be established. This case is analogous to images related by rotation about the center of projection. We will return to this condition in Section 7.

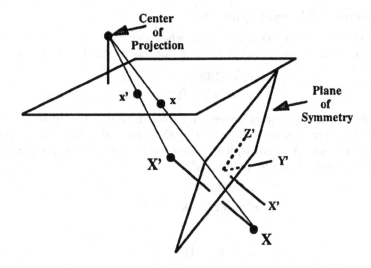

Fig. 3. The coordinate system for bi-lateral symmetry.

Epipolar Geometry The matrix for the skew test in this case is, from equation (15),

$$[R\Gamma R^T t]_\times R\Sigma R^T$$

Applying the identity (14) simplifies this to

$$R[\Gamma R^T t]_\times \Sigma R^T$$

This is a skew matrix since, $[\Gamma R^T t]_\times$ is a matrix of the form

$$\begin{bmatrix} 0 & 0 & 0 \\ 0 & 0 & -x \\ 0 & x & 0 \end{bmatrix}$$

and post multiplying by Σ maintains this skew form (the rotations simply rotate the quadratic form vectors). Consequently, the correspondences are auto-epipolar.

7 Non-Epipolar Correspondence Structures

We reserve the terminology "epipolar geometry" to those cases of repeated structure where the equivalent cameras, P_a and P_b, actually have distinct centers of projection. There are, however, important cases of repeated structures where there is no translation between the centers.

7.1 Example - Bilateral Symmetry

Consider the case of bilateral symmetry when the plane of symmetry passes through the center of projection of P_a. The cameras in standard form become,

$$P_a = [I|0]$$
$$P_b = [KR\Sigma R^T K^{-1}|0]$$

There is no epipolar geometry defined, however there is still a correspondence structure. The correspondence is defined by the relationship between the image projections of S and S'. That is, if we define the image projection of a point in S as x and the corresponding point as x' then,

$$x = [I|0] X$$
$$x' = [KR\Sigma R^T K^{-1}|0] X$$

Thus,

$$p' = Tp$$

where $T = [KR\Sigma R^T K^{-1}]$. So x and x' are related by a planar projective transformation. However, this transformation is not an arbitrary 3×3 matrix and there results a convenient correspondence structure [8].

First, note that $T^2 = I$, so T has eigen-values ± 1, this is a two-cyclic homography. Further, it is clear from the special case when $RK = I$, that T has eigen-values $\{-1, 1, 1\}$ (i.e. there is a degenerate eigenvalue) because in this case $T = \Sigma$. Since eigen-values are preserved by a similarity transformation this is true of T in general, and T is known as a planar harmonic homology [11].

7.2 Planar Homology

Eigen-vectors of a projective transformation determine the fixed points and fixed lines of the transformation. If two eigen-vectors have the same eigen-value then they define a line of fixed points. The fixed lines and points for a planar-homology are shown in Figure 4.

As shown by Springer, these eigenvalues define a pencil of fixed lines all intersecting at a fixed point called the *center* of the homology. The center is the fixed point corresponding to the eigen-value $\lambda = -1$. There is one line of the pencil which passes through any given point. This pencil defines the correspondences between image points which are corresponding projections of S and S'. That is, each line of the pencil is fixed under the transformation which carries x to x'. Therefore, given that x is on a line l of the pencil, then x' is on the same line.

A final interesting example of planar homology is provided by the case of a rotationally symmetric object. In this case we can consider that the outline curve on the object surface is a bilaterally symmetric pair with the plane of symmetry passing always through the center of projection. Even if the plane of symmetry is arbitrarily rotated about the center, the relationship between the two halves of the occluding boundary in the image is just a planar homology and the resulting image structure can be used to find corresponding image points on each side of the symmetry plane.

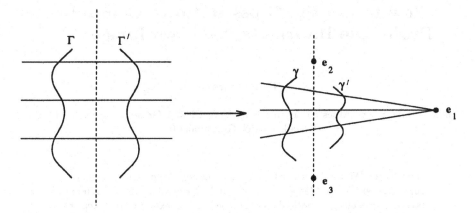

Fig. 4. Under a projective transformations parallel object correspondences converge to a vanishing point. Corresponding points are related in this case by a particular projective transformation, T, called a planar-homology. Two of the eigenvalues of T, corresponding to e_2 and e_3, are equal. The third, corresponding to e_1, is distinct and non-zero. The line $e_2 \times e_3$ is a line of fixed points. Corresponding points, x' and x, are collinear with e_1. e_1 defines a pencil of fixed lines.

References

1. Faugeras, O., "What can be Seen in Three Dimensions with an Uncalibrated Stereo Rig?" *Proc. of ECCV*, p.563-578, 1992.
2. Faugeras, O., Luong, Q.T., and Maybank, S.J., "Camera Self-Calibration: Theory and Experiments," *Proc. of ECCV*, 321-334, 1992.
3. Hartley, R.I., Gupta, R. and Chang, T., "Stereo from Uncalibrated Cameras," *Proc. of CVPR*, p.761-764, 1992.
4. Hartley, R.I., "Cheirality invariants", *Proc. DARPA IU Workshop*, 745–753, 1993.
5. Hartley, R.I., "Self-calibration of stationary cameras," *Proc. of ECCV*, 1994.
6. Luong, Q.T. and Vieville, T., "Canonic representations for the geometries of multiple projective views," *Tech. Rep.* ucb/csd-93-772, University of California, Berkeley, USA, 1993.
7. Moons, T., Van Gool, L., Van Diest, M. and Oosterlinck, A., "Affine structure from perspective image pairs under relative translations between object and camera," University of Leuven Report No. KUL/ESTAT/MI2/9306, 1993.
8. Mukherjee, D.P., Zisserman, A. and Brady, J.M., "Shape from Symmetry - Detecting and Exploiting Symmetry in Affine Images", Univ. of Oxford, Dept. Eng. Sci. Report No. OUEL 1988/93. To appear, *Proc. Royal Soc.*, 1994.
9. Mundy, J.L. and Zisserman, A. (editors), *"Geometric Invariance in Computer Vision,"*, MIT Press, Cambridge Ma, 1992.
10. Rothwell, C.A., Forsyth, D.A., Zisserman, A. and Mundy, J.L. "Extracting Projective Structure from Single Perspective Views of 3D Point Sets", *ICCV*, 1993.
11. Springer, C., "Geometry and Analysis of Projective Spaces," W.H. Freeman and Company, 1964.

How to use the Cross Ratio to Compute Projective Invariants from two Images *

Patrick Gros

LIFIA - INRIA Rhône-Alpes 46, avenue Félix Viallet 38031 Grenoble Cedex 1 - France
E-mail: Patrick.Gros@imag.fr

Abstract. We are interested in the applications of invariant theory to computer vision problems. A survey and clarification of the different invariant calculation methods are detailed in our extented technical report [1]. In this paper, we concentrate on 3D invariants from pairs of images instead of invariants related to the planar projective transformations from monocular image, that have been already largely studied by many people. Especially, invariants of different configurations coming from different combinations of 3D points, 3D lines, and conics are under consideration, and the stabilities of the invariants computed differently are compared. We conclude by showing to what extent these invariant measures can be used for recognition and indexing.

1 Introduction

Invariant theory is a very classical mathematical theory. Some of its results date from antiquity and the major contributions are from the last century. The first use of this theory in computer vision was for the development of robust pattern recognition systems widely used in industry [2, 3]. These algorithms needed good conditions of luminosity and contrast (black objects on white backgrounds for example), only one totally visible object per image and the use of invariants like the ratio of the surface of a plane object to the square of its perimeter (such a ratio is invariant under similarity).

More recent works involve the use of local invariants which are associated with small topological features. These invariants may be angles and length ratios associated with two concurrent lines [4], affine coordinates associated with four points [5, 6], cross ratios associated with 5 lines or with 2 conics [7], differential quantities computed at every point of a curve [8, 9] or a combination of algebraic and differential quantities [7, 10, 11]. Thus it is now possible to find metrical and quantitative tokens in images like distances, length ratios or cross ratios, tokens which are natural complements for topological and qualitative ones used in many algorithms of vision: graph isomorphisms, research of facets, polygons, patterns...

---

* This work has been sponsored by the "Ministère de Recherche et de la Technologie" and by the "Centre National de la Recherche Scientifique" through the ORASIS project as part of the PRC Communication Homme–Machine and funded by CEC through ESPRIT–BRA 6448 (the VIVA project).

There are two major fields of work within the new considerations on invariants in computer vision:

- precise study of the invariants: robustness, and numerical stability of the invariants, computation of new invariants associated with curves or with 3D configurations of points, lines, and conics [1];
- practical use of these invariants to solve vision problems; an interest clearly shown by Mohr *et al.* [12], Forsyth *et al.* [13], and Kapur *et al.* [14].

More generally, one will find a state of the art approach in [15] for both mathematical aspects and applications. These applications concern difficult basic problems of vision and seem to be a new profitable way to solve them. As invariants are numerical quantities associated with topological features, they can be used to index models or images in a large data base and to recognize an object represented on an image using this data base [6, 7]. Given a model of the transformation induced by a camera, invariants allow robust measurements to be made in images. These measures are useful for point matching [4], relative positioning of 3D features with respect to reference points and predicting the position of points in a new image when their projection is known in other images [16, 17, 12], shape reconstruction [18] and epipolar geometry reconstruction [19]. They can be integrated in 2D or 3D models and give additional constraints during the verification stage of a recognition system [20]. These examples of applications clearly show the interest of using invariants in computer vision.

This paper deals with the problem of computing 3D invariants from two 2D images. It provides invariants for many configurations of 3D lines, conics, and points and shows the way to compute these invariants directly from the two images without any 3D reconstruction. Section 2 is devoted to a coplanarity test and to its inversion, which is intensively used in the latter. Section 3 describes the invariants associated with many different configurations. Section 4 provides experimental results on both artificial and real data and especially shows the robustness of 3D invariants with respect to image noise. Experiments are conducted for testing coplanarity and testing the discrimination capacities of invariants with noisy data. Experiments on real data prove the validity of the simulation results.

2 A Coplanarity Test

[2] Let us suppose that we have two images and that we know the epipolar geometry between these two images. Given the projections of any four points onto these images, it is possible to determine whether the four 3D points are coplanar or not.

Let A, B, C, and D be the four 3D points and a_1, b_1, c_1, and d_1, and a_2, b_2, c_2, and d_2 be their projections onto the two images (see Fig. 1). Let e_1 and e_2 be

---

[2] This test is due to Roger Mohr and the method was published by Faugeras [19], but no experimentation was provided.

the epipoles in the images. We suppose that the projections are not merged with the epipoles and that they are labeled in such a way that (a_1, c_1, e_1), (b_1, d_1, e_1), (a_2, c_2, e_2), and (b_2, d_2, e_2) are not collinear.

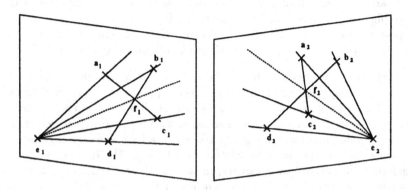

Fig. 1. A coplanarity test.

We denote $f_1 = (a_1c_1) \cap (b_1d_1)$, and $f_2 = (a_2c_2) \cap (b_2c_2)$. A, B, C, and D are coplanar if and only if the two pencils of lines $(e_1a_1, e_1b_1, e_1c_1, e_1d_1, e_1f_1)$, and $(e_2a_2, e_2b_2, e_2c_2, e_2d_2, e_2f_2)$ define the same cross ratios, i.e.:

$$\frac{|e_1a_1c_1||e_1b_1f_1|}{|e_1a_1f_1||e_1b_1c_1|} = \frac{|e_2a_2c_2||e_2b_2f_2|}{|e_2a_2f_2||e_2b_2c_2|} \tag{1}$$

where $|xyz|$ is the determinant of the coordinates of the points x, y, and z.

As a matter of fact, if they are coplanar, the two lines (AC) and (BD) intersect one another at a point F, and f_1 and f_2 are the projections of that point F onto the images. According to the epipolar lines properties, the two pencils of lines $(e_1a_1, e_1b_1, e_1c_1, e_1d_1, e_1f_1)$, and $(e_2a_2, e_2b_2, e_2c_2, e_2d_2, e_2f_2)$ are homographic and define the same cross ratios.

If A, B, C, and D are not coplanar, let us suppose that A, B, and C are fixed and that D is moving along its view line with respect to the first image. a_1, b_1, c_1, and d_1 are fixed, so is f_1. In the second image, a_2, b_2, and c_2 are fixed and d_2 is moving along its epipolar line. As a_2, c_2, and e_2 are not collinear, (a_2, c_2) is not an epipolar line and f_2 does not remain on the same epipolar line. The two pencils of lines are no longer homographic: they do not define the same cross ratios.

2.1 Construction of coplanar points.

There are two ways to use this test. First, to test whether four points are coplanar or not when only their projections onto two images are known. One has just to construct the points f_1 and f_2 and to verify that the two pencils of lines define the same cross ratios.

Second it permits the construction of coplanar points. Suppose that we know the projections onto two images of three points A, B, and C and of one straight line L. Let a_1, b_1, c_1, l_1, a_2, b_2, c_2, and l_2 be these projections. If the epipolar geometry is known, if (a_1, c_1, e_1), (b_1, d_1, e_1), (a_2, c_2, e_2), and (b_2, d_2, e_2) are not collinear and if l_1 and l_2 do not pass through e_1 and e_2 respectively, it is therefore possible to compute the projections of the point D of L which is coplanar with A, B, and C.

First method. A first method to compute these intersection points just consists in inverting the coplanarity test.

1. Let e_1 and e_2 be the two epipoles and d_1 be any point of l_1 (see Fig. 1). We can compute the cross ratio k of the pencil of lines $(e_1 a_1, e_1 b_1, e_1 c_1, e_1 f_1)$.

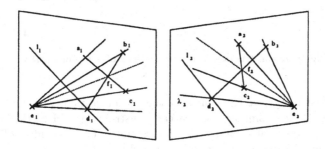

Fig. 2. Construction of coplanar points.

2. This cross ratio define a single line λ_2 passing through e_2 such that the cross ratio of the pencil $(e_2 a_2, e_2 b_2, e_2 c_2, \lambda_2)$ is k.
3. Let d_2 be the intersection of λ_2 and l_2, and f_1, f_2 be those of $(a_1 c_1)$ and $(b_1 d_1)$, and $(a_2 c_2)$ and $(b_2 d_2)$ respectively.
4. According to the coplanarity test, d_1 and d_2 are the projection of a point D of L coplanar with A, B, and C if and only if the cross ratios of $(e_1 a_1, e_1 b_1, e_1 c_1, e_1 f_1)$ and $(e_2 a_2, e_2 b_2, e_2 c_2, e_2 f_2)$ are equal.

We therefore have to solve one equation with one unknown: the coordinate of d_1 on l_1. Unfortunately, this equation is quadratic. One solution is the true solution, the other one corresponds to the case where $(b_1 l_1)$ passes through the epipole. To avoid this nonlinearity, the following constructive method can be used.

Second method. Given the projections of five 3D points A, B, C, D, and E into two images, we look for the projections into these two images of the point J which belongs to the line (DE) and which is coplanar with A, B, and C (see Fig. 3). We suppose that we know the epipolar geometry between the two images. The view plane of (DE) with respect to the first image respectively cuts (AB) and (BC) in F and G. The lines (FG) and (DE) intersect each other at a point coplanar with A, B, and C: it is J.

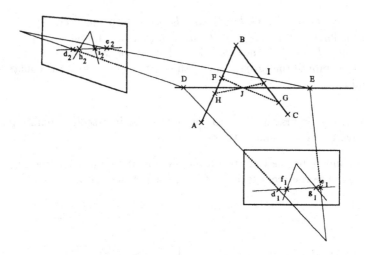

Fig. 3. Reconstruction of the projections of 3D points: 3D view.

In the first image, we can construct the two projections of F and G: f_1 and g_1 (see Fig. 4). In a similar way we can construct h_2 and i_2 the projections in the second image of H and I the intersections of (AB) and (BC) with the view plane of (DE) with respect to the second image. With the help of epipolar geometry, we can construct $h_1, i_1, f_2,$ and g_2. Then we have $(FG) \cap (HI) = J$, $(f_1g_1) \cap (h_1i_1) = j_1$, and $(f_2g_2) \cap (h_2i_2) = j_2$. They are the points we are looking for.

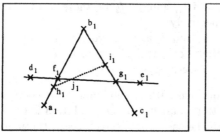
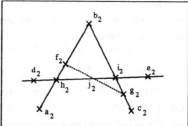

Fig. 4. Reconstruction of the projections of 3D points: the two images.

The corresponding computations may be done very easily in vectorial formalization using projective coordinates. The coordinates of the straight line defined by two points are the cross product of the coordinates of these two points. For example the coordinates of (e_1d_1) are $e_1 \times d_1$.

If we denote by F the fundamental matrix, we have:

$$f_1 = (d_1 \times e_1) \times (b_1 \times a_1) \text{ et } f_2 = (b_2 \times a_2) \times F.f_1$$
$$g_1 = (d_1 \times e_1) \times (b_1 \times c_1) \text{ et } g_2 = (b_2 \times c_2) \times F.g_1 \qquad (2)$$

$$h_2 = (d_2 \times e_2) \times (b_2 \times a_2) \text{ et } h_1 = (b_1 \times a_1) \times F^T . h_2$$
$$i_2 = (d_2 \times e_2) \times (b_2 \times c_2) \text{ et } i_1 = (b_1 \times c_1) \times F^T . i_2$$

and eventually:

$$j_1 = (h_1 \times i_1) \times (f_1 \times g_1) = (h_1 \times i_1) \times (d_1 \times e_1)$$
$$j_2 = (f_2 \times g_2) \times (h_2 \times i_2) = (f_2 \times g_2) \times (d_2 \times e_2) \tag{3}$$

3 Computation of 3D Invariants from Two Images

In [1], we show how to use the cross ratio to find invariants in planar problems. The same methodology may be used in 3D. For some configurations of points and straight lines in 3D, we can interpret the existing invariants with respect to 3D collineations in terms of cross ratios. Furthermore, if we do not know the position of these 3D elements but only their projections onto two images and if the epipolar geometry is known, it is often possible to compute the cross ratios from these images.

The possible applications in vision are very large: when two or more images of the same object are available, if these images have already been matched, one can compute the epipolar geometry, find the image points which correspond to 3D coplanar points using the coplanarity test, and compute 3D invariants. These invariants are useful for projective reconstruction of the 3D points, to modelize geometrically and not only topologically an object, to index these models in a large data base, to match such a model with a new image...It should be noticed that all this can be done with images taken with one or more uncalibrated cameras. The only assumption is that these cameras realize a perspective projection.

In this section, we consider only points, lines, and conics, because they can be easily observed in images, which is not the case with planes. We remind the reader that the 3D collineation group is a manifold of dimension 15 (a collineation is defined by a 4×4 matrix up to a scale factor).

3.1 Case of six points

Consider 6 points in a 3D space. Each point is characterized by four homogeneous coordinates defined up to a scale factor: it therefore has three degrees of freedom, and this 6-point configuration has 18 degrees of freedom. Thus, 18 is the dimension of configuration space. As the transformation group has dimension 15, there are 3 invariants for this problem.

Let A, B, C, D, E, and F be 6 points. We can construct three new points in a projectively invariant way: $D' = (EF) \cap (ABC)$, $E' = (DF) \cap (ABC)$, and $F' = (DE) \cap (ABC)$, where (ABC) represents the plane containing the three points A, B, and C. The points A, B, C, D', E', and F' are coplanar; four of them form a projective basis and the two others have two projective coordinates in this basis, i.e. they define four cross ratios. Three of them are independent: they are the invariants of the problem.

In the case where we know only the projections of the six points A, B, C, D, E, and F onto two images, computing the projections onto these images of points D', E', and F' is possible using the coplanarity test. The cross ratios defined by coplanar points are invariant under projective projections. The three independent invariants of the problem can therefore be computed from the two images.

3.2 Case of one straight line and four points

A straight line in 3D has four degrees of freedom. A configuration of one line and 4 points has therefore 16 degrees of freedom and one invariant under the collineation group action.

Given any configuration, three among the four points of the configuration define a plane which intersect the straight line of the configuration in one point. As there are four different subsets of three points, we can construct four points along a the line: these four points define a cross ratio.

As in the previous case, the coplanarity test allows us to compute this cross ratio from two images of the configuration.

3.3 Case of two straight lines and three points

A configuration of two straight lines and three points has $2 \times 4 + 3 \times 3 = 17$ degrees of freedom and hence two invariants. The three points define a plane which intersects the two lines: that gives 5 coplanar points which define 2 independent cross ratios. These cross ratios may be computed from two images of the configuration using the coplanarity test.

3.4 Case of three straight lines and two points

This kind of configuration has $3 \times 4 + 2 \times 3 = 18$ degrees of freedom, that is to say three invariants. Let P_1, P_2, D_1, D_2, and D_3 be the two points and the three lines of a configuration.

We construct four planes π_1, π_2, π_3, and π_4 as follows: they contain respectively D_1 and P_1, D_1 and P_2, D_2 and P_1, and D_2 and P_2. These four planes intersect D_3 in four points which define a cross ratio.

By circular permutation on the subscripts of the lines, we obtain three cross ratios, which can, once again, be obtained using the coplanarity test. This implies that none of the projections of the three lines pass through one of the epipoles. With this assumption, we can determine the projections of each point of the three straight lines, and the construction of the coplanarity test is possible.

3.5 Case of four straight lines, two of them being coplanar

In this case, a configuration is composed of 2 coplanar straight lines and any two other lines. Two coplanar lines have 7 degrees of freedom, and the full configuration has 15 degrees of freedom.

An invariant may be easily constructed: the two coplanar lines define a plane which intersects the two other lines. We obtain two lines and two points in the same plane, and there is an invariant. The transformation group and the configuration set have the same dimension, and the existence of an invariant is due to an isotropy group.

Like the previous cases, the invariant cross ratio of this problem is computable from two images of the configuration if the epipolar geometry is known.

A particular subcase consists of two pairs of coplanar straight lines. Each pair defines a plane. The intersection of these planes is a line which meets the four lines in four points, which are therefore collinear: this gives a cross ratio.

3.6 Case of any four straight lines in general position

This case is much more complex than the previous ones. As any four lines have 16 degrees of freedom, there should be at least one invariant. A geometric construction of invariant cross ratios is possible. Here are the different steps of the construction:

1. The fact that a line is included in a quadric gives 3 constraints that must be verified by that quadric. Let A and B be any two points and Q a quadric of equation: $ax^2 + by^2 + cy^2 + dyz + exz + fxy + gx + hy + iz + j = 0$. Suppose the straight line (AB) is included in Q: any point of (AB) may be written $P = \lambda A + B$ ($P = A$ if λ is infinite). We have:

$$(\forall \lambda \quad P \in Q) \implies 0 = a(\lambda x_A + x_B)^2 + b(\lambda y_A + y_B)^2 + c(\lambda z_A + z_B)^2 \qquad (4)$$
$$+ d(\lambda y_A + y_B)(\lambda z_A + z_B) + e(\lambda x_A + x_B)(\lambda z_A + z_B)$$
$$+ f(\lambda x_A + x_B)(\lambda y_A + y_B) + g(\lambda x_A + x_B) + h(\lambda y_A + y_B) + i(\lambda z_A + z_B) + j$$

Expressing that the three terms in λ^2, λ^1 and λ^0 vanish gives the three constraints.

2. As a quadric is defined by 10 coefficients up to a scale factor, the fact that three lines belong to a quadric gives 9 constraints and completely define this quadric. As this quadric contains real straight lines, it is a ruled quadric, i.e., a hyperboloid of one sheet or a hyperbolic paraboloid.

3. A ruled quadric contains two families of generators (i.e., straight lines included in this quadric). A single line of each family passes through each point of the quadric. Two lines of the same family never intersect one another, but a line of one of the families intersects all the lines of the other family.

4. Four lines of the same family of generators on a quadric define a cross ratio. As a matter of fact, any line D of the other family intersects these four lines at four collinear points. These points define a cross ratio which does not depend on D, but only on the four initial lines.

5. We consider any four straight lines in a 3D space such that no two of them are coplanar (see Section 3.5 otherwise). Three of them define a ruled quadric. As these lines do not intersect each other (they are not coplanar), they belong to the same family F_1 of generators. The fourth line intersects the quadric in

two points P_1 and P_2. Through each of these points pass a line belonging to the generator family F_1. We obtain five lines of the same generator family, i.e. two cross ratios.

6. We can make permutations on the lines used to define the quadric, and we obtain 8 cross ratios. Two questions remain: how many of these cross ratios are independent? Are these cross ratios computable from two images of the four lines, the epipolar geometry being known?

This proof shows that there exist two lines, L_1 and L_2 which meet any four lines. This defines four points of intersection on each of these two lines and hence two cross ratios.

Conversely, there exist only two such lines. If a third one, L_3, has also met the four lines, it would have met the quadric Q in three points, and then it would have been included in Q; it would have met the fourth line in P_1 or P_2 and would have been equal to one of the two first lines L_1 or L_2 according to the properties of generator families.

Hartley [21] independently investigated the invariants of four lines and he demonstrated a few more results: the two cross ratios found are independent and completely characterize the set of four lines up to a 3D collineation. Intuitively, the independence is quite clear. The fourth line may move in such a way that P_1 remains in the same place and P_2 moves on the quadric: one of the cross ratio remains unchanged, and the other one varies.

As four lines have 16 degrees of freedom and as we found 2 invariants, there should exist an isotropy subgroup of dimension 1. With the reference points chosen such that the equations of L_1 and L_2 are $x = y = 0$ and $z = t = 0$, the isotropy subgroup contains the transformations represented by matrices of the form $diag(\alpha, \alpha, \beta, \beta)$ where α and β are any two constants.

3.7   Case of conics, points, and lines

Case of one conic and three points. A conic in 3D is defined by 8 parameters: 3 to define the plane in which the conic lies, and 5 to define the conic in that plane. Each point has 3 parameters and the whole configuration has 17 parameters. That is, $\dim E = 8 + 3 \times 3 = 17$, $\dim G = 15$. There exist at least two invariants.

The three points define three lines which meet the plane defined by the conic in three collinear points. The line, which these points belong to, meets the conic in two points and we obtain thus five collinear points that allow us to compute two cross ratios.

Other cases. In the case of one conic, two points, and one line, the two points define a line, and thus we have two lines which intersect the conic plane in two points. That defines a line which intersects the conic in two points: we therefore obtain four collinear points and we can compute a cross ratio. To find the two other invariants, we consider the pencil of planes defined by the line of the configuration. We can get five particular planes in this pencil: two planes are tangent to the conic, two go through the two configuration points and one goes through the point of intersection between the conic plane and the line defined by the two points. Five planes in a pencil define two cross ratios.

In the same way, we can find respectively one invariant for one conic and two lines $(1 = (8 + 2 \times 4) - 15)$, one for two conics $(1 = 2 \times 8 - 15)\ldots$

4 Experimental Results

4.1 Introduction

In this section we show results on both simulated and real data. The simulated data allow to study quantitatively the effect of noise on the numerical results. Some results on real images are also shown.

For the simulated images, noise is uniform. This choice was done to control precisely noise amplitude. With a Gaussian noise, the variance may change, but any value of noise is always possible since its probability never vanishes. Furthermore some of the image noise is uniform such as discretization noise.

Many of the tests done lead to compare cross ratios. The appendix explains the method that we have used to do such comparisons.

The computation of the epipolar geometry, i.e. the fundamental matrix and the two epipoles of a pair of images, can be efficiently done if we consider each matrix entries as an unknown with no other constraints. This leads to a system of linear homogeneous equations that can be solved using a singular value decomposition method [22, SVD] in the least squares sense. Unfortunately, this linear solution without constraints is sometimes far away from the real solution in practice. Nonlinear iterative methods are necessary to obtain better estimations, as it has been reported in [23].

Our method to compute the epipolar geometry is to get a first solution by the SVD linear method and to improve it by a nonlinear least-squares method, based on Levenberg-Marquardt's algorithm. The error function is the same as that proposed in [23]: it is defined as the sum of the squares of the distance of a point to its epipolar line. The constraint of rank 2 of the fundamental matrix is directly imposed to the matrix representation, as it is done in [23].

4.2 The coplanarity test with simulated data

The coplanarity test is studied with simulated data. This test provides a way to detect image points which correspond to 3D coplanar points. The search for such points may be used to compute 2D invariants associated with some particular point configurations, or to choose a projective basis for uncalibrated projective reconstruction [19, 24]. In the latter, the test needs only to be a necessary test.

The three stages of the experimentation are the following: computation of coplanarity thresholds, study of coplanar configurations, study of any configurations.

Computation of coplanarity thresholds. The aim of this first stage is to compute a coplanarity threshold for each level of noise. The configuration will be considered coplanar if the "distance" between its two projections into two images is smaller than this threshold. The experiment is set as follows: 2500 configurations of four coplanar points are uniformly chosen in the cube $[10, 246]^3$. All these points are projected onto two images. The motion of the camera between the two images is a rotation of 30 degrees. Some noise is added to the the position of these projected points and the epipolar geometry is computed.

Some of the projected configurations are degenerated and therefore are eliminated. That is the case of the projected configurations having points less than 10 pixels apart and of those which are almost collinear. The test is computed for the remaining configurations. Each configuration provides a pencil of five lines passing through the epipole in each image, and defines five cross ratios. The corresponding cross-ratios are compared and the result of the test is the sum of the five differences.

Fig. 5 shows the minimum, mean and maximum values obtained at each noise level. The maximum values appear not to be very significative, but correspond to isolated configurations. The mean value does not grow fast with noise: that shows the robustness of the test.

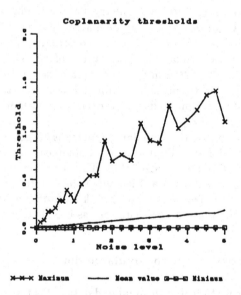

Fig. 5. Coplanarity test applied to coplanar point projections.

Testing configurations. We use three values of thresholds for the test: the mean value m computed in the previous paragraph, $1.5 \times m$, and $2 \times m$. Fig. 6(left) shows the percentage of coplanar configurations giving a positive result, i.e., considered as coplanar according to the test. Fig. 6(right) show the percentage of positive results obtained with 2500 non coplanar configurations. These percentages are not equal to zero because some configurations are almost coplanar, and because of image noise. Table 1 summarises all the results.

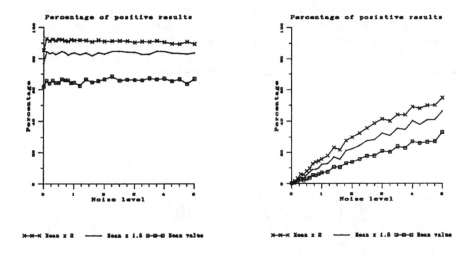

Fig. 6. Percentage of positive results for coplanar configurations (left) and for any configurations (right)

Level	Thresholds								
of	mean			mean ×1.5			mean ×2		
noise	Value	Copl	Any	Value	Copl	Any	Value	Copl	Any
0.0	1.5e-05	61.8	0.06	2.25e-5	76.9	0.06	3e-5	85.4	0.06
0.5	0.017	64.2	3.0	0.026	83.6	5.47	0.034	92.3	7.95
1.0	0.033	64.4	7.0	0.049	83.8	12.2	0.065	91.6	15.8
2.0	0.069	66.7	13.8	0.10	83.0	22.3	0.14	91.1	29.8
3.0	0.11	66.0	20.9	0.16	84.1	32.4	0.21	90.4	41.2
4.0	0.14	67.1	26.9	0.21	84.6	40.2	0.28	90.6	48.9
5.0	0.18	67.0	33.0	0.27	83.7	46.3	0.37	89.5	54.7

Table 1. Results of the coplanarity test: percentage of positive results for coplanar and non coplanar configurations at several levels of noise.

In conclusion one can see that the test works well if one eliminates the degenerate cases of points almost lying on the line going through the epipole. This is not surprising since it is a case for which the test is not valid. Otherwise the test is necessary but not sufficient to detect the projections of coplanar points.

This insufficiency is due to the image noise. Nevertheless, it allows an efficient reduction of the potential candidates of four point sets to coplanarity.

4.3 The coplanarity test with real data

In this paragraph the coplanarity test is used with two real images of a wood house (Fig. 7). We consider some of the corners of these images. These corners are numbered as shown on Fig. 7. From each image, 29 corners are extracted and matched. From the 23,751 possible sets of four points, 17,745 of them remain when the unstable configurations have been filtered out.

Fig. 7. Two images of a wooden house and numbering of the image corners.

An experimental study of the test with real data does not show any natural coplanarity threshold. Some of the configurations giving the smallest results to the test are shown on Table 2. Some of the results, in the left part of the table, are difficult to evaluate, because the planarity of the 3D configuration is not clear.

Corner numbers	Result	Corner numbers	Result
2 24 25 28	0.000250446	0 5 12 17	0.00026739
0 11 15 27	0.000313107	2 10 14 17	0.000313721
7 11 12 20	0.000345824	1 8 10 15	0.000314295
		3 10 12 15	0.000347512
		1 2 10 17	0.000366849
		1 2 14 17	0.000370531
		7 16 19 24	0.00039199
		0 1 10 14	0.000396603

Table 2. Results obtained for a few configurations.

Another way to use the test is to look at all the configurations having three corners in common, as shown on Table 3. When the configurations are ordered

according to their result with respect to the test, it is easy to separate the
coplanar configurations from the other ones, as indicated by the line in each
column. The only problem is that the corresponding threshold is not the same
in all cases. This is a real limitation for the test, which also require a good
accuracy for the point positions, which is not always available.

Common corners 5, 8	14	Common corners 21, 23	28
4th corner	Result	4th corner	Result
0	0.00123847	18	0.00114258
3	0.00142479	12	0.00336455
17	0.00144425	24	0.00361946
1	0.00161304	16	0.0062559
15	0.00307953	19	0.00675905
18	0.00347562	9	0.00860071
2	0.00444478	14	0.00919245
7	0.00576232	22	0.0108486
23	0.0076242	4	0.0158454
4	0.00886061	7	0.0282956
13	0.0133648	5	0.038735
19	0.0157966	2	0.0424568
27	0.0165858	3	0.0453531
9	0.0214658	0	0.0480963
25	0.0353054	25	0.0503932
26	0.0383085	26	0.0510969
21	0.044384	10	0.0540821
11	0.0544166	20	0.0553584
6	0.0563005	6	0.058392
		8	0.0588166
		1	0.0643018
		11	0.0665695
		17	0.0715031

Table 3. Results obtained by the configurations containing the corners numbered 5, 8
and 14 and those containing the corner numbered 21, 23 and 28.

A detailled study of the results shows that the coplanarity test is very reliable
when the points are precisely extracted. Problems occur for example with T-
junctions (where a object occludes partially another), or curvature maxima of
curves considered as corners. Elsewhere, the results depend on the precision of
the corners as it was the case with the simulated data.

4.4 The invariant of two pairs of coplanar lines

Results with simulated data. 450 points are uniformly chosen in a cube, and
segments are drawn between the points 0 and 1, 1 and 2, afterwards between
3 and 4, 4 and 5...in order to form pairs of coplanar lines. These points are

projected onto two images, some noise is added to the point projections and the epipolar geometry is computed from these data.

The 22 350 configurations of two pairs of coplanar lines are then filtered to eliminate configurations having segments that are too short, or accidental collinearities or coplanarities. The invariants associated to each configuration are then compared to the corresponding invariants computed from the 3D exact data. The results are shown on Fig. 8(left).

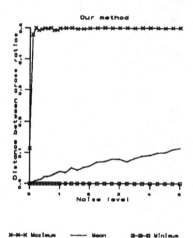 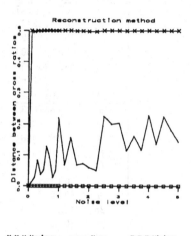

Fig. 8. Comparison between the computation done from the images and that done from the 3D data (left). Comparison between the computation done from the reconstructed scene and that done from the 3D initial data (right).

To be able to evaluate our invariant computation method, let us use another method. From the same noised image data we reconstruct the scene using the projective reconstruction method described in [19]. The invariants are thus computed from the reconstructed scene, and compared to those computed from the initial 3D data. The obtained results are shown on Fig. 8(right). The two curves of Fig. 8 have similar aspects, but our method appears to be less sensitive to noise and more stable.

Results with real data. We present here results on real data. Fig. 9 represents three images of the same object: it is a dihedron with triangles painted on both sides. Contours were extracted from these three images and were approximated by segments numbered as in Fig. 9. The two following pairs of images were studied: the two first images, and the two last ones. For each of these pairs, the correspondence between points, the epipolar geometry and some invariants of pairs of coplanar lines were computed.

Table 10 shows the results: the (i, j) element of the table gives the difference of

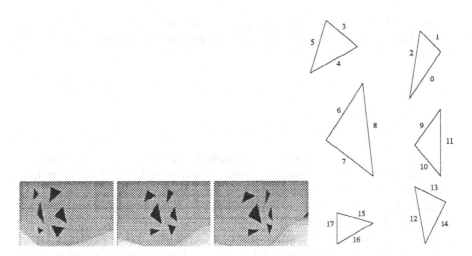

Fig. 9. Three images of a dihedron and segment numbering.

the invariants of S_i computed from the images 1 and 2, and S_j computed from the images 2 and 3. This difference is computed as mentioned in the beginning of the section 4. We use the following sets of lines: $S_1 = \{0, 2, 3, 5\}$, $S_2 = \{1, 2, 15, 16\}$, $S_3 = \{3, 5, 9, 11\}$, $S_4 = \{3, 5, 12, 14\}$, $S_5 = \{7, 8, 12, 14\}$, $S_6 = \{9, 11, 15, 17\}$ and $S_7 = \{12, 13, 15, 17\}$.

	S_1	S_2	S_3	S_4	S_5	S_6	S_7
S_1	**0.000766**	0.035241	0.046054	0.011993	0.082378	0.097035	0.007931
S_2	0.034279	**0.000195**	0.081099	0.047038	0.117423	0.132080	0.027115
S_3	0.037669	0.072144	**0.00915**	0.024910	0.045474	0.060131	0.044834
S_4	0.018515	0.052989	0.028305	**0.005756**	0.064629	0.079286	0.025679
S_5	0.079718	0.114193	0.032898	0.066960	**0.003425**	0.018082	0.086883
S_6	0.106032	0.140507	0.059212	0.093273	0.022888	**0.008231**	0.113197
S_7	0.007940	0.026535	0.054760	0.020699	0.091083	0.105573	**0.000775**

Fig. 10. Differences between invariants.

The invariants appear to be good discriminators. The only ambiguities are the entries (1, 7) and (7, 1) of the table. As in the two last paragraphs, invariants constitute a necessary but non sufficient test of recognition. Non sufficiency may be due to image noise or more probably to the fact that different configurations may be deduced one from the other by a homography: therefore they have equal invariants and may not be distinguished by this method.

Two points have to be noticed: first the test used with real data works better than used with simulated data. This is due to the simulated data which contain degenerate or almost degenerate cases. Because of the noise and of numerical approximations, such degenerate cases are probable with a random generator of data. These cases do not occur so frequently in practice.

Second the invariants of 2 pairs of coplanar lines do not depend from dihedron angle. Then these invariants could be used for the recognition of articulated objects.

5   Conclusion

In this paper, we showed a way to approach the problem of finding invariants. It consists in looking for particular invariants related to the canonical invariant of the considered transformation.

Even if this method is not as general as an algebraic method for example, it easily finds the invariants of a problem in many cases, and it provides an immediate geometrical interpretation of these invariants. The use of this method should therefore be given first priority, even if the results are possibly to be completed with other methods.

In the last part, we showed how this last method is usable in 3D vision problems like recognition. These applications of this method are due to the fact that 3D invariants like cross ratios can be computed directly from 2D images without any reconstruction, if point matching and epipolar geometry between the two images are known. As they may be computed on local features, they may be used in case of partial occlusion. Some of them are also usable for articulated objects.

The experimental results show that the cross ratio is not too sensitive to noise if the degenerate cases are eliminated. In any case these degenerate cases are not very frequent. The discriminating character of the cross ratio is dependent on image noise and in a practical use, the test of coplanarity presented in the paper is only necessary. The experiments on real data prove the validity of the results on simulated data.

Appendix: a Distance between Cross Ratios

Many of the tests done in this paper lead to compare cross ratios. To do so, we used the method of the random cross ratios [25]. Four points are uniformly chosen on a line and their cross ratio is computed. Then the density of the cross ratio values on the real line is computed, as shown on Fig. 11, and then the corresponding partition function F, shown on Fig. 12.

To compare two cross ratios x and y, we compute their "difference", i.e. $|F(x) - F(y)|$, their distance with respect to the partition function. As the point at infinity plays the same role as all the other real points, we have to consider the two possible ways to go from x to y: the real way, and the way going through the point at infinity. In conclusion, the distance between cross ratios is $\min(|F(x) -$

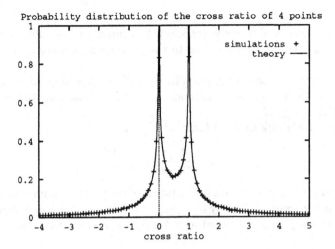

Fig. 11. Cross ratio density function.

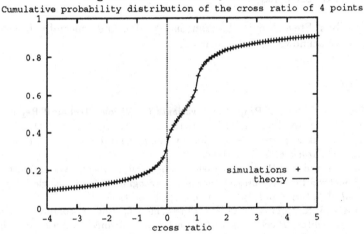

Fig. 12. Cross ratio partition function.

$F(y)|, 1 - |F(x) - F(y)|)$, where:

$$F(x) = \begin{cases} F1(x) + F3(x) & \text{if } x < 0 \\ 1/3 & \text{if } x = 0 \\ 1/2 + F2(x) + F3(x) & \text{if } 0 < x < 1 \\ 2/3 & \text{if } x = 1 \\ 1 + F1(x) + F2(x) & \text{if } 1 < x \end{cases}$$

$$F1(x) = \frac{1}{3}\left(x(1-x)\ln\left(\frac{x-1}{x}\right) - x + \frac{1}{2}\right)$$

$$F2(x) = \frac{1}{3}\left(\frac{x - x\ln(x) - 1)}{(x-1)^2}\right)$$

$$F3(x) = \frac{1}{3}\left(\frac{(1-x)\ln(1-x) + x}{x^2}\right)$$

For more details, see [25].

Such a method is absolutely necessary to compare cross ratio values. For example 0 is as far from 1 as ∞ due to the symmetric properties of the cross ratio.

Maybank [26] have worked independently with a different probability distribution, but he finds a partition function qualitatively and quantitatively very closed to that of Fig. 12.

One could also think to use a function such as:

$$ f : \quad x \longmapsto \frac{4}{27} \frac{\left(x^2 - x + 1\right)^3}{x^2(1 - x)^2} $$

This function is invariant under a permutation of the points defining the cross ratio. On the other hand, a quantity like $|f(a) - f(b)|$ has no particular significance and this function f cannot be used as a distance between cross-ratios.

Acknowledgements

Robert Collins, Steve Maybank, Françoise Veillon and especially Roger Mohr are gratefully acknowledged for their comments.

References

1. P. Gros and L. Quan. Projective Invariants for Vision. Technical Report RT 90 IMAG - 15 LIFIA, LIFIA–IRIMAG, Grenoble, France, December 1992.
2. M.K. Hu. Visual pattern recognition by moment invariants. IEEE *Trans. on Information Theory*, 8:179–187, 1962.
3. B. Bamieh and R.J.P. de Figueiredo. A general moment-invariants/attributed-graph method for three-dimensional object-recognition from a single image. IEEE *Journal of Robotics and Automation*, 2(1):31–41, 1986.
4. P. Gros and R. Mohr. Automatic object modelization in computer vision. In H. Bunke, editor, *Proceedings of the workshop "Advances in Structural and Syntactic Pattern Recognition", Bern, Switzerland*, volume 5 of *Series on Machine Perception and Artificial Intelligence*, pages 385–400. World Scientific, August 1992.
5. Y. Lamdan, J. T. Schwartz, and H. J. Wolfson. Affine invariant model-based object recognition. IEEE *Journal of Robotics and Automation*, 6:578–589, 1990.
6. H.J. Wolfson. Model-based object recognition by geometric hashing. In O. Faugeras, editor, *Proceedings of the 1st European Conference on Computer Vision, Antibes, France*, pages 526–536. Springer-Verlag, April 1990.
7. C.A. Rothwell, A. Zisserman, D.A. Forsyth, and J.L. Mundy. Canonical frames for planar object recognition. In G. Sandini, editor, *Proceedings of the 2nd European Conference on Computer Vision, Santa Margherita Ligure, Italy*, pages 757–772. Springer-Verlag, May 1992.
8. I. Weiss. Projective invariants of shapes. In *Proceedings of DARPA Image Understanding Workshop, Cambridge, Massachusetts, USA*, pages 1125–1134, 1988.
9. I. Weiss. Noise-resistant invariant of curves. In *Proceeding of the DARPA–ESPRIT workshop on Applications of Invariants in Computer Vision, Reykjavik, Iceland*, pages 319–344, 1991.

10. L. Van Gool, P. Kempenaers, and A. Oosterlinck. Recognition and semi-differential invariants. In *Proceedings of the Conference on Computer Vision and Pattern Recognition, Maui, Hawaii, USA*, pages 454–460, June 1991.

11. L. Van Gool, L.T. Moons, E. Pauwels, and A. Oosterlinck. Semi-Differential Invariants. In J. Mundy and A. Zisserman, editors, *Geometric Invariance in Computer Vision*, pages 157–192. MIT Press, 1992.

12. R. Mohr, L. Morin, and E. Grosso. Relative positioning with poorly calibrated cameras. In *Proceeding of the* DARPA–ESPRIT *workshop on Applications of Invariants in Computer Vision, Reykjavik, Iceland*, pages 7–45, March 1991.

13. D. Forsyth, J. Mundy, and A. Zisserman. Transformationnal invariance - a primer. In *Proceedings of the British Machine Vision Conference, Oxford, England*, pages 1–6, September 1990.

14. D. Kapur and J. L. Mundy. Fitting affine invariant conics to curves. In *Proceeding of the* DARPA–ESPRIT *workshop on Applications of Invariants in Computer Vision, Reykjavik, Iceland*, pages 209–233, March 1991.

15. J.L. Mundy and A. Zisserman, editors. *Geometric Invariance in Computer Vision.* MIT Press, Cambridge, Massachusetts, USA, 1992.

16. R. Mohr, L. Morin, C. Inglebert, and L. Quan. Geometric solutions to some 3D vision problems. In J.L. Crowley, E. Granum, and R. Storer, editors, *Integration and Control in Real Time Active Vision,* ESPRIT BRA Series. Springer-Verlag, 1991.

17. R. Mohr and L. Morin. Relative positioning from geometric invariants. In *Proceedings of the Conference on Computer Vision and Pattern Recognition, Maui, Hawaii, USA*, pages 139–144, June 1991.

18. J.J. Koenderink and A. J. van Doorn. Affine structure from motion. Technical report, Utrecht University, Utrecht, The Netherlands, October 1989.

19. O. Faugeras. What can be seen in three dimensions with an uncalibrated stereo rig? In G. Sandini, editor, *Proceedings of the 2nd European Conference on Computer Vision, Santa Margherita Ligure, Italy*, pages 563–578. Springer-Verlag, May 1992.

20. D. Forsyth, J.L. Mundy, A. Zisserman, C. Coelho, A. Heller, and C. Rothwell. Invariant descriptors for 3D object recognition and pose. IEEE *Transactions on PAMI*, 13(10):971–991, October 1991.

21. R. Hartley. Invariants of lines in space. In *DARPA Image Understanding Workshop*, pages 737–744, 1993.

22. W.H. Press, B.P. Flannery, S.A. Teukolsky, and W.T. Vetterling W.T. *Numerical Recipes in C.* Cambridge University Press, 1988.

23. O.D. Faugeras, Q.T. Luong, and S.J. Maybank. Camera Self-Calibration: Theory and Experiments. In G. Sandini, editor, *Proceedings of the 2nd European Conference on Computer Vision, Santa Margherita Ligure, Italy*, pages 321–334. Springer-Verlag, May 1992.

24. R. Mohr, F. Veillon, and L. Quan. Relative 3D reconstruction using multiple uncalibrated images. In *Proceedings of the Conference on Computer Vision and Pattern Recognition, New York, USA*, pages 543–548, June 1993.

25. K. Åström and L. Morin. Random cross ratios. Technical Report RT 88 IMAG - 14 LIFIA, LIFIA–IRIMAG, October 1992.

26. S.J. Maybank. Classification based on the Cross Ratio. In *Proceeding of the* DARPA–ESPRIT *workshop on Applications of Invariants in Computer Vision, Azores, Portugal*, pages 113–132, October 1993.

On Geometric and Algebraic Aspects of 3D Affine and Projective Structures from Perspective 2D Views*

Amnon Shashua

Massachusetts Institute of Technology
Artificial Intelligence Laboratory
Center for Biological Computational Learning
Cambridge, MA 02139

Abstract. This paper investigates the differences — conceptually and algorithmically — between affine and projective frameworks for the tasks of visual recognition and reconstruction from perspective views. The study is made by first proposing an affine framework for perspective views, captured by a single remarkably simple equation, which is based on a viewer-centered invariant we call *relative affine structure*. Via corollaries of the main result we make connections to previous work and show that Euclidean, affine and projective structure representations can be obtained by simple specializations and generalizations of our main results.

1 Introduction

The geometric relation between objects (or scenes) in the world and their images, taken from different viewing positions by a pin-hole camera, has many subtleties and nuances and has been the subject of research in computer vision since its early days. Two major areas in computer vision have been shown to benefit from an analytic treatment of the 3D to 2D geometry: visual recognition and reconstruction from multiple views (as a result of having motion sequences or from stereopsis).

A recent approach with growing interest in the past few years is based on the idea that non-metric information, although weaker than the information provided by depth maps and rigid camera geometries, is nonetheless useful in the sense that the framework may provide simpler algorithms, camera calibration is not required, more freedom in picture-taking is allowed — such as taking pictures of pictures of objects, and there is no need to make a distinction between orthographic and perspective projections. The list of contributions to this framework include (though not intended to be complete) [15, 28, 41, 42, 10, 22, 1, 4, 30, 31, 21, 39, 25, 5, 6, 18, 29, 14, 13, 7, 24, 2, 23, 3, 37] — and directly relevant to this paper are the work described in [15, 4, 31].

We investigate the intrinsic differences — conceptually and algorithmically — between an affine framework for recognition/reconstruction and a projective

---

* This paper is a revised version of MIT, AI Memo 1405, bearing the same title.

framework. Although the distinction between affine and projective spaces, and between affine and projective properties, is perfectly clear from classic studies in projective and algebraic geometries, as can be found in [9, 26, 27], it is less clear how these concepts relate to reconstruction from multiple views. In other words, given a set of views, under what conditions can we expect to recover affine invariants? what is the benefit from recovering projective invariants over affine? are there tasks, or methodologies, for which an affine framework is completely sufficient? what are the relations between the set of views generated by a pinhole camera and the set of all possible projections $\mathcal{P}^3 \mapsto \mathcal{P}^2$ of a particular object? These are the kinds of questions for which the current literature does not provide satisfactory answers.

In the course of addressing these questions we derive a new invariant, which is in the middle ground between affine and projective. The invariant, referred to as *relative affine*, is a result of choosing a representation $\mathcal{R}_o$ of space in which an arbitrarily chosen plane π (determined by three corresponding points across two views) is the plane at infinity — with respect to $\mathcal{R}_o$. It is then shown that all other representations of space, generated by general uncalibrated camera motion, can be described by an element of the affine group applied to $\mathcal{R}_o$. If the plane π happens to be the plane at infinity with respect to our world coordinate system (i.e., really at infinity), then the invariant is simply the affine structure of the scene, and if the projection center is at infinity, then the invariant is simply the affine structure described by [15]. Thus, we derive a description of structure relative to a reference plane and the projection center of one of our cameras. We show that this description of structure leads to an extremely simple equation, requires fewer corresponding points than a projective invariant, and is completely sufficient to familiar visual tasks including visual recognition by alignment (i.e., to the task of re-projection, or image transfer), and 3D reconstruction with respect to a viewer coordinate frame.

We then extend the relative affine framework to projective. This introduces a second plane, and is equivalent of replacing the role of the camera center as a basis point with a fifth scene point. Thus we obtain an object-based invariant, and that has applications as well. The projective result is a refinement on previous work [31, 4] and is shown here for three reasons: (i) one can capture the result in a single simple equation, (ii) the result is a natural extension of the relative affine framework, and (iii) the derivation does not involve the epipoles in a direct manner (as in [31, 4]), thus may yield accurate estimation of invariants in certain industrial applications.

Further work along these lines, and more details, are contained in results published after this workshop, and can be found in [33, 32, 35, 36].

2   Notations

We consider object space to be the three-dimensional projective space $\mathcal{P}^3$, and image space to be the two-dimensional projective space $\mathcal{P}^2$. An object (or scene) is modeled by a set of points and let $\psi_i \subset \mathcal{P}^2$ denote views (arbitrary), indexed by

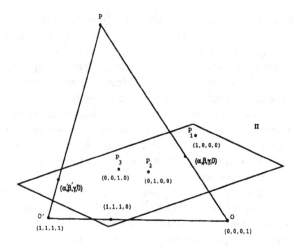

Fig. 1.

i, of the object. Given two views with projection centers $O, O' \in \mathcal{P}^3$, respectively, the epipoles are defined as the intersection of the line $\overline{OO'}$ with both image planes. Because the image plane is finite, we can assign, without loss of generality, the value 1 as the third homogeneous coordinate to every *observed* image point. When only two views ψ_o, ψ_1 are discussed, then points in ψ_o are denoted by p, their corresponding points in ψ_1 are denoted by p', and the epipoles are $v \in \psi_o$ and $v' \in \psi_1$. The symbol $\cong$ denotes equality up to a scale, GL_n stands for the group of $n \times n$ matrices, and PGL_n is the group defined up to a scale.

3 Relative Affine Structure and Invariant From Two Perspective Views

As mentioned in the introduction, we need five reference points in order to represent space as seen from two uncalibrated cameras. The key idea is to have one of the cameras as part of the reference frame, which we will show gives rise to an affine invariant. Our construction starts by assigning a frame of reference of three scene points and the two camera centers. This frame is sufficient for generating an invariant (which we show is affine) up to an unknown uniform scale. A fourth scene point is then required for setting the scale. Since one of the cameras is arbitrary, we are left with four scene reference points and one camera center (camera center of the reference view). We will discuss theoretical implications and relations to other results later in this section.

Let P_1, P_2, P_3 be three object points projecting onto corresponding points $p_j, p'_j, j = 1, 2, 3$, in the two views. We assign the coordinates $(1, 0, 0, 0), (0, 1, 0, 0)$ and $(0, 0, 1, 0)$ to P_1, P_2, P_3, respectively. For later reference, the plane passing through P_1, P_2, P_3 will be denoted by π_1. Let O be the projection center of the first camera, and O' the projection center of the second camera. We assign the coordinates $(0,0,0,1),(1,1,1,1)$ to O, O', respectively (see Figure 1). This choice of representation is always possible because the two cameras are part of $\mathcal{P}^3$. By construction, the point of intersection of the line $\overline{OO'}$ with π_1 has the coordinates $(1,1,1,0)$. Note that π_1 is the plane $x_3 = 0$ (the plane at infinity with respect to this representation), thus the linear combination of O and O' with $x_3 = 0$ must be a multiple of $(1,1,1,0)$.

Let P be some object point projecting onto p, p'. The line $\overline{OP}$ intersects π_1 at the point $(\alpha, \beta, \gamma, 0)$. The coordinates α, β, γ can be recovered by projecting the image plane onto π_1, as follows. Given the epipoles v and v', we have by our choice of coordinates that p_1, p_2, p_3 and v are projectively (in $\mathcal{P}^2$) mapped onto $e_1 = (1,0,0), e_2 = (0,1,0), e_3 = (0,0,1)$ and $e_4 = (1,1,1)$, respectively. Therefore, there exists a unique element $A_1 \in PGL_3$ that satisfies $A_1 p_j \cong e_j$, $j = 1, 2, 3$, and $A_1 v = e_4$. Note that we have made a choice of scale by setting $A_1 v$ to e_4, this is simply for convenience as will be clear later on. Let $A_1 p = (\alpha, \beta, \gamma)$.

Similarly, the line $\overline{O'P}$ intersects π_1 at $(\alpha', \beta', \gamma', 0)$. Let $A_2 \in PGL_3$ be defined by $A_2 p'_j \cong e_j$, $j = 1, 2, 3$, and $A_2 v' = e_4$. Let $A_2 p' = (\alpha', \beta', \gamma')$. Since P can be described as a linear combination of two points along each of the lines $\overline{OP}$, and $\overline{O'P}$, we have the following equation:

$$
P \cong \begin{pmatrix} \alpha \\ \beta \\ \gamma \\ 0 \end{pmatrix} - k \begin{pmatrix} 0 \\ 0 \\ 0 \\ 1 \end{pmatrix} = \mu \begin{pmatrix} \alpha' \\ \beta' \\ \gamma' \\ 0 \end{pmatrix} - s \begin{pmatrix} 1 \\ 1 \\ 1 \\ 1 \end{pmatrix},
$$

from which it immediately follows that $k = s$. Note that since only ratios of coordinates are significant in $\mathcal{P}^n$, k is determined up to a uniform scale, and any point $P_o \notin \pi_1$ can be used to set a mutual scale for all views — by setting an appropriate scale for v', for example. The value of k can easily be determined from image measurements as follows: we have

$$
\mu \begin{pmatrix} \alpha' \\ \beta' \\ \gamma' \end{pmatrix} = \begin{pmatrix} \alpha \\ \beta \\ \gamma \end{pmatrix} + k \begin{pmatrix} 1 \\ 1 \\ 1 \end{pmatrix}.
$$

Multiply both sides by A_2^{-1} for which we get

$$
\mu p' = Ap + kv',
$$

where $A = A_2^{-1} A_1$. Note that $A \in PGL_3$ is a collineation (homography) between the two image planes, due to π_1, determined by $p'_j \cong Ap_j$, $j = 1, 2, 3$, and $Av = v'$ (therefore, can be recovered directly without going through A_1, A_2). Similar proofs that a homography of a plane can be recovered from three points and the epipoles are found in [31, 25].

Since k is determined up to a uniform scale, we need a fourth correspondence p_o, p'_o, and let A, or v', be scaled such that $p'_o \cong Ap_o + v'$. Then k is an affine invariant, which we will refer to as "relative affine structure". Furthermore, $(x, y, 1, k)$ are the homogeneous coordinates representation of P, and the

3×4 matrix $[A, v']$ is a camera transformation matrix between the two views. We have, thus, arrived to the following result:

Theorem 1 Relative Affine Structure. *Let π_1 be some arbitrary plane and let $P_j \in \pi_1$, $j = 1, 2, 3$ projecting onto p_j, p'_j in views ψ_o, ψ_1, respectively. Let $p_o \in \psi_o$ and $p'_o \in \psi_1$ be projections of $P_o \notin \pi_1$. Let $A \in PGL_3$ be a homography of $\mathcal{P}^2$ determined by the equations $Ap_j \cong p'_j$, $j = 1, 2, 3$, and $Av \cong v'$, scaled to satisfy the equation $p'_o \cong Ap_o + v'$. Then, for any point $P \in \mathcal{P}^3$ projecting onto $p \in \psi_o$ and $p' \in \psi_1$, we have*

$$\boxed{p' \cong Ap + kv'} \tag{1}$$

The coefficient $k = k(p)$ is independent of ψ_1, i.e., is invariant to the choice of the second view, and the coordinates of P are $(x, y, 1, k)$.

The key idea in Theorem 1 was to use both camera centers as part of the reference frame in order to show that the transformation between an arbitrary representation $\mathcal{R}_o$ of space as seen from the first camera and the representation $\mathcal{R}$ as seen from any other camera position, can be described by an element of the affine group. In other words, we have chosen an arbitrary plane π_1 (determined uniquely by the choice of three corresponding points and the epipoles) and made a choice of representation $\mathcal{R}_o$ in which π_1 is the plane at infinity (i.e., π_1 was mapped to infinity — not an unfamiliar trick, especially in computer graphics). The representation $\mathcal{R}_o$ is associated with $[x, y, 1, k]$ where k vanishes for all points coplanar with π_1, which means that π is the plane at infinity under the representation $\mathcal{R}_o$. What was left to show is that π_1 remains the plane at infinity under all subsequent camera transformations, and therefore k is an affine invariant. Because k is invariant relative to the representation $\mathcal{R}_o$ we named it "relative affine structure"; this should not be confused with the term "relative invariants" used in classical invariant theory (multiplied by a power of the transformation determinant, as opposed to "absolute invariants").

Certain corollaries and connections to previous results can be readily made. First, we rewrite k as follows: if we denote the point of intersection of the line $\overline{OP}$ with π_1 by $\tilde{P}$, we have,

$$k = \frac{\frac{P - \tilde{P}}{P - O}}{\frac{P_o - \tilde{P}_o}{P_o - O}}. \tag{2}$$

In other words, k can be described as a ratio of of distances of P from the reference plane π_1 and from the camera center O, normalized by a fixed ratio of P_o from the reference plane and O. Two immediate corollaries arise by considering the special cases when O is at infinity, or when π_1 is at infinity with respect to the Euclidean frame (world coordinate system). When O is at infinity, we have the case of parallel projection, and the terms involving O (i.e., depth) cancel out, and we are left with

$$k = \frac{P - \tilde{P}}{P_o - \tilde{P}_o},$$

which is precisely the way shape was described in [15] (see also [28, 29]). In the second view, if it is orthographic, then the two trapezoids $P, \tilde{P}, p', Ap$ and $P_o, \tilde{P}_o, p'_o, Ap_o$ are similar, and from similarity of trapezoids we obtain

$$\frac{P - \tilde{P}}{P_o - \tilde{P}_o} = \frac{p' - Ap}{p'_o - Ap_o},$$

which, again, is the expression described in [15]. Similarly, when π_1 is at infinity the terms involving the distance to π_1 cancel out, leaving us with:

$$k = \frac{P_o - O}{P - O},$$

which is inverse depth, i.e., the affine structure of the scene [4, 24, 20] (it would be Euclidean, if in addition the camera was internally calibrated). We have arrived to the following corollary:

Corollary 2. *The relative affine structure of the scene, described in Theorem 1, reduces to the affine structure of the scene in the case of parallel projection [15], and in the case the reference plane happens to be the plane at infinity[4, 24, 20].*

Theorem 1 shows the connection between the epipole v', a homography A due to some arbitrary plane, and the relative affine structure k. A similar connection can be made between the "fundamental" matrix [4, 5] the epipole and the homography, as follows: Let $p \in \psi_0, p' \in \psi_1$ be two corresponding points, and let l, l' be their corresponding epipolar lines, i.e., $l \cong p \times v$ and $l' \cong p' \times v'$. Since lines are projective invariants, then any point along l is mapped by A to some point along l'. Thus, $l' \cong v' \times Ap$, and because p' is incident to l', we have $p'^\top (v' \times Ap) = 0$, or equivalently: $p'^\top [v']Ap = 0$, or $p'^\top Fp = 0$, where $F = [v']A$, and $[v']$ is the skew-symmetric matrix defined by $[v']w = v' \times w$ for any vector w. Thus, the fundamental matrix F can be written as a product of the skew-symmetric matrix representing the translational component of camera motion, and the homography A due to some arbitrary plane π_1. This is similar to the decomposition of the "essential matrix" [17] as $E = [v']R$, where R is the rotational component of the (rigid) camera displacement. Since R is a particular case of a homography (corresponds to the case where π_1 is the plane at infinity, see [35]), we can see how the essential matrix generalizes in the projective case to become the fundamental matrix. A similar generalization was derived in [10] by showing that the product $[v']R$ remains fixed if we add to R an element that vanishes as a product with $[v']$ (these two generalizations of E are unified in [35]). The product $[v']A$ also connects to two other known results. First, we see that given a homography, the epipole v' follows by having two corresponding points coming from scene points not coplanar with π_1 — an observation that was originally made by [16]. Second, in the case of parallel projection we have A becoming a 2D affine transformation (third row is a multiple of $(0, 0, 1)$), and the third element of v' vanishes. By substitution, the product $[v']A$ reduces to the expression given in [11]. Taken together, we have the following corollary:

Corollary 3. *The "essential" matrix $E = [v']R$ is a particular case of a generalized matrix $F = [v']A$. The product $[v']A$ embodies the results of recovering the epipoles from a planar patch [16] and the epipolar expression in the orthographic case [11].*

Finally, consider the set of S views obtained from the mapping $\mathcal{P}^3 \mapsto \mathcal{P}^2$. The views obtained by an internally calibrated camera (which we will refer to as a "rigid camera") are clearly a subset of S. The set S, for example, contains images that are obtained by taking views of views of an object. The question we address next is whether the relative affine framework is completely realizable by a rigid camera taking views and views of views of an object. This question was addressed originally in [13] but assuming only orthographic views. A more general result is expressed in the following corollary:

Corollary 4. *Given an arbitrary camera position with coordinate frame representation $\mathcal{R}_o$, then the remaining representations $\mathcal{R}$ of $\mathcal{P}^3$ are obtained by an element of the affine group applied to $\mathcal{R}_o$, and are realizable by a rigid motion of the camera frame from its initial position, if in addition to taking pictures of the object we allow any finite sequence of pictures of pictures to be taken as well.*

The proof has a trivial and a less trivial component. The trivial components include, first, the fact that $\mathcal{R}$ is affinely related to $\mathcal{R}_o$ (directly shown in Theorem 1), and secondly, that an affine motion of the camera frame can be decomposed into a rigid motion followed by some arbitrary collineation in $\mathcal{P}^2$. The less trivial component is to show that any collineation in $\mathcal{P}^2$ can be created by a finite sequence of views of a view where only rigid motion of the camera frame is allowed. The details can be found in the Appendix.

We consider next the relationship between the relative affine structure and the projective structure of the scene [4, 10, 31, 19]. By adding a second reference plane we can represent a projective invariant as a function of two homographies, rather than a homography and the epipole. The theoretical and practical differences between the projective and relative affine results will be discussed in Sections 4 and 5, but first, we address the algorithmic aspect of the relative affine framework.

3.1 Two Algorithms: Re-projection and Relative Affine Reconstruction from Two Perspective Views

On the practical side, we have arrived to a remarkably simple algorithm for projective reconstruction of the scene from two perspective/orthographic views (with an uncalibrated camera), and an algorithm for generating novel views of a scene (re-projection). For reconstruction we follow these steps:

1. Recover epipoles v, v' using the relation $p'^{\top} F p = 0$. The epipoles follow from $Fv = 0$ and $F^{\top}v' = 0$ [4]. The latter readily follows from Corollary 3 as $[v']Av \cong [v']v' = 0$ and $A^{\top}[v']^{\top}v' = -A^{\top}[v']v' = 0$.

2. Recover the matrix A that satisfies $Ap_j \cong p'_j$, $j = 1, 2, 3$, and $Av \cong v'$. This requires a solution of a linear system of eight equations (see, for example, Appendices in [21, 29, 30] for details).

3. Set the scale of v' by using a fourth corresponding pair p_o, p'_o such that $p'_o \cong Ap_o + v'$.

4. For every corresponding pair p, p' recover the affine depth k that satisfies $p' \cong Ap + kv'$. As a technical note, k can be recovered in a least-squares fashion by using cross-products:

$$k = \frac{(p' \times v')^T (Ap \times p')}{\| p' \times v' \|^2}.$$

Note that the reconstructed representation $[x, y, 1, k]$ is projective, not affine, because it its related to the Euclidean representation by an element of the projective group (i.e., the relation between the chosen representation $\mathcal{R}_o$ and the Euclidean representation is projective). Note also that k is invariant as long as we use the first view as a reference view, i.e., compute k between a reference view p and any other view. The invariance of k can be used to "re-project" the object onto corresponding points p'' in any third view ψ_2, as follows. We observe:

$$p'' \cong Bp + kv'',$$

for some matrix B and epipole v''. One can solve for B and v'' by observing six corresponding points between the first and third view. Each pair of corresponding points p_j, p''_j contributes two equations:

$$b_{31}x_j x''_j + b_{32}y_j x''_j + k_j v''_3 x''_j + x''_j = \\ b_{11}x_j + b_{12}y_j + b_{13} + k_j v''_1,$$

$$b_{31}x_j y''_j + b_{32}y_j y''_j + k_j v''_3 y''_j + y''_j = \\ b_{21}x_j + b_{22}y_j + b_{23} + k_j v''_2,$$

where $b_{33} = 1$ (this for setting an arbitrary scale because the system of equations is homogeneous — of course this prevents the case where $b_{33} = 0$, but in practice this is not a problem; also one can use principal component analysis instead of setting the value of some chosen element of B or v''). The values of k_j are found from the correspondences p_j, p'_j, $j = 1, ..., 6$ (note that $k_1 = k_2 = k_3 = 0$). Once B, v'' are recovered, we can find the location of p''_i for any seventh point p_i, by first solving for k_i from the equation $p'_i \cong Ap_i + k_i v'$, and then substituting the result in the equation $p''_i \cong Bp_i + k_i v''$.

4 Projective Structure and Invariant From Two Perspective Views

Relative affine structure required the construction of a single reference plane, and for that reason it was necessary to require that one view remained fixed to

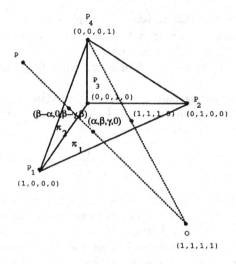

Fig. 2.

serve as a reference view. To permit an invariant from any pair of views of $\mathcal{S}$, we should, by inference, design the construction such that the invariant be defined relative to two planes. By analogy, we will call the invariant "projective depth" [31]. This is done as follows.

We assign the coordinates $(1,0,0,0), (0,1,0,0)$ and $(0,0,1,0)$ to P_1, P_2, P_3, respectively. The coordinates $(0,0,0,1)$ are assigned to a fourth point P_4, and the coordinates $(1,1,1,1)$ to the projection center of the first camera O (see Figure 2). The plane passing through P_1, P_2, P_3 is denoted by π_1 (as before), and the plane passing through P_1, P_3, P_4 is denoted by π_2. Note that the line $\overline{OP_4}$ intersects π_1 at $(1,1,1,0)$, and the line $\overline{OP_2}$ intersects π_2 at $(1,0,1,1)$.

As before, let A_1 be the collineation from the image plane to π_1 by satisfying $A_1 p_j \cong e_j, \; j = 1, ..., 4$, where $e_1 = (1,0,0), e_2 = (0,1,0), e_3 = (0,0,1)$ and $e_4 = (1,1,1)$. Similarly, let E_1 be the collineation from the image plane to π_2 by satisfying $E_1 p_1 \cong e_1, E_1 p_2 \cong e_4, E_1 p_3 \cong e_2$ and $E_1 p_4 \cong e_3$. Note that if $A_1 p = (\alpha, \beta, \gamma)$, then $E_1 p \cong (\beta - \alpha, \beta - \gamma, \beta)$. We have therefore, that the intersection of the line $\overline{OP}$ with π_1 is the point $P_{\pi_1} = (\alpha, \beta, \gamma, 0)$, and the intersection with π_2 is the point $P_{\pi_2} = (\beta - \alpha, 0, \beta - \gamma, \beta)$. We can express P and O as a linear combination of those points:

$$
P \cong \begin{pmatrix} \alpha \\ \beta \\ \gamma \\ 0 \end{pmatrix} + \kappa \begin{pmatrix} \beta - \alpha \\ 0 \\ \beta - \gamma \\ \beta \end{pmatrix},
$$

$$\begin{pmatrix} 1 \\ 1 \\ 1 \\ 1 \end{pmatrix} \cong \begin{pmatrix} \alpha \\ \beta \\ \gamma \\ 0 \end{pmatrix} + \kappa' \begin{pmatrix} \beta - \alpha \\ 0 \\ \beta - \gamma \\ \beta \end{pmatrix}$$

Consider the cross ratio κ/κ' of the four points $O, P_{\pi_1}, P_{\pi_2}, P$. Note that $\kappa' = 1$ independently of P, therefore the cross ratio is simply κ. Thus, κ is invariant up to a uniform scale, and any fifth object point P_o (not lying on any face of the tetrahedron P_1, P_2, P_3, P_4) can be assigned $\kappa_o = 1$ by choosing the appropriate scale for A_1 (or E_1). This has the effect of mapping the fifth point P_o onto the projection center ($P_o \cong (1,1,1,1)$). We have, therefore, that κ (normalized) is a projective invariant, which we call "projective depth". We show next how κ can be computed from image measurements alone, given a second view.

Let A be the homography between the two image planes due to π_1, and similarly, let E be the homography due to π_2. We have that the projections of P_{π_1} and P_{π_2} onto the second image are captured by Ap and Ep, respectively. Denote by v' the location of the epipole in view ψ_1 (the projection of O onto ψ_1). Therefore, the cross ratio of $O, P_{\pi_1}, P_{\pi_2}, P$ is equal to the cross ratio of v', Ap, Ep, p', which is computed as follows:

$$p' \cong Ap + sEp,$$
$$v' \cong Ap + s'Ep,$$

then $k = s/s'$, up to a uniform scale factor (which is set using a fifth point). Here we can also show that s' is a constant independent of p, as follows: Let q be an arbitrary point in ψ_o. Then,

$$v' \cong Aq + s'_q Eq.$$

Let H be a matrix defined by $H = A + s'_q E$. Then, $v' \cong Hv$ and $v' \cong Hq$. This could happen only if $v' \cong Hp$, for all p, and $s' = s'_q$. We have obtained a very simple algorithm for recovering a projective invariant from two perspective (orthographic) views:

$$p' \cong Ap + kEp,$$

where A and E are described above, and k is invariant up to a uniform scale, which can be set by observing a fifth correspondence p_o, p'_o, i.e., set the scale of E to satisfy $p'_o \cong Ap_o + Ep_o$. We have arrived to the following result, which is a refinement on the general result made in [4] that five corresponding points and the corresponding epipoles are sufficient for reconstruction up to a collineation in $\mathcal{P}^3$:

Theorem 5. *Let π_1 and π_2 be two arbitrary and distinct planes in $\mathcal{P}^3$ each projecting onto both image planes $\psi_o, \psi_1 \subset \mathcal{P}^2$, and let $A, E \in PGL_3$ be the two projective mappings (homographies) $\psi_o \mapsto \psi_1$ due to π_1 and π_2, respectively. Let A (or E) be scaled to satisfy*

$$p'_o \cong Ap_o + Ep_o,$$

where $p_o \in \psi_o$ and $p'_o \in \psi_1$ are corresponding points which are the projections of $P_o \notin \pi_1, \pi_2$. Then, for any corresponding pair $p \in \psi_o$ and $p' \in \psi_1$ coming from a point $P \in \mathcal{P}^3$, we have:

$$p' \cong Ap + kEp \qquad (3)$$

where the scalar k is a projective invariant (is independent of the positions of the two cameras and their internal parameters).

The geometric description of Equation 3 and its proof can be described as follows. Take any point O in space and consider the line $\overline{OP}$ and the line $\overline{OP_o}$. Each of these lines intersects the two reference planes at two points (in general), therefore we can measure a cross ratio along each of the two lines. For example, the line $\overline{OP}$ intersects the planes at P_{π_1} and P_{π_2}, and the cross ratio is $< P, O, P_{\pi_1}, P_{\pi_2} >$. The value of κ is the ratio between the two cross ratios along the lines $\overline{OP}$ and $\overline{OP_o}$ respectively. The value of κ remains unchanged regardless of the choice of O, and furthermore, under any projective transformation of the scene. In particular, the point O can coincide with P_o, and thus, we can describe the relative shape of an arbitrary point P in space relative to two arbitrary planes π_1, π_2 and a unit point P_o as the cross ratio along the ray $\overline{PP_o}$. In [35] it is also shown that κ is equal to the ratio of two relative affine structures, one with respect to π_1, and the other with respect to π_2.

In practical terms, the difference between a full projective framework [4, 10, 31, 19] and the relative affine framework can be described as follows. In a full projective framework, if we denote by f the invariance function acting on a pair of views indexed by a fixed set of five corresponding points, then $f(\psi_i, \psi_j)$ is fixed for all i, j. In a relative affine framework, if we denote f_o as the invariance function acting on a fixed view ψ_o and an arbitrary view ψ_i and indexed by a fixed set of four corresponding points, then $f_o(\psi_o, \psi_i)$ is fixed for all i. Therefore, a projective invariant, such as the one described here, is worthwhile computing for tasks for which we do not have a fixed reference view available. Worthwhile because projective depth requires an additional corresponding point, and requires slightly more computations (recover the matrix E in addition to A). Such a task, for example, is to update the reconstructed structure from a moving stereo rig. At each time instance we are given a pair of views from which projective depth can be computed (projective coordinates follow trivially), and since both cameras are changing their position from one time instant to the next, we cannot rely on an affine invariant.

5 Summary

We have discussed the range of structure descriptions entailed by Euclidean, affine and projective frameworks from the perspective of a new framework we call relative affine. Our main results were contained in Theorems 1 and 5 and corollaries in between. A relative affine invariant reduces to the affine structure when the camera center is at infinity or when the reference plane is at infinity. The ratio of two relative affine invariants, each with respect to a distinct reference plane, is a projective invariant. Both the relative affine and the projective were captured by a single simple equation relating the invariant to the epipole and a homography, or two homographies, respectively. The distinction between the two is not only useful for theoretical reasons, but as we saw in Section 3.1 there are certain tasks for which a relative affine invariant is completely sufficient. These tasks include recognition by alignment, and reconstruction relative to a viewer-based coordinate frame (i.e., a reference view is available). We have seen that from a theoretical standpoint, a projective invariant, such as projective-depth κ in Equation 3, is really necessary when a reference view is not available. For example, assume we have a sequence of n views $\psi_o, \psi_1, ..., \psi_{n-1}$ of a scene and we wish to recover its 3D structure. An affine framework would result if we choose one of the views, say ψ_o, as a reference view, and compute the structure as seen from that camera location given the correspondences $\psi_o \implies \psi_i$ with all the remaining views — this is a common approach for recovering metric structure from a sequence. Because relative affine structure is invariant, we have $n - 1$ occurrences of the same measurement k for every point, which can be used as a source of information for a least-squares solution for k (see [35]). Now consider the projective framework. Projective-depth κ is invariant for any two views ψ_i, ψ_j of the sequence. We have therefore $n(n - 1)$ occurrences of κ which is clearly a stronger source of information for obtaining an over-determined solution. The conclusion from this example is that a projective framework has practical advantages over the relative affine, even in cases where a relative affine framework is theoretically sufficient. There are other practical considerations in favor of the projective framework. In the relative affine framework, the epipole v' plays a double role — first for computing the homography A, and then for computing the relative affine structure of all points of interest. In the projective framework, the epipoles are used only for computing the homographies A and E but not used for computing κ. This difference has a practical value as one would probably like to have the epipoles play as little a role as possible because of the difficulty in recovering their location accurately in the presence of noise. In industrial applications, for example, one may be able to set up a frame of reference of two planes with four coplanar points on each of the planes. Then the homographies A and E can be computed without the need for the epipoles, and thus the entire algorithm, expressed in Equation 3, can proceed without recovering the epipoles at all.

Finally, the relative affine result has proven useful for derivation of other results and applications, some of which can be found in [36, 34, 32]. More details and experimental results on the material presented in this paper can be found in [33, 35].

A Appendix Proof of Corollary

Corollary *Given an arbitrary camera position with coordinate frame representation $\mathcal{R}_o$, then the remaining representations $\mathcal{R}$ of $\mathcal{P}^3$ are obtained by an element of the affine group applied to $\mathcal{R}_o$, and are realizable by a rigid motion of the camera frame from its initial position, if in addition to taking pictures of the object we allow any finite sequence of pictures of pictures to be taken as well.*

Lemma 6. *The set of representations $\mathcal{R}$ which are affinely related to an initial representation $\mathcal{R}_o$ can be generated by a rigid camera motion, starting from some fixed initial position, followed by some collineation in $\mathcal{P}^2$.*

Proof: We have shown that any view ψ can be generated by satisfying Equation 1, reproduced below:

$$p' \cong Ap + kv'.$$

Note that $k = 0$ for all $P \in \pi_1$. The plane π_1 is at infinity with respect to $\mathcal{R}_o$, but not with respect to the world coordinate frame. Thus, we map $\mathcal{R}_o$ to a world coordinate representation by sending π_1 to infinity: Let $M \in GL_4$ be defined as

$$M = \begin{bmatrix} 1 & 0 & 0 & 0 \\ 0 & 1 & 0 & 0 \\ 0 & 0 & 1 & 0 \\ 1 & 1 & 1 & 1 \end{bmatrix}.$$

We have:

$$p' \cong Ap + kv'$$

$$= [A, v'] \begin{pmatrix} x \\ y \\ 1 \\ k \end{pmatrix}$$

$$\cong [A, v']M^{-1} \begin{pmatrix} x_b \\ y_b \\ z_b \\ 1 \end{pmatrix}$$

$$= S \begin{pmatrix} x_b \\ y_b \\ z_b \end{pmatrix} + u,$$

where $x_b = x/(x+y+1+k)$, $y_b = y/(x+y+1+k)$ and $z_b = 1/(x+y+1+k)$. Let R be a rotation matrix in 3D, and let B denote a collineation in $\mathcal{P}^2$, i.e., $B \in GL_3$, and let w be some vector in 3D. Then, we must show that

$$p' \cong BR \begin{pmatrix} x_b \\ y_b \\ z_b \end{pmatrix} + Bw.$$

For every R, B and w, there exists S and u that produce the same image, simply be setting $S = BR$ and $u = Bw$. We must also show that for every S and u there exists R, B and w that produce the same image: Since S is of full rank (because A is), then the claim is true by simply setting $B = SR^T$ and $w = B^{-1}u$, for any arbitrary orthogonal matrix R. In conclusion, any view ψ can be generated by some rigid motion R, w starting from a fixed initial position, followed by some collineation B of the image plane. []

We need to show next that any collineation in $\mathcal{P}^2$ can be expressed by a finite sequence of views taken by a rigidly moving camera, i.e., calibrated camera. It is worthwhile noting that the equivalence of projective transformations (an algebraic concept) with a finite sequence of projections of the plane onto itself (a geometric concept) is fundamental in projective geometry. For example, it is known that any projective transformation of the plane can be obtained as the resultant of a finite sequence of projections [40, Thm. 10, pp. 74]. The question, however, is whether the equivalence holds when projections are restricted to what is generally allowed in a rigidly moving camera model. In other words, in a sequence of projections of the plane, we are allowed to move the projection center anywhere in $\mathcal{P}^3$; the image plane is allowed to rotate around the new location of the projection center and scale its distance from it along a distinguishable axis (scaling focal length along the optical axis). What is not allowed, for example, is tilting the image plane with respect to the optical axis (that has the effect of changing the location of the principal point and the image scale factors — all of which should remain constant in a calibrated camera). Without loss of generality, the camera is set such that the optical axis is perpendicular to the image plane, and therefore when the projection center is an ideal point the projecting rays are all perpendicular to the plane, i.e., the case of orthographic projection.

The equivalence between a sequence of perspective/orthographic views of a plane and projective transformations of the plane is shown by first reducing the problem to scaled orthographic projection by taking a sequence of two perspective projections, and then using a result of [38, 12] to show the equivalence for the scaled orthographic case. The following two auxiliary propositions are used:

Lemma 7. *There is a unique projective transformation of the plane in which a given line u is mapped onto an ideal line (has no image in the real plane) and which maps non-collinear points A, B, C onto given non-collinear points A', B', C'.*

Proof: This is standard material (cf. [8, pp. 178]). []

Lemma 8. *There is a scaled orthographic projection for any given affine transformation of the plane.*

Proof: follows directly from [38, 12] showing that any given affine transformation of the plane can be obtained by a unique (up to a reflection) 3D similarity transform of the plane followed by an orthographic projection. []

Lemma 9. *There is a finite sequence of perspective and scaled orthographic views of the plane, taken by a calibrated camera, for any given projective transformation of the plane.*

Proof: The proof follows and modifies [8, pp. 179]. We are given a plane α and a projective transformation T. If T is affine, then by Lemma 8 the proposition is true. If T is not affine, then there exists a line u in α that is mapped onto an ideal line under T. Let A, B, C be three non-collinear points which are not on u, and let their image under T be A', B', C'. Take a perspective view onto a plane α' such that u has no image in α' (the plane α' is rotated around the new projection center such that the plane passing through the projection center and u is parallel to α'). Let A_1, B_1, C_1 be the images of A, B, C in α'. Project α' back to α by orthographic projection, and let A_2, B_2, C_2 be the image of A_1, B_1, C_1 in α. Let F be the resultant of these two projections in the stated order. Then F is a projective transformation of α onto itself such that u has no image (in the real plane) and A, B, C go into A_2, B_2, C_2. From Lemma 8 there is a viewpoint and a scaled orthographic projection of α onto α'' such that A_2, B_2, C_2 go into A', B', C', respectively. Let L be the resultant of this projection (L is affine). $\hat{T} = FL$ is a projective transformation of α such that u has no image and A, B, C go into A', B', C'. By Lemma 7, $T \cong \hat{T}$. $\square$

Proof of Proposition: follows directly from Lemma 6 and Lemma 9. $\square$

References

1. E.B. Barrett, M.H. Brill, N.N. Haag, and P.M. Payton. Invariant linear methods in photogrammetry and model-matching. In J.L. Mundy and A. Zisserman, editors, *Applications of invariances in computer vision.* MIT Press, 1992.

2. R. Cipolla, Y. Okamoto, and Y. Kuno. Robust structure from motion using motion parallax. In *Proceedings of the International Conference on Computer Vision*, pages 374–382, Berlin, Germany, May 1993.

3. S. Demey, A. Zisserman, and P. Beardsley. Affine and projective structure from motion. In *Proceedings of the British Machine Vision Conference*, October 1992.

4. O.D. Faugeras. What can be seen in three dimensions with an uncalibrated stereo rig? In *Proceedings of the European Conference on Computer Vision*, pages 563–578, Santa Margherita Ligure, Italy, June 1992.

5. O.D. Faugeras, Q.T. Luong, and S.J. Maybank. Camera self calibration: Theory and experiments. In *Proceedings of the European Conference on Computer Vision*, pages 321–334, Santa Margherita Ligure, Italy, June 1992.

6. O.D. Faugeras and S. Maybank. Motion from point matches: Multiplicity of solutions. *International Journal of Computer Vision*, 4:225–246, 1990.

7. O.D. Faugeras and L. Robert. What can two images tell us about a third one? Technical Report INRIA, France, 1993.

8. D. Gans. *Transformations and Geometries.* Appleton-Century-Crofts, New York, 1969.

9. J. Harris. *Algebraic Geometry, A First Course.* Springer-Verlag, Graduate Texts in Mathematics., 1992.

10. R. Hartley, R. Gupta, and T. Chang. Stereo from uncalibrated cameras. In *Proceedings IEEE Conf. on Computer Vision and Pattern Recognition*, pages 761–764, Champaign, IL., June 1992.

11. T.S. Huang and C.H. Lee. Motion and structure from orthographic projections. *IEEE Transactions on Pattern Analysis and Machine Intelligence*, PAMI-11:536–540, 1989.

12. D.P. Huttenlocher and S. Ullman. Recognizing solid objects by alignment with an image. *International Journal of Computer Vision*, 5(2):195–212, 1990.

13. D.W. Jacobs. *Recognizing 3-D objects from 2-D images*. PhD thesis, M.I.T Artificial Intelligence Laboratory, September 1992.

14. D.W. Jacobs. Space efficient 3D model indexing. In *Proceedings IEEE Conf. on Computer Vision and Pattern Recognition*, pages 439–444, 1992.

15. J.J. Koenderink and A.J. Van Doorn. Affine structure from motion. *Journal of the Optical Society of America*, 8:377–385, 1991.

16. C.H. Lee. Structure and motion from two perspective views via planar patch. In *Proceedings of the International Conference on Computer Vision*, pages 158–164, Tampa, FL, December 1988.

17. H.C. Longuet-Higgins. A computer algorithm for reconstructing a scene from two projections. *Nature*, 293:133–135, 1981.

18. R. Mohr, L. Quan, F. Veillon, and B. Boufama. Relative 3D reconstruction using multiple uncalibrated images. Technical Report RT 84-IMAG, LIFIA — IRIMAG, France, June 1992.

19. R. Mohr, F. Veillon, and L. Quan. Relative 3d reconstruction using multiple uncalibrated images. In *Proceedings IEEE Conf. on Computer Vision and Pattern Recognition*, pages 543–548, New York, NY, June 1993.

20. T. Moons, L. Van Gool, M. Van Diest, and E. Pauwels. Affine reconstruction from perspective image pairs. *In these proceedings*.

21. J. Mundy and A. Zisserman. Appendix — projective geometry for machine vision. In J. Mundy and A. Zisserman, editors, *Geometric invariances in computer vision*. MIT Press, Cambridge, 1992.

22. J.L. Mundy, R.P. Welty, M.H. Brill, P.M. Payton, and E.B. Barrett. 3-D model alignment without computing pose. In *Proceedings Image Understanding Workshop*, pages 727–735. Morgan Kaufmann, San Mateo, CA, January 1992.

23. Q.T.Luong and O.D. Faugeras. Determining the fundamental matrix with planes: Instability and new algorithms. In *Proceedings IEEE Conf. on Computer Vision and Pattern Recognition*, pages 489–494, New York, NY, June 1993.

24. L. Quan. Affine stereo calibration for relative affine shape reconstruction. In *Proceedings of the British Machine Vision Conference*, pages 659–668, 1993.

25. L. Robert and O.D. Faugeras. Relative 3D positioning and 3D convex hull computation from a weakly calibrated stereo pair. In *Proceedings of the International Conference on Computer Vision*, pages 540–544, Berlin, Germany, May 1993.

26. J.G. Semple and G.T. Kneebone. *Algebraic Projective Geometry*. Clarendon Press, Oxford, 1952.

27. J.G. Semple and L. Roth. *Introduction to Algebraic Geometry*. Clarendon Press, Oxford, 1949.

28. A. Shashua. Correspondence and affine shape from two orthographic views: Motion and Recognition. A.I. Memo No. 1327, Artificial Intelligence Laboratory, Massachusetts Institute of Technology, December 1991.

29. A. Shashua. *Geometry and Photometry in 3D visual recognition*. PhD thesis, M.I.T Artificial Intelligence Laboratory, AI-TR-1401, November 1992.

30. A. Shashua. Projective structure from two uncalibrated images: structure from motion and recognition. A.I. Memo No. 1363, Artificial Intelligence Laboratory, Massachusetts Institute of Technology, September 1992.

31. A. Shashua. Projective depth: A geometric invariant for 3D reconstruction from two perspective/orthographic views and for visual recognition. In *Proceedings of*

the International Conference on Computer Vision, pages 583–590, Berlin, Germany, May 1993.

32. A. Shashua. Algebraic functions for recognition. *IEEE Transactions on Pattern Analysis and Machine Intelligence*, 1994. in press.

33. A. Shashua. Projective structure from uncalibrated images: structure from motion and recognition. *IEEE Transactions on Pattern Analysis and Machine Intelligence*, 1994. in press.

34. A. Shashua. Trilinearity in visual recognition by alignment. In *Proceedings of the European Conference on Computer Vision*, Stockholm, Sweden, May 1994.

35. A. Shashua and N. Navab. Relative affine structure: Theory and application to 3d reconstruction from perspective views. In *Proceedings IEEE Conf. on Computer Vision and Pattern Recognition*, Seattle, Washington, 1994.

36. A. Shashua and S. Toelg. The quadric reference surface: Applications in registering views of complex 3d objects. In *Proceedings of the European Conference on Computer Vision*, Stockholm, Sweden, May 1994.

37. R. Szeliski and S.B. Kang. Recovering 3D shape and motion from image streams using non-linear least squares. Technical Report D.E.C., December 1992.

38. S. Ullman. Aligning pictorial descriptions: an approach to object recognition. *Cognition*, 32:193–254, 1989. Also: in MIT AI Memo 931, Dec. 1986.

39. S. Ullman and R. Basri. Recognition by linear combination of models. *IEEE Transactions on Pattern Analysis and Machine Intelligence*, PAMI-13:992—1006, 1991. Also in M.I.T AI Memo 1052, 1989.

40. O. Veblen and J.W. Young. *Projective Geometry, Vol. 1*. Ginn and Company, 1910.

41. D. Weinshall. Model based invariants for 3-D vision. *International Journal of Computer Vision*, 10(1):27–42, 1993.

42. D. Weinshall and C. Tomasi. Linear and incremental acquisition of invariant shape models from image sequences. In *Proceedings of the International Conference on Computer Vision*, pages 675–682, Berlin, Germany, May 1993.

The Double Algebra: An Effective Tool for Computing Invariants in Computer Vision

Stefan Carlsson

Computational Vision and Active Perception Laboratory (CVAP)
NADA-KTH, Stockholm, Sweden
stefanc@bion.kth.se

Abstract. The double algebra is a system for computations involving subspaces of a general finite dimensional vector space. If this vector space is taken as projective 3-space, the operations of the double algebra can be interpreted as joins and intersections of points, lines and planes. All computations are coordinate free and invariant over linear transformations. The double algebra is therefore a very effective tool for computation of linear invariants of geometric configurations. In this paper we show how to compute linear invariants of general configurations points and lines observed in two images and polyhedral configurations observed in one image. For these cases we derive directly explicit expression of the invariants without reconstructing individual points and lines.

1 Introduction

The basic problem facing automatic visual recognition systems is the variability of the image an object can produce due to changes in viewpoint and intrinsic camera parameters. This is the main motivation behind the interest in computing geometric invariants for objects. For planar objects and linear imaging, images of the same object will be related by a projective transformation. Representing the object by projective invariants, i.e. linear invariants in homogeneous image coordinates, will then make the recognition immune to changes in camera viewpoint and intrinsic parameters [10]. For general objects in 3-D, no invariants can be computed from one single image [3]. The problem of computing invariants in this case can be said to be under constrained. By introducing extra constraints such as mutual co-planarity of several object points or observations in more than one image, it is possible to compute linear invariants for objects in projective 3-space from observed projected image coordinates.

The problem of computing linear invariants from multiple images for general objects in 3-D has been addressed in several recent works, [2, 5, 6, 7, 8, 13]. The methods used in these works are often based on a combination of algebraic and constructive geometric techniques. Linear invariants in projective 3-space can be computed from 6 points using determinants of homogeneous coordinates:

$$I = \frac{|u_1\ u_2\ u_3\ u_4|\ |u_4\ u_5\ u_2\ u_6|}{|u_1\ u_2\ u_4\ u_5|\ |u_3\ u_4\ u_2\ u_6|} \tag{1}$$

If the same expression is computed using the coordinates after a linear transformation, $u' = T\ u$, the determinant of the transformation matrix can be factored: $|u_1'\ u_2'\ u_3'\ u_4'| = |T|\ |u_1\ u_2\ u_3\ u_4|$ and therefore cancelled, leaving the expression invariant.

The techniques for computing invariants in the case of multiple images and also in the case of polyhedral scenes observed in one image, [14] [12] are based on reconstruction of individual points and lines up to a projective transform. In this paper we will present a more general technique for computation of invariants from single and multiple images, of points and lines in 3-D where the invariants are computed without this individual reconstruction. This technique will be based on the double algebra as defined in [1]. The double algebra can be seen as an algebra of geometric incidence relations. In eucledian 3-space these incidences take the form of intersections between e.g. a line and a plane, or the joining of two points by a line. In projective space, points , lines and planes are represented by linear subspaces. The double algebra is therefore a system for computations involving subspaces of a general finite dimensional vector space. In the double algebra all relations and entities are invariant over linear transformations. This means that all computations are coordinate free and we are lead very quickly to the computation of linear invariants.

Historically, the double algebra is a modern version of the 19:th century Grassman-algebra. For the closer relation with Grassman-algebra the reader is referred to the introduction in [1].

2 The Double Algebra

Vision starts with projection to an image plane in eucledian 3-space. Using the standard pinhole model of a camera, a line of sight to a point in space is defined as the unique line passing through the point and the projection point of the camera. The image point is defined as the intersection of this line with the image plane. This example actually contains the basic ingredients of the double algebra.

Two points can be joined to give a line and a line can intersect or meet a plane to give a point. The operations of join and meet in eucledian 3-space can be used to define new points, lines and planes by pairwise combination. In projective 3-space a point (x, y, z) is represented by the homogeneous vector $a = w(x, y, z, 1)$ with w being an arbitrary scalar. This is a one-dimensional subspace of projective 3-space, the linear span of the vector a, which we denote by $S(a)$. The line passing through two points (a, b) in projective 3-space corresponds to the subspace given

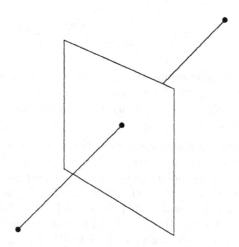

Fig. 1. The standard pinhole camera model

by the linear span of (a, b) denoted $S(a, b)$, and a plane passing through three points (a, b, c) corresponds to the linear span $S(a, b, c)$.

The operation of join of points, lines and planes in eucledian 3 space will correspond to joint linear spans and the meet operation corresponds to intersections of their corresponding subspaces in projective 3-space. This can be summarized in the following scheme where the join operation is denoted $\vee$ and the meet operation $\wedge$. (Note that in standard exterior algebra the $\wedge$ sign is actually used for exterior product which in the double algebra corresponds to the join operation.)

Eucledian 3-space		**Projective 3-space**	
	join		
point $\vee$ point $\rightarrow$ line		$S(a) \vee S(b)$	$\rightarrow S(a, b)$
point $\vee$ line $\rightarrow$ plane		$S(a) \vee S(b, c)$	$\rightarrow S(a, b, c)$
	meet		
line $\wedge$ plane $\rightarrow$ point		$S(a, b) \wedge S(c, d, e)$	$\rightarrow S(a, b) \cap S(c, d, e)$
plane $\wedge$ plane $\rightarrow$ line		$S(a, b, c) \wedge S(d, e, f)$	$\rightarrow S(a, b, c) \cap S(d, e, f)$

In general the join and meet operations are defined for a finite dimensional vector space V. If $\bar{A}$ and $\bar{B}$ denote disjoint subspaces, i.e. $\bar{A} \cap \bar{B} = 0$ the join operation is defined as:

$$\bar{A} \vee \bar{B} \;=\; \bar{A} + \bar{B} \tag{2}$$

Where $\bar{A} + \bar{B}$ means the least subspace which contains both $\bar{A}$ and $\bar{B}$. The meet

join

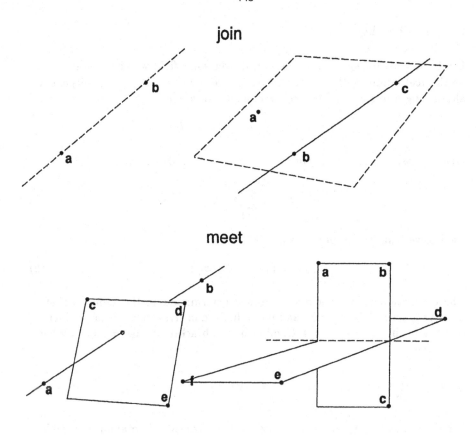

meet

Fig. 2. The join and meet operations in eucledian 3-space

operation is defined as:

$$\bar{A} \wedge \bar{B} = \bar{A} \cap \bar{B} \qquad (3)$$

provided $\bar{A} \cup \bar{B} = V$

The double algebra is a system for computations with subspaces of a finite dimensional vector space. In this algebra subspaces are represented by *extensors*, which are objects constructed from the elements of the vector space. The join and meet of extensors produce new extensors. On the vector space is defined a non-degenerate altrnating linear form called the *bracket* by which the extensors are defined. All computations and relations derived are coordinate free and therefore independent of the choice of reference system. This property will lead us very quickly to computations of linear invariants. This chapter will be a brief review of the double algebra as defined in [1]. For proofs and more detailed treatment we refer the reader to this reference and the related works [4, 11, 15], which also contain applications to projective geometry.

2.1 The bracket

Let V be a vector space of dimension n over some field which we will take to be the real numbers R. A *bracket* over the vector space V is a non-degenerate alternating n-linear form defined over the vector space:

$$x_1 \ldots x_n \longrightarrow [x_1 \ldots x_n] \in R \tag{4}$$

Given a basis $e_1 \ldots e_n$ of V with $[e_1 \ldots e_n] = 1$ and vectors:

$$x_i = \sum_{j=1}^{n} x_{ij} \, e_j \tag{5}$$

the bracket can be computed as a determinant:

$$[x_1 \ldots x_n] = \det(x_{ij}) \tag{6}$$

The distinction between a bracket and a determinant in the same as that of inner product in hilbert space and its evaluation in terms of sums of products of coordinates in a specific basis. Computing the bracket as a determinant is basis dependent.

2.2 The join

For elements $x_1^i \ldots x_k^i$ in the vector space V we consider formal linear combinations:

$$\sum_i w_i \, x_1^i \ldots x_k^i \tag{7}$$

The definition of the bracket can be extended to linear combinations of n elements by:

$$[\sum_i w_i \, x_1^i \ldots x_n^i] = \sum_i w_i \, [x_1^i \ldots x_n^i] \tag{8}$$

Given elements $y_{k+1} \ldots y_n$ in V We can define an equivalence relation on linear combinations of vector sequences:

$$\sum_i w_i \, a_1^i \ldots a_k^i \sim \sum_i v_i \, b_1^i \ldots b_k^i \tag{9}$$

if for all choices of elements $y_{k+1} \ldots y_n$ in V we have:

$$\left[\sum_i w_i \, a_1^i \ldots a_k^i, y_{k+1} \ldots y_n \right] = \left[\sum_i v_i \, b_1^i \ldots b_k^i, y_{k+1} \ldots y_n \right] \qquad (10)$$

A sequence $A = a_1 \ldots a_k$ of elements in V is called an *extensor* of step k. To every extensor we can associate the subspace of V given by the span of $a_1 \ldots a_k$ which we will denote by $\bar{A}$. Note that the equivalence relation imply that extensors inherit properties from the bracket. E.g. $a_1 \ldots a_k$ is non-zero if and only if the a_i form a linearly independent set and $a_1 \ldots a_k = w \, b_1 \ldots b_k$ for some w, if sequences $a_1 \ldots a_k$ and $b_1 \ldots b_k$ span the same subspace. The association between an extensor and a subspace is therefore defined only up to an arbitrary scale factor.

Given two extensors A and B of step k and l respectively with $k + l \leq n$ the *join* is defined as:

$$A \vee B = a_1 \ldots a_k \vee b_1 \ldots b_l = a_1 \ldots a_k, \, b_1 \ldots b_l \qquad (11)$$

If $\bar{A} + \bar{B}$ denotes the least subspace containing both $\bar{A}$ and $\bar{B}$ we have the relation:

$$\overline{A \vee B} = \bar{A} + \bar{B} \qquad (12)$$

2.3   The meet

The meet between two extensors $A = a_1 \ldots a_j$ and $B = b_1 \ldots b_k$ with $j + k > n$, is a new extensor and should correspond to the intersection of their associated subspaces.

$$\overline{A \wedge B} = \bar{A} \cap \bar{B} \qquad (13)$$

This will be achieved if the meet operation is defined as:

$$A \wedge B = \sum_\sigma sign(\sigma) \, [\, a_{\sigma(1)} \ldots a_{\sigma(n-k)} \, b_1 \ldots b_k \,] \, a_{\sigma(n-k+1)} \cdots a_{\sigma(j)} \qquad (14)$$

The sum is taken over all permutations σ of $\{1, 2 \ldots j\}$ such that $\sigma(1) < \sigma(2) < \ldots < \sigma(d-k)$ and $\sigma(d-k+1) < \sigma(d-k+2) < \ldots < \sigma(j)$

If A is an extensor of step k and B an extensor of step l, the meet is associative distributive over addition and anti commutative with the rule:

$$A \wedge B = (-1)^{(n-k)(n-l)} B \wedge A$$

As an example we can take the meet of two 3-extensors in a 4 dimensional vector space:

$$a_1 \, a_2 \, a_3 \, \wedge \, b_1 \, b_2 \, b_3 \, =$$

$$= [\, a_1 \, b_1 \, b_2 \, b_3 \,]\, a_2 \, a_3 \, - [\, a_2 \, b_1 \, b_2 \, b_3 \,]\, a_1 \, a_3 \, + [\, a_3 \, b_1 \, b_2 \, b_3 \,]\, a_1 \, a_2 \quad (15)$$

If the vectors a_i and b_i are in projective 3-space this equation gives the extensor representation of the line of intersection between the planes containing the points $a_1 \, a_2 \, a_3$ and $b_1 \, b_2 \, b_3$ respectively.

3   The Pinhole Camera

The aim of this paper is to express linear invariants of points and lines in projective 3-space in terms of observed image coordinates. We will therefore start with analyzing projective imaging using the standard pinhole camera model fig. 3. In this model a point u in projective 3-space is projected to an image plane by a projection point a_0. The projected point a' on the image plane is then given by the intersection of the line $a_0 \, u$ with the plane. The plane is defined by three arbitrary non-collinear points a_1, a_2, a_3 The projected point can therefore be ¡expressed using the meet as:

$$a' = a_1 \, a_2 \, a_3 \, \wedge \, a_0 \, u \; =$$

$$= [\, a_0 \, a_2 \, a_3 \, u \,]\, a_1 \, + [\, a_0 \, a_3 \, a_1 \, u \,]\, a_2 \, + [\, a_0 \, a_1 \, a_2 \, u \,]\, a_3 \tag{16}$$

Observations in an image will be made in a eucledian coordinate system which can be constructed by selection of three non-collinear points in the image. For this we can take the image plane defining points a_1, a_2, a_3. If we let $\bar{a}_1$, $\bar{a}_2$, $\bar{a}_3$ be their corresponding coordinates in eucledian 3-space we take $\bar{a}_1$ as the origin of the image coordinate system with axis defined by vectors $\bar{a}_2 - \bar{a}_1$ and $\bar{a}_3 - \bar{a}_1$. The eucledian coordinates of the projected point a' is denoted $\bar{a}'$. In the image coordinate system it will have coordinates x, y according to:

$$\bar{a}' = \bar{a}_1 + x\,(\bar{a}_2 - \bar{a}_1) + y\,(\bar{a}_3 - \bar{a}_1) = (1 - x - y)\,\bar{a}_1 + x\,\bar{a}_2 + y\,\bar{a}_3 \tag{17}$$

If we take the 4-vectors $\begin{pmatrix} \bar{a}_1 \\ 1 \end{pmatrix}$, $\begin{pmatrix} \bar{a}_2 \\ 1 \end{pmatrix}$ and $\begin{pmatrix} \bar{a}_3 \\ 1 \end{pmatrix}$ as a basis we can express the projected point a' using homogeneous coordinates w_i in projective as:

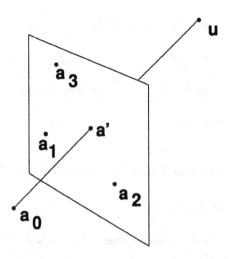

Fig. 3. Four points a_0, a_1, a_2, a_3 define a pinhole camera

$$a' = w_1 \begin{pmatrix} \bar{a}_1 \\ 1 \end{pmatrix} + w_2 \begin{pmatrix} \bar{a}_2 \\ 1 \end{pmatrix} + w_3 \begin{pmatrix} \bar{a}_3 \\ 1 \end{pmatrix} = w_1\, a_1 + w_2\, a_2 + w_3\, a_3 \quad (18)$$

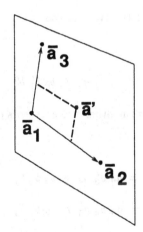

Fig. 4. Image coordinate system defined by eucledian coordinates.

The homogeneous coordinates are the determined up to a scale factor by the eucledian coordinates and they are related to the object and camera defining points as:

$$w_1 = w\,(1 - x - y) \; = \; [\; a_0 \; a_2 \; a_3 \; u \;]$$

$$w_2 = w\,x \qquad\qquad = \; [\; a_0 \; a_3 \; a_1 \; u \;] \tag{19}$$

$$w_3 = w\,y \qquad\qquad = \; [\; a_0 \; a_1 \; a_2 \; u \;]$$

where w is an arbitrary scalar.

4 Linear Invariants from Observations in Two Images

4.1 Invariants of six points

Using bracket notation the linear invariant of 6 points in P^3, which was discussed in the introduction, is:

$$I \; = \; \frac{|u_1 \; u_2 \; u_3 \; u_4| \; |u_4 \; u_5 \; u_2 \; u_6|}{|u_1 \; u_2 \; u_4 \; u_5| \; |u_3 \; u_4 \; u_2 \; u_6|} \tag{20}$$

The basic building block in this invariant is the 4-point bracket $[u_i \; u_j \; u_k \; u_l]$ We will now show how these brackets can be computed using the methods of the double algebra.

Looking at figure 5 we see that the two-extensor $u_1 \; u_2$ can be expressed using the meet operation as:

$$u_1 \; u_2 \; = \; a_0 \; a_1' \; a_2' \; \wedge \; b_0 \; b_1' \; b_2' \tag{21}$$

In the same way we can express the other two-extensors occurring in the expression for the invariant as:

$$u_3 \; u_4 \; = \; a_0 \; a_3' \; a_4' \; \wedge \; b_0 \; b_3' \; b_4'$$

$$u_4 \; u_5 \; = \; a_0 \; a_4' \; a_5' \; \wedge \; b_0 \; b_4' \; b_5'$$

$$u_2 \; u_6 \; = \; a_0 \; a_2' \; a_6' \; \wedge \; b_0 \; b_2' \; b_6'$$

$$\tag{22}$$

We can now form the bracket and use the anti-commutativity property of the meet operation:

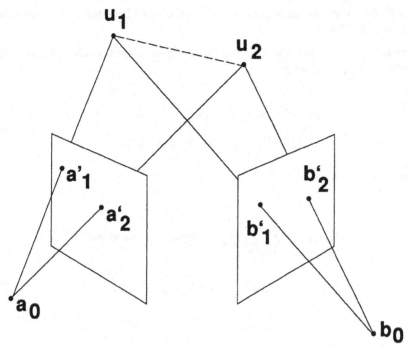

Fig. 5. Two points projected in two frames

$$[u_1\ u_2\ u_3\ u_4] = u_1\ u_2 \wedge u_3\ u_4 =$$

$$= a_0\ a_1'\ a_2' \wedge b_0\ b_1'\ b_2' \wedge a_0\ a_3'\ a_4' \wedge b_0\ b_3'\ b_4' =$$

$$= -\ a_0\ a_1'\ a_2' \wedge a_0\ a_3'\ a_4' \wedge b_0\ b_1'\ b_2' \wedge b_0\ b_3'\ b_4' =$$

$$= -([a_0\ a_1'\ a_2'\ a_3']\ a_0\ a_4' - [a_0\ a_1'\ a_2'\ a_4']\ a_0\ a_3') \wedge ([b_0\ b_1'\ b_2'\ b_3']\ b_0\ b_4' - [b_0\ b_1'\ b_2'\ b_4']\ b_0\ b_3') =$$

$$= [a_0\ a_1'\ a_2'\ a_3']\ [b_0\ b_1'\ b_2'\ b_3']\ [a_0\ b_0\ a_4'\ b_4'] + [a_0\ a_1'\ a_2'\ a_4']\ [b_0\ b_1'\ b_2'\ b_4']\ [a_0\ b_0\ a_3'\ b_3'] -$$

$$- [a_0\ a_1'\ a_2'\ a_3']\ [b_0\ b_1'\ b_2'\ b_4']\ [a_0\ b_0\ a_4'\ b_3'] - [a_0\ a_1'\ a_2'\ a_4']\ [b_0\ b_1'\ b_2'\ b_3']\ [a_0\ b_0\ a_3'\ b_4']$$

$$(23)$$

The expression for the bracket $[u_1\ u_2\ u_3\ u_4]$ is built from brackets of three different kinds:

$$[a_0\ a_i'\ a_j'\ a_k'], \qquad [b_0\ b_i'\ b_j'\ b_k'], \qquad [a_0\ b_0\ a_i'\ b_j']$$

We will now show how these brackets can be expressed in terms of the observable image coordinates.

Expressing a' and b' in terms of their homogeneous image coordinates and image plane defining points we get:

$$a'_i = \alpha_{i,1}\, a_1 + \alpha_{i,2}\, a_2 + \alpha_{i,3}\, a_3$$

$$b'_i = \beta_{i,1}\, b_1 + \beta_{i,2}\, b_2 + \beta_{i,3}\, b_3 \tag{24}$$

Using this we have:

$$[a_0\ a'_i\ a'_j\ a'_k] = \sum_{l=1}^{3}\sum_{m=1}^{3}\sum_{n=1}^{3}\alpha_{i,l}\,\alpha_{j,m}\,\alpha_{k,n}\,[a_0\ a_l\ a_m\ a_n] =$$

$$= [a_0\ a_1\ a_2\ a_3]\,|\alpha_i\ \alpha_j\ \alpha_k| \tag{25}$$

and:

$$[b_0\ b'_i\ b'_j\ b'_k] = \sum_{l=1}^{3}\sum_{m=1}^{3}\sum_{n=1}^{3}\beta_{i,l}\,\beta_{j,m}\,\beta_{k,n}\,[b_0\ b_l\ b_m\ b_n] =$$

$$= [b_0\ b_1\ b_2\ b_3]\,|\beta_i\ \beta_j\ \beta_k| \tag{26}$$

For the brackets of type $[a_0\ b_0\ a'_i\ b'_j]$ we get:

$$[a_0\ b_0\ a'_i\ b'_j] = \sum_{m=1}^{3}\sum_{n=1}^{3}\alpha_{i,m}\,\beta_{j,n}\,[a_0\ b_0\ a_m\ b_n] =$$

$$= (\alpha_{i,1}\ \alpha_{i,2}\ \alpha_{i,3}) \begin{pmatrix} [a_0\ b_0\ a_1\ b_1] & [a_0\ b_0\ a_1\ b_2] & [a_0\ b_0\ a_1\ b_3] \\ [a_0\ b_0\ a_2\ b_1] & [a_0\ b_0\ a_2\ b_2] & [a_0\ b_0\ a_2\ b_3] \\ [a_0\ b_0\ a_3\ b_1] & [a_0\ b_0\ a_3\ b_2] & [a_0\ b_0\ a_3\ b_3] \end{pmatrix} \begin{pmatrix} \beta_{j,1} \\ \beta_{j,2} \\ \beta_{j,3} \end{pmatrix} =$$

$$= \alpha_i^T\ \mathbf{F}\ \beta_j \tag{27}$$

where $\mathbf{F}$ is the matrix with elements $[a_0\ b_0\ a_i\ b_j]$

Expressing the brackets of eq. 23 in terms of image coordinates and the matrix **F** we get.

$$[u_1 \ u_2 \ u_3 \ u_4] \ = \ [a_0 \ a_1 \ a_2 \ a_3] \ [b_0 \ b_1 \ b_2 \ b_3] \ Q(\alpha_1 \ldots \alpha_4, \beta_1, \ldots \beta_4, \mathbf{F}) \quad (28)$$

where:

$$Q(\alpha_1 \ldots \alpha_4, \beta_1, \ldots \beta_4, \mathbf{F}) \ =$$

$$= \ |\alpha_1 \ \alpha_2 \ \alpha_3| \ |\beta_1 \ \beta_2 \ \beta_3| \ \alpha_4^T \ \mathbf{F} \ \beta_4 \ + \ |\alpha_1 \ \alpha_2 \ \alpha_4| \ |\beta_1 \ \beta_2 \ \beta_4| \ \alpha_3^T \ \mathbf{F} \ \beta_3 \ -$$

$$- \ |\alpha_1 \ \alpha_2 \ \alpha_3| \ |\beta_1 \ \beta_2 \ \beta_4| \ \alpha_4^T \ \mathbf{F} \ \beta_3 \ - \ |\alpha_1 \ \alpha_2 \ \alpha_4| \ |\beta_1 \ \beta_2 \ \beta_3| \ \alpha_3^T \ \mathbf{F} \ \beta_4 \ =$$

$$= \ (\ |\alpha_1 \ \alpha_2 \ \alpha_3| \ \alpha_4 - |\alpha_1 \ \alpha_2 \ \alpha_4| \ \alpha_3 \ )^T \ \mathbf{F} (\ |\beta_1 \ \beta_2 \ \beta_3| \ \beta_4 - |\beta_1 \ \beta_2 \ \beta_4| \ \beta_3 \ ) \ =$$

$$= \ (\ \alpha_1 \ \alpha_2 \ \wedge \ \alpha_3 \ \alpha_4 \ )^T \ \mathbf{F} \ (\ \beta_1 \ \beta_2 \ \wedge \ \beta_3 \ \beta_4 \ ) \ =$$

$$= \ \alpha_{12\_34}^T \mathbf{F} \ \beta_{12\_34}$$

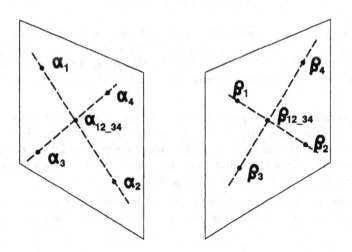

Fig. 6. The points of intersection α_{12_34} and β_{12_34}

where the vectors α_{12_34} and β_{12_34} are the coordinates of the intersection of the line $\alpha_1 \ \alpha_2$ with $\alpha_3 \ \alpha_4$ and $\beta_1 \ \beta_2$ with $\beta_3 \ \beta_4$ respectively.

The 4-point bracket can then be written:

$$[u_1 \ u_2 \ u_3 \ u_4] \ = \ [a_0 \ a_1 \ a_2 \ a_3] \ [b_0 \ b_1 \ b_2 \ b_3] \ \alpha_{12\_34}^T \ \mathbf{F} \ \beta_{12\_34} \quad (29)$$

Repeating this procedure for the other brackets in the expression for the 6-point invariant we get:

$$I = \frac{[u_1\ u_2\ u_3\ u_4]\ [u_4\ u_5\ u_2\ u_6]}{[u_1\ u_2\ u_4\ u_5]\ [u_3\ u_4\ u_2\ u_6]} = \frac{\alpha_{12\_34}^T\ \mathbf{F}\ \beta_{12\_34}\quad \alpha_{45\_26}^T\ \mathbf{F}\ \beta_{45\_26}}{\alpha_{12\_45}^T\ \mathbf{F}\ \beta_{12\_45}\quad \alpha_{34\_26}^T\ \mathbf{F}\ \beta_{34\_26}}$$

$$(30)$$

We see that the fundamental matrix $\mathbf{F}$ plays a dominant role in this expression. This matrix contains information about intrinsic and extrinsic camera parameters and it can be computed from known point matches using the geometric constraints of the two-camera system.

4.2 The epipolar constraint

The points $a_0\ b_0\ a_i'\ b_i'$ all lie in the same epipolar plane. We therefore have:

$$[a_0\ b_0\ a_i'\ b_i'] = \alpha_i^T\ \mathbf{F}\ \beta_i = 0 \qquad (31)$$

which is the epipolar constraint. Given at least 8 points the elements of the matrix $\mathbf{F}$ can be computed up to an arbitrary scale factor by solving the linear system of eq. 31 The matrix $\mathbf{F}$ is the fundamental matrix, defined in [6], and generalizes the essential matrix [9] to the case of unknown intrinsic camera parameters.

An important projective property of four points is whether they are coplanar. The intersection points α_{12_34} and β_{12_34} will then be in projective correspondence. Co-planarity means that their bracket vanishes, and from eq. 29 we see that this is the case if the points of intersection α_{12_34} and β_{12_34} are in projective correspondence, i.e. we will have: $\alpha_{12\_34}^T\ \mathbf{F}\ \beta_{12\_34} = 0$

The intersections of the line between projection points a_0 and b_0 with the image planes are known as the epipolar points, e_a and e_b. They can be computed as:

$$e_a = a_1\ a_2\ a_3 \wedge a_0\ b_0 = [a_0\ b_0\ a_2\ a_3]\ a_1 + [a_0\ b_0\ a_3\ a_1]\ a_2 + [a_0\ b_0\ a_1\ a_2]\ a_3 \qquad (32)$$

Since e_a lies in the plane $a_0\ b_0\ b_i$ for arbitrary b_i. we have:

$$e_a \vee a_0\ b_0\ b_i = 0 \qquad (33)$$

Developing this expression we get:

$$[a_0\ b_0\ a_1\ b_i]\ [a_0\ b_0\ a_2\ a_3] + [a_0\ b_0\ a_2\ b_i]\ [a_0\ b_0\ a_3\ a_1] + [a_0\ b_0\ a_3\ b_i]\ [a_0\ b_0\ a_1\ a_2] = 0$$

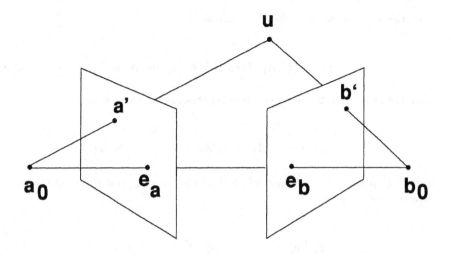

Fig. 7. Epipolar points, and plane

If we take this equation for $i = 1, 2, 3$ we get:

$$\mathbf{F}^T \, \epsilon_a \; = \; 0 \tag{34}$$

I.e. the vector ϵ_a which is the image coordinate vector of the epipolar point e_a in the a-plane, is the null-pace of the matrix $\mathbf{F}^T$.

4.3 Invariants of four lines

A line in projective space P^3 can be represented by a two-extensor $u^{(1)} \, u^{(2)}$ where $u^{(1)}$ and $u^{(2)}$ represent arbitrary points on the line. Given four lines:

$$L_i \; = \; u_i^{(1)} \, u_i^{(2)} \qquad i = 1 \ldots 4 \tag{35}$$

we can define a linear invariant as:

$$\frac{[L_1 \, L_2] \, [L_3 \, L_4]}{[L_1 \, L_3] \, [L_2 \, L_4]} \; = \; \frac{[u_1^{(1)} \, u_1^{(2)} \, u_2^{(1)} \, u_2^{(2)}] \, [u_3^{(1)} \, u_3^{(2)} \, u_4^{(1)} \, u_4^{(2)}]}{[u_1^{(1)} \, u_1^{(2)} \, u_3^{(1)} \, u_3^{(2)}] \, [u_2^{(1)} \, u_2^{(2)} \, u_4^{(1)} \, u_4^{(2)}]} \tag{36}$$

The lines L_i project to lines A_i, B_i in the two images. They are then related as:

$$L_i \; = \; a_0 \, A_i \, \wedge \, b_0 \, B_i \qquad i = 1 \ldots 4 \tag{37}$$

Using this relation we have for the bracket:

$$[L_1 \; L_2] \;=\; (a_0 \; A_1 \; \wedge \; b_0 \; B_1) \; \wedge \; (a_0 \; A_2 \; \wedge \; b_0 \; B_2) \tag{38}$$

Using the anti-commutativity of the meet this can be written as:

$$[L_1 \; L_2] \;=\; -\; a_0 \; A_1 \; \wedge \; a_0 \; A_2 \; \wedge \; b_0 \; B_1 \; \wedge \; b_0 \; B_2 \tag{39}$$

By picking points $a_i^{(1)}, a_i^{(2)}$ and $b_i^{(1)}, b_i^{(2)}$ on the lines A_i and B_i respectively as representatives we get:

$$A_i \;=\; a_i^{(1)} \; a_i^{(2)} \qquad B_i \;=\; b_i^{(1)} \; b_i^{(2)} \qquad i \;=\; 1 \ldots 4 \tag{40}$$

and for the bracket:

$$[L_1 \; L_2] \;=\; -\; a_0 \; a_1^{(1)} \; a_1^{(2)} \; \wedge \; a_0 \; a_2^{(1)} \; a_2^{(2)} \; \wedge \; b_0 \; b_1^{(1)} \; b_1^{(2)} \; \wedge \; b_0 \; b_2^{(1)} \; b_2^{(2)} \tag{41}$$

We see that this expression is of the same type as that of eq. 23 In both cases we are dealing with four points in each image. The only difference is that the points are no longer in projective correspondence. This property was however not relevant for the derivation of the expression for the 4-point bracket. The derivation for the 4-point bracket can therefore be carried over to the 2-line case directly, and we have for the 2-line bracket:

$$[L_1 \; L_2] \;=\; [a_0 \; a_1 \; a_2 \; a_3] \; [b_0 \; b_1 \; b_2 \; b_3] \; \alpha_{1\_2}^T \; \mathbf{F} \; \beta_{1\_2} \tag{42}$$

where α_{1_2} and β_{1_2} are the image coordinates of the points of intersection of the lines $A_1 \; A_2$ and $B_1 \; B_2$ respectively, i.e:

$$\alpha_{1\_2} \;=\; \alpha_1^{(1)} \; \alpha_1^{(2)} \; \wedge \; \alpha_2^{(1)} \; \alpha_2^{(2)} \qquad \beta_{1\_2} \;=\; \beta_1^{(1)} \; \beta_1^{(2)} \; \wedge \; \beta_2^{(1)} \; \beta_2^{(2)} \tag{43}$$

with $\alpha_1^{(1)} \; \alpha_1^{(2)}$ and $\beta_1^{(1)} \; \beta_1^{(2)}$ being the image coordinates of the points $a_1^{(1)} \; a_1^{(2)}$ and $b_1^{(1)} \; b_1^{(2)}$ on the lines.

For the 4-line invariant we get:

$$\frac{[L_1 \; L_2] \; [L_3 \; L_4]}{[L_1 \; L_3] \; [L_2 \; L_4]} \;=\; \frac{\alpha_{1\_2}^T \; \mathbf{F} \; \beta_{1\_2} \quad \alpha_{3\_4}^T \; \mathbf{F} \; \beta_{3\_4}}{\alpha_{1\_3}^T \; \mathbf{F} \; \beta_{1\_3} \quad \alpha_{2\_4}^T \; \mathbf{F} \; \beta_{2\_4}} \tag{44}$$

4.4 Combinations of points and lines

Invariants can be defined from combinations of points and lines. The basic unit in the construction of these invariants is the bracket computed from two points and one line:

$$[u_1 \ u_2 \ L_1] \tag{45}$$

from eq. 21 we have

$$u_1 \ u_2 \ = \ a_0 \ a_1' \ a_2' \ \wedge \ b_0 \ b_1' \ b_2' \tag{46}$$

and for the line we have

$$L_1 \ = \ a_0 \ A_1 \ \wedge \ b_0 \ B_1 \ = \ a_0 \ a_1^{(1)} \ a_1^{(2)} \ \wedge \ b_0 \ b_1^{(1)} \ b_1^{(2)} \tag{47}$$

which gives :

$$[u_1 \ u_2 \ L_1] \ = \ a_0 \ a_1' \ a_2' \ \wedge \ b_0 \ b_1' \ b_2' \ \wedge \ a_0 \ a_1^{(1)} \ a_1^{(2)} \ \wedge \ b_0 \ b_1^{(1)} \ b_1^{(2)} \tag{48}$$

As in the two line case we see that this expression is of the same type as that of eq. 23 The derivations leading to the bracket expression for four points can then be carried over directly and we get:

$$[u_1 \ u_2 \ L_1] \ = \ [a_0 \ a_1 \ a_2 \ a_3] \ [b_0 \ b_1 \ b_2 \ b_3] \ \alpha_{12\_1}^T \ \mathbf{F} \ \beta_{12\_1} \tag{49}$$

where α_{12_1} and β_{12_1} are the image coordinates of the points of intersection of the line A_1 with the line through the points α_1 and α_2 and the intersection of the line B_1 with the line through the points β_1 and β_2 respectively, i.e:

$$\alpha_{12\_1} \ = \ \alpha_1 \ \alpha_2 \ \wedge \ \alpha_2^{(1)} \ \alpha_2^{(2)} \qquad \beta_{12\_1} \ = \ \beta_1 \ \beta_2 \ \wedge \ \beta_2^{(1)} \ \beta_2^{(2)} \tag{50}$$

Invariants for sets of points and lines can now be constructed using the bracket expressions of the type $[u_i \ u_j \ L_k]$ and $[L_i \ L_j]$ as building blocks. Examples are:

3 lines and 2 points

$$\frac{[L_1 \ L_2] \ [u_1 \ u_2 \ L_3]}{[L_1 \ L_3] \ [u_1 \ u_2 \ L_2]} = \frac{\alpha_{1\_2}^T \ \mathbf{F} \ \beta_{1\_2} \ \ \alpha_{12\_3}^T \ \mathbf{F} \ \beta_{12\_3}}{\alpha_{1\_3}^T \ \mathbf{F} \ \beta_{1\_3} \ \ \alpha_{12\_2}^T \ \mathbf{F} \ \beta_{12\_2}}$$

2 lines and 4 points

$$\frac{[u_1 \ u_2 \ L_1] \ [u_3 \ u_4 \ L_2]}{[u_1 \ u_2 \ L_2] \ [u_3 \ u_4 \ L_1]} = \frac{\alpha_{12\_1}^T \ \mathbf{F} \ \beta_{12\_1} \ \ \alpha_{34\_2}^T \ \mathbf{F} \ \beta_{34\_2}}{\alpha_{12\_2}^T \ \mathbf{F} \ \beta_{12\_2} \ \ \alpha_{34\_1}^T \ \mathbf{F} \ \beta_{34\_1}} \qquad (51)$$

2 lines and 3points

$$\frac{[u_1 \ u_2 \ L_1] \ [u_2 \ u_3 \ L_2]}{[u_1 \ u_2 \ L_2] \ [u_2 \ u_3 \ L_1]} = \frac{\alpha_{12\_1}^T \ \mathbf{F} \ \beta_{12\_1} \ \ \alpha_{23\_2}^T \ \mathbf{F} \ \beta_{23\_2}}{\alpha_{12\_2}^T \ \mathbf{F} \ \beta_{12\_2} \ \ \alpha_{23\_1}^T \ \mathbf{F} \ \beta_{23\_1}}$$

5   Linear Invariants from one Image

Given observations in just one image extra constraints have to be imposed on point and line sets in 3-D in order to compute invariants. For the case of polyhedral scenes, methods have been presented [12] [14] that compute 3-D structure up to a projective transformation. In this section we will show how to use the double algebra for the direct computation of linear invariants of polyhedral scenes without any prior projective reconstruction.

Consider four coplanar points $u_1 \ldots u_4$ in projective 3-space. The coplanar lines $u_1 \ u_2$ and $u_3 \ u_4$ will intersect in a point u_{12_34} given by:

$$u_{12\_34} = u_1 \ u_2 \ \wedge \ u_3 \ u_4 \ u_s = [u_1 \ u_2 \ u_4 \ u_s] \ u_3 - [u_1 \ u_2 \ u_3 \ u_s] \ u_4 \quad (52)$$

where u_s is an arbitrary point not contained in the plane $u_1 \ldots u_4$ The points u_i project to points a_i' in the image defined as previously by the points $a_0 \ a_1 \ a_2 \ a_3$.

$$a_i' = a_0 \ u_i \ \wedge \ a_1 \ a_2 \ a_3 \qquad (53)$$

For the point u_{12_34} we get:

$$a_{12\_34}' = a_0 \ u_{12\_34} \ \wedge \ a_1 \ a_2 \ a_3 =$$

$$= \ a_0 \ [u_1 \ u_2 \ u_4 \ u_s] \ u_3 \ \wedge \ a_1 \ a_2 \ a_3 - a_0 \ [u_1 \ u_2 \ u_3 \ u_s] \ u_4 \ \wedge \ a_1 \ a_2 \ a_3 = (54)$$

$$= \ [u_1 \ u_2 \ u_4 \ u_s] \ a_3' - [u_1 \ u_2 \ u_3 \ u_s] \ a_4'$$

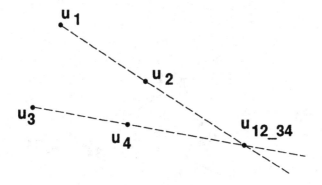

Fig. 8. Four coplanar points in 3-D

The points a_i' can be expressed using homogeneous image coordinate vectors α_i as:

$$a_i' = \alpha_{i,1}\, a_1 + \alpha_{i,2}\, a_2 + \alpha_{i,3}\, a_3 \tag{55}$$

Using this and eq. 54 we get:

$$\alpha_{12\_34} = [u_1\ u_2\ u_4\ u_s]\, \alpha_3 - [u_1\ u_2\ u_3\ u_s]\, \alpha_4 \tag{56}$$

The image coordinates α_{12_34} of the intersection point can also be expressed using the projected image coordinates as:

$$\alpha_{12\_34} = \alpha_1\, \alpha_2 \wedge \alpha_3\, \alpha_4 = [\alpha_1\ \alpha_2\ \alpha_4]\, \alpha_3 - [\alpha_1\ \alpha_2\ \alpha_3]\, \alpha_4 \tag{57}$$

From which we get:

$$\frac{[u_1\ u_2\ u_4\ u_s]}{[u_1\ u_2\ u_3\ u_s]} = \frac{[\alpha_1\ \alpha_2\ \alpha_4]}{[\alpha_1\ \alpha_2\ \alpha_3]} \tag{58}$$

If we have two more points u_5 and u_6 such that the line $u_5\ u_6$ is coplanar with the line $u_3\ u_4$ we can in the same way derive the relation:

$$\frac{[u_5\ u_6\ u_4\ u_t]}{[u_5\ u_6\ u_3\ u_t]} = \frac{[\alpha_5\ \alpha_6\ \alpha_4]}{[\alpha_5\ \alpha_6\ \alpha_3]} \tag{59}$$

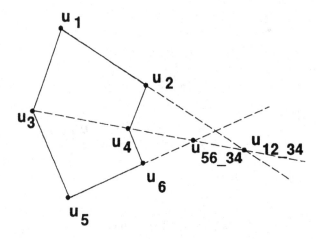

Fig. 9. Polyhedral configuration of 6 points

where u_t is an arbitrary point not contained in the plane $u_3\ u_4\ u_5\ u_6$. If we choose $u_s = u_5$ and $u_t = u_2$ we get the linear invariant:

$$\frac{[u_1\ u_2\ u_4\ u_5]\ [u_5\ u_6\ u_3\ u_2]}{[u_1\ u_2\ u_3\ u_5]\ [u_5\ u_6\ u_4\ u_2]} = \frac{[\alpha_1\ \alpha_2\ \alpha_4]\ [\alpha_5\ \alpha_6\ \alpha_3]}{[\alpha_1\ \alpha_2\ \alpha_3]\ [\alpha_5\ \alpha_6\ \alpha_4]} \tag{60}$$

This invariant can be shown to be algebraically related to the cross ratio of the four collinear points $u_3\ u_4\ u_{12\_34}\ u_{56\_34}$ which has been observed earlier [16] as a way to compute an invariant from this configuration.

Summary

This paper has been an introduction to the double algebra with application to the problem of computing linear invariants for general configurations of points and lines in projective 3-space based on observations in two images and polyhedral configurations based on observations in one image. For various combinations of points and lines we get explicit expressions for the linear invariants involving image coordinates and the fundamental matrix. The strength of the double algebra lies in the fact that it replaces geometric constructions with algebraic operations. The coordinate free and linearly invariant form of all expressions permits us to compute the invariants directly without reconstruction of the individual points and lines up to a projective transformation.

Acknowledgements

I would like to thank Lars Svensson of the Royal Institute of Technology for introducing me to, and discussions on, the double algebra. This work was part of Esprit Basic Research Action 6448, VIVA, with support from Swedish NUTEK.

References

1. M. Barnabei, A. Brini and G-C. Rota, (1985), On the exterior calculus of invariant theory, J. of Algebra, vol. 96, pp 120-160.
2. E.B. Barrett, P.M. Payton, N.N. Haag, and M.H. Brill, M.H. (1991), General methods for determining projective invariants in imagery. CVGIP-IU 53, pp. 46-65.
3. J. B. Burns, R. S. Weiss and E.M. Riseman, (1993), View variation of point-set and line-segment features, IEEE Trans. on Pattern Analysis and Machine Intelligence, 15, pp 51-68.
4. P. Doubilet, G-C. Rota and J. Stein, (1974), On the foundations of combinatorial theory: IX Combinatorial methods in invariant theory. Studies in Applied Mathematics, Vol. 53, pp. 185-216.
5. O.D. Faugeras, (1992), What can be seen in three dimensions with an un calibrated stereo rig?, Proc. 2:nd ECCV, pp. 563-578.
6. O.D. Faugeras, Q.T. Luong, and S.J. Maybank, (1992), Camera self- calibration: Theory and experiments, Proc. 2:nd ECCV, pp. 321-334.
7. P. Gros and L. Quan, (1992), Projective Invariants for Vision, Technical report: RT 90 IMAG-15 LIFIA
8. R.I. Hartley, Estimation of relative camera positions for un-calibrated cameras, Proc. 2:nd ECCV, pp. 579-587.
9. C. Longuet-Higgins, (1981), A computer algorithm for reconstructing a scene from two projections, Nature, vol 293, pp. 133-135.
10. Mundy, Zisserman (eds) (1992), Geometric Invariance in Computer Vision, MIT-Press.
11. G-C. Rota and J. Stein, (1976), Applications of cayley algebras, Accademia Nazionale dei Lincei atti dei Convegni Lincei 17, Colloquio Internazionale sulle Teorie Combinatoire, Tomo 2, Roma.
12. C.A. Rothwell, D.A. Forsyth, A.P. Zisserman, J.L. Mundy (1993) Extracting Projective Structure from Single Perspective Views of 3-D Point Sets Proc. of 4:th ICCV, pp. 573-582.
13. A. Shashua, (1993), Projective depth: A Geometric Invariant for 3-D Reconstruction From Two Perspective/Orthographic Views and for Visual recognition, Proc 4:th ICCV, pp. 583-590.
14. G. Sparr, (1992), Depth Computations from Polyhedral Images, Image and Vision Computing, vol. 10, no. 10, pp. 683-688.
15. L. Svensson (1993), On the use of the double algebra in computer vision, Technical. rep. TRITA-NA-P9310
16. A. Zisserman (personal communication)

Matching Perspective Views
of Parallel Plane Structures *

Luc Van Gool, Theo Moons, Marc Van Diest, and Eric Pauwels

Katholieke Universiteit Leuven, ESAT – MI2,
Kard. Mercierlaan 94, B-3001 LEUVEN, Belgium

Abstract. Within an invariance framework, the recognition of plane objects under general viewpoints and perspective projection calls for the extraction of two-dimensional projective invariants. If the possible poses of the object are constrained with respect to the camera, however, simpler groups than the projective transformations become relevant, and consequently, simpler invariants exist. Several such special types of pose constraints are discussed – all amount to the object plane remaining parallel to its original orientation – and the corresponding groups are outlined. For each group a number of invariants are derived to illustrate the gain in simplicity.

1 Introduction

1.1 Rationale

In recent years, a gamut of papers have focused on invariant based recognition and description of plane shapes under perspective projection. As long as the relative orientation and position of the objects with respect to the camera are arbitrary, invariance under all projective transformations has to be dealt with.

In this paper, it is shown for a specific type of constraints on the possible relative poses of the objects and the camera that they simplify the recognition. This follows from the fact that no longer the group of projective transformations has to be dealt with, but rather subgroups thereof. These subgroups are governed by fewer parameters and consequently their invariants are simpler to compute and need fewer data. The basic restriction is that *the object plane remains parallel to itself under the three-dimensional (3D) motion.* Three types of 3D motions of the observed plane objects, each obeying this *parallelism constraint* are considered:

1. rotations about an axis perpendicular to the object plane combined with general translations,
2. general translations, and
3. translations in the object plane.

---

* Theo Moons and Eric Pauwels were supported by the Belgian National Fund for Scientific Research (N.F.W.O.). The support by Esprit BRA 6448 VIVA and the cofinancing support by the Flemish government are gratefully acknowledged.

A further distinction is made between situations where the orientation or the orientation and position of the vanishing line for the object plane – henceforth referred to as *the horizon* – is known. As explained later, knowledge about the horizon amounts to having information about the relative orientation of the camera and the object plane and v.v.. Of course, this observation is not new.

The work is related to recent contributions dealing with objects lying in a plane for which the vanishing line is known [CB1] or moving in a fixed plane with respect to the camera [TBS1]. Links with the former work are especially strong. Besides the quest of simpler invariants for simpler, constrained motions, additional justification for the reported work is two-fold:

1. results are obtained for cases where the horizon for the object plane is known only partially (i.e. its orientation only), and
2. if the horizon is known, going to an affine situation by moving the line to infinity and transforming a complete image, the majority of points might remain unused in subsequent processing and the corresponding effort is wasted. Hence, methods working on the image data of interest directly can be useful.

Object symmetry in plane shapes is another but related situation where the symmetric half of a pattern is mapped onto its other half by a "motion" that is of a restricted nature (it e.g. stays in the object plane). Looking at a perspectively skewed symmetry, the special nature of the symmetry transformation can be capitalized on to find simpler invariants [MZB1, Vea2]. The symmetry case will not be considered here.

Applications of the parallelism constraint are legion. Especially surveillance type of problems are often such that objects moving on a ground plane have to be detected, tracked, or recognized. Operations to be carried out on workpieces transported on a conveyor belt are a second important class of applications where the conditions imposed in the paper are frequently met. The results are also relevant for finding point correspondences when applying the affine reconstruction from a translating camera introduced by the authors in another chapter of the book. In accordance with the bulk of such applications, *it will be assumed that a single camera with fixed parameters (e.g. focal length) is used.*

1.2   Camera Model and Image Deformations

The deformations on the image plane induced by three-dimensional Euclidean motions (rotations + translations) of a plane shape under perspective projection are known to be two-dimensional projective transformations. Although it is not our intention to reiterate this result, the influence of projection is discussed briefly, in order to investigate how the parameters of the motion and the contour plane end up in the expressions of these projective deformations.

The pinhole camera model is used, as shown in Fig. 1. The point **X** with three-dimensional coordinates $(X, Y, Z)^t$ has for the coordinates of its image projection $(x, y)^t$

$$x = f\frac{X}{Z} \qquad \text{and} \qquad y = f\frac{Y}{Z} \ .$$

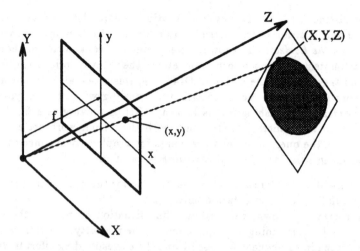

Fig. 1. Pinhole camera model: f *is the focal length,* X, Y, Z *are coordinates in the world coordinate frame and* x, y *coordinates in the image coordinate frame. The contour under scrutiny is supposed to be planar as shown in the figure.*

Because the point $(X, Y, Z)^t$ lies in the contour plane, say $mX + nY + oZ + p = 0$, Z can be expressed as a function of (x, y) as

$$Z = \frac{-pf}{mx + ny + of} \ .$$

Assume that the curve undergoes an arbitrary three-dimensional motion (rotation + translation):

$$\mathbf{X'} = R\,\mathbf{X} + T$$

with primes here and in the sequel denoting corresponding quantities after the motion and with R a rotation matrix and T a translation vector:

$$R = \begin{pmatrix} r_{11} & r_{12} & r_{13} \\ r_{21} & r_{22} & r_{23} \\ r_{31} & r_{32} & r_{33} \end{pmatrix} \qquad \text{and} \qquad T = \begin{pmatrix} t_1 \\ t_2 \\ t_3 \end{pmatrix} .$$

Considering that

$$\begin{cases} x = f\frac{X}{Z}, \\ y = f\frac{Y}{Z}, \end{cases} \qquad \text{and} \qquad \begin{cases} x' = f\frac{X'}{Z'}, \\ y' = f\frac{Y'}{Z'}, \end{cases}$$

one finds

$$x' = f \frac{(r_{11} - \frac{t_1}{p}m)x + (r_{12} - \frac{t_1}{p}n)y + (r_{13} - \frac{t_1}{p}o)f}{(r_{31} - \frac{t_3}{p}m)x + (r_{32} - \frac{t_3}{p}n)y + (r_{33} - \frac{t_3}{p}o)f} \ ,$$

$$y' = f \frac{(r_{21} - \frac{t_2}{p}m)x + (r_{22} - \frac{t_2}{p}n)y + (r_{23} - \frac{t_2}{p}o)f}{(r_{31} - \frac{t_3}{p}m)x + (r_{32} - \frac{t_3}{p}n)y + (r_{33} - \frac{t_3}{p}o)f} \ .$$

(1)

This is a two-dimensional projective transformation, i.e. a transformation of the type

$$x' = f \frac{p_{11}x + p_{12}y + p_{13}f}{p_{31}x + p_{32}y + p_{33}f}$$

$$y' = f \frac{p_{21}x + p_{22}y + p_{23}f}{p_{31}x + p_{32}y + p_{33}f}$$

(2)

or with $N = p_{31}x + p_{32}y + p_{33}f = (r_{31} - \frac{t_3}{p}m)x + (r_{32} - \frac{t_3}{p}n)y + (r_{33} - \frac{t_3}{p}o)f$

$$\begin{pmatrix} x' \\ y' \\ 1 \end{pmatrix} = \frac{1}{N} \begin{pmatrix} f(r_{11} - \frac{t_1}{p}m) & f(r_{12} - \frac{t_1}{p}n) & f^2(r_{13} - \frac{t_1}{p}o) \\ f(r_{21} - \frac{t_2}{p}m) & f(r_{22} - \frac{t_2}{p}n) & f^2(r_{23} - \frac{t_2}{p}o) \\ (r_{31} - \frac{t_3}{p}m) & (r_{32} - \frac{t_3}{p}n) & f(r_{33} - \frac{t_3}{p}o) \end{pmatrix} \begin{pmatrix} x \\ y \\ 1 \end{pmatrix} \ .$$

Replacing the rotation matrix by an arbitrary 3×3 matrix, thereby replacing the three-dimensional motion of **X** by an arbitrary three-dimensional affine transformation, one would still find projective transformations between the different projections of a shape. Nevertheless, the projective transformations are the smallest group containing all the deformations (1) (perspectivities don't form a group). In the sequel, additional constraints on the object motion will be shown to single out proper subgroups of the projective transformations. The lower number of independent parameters for these subgroups results in simpler invariant descriptions.

1.3 Projective Invariants

In the sequel, **x** is shorthand notation for the image coordinates $(x, y)^t$ of a point **X** with 3D coordinates $(X, Y, Z)^t$. Subscripts as in $\mathbf{x}_i$ are used as identification tags for specific points, referred to as *reference points*. Moreover, N is also in the sequel defined as

$$p_{31} \ x + p_{32} \ y + p_{33} \ f$$

and similarly N_i denotes $p_{31} x_i + p_{32} y_i + p_{33} f$. If the point **X** is lying on a curve, the image projection of that point, the image point **x**, will lie on the image projection of the curve, i.e. a curve in the image. If we parameterize this image curve with some parameter t, then $\mathbf{x}^{(j)}$ will denote $(\frac{d^j x}{dt^j}, \frac{d^j y}{dt^j})^t$. As mentioned earlier, primes will denote values after a motion has taken place, e.g. $\mathbf{x}'$ represents the image projection of a point **x** after the corresponding projective deformation of the projected object shape.

The kind of invariants that are considered here, are all composed of a number of basic building blocks. For the general group of projective transformations, building blocks take the form of determinants. The following building blocks change in quite a simple manner under a projective transformation:

$$|x' - x_i' \; x' - x_j'| = \frac{|P|}{N N_i N_j} \; |x - x_i \; x - x_j| \; ,$$

$$|x' - x_i' \; x^{(1)'}| = \frac{|P|}{N^2 N_i} \; |x - x_i \; x^{(1)}| \; ,$$

$$|x^{(1)'} \; x^{(2)'}| = \frac{|P|}{N^3} \; |x^{(1)} \; x^{(2)}| \; .$$

with

$$|P| = \begin{vmatrix} p_{11} & p_{12} & p_{13} \\ p_{21} & p_{22} & p_{23} \\ p_{31} & p_{32} & p_{33} \end{vmatrix} \; .$$

The problem of finding invariants has now become one of eliminating the above factors. An example of such an invariant for the projective group is what sometimes is referred to as a 5-point cross-ratio:

$$\frac{|x - x_1 \; x - x_3| \; |x_2 - x_3 \; x_2 - x_4|}{|x - x_2 \; x - x_3| \; |x_1 - x_3 \; x_1 - x_4|} \tag{3}$$

where all the factors appearing after the application of a projective transformation can be checked to cancel out each other. The way such invariant is used is that x_1, x_2, x_3, and x_4 are some easily distinguishable fixed reference points in the scene which enable the above invariant to be calculated for each additional arbitrary point x. As an example, Fig. 2 shows a pair of views of a basket, one before and one after the basket translated. On these images, a number of points were indicated manually, using a mouse. No special efforts were made to obtain high precision (e.g. points were *not* extracted as the intersections of fitted lines or using sophisticated corner detectors). The points indicated by the numbers 1, 2, 3 and 4 were used as reference points, and the values of invariant (3) were computed for the other points in both images. The results are given in Table 1. Notice the large difference in the values for points no. 9 and 10. This was to be expected, since point no. 9 does not belong to the plane defined by the points 1, 2, 3 and 4; whereas point no. 10 is not even translated with respect to the camera. Several other invariants and invariant parameters can be constructed combining the building blocks in different ways. For a more detailed discussion the reader is referred to [BBP1, Vea1, Vea3].

1.4 The Horizon

The horizon line of a plane (containing the vanishing points of lines parallel to the plane) is the intersection of the parallel plane containing the projection center and the image plane, i.e. the intersection of $mX + nY + oZ = 0$ and $Z = f$, yielding

$$mx + ny + of = 0 \; .$$

Fig. 2. *Pair of views of a translated basket, taken with a static camera.*

Table 1. *The values of invariant (3) for the images shown in Fig. 2. The points numbered 1, 2, 3 and 4 are used as reference points.*

point	view 1	view 2
5	−0.189	−0.181
6	−0.004	−0.006
7	0.140	0.142
8	−0.006	−0.001
9	−0.148	−0.016
10	−2.300	−0.503

The position of the horizon depends on the focal length f. If the horizon is not known *a priori*, several methods for its extraction have been propounded [SCC1, Tea1].

It is clear that there is a very direct relation between this equation for the horizon and the equation of the object plane. Depending on whether the orientation and position or only the orientation of the horizon is known, the relative pose of the camera is known to different degrees. Once the orientation of the horizon is known, i.e. m/n can be determined, the relative camera vs. object plane tilt is known. The distance of the horizon to the intersection of the optical axis with the image plane – coined the *image optic center* – is directly related to the slant, but the slant cannot be extracted from the horizon's equation, except when the focal length f has been determined and o and f in the equation's term of can be disentangled. The focal length will be assumed to be unknown. Hence, the 3D position of the object plane can not be determined from the horizon, a "deprojection" to a perpendicular view can not be produced, and Euclidean reconstruction up to a scale is impossible from a single view.

2 Rotations in the Plane and Translations

The most general situation that will be considered is one of a plane object that can undergo arbitrary 3D translations and a rotation in the object plane. This amounts to allowing arbitrary motions in the object plane followed by a translation of the object out of the plane. This situation can be reversed in the sense of having an observer looking at a plane under a fixed slant and tilt angle, and who might rotate about an axis perpendicular to the plane and translate.

2.1 Knowing the Horizon's Orientation

If only the orientation of the horizon is known (i.e. m/n), the resulting transformation group still is 8D and one has to use the 5-point cross ratio type of invariants.

2.2 Knowing the Horizon's Orientation and Position

If the orientation and position of the horizon are known, then it can be moved to infinity. The resulting scene only has affine deformations then. Hence, 4 points suffice to extract an invariant. The knowledge of the horizon can be exploited more directly, however. Adding the horizon line to the 4 points in the scene suffices for the extraction of a complete set of 2 independent projective invariants. This suggests that the complete knowledge of the horizon yields a 6 dimensional subgroup of the projective transformations. This is proven in [Vea4]. Here, this claim is corroborated by looking at a simple example where the horizon is known: horizontal planes. In that case, the horizon is given by $y = 0$. This is one of the cases where the subgroup can be made explicit rather easily. If the relative motion of the object and the cameras includes a general translation and a rotation about a vertical axis, and denoting

$$C = \cos\theta \qquad\qquad S = \sin\theta$$

with θ the angle of rotation, we find for the image coordinate transformation

$$x' = f \frac{Cx - \frac{t_1}{p}ny + Sf}{-Sx - \frac{t_3}{p}ny + Cf} \qquad \text{and} \qquad y' = \frac{(1 - \frac{t_2}{p}n)y}{-Sx - \frac{t_3}{p}ny + Cf} \; ;$$

or, concisely,

$$x' = \frac{ax + by + c}{dx + ey + g}, \qquad \text{and} \qquad y' = \frac{hy}{dx + ey + g}.$$

The latter equation defines a 3-D group. The pair of equations lead to a 6-D group, although it might seem only 5-D when looking at the original equations, since it seems that $a = g$. This, however, is a property which is not preserved under the composition of such transformations. For invariants without derivatives we therefore need at least 4 points. This result can be generalized to other situations where the horizon is known.

The horizon has the nice feature to remain invariant under the envisaged motions of the object and once found no further search as for the reference points is needed. An example of an invariant for 4 points and the horizon (i.e. 4 points and a line) is

$$\frac{|\mathbf{x} - \mathbf{x_1} \; \mathbf{x} - \mathbf{x_3}| \, (mx_2 + ny_2 + of)}{|\mathbf{x} - \mathbf{x_2} \; \mathbf{x} - \mathbf{x_3}| \, (mx_1 + ny_1 + of)} \tag{4}$$

Note that $mx_i + ny_i + of$ is the (signed) distance of the point $\mathbf{x_i}$ to the horizon (when measured in the image). This invariant was computed for the images in Fig. 2, with the points 1, 2 and 3 as reference points. The horizon, found by calculating the intersections of parallel lines in the scene, is given by $0.046x + y - 2191 = 0$, and is almost horizontal. Table 2 shows the results. Note again the different values for points no. 9 and 10.

Table 2. *The values of invariant (4) for the images shown in Fig. 2. The points numbered 1, 2 and 3 are used as reference points.*

point	view 1	view 2
4	0.999	0.999
5	−0.189	−0.181
6	−0.004	−0.006
7	0.140	0.142
8	−0.006	−0.001
9	−0.148	−0.016
10	−2.297	−0.503

Alternatively, if the point x_3 can be chosen to lie on the horizon, this expression can be rewritten as

$$
\frac{|x - x_1 \quad x - x_3|\ (m(x_2 - x_3) + n(y_2 - y_3))}{|x - x_2 \quad x - x_3|\ (m(x_1 - x_3) + n(y_1 - y_3))}
\tag{5}
$$

The horizon point should move rigidly with the object and such point could in principle be found by intersecting the horizon with a tangent line at a reference point. Table 3 shows the values of this invariant for the images in Fig. 2, using 1 and 2 as reference points. As the reference point belonging to the horizon, the intersection with the horizon of the line joining the points 1 and 2 (long edge) and of the line joining 2 and 3 (short edge) were used respectively. Note how the values for the long edge invariant are all close to 1. This is because the reference point on the horizon is collinear with those of the scene. Therefore, the quotient of the determinants in (5) equals the (signed) ratio of the distances from the horizon point to point 1 and point 2. The remaining factor − the quotient of the signed distances of x_2 and x_1 to the horizon − equals the reciprocal of this ratio. Hence, the long edge invariant is trivial with constant value 1. The huge (absolute) values of the short edge invariant for point no. 3 (not to be mistaken for x_3) are due to the fact that this point belongs to the line defining the reference point on the horizon, thus rendering zero the first determinant in the denominator. In both cases, the other values of the invariants are stable, except for the points 9 and 10, as was to be expected.

The above construction is equivalent to using four points and the first derivative in one of them (i.e. using the orientation of the horizon at x_3). This yields 10 data vs. 9 parameters and the counting argument predicts the existence of at least one invariant.

Similarly,

$$
\frac{|x - x_1 \quad x - x_3|\ (m(x_2 - x_4) + n(y_2 - y_4))}{|x - x_2 \quad x - x_3|\ (m(x_1 - x_4) + n(y_1 - y_4))}
\tag{6}
$$

is an invariant when x_4 instead of x_3 is a point on the horizon. In this case enough information is available to obtain two independent invariants. Note how

Table 3. *The values of invariant (5) for the images shown in Fig. 2. Points 1 and 2 were used as reference points in the scene; the intersection of the line joining the points 1 and 2 (long edge) resp. of the line joining 2 and 3 (short edge) with the horizon served as the reference point belonging to the horizon.*

point	long edge		short edge	
	view 1	view 2	view 1	view 2
3	0.996	0.996	4851.240	−330.245
4	0.996	0.996	−0.001	−0.002
5	0.991	0.991	−1.158	−1.158
6	0.992	0.993	−1.147	−1.145
7	0.992	0.993	−0.834	−0.836
8	0.991	0.992	−0.834	−0.832
9	1.009	1.011	0.221	0.250
10	1.004	1.008	−0.514	−0.029

in that case the first part of the invariant is the affine invariant ratio of areas defined by four arbitrary points, followed by a factor that compensates for the perspective effects. Knowing the horizon suffices to switch to affine concepts provided such compensation of perspective foreshortening is taken care of. This ability to get very close to the affine situation doesn't come as a surprise [CB1, LTD1, Zea1]. In Table 4 the values of this invariant are given for the images in Fig. 2. Points 1, 2 and 3 were used as reference points in the scene; and, as before, the intersection of the horizon with the line joining 1 and 2 (long edge), resp. 2 and 3 (short edge), were used as reference point on the horizon. Since only the value of the determinant factors changes from point to point, the long edge and short edge invariants are the same.

Table 4. *The values of invariant (6) for the images shown in Fig. 2. Points 1, 2 and 3 were used as reference points in the scene; and the intersection of the horizon with the line joining 1 and 2 (long edge), served as reference point on the horizon.*

point	view 1	view 2
4	0.999	0.999
5	−0.189	−0.181
6	−0.004	−0.006
7	0.140	0.142
8	−0.006	−0.001
9	−0.148	−0.016
10	−2.297	−0.503

3 General Translations

In this section arbitrary, three-dimensional relative translations between object and camera are considered. If no rotation is applied, but only translations, then $r_{ij} = \delta_{ij}$, with δ_{ij} the Kronecker delta and the projective transformation matrix is

$$\begin{pmatrix} f(1 - \frac{t_1}{p}m) & f(-\frac{t_1}{p}n) & f^2(-\frac{t_1}{p}o) \\ f(-\frac{t_2}{p}m) & f(1 - \frac{t_2}{p}n) & f^2(-\frac{t_2}{p}o) \\ (-\frac{t_3}{p}m) & (-\frac{t_3}{p}n) & f(1 - \frac{t_3}{p}o) \end{pmatrix}$$

This specification of the transformations studied is not relevant in itself though. It has to be checked what the smallest transformation group is which contains all such transformations and their compositions, given that f, m, n, and o are to be considered fixed but arbitrary numbers and t_1, t_2, t_3, and p have to be considered variable.

3.1 Knowing the Horizon's Orientation

First, suppose the orientation of the horizon is known. In this case m/n is known and as can be checked

$$\frac{p_{31}}{p_{32}} = \frac{m}{n} \ .$$

This constraint survives scaling and composition, thereby lowering the number of independent parameters. A direct proof of such constraints is rather cumbersome though. As shown in [Vea4] the resulting group is 6D and its explicit representation shows that the above constraint holds for all transformations in the group. Again, the 6D-claim can be corroborated by considering a simpler case. If the object plane is known to be purely slanted and therefore $m/n = 0$, the lower dimension of the resulting transformation group is particularly obvious:

$$x' = f\frac{x + t_1\frac{n}{p}y - t_1\frac{o}{p}f}{-t_3\frac{n}{p}y + (1 - t_3\frac{o}{p})f} \quad \text{and} \quad y' = f\frac{(1 - t_2\frac{n}{p})y - t_2\frac{o}{p}f}{-t_3\frac{n}{p}y + (1 - t_3\frac{o}{p})f} \ ;$$

or transformations of the form

$$x' = \frac{ax + by + e}{dy + g} \quad \text{and} \quad y' = \frac{cy + h}{dy + g} \ .$$

The y-transformations form a group in their own right, which is 3-D. The global transformations form a 6-D group. In either case, information from at least 4 points has to be combined for the construction of an invariant. For planes with a known tilt (i.e. when the orientation of the horizon is known as assumed here), it suffices to rotate the image to create the circumstances just discussed. Hence, it seems natural to expect the subgroup to be 6D indeed.

Since the group governing this problem has a dimension of 6, a pair of independent invariants using four points has to exist. These invariants are found using the additional building block

$$m(x_i' - x_j') + n(y_i' - y_j') = \frac{f^2}{N_i N_j} \frac{p - t_1 m - t_2 n - t_3 o}{p} \, (m(x_i - x_j) + n(y_i - y_j))$$

which looks quite familiar by now. Furthermore, in the case of general translations

$$|P| = f^3 \left(\frac{p - t_1 m - t_2 n - t_3 o}{p} \right)$$

and therefore

$$m(x_i' - x_j') + n(y_i' - y_j') = \frac{|P|}{f N_i N_j} \, (m(x_i - x_j) + n(y_i - y_j)).$$

A pair of invariants is

$$\frac{(m(x - x_1) + n(y - y_1))(m(x_2 - x_3) + n(y_2 - y_3))}{(m(x - x_2) + n(y - y_2))(m(x_1 - x_3) + n(y_1 - y_3))} \tag{7}$$

and

$$\frac{|\mathbf{x} - \mathbf{x_1} \; \mathbf{x} - \mathbf{x_2}| \, (m(x_1 - x_3) + n(y_1 - y_3))}{|\mathbf{x} - \mathbf{x_1} \; \mathbf{x} - \mathbf{x_3}| \, (m(x_1 - x_2) + n(y_1 - y_2))}. \tag{8}$$

Notice the close resemblance of the first expression to the cross-ratio. In fact, it is a cross-ratio not of positions of points along a line but of distances of points to the horizon. Table 5 show the values of these two invariants for the images in Fig. 2. Points no. 1, 2 and 3 again are used as reference points. Notice how invariant (7) takes the same values for the points 9 and 10 in both images. This is because the performed translation was (almost) parallel to the horizon. Observe also the comparatively huge (absolute) values invariant (8) assumes at points 6 and 8. The reason is that these points are collinear with 1 and 3, which implies that the denominator $|\mathbf{x} - \mathbf{x_1} \; \mathbf{x} - \mathbf{x_3}|$ becomes zero. The almost-collinearity of points 5 and 7 explains the relatively low precision for their invariants.

3.2 Knowing the Horizon's Orientation and Position

If not only the orientation of the horizon, but also its position is known, then a 3D group emerges (for a formal proof see [Vea4]). Again, to get a feel for the situation, it is useful to consider a simple case. If the object plane is known to be horizontal, then both the orientation and position of the horizon are known: $y = 0$ and $m = o = 0$. The emerging subgroups are salient in this case:

$$x' = f \frac{x - t_1 \frac{p}{n} y}{-t_3 \frac{p}{n} y + f} \qquad \text{and} \qquad y' = f \frac{(1 - t_2 \frac{p}{n}) y}{-t_3 \frac{p}{n} y + f} \; ;$$

Table 5. *The values of invariants (7) and (8) for the images shown in Fig. 2. Points 1, 2 and 3 are used as reference points.*

<table>
<tr><td colspan="3" align="center">invariant (7)</td><td colspan="3" align="center">invariant (8)</td></tr>
<tr><th>point</th><th>view 1</th><th>view 2</th><th>point</th><th>view 1</th><th>view 2</th></tr>
<tr><td>4</td><td>−0.372</td><td>−0.363</td><td>4</td><td>1.522</td><td>1.520</td></tr>
<tr><td>5</td><td>−1.145</td><td>−1.142</td><td>5</td><td>−7.797</td><td>−8.245</td></tr>
<tr><td>6</td><td>−1.468</td><td>−1.433</td><td>6</td><td>−443.704</td><td>−314.651</td></tr>
<tr><td>7</td><td>−0.929</td><td>−0.919</td><td>7</td><td>10.591</td><td>10.462</td></tr>
<tr><td>8</td><td>−0.760</td><td>−0.750</td><td>8</td><td>−214.671</td><td>−961.807</td></tr>
<tr><td>9</td><td>0.119</td><td>0.123</td><td>9</td><td>3.789</td><td>25.735</td></tr>
<tr><td>10</td><td>0.073</td><td>0.059</td><td>10</td><td>1.179</td><td>1.429</td></tr>
</table>

or transformations of the form

$$x' = \frac{ax + by}{dy + a} \quad \text{and} \quad y' = \frac{cy}{dy + a} \ .$$

These transformations form a group, which is 3D, The y-transformations form a 2D group in their own right. The 3D group requires at least 2 points for an invariant.

Potential new building blocks for the general case with known horizon can be checked to be

$$\begin{vmatrix} x'_i & x'_j \\ y'_i + \frac{of}{n} & y'_j + \frac{of}{n} \end{vmatrix} = \frac{f^2}{N_i N_j} \frac{p - t_1 m - t_2 n - t_3 o}{p} \begin{vmatrix} x_i & x_j \\ y_i + \frac{of}{n} & y_j + \frac{of}{n} \end{vmatrix}$$

$$= \frac{|P|}{f N_i N_j} \begin{vmatrix} x_i & x_j \\ y_i + \frac{of}{n} & y_j + \frac{of}{n} \end{vmatrix}$$

and

$$m x' + n y' + o f = \frac{f}{N} \frac{p - t_1 m - t_2 n - t_3 o}{p} (m x + n y + o f)$$

$$= \frac{|P|}{f^2 N} (m x + n y + o f) \ .$$

Using the first type the following invariant is found:

$$\frac{\begin{vmatrix} x & x_1 \\ y + \frac{of}{n} & y_1 + \frac{of}{n} \end{vmatrix}}{m(x - x_1) + n(y - y_1)} \tag{9}$$

The values of this invariant for the indicated points in the images of Fig. 2 are shown in Table 6. Point no. 1 is used as reference point. Observe that the differences between corresponding values for the two views are larger than in the previous examples. This is caused by the rather poor estimate that was used for the position of the optic center in the image. Indeed, it should be emphasized that *the knowledge of the image optic center is crucial for being able to use these building blocks.* In contrast to most other building blocks obtained so far, the absolute position of points in the image matters, since expressions are not solely composed of coordinate differences (or coordinate derivatives for that matter). A certain degree of calibration is therefore required. The central point of the image is not necessarily the best estimate of the true image optic center. The same remarks hold for all other invariants to be derived which can not be expressed as a function of coordinate differences and derivatives only.

Table 6. *The values of invariant (9) for the images shown in Fig. 2. Point 1 is used as reference point.*

point	view 1	view 2
2	−2085.9	−2015.8
3	−334.0	−286.5
4	3023.0	3039.5
5	−533.2	−473.5
6	−337.9	−291.9
7	−151.3	−103.7
8	−342.1	−288.3
9	294.1	−216.5
10	9439.7	3748.5

A way around this problem is easy to find though. Knowing the horizon and knowing that under general translations the points on the horizon stay put, the equivalence of the above invariant with the following types of invariants can be shown:

$$\frac{|\mathbf{x} - \mathbf{x}_1 \ \mathbf{x} - \mathbf{x}_2|}{m(x - x_1) + n(y - y_1)} \tag{10}$$

with $\mathbf{x}_2$ on the horizon, and

$$\frac{|\mathbf{x} - \mathbf{x}_1 \ \mathbf{x} - \mathbf{x}_2|}{|\mathbf{x} - \mathbf{x}_1 \ \mathbf{x} - \mathbf{x}_3|} \tag{11}$$

with $\mathbf{x}_2$ and $\mathbf{x}_3$ on the horizon. Both expressions are combinations of building blocks met earlier. Taking into account that for points on the horizon $mx + ny + of = 0$ and hence

$$N = -t_3\frac{m}{p}x - t_3\frac{n}{p}y + (1 - t_3\frac{o}{p})f = f,$$

it is easy to check that both (10) and (11) are invariant. Using the fact that both $\mathbf{x}_2$ and $\mathbf{x}_3$ lie on the horizon and therefore $m(x_2 - x_3) + n(y_2 - y_3) = 0$, it is not difficult to show that (11) can be rewritten as

$$\frac{|\mathbf{x}-\mathbf{x_1}\ \mathbf{x}-\mathbf{x_2}|}{|\mathbf{x}-\mathbf{x_1}\ \mathbf{x}-\mathbf{x_3}|} = 1 + \frac{|\mathbf{x}-\mathbf{x_1}\ \mathbf{x_3}-\mathbf{x_2}|}{|\mathbf{x}-\mathbf{x_1}\ \mathbf{x}-\mathbf{x_3}|}$$

$$1 + \frac{(\mathbf{x_2}-\mathbf{x_3})}{n}\ \frac{m(x-x_1)+n(y-y_1)}{|\mathbf{x}-\mathbf{x_1}\ \mathbf{x}-\mathbf{x_3}|} \ .$$

This shows the equivalence of the two types of image optic center insensitive invariants. Next we show the relation between (10) and (9), using the relation $y_2 = -(m/n)x_2 - (of/n)$ on the coordinates of the horizon point $\mathbf{x_2}$:

$$\frac{|\mathbf{x}-\mathbf{x_1}\ \mathbf{x}-\mathbf{x_2}|}{m(x-x_1)+n(y-y_1)} = \frac{(x-x_1)(y-y_2)-(y-y_1)(x-x_2)}{m(x-x_1)+n(y-y_1)}$$

$$= \frac{\begin{vmatrix} x & x_1 \\ y+\frac{of}{n} & y_1+\frac{of}{n} \end{vmatrix}}{m(x-x_1)+n(y-y_1)} + \frac{x_2}{n}.$$

The two alternative types of invariants (10) and (11) are composed of coordinate differences solely. As a conclusion, the requirement to know the image optic center can be circumvented with negligible effort by using points on the horizon.

Tables 7 and 8 contain the values of (10) and (11) for the images shown in Fig. 2. In both cases, point no. 1 was used as the reference point in the scene, and as reference points on the horizen the intersections of the horizon with the line joining points 1 and 2, and with the line joining 2 and 3 were chosen. Observe that, in both cases, the values for the points 3, 6 and 8 are (almost) the same. This happens because both invariants should admit the same value for all points lying on a line through point no. 1 (i.e. the reference point in the scene), as can easily be verified. Also note that the second invariant (Table 8) should have zero value for point no. 2, because it is collinear with point 1 and the point on the horizon of the long edge — thus resulting in a zero numerator for (11). Furthermore, the denominator of (11) becomes zero for point no. 4, since it lies on the line connecting point 1 and the point on the horizon of the short edge. This explains the comparatively huge (absolute) value of the invariant in this point.

4 Translations in the Plane

This is the most constrained type of motion considered. The object may only translate in its plane or, equivalently, the camera may only translate parallel to the object plane. The translation parameters obey the constraint

$$mt_1 + nt_2 + ot_3 = 0 \ .$$

Also note that

$$|P| = \begin{vmatrix} (1-t_1\frac{m}{p})f & -t_1\frac{n}{p}f & -t_1\frac{o}{p}f^2 \\ -t_2\frac{m}{p}f & (1-t_2\frac{n}{p})f & -t_2\frac{o}{p}f^2 \\ -t_3\frac{m}{p} & -t_3\frac{n}{p} & (1-t_3\frac{o}{p})f \end{vmatrix} = f^3(1-t_1\frac{m}{p}-ft_2\frac{n}{p}-t_3\frac{o}{p}) = f^3$$

Table 7. *The values of invariant (10) for the images shown in Fig. 2. Point 1 was used as reference point in the scene, and the intersection of the line joining the points 1 and 2 (long edge) (resp. of the line joining 2 and 3 (short edge)) with the horizon served as the reference point belonging to the horizon.*

point	long edge		short edge	
	view 1	view 2	view 1	view 2
2	−10	−9	−4452	−4407
3	1513	1494	−2929	−2904
4	4430	4384	−12	−15
5	1340	1331	−3102	−3067
6	1509	1489	−2933	−2909
7	1671	1653	−2771	−2746
8	1506	1492	−2936	−2906
9	2059	1554	−2384	−2844
10	10007	5000	5565	601

Table 8. *The values of invariant (11) for the images shown in Fig. 2. Point 1 is used as reference point in the scene, and the intersection points of the horizon with the line joining the points 1 and 2 and with the line joining 2 and 3 respectively, served as the reference points belonging to the horizon.*

point	view 1	view 2
2	0.002	0.002
3	−0.516	−0.514
4	−374.825	−299.377
5	−0.432	−0.434
6	−0.515	−0.512
7	−0.603	−0.602
8	−0.513	−0.513
9	−0.864	−0.547
10	1.798	8.314

in that case. The composition rule for the transformations becomes quite simple. The effect in the image of applying two subsequent translations $(t_1, t_2, t_3)^t$ and

$(t'_1, t'_2, t'_3)^t$ is captured by the matrix

$$f \begin{pmatrix} f(1 - \frac{t_1+t'_1}{p}m) & f(-\frac{t_1+t'_1}{p}n) & f^2(-\frac{t_1+t'_1}{p}o) \\ f(-\frac{t_2+t'_2}{p}m) & f(1 - \frac{t_2+t'_2}{p}n) & f^2(-\frac{t_2+t'_2}{p}o) \\ (-\frac{t_3+t'_3}{p}m) & (-\frac{t_3+t'_3}{p}n) & f(1 - \frac{t_3+t'_3}{p}o) \end{pmatrix} =$$

$$\begin{pmatrix} f(1 - \frac{t'_1}{p}m) & f(-\frac{t'_1}{p}n) & f^2(-\frac{t'_1}{p}o) \\ f(-\frac{t'_2}{p}m) & f(1 - \frac{t'_2}{p}n) & f^2(-\frac{t'_2}{p}o) \\ (-\frac{t'_3}{p}m) & (-\frac{t'_3}{p}n) & f(1 - \frac{t'_3}{p}o) \end{pmatrix} \begin{pmatrix} f(1 - \frac{t_1}{p}m) & f(-\frac{t_1}{p}n) & f^2(-\frac{t_1}{p}o) \\ f(-\frac{t_2}{p}m) & f(1 - \frac{t_2}{p}n) & f^2(-\frac{t_2}{p}o) \\ (-\frac{t_3}{p}m) & (-\frac{t_3}{p}n) & f(1 - \frac{t_3}{p}o) \end{pmatrix}$$

4.1 Knowing the Horizon's Orientation

If the orientation m/n is known, the resuling transformation group is 5D. The following constraints can be seen to survive composition and to be insensitive to matrix scaling (projective transformations!):

$$\frac{p_{31}}{p_{32}} = \frac{p_{13}\,p_{21}}{p_{12}\,p_{23}} = \frac{m}{n} \qquad \text{and} \qquad \left(p_{11} - p_{12}\frac{p_{31}}{p_{32}}\right)^3 = |P|$$

Finding invariants again proceeds through first finding building blocks, which in this case we borrow from earlier sections, but the behaviour of which is simplified. In particular,

$$m(x'_i - x'_j) + n(y'_i - y'_j) = \frac{f^2}{N_i N_j}\,(m(x_i - x_j) + n(y_i - y_j))$$

$$= \frac{|P|}{fN_i N_j}\,(m(x_i - x_j) + n(y_i - y_j))$$

As 3-point invariant one finds

$$\frac{|x - x_1 \; x - x_2|^2}{(m(x - x_1) + n(y - y_1))\,(m(x - x_2) + n(y - y_2))\,(m(x_1 - x_2) + n(y_1 - y_2))}\,.$$

4.2 Knowing the Horizon's Orientation and Position

If additionally to the orientation also the position of the horizon is known, moving this line to infinity would result in the motions becoming pure translation and the relevant group to be of dimension 2. A subgroup of that dimension is found indeed, as proven in [Vea4]. Again, this claim is corroborated by considering the simple case of horizontal planes. In that case, the image coordinate transformations simplify to

$$x' = f\frac{x - t_1 ky}{-t_3 ky + f} \qquad \text{and} \qquad y' = f\frac{y}{-t_3 ky + f}\,;$$

or transformations of the form

$$x' = \frac{ax + by}{dy + a} \quad \text{and} \quad y' = \frac{ay}{dy + a} \; .$$

We have the choice of working with the transformation group working on the ys (1-D) or with the transformation pair, which also forms a group (2-D). The number of points required is the same in either case. Nevertheless, the second choice will yield two invariants, whereas the first choice leaves one with a single invariant. As an additional building block we use

$$mx'_i + ny'_i + of = \frac{f}{N_i}(mx + ny + of)$$

As 2-point invariants we find

$$\frac{m(x_2 - x_1) + n(y_2 - y_1)}{(mx_2 + ny_2 + of)\,(mx_1 + ny_1 + of)} = \frac{1}{mx_1 + ny_1 + of} - \frac{1}{mx_2 + ny_2 + of}$$

and

$$\frac{\begin{vmatrix} x_1 & x_2 \\ y_1 + \frac{of}{n} & y_2 + \frac{of}{n} \end{vmatrix}}{(mx_1 + ny_1 + of)\,(mx_2 + ny_2 + of)} \quad \text{or} \quad \frac{\begin{vmatrix} x_1 & x_2 \\ y_1 + \frac{of}{n} & y_2 + \frac{of}{n} \end{vmatrix}}{m(x_2 - x_1) + n(y_2 - y_1)} \; .$$

as a second invariant. Note that this last invariant also is invariant under general translations (cfr. previous case). To check whether the translation doesn't leave the plane, an invariant of the first type should be used. As in other cases where these building blocks were used, the image optic center should be known. Again, this problem can be circumvented by using points on the horizon, which as before stay put and are ideal for use as reference points. Assuming that x_2 is a point on the horizon, an example invariant is given by

$$\frac{m(x - x_1) + n(y - y_1)}{(m(x - x_2) + n(y - y_2))\,(m(x_1 - x_2) + n(y_1 - y_2))}$$

5 Remarks and Conclusions

In a number of cases of particular practical importance, the invariants become very simple. These cases include purely slanted planes ($m/n = 0$), horizontal ($m/n = o/n = 0$), and vertical ($n/m = o/m = 0$) planes. For instance, in the case of a horizontal plane building blocks are

$$(y_i - y_j) \quad \text{instead of} \quad m(x_i - x_j) + n(y_i - y_j)$$

$$y \quad \text{instead of} \quad mx + ny + of$$

$$\begin{vmatrix} x_i & x_j \\ y_i & y_j \end{vmatrix} \quad \text{instead of} \quad \begin{vmatrix} x_i & x_j \\ y_i + \frac{of}{n} & y_j + \frac{of}{n} \end{vmatrix}$$

Although the use of coordinate derivatives was hinted at, this idea was not pursued further. Examples of differential and semi-differential invariants using derivatives are easy to find, both to realize invariance with less points and to obtain invariant parameters. It is for instance not difficult to check that for pure, but arbitrary translations

$$m\frac{dx'}{dt} + n\frac{dy'}{dt} = \frac{f^2}{N^2}\frac{p - t_1 m - t_2 n - t_3 o}{p}\left(m\frac{dx}{dt} + n\frac{dy}{dt}\right)$$

is a useful building block based on derivatives. An example of an invariant parameter requiring first order derivatives only is given by

$$\int \text{abs}\left(\frac{(m(dx/dt) + n(dy/dt))\,(m(x_1 - x_2) + n(y_1 - y_2))}{(m(x - x_1) + n(y - y_1))\,(m(x - x_2) + n(y - y_2))}\right)\,dt \ .$$

Points on the horizon can be called upon to simplify expressions as before. For instance, with $\mathbf{x_1}$ on the horizon

$$\frac{|\mathbf{x} - \mathbf{x_1}\,\mathbf{x}^{(1)}|}{m(dx/dt) + n(dy/dt)}$$

is an invariant under arbitrary translations, indicating the distance between the horizon point $\mathbf{x_1}$ and the intersection of the tangent line at $\mathbf{x}$ with the horizon. Constraining the translation to be parallel to the object plane

$$\int \frac{|\mathbf{X}^{(1)}\,\mathbf{X}^{(2)}|^{2/3}}{m(dx/dt) + n(dy/dt)}dt$$

can be used as a differential, invariant parameter, and using a point $\mathbf{x_1}$ on the horizon

$$\int \text{abs}\left(\frac{m(dx/dt) + n(dy/dt)}{(m(x - x_1) + n(y - y_1))^2}\right)\,dt$$

is an invariant parameter.

In summary, it was shown that the recognition of plane shapes can be simplified if constraints are imposed on the allowable motions. Several types of applications might benefit, including surveillance and machine vision for parts transported on conveyors. Several subgroups were identified and the advantages of knowing the horizon were highlighted. Special but important cases such as purely slanted or horizontal planes have particularly simple invariants. Also the semi-differential framework [VKO1, BBP1, Vea1] was shown to be useful.

References

[BBP1] M. Brill, E. Barrett, and P. Payton, Projective invariants for curves in two and three dimensions, in *Geometric Invariance in Computer Vision*, eds. Mundy & Zisserman, pp.193-214, MIT Press, 1992.

[CB1]   R. Collins and J. Beveridge, Matching perspective views of coplanar structures using projective unwarping and similarity matching, Conf. Computer Vision Pattern Recognition, pp.240-245, 1992.

[LTD1] R. Lotufo, B. Thomas, and E. Dagless, Road following algorithm using a panned plan-view transformation, Proc. 1st ECCV, pp.231-235, 1990.

[MZB1] D. Mukherjee, A. Zisserman, and M. Brady, Shape from symmetry – detecting and exploiting symmetry in affine images, Techn. Report Univ. of Oxford, OUEL 1988/93, 1993.

[SCC1] M. Straforini, C. Coelho, and M. Campani, Extraction of vanishing points from images of indoor and outdoor scenes, Image and Vision Computing, Vol.11, No.2, pp.91-99, march 1993.

[Tea1] A. Tai, J. Kittler, M. Petrou, and T. Windeatt, Vanishing point detection, Image and Vision Computing, Vol.11, No.4, pp.240-245, 1993.

[TBS1] T. Tan, K. Baker, and G. Sullivan, 3D structure and motion estimation from 2D image sequences, Image and Vision Computing, vol.11, no.4, pp.203-210, 1993.

[VKO1] L. Van Gool, P. Kempenaers. and A. Oosterlinck, Recognition and semi-differential invariants, Proc. CVPR, pp. 454-460, june 1991

[Vea1] L. Van Gool, T. Moons, E. Pauwels, and A. Oosterlinck, Semi-differential invariants, in *Geometric Invariance in Computer Vision*, eds. Mundy & Zisserman, pp.157-192, MIT Press, 1992.

[Vea2] L. Van Gool, T. Moons, D. Ungureanu, and A. Oosterlinck, The characterization and detection of skewed symmetry, Kath. Univ. Leuven, Techn. Report KUL/ESAT/MI2/9304, 1993, accepted for publication in CVGIP:IU.

[Vea3] L. Van Gool, T. Moons, E. Pauwels, and J. Wagemans, Invariance from the Euclidean geometer's perspective, accepted for publication in Perception.

[Vea4] L. Van Gool, T. Moons, M. Van Diest, and E. Pauwels, Perspective matching and tracking of moving plane structures with constant object plane orientation, Kath. Univ. Leuven, Techn. Report KUL/ESAT/MI2/9305, 1993.

[Zea1] T. Zielke, K. Storjohann, H. Mallot, and W. von Seelen, Adaptive computer vision systems to the visual environment: topographic mapping, Proc. 1st ECCV 90, pp. 613-615, 1990.

Invariants for Recovering Shape from Shading

Isaac Weiss[*]

Center for Automation Research,
University of Maryland, College Park, MD 20742 USA

Abstract. The image formed by shading depends on many variables, including the shape of the object, the lighting characteristics, the imaging system, etc. Most of these variables are not known in advance, so the calculation of shape from shading is difficult. The problem could be greatly simplified if we could find invariants of the situation, namely quantities that stay constant as some of the unknown variables change. In this paper we apply known methods of mathematical physics to finding invariants of physical imaging processes. These methods take advantage of various symmetries, which can be part of a model-based approach to recognition. We concentrate on the shape from shading problem, but the methods have a much wider applicability.

1 Introduction

The formation of images involves two components: a geometrical component involving the shape of the object and the geometry of the imaging system, and a physical component. The latter can take many forms, since the imaging sensor may be visible light, infrared, radar, sonar, etc. In these physical processes we measure some physical quantity such as grey level, intensity, or wavelength, and from it we have to infer the geometry of the object.

Both the geometrical and the physical components contain unknown quantities which have to be eliminated before an object can be identified. The geometric component includes, for example, the point of view from which the image was taken, and there is a large set of possible viewpoints which can complicate object recognition. The physical process has even more unknowns; in the shading example, we have surface reflectance, the light intensity and its spatial distribution, the characteristics of the imaging system, etc. Infrared imaging depends on the surface temperature, and sonar depends on the transmission coefficient of the conducting medium. All these unknowns greatly complicate the recognition task.

One way of simplifying the problem is the use of invariants, namely quantities that stay constant as some of the unknown variables change. Research on invariants so far has concentrated on *geometrical* invariants, which are invariant

---

[*] The author is grateful for the support of the Air Force Office of Scientific Research under Grant F49620-92-J-0332, and of the Advanced Research Projects Agency (ARPA Order No. 8459) and the U.S. Army Topographic Engineering Center under Contract DACA76-92-C-0009.

to some geometrical property of the imaging process. For example, considerable work has been done [Weiss, 1988; Mundy and Zisserman, 1992; Weiss, 1992, 1993] on finding properties of the geometrical shape that are invariant to change in the point of view. However, the physical processes contain many more unknowns as described above and the problem is more difficult.

Invariants of physical processes are a well studied subject in modern physics and there are various methods of finding them. Simple examples are the laws of conservation of energy and momentum, which are in fact invariants of the laws of motion. In this paper we adapt some of these methods for application to computer vision. We concentrate on the shading problem as an example, but similar methods can be applied to other imaging processes.

2   The Shape from Shading Equations

In the shape from shading problem, we have the data in the form of the image brightness $E(x, y)$, from which the characteristics of the scene have to be inferred. These characteristics include many unknowns, such as the shape of the object, the surface reflectance, the lighting, etc. As a way of simplifying the problem, the "reflectance map" was introduced by Horn [1986]. This is a function $R(p, q)$ that represents the amount of light falling on the image. It contains only the two unknowns p, q which represent the slopes of the surface in the x and y directions. It is assumed that this function is known, i.e. that the light distribution and other factors are already built into R, and the only unknowns are the slopes of the object at each point x, y. Assuming that the image brightness is equal to the amount of light falling on the image (with a normalization factor built into E), we have the image irradiance equation

$$E(x, y) = R(p, q) \tag{1}$$

This deceptively simple looking equation is in fact a complicated partial differential equation, because p, q are the derivatives of the surface height z with respect to x, y, namely $p = z_x, q = z_y$. This equation can be solved by the method of *characteristics*, which is quite commonly used for first order partial differential equations. In this method, we assume that we have some known initial conditions on an appropriate subspace of the space of interest, and grow the solution from there. For example, if we need to solve an equation in the plane, we need initial conditions along some curve in the plane. Starting from each point on this initial curve, we can advance in small (infinitesimal) steps in the plane, growing a *characteristic curve* there (fig. 1). The directions of the steps, and thus the characteristic curves, are determined by the given equation. The collection of all the characteristic curves, starting from all points on the initial curve, is the solution of the equation.

In our case we have a four-dimensional space for the unknowns x, y, p, q, and instead of curves we talk about *strips* in the 4-D space. These strips are projected as curves on the x, y plane, with known values of p, q at each curve point x, y. Thus we need an initial curve $\Gamma(x, y)$ in the plane on which p, q are known, and

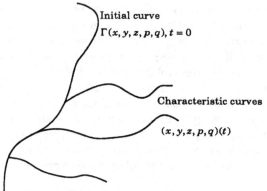

Fig. 1. Method of characteristics

from it we will grow characteristic curves in the plane on which p, q are known. These are equivalent to characteristic strips in the x, y, p, q space.

The equations used to grow the characteristics are in our case

$$\dot{x} = R_p \qquad \dot{y} = R_q$$

$$\dot{p} = E_x \qquad \dot{q} = E_y \qquad (2)$$

We have t as a parameter along the curves and the dot means differentiation with respect to t. These equation are derived in [Horn 1986]. We will later derive a somewhat generalized version. We have four coupled first order differential equations that are easy to integrate numerically. We also have an additional equation that can be integrated after the above equations are solved:

$$\dot{z} = pRp + qRq$$

The problem remains of finding the initial conditions. We can define an arbitrary initial curve $\Gamma(x, y)$, but we also need the values of p, q at each point on it. Thus we need some additional constraints.

One constraint can be obtained from the equation of the curve Γ itself. If the curve is parametrized by η, we have

$$\frac{\partial z}{\partial \eta} = p \frac{\partial x}{\partial \eta} + q \frac{\partial y}{\partial \eta}$$

which relates the three unknowns $p, q, \partial z/\partial \eta$ to the two known quantities $\partial x/\partial \eta$, $\partial y/\partial \eta$. However, this is not enough to solve the problem. We need more constraints, and there is no general way of obtaining them.

This where invariants can come to the rescue. Our goal is to use invariants as constraints that will replace most of the initial conditions, so that we can build the characteristic curves without a need for initial conditions. them. As it turns out, such invariant constraints do exist if the irradiance equation possesses *symmetries* with respect to some coordinate transformations such as translation or rotation. These symmetries are quite common and will enable us to solve the shading problem in many cases.

For our subsequent treatment of invariants, we now recast the four equations (2) in a different form which is more suitable for being handled by the calculus of variations. We define the Hamiltonian function H as

$$H = R - E = R(p, q) - E(x, y)$$

The characteristic equations (2) can now be written in the form of Hamilton's equations:

$$\dot{x} = \frac{\partial H}{\partial p} \qquad \dot{y} = \frac{\partial H}{\partial q} \tag{3}$$

$$\dot{p} = -\frac{\partial H}{\partial x} \qquad \dot{q} = -\frac{\partial H}{\partial y} \tag{4}$$

This form is similar to the one used to describe physical processes, and make it possible to use the available knowledge in mathematical physics about invariants of such processes. It should be noted, however, that the similarity is only an analogy here, since our p, q are purely geometrical entities (slopes) while in physics they represent momentum.

Another advantage of the Hamiltonian representation is that it enables us to deal with a more general irradiance equation than the one given in (1). We have generalized the reflectance function $R(p, q)$ in that equation in two ways: a) adding dependence on x, y, taking into account changes in surface reflectance; b) defining p, q as more general variables then the slopes, e.g. angles or components of a normal vector. This is valuable because the reflectance laws are simpler (and more evidently symmetric) in terms of such variables.

In the remainder of this section, we present a proof of the Hamilton equations (3),(4) in a treatment which is more general then that in [Horn 1986] and accommodates the above generalizations.

Moving along an infinitesimal vector dx, dy in the plane, the surface variables p, q change according to

$$dp = p_x dx + p_y dy \qquad dq = q_x dx + q_y dy$$

or in a matrix form

$$\begin{pmatrix} dp \\ dq \end{pmatrix} = A \begin{pmatrix} dx \\ dy \end{pmatrix} \tag{5}$$

with

$$A = \begin{pmatrix} p_x & p_y \\ q_x & q_y \end{pmatrix}$$

This holds for any kind of variables p, q. If p, q are the slopes, then A is equal to the Hessian matrix (not to be confused with the Hamiltonian H, a scalar):

$$H = \begin{pmatrix} z_{xx} & z_{xy} \\ z_{xy} & z_{yy} \end{pmatrix}$$

From eq. (5) it is easy to derive the relation between the "inverse" differential operators, e.g. by the chain differentiation rule, and obtain

$$\begin{pmatrix} \frac{\partial}{\partial p} \\ \frac{\partial}{\partial q} \end{pmatrix} = A^{-1} \begin{pmatrix} \frac{\partial}{\partial x} \\ \frac{\partial}{\partial y} \end{pmatrix}$$

This relation enables us to differentiate with respect to p, q when the function has the arguments x, y. The Hamiltonian is a function of four variables, $H(x, y, p, q)$, and by the irradiance equation (1) it vanishes on a 2-D subspace defined by $p(x, y)$, $q(x, y)$. We can now use the above relation to differentiate H in this subspace. Differentiating H respect to p, q and equating to 0 we obtain

$$\begin{pmatrix} \frac{\partial H}{\partial p} \\ \frac{\partial H}{\partial q} \end{pmatrix} + A^{-1} \begin{pmatrix} \frac{\partial H}{\partial x} \\ \frac{\partial H}{\partial y} \end{pmatrix} = 0$$

(The first term differentiates with respect to p, q directly and the second term does it indirectly through x, y). Thus we can write

$$\begin{pmatrix} \frac{\partial H}{\partial p} \\ \frac{\partial H}{\partial q} \end{pmatrix} = -A^{-1} \begin{pmatrix} \frac{\partial H}{\partial x} \\ \frac{\partial H}{\partial y} \end{pmatrix} \tag{6}$$

We now have a system of equations (5),(6). The matrix A can be eliminated from it by defining the infinitesimal step along a characteristic curve as

$$\begin{pmatrix} dx \\ dy \end{pmatrix} = \begin{pmatrix} \frac{\partial H}{\partial p} \\ \frac{\partial H}{\partial q} \end{pmatrix} dt \tag{7}$$

This can be substituted in (5), followed by (6), namely

$$\begin{pmatrix} dp \\ dq \end{pmatrix} = A \begin{pmatrix} \frac{\partial H}{\partial p} \\ \frac{\partial H}{\partial q} \end{pmatrix} dt = -AA^{-1} \begin{pmatrix} \frac{\partial H}{\partial x} \\ \frac{\partial H}{\partial y} \end{pmatrix} dt$$

to finally obtain

$$\begin{pmatrix} dp \\ dq \end{pmatrix} = - \begin{pmatrix} \frac{\partial H}{\partial x} \\ \frac{\partial H}{\partial y} \end{pmatrix} dt$$

This and eq. (7) are equivalent to the Hamilton equations (4),(3).

3 Invariants and Symmetries

In this section we derive the relation between symmetries of the Hamiltonian with respect to coordinate transformations, on the one hand, and invariants, or conservation laws, on the other.

The Hamilton equations are four first-order differential equations in the four unknowns x, y, p, q. We want to obtain a system of two second-order equations in the two variables x, y only. This will make the geometrical dependence on the coordinates more transparent and allow us to make use of the symmetry properties. To do this we use the Legendre transformation.

The Legendre transformation is defined (in 1-D) as follows. Given a function $F(x)$, we want to define a new variable, the derivative $\xi = dF/dx$, and transform F to a function of this new variable. A straightforward way of doing this is simply to invert $\xi(x)$ to obtain $x(\xi)$ and substitute it in $F(x)$. However, this will cause a loss of mathematical information, because $F(x)$ may contain constants (or functions of variables other than x) which would be lost in the differentiation. The standard way to avoid this problem is to define a new function $\bar{F}$ as

$$\bar{F} = x\xi(x) - F(x) \tag{8}$$

and then substitute $x(\xi)$ for x in $\bar{F}$ to obtain $\bar{F}(\xi)$. This is the *Legendre transformation*.

The Legendre transformation is reversible. First, the derivative of $\bar{F}(\xi)$ with respect to the new variable ξ is equal to the original variable x, since from eq. (8) we have

$$d\bar{F} = x\,d\xi + \xi\,dx - \frac{dF}{dx}dx = x\,d\xi$$

Thus, performing the Legendre transformation on $\bar{F}$ gives back the original F:

$$\xi\frac{\bar{F}}{d\xi} - \bar{F} = \xi x - \bar{F} = F$$

The higher-dimensional generalization is straightforward.

The Legendre transformation of a Hamiltonian is called a Lagrangian:

$$L = p_i\frac{\partial H}{\partial p_i} - H \tag{9}$$

with $p_i = p, q$ in our case.

To complete the transformation, the variables p, q have to be replaced by the derivatives $\frac{\partial H}{\partial p}$ and $\frac{\partial H}{\partial q}$. These derivatives are replaced in turn by the quantities $\dot{x}, \dot{y}$, because of eqs. (3). To do that, we have to calculate the quantities $\dot{x}, \dot{y}$ as functions of x, y, p, q, invert the system to obtain q, p as functions of $\dot{x}, \dot{y}, x, y$, and substitute in the Lagrangian:

$$L(x, y, \dot{x}, \dot{y}) = p(x, y, \dot{x}, \dot{y})\dot{x} + q(x, y, \dot{x}, \dot{y})\dot{y} - H(x, y, \dot{x}, \dot{y})$$

with the Hamiltonian part being

$$H(x, y, \dot{x}, \dot{y}) = R(p(\dot{x}, \dot{y}, x, y), q(\dot{x}, \dot{y}, x, y)) - E(x, y)$$

We can see that this inversion affects only the R part of the Hamiltonian and not the E part. For most practical purposes the inversion will not have to be performed.

Since we have transformed from the Hamiltonian to the Lagrangian and changed our independent variables, the Hamilton equations (3),(4) are also transformed. We have already made use of eqs. (3); the remaining equations, (4), transform to the two Euler-Lagrange equations

$$\frac{d}{dt}\frac{\partial L}{\partial \dot{x}} = \frac{\partial L}{\partial x} \qquad \frac{d}{dt}\frac{\partial L}{\partial \dot{y}} = \frac{\partial L}{\partial y} \tag{10}$$

The equivalence of these equations to the Hamilton form can be easily seen if we recall the reversibility of the Legendre transformation, namely that the derivatives of L with respect to the new variables $\dot{x}, \dot{y}$ are equal to the original variables p, q.

We can now apply the methods of the calculus of variations to the Lagrangian to find invariants.

4   Noether's Theorem

The main result concerning invariants of Euler-Lagrange-type equations is the Noether theorem [Lovelock and Rund 1975]. It states that if the Lagrangian is symmetric (invariant) with respect to a particular transformation of the coordinates, then there exists a quantity that remains unchanged as the parameter t changes. This is an invariant, or a conserved quantity, of the Lagrangian, or equivalently, an invariant of the corresponding equations. The form of this invariant is also given, in terms of the coefficients of the coordinate transformation.

In the classical example, energy and momentum are invariants of the equations of motion, namely they are constant as the time t changes. Energy conservation results from symmetry of the equations of motion with respect to translation in time, while momentum conservation results from symmetry of the motion equations with respect to translation in space. Similarly, conservation of angular momentum results from a rotational symmetry of the equations. (By symmetry we mean that the form of the *equation* is symmetric with respect to the transformation. The *solution* is not generally symmetric and depends on the initial conditions).

We deal with a transformation of the coordinates and t, having r parameters w^s, $s = 1 \ldots r$. For example, the rotation group in the plane has one parameter, the angle θ. This coordinate transformation can be written as

$$\bar{x}^i = x^i + \zeta_s^i dw^s, \qquad \bar{t} = t + \xi_s dw^s \tag{11}$$

with ζ_s^i, ξ_s being some coefficients characterizing the transformation. They generally depend on x^i, t. The summation convention is used. (In the planar case x^i is x, y).

Theorem (Noether). *If the Lagrangian L is invariant under the transformation (11), and it satisfies the Euler-Lagrange equations (10), then the following r quantities are invariant along t:*

$$\theta_s = -L\xi_s - \frac{\partial L}{\partial \dot{x}^i}(\zeta_s^i - \dot{x}^i \xi_s) \tag{12}$$

Namely, they satisfy the conservation law

$$\frac{d\theta_s}{dt} = 0$$

By the Legendre transformation of R these invariants can also be written as

$$\theta_s = H\xi_s - p_i\zeta_s^i \tag{13}$$

with $p_i = \partial L/\partial \dot{x}^i$. Thus we can write invariants in terms of the original Hamiltonian and original variables p, q. The symmetry properties of the Lagrangian are the same as those of the Hamiltonian, because the additional term $p_i\frac{\partial H}{\partial p_i}$ is a scalar product of covariant and contravariant vectors.

The Lagrangian is often not fully invariant to the coordinate transformation and may contain terms that depend on the transformation. For example, momentum is not conserved in the presence of external forces. This is expressed by a term in the Lagrangian which is not symmetric. However, one can still write a meaningful conservation law that relates the change of momentum in time to the non-symmetric part of the Lagrangian. In the general case this can be written as follows:

$$\frac{d\theta_s}{dt} = -\frac{\partial L}{\partial w^s} \tag{14}$$

Combining the above equations with eq. (13) we obtain the following equations for change in the invariants

$$\frac{d}{dt}(p_i\zeta_s^i - H\xi_s) = \frac{\partial L}{\partial w^s} \tag{15}$$

In conclusion, to find invariant constraints, we have to find coordinate transformations which leave L unchanged and substitute the coefficients ξ, ζ of such transformations in the above equation.

5 Invariants of Shading

Here we use the above formulas to find invariants for the shading problem. In the shading case the parameter t above is a parameter along the characteristic curves, and so we look for invariants that stay constant along these curves. The Lagrangian contains the two functions R, E. The E is known (the image brightness) and in general will not be symmetric. This part is analogous the the external forces in a physical situation. However, this part does not pose a problem because it is known from the image. R represents the properties of the object and the light; this is the part whose symmetry is helpful. Thus, when R possesses a symmetry, the invariants will change according to the change in the known E only, and will not be affected by R. We can now write the change in the invariants from eqs. (9),(15) as, using $H = 0$:

$$\frac{d}{dt}(p_i\zeta_s^i) = \frac{\partial}{\partial w^s}(p_i\frac{\partial R}{\partial p_i} + E - R) \tag{16}$$

For a symmetric R, all the R-related terms vanish:

$$\frac{d}{dt}(p_i\zeta_s^i) = \frac{\partial E}{\partial w^s} = \frac{\partial E}{\partial x^i}\zeta_s^i \tag{17}$$

with the rhs being a known quantity. The last equality holds for any function of x^i (but not of $\dot{p}^i, x^i, t$)

$$\frac{\partial}{\partial w^s} = \frac{\partial}{\partial x^i}\zeta_s^i \tag{18}$$

An interesting property here is that we do not need to know the exact details of R to find the forms of various invariants. The symmetry properties are sufficient.

A simpler form of the invariant constraint can be obtained which eliminates the E term from (16). Expanding the E term of (16) using (18) we obtain

$$\dot{p}_i\zeta_s^i + p_i\dot{\zeta}_s^i = \frac{\partial E}{\partial x_i}\zeta_s^i + \frac{\partial R'}{\partial w^s}$$

with R' containing all the R-related terms. We can subtract from the above the shading equations (2) multiplied by ζ_s^i and obtain

$$p_i\dot{\zeta}_s^i = \frac{\partial R'}{\partial w^s} \tag{19}$$

The rhs vanishes for a symmetric R. This is because R' is a Legendre transformation of R and has the same symmetries.

It is clear that our job now is to find transformations under which the reflectance function R, or the underlying situation that it describes, is symmetric. The coefficients ζ_s^i of this transformation will then be substituted into eq. (17) (or (19)) above to find the invariant constraints. These constraints will then be used to almost eliminate the need for initial conditions for the characteristic equations.

We will now examine several symmetries of the reflectance function and the invariants that they induce.

5.1 Translation in Space

The reflectance function as written in (1) used the assumption that the light source does not vary spatially, but only depends on angles. The dependence on the shape itself is also through angles, i.e. there is no spatial change in the reflectance coefficient. Thus $R(p, q)$ is translationally symmetric and we can deduce the translation invariants. In this case the transformation variables w^s are the translations $\Delta x, \Delta y$ and the transformation is

$$\bar{x} = x + \Delta x \qquad \bar{y} = y + \Delta y$$

so we have

$$\zeta_1^1 = \zeta_2^2 = 1 \qquad \zeta_1^2 = \zeta_2^1 = 0$$

From eq. (17) we obtain

$$\dot{p}_1 = \frac{\partial E}{\partial x} \qquad \dot{p}_2 = \frac{\partial E}{\partial y}$$

The above equations are identical to the shading equations (2) that we started with, so there is nothing new gained here (except some insight).

In a physical analogy, the above equation represents the change in momentum under the influence of a potential $-E$, whose derivatives provide the external force.

5.2 Rotation around an Axis Perpendicular to the Image

Rotational symmetry of the equations can occur in several cases. In the simplest case, the light source illuminates the object in a direction along the camera axis, and is symmetric. Then R does not depend on the orientation around the symmetry axis. The transformation variable here is the rotation angle θ. Rather than calculate the ζ_s^i we follow the physical analogy and write the invariant equation as a change in the angular momentum under the influence of an external torque. Accordingly, eq. (17) takes the form

$$\frac{d}{dt}(\mathbf{x} \times \mathbf{p}) = \frac{\partial E}{\partial \theta} = \mathbf{x} \times \frac{\partial E}{\partial \mathbf{x}} \tag{20}$$

The rhs represents rotation because of eq. (18):

$$\frac{\partial}{\partial \theta} = \mathbf{x} \times \frac{\partial}{\partial \mathbf{x}} = x \frac{\partial}{\partial y} - y \frac{\partial}{\partial x}$$

It is assumed here that all the vectors above are in the plane. Since the light source is at infinity, the location of the symmetry axis can be arbitrary. The above equation can be simplified by eliminating E using the linear momentum conservation law, eqs. (2). (This was done for the general case in eq. (19).) From (20) we have

$$\dot{\mathbf{x}} \times \mathbf{p} + \mathbf{x} \times \dot{\mathbf{p}} = \mathbf{x} \times \frac{\partial E}{\partial \mathbf{x}}$$

The last two terms above are equal because of eqs. (2), so we are left with

$$\dot{\mathbf{x}} \times \mathbf{p} = 0 \tag{21}$$

The meaning of the above equation is different from the physics analog. There, the momentum $\mathbf{p}$ is proportional to $\dot{\mathbf{x}}$ so this equation is an identity. However, in our situation $\mathbf{p}$ is not a momentum and the above equation contains a meaningful invariant constraint. It means that the direction of the characteristic curve is parallel to the gradient of the surface, for a circular light source.

5.3   Circular Object

In this case, the object is circularly symmetric, while the light source is not. R itself can always be made symmetric by requiring that the light source be attached to the coordinate system and move along with it when it rotates. For a general object such a movement will create a new image with an unknown relationship to the one at hand, since the object is illuminated from different directions. However, if the object is symmetric, then the new image will be indistinguishable from the old one and $E(x, y)$ will be unchanged as a function of the rotation angle θ. The invariant equation (20) now reduces to

$$\frac{d}{dt}(xq - py) = 0$$

with the origin lying on the symmetry axis.

5.4   Rotation around a General Axis

The previous cases are easily generalized to arbitrary rotations. This means that the light source has a rotational symmetry around an arbitrary, and *unknown*, axis. As before, the surface reflectance properties are unknown too.

Given a scalar function $E(x, y, z)$ and an axis in the direction of the unit vector n_x^a, n_y^a, n_z^a, the change in E when rotated around the axis can be written as $\mathbf{n}^a \cdot \mathbf{x} \times \frac{\partial E}{\partial \mathbf{x}}$. This can also be written as a determinant

$$\frac{\partial}{\partial \theta} = \mathbf{n}^a \cdot \mathbf{x} \times \frac{\partial}{\partial \mathbf{x}} = \begin{vmatrix} n_x^a & n_y^a & n_z^a \\ x & y & z \\ \frac{\partial}{\partial x} & \frac{\partial}{\partial y} & \frac{\partial}{\partial z} \end{vmatrix}$$

This can be easily derived from eq. (18).

The angular momentum around the axis $\mathbf{n}^a$ is given by $\mathbf{n}^a \cdot \mathbf{x} \times \mathbf{p}$, so the invariant constraint is now

$$\frac{d}{dt}(\mathbf{n}^a \cdot \mathbf{x} \times \mathbf{p}) = \mathbf{n}^a \cdot \mathbf{x} \times \frac{\partial E}{\partial \mathbf{x}} \tag{22}$$

The geometrical meaning of this constraint is similar to the one in the last case. Looking at the vector components of the above equation, we see that the z component is equal to eq. (20), multiplied by n_z^a. Therefore this component is the same invariant constraint as in the restricted case of a perpendicular axis. The other components vanish. The simpler form (21) is also obtained in the same way. Geometrically this means that the characteristics are parallel to the surface gradient, when the illumination is rotationally symmetric around an *arbitrary* axis.

6 General Illumination

Even in the general case there are still internal symmetries of the problem that can be exploited to find invariants. Most importantly, we have the following properties for most surfaces: a) a surface element can be rotated around an axis normal to it without changing its reflectance, b) the physical reflectance law depends only on the difference between the directions of the normal, on the one hand, and incident and emanating rays, on the other, rather than on each direction independently. We can use these symmetries to find general invariants.

We take advantage of the fact that our treatment can handle a more general form of the reflectance function R. This function is created by combining the reflectance of light falling from all directions. Therefore we can write R as

$$R(\mathbf{n}) = \int r((\mathbf{n} - \mathbf{n}_e) \cdot (\mathbf{n} - \mathbf{n}_i)) s(\mathbf{n}_i) d\mathbf{n}_i \tag{23}$$

$\mathbf{n}$ here is the surface normal (replacing the slopes p, q), $\mathbf{n}_i$ are the unit vectors in the directions of the incident light, and $\mathbf{n}_e$ is in the direction of the light emanating from the surface (or the direction of the viewer's camera axis). r represents the physical law of the surface reflectance and s is the intensity of the light falling from a particular direction $\mathbf{n}_i$.

We can see that r is invariant to translation and rotation of the coordinates and to rotation of the surface element. The source of asymmetries is the illumination s. When the illumination is rotationally symmetric around some axis, than rotation around that axis will not change the functional form of the above R and the invariant constraint (21) holds. When the source is not symmetric, then the more general equation (19) has to be used. We obtain

$$\mathbf{n}^a \cdot \dot{\mathbf{x}} \times \mathbf{p} = \frac{\partial R'}{\partial \theta} \tag{24}$$

This is a general invariant equation for general illumination.

The rhs is now unknown because it depends on the unknown $\mathbf{n}$. We can get some insight into it by looking at the structure of R written before, eq. (23). Rotation of R changes only the illumination factor, $s(\mathbf{n}_i)$. To see this we notice that $\mathbf{n}_i$ is a dummy index and we can choose to rotate it along with $\mathbf{n}$. This makes the scalar product r invariant, while $d\mathbf{n}_i$ is invariant because the Jacobian of the rotation is 1. The domain of integration is also unchanged. The transition from R to R' preserves the invariance. We can thus write

$$\frac{\partial R'}{\partial \theta} = \int \left(\mathbf{n} \cdot \frac{\partial r}{\partial \mathbf{n}} - r \right) \frac{\partial s(\mathbf{n}_i)}{\partial \theta} d\mathbf{n}_i$$

In many practical situations the light source deviates only mildly from perfect rotational symmetry, so the above equation can be approximation by 0. In this case we again obtain eq. (21), but this time as a *quasi-invariant* constraint rather than a strictly invariant one. It should be noted that the invariants constraints here are *local*. That is, The axis of symmetry does not have to be the same throughout the scene. At each particular neighborhood we can have one dominant light source which is rotationally symmetric around some (unknown) axis in that neighborhood, and it will change over slowly to another light source as we move to a different neighborhood. The constraint (21) will still hold as a quasi-invariant throughout the image.

7 Recovering the Shape

The constraints derived above can be used to recover the shape, up to a few constants. We use here the example developed above of a rotationally symmetric light source with an arbitrary axis of symmetry. Unlike previous works (e.g. Oliensis and Dupuis, (1993)), the light source direction is *unknown*. Also, we make no assumptions on the surface reflectance properties. Other kinds of symmetry can be similarly applied.

In the unconstrained case, the method of characteristics needs an initial curve on which all variables are known. In our case, however, we need only one initial *point* with known $\mathbf{p}$. From this point we can recover the whole surface. To find an initial point we can follow, for example, the usual methods that look for a singular point such as the point with maximum brightness. We suspect that for a well behaved system of equations, the general appearance of the reconstructed shape will not depend too much on the initial conditions at the starting point.

The method outlined below is probably not optimal. It is only meant to demonstrate the feasibility of the recovery of shape using an invariant constraint. Numerical analysis techniques can be used to analyze the numerical errors in the process and improve on it.

From the given starting point, we can grow one characteristic curve. Normally, the system of equations does not give us any way of growing the solution going in *perpendicular* to a characteristic, and we need to grow each characteristic separately from it own initial point. However, our constraint does enable us to propagate from one characteristic to another, so the one known characteristic is sufficient. The key property that enables us to reconstruct the rest of the shape is the fact that the characteristic curves are perpendicular to the surface elevations, namely the curves of constant height z. This follows from the invariant constraint (21) which results from our symmetry assumption. This constraint means that the surface gradient $\mathbf{p}$ is parallel to the characteristic, with direction $\dot{\mathbf{x}}$. Since the elevation is perpendicular to the gradient, it is also perpendicular to the characteristic.

Since we have one characteristic, we know the values of all variables $\mathbf{x}, \mathbf{p}, z$ along it. We can now pick any point $\mathbf{x}_1$ along it, and move in perpendicular to the characteristic, namely along an elevation. We move a small distance to a point $\mathbf{x}_1 + \Delta\mathbf{x}$. We assume as a first approximation that this new point has the same gradient $\mathbf{p}_1$ as a previous one. This gradient value, along with the new point's coordinates $\mathbf{x}_1 + \Delta\mathbf{x}$, can serve as the initial conditions for growing a new characteristic.

This new characteristic is only a first approximation. It has an error of order $O(h)$, with h being the step size. We need to reduce the error to order $O(h^2)$ so the accumulation of error when building further characteristics will be acceptable. To do that, we recalculate the elevations by linking points of the same height z on the two characteristics. As the elevations have to be perpendicular to both characteristics, they are now curved and we can calculate their curvature. Assuming the curvature is nearly constant in a small vicinity, we can recalculate the elevation around the point x_1 that we started with, from knowledge of the other elevations in the vicinity. We can now recalculate the position of $x_1 + \Delta x$ along the recalculated elevation, going from x_1. As the other elevations in the vicinity of this recalculated point are also better known now, we can find a new gradient $p_1 + \Delta p$ there. We thus have a better starting point for the second characteristic, and we rebuild it. We can repeat the process, and for a small h it is likely to converge rapidly. An analytic process can also be developed based on the above principles.

Having found the second characteristic, we can proceed from it in the same way to find the rest of the surface. The process is local and there is no global minimization problem.

8 Conclusions

Although the paper is supposed to conclude here, this is really only the beginning. We have laid the groundwork for a general method of finding physical invariants of images, based on symmetries in either the scene or the fundamental imaging process itself. Such symmetries are quite prevalent in the real world and can form the basis for a model based system of image reconstruction. Our goal is now to apply the general framework to specific examples, both analytically and numerically, and to extend the class of symmetries that we can handle.

References

Horn, B.K.P.: Robot Vision, MIT Press (1986)

Lovelock, D. and Rund, H.: Tensors, Differential Forms, and Variational Principles, Dover (1975)

Mundy, J.L. and Zisserman, A., Eds: Geometric Invariance in Machine Vision, MIT Press (1992)

Oliensis, J. and Dupuis, P.: Provably convergent algorithms for shape from shading. Proc. DARPA Image Understanding Workshop, Washington, D.C. (April 1993) 1121–1130

Weiss, I.: Projective invariants of shapes. Proc. DARPA Image Understanding Workshop, Cambridge, MA (April 1988) 1125–1134

Weiss, I.: Noise resistance invariants of curves. IEEE T-PAMI 15 (Sept. 1992) 943-948

Weiss, I.: Geometric invariants and object recognition. International Journal of Computer Vision 10:3 (June 1993) 201-231

Fundamental Difficulties with Projective Normalization of Planar Curves *

Kalle Åström

Dept. of Mathematics, Lund Institute of Technology, Box 118, S-221 00 Lund, Sweden

Abstract. In this paper projective normalization and projective invariants of planar curves are discussed. It is shown that there exists continuous affine invariants. It is shown that many curves can be projected arbitrarily close to a circle in a strengthened Hausdorff metric. This does not infer any limitations on projective invariants, but it is clear that projective normalization by maximizing compactness is unsuitable. It is also shown that arbitrarily close to each of a finite number of closed planar curves there is one member of a set of projectively equivalent curves. Thus there can not exist continuous projective invariants, and a projective normalisation scheme can not have both the properties of continuity and uniqueness. Although uniqueness might be preferred it is not essential for recognition. This is illustrated with an example of a projective normalization scheme for non-algebraic, both convex and non-convex, curves.

1 Model Based Vision Using Invariants

The pinhole camera is often an adequate model for projecting points in three dimensions onto a plane. Using this model it is straightforward to predict the image of a collection of objects in specified positions. The inverse problems, to identify and to determine the three-dimensional positions of possible objects from an image, are however much more difficult. Traditionally recognition has been done by matching each model in a model data base with parts of the image. Recently, model based recognition using viewpoint invariant features of planar curves and point configurations has attracted much attention, cf. [MZ1]. Invariant features are computed directly from the image and used as indices in a model data base. This gives algorithms which are significantly faster than the traditional methods. These techniques cannot, however, be used to recognise general curves or point features in three dimensions by means of one single image. Additional information, e.g. that the object is planar, is needed. For point configurations the reason is that only trivial invariants exist in the general case, as is shown in [BW1]. In this paper it is shown that there are some fundamental limitations also for planar curves.

---

* The work has been supported by the Swedish National Board for Technical and Industrial Development (NUTEK). The work is done within the ESPRIT–BRA project VIVA.

The paper is organized as follows. In Section 2 the notation is introduced. Normalization schemes are discussed in a general framework and their relation to invariants, recognition and pose determination are given. A classical normalization scheme under affine transformations based on moments is presented in Section 3. The key observation is that this normalization scheme is continuous in the Hausdorff metric. In Section 4 it is shown that every curve in a large class can be projectively transformed into a curve arbitrarily close to a circle in a strengthened Hausdorff metric. A direct consequence is that projective normalization by maximizing compactness is inherently difficult and the normalized curve will depend crucially on how the boundary curve is represented. A somewhat surprising fact is shown in Section 5. Given a finite number of closed planar curves $\Gamma_1, \ldots, \Gamma_m$ it is possible to construct another set of planar curves $D_1, \ldots, D_m$ which are projectively equivalent and in which D_i in the Hausdorff metric is arbitrarily close to Γ_i, $i = 1, \ldots, m$. One consequence is that there exists no non-constant continuous projective invariants from the set of planar curves to the real line. Another consequence is that normalization schemes on closed planar curves can not both be continuous in this metric and give a unique representative from each equivalence class. In Section 6 a normalization scheme for non-algebraic, both convex and non-convex curves is presented and illustrated. This scheme is by no means perfect, but it illustrates that uniqueness can be sacrificed for continuity.

2 Preliminaries

This section contains some preliminaries and notations. First the problem of extracting geometrical features from an image is briefly discussed. The main idea is that it is possible to find small regions, despite occlusion and changes in lighting. The idea of using normalization to find invariants is then described and some notations are introduced.

2.1 Extraction of Curves

A grayscale image contains large amounts of information. The main idea of invariant based recognition is to throw away information that varies with lighting, occlusion and viewpoint, and to keep invariant features that allow recognition. The first step in this process is to extract geometrical features in the image. This can be done by algorithms for edge extraction and segmentation, cf. Figure 1. In this figure concavities are extracted from the outline of a spanner. In this paper we discuss the possibility of finding stable viewpoint invariant features of regions or closed curves.

2.2 Using Normalization to Find Invariants

A group G, in this paper the planar affine or projective group, is said to act on a set Ω if there exists a mapping $(G, \Omega) \ni (g, \omega) \longrightarrow g(\omega) \in \Omega$ with properties

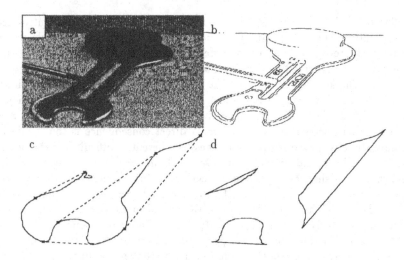

Fig. 1. 1a: A grayscale image of a scene with a roughly planar object. 1b: Edges are extracted using a Canny-Deriche edge detector. 1c: Distinguished points on one edge are used to segment a curve into pieces in a projectively invariant way. 1d: Distinguished points and lines can also be used to extract small regions in a projectively invariant way. Three such regions are shown in the figure.

$1(\omega) = \omega$, $\forall \omega \in \Omega$ and $g_1(g_2(\omega)) = (g_1 g_2)(\omega)$, $\forall \omega \in \Omega$, $\forall g_1, g_2 \in G$. The notation for group action is either $g\omega$ or $g(\omega)$.

Two elements ω_1 and ω_2 are said to have the same shape if $\omega_1 = g\omega_2$ for some transformation $g \in G$. This is an equivalence relation, because of the group structure of G. We write

$$\omega_1 \sim \omega_2 \iff \exists g \in G, \quad \omega_1 = g\omega_2 . \tag{1}$$

The equivalence relation divides Ω into disjoint equivalence classes. Denote the equivalence class containing ω by $G\omega = \{g\omega | g \in G\}$.

Let $T : \Omega \longrightarrow W$ be a function defined on Ω with values in some feature set W. This function is called an *invariant* if $\omega_1 \sim \omega_2 \implies T(\omega_1) = T(\omega_2)$ and a *complete invariant* if $\omega_1 \sim \omega_2 \iff T(\omega_1) = T(\omega_2)$.

A *normalization scheme* is simply a choice of *normal* reference frames. Let Ω_P denote this set of normal elements. One common construction is $\Omega_P = \{\omega | P(\omega) = 0\}$, where $P : \Omega \to R^n$ is some function. Another construction is to let Ω_P be those elements which maximize some feature in its equivalence class. For each element ω let the corresponding equivalence class $G\omega$ be represented by its normal elements, i.e. by

$$T(\omega) = G\omega \cap \Omega_P . \tag{2}$$

In the sequel we will say that a normalization scheme has the *uniqueness property* if there is only one normal reference frame, i.e. $G\omega \cap \Omega_P$ has only one element. A normalization scheme is called *continuous* if the normal reference frames depend continuously on ω. Assume that we have uniqueness in the normalization scheme. Any element ω_1 can then be uniquely factorized as

$$\omega_1 = g_1 \omega_1^{inv}, \tag{3}$$

with $g_1 \in G$ and $\omega_1^{inv} = T(\omega_1)$.

Isotropy, cf. [Wi1, Gå1], and maximal compactness, cf. [BY1] are two examples of affine normalization of planar curves. These two ideas give the same normal reference frames. This reference frame is unique up to similarity transformations.

2.3 Notations

A *rectifiable* curve is a continuous parametric curve with finite arclength. Let $\mathcal{C}$ be the set of all closed rectifiable curves. For such curves it is possible to calculate the arclength l and the area A enclosed by the curve. It is a well known fact from the calculus of variations that $l(C)^2/A(C) \geq 4\pi$, with equality if and only if C is a circle. For a specific curve $C \in \mathcal{C}$, let P_C be the set of projective transformations that sends C into $\mathcal{C}$. In other words such transformations do not send any of the points of C to infinity. Two images of the same planar curve, caught by a pinhole camera, are related by such a transformation. Two metrics on $\mathcal{C}$ are defined by

$$d(C_1, C_2) = \max_{z_1 \in C_1} \min_{z_2 \in C_2} ||z_1 - z_2|| + \max_{z_2 \in C_2} \min_{z_1 \in C_1} ||z_1 - z_2|| \tag{4}$$

and

$$\tilde{d}(C_1, C_2) = \max_{z_1 \in C_1} \min_{z_2 \in C_2} ||z_1 - z_2|| +$$
$$\max_{z_2 \in C_2} \min_{z_1 \in C_1} ||z_1 - z_2|| + |l(C_1) - l(C_2)|. \tag{5}$$

Here $||x||$ is the euclidean norm. The first metric is the ordinary Hausdorff metric. The second one is a strengthened version, the modification being that also the arclengths should be compared. These metrics will be used to compare two projected curves in the image plane. Due to digitization effects and other errors in the image plane, it is difficult to discriminate two image curves that are close in this metric. Every point on each curve is close to some point on the other curve and the arclengths are almost equal.

Let Ω be the class of all compact sets $\omega \subset R^2$ with positive area, whose boundary $C = \partial\omega$ is in $\mathcal{C}$. Two elements of Ω are compared using the above metrics on the boundary, i.e. we define $d(\omega_1, \omega_2) = d(\partial\omega_1, \partial\omega_2)$. Let moments be defined as

$$m_0(\omega) = \int_{x \in \omega} dx_1 dx_2$$
$$m_1(\omega)_i = \int_{x \in \omega} x_i \, dx_1 dx_2$$
$$m_2(\omega)_{ij} = \int_{x \in \omega} x_i x_j \, dx_1 dx_2$$
$$m_3(\omega)_{ijk} = \int_{x \in \omega} x_i x_j x_k \, dx_1 dx_2$$

Notice that m_0 is a scalar, m_1 a vector and m_2 a matrix. The moments depend continuously on ω in the metrics above.

The planar affine transformation group G_a and the planar projective transformation group G_p are used. For simplicity we will talk somewhat losely about G_p acting on Ω.

Once in a normal reference frame any feature is invariant. Moments and Fourier coefficients can be used for curves and regions. In our experiments we have divided the plane in sectors and used the area of a region in each sector as a feature, see [Ås2, Ås3]. This has been quite effective.

Assume that d is a metric on Ω. Assume also that we have a normalization scheme with uniqueness. Then a G-invariant metric on the class of shapes is defined by

$$d_G(\omega_1, \omega_2) = d(T(\omega_1), T(\omega_2)) \qquad (6)$$

Rotationally symmetric shapes are difficult to normalize with respect to rotations. Any rotational normalization scheme will have trouble with shapes that are close to rotational symmetry. On the other hand rotations do not affect Euclidean distance between a pair of points. It is therefore possible to define a metric on shapes with respect to the group G_{rot} of rotational transformations

$$G_{rot} = \{g = \begin{pmatrix} \cos(\theta) & -\sin(\theta) \\ \sin(\theta) & \cos(\theta) \end{pmatrix} | \theta \in R\}$$

acting on R^2 by left multiplication. The following induced Hausdorff metric will do

$$d_{rot}(\omega_1, \omega_2) = \min_{g \in G_{rot}} d(g\omega_1, \omega_2) \qquad (7)$$

3 Existence of Continuous Affine Invariants

The following affine normalization scheme is based on the well known principle of moments of inertia. The key issue here is that the normalization scheme is continuous in the Hausdorff metric. The results below generate corresponding results for the closed boundary curves of such regions. A typical example is an extracted concavity as in Figure 1.

The moments change in a simple way when a region is transformed affinely. For instance we have

$$
\begin{array}{llll}
m_1(\omega + b) = \int_{y \in \omega + b} y \, dy = & \int_{x \in \omega} (x + b) \, dx & = m_1(\omega) + bm_0(\omega) \\
m_1(A\omega) = \int_{y \in A\omega} y \, dy = & \int_{x \in \omega} Ax |\det A| \, dx & = |\det(A)| A m_1(\omega) \\
m_2(A\omega) = \int_{y \in A\omega} yy^T \, dy = \int_{x \in \omega} Ax(Ax)^T |\det A| \, dx & = A m_2(\omega) A^T |\det(A)|
\end{array}
$$

It is therefor easy to use the moments to select representatives from each equivalence class.

Theorem 1. *Given $\omega \in \Omega$, there is an orientation preserving affine transformation $x \mapsto Ax + b$ unique up to rotations that transforms ω into a region $\omega' \in \Omega_P$, where*

$$\Omega_P = \{\omega \mid \quad m_0(\omega) = 1, \quad m_1(\omega) = 0, \quad m_2(\omega) = aI, \quad a \in R\}. \qquad (8)$$

Furthermore the complete invariant $T(\omega) = G_{aff}\omega \cap \Omega_P$ is a continuous mapping from (Ω, d) to $(\Omega/G_{rot}, d_{rot})$.

Proof. First translate so that the center of mass is at the origin. The condition $m_1(\omega + b) = 0$ gives

$$m_1(\omega + b) = m_1(\omega) + bm_0(\omega) = 0.$$

Since $m_0(\omega) \neq 0$, b is uniquely determined as

$$b = -\frac{m_1(\omega)}{m_0(\omega)}.$$

Assuming that $m_1(\omega) = 0$, A has to be chosen so that the second moment is the identity matrix. Observe that $m_1(\omega) = 0$ implies that $m_1(A\omega) = 0$, i.e. the mass center is not affected by multiplication with A. The condition

$$m_2(A\omega) = |\det(A)|Am_2(\omega)A^T = aI$$

gives

$$m_2(\omega) = BB^T a|\det(B)|$$

with $B = A^{-1}$. Let $|B|$ be the positive square root of the positive definite matrix BB^T, i.e. $|B|^2 = BB^T$. Then $|B|$ is a scalar multiple of $\sqrt{m_2(\omega)}$. The matrix A is thus given as

$$A = |B|^{-1}.$$

It is determined uniquely up to rotation and scale. Finally fix the scale by $m_0(\omega') = 1$. It is easy to see that all transformations are continuous in the Hausdorff metric.

The normalization scheme based on (8) has the following properties.

- Uniqueness. In (3), g and ω^{inv} are unique up to rotation.
- Continuity. Both g and ω^{inv} depend continuously on ω.
- Easy to compute. As can be seen from the proof of Theorem 1, the transformation g can be directly computed from the moments of order 0, 1 and 2 of the region ω.
- Robust to digitization errors.
- No distinguished points are needed.

This scheme can be very useful in the recognition of planar curve segments, obtained from concavities. The affine approximation is often valid since these concavities often occupy a small region in the image. It can be seen that the method has good robustness properties, in comparison with maximum compactness and weak isotropy.

4 Inherent Difficulties in Maximizing Compactness

Let $\tilde{C} \subset C$ consist of those curves in $\tilde{C}$ such that the boundary of the convex hull has at least one smooth, curved part. In this section it will be proved that all curves C can be projectively transformed into a curve arbitrarily close to a circle even in the strengthened Hausdorff metric $\tilde{d}$. This fact does not by itself have any implications on the existence of projective invariants.

Theorem 2. *Let C_0 be a circle of radius one. Then*

$$C \in \tilde{C} \Longrightarrow \inf_{p \in P_C} \tilde{d}(p(C), C_0) = 0.$$

One interpretation of this theorem is that comparing the images of C from some sequence of projective viewpoints, these images look more and more like a circle. As will be seen in the proof below the projective transformations involved when approaching the limit are quite extreme, but still non-singular.

Proof. Choose a point $a \in C$ so that C is smooth at a, and so that the tangent at a intersects C only at a. Choose a coordinate system with origin at a, with x-axis along the tangent, and so that the curvature at a equals one.

The idea of the proof is to construct a sequence of transformations $(p_n)_1^\infty$ so that $p_n(C) \longrightarrow C_0$ as $n \longrightarrow \infty$, in the metric $\tilde{d}$. The image of a part of the curve around a will form the main part of C_0, and the remaining part of C will be mapped into a neighbourhood of one particular point of C_0.

The transformations $p_n, n > 0$ are defined by

$$p_n(x, y) = \left(\frac{2nx}{(n^2 - 1)y + 2}, \frac{2n^2 y}{(n^2 - 1)y + 2} \right). \tag{9}$$

We will also use the ellipses

$$C_\epsilon = \{((1 + \epsilon) \cos t, \sin t + 1) | t \in \mathcal{R}\}, \quad \epsilon > -1 \tag{10}$$

with center at the point $(0, 1)$, axis of length $1 + \epsilon$ in the x-direction and of length 1 in the y-direction. In particular, C_0 is the unit circle $x^2 + (y - 1)^2 = 1$. These ellipses intersect twice at $(0, 0)$ and twice at $(0, 2)$.

One can easily verify, e.g. using homogeneous coordinates, that the family $(p_n)_1^\infty$ has the following properties:

$$p_1 = \text{identity} \tag{11}$$
$$p_a \circ p_b = p_{ab} \tag{12}$$
$$p_n(C_\epsilon) = C_\epsilon \tag{13}$$
$$p_n(0, 0) = (0, 0) \tag{14}$$
$$p_n(0, 2) = (0, 2) \tag{15}$$

By (13), the transformations p_n reparametrise the ellipses C_ϵ. It will be seen that if $n > 1$ a vicinity around $(0,0)$ expands and a vicinity around $(0,2)$ contracts. More precisely, by rewriting (9) as

$$p_n(x,y) = \left(\frac{2nx}{(n^2-1)y+2}, 2 + \frac{2y-4}{(n^2-1)y+2} \right), \tag{16}$$

it follows that for every compact region D in the open half plane $\{(x,y)|\ y > 0\}$,

$$\sup_D |p_n(x,y) - (0,2)| \leq K/n, \tag{17}$$

for some constant K. Hence $(p_n)_1^\infty$ is uniformly convergent to $(0,2)$ on D. Since the jacobians of p_n are uniformly bounded by $O(1/n)$ on D, it also follows that the transformations p_n are uniformly Lipschitz continuous on D, i.e.

$$|p_n(x_1,y_1) - p_n(x_2,y_2)| \leq K/n|(x_1,y_1) - (x_2,y_2)|,$$
$$\forall(x_1,y_1) \in D, \forall(x_2,y_2) \in D, \forall n \tag{18}$$

The inverse projective transformation p_n^{-1} is equal to p_n after the change of variables $x \mapsto -x, y \mapsto 2 - y$, which exchanges the points $(0,0)$ and $(0,2)$. Thus the inverse transformations p_n^{-1} also have the contractive properties (17) and (18) in every compact region D in the open half plane $\{(x,y)|\ y < 2\}$.

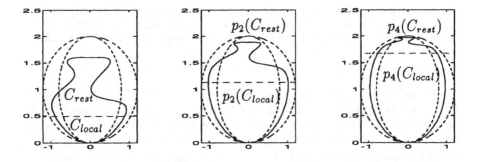

Fig. 2. The curve is split into two parts. A local part C_{local} belongs to the region bounded by the line and the two ellipses. C_{rest} is the complementary part of C.

Take $\epsilon > 0$, and let C_{local} be the connected component of C in a neighbourhood of $(0,0)$, that lies between the ellipses C_ϵ and $C_{-\epsilon}$, cf. Figure 2. Since the curve $p_n(C_{local})$ lies between the ellipses, the following inequalities hold,

$$1 - \epsilon < |(u,v) - (0,1)| < 1 + \epsilon, \quad \forall(u,v) \in p_n(C_{local}), \forall n.$$

The rest of the curve, $C_{rest} = C \setminus C_{local}$, is compact and belongs to the upper half plane. By the uniform convergence (17), for each $\epsilon > 0$ we can choose n so that all points of $p_n(C_{rest})$ lie within the distance ϵ from C_0, cf. Figure 2. Hence

$$\lim_{n \to \infty} \left(\max_{z_1 \in p_n(C)} \min_{z_2 \in C_0} \|z_1 - z_2\| + \max_{z_1 \in C_0} \min_{z_2 \in p_n(C)} \|z_1 - z_2\| \right) = 0 \qquad (19)$$

By this, one has control on the first two terms in the definition of $\tilde{d}$. A consequence that will be used below, is that $\lim_{n \to \infty} A(p_n(C)) = \pi$.

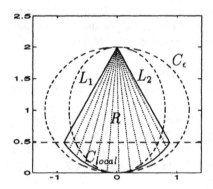 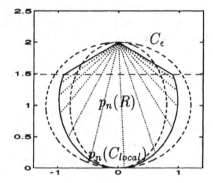

Fig. 3. The local part C_{local} together with two line segments form the boundary of a convex region R. The ellipse C_ϵ circumvents the convex region $p_n(R)$ for all n. For every n the transformed region $p_n(R)$ is convex and belongs to the interior of the ellipse C_ϵ.

It remains to consider the third term in $\tilde{d}$. The curve C is smooth around $(0,0)$, so it is possible to choose C_{local} so small that together with the lines L_1 and L_2 from the endpoints of C_{local} to $(0,2)$, it forms the boundary of a convex region R, cf. Figure 3. Since the shortest path circumventing a bounded region is the boundary of its convex hull, and since $p_n(C_{local})$ is part of the boundary of the convex region $p_n(R)$, we can deduce that $l(p_n(C_{local})) < l(C_\epsilon)$ for all n. By comparison with a circle of radius $1 + \epsilon$ we get $l(C_\epsilon) < 2\pi(1+\epsilon)$. Since C_{rest} lies in a compact subset of the open upper half plane, by means of (18) we have

$$\limsup_{n \to \infty} l(p_n(C)) \leq \limsup_{n \to \infty} l(p_n(C_{local})) + \limsup_{n \to \infty} l(p_n(C_{rest})) \leq 2\pi(1 + \epsilon) + 0.$$

Hence $\limsup_{n \to \infty} l(p_n(C)) \leq 2\pi$. Since $l(p_n(C))^2 / A(p_n(C)) \geq 4\pi$, it follows that $\liminf_{n \to \infty} l(p_n(C)) \geq 2\pi$. Hence $\lim_{n \to \infty} l(p_n(C)) = 2\pi$, which concludes the proof.

An immediate corollary is

Corollary 3.

$$C \in \tilde{C} \Longrightarrow \inf_{p \in P_C} \frac{l(p(C))^2}{A(p(C))} = 4\pi$$

It has been proposed, e.g. in [BS1], to base a canonical representation $\bar{p}(C)$ of the curve C on the transformation $\bar{p}$ that minimizes the inverse compactness measure $l(p(C))^2/A(p(C))$. According to the corollary, the minimum is not attained if $C \in \tilde{C}$. This canonical representation is thus only well defined for curves that do not have a smooth and curved part on the convex hull, e.g. for polygons. It is, however, still possible that the local minima could be used, even for curves in $\tilde{C}$.

5   Non-Existence of Continuous Projective Invariants

In the proof of Theorem 2 one notices that the main part of the curve is squeezed into a neighbourhood of a point. For large n, the curve $p_n(C)$ looks like a circle, but has a small ripple that corresponds to the main part of the curve C. It turns out that if we slightly perturb the curve $p_n(C)$ outside this ripple and then do the inverse projective transformation, the new curve is almost identical to the original one. A consequence is the following somewhat surprising theorem.

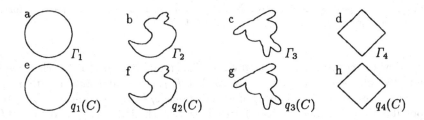

Fig. 4. The four upper curves are not projectively equivalent, but the four lower ones are.

Theorem 4. *Given* $\Gamma_1, \ldots, \Gamma_m \in C$. *To every* $\epsilon > 0$, *there exist a curve* C *and projective transformations* $q_1, \ldots, q_m$ *so that*

$$\tilde{d}(q_i(C), \Gamma_i) < \epsilon, \qquad i = 1, \ldots, m.$$

The theorem is illustrated in Figure 4. Note that the curves Γ_i do not have to be smooth.

Proof. Since there is a smooth curve arbitrarily close to every curve fulfilling the assumptions above, it is no restriction to assume that the curves $\Gamma_1, \ldots, \Gamma_m$ are smooth and therefore in $\widetilde{C}$. To each Γ_j associate a point P_j on C_0, a rectangle D_j and a sector S_j, according to Figure 5, where the sectors S_j are supposed to be pairwise disjoint.

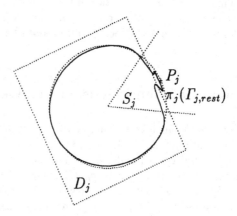

Fig. 5. Illustration of $\pi_j(\Gamma_j)$. After applying a projective transformation π_j to the curve Γ_j, the part in sector S_j will be glued with other corresponding parts to form a curve that approximates $\pi_j(\Gamma_j)$ for every $j = 1, \ldots, m$.

Now the construction in the proof of Theorem 2 is used to cut each curve Γ_j into two pieces $\Gamma_{j,local}$, and $\Gamma_{j,rest}$, so that $\Gamma_{j,local}$ has arclength less than $\epsilon/2$. Hence all points of $\Gamma_{j,local}$ is at most a distance $\epsilon/4$ from a point in $\Gamma_{j,rest}$. It is possible to find projective transformations π_j such that $\pi_j(\Gamma_j)$ is at most $1/m$ from C_0 in the $\tilde{d}$-metric, and

$$\pi_j(\Gamma_{j,local}) \subset D_j \qquad (20)$$

$$\pi_j(\Gamma_{j,rest}) \subset (\cap_{i \neq j} D_i) \cap S_j \qquad (21)$$

$$l(\pi_j(\Gamma_{j,rest})) < 1/m \qquad (22)$$

Since the inverse projection $q_j = \pi_j^{-1}$ has the contractive property (18), it can be chosen so that the it shrinks all curves in D_j of arclength less than a constant M, which will be specified later, into a curve with arclength less than $\epsilon/2$.

Let C be constructed by gluing the patches $\pi_j(\Gamma_{j,rest})$, the line segments obtained by radially connecting the endpoints of $\pi_j(\Gamma_{j,rest})$ with C_0, for all j, and the intermediate arcs of C_0. Both $C \setminus \pi_j(\Gamma_{j,rest})$ and $\pi_j(\Gamma_{j,local})$ are in D_j. Since C is a patch of m curves each with arclength less than $1/m$, of parts of the unit circle, and of $2m$ radial line segments of length less than $1/m$, the total arclength of $C \setminus \pi_j(\Gamma_{j,rest})$ is certainly less than $M = 1 + 2\pi + 2$. By the choice of q_j, this means that the curve $q_j(C \setminus \pi_j(\Gamma_{j,rest}))$ has arclength less than $\epsilon/2$. It is then clear that

$$\tilde{d}(q_j(C \setminus \pi_j(\Gamma_{j,rest})), \Gamma_{j,local}) < \epsilon.$$

The remaining part of C is $\pi_j(\Gamma_{j,rest})$, which is mapped identically into $\Gamma_{j,rest}$ by q_j. Hence $\tilde{d}(q_j(C), \Gamma_j) < \epsilon$.

The construction of C and q_i in the proof can be done by explicit formulas. Note that the transformations q_j are physically realisable in the pinhole camera model. An algorithm based on the proof have been implemented in MATLAB. Figure 4 has been constructed using this algorithm. Figure 6 shows what the mixed curve C looks like from eight different viewpoints. Observe that these eight different views are all projectively equivalent. Notice the kind of extreme, but non-singular, projective transformations that are involved.

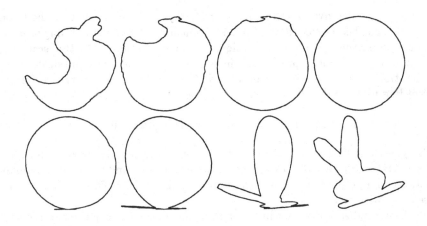

Fig. 6. Eight projectively equivalent views of the same planar curve. The duck transforms into a circle and then into a rabbit.

The theorem is in itself somewhat surprising and unintuitive at first, but it is a simple trick of hiding a shape along the convex hull of another shape. The reason it works is the use of extreme, but non-singular, projective transformations. The consequences are perhaps more important.

Corollary 5. *Let T be a projectively invariant mapping from the set of closed continuous curves with finite arc-length to a Hausdorff topological feature space, e.g. the real line, then T maps all curves at which it is continuous onto the same value.*

Proof. Assume to the contrary that $r_1 = T(\Gamma_1) \neq r_2 = T(\Gamma_2)$. Since the feature space is Hausdorff it is possible to find disjoint open sets $O_1 \ni r_1$ and $O_2 \ni r_2$. According to Theorem 4 the inverse images $T^{-1}(O_1)$ and $T^{-1}(O_2)$, which are open sets around Γ_1 and Γ_2, contain a projectively equivalent pair of curves, contradicting the assumption.

Suppose that we have a continuous projective normalization scheme that gives a unique representative from each equivalence class. It would then be possible to construct a continuous and non-constant projective invariant mapping from the set of curves with the Hausdorff metric to the real line. This is impossible according to Corollary 5. The conclusion is that *projective normalization schemes on the set of planar curves cannot both be continuous and give a unique representative from each equivalence class.* Either continuity or uniqueness has to be sacrificed.

6   Projective Normalization

Global projective invariants of curves are tricky. No matter what method you use, distinguished points, fitting ellipses, moments, projective smoothing or maximum compactness, you get non-uniqueness or discontinuity. In this section a normalization scheme is presented which might be useful. Only physically realisable transformations will be considered. Choose the normal reference frames according to

$$\Omega_P = \{\omega| \quad m_0(\omega) = 1, m_2(\omega) = aI, m_3(\omega) = 0, a \in R\} \tag{23}$$

This gives a normalization scheme with several representatives from each equivalence class. One way of locking the rotation is to demand that the maximum distance of a point in ω to the origin occurs at the x_1-axis. This method can be used also with convex curves.

The normalization scheme has been implemented and an experimental session will be presented. In this experiment, gray-scale images of roughly planar objects are taken with a digital camera. Polygon approximations of contours in the image are obtained using a Canny-Deriche edge detector. These curves are then normalized according to the proposed method, see Figure 7. Notice the good performance in Figures 7b and 7c. The three normalized curves lie practically on top of each other in spite of possible nonlinearities in the camera, errors in segmentation and in edge detection. The rabbit covered roughly 150×200 pixels in the image.

7   Discussion

Theorem 2 states that every smooth and closed rectifiable curve can be transformed arbitrarily close to a circle by means of a projective transformation,

  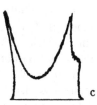

Fig. 7. Three images of rabbits, cf. Figure 7a, are normalized into a reference frame in which their third moment tensor is zero and the second moment matrix is the identity, cf. Figure 7b The same normalization is applied to the three regions enclosed by a bitangent and part of a contour, cf. Figure 7c

which is not affine. This fact does not per se have any implications on invariants, but we draw the conclusion that one should be careful when maximizing compactness over projective transformations.

The argument is similar to the trivial observation that one should not try to normalize curves under similarity transformations by minimizing area enclosed by the curve, since every rectifiable curve can be transformed arbitrarily close to a point simply by shrinking it.

It is also easy to see that every rectifiable curve can be transformed arbitrarily close in the Hausdorff metric to a line segment by means of an affine transformation, but we know from Theorem 1 that there are continuous affine invariant features of closed rectifiable curves.

Theorem 4 on the other hand has no counterpart in the similarity or affine cases. The reason is that affine transformations act in the same way around every point. It is not possible to contract one part of the curve and expand another. Given two curves of different affine shape it is not possible to construct a third curve and two affine transformations so both images of the third curve are arbitrarily close to the respective original.

A direct consequence of Theorem 4 is that there are no non-trivial stable projective invariants for closed planar curves. More precisely, every continuous and projectively invariant mapping from the set of closed rectifiable planar curves to the real line has to be constant. This means that a projective normalization scheme cannot both be continuous and give a unique representative from each projective equivalence class of curves. It is however possible that continuity can be achieved by sacrificing uniqueness as in Section 6, see also [5,8,11]. The perspective effects are usually small under normal viewing conditions. This fact should be possible to use in recognition algorithms.

The use of differential invariants has been proposed for recognition of planar curves. These are however very sensitive to noise. Therefore pre-smoothing of the curves is often necessary. Recently curve evolution schemes have been constructed that are both smoothing and invariant under similarity or affine transformations, cf. [ST1, ST2]. Projectively invariant curve evolution is currently under investigation. In light of Theorem 4 it is apparent that it is impossible to have a process that both commutes with projective transformations and smooths out small errors. When dealing with projective equivalence of planar curves it is impossible to discriminate between shapes on differents scales. What is small scale detail from one view-point is large scale shape from another.

Acknowledgements

I would like to thank my supervisor Gunnar Sparr for inspiration and guidance. I would also like to thank my fellow students Anders Heyden and Carl-Gustav Werner for their help. The paper has been inspired by participation in the ESPRIT-project VIVA, in particular it is heavily influenced by the recognition system that has been developed at Oxford, cf. [Ro1].

References

[BM1] Blake, A., Marinos, C., Shape from Texture: Estimation, Isotropy and Moments. *Artificial Intelligence, Vol 45, p. 332-380*, 1990.

[BS1] Blake, A., Sinclair, D., On the projective normalisation of planar shape, *Technical Report OUEL, Oxford, Great Britain*, 1992.

[BY1] Brady, M., Yuille, A., An Extremum Principle for Shape from Contour, *PAMI-6, No 3, p. 288-301*, 1984.

[BW1] Burns J. B., Weiss R. S., Riseman E. M., The Non-existence of General-case View-Invariants, *Geometrical Invariance in Computer Vision* Mundy, J. L. and Zisserman, A. editors, MIT Press 1992.

[Ca1] S. Carlsson, 'Projectively Invariant Decomposition and Recognition of Planar Shapes' *Proc. 4th ICCV, Berlin, p 471-475* May 1993.

[DH1] Duda, R. O. and Hart, P. E., Pattern Classification and Scene Analysis, *Wiley-Interscience*, 1973.

[Gå1] Gårding, J.: Shape from Surface Markings. Ph. D. thesis, Dept. of Numerical Analysis and Computer Science, Royal Institute of Technology, Stockholm, Sweden (1991)

[GM1] Van Gool, L., Moons, T., Pauwels, E. and Oosterlinck, A., Semi-differential Invariants, *ESPRIT/DARPA Invariants Workshop, Reykjavik, Iceland, pages 359-386* 1991.

[Gr1] Gros, P., and Quan L.: Projective Invariants for Vision. Technical Report RT 90 IMAG - 15 LIFIA, LIFIA-IRIMAG, Grenoble, France (1992).

[LS1] Lamdan, Y., Schwartz, J. T., and Wolfson, H. J., Affine Invariant Model-based Object Recognition, *IEEE Journal of Robotics and Automation, 6:578-589*, 1990.

[MZ1] Mundy, J. L., and Zisserman A. (editors), Geometric invariance in Computer Vision, *MIT Press, Cambridge Ma, USA*, 1992.

[PM1] Perona, P., and Malik, J., Scale-space and edge detection using anisotropic diffusion, *IEEE trans. Pattern Anal. Machine Intell. 12, pp 629-639*, 1990.

[Ro1] Rothwell, C. A., Zisserman, A., Forsyth, D. A., and Mundy, J. L., Canonical Frames for Planar Object Recognition, *Proc. of the Second European Conference of Computer Vision, Genova, Italy, pages 757-772* 1992.

[ST1] Sapiro, G., and Tannenbaum A., On invariant curve evolution and image analysis, *to appear in Indiana University Journal of Mathematics* 1993.

[ST2] Sapiro, G., and Tannenbaum A., On affine invariant scale-space, *to appear in Journal of Functional analysis* 1993.

[We1] Weiss, I., Noise-resistant Invariants of Curves, *ESPRIT/DARPA Invariants Workshop, Reykjavik, Iceland, pages 319-344* 1991.

[Wi1] Witkin, A. P.: Recovering Surface Shape and Orientation from Texture. J. of Artificial Intelligence **17** (1981) 17-45

[Ås1] Åström, K., A Correspondence Problem in Laser-Guided Navigation, *Proc. Swedish Society for Automated Image Analysis, Uppsala, Sweden, pages 141-144,* 1992.

[Ås2] Åström, K., Affine Invariants of Planar Sets, *Proc. 8th Scandinavian Conference on Image Analysis, Tromsö, Norway* 1993.

[Ås3] Åström, K.: Object Recognition using Affine and Projective Invariants of Planar Sets. CODEN:LUFTD2/TFMA-3002/5002-SE, Lund, Sweden (1993)

Invariant Size Functions

Alessandro Verri and Claudio Uras

Dipartimento di Fisica dell'Università di Genova
Via Dodecaneso 33, 16146 Genova, Italy

Abstract. Size functions are integer valued functions of two real variables which represent metric and topological properties of visual shape. In this paper size functions invariant for transformations of increasing generality are presented and discussed. Experiments on synthetically generated and real images show that by means of size functions invariant for Euclidean, affine, or projective transformations it is possible to identify similar shapes and distinguish between different shapes independently of the observer viewpoint. Since size functions are inherently robust against small qualitative and quantitative changes in the apparent shape of the viewed objects, it is concluded that size functions can be useful for viewpoint invariant recognition of natural shapes.

1 Introduction

In the past few years the study of invariants for shape representation and object recognition has received increasing attention from the computer vision community (see [FMZ, VMP, RFZ, Ca] for example). With almost no exception the literature on the subject is dedicated to problems in which an exact model of the observed objects is available.

Recently, the description of shapes by means of integer valued functions of two real variables, named *size functions*, has been proposed [Fr1, Fr2, VUF]. Unlike more traditional approaches, size functions encode information on both qualitative and quantitative properties of the viewed objects and appear to be well suited for the representation and recognition of shapes for which a precise mathematical model can be difficult, if not impossible, to obtain [UV1, UV2].

This paper shows that it is possible to design size functions invariant for Euclidean, affine, or projective transformations. The proposed "invariant" size functions are computed from the outline of planar (or almost planar) shapes and have the appealing property of being both viewpoint independent and stable against small changes in the apparent shape. In some cases the desired invariance is obtained through the use of suitable reference points, like the center of mass, inflections, and cusps. More general methods for the design and computation of invariant size functions will be considered in a forthcoming paper.

The paper is organized as follows. In Sect. 2 the theory of size functions is reviewed. In Sect. 3 a size function invariant for Euclidean transformations,

---

* This work has been partially funded by the EEC B.R.A. project VIVA.

which was already presented in [VUF], is discussed and tested on real images. Size functions invariant for affine and perspective transformations are introduced in Sect. 4 and 5 respectively. In both sections experimental results on synthetically generated planar shapes and real images of not exactly planar objects (leaves) are reported. Finally, Sect. 6 highlights the directions of future research in the area of invariant size functions and summarizes the obtained results.

2 Metric Homotopies and Size Functions

In this section an overview of the main concepts and results of the theory of size functions is presented. For a formal introduction to the theory see [Fr1, Fr2, Fr3]. Let us first establish some basic notation.

2.1 Definitions

In what follows a shape is an n-dimensional, compact, boundaryless, piecewise C^∞ submanifold $\mathcal{M}$ of a Euclidean space E^m ($n < m$). The curve α identified by the solid line in Fig.1(a) is an example of shape with $n = 1$, $m = 2$, and E^2 equal to the real plane. Let us denote with $\mathcal{M}^k$ the set of ordered k-tuples of points p_i of $\mathcal{M}$, $i = 1, ..., k$, and let p be a generic point in $\mathcal{M}^k$. The important concept of measuring function can now be defined.

Definition 1. A *measuring function* is a continuous function

$$\varphi : \mathcal{M}^k \to \mathbb{R}.$$

For example, the continuous function $D_a : \alpha \to \mathbb{R}$ in Fig.1(a), which measures the Euclidean distance of a point on α from the point a, is a measuring function with $k = 1$.

The notion of measuring function leads to the key concept of metric homotopy.

Definition 2. A *metric $H(\varphi \leq y)$-homotopy* between p and q in $\mathcal{M}^k$ is a continuous function $H : [0, 1] \to \mathcal{M}^k$ such that

- $H(0) = p$, $H(1) = q$;
- $\varphi[H(\tau)] \leq y$ $\forall \tau \in [0, 1]$.

We write $p \simeq_{\varphi \leq y} q$, if such a metric homotopy exists, or if $p = q$. It can easily be seen that a $H(\varphi \leq y)$-homotopy is an equivalence relation. Therefore $\mathcal{M}^k$ is naturally partitioned into equivalence classes modulo the $H(\varphi \leq y)$-homotopy. The relevance of the concept of metric $H(\varphi \leq y)$-homotopy, in the special case $\varphi = D_a$, is illustrated by means of the dotted circles of center a and radii r_1 and r_2 drawn in Fig.1(a). Since there exists a trajectory on α from p to q, trajectory which is entirely contained in the circle of radius r_1, then $p \simeq_{D_a \leq r_1} q$. Instead,

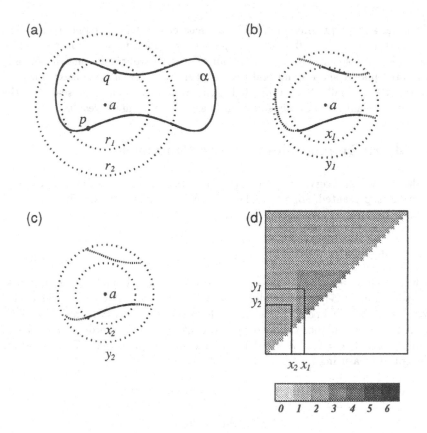

Fig. 1. An example of metric homotopy and size function. (*a*). Since there is a trajectory on α from p to q which is entirely contained inside the circle of radius r_1, then $p \simeq_{D_a \leq r_1} q$. Conversely, since there is no such trajectory inside the circle of radius r_2, then $p \not\simeq_{D_a \leq r_2} q$. (*b*) and (*c*). The dotted lines mark the portions of α with $D_a \leq y_1$ and $D_a \leq y_2$, the solid lines the portions with $D_a \leq x_1$ and $D_a \leq x_2$ respectively. Therefore, $l_{D_a}(\alpha)(x_1, y_1) = 2$ and $l_{D_a}(\alpha)(x_2, y_2) = 1$. (*d*). Grey value coded diagram of the size function $l_{D_a}(\alpha)(x, y)$. The x and y variables range in the horizontal and vertical axis respectively between $D_a^{\min}$ and $D_a^{\max}$ with $x \leq y$. Below: the grey value coding of the size function.

there is no trajectory from p to q entirely contained in the circle of radius r_2, and thus $p \not\simeq_{D_a \leq r_2} q$.

A metric homotopy has two general properties. Let $\varphi^{\min}$ and $\varphi^{\max}$ be the minimum and maximum of the measuring function φ over $\mathcal{M}^k$ respectively. First, there is no metric homotopy between any pair of points for $y < \varphi^{\min}$. Second, all the points are metric homotopic for $y \geq \varphi^{\max}$.

Let now $\mathcal{M}^k(\varphi \leq x)$ be the set of points p in $\mathcal{M}^k$ with $\varphi(p) \leq x$. We have the following definition of size function.

Definition 3. The size function $l_\varphi(\mathcal{M}) : \mathbb{R}^2 \to N \cup \{+\infty\}$ can be defined as

$$(x, y) \hookrightarrow \begin{cases} \#(\mathcal{M}^k(\varphi \le x)/ \simeq_{\varphi \le y}) \text{ if finite,} \\ \\ +\infty \text{ otherwise.} \end{cases}$$

Intuitively, $l_\varphi(\mathcal{M})(x, y)$ equals the number of connected components of the set of points of $\mathcal{M}^k$ with $\varphi \le y$ which contain at least a point with $\varphi \le x$. The notion of size function is further exemplified in Fig.1(b) and (c), where $\varphi = D_a$, and in Fig.2(b) and (c) where, $\varphi = D_2$. From Fig.1(b) the size function $l_{D_a}(\alpha)(x_1, y_1)$ equals 2 since both of the two connected components of the set of points with $D_a \le y_1$ (that is, the points which lie within the circle of center a and radius y_1), contain at least a point with $D_a \le x_1$ (that is, a point which lies inside the circle of radius x_1). Instead, $l_{D_a}(\alpha)(x_2, y_2) = 1$ since only one of the two connected components of the set of points with $D_a \le y_2$ in Fig.1(c) contains a point with $D_a \le x_2$. The grey value coded diagram of the size function $l_{D_a}(\alpha)$, with $D_a^{\max} \le x \le y \le D_a^{\max}$, is shown in Fig.1(d).

Let us now list the main properties of size functions.

2.2 Main Properties

First, if $T_\varphi(\mathcal{M}) = \{(x, y) : \varphi^{\min} \le x \le y \le \varphi^{\max}\}$ and φ is the measuring function, a basic result of the theory of size functions ensures that the value of the size function $l_\varphi(\mathcal{M})$, within the triangular region $T_\varphi(\mathcal{M})$ and for many well behaved measuring functions φ, is always finite and strictly positive [Fr2]. An important consequence of this result is that all the interesting information on the viewed shape lies within a region of finite area, the triangle $T_\varphi(\mathcal{M})$.

Second, $l_\varphi(\mathcal{M})(x, y)$ is nonincreasing with y and nondecreasing with x (see Fig.1(d) for example). These monotonicity properties can be used to compute a size function over a discrete mesh of points in $T_\varphi(\mathcal{M})$ and interpolate the intermediate values [Fr2].

Third, different measuring functions, in general, induce different size functions of the same shape. This property, which is very useful in order to produce a richer shape representation, is illustrated in Fig.2. Let us define the measuring function $D_2 : \mathcal{M}^2 \to \mathbb{R}$ as the Euclidean distance between ordered pairs of points of $\mathcal{M}$. In Fig.2(a), in which the same curve α of Fig.1 is displayed, some pairs of points of α are marked. Let $D_2(p_1, p_2) = l_1$, $D_2(q_1, q_2) = l_2$, and $D_2(r_1, r_2) = l_3$. It is evident that $D_2^{\min} = 0$ (for example, $D_2(s_1, s_2) = 0$) and $D_2^{\max} = l_3$. The diagram of the induced size function $l_{D_2}(\alpha; x, y)$ with $0 \le x \le y \le l_3$ is reproduced in Fig.2(b). For $l_1 \le x \le y < l_2$ the size function $l_{D_2}(\alpha)$ equals 3 because the pairs (s_1, s_2), (p_1, p_2), and (p_2, p_1) belong to three different equivalence classes modulo the $H(D_2 \le l_2)$-homotopy.

Fourth, the notion of size function can be formally extended to the discrete case. For an exhaustive and rigorous treatment of the subject see [Fr2]. Since the present research is restricted to the analysis of measuring functions defined on single points of one-dimensional planar contours, let us briefly discuss this special

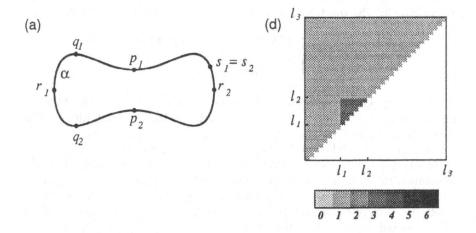

Fig. 2. An example of size function induced by the measuring function D_2. (a). The shape α and some pairs of points relevant to the computation of l_{D_2}. (b). Grey value coded diagram of the size function $l_{D_2}(\alpha)(x, y)$. The x and y variables range in the horizontal and vertical axis respectively between $D_2^{\min}$ and $D_2^{\max}$ with $x \le y$. Below: the grey value coding of the size function.

case. In order to extend the notion of size function to a set of ordered points p^i, $i = 1, ..., N$, which approximate a planar curve, a few preliminary definitions are needed. Let G be the undirected graph whose nodes are the points p^i and whose edges connect the pairs (p^i, p^{i+1}) for $i = 1, ..., N - 1$ (if the curve is closed, p^N is also connected with p^1). The measuring function φ is defined on the nodes of G, and $\mathcal{M}(\varphi \le x)$ is $G_{\varphi \le x}$, or the subgraph of G whose nodes are the points with $\varphi \le x$. The size function can now be defined as the number of connected components of the graph $G_{\varphi \le y}$ which contain at least one vertex with $\varphi \le x$.

Under rather general hypotheses, it can be shown [Fr2] that (i) with the exceptions of regions around the discontinuities the size functions computed in the discrete approximation and in the continuous case coincide, and (ii) in the limit of $N \to \infty$, the area of these regions vanishes. A description of the algorithm which has been used in the paper for the computation of the presented size functions can be found in [UV2].

A final fundamental property of the presented theory is that a size function inherits the invariant properties of the underlying measuring function. In the rest of the paper size functions invariant for Euclidean, affine, and perspective transformations are presented and discussed. In order to evaluate quantitatively the effectiveness of the proposed size functions for shape representation, a distance between shapes in terms of size functions must first be defined. Let us conclude this section by recalling the definition of distance between size functions proposed in [UV1]. This distance function will be used throughout the paper to identify or distinguish shapes in terms of the computed size functions.

2.3 A Similarity Measure between Size Functions

Figure 3 shows the size functions l_{D_c} relative to the contours displayed in the lower right corners. The measuring function D_c is the distance of a point on the contour from the point c, the center of mass of the contour. The contours are the outlines of two sassafras ((a) and (b)) and two sweetgum ((c) and (d)) leaves. Clearly, an appropriate distance function should be small between the size functions of (a) and (b), and (c) and (d), and large otherwise.

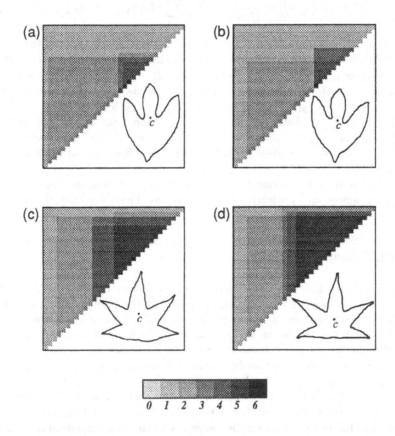

Fig. 3. Measuring the distance between shapes by means of size functions. (a), (b), (c), and (d). The size functions l_{D_c} relative to the contours displayed in the lower right corners. The contours are the outlines of two sassafras ((a) and (b)) and sweetgum ((c) and (d)) leaves. The x and y variables range in the horizontal and vertical axis respectively between $D_c^{\min}$ and $D_c^{\max}$ with $x \leq y$. Below: the grey value coding of the size functions.

To this purpose let α_1 and α_2 be the point sets which sample two shapes, and $\varphi^{\min}(\alpha_i)$ and $\varphi^{\max}(\alpha_i)$ the minimum and maximum of φ on α_i, for $i = 1, 2$.

Let us translate and scale φ by defining

$$\hat{\varphi} = \frac{\varphi - \varphi^{\min}(\alpha_i)}{\varphi^{\max}(\alpha_i) - \varphi^{\min}(\alpha_i)} \tag{1}$$

on α_i, for $i = 1, 2$. Then, $0 \le \hat{\varphi} \le 1$ and a distance d between the size functions $l_{\hat{\varphi}}(\alpha_1)$ and $l_{\hat{\varphi}}(\alpha_2)$ can be defined as

$$d\left(l_{\hat{\varphi}}(\alpha_1), l_{\hat{\varphi}}(\alpha_2)\right) = \frac{2}{R(R-1)} \sum_{i=1}^{R-1} \sum_{j=1}^{R-i} \mid \bar{l}_{\hat{\varphi}}(\alpha_1)_{i,j} - \bar{l}_{\hat{\varphi}}(\alpha_2)_{i,j} \mid \tag{2}$$

The distance d is simply the normalized sum of the absolute value of the point-wise differences between size functions $l_{\hat{\varphi}}(\alpha_1)$ and $l_{\hat{\varphi}}(\alpha_2)$ regarded as triangular matrices $\bar{l}_{\hat{\varphi}}(\alpha_1)_{i,j}$ and $\bar{l}_{\hat{\varphi}}(\alpha_2)_{i,j}$ with $i = 1, ..., R-1$ and $j = 1, ..., R-i$. The normalization factor is chosen so that $d(l_{\hat{\varphi}}(\alpha_1), l_{\hat{\varphi}}(\alpha_2)) = 1$ if, on average, the triangular matrices $\bar{l}_{\hat{\varphi}}(\alpha_1)$ and $\bar{l}_{\hat{\varphi}}(\alpha_2)$ differ by 1 at each entry.

For example, the distances between the size functions of Fig.3(a) and (b), and Fig.3(c) and (d), computed by means of (2), are 0.17 and 0.26 respectively. Instead, the distance between any other pair of size functions of Fig.3 is larger than 0.91.

We are now in a position to discuss and test size functions invariant for Euclidean, affine, and projective transformations. First, the case of Euclidean transformation is considered.

3 Euclidean Invariance

In this section a size function invariant for Euclidean transformation is considered. The measuring function D_a described in the previous section is only invariant for rotation on the image plane around the point a. Consequently, the induced size function fails to be invariant even for a simple translation of the viewed shape. In order to enforce invariance for a broader, and more interesting, class of transformations, a possible strategy is to measure the distance of the contour points from a point endowed with suitable invariance properties.

If the point a is the center of mass c of the contour, as in the example of Fig.3, the measuring function D_c and the induced size function l_{D_c} are invariant for rotation and translation over the image plane, and thus Euclidean invariance, is readily obtained. This invariance property is illustrated in Fig.4(a) and (b). Figures 4(a) and (b) show the size functions of the same shape up to unknown Euclidean and scaling transformations (the actual shapes are displayed in the corresponding lower right corners). The invariance for scaling is simply ensured by proper normalization of the minimum and maximum value of the measuring function given by (1). As expected, the diagrams of Fig.4(a) and (b) are indistinguishable.

A striking feature of the presented scheme is tolerance to noise. This can be appreciated by looking at the diagrams of the size functions of Fig.4(c) and (d). In the case of Fig.4(c) a small perturbation, 1% of the shape diameter, was added

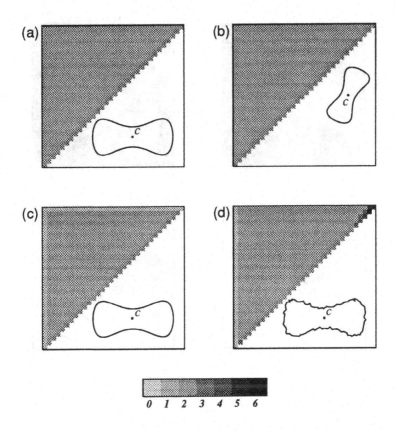

Fig. 4. Euclidean invariance and tolerance to noise of l_{D_c}. (a), (b), (c), and (d). The size functions of the contours displayed in the corresponding lower right corners. Below: the grey value coding of the size functions.

to the coordinates of the center of mass, while in the case of Fig.4(d) a much larger amount of noise was added to the coordinates of the curve points. The resulting shapes and centers of mass are displayed in the lower right corners of Fig.4(c) and (d) respectively. By inspection of the size functions of Fig.4(c) and (d), it can easily be seen that l_{D_c} is almost unaffected by noise (the distances of the size functions of Fig.4(c) and (d) from the size function of Fig.4(a), computed by means of (2), are 0.12 and 0.07 respectively).

An example on real images is shown in Fig.5. Figures 5(a) and (b) show two leaves of the same species. Since the two leaves were rather similar and the viewing camera was nearly orthogonal to the supporting plane, the images of Fig.5(a) and (b), apart from an unknown scaling factor, can be thought of as equivalent, or "nearly equivalent", up to a Euclidean transformation. The equivalence cannot be expected to be perfect due to small differences in the shape of the two leaves and inaccurate camera calibration.

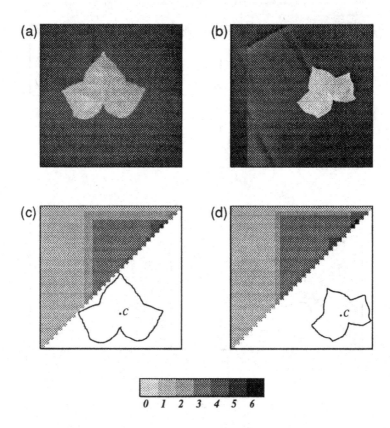

Fig. 5. Euclidean invariance. (a) and (b). Images of two ivy leaves. (c) and (d). The size functions l_{D_c} relative to the contours of the leaves of (a) and (b) respectively. The x and y variables range in the horizontal and vertical axis respectively between D_c^{min} and D_c^{max} with $x \leq y$. Below: the grey value coding of the size functions.

Figures 5(c) and (d) show the size functions computed on the contours of the leaves of Fig.5(a) and (b) and induced by the measuring function D_c. The contours, extracted by means of standard edge detection, contour following, and thresholding techniques, are displayed in the corresponding lower right corners. From Fig.5(c) and (d), it can easily be seen that the representations of the viewed leaves in terms of the size function l_{D_c} are very similar. Correspondingly, the distance between the two size functions, computed by means of (2), is 0.09.

Let us now introduce size functions invariant for a broader class of transformations.

4   Affine Invariance

In the case of planar objects, Euclidean transformations are well suited to describe shape changes in images taken from different viewpoints only if the optical axis of the viewing camera is orthogonal, or nearly orthogonal, to the object plane. When this assumption is violated, but the size of the observed object is small compared to the distance of the viewing camera, different images of the same object can be considered "nearly equivalent" up to an unknown affine transformation.

Let us now describe a measuring function which will be used to produce size functions invariant for affine transformations. The key idea is the affine invariance of the ratio of the lengths of two collinear segments, as illustrated in Fig.6(a). Let r be the line through the center of mass c and a generic point p of the contour of Fig.6(a). Of all the intersections q_i between r and the contour, let q_1 be the furthest from p. The ratio

$$LR(p) = \frac{\overline{pc}}{\overline{pq_1}} \quad ,$$

where $\overline{pc}$ and $\overline{pq_1}$ are the distances between p and c and between p and q_1 respectively, is an affine invariant measure at p. As p varies across the contour, an affine measuring function $LR(p)$ is obtained. For the sake of completeness, the diagram of the measuring function LR, relative to the contour of Fig.6(a), is reproduced in Fig.6(b).

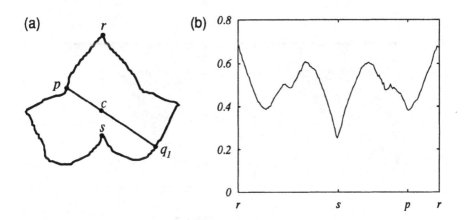

Fig. 6. Affine invariant measuring function. (a). Since c is the center of mass of the contour, the ratio between the distance from p to c and the distance between from p to q_1 is invariant for affine transformation. (b). Diagram of the measuring function LR plotted against the contour points.

The affine invariance of the size function l_{LR}, induced by the measuring function LR, is shown in Fig.7. Figures 7(a) and (b) show the images of two ivy leaves taken from very different viewing angles but at a considerable distance from the supporting table (more than 1 meter).

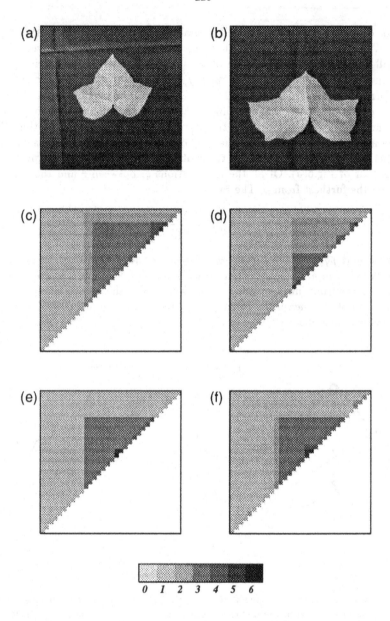

Fig. 7. Affine invariant size function. (a) and (b). Images of two ivy leaves taken from very different viewpoints. (c) and (d). Euclidean invariant size functions l_{D_e} of the contours of the leaves of (a) and (b). (e) and (f). Affine invariant size functions l_{LR} of the same contours. The x and y variables in $(c-f)$ range in the horizontal and vertical axis respectively between the minimum and maximum value of the corresponding measuring function, with $x \leq y$. Below: the grey value coding of the size functions.

The size functions l_{D_c} relative to the contours of the leaves of Fig.7(a) and (b) are reproduced in Fig.7(c) and (d) respectively. It can easily be seen that since the "distance from the center of mass" is Euclidean invariant but not affine invariant, the obtained size functions are very different. Correspondingly, the distance between the size functions of Fig.7(c) and (d), computed by means of (2), is 0.38. Instead, Fig.7(e) and (f) reproduce the diagrams of the size function l_{LR} relative to the leaves of Fig.7(a) and (b) respectively. By a simple inspection of Fig.7(e) and (f), it is evident that the obtained affine invariant descriptions are very similar. Quantitatively, this is confirmed by the fact that the distance between the size functions of Fig.7(e) and (f), estimated with (2), is 0.03.

Size functions can also be usefully employed in the analysis of shapes which contain straight edges. In the following example the same size function l_{LR} was used to decide whether two polygons were equivalent up to an unknown affine transformation. Figures 8(a) and (b) show the size functions l_{LR} of the two quadrilaterals displayed in the corresponding lower right corners. The quadrilateral of Fig.8(b) was obtained by first applying a random affine transformation, and then adding noise to the coordinates of the vertices of the quadrilateral in Fig.8(a). Even in the presence of noise, the affine equivalence between the two quadrilaterals can be concluded from the similarity of the obtained size functions (the distance between the size functions of Fig.8(a) and (b), computed with (2), is 0.02). Conversely, the size functions l_{LR}, shown in Fig.8(c) and (d) and relative to the quadrilaterals displayed in the lower right corners, are very different (the distance between the size functions of Fig.8(c) and (d), computed with (2), is 0.49). This agrees with the fact that there is no affine transformation which can account for the shape changes between the quadrilaterals of Fig.8(c) and (d).

The affine invariance of the size function l_{LR} was obtained by making use of a reference point, the center of mass c of the shape. This is not always the case. For example, let us introduce an affine invariant size function, not based on reference points and well suited for the representation of polygons. This size function can be defined as follows.

First the vertices of the polygonal contour γ are located by checking the local orientation of the lines through adjacent points of the randomly sampled contour. As a result the sampled points which correspond to the vertices are determined. Then, for each point p of the polygonal contour γ, the triangle $p_1 p p_2$ is constructed, with p_1 and p_2 the vertices that immediately precede and follow the point p along the contour in the counterclockwise direction. An affine invariant measure $AR : \gamma \rightarrow \mathbb{R}$ can be defined in p as

$$AR(p) = \frac{area(p_1 p p_2)}{area(\gamma)} \quad,$$

where $area(\gamma)$ is positive by definition and $area(p_1 p p_2)$ is positive if in the triangle $p_1 p p_2$ the points p_1, p, p_2 are ordered clockwise, negative otherwise. Clearly, $AR(p) = 0$ if and only if p is not a vertex of γ. As p varies across the contour, an affine invariant measuring function $AR(p)$ is obtained.

The size functions l_{AR}, for the same polygons of Fig.8, are displayed in Fig.9. Again the affine "similarity" of the two quadrilaterals displayed in the lower right

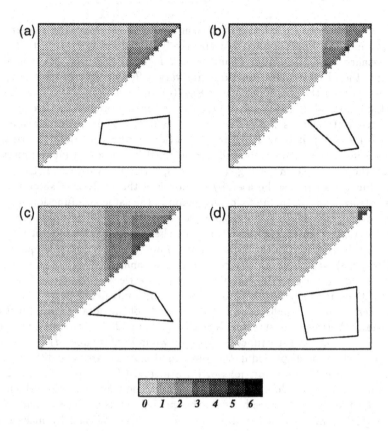

Fig. 8. $(a - d)$. The affine invariant size functions l_{LR} relative to the quadrilaterals displayed in the lower right corners. The x and y variables range in the horizontal and vertical axis respectively between $LR^{\min}$ and $LR^{\max}$ with $x \leq y$. Below: the grey value coding of the size functions.

corners of Fig.9(a) and (b) can be concluded from the similarity of the obtained size functions (the distance between the size functions l_{AR} in Fig.9(a) and (b), computed with (2), is 0.03). Similarly, the fact that the quadrilaterals of Fig.9(c) and (d) are not related by an affine transformation can be inferred from the clear difference between the computed size functions (the distance between the size functions l_{AR} in Fig.9(c) and (d), computed with (2), is 1.35).

In conclusion, it can be thought that the size functions l_{LR} and l_{AR} induce different metrics in the world of polygonal contours. Both metrics, however, agree on the sets of affinely related polygons.

Let us now consider the more general case of projective transformation.

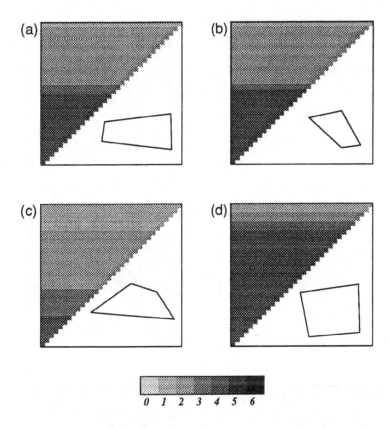

Fig. 9. $(a - d)$. The affine invariant size functions l_{AR} relative to the quadrilaterals displayed in the lower right corners. The x and y variables range in the horizontal and vertical axis respectively between AR^{min} and AR^{max} with $x \le y$. Below: the grey value coding of the size functions.

5 Projective Invariance

In the most general case, shape deformations due to viewpoint changes can only be described by projective transformations. It is not difficult to produce examples in which the affine approximation is definitely inadequate. Figures $10(a)$ and (b) show the affine invariant size functions l_{LR} relative to the shapes displayed in the lower right corners.

The shape of Fig.10(b) was obtained by applying a "strong" projective transformation to the shape of Fig.10(a), which can be thought of as lying on a plane parallel to the image plane. The fact that the affine invariant size function l_{LR} is unable to capture the equivalence between the two shapes can be easily appre-

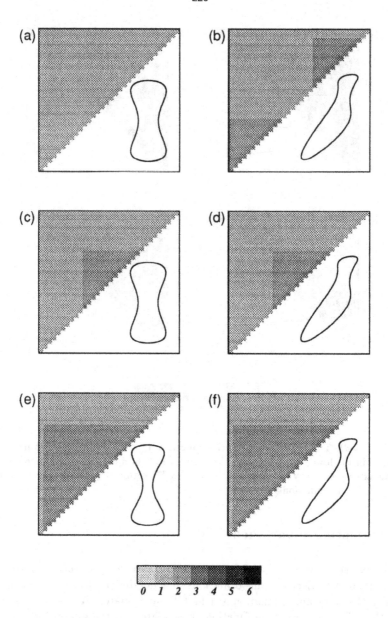

Fig. 10. Projective invariant size function. (a) and (b). Affine invariant size functions l_{LR} relative to the shapes displayed in the lower right corners. The x and y variables range in the horizontal and vertical axis respectively between the l_{LR}^{min} and 0.75, with $x \leq y$. (c) and (d). Projective invariant size function l_{CR} relative to the same shapes of (a) and (b). (e) and (f). Projective invariant size functions l_{CR} relative to the shapes displayed in the lower right corners. The x and y variables in $(c - f)$ range in the horizontal and vertical axis respectively between the minimum and maximum value of the corresponding measuring function, with $x \leq y$. Below: the grey value coding of the size functions.

ciated from the size functions of Fig.10(a) and (b). Actually, the size function of Fig.10(a) is trivial since the measuring function LR is constant.

Instead, if the projective invariant measuring function CR is used, the two almost indistinguishable size functions displayed in Fig.10(c) and (d) can be obtained (the same shapes are again displayed in the lower right corners of Fig.10(c) and (d) for ease of reference). Given the strong perspective deformation between the original and the projectively transformed shape of Fig.10(c) and (d), it is legitimate to ask whether, or not, the remarkable similarity of the obtained size functions is due to a lack of descriptive power of the employed measuring function CR. Before going into the details of the design of the measuring function CR, let us argue, by means of a further example, that this is not the case.

Figures 10(e) and (f) show the size functions l_{CR} relative to the shapes displayed in the lower right corners. The shape of Fig.10(e) is qualitatively similar to the shape of Fig.10(c). Quantitatively, the two shapes differ by the relative width of the narrowing. The size functions reproduced in Fig.10(e) and (f) are almost identical as again the shape of Fig.10(f) was obtained by applying a projective transformation to the shape of Fig.10(e). The qualitative similarity of the shapes of Fig.10(c) and (e) agrees with the qualitative similarity of the corresponding size functions l_{CR}. However, the obtained size functions are quantitatively different as can be appreciated by the fact that their distance, computed by means of (2), is 0.40.

Let us now describe the projective invariant measuring function CR. By using projectively invariant points, or reference points, four collinear points can be associated with each single contour point. This is illustrated in Fig.11(a). First, the four inflections m, n, p, and q of the shape of Fig.11(a) (the same shape of Fig.10(a)) are selected as reference points. Then, the two triplets of projectively invariant collinear points, (m, n, r) and (p, q, r), are determined by intersecting the lines through m and n and through p and q, where r is the point of intersection. Finally, if t is the intersection between the line through s and p, the points m, n, r, and t, are collinear and the number

$$ CR(s) = \left| \frac{(\overline{mr} \cdot \overline{nt})}{(\overline{mt} \cdot \overline{nr})} \right| $$

is a projective invariant measure at s. As s varies across the contour, a projective measuring function CR(s) is obtained. The diagram of the measuring function CR is shown in Fig.11(b). The function CR is considered in the range between 0 and 1.5 in which it was found to yield significant information on the shape contour.

Figures 11(c) and (d) reproduce the geometrical construction and the diagram of the measuring function CR as in Fig.11(a) and (b), but relative to the shape of Fig.11(c) (the same shape of Fig.10(e)). By comparing the diagrams of Fig.11(b) and (d) it can be seen that the measuring function CR is sensitive to the different narrowing of the shapes of Fig.11(a) and (c).

Clearly, the definition of the measuring function CR involves several arbitrary choices. First, the selection and labeling of the reference points. In the

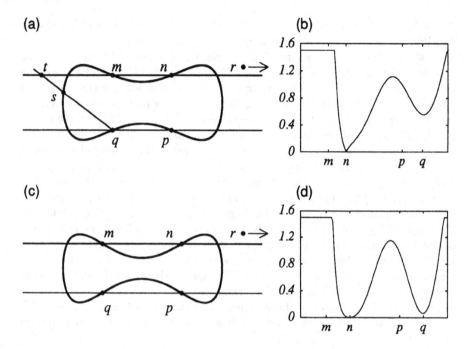

Fig. 11. Projective invariant measuring function. (a). the points m, n, r, and t are collinear. The point r, in this specific view of the planar shape, lies at infinity in the direction of the lines through m and n, and p and q. (b). Diagram of the measuring function CR relative to the contour of (a). (c) and (d). As in (a) and (b) but relative to a slightly different contour.

computation of the size functions of Fig.10, the inflection points were determined by means of numerical differentiation and labeled by hand. Second, the choice of the triplet of projectively invariant collinear points. Third, the choice of the reference point used to determine the fourth collinear point. Fourth, the choice of the cross ratio of the four collinear points. While the last three choices, at least in the analysis of shapes like those of Fig.10, are essentially equivalent and do not lead to qualitatively different results, the choice and labeling of the reference points is crucial. This is illustrated by the following last example, which presents a preliminary result on real images.

The projective invariant size function l_{CR} is used to produce the results shown in Fig.12. Figures 12(a) and (b) display two very different images of the same ivy leaf and Fig.12(c) and (d) the corresponding size functions l_{LR}.

From Fig.12(c) and (d), it is evident that the representation which can be obtained by means of the affine invariant size function l_{LR} is inadequate. This is not surprising since the camera was very close to the viewed scene. Instead, Fig.12(e) and (f) show that the projective invariant size functions l_{CR} are very similar. In this example, the four selected reference points (shown in Fig.12(a)

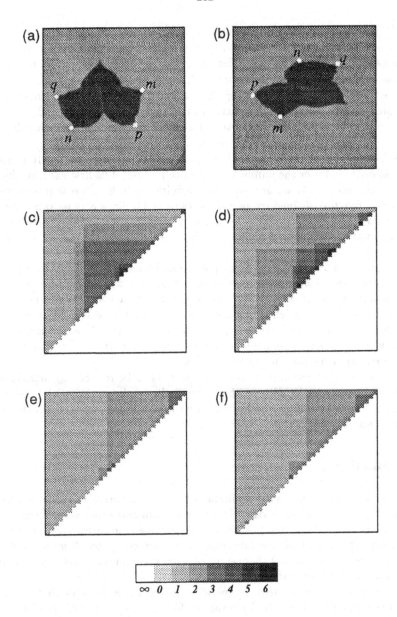

Fig. 12. An example on real images. (a) and (b). Two images of the same ivy leaf taken from very different viewpoints. (c) and (d). Affine invariant size functions l_{LR} relative to the leaf contour in (a) and (b), respectively. (e) and (f). Projective invariant size functions l_{CR} relative to the leaf contour in (a) and (b). The x and y variables in ($c-f$) range in the horizontal and vertical axis respectively between the minimum and maximum value of the corresponding measuring function, with $x \leq y$. Below: the grey value coding of the size functions.

and (*b*)) were cusps of the leaf contour, selected and matched by hand. By inspection, it can easily be seen that the ordering of the reference points along the contours of Fig.10 and Fig.12 is different. Let us now comment on the relevance of these preliminary results on future work.

The diagrams of Fig.10 and Fig.12 indicate that size functions able to encode projectively invariant information can actually be produced. Undoubtedly, however, the proposed size function is based on the use of a large number of reference points, perhaps too large to be of practical use.

Before discussing a couple of research directions that are currently investigated in order to lower the number of reference points, let us first explain why at least 4 reference points are needed in the definition of CR, a "cross ratio based" measuring function defined on single points ($k = 1$). Since a cross ratio can be associated with at least 5 points in general position, a "cross ratio based" measuring function defined on k-tuples of points, needs at least $r = 5 - k$ reference points.

The minimal number of reference points can be reduced by considering measuring functions based on k-tuples of points with $k > 1$. With this strategy, for example, a "cross ratio based" measuring function which makes no use of reference points can be defined on k-tuples of points with $k \geq 5$. Since memory allocation and run time increase at least with N^k, where N is the number of points which sample the shape (typically $100 \leq N \leq 200$), the bound $k \geq 5$, in the current implementation, is not practical.

Alternatively, the number of reference points can be reduced by introducing differential invariants [VMP]. At the moment the implementation of measuring functions based on differential invariants with $k = 2$ and no need of reference points is under study.

6 Conclusion

Size functions are integer valued functions of two real variables which represent metric and topological properties of visual shape. In this paper several size functions invariant for Euclidean, affine, and projective transformations have been presented. The described size functions, which are computed from the outline of planar (or almost planar) shapes, make often use of suitable reference points, like the center of mass, inflections, or cusps.

Experiments on synthetically generated and real images show that the presented size functions are actually invariant for the desired transformations and able to produce representations which can be used to identify similar shapes and distinguish between different shapes. Since size functions are inherently robust against small changes in the apparent shape of the viewed objects, the results presented in this paper indicate that size functions are likely to be very useful for viewpoint invariant representation and recognition of natural shapes.

In conclusion, let us briefly mention the main open problems in the study of invariant size functions. Although some interesting results have been obtained, much work remains to be done especially in the case of affine and projective transformations. First, the stability of the proposed size functions against inaccurate localization of the reference points and the use of more robust reference points have to be explored. Second, methods for the definition of invariant size functions which are not based on the reference points must be thoroughly investigated. Since these methods are bound to be based on the design of measuring functions defined on k-tuples of points with $k > 1$, the problem of computing efficiently a size function for relatively high values of k must also be addressed.

We are grateful to Giulia Piccioli, Pietro Parodi, Enrico De Micheli, and Theo Moons for useful discussions. The images from which the contours of Fig.3 were extracted are due to the courtesy of Lawrence Chachere. The quadrilaterals of Figs.8 and 9 were kindly provided by Johan Wagemans. Laura Giovanelli checked the English.

References

[Ca]   Carlsson, S.: Projectively invariant decomposition and recognition of planar shapes. Proc. of the 4th Int. Conf. Comput. Vision. Berlin, Germany, (1993) 471-475.

[FMZ]   Forsyth, D.A., Mundy, J.L., Zisserman, A., Coelho, C., Heller, A., Rothwell, C.A.: Invariant descriptors for 3D object recognition and pose. PAMI-13 10 (1991) 971-991.

[Fr1]   Frosini, P.: A distance for similarity classes of submanifolds of a Euclidean space. Bull. Austral. Math. Soc. 42 (1990) 407-416.

[Fr2]   Frosini, P.: Discrete computation of size functions. Journal of Combinatorics, Information and System Sciences, in press (1993)

[Fr3]   Frosini, P.: Metric homotopies. Submitted for publication (1994).

[RFZ]   Rothwell, C.A., Forsyth, D.A., Zisserman, A., Mundy, J.L.: Extracting projective structure from single perspective views of 3D point sets. Proc. of the 4th Int. Conf. Comput. Vision. Berlin, Germany, (1993) 573-582.

[UV1]   Uras, C., Verri, A.: Studying shape through size functions. In: O, Y., Toet, A., Foster, D., Heijmans, H., Meer, P. (eds.), Shape in Picture, NATO ASI Series F Vol. 126, Springer-Verlag, Berlin Heidelberg, (1994) pp. 81-90.

[UV2]   Uras, C., Verri, A.: On the recognition of the alphabet of the sign language through Size Functions. Submitted for publication (1994).

[VMP]   Van Gol, L.J., Moons, T., Pauwels, E.J., Oosterlinck, A.: Semi-differential invariants. In: Mundy, J., Zisserman, A. (eds.), Geometric Invariants in Computer Vision, MIT Press, Cambridge, Massachusetts, (1992) pp. 193-214.

[VUF]   Verri, A., Uras, C., Frosini, P., Ferri, M.: On the use of size functions for shape analysis. Biol. Cybern. 70 (1993) 99-107.

Recovery

Euclidean Reconstruction from Uncalibrated Views *

Richard I. Hartley

G.E. CRD, Schenectady, NY, 12301.
Email : hartley@crd.ge.com

Abstract. The possibility of calibrating a camera from image data alone, based on matched points identified in a series of images by a moving camera was suggested by Mayband and Faugeras. This result implies the possibility of Euclidean reconstruction from a series of images with a moving camera, or equivalently, Euclidean structure-from-motion from an uncalibrated camera. No tractable algorithm for implementing their methods for more than three images have been previously reported. This paper gives a practical algorithm for Euclidean reconstruction from several views with the same camera. The algorithm is demonstrated on synthetic and real data and is shown to behave very robustly in the presence of noise giving excellent calibration and reconstruction results.

1 Introduction

The possibility of calibrating a camera based on the identification of matching points in several views of a scene taken by the same camera has been shown by Maybank and Faugeras ([13, 4]). Using techniques of Projective Geometry they showed that each pair of views of the scene can be used to provide two quadratic equations in the five unknown parameters of the camera. A method of solving these equations to obtain the camera calibration has been reported in [13, 4, 12] based on directly solving these quadratic equations using continuation. It has been reported however that this method requires extreme accuracy of computation, and seems not to be suitable for routine use. In addition with large numbers of cameras (more than three or four) this method threatens to be unworkable.

In this paper a method is given based partly on the well known Levenberg-Marquardt (LM) parameter estimation algorithm, partly on new non-iterative algorithms and partly on techniques of Projective Geometry for solving this self-calibration problem. This algorithm has the advantage of being applicable to large numbers of views, and in fact performs best when many views are given. As a consequence, the algorithm can be applied to the structure-from-motion problem to determine the structure of a scene from a sequence of views with the same uncalibrated camera. Indeed, since the calibration of the camera may be

---

* The research described in this paper has been supported by DARPA Contract #MDA972-91-C-0053

determined from the correspondence data, it is possible to compute a Euclidean reconstruction of the scene. That is, the scene is reconstructed, relative to the placement of one of the cameras used as reference, up to an unknown scaling.

The algorithm is demonstrated on real and synthetic data and is shown to perform robustly in the presence of noise.

2   The Camera Model

A commonly used model for perspective cameras is that of projective mapping from 3D projective space, $\mathcal{P}^3$, to 2D projective space, $\mathcal{P}^2$. This map may be represented by a 3×4 matrix, M of rank 3. The mapping from $\mathcal{P}^3$ to $\mathcal{P}^2$ takes the point $\mathbf{x} = (x, y, z, 1)^\top$ to $\mathbf{u} = M\mathbf{x}$ in homogeneous coordinates.

The matrix M may be decomposed as $M = K(R| - Rt)$, where $\mathbf{t}$ represents the location of the camera, R is a rotation matrix representing the orientation of the camera with respect to an absolute coordinate frame, and K is an upper triangular matrix called the *calibration matrix* of the camera. Given a matrix M it is a very simple matter to obtain this decomposition, using the QR-decomposition of matrices.

The entries of the matrix K may be identified with certain physically meaningful quantities known as internal camera parameters. Indeed, K may be written as

$$K = \begin{pmatrix} k_u & s & p_u \\ 0 & k_v & p_v \\ 0 & 0 & 1 \end{pmatrix} \tag{1}$$

where

- k_u is the magnification in the u coordinate direction
- k_v is the magnification in the v coordinate direction
- p_u and p_v are the coordinates of the principal point
- s is a skew parameter corresponding to a skewing of the coordinate axes.

Note that K is non-singular. This follows from the requirement that M should have rank 3.

3   The Euclidean Reconstruction Problem

The reconstruction problem to be solved in this paper will now be described. Consider a situation in which a set of 3D points $\mathbf{x}_j$ are viewed by a set of N cameras with matrices M_i numbered from 0 to $N - 1$. Denote by $\mathbf{u}_j^i$ the coordinates of the j-th point as seen by the i-th camera. Given the set of coordinates $\mathbf{u}_j^i$ it is required to find the set of camera matrices, M_i and the points $\mathbf{x}_j$. This is the reconstruction problem. A *reconstruction* based on a set of image correspondences $\{\mathbf{u}_j^i\}$ consists of a set of camera matrices M_i and points $\mathbf{x}_j$ such that $M_i\mathbf{x}_j \approx \mathbf{u}_j^i$. (The notation $\approx$ denotes equality up to a non-zero scale factor.) For compactness we denote the reconstruction by the pair ($\{M_i\}, \{\mathbf{x}_j\}$). Without further restriction on the M_i or $\mathbf{x}_j$, such a reconstruction is called a projective reconstruction, because the points $\mathbf{x}_j$ may differ by an arbitrary 3D projective transformation from the *true* reconstruction ([3, 5]). A reconstruction that is known to differ from the true reconstruction by at most a 3D affine transformation is called an affine reconstruction, and one that differs by a Euclidean transformation from the true reconstruction is called a Euclidean reconstruction. The term Euclidean transformation will be used in this paper to mean a similarity transform, namely the composition of a rotation, a translation and a uniform scaling.

According to the result of Maybank and Faugeras ([13]) if all the cameras have the same calibration then the calibration matrix K may be determined, and is at least locally unique. (Whether this is true for exactly three views was left somewhat ambiguous in [13] but was clarified by Luong ([12])). Consequently, we assume in this paper that all cameras have the same calibration, so that $M_i = K(R_i \mid -R_i\mathbf{t}_i)$, where each R_i is a rotation matrix and K is an upper-triangular matrix, the common calibration matrix of all the cameras. We attempt to retrieve M_i and $\mathbf{x}_j$ from a set of image correspondences $\mathbf{u}_j^i$. The points $\mathbf{x}_j$ and the camera matrices, M_i can not be determined absolutely. Instead it is required to determine them up to a Euclidean transformation. In order to constrain the solution, it may be assumed that $R_0 = I$ and $\mathbf{t}_0 = 0$. The solution may then be determined up to scaling.

Because of Maybank and Faugeras's result, with more than three views any reconstruction for which all the camera matrices M_i have the same calibration is virtually assured of being the true reconstruction, or at least differing by at most a Euclidean transformation – it is a Euclidean reconstruction.

This paper, therefore gives an algorithm for computing a Euclidean reconstruction of a scene based only on image correspondence data from uncalibrated cameras. An alternative method for Euclidean reconstruction that uses extra Euclidean constraints is reported in [2].

4 Levenberg Marquardt Minimization

The Levenberg-Marquardt (LM) algorithm is a well known algorithm for parameter estimation ([15]). However, since it is such an important ingredient of our reconstruction method, it is described here in detail.

4.1 Newton Iteration

Given a hypothesized functional relation $\mathbf{y} = f(\mathbf{x})$ where $\mathbf{x}$ and $\mathbf{y}$ are vectors in some Euclidean spaces R^m and R^n, and a measured value $\hat{\mathbf{y}}$ for $\mathbf{y}$, we wish to find the vector $\hat{\mathbf{x}}$ that most nearly satisfies this functional relation. More precisely, we seek the vector $\hat{\mathbf{x}}$ satisfying $\hat{\mathbf{y}} = f(\hat{\mathbf{x}}) + \hat{\epsilon}$ for which $||\hat{\epsilon}||$ is minimized. The method of Newton iteration starts with an initial estimated value $\mathbf{x}_0$, and proceeds to refine the estimate under the assumption that the function f is locally linear. Let $\hat{\mathbf{y}} = f(\mathbf{x}_0) + \epsilon_0$. We assume that the function f is approximated at $\mathbf{x}_0$

by $f(\mathbf{x}_0 + \Delta) = f(\mathbf{x}_0) + J\Delta$, where J is the linear mapping represented by the Jacobian matrix $J = \partial \mathbf{y}/\partial \mathbf{x}$. Setting $\mathbf{x}_1 = \mathbf{x}_0 + \Delta$ leads to $\hat{\mathbf{y}} - f(\mathbf{x}_1) = \hat{\mathbf{y}} - f(\mathbf{x}_0) - J\Delta = \epsilon_0 - J\Delta$. It is required to minimize $\|\epsilon_0 - J\Delta\|$. Solving for Δ is a linear minimization problem that can be solved by the method of normal equations. The minimium occurs when $J\Delta - \epsilon_0$ is perpendicular to the row space of J, which leads to the so-called *normal equations* $J^\top(J\Delta - \epsilon_0) = 0$ or $J^\top J\Delta = J^\top \epsilon_0$. Thus, the solution is obtained by starting with an estimate $\mathbf{x}_0$ and computing successive approximations according to the formula

$$\mathbf{x}_{i+1} = \mathbf{x}_i + \Delta_i$$

where Δ_i is the solution to the normal equations

$$J^\top J \Delta_i = J^\top \epsilon_i \ .$$

Matrix J is the Jacobian $\partial \mathbf{y}/\partial \mathbf{x}$ evaluated at $\mathbf{x}_i$ and $\epsilon_i = \hat{\mathbf{y}} - f(\mathbf{x}_i)$ One hopes that this algorithm will converge to the required least-squares solution $\hat{\mathbf{x}}$. Unfortunately, it is possible that this iteration procedure converges to a local minimum value, or does not converge at all. The behaviour of the iteration algorithm depends very strongly on the initial estimate $\mathbf{x}_0$.

4.2 Levenberg-Marquardt Iteration

The Levenberg-Marquardt (abbreviated LM) iteration method is a slight variation on the Newton iteration method. The normal equations $N\Delta = J^\top J\Delta = J^\top \epsilon$ are replaced by the *augmented normal equations* $N'\Delta = J^\top \epsilon$, where $N'_{ii} = (1 + \lambda)N_{ii}$ and $N'_{ij} = N_{ij}$ for $i \neq j$. The value λ is initially set to some value, typically $\lambda = 10^{-3}$. If the value of Δ obtained by solving the augmented normal equations leads to a reduction in the error, then the increment is accepted and λ is divided by 10 before the next iteration. On the other hand if the value Δ leads to an increased error, then λ is multiplied by 10 and the augmented normal equations are solved again, this process continuing until a value of Δ is found that gives rise to a decreased error. This process of repeatedly solving the augmented normal equations for different values of λ until an acceptable Δ is found constitutes one iteration of the LM algorithm.

4.3 Implementation

Based on the implementation of the LM algorithm in [15] I have coded a general minimization routine. To use this algorithm in the simplest form it is necessary only to provide a routine to compute the function being minimized, a goal vector $\hat{\mathbf{y}}$ of observed or desired values of the function and an initial estimate $\mathbf{x}_0$. If desired, it is possible to provide a function to compute the Jacobian matrix J. If a null function is specified, then the differentiation is done numerically. Numerical differentiation is carried out as follows. Each independent variable x_i is incremented in turn to $x_i + \delta$, the resulting function value is computed using the routine provided for computing f and the derivative is computed as a ratio.

The value δ is set to the maximum of $|10^{-4} * x_i|$ and 10^{-6}. This choice seemingly gives a good approximation to the derivative. In practice, I have seen almost no disadvantage in using numerical differentiation, though for simple functions f I prefer to provide a routine to compute J, partly for aesthetic reasons, partly because of a possible slightly improved convergence and partly for speed.

As an alternative to all the dependent variables being equally weighted, it is possible to provide a weight matrix specifying the weights of the dependent variables $\mathbf{y}$. This weight matrix may be diagonal specifying independent weights for each of the y_i, or else it may be symmetric, equal to the inverse of the covariance matrix of the variables y_i. If C is the covariance matrix of $\mathbf{y}$, then the normal equations become $J^\top C^{-1} J \Delta_i = J^\top C^{-1} \epsilon_i$.

4.4 Sparse Methods in LM Scene Reconstruction

In pose estimation and scene reconstruction problems involving several cameras the LM algorithm is appropriately used to find a least-squares solution. In cases where the camera parameters and the 3D locations of the points are to be found simultaneously the Jacobian matrix, J has a special block structure. This block structure gives rise to a sparse block structure of the normal equations. It is possible to take advantage of this to achieve an enormous simplification in the solution of the normal equations. This method is described in [17] but is presented here for the convenience of the reader.

In the case of scene reconstruction, the variable parameters fall into two classes, namely the camera parameters and the coordinates of the points $\mathbf{x}_j$. Altering the coordinates of a point $\mathbf{x}_j$ will cause a change in the coordinates of each point $\mathbf{u}_j^i$ with the same index j as the point. Similarly, altering the parameters of a camera M_i will lead to a change in the points $\mathbf{u}_j^i$ with the same index i as the camera. Consequently, the matrix J of partial derivatives of the dependent parameters with respect to the independent parameters has a particular sparse structure as shown in the following diagram.

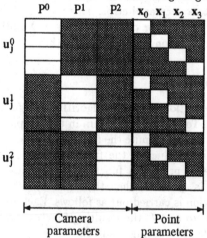

Camera parameters   Point parameters

The diagram shows the case for three camera and four points, but the general scheme is easily extended to any number of points and cameras. In the case where certain of the parameters are set to fixed values (for instance, the camera M_0 may be fixed to the value $(I \mid 0)$) then the corresponding columns are missing from the matrix. In addition, in the cases where some points are not visible in some views, then the corresponding rows are missing from the matrix. This all makes very little difference to the following discussion.

Because of the structure of the matrix J, the normal equations $J^T J \Delta = J^T \epsilon$ has a special block structure as follows:

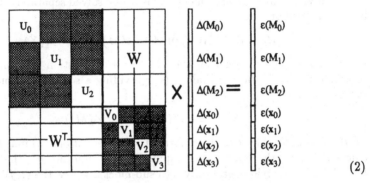

$$(2)$$

It is possible to give specific formulae for each of the blocks in the normal equations. Specifically, let $D(\mathbf{u}_j^i, M_i)$ represent the matrix of partial derivatives of the coordinates of the image point $\mathbf{u}_j^i$ with respect to the parameters of the matrix M_i. Similarly, let $D(\mathbf{u}_j^i, \mathbf{x}_j)$ be the matrix of partial derivatives of the coordinates of $\mathbf{u}_j^i$ with respect to the coordinates of the point $\mathbf{x}_j$. Further, write $\epsilon(\mathbf{u}_j^i)$ to represent the current residual error in the point $\mathbf{u}_j^i$ Then, we may write

$$U_i = \sum_j D(\mathbf{u}_j^i, M_i)^T D(\mathbf{u}_j^i, M_i)$$

$$V_j = \sum_i D(\mathbf{u}_j^i, \mathbf{x}_j)^T D(\mathbf{u}_j^i, \mathbf{x}_j)$$

$$W_{ij} = D(\mathbf{u}_j^i, M_i)^T D(\mathbf{u}_j^i, \mathbf{x}_j) \tag{3}$$

$$\epsilon(M_i) = \sum_j D(\mathbf{u}_j^i, M_i)^T \epsilon(\mathbf{u}_j^i)$$

$$\epsilon(\mathbf{x}_j) = \sum_i D(\mathbf{u}_j^i, \mathbf{x}_j)^T \epsilon(\mathbf{u}_j^i)$$

The normal equations (2) may be written in the form

$$\begin{pmatrix} U & W \\ W^T & V \end{pmatrix} \begin{pmatrix} \Delta(M) \\ \Delta(X) \end{pmatrix} = \begin{pmatrix} \epsilon(M) \\ \epsilon(X) \end{pmatrix}$$

where each of the matrices U, V and the vectors $\Delta(M)$, $\Delta(X)$, $\epsilon(M)$ and $\epsilon(X)$ is itself made up of subblocks.

We assume that V is invertible, and multiply each side of the normal equations on the left by the matrix

$$\begin{pmatrix} I & -WV^{-1} \\ 0 & I \end{pmatrix}$$

The resulting set of equations

$$\begin{pmatrix} U - WV^{-1}W^\mathsf{T} & 0 \\ W^\mathsf{T} & V \end{pmatrix} \begin{pmatrix} \Delta(M) \\ \Delta(X) \end{pmatrix} = \begin{pmatrix} \epsilon(M) - WV^{-1}\epsilon(X) \\ \epsilon(X) \end{pmatrix} \tag{4}$$

may be divided into two sets of equations, to be solved separately. From the top half of (4), one obtains

$$(U - WV^{-1}W^\mathsf{T})\Delta(M) = \epsilon(M) - WV^{-1}\epsilon(X) \tag{5}$$

which may be solved to get $\Delta(M)$. The resulting solution may then be substituted back into the bottom half of (4) providing a set of equations $V\Delta(X) = \epsilon(X) - W^\mathsf{T}\Delta(M)$, or

$$\Delta(X) = V^{-1}(\epsilon(X) - W^\mathsf{T}\Delta(M)) . \tag{6}$$

Because of the block-diagonal form of V, the equations (5) may be computed efficiently using the quantities computed in (3). Specifically, the matrix $A = U - WV^{-1}W^\mathsf{T}$ divides naturally into sub-blocks, where the (i, j)-th sub-block is the matrix

$$A_{ij} = \delta_{ij} U_i - \sum_k W_{ik} V_k^{-1} W_{jk}{}^\mathsf{T} \tag{7}$$

The vector $\mathbf{b} = \epsilon(M) - WV^{-1}\epsilon(X)$ also divides into blocks of the form

$$\mathbf{b}_i = \epsilon(M_i) - \sum_j W_{ij} V_j^{-1} \epsilon(\mathbf{x}_j) \tag{8}$$

Matrix A and the vector $\mathbf{b}$ may be computed directly, without needing to compute and store either the matrix J, or the the normal equations (2). The amount of computation required is linear in the number of points $\mathbf{x}_j$ involved, and also linear in the total number of observed points $\mathbf{u}_j^i$.

Similarly, the back-substitution given by (9) may be done block-by-block as follows :

$$\Delta(\mathbf{x}_j) = V_j^{-1}(\epsilon(\mathbf{x}_j) - \sum_i W_{ij}{}^\mathsf{T} \Delta(M_i)) \tag{9}$$

The back substitution also requires computation time linear in the number of points involved.

The above algorithm was described for the case of Newton iteration. It is easy to see how to extend this to LM iteration. One needs simply to augment the matrix $J^\mathsf{T} J$, which comes down to augmenting the matrices U_i and V_j in Fig 2. Augmenting the matrices V_j will help to ensure that they are invertible, even in degenerate cases where V_j is singular. This effect of augmenting the normal equations is the reason that it is not essential to avoid over-parametrization of the minimization problem.

This method is easily extended in many ways :

1. To allow different weightings to errors in the different measured image points $\mathbf{u}_j^i$.
2. To allow estimated values (with confidence weightings) to be provided for individual camera or point parameters.
3. To allow for relations to be specified between the parameters of different cameras, such as specifying that two cameras have the same focal length, or that a set of cameras all lie in a straight line.

Using these sparse methods, it is possible to solve systems where there are thousands of point correspondences. In fact, I have solved in reasonable time systems in which more than 5000 point correspondences were given. If such a system were solved using the complete normal equations, then the dimension of the system of normal equations would be greater than 15000×15000, and solving it using usual methods (for instance Gaussian elimination) would be out of the question.

5 Reconstruction by Direct Levenberg-Marquardt Iteration

A direct approach to the Euclidean reconstruction problem is to solve directly for the unknown camera matrices, $M_i = K(R_i \mid -R_i t_i)$ and points $\mathbf{x}_j$. In particular, we search for M_i of the required form, and $\mathbf{x}_j$ such that $\hat{\mathbf{u}}_j^i = M_i \mathbf{x}_j$ and such that the squared error sum

$$\sum_{i,j} d(\hat{\mathbf{u}}_j^i, \mathbf{u}_j^i)^2$$

is minimized, where $d(*, *)$ represents Euclidean distance. Using this minimization criterion relies on an assumption that measurement errors are caused by errors in measurement of the pixel locations of the $\mathbf{u}_j^i$, and that these errors are independent and gaussian. This problem may be formulated in the form $\mathbf{y} = f(\mathbf{x})$, where the independent variables $\mathbf{x}$ comprise the 3D coordinates of each of the points $\mathbf{x}$ in space, the rotations R_i of each of the cameras and the common calibration matrix K. The dependent variables $\mathbf{y}$ comprise the image coordinates $\mathbf{u}_j^i$.

There are various methods of parametrizing the rotations. Horn ([8, 9]) uses quaternions to do this. I prefer to parametrize rotations using Eulerian angles. This has the advantage that a rotation is parametrized by the minimum of three parameters, instead of four using quaternions. To avoid problems of singularities in the representation of rotations by Eulerian angles, rotations are parametrized as incremental rotations with respect to the present "base rotation". Thus, each R_i is represented as a product $R_i = X_i \Delta(\theta_i, \phi_i, \kappa_i)$, where $\Delta(\theta_i, \phi_i, \kappa_i)$ is the rotation represented by Eulerian angles θ_i, ϕ_i and κ_i. Initially, X_i is set to the initial estimate of the rotation, and θ_i, ϕ_i and κ_i are all set to zero (and hence Δ is the identity mapping). At the end of each LM iteration X_i is set to the product $X_i \Delta(\theta_i, \phi_i, \kappa_i)$, and θ_i, ϕ_i and κ_i are reset to zero.

Such an approach to Euclidean scene reconstruction will work perfectly well, *provided the initial estimate is sufficiently close.* With arbitrary or random guesses at initial values of the parameters it usually fails dismally. The problem as posed is similar to the relative placement problem. This problem was given a robust solution by Horn ([8, 9]) In fact the algorithm given in [8] amounts essentially to Newton iteration by solving the normal equations, using the method of back-substitution mentioned in Section 4.4, and parametrizing rotations as quaternions. Horn avoids the need for an informed initial guess by iterating from each of a number of equally spaced or random rotations and selecting the best solution. The problem considered by Horn differs from the problem considered here in that we are considering uncalibrated cameras, and we wish to be able to solve for a large number of cameras at once. Thus, there is an unknown calibration matrix that must be estimated. Furthermore, instead of one rotation, we have several. With more than a small number of cameras the idea of sampling the rotation space is unworkable.

In short, direct iteration may be used to refine a solution found by other techniques, but can not be used on its own.

6   Projective Reconstruction

Instead of attempting a direct reconstruction, calibration and pose estimation as in the previous section, we use a two-step approach. In the first step, a projective reconstruction of the scene is computed, dropping the assumption that the images are all taken with the same camera. The scene configuration obtained in this manner will differ from the true configuration by a 3D projective transformation. In the second step, this projective transform is estimated. The advantage of proceeding in this manner is that projective reconstruction is relatively straightforward. Then step two, the estimation of the correct 3D transformation, comes down to solving an 8-parameter estimation problem, which is far more tractable than the original problem. Nevertheless, the estimation of the 3D transformation is itself carried out in several sub-steps.

For the present, we drop the assumption that all the cameras have the same calibration. The basic fact about projective reconstruction is the theorem ([3, 5]) that any two reconstructions of a scene from a set of (sufficiently many) image correspondences in images taken with uncalibrated cameras differ by a 3D projective transformation. In particular a solution in which all the cameras have the same calibration must differ by a projective transformation from any other solution in which the cameras are possibly different.

Various methods of projective reconstruction from two or more views have been given previously ([3, 5, 14]). The method given in [5] is a straight-forward non-iterative construction method from two views. Where high precision is required, it should be followed by iterative refinement. Mohr et. al. ([14]) have reported a direct LM approach to projective reconstruction. However, with my recoding of their algorithm I have been unable to obtain reliable convergence in all cases. Therefore, I shall describe a different (although similar) approach, also based on LM iteration.

As usual, we assume that errors in the data are manifested as errors in measurement of the pixel locations of the $\mathbf{u}_j^i$, and that these errors are independent and gaussian. As with Euclidean reconstruction, the problem is to find the camera matrices, M_i and points $\mathbf{x}_j$ such that $\hat{\mathbf{u}}_j^i = M_i \mathbf{x}_j$ and such that the squared error sum

$$\sum_{i,j} d(\hat{\mathbf{u}}_j^i, \mathbf{u}_j^i)^2$$

is minimized. Without loss of generality (and without changing the value of the error expression) it may be assumed that the first camera has matrix $M_0 = (I \mid 0)$. This least-squares minimization problem is different from the one described in Section 5. The problem is formulated in the form $\mathbf{y} = f(\mathbf{x})$ where the set of independent variables $\mathbf{x}$ comprise the 3D coordinates of all the points in space and the entries of the camera matrices M_i for $i > 0$. The dependent variables $\mathbf{y}$ are the image coordinates.

The main difference between my algorithm and that of Mohr et. al. is that whereas they fix the locations of five points in space, I fix the location and the orientation of one of the cameras. In particular, I set $M_0 = (I \mid 0)$. In the algorithm of Mohr et. al. a check is necessary to make sure that the five points chosen are not in fact coplanar. Such a check is not necessary in my algorithm. Setting $M_0 = (I \mid 0)$ still leaves three degrees of freedom. The LM method easily handles systems with redundant parameters, however, so this is not a problem. If desired, however, it is possible to constrain the solution completely by specifying three arbitrary points to lie on the plane at infinity. In doing this it is necessary to check that the points are not collinear, or coplanar with the camera centre of M_0, which may be done easily be choosing three points that do not map to collinear points in the image corresponding to M_0.

This method will not converge, however, if a good initial estimate is not known. Fortunately, there exist linear methods for computing an initial reconstruction. The strategy is as follows. We use two of the views to compute a projective reconstruction of those points seen in the two images. The locations of these points and their images in the other views are used to solve one by one for the positions of the other cameras (in the arbitrary projective frame of the initial reconstruction). The 3D locations of additional points may be computed as soon as the camera parameters are known for two cameras in which these points are visible.

In particular, let F be the fundamental matrix for a pair of cameras. If F factors as a product $F = [\mathbf{p}']_\times M$, then the matrices $(I \mid 0)$ and $(M|\mathbf{p}')$ are one choice of a pair of camera matrices for the two cameras. Let $\mathbf{u} \leftrightarrow \mathbf{u}'$ be a pair of matched points in the two images, then it may be shown ([7]) that the point $M\mathbf{u}$ lies on the epipolar line $\mathbf{u}' \times \mathbf{p}'$ in the second image ($\mathbf{p}'$ is the epipole). If in particular $M\mathbf{u} = \beta\mathbf{u}' - \alpha\mathbf{p}'$ then the corresponding object space point $\mathbf{x}$ is $\begin{pmatrix} \mathbf{u} \\ \alpha \end{pmatrix}$. It is easily verified that this point maps onto $\mathbf{u}$ and $\mathbf{u}'$ in the two images.

Using this method we may reconstruct the points seen in these two images. This initial reconstruction from two views may be refined by LM iteration if required. In fact this is done in our implementation.

Given this initial reconstruction of a subset of the points visible in the first two images, it is now possible to compute directly the camera matrix for any other cameras in which at least six of these points are visible. This is done using the direct linear transformation (DLT) method as described by Sutherland ([19]). The order in which the camera matrices are computed is done so as to maximize the number of already reconstructed points seen by each camera in turn.

After all the camera matrices and 3D point locations have been computed in this way, the LM camera modelling program is run to refine the camera matrices and the point locations as already described.

7 Converting Projective to Euclidean Reconstruction

Once we have a projective reconstruction of the imaging geometry any other reconstruction (including a desired Euclidean reconstruction) may be obtained by applying a 3D projective transformation. In particular, if $(\{M_i\}, \{x_j\})$ is a projective reconstruction, then any other reconstruction is of the form $(\{M_i H^{-1}\}, \{Hx_j\})$ where H is a 4×4 non-singular matrix. We seek such a matrix H such that the transformed camera matrices $M_i H^{-1}$ all have the same (yet to be determined) calibration matrix, K. In other words, we seek H such that $M_i H^{-1} = K(R_i \mid -R_i t_i)$ for all i, where each R_i is a rotation matrix and K is the common upper-triangular calibration matrix.

Without loss of generality, we may make the additional restriction that the zeroeth camera remains located at the origin and that R_0 is the identity. Since in the original projective reconstruction $M_0 = (I \mid 0)$, it follows that H^{-1} may be assumed to have the restricted form

$$H^{-1} = \begin{pmatrix} K & \mathbf{0} \\ \mathbf{v}^\mathsf{T} & \alpha \end{pmatrix} .$$

Since the constant α represents scaling in 3-space, we may further assume that $\alpha = 1$. Equivalently, since K is non-singular, we may (and shall) rather assume that H^{-1} has the form

$$H^{-1} = \begin{pmatrix} K & 0 \\ -\mathbf{v}^\mathsf{T} K & 1 \end{pmatrix} = \begin{pmatrix} I & 0 \\ -\mathbf{v}^\mathsf{T} & 1 \end{pmatrix} \begin{pmatrix} K & 0 \\ 0 & 1 \end{pmatrix} \tag{10}$$

Now, writing each $M_i = (A_i \mid -A_i t_i)$ and multiplying out leads to a requirement that

$$A_i(I + t_i \mathbf{v}^\mathsf{T})K \approx KR_i \tag{11}$$

for some rotation matrix R_i. Our goal is to find K and $\mathbf{v}$ to satisfy this set of conditions. Recall that K is upper triangular, and we may further assume that K_{33} equals 1, hence K contains five unknown entries. The vector $\mathbf{v}$ has a further three unknown entries. In total, it is required to estimate these eight unknown parameters.

Of course, for inexact data, the equations (11) will not be satisfied exactly, and so we will cast this problem as a least-squares minimization problem that may be solved using LM. In particular, given values for K and $\mathbf{v}$, we compute the expression $A_i(I + \mathbf{t}_i\mathbf{v}^\mathsf{T})K$ for each i (remembering that A_i and $\mathbf{t}_i$ are known). Taking the QR decomposition of this matrix, we obtain upper-triangular matrices K_i' such that

$$A_i(I + \mathbf{t}_i\mathbf{v}^\mathsf{T})K = K_i'R_i \ . \tag{12}$$

Subsequently, we compute the matrices $X_i = K^{-1}K_i'$ for all i. Since we have assumed that $M_0 = (A_0 \mid -A_i\mathbf{t}_i) = (I \mid 0)$, it follows that $X_0 = I$. Furthermore, if K and $\mathbf{v}$ satisfy the desired condition (11) then $K_i' \approx K$ for all $i > 0$, and so $X_i \approx I$. Accordingly, we seek to minimize the extent by which X_i differs from the identity matrix. Consequently, we multiply each X_i by a normalizing factor α_i chosen so that the sum of squares of diagonal entries of $\alpha_i X_i$ equals 3, and so that $\det \alpha_i X_i > 0$. Now, we seek K and $\mathbf{v}$ to minimize the expression

$$\sum_{i>0} \|\alpha_i X_i - I\|^2 \tag{13}$$

Note that each $\alpha_i X_i - I$ is an upper-triangular matrix. This minimization problem fits the general form of LM estimation of a fuction $f : R^8 \mapsto R^{6(N-1)}$ where N is the total number of cameras. The function f maps the eight [2] variable entries of K and $\mathbf{v}$ to the diagonal and above-diagonal entries of $\alpha_i X_i - I$ for $i > 0$. Since this minimization problem involves the estimation of 8 parameters only, it is obviously a great improvement over the original problem as stated in Section 3 that required the simultaneous estimation of the matrix K, the $N-1$ rotation matrices R_i for $i > 0$ and the 3D point coordinates of all points $\mathbf{x}_j$.

It turns out still to be impractical to solve this minimization problem without a good initial guess at K and $\mathbf{v}$. It is possible to take a good prior guess at K if some knowledge of the camera is available. On the other hand, it is difficult to guess the vector $\mathbf{v}$, so it will be necessary to find some way to obtain an initial estimate for $\mathbf{v}$. It will turn out that if $\mathbf{v}$ is known, then the calibration matrix K can be computed by a straight-forward non-iterative algorithm, so there is no need to guess K.

8 Euclidean From Affine Reconstruction

With H^{-1} of the form (10) matrix H may be written as

$$H = \begin{pmatrix} K^{-1} & 0 \\ 0 & 1 \end{pmatrix} \begin{pmatrix} I & 0 \\ \mathbf{v}^\mathsf{T} & 1 \end{pmatrix} \ .$$

The right-hand one of these two matrices represents a transformation that moves the plane at infinity, whereas the second one is an affine transformation,

---

[2] It is possible to assume certain restrictions on the entries of K, such as that skew is zero and that the pixels are square, thereby diminishing the number of variable parameters

not moving the plane at infinity. In fact, if $\mathbf{x}$ is a point being mapped to infinity by the transformation H, then $(\mathbf{v}^\top 1)\mathbf{x} = 0$. So $(\mathbf{v}^\top 1)$ represents the plane that is mapped to the plane at infinity by H.

We will now suppose that by some magic we have been able to determine $\mathbf{v}$. This means, in effect that we know the position of the plane at infinity in the reconstruction. Otherwise stated, we have been able to determine the structure up to an affine transformation. We will now present a simple non-iterative algorithm for the determination of K, and hence of the Euclidean structure.

Equation (11) may be written as $B_i K = K R_i$ where $B_i = \alpha_i A_i (I + \mathbf{t}_i \mathbf{v}^\top)$, and the constant factor α_i is chosen so that $\det B_i = 1$. Matrix B_i is known since A_i, $\mathbf{t}_i$ and $\mathbf{v}$ are assumed known. The equation $B_i K = K R_i$ may be written as $K^{-1} B_i K = R_i$. In other words, each B_i is the conjugate of a rotation matrix, the conjugating element being the same in each case – the calibration matrix K. For any non-singular matrix X, let $X^{-\top}$ be the inverse transpose of X. For a rotation matrix R, we have $R = R^{-\top}$. From the equation $R_i = K^{-1} B_i K$ it follows by taking inverse transposes that $R_i = K^\top B_i^{-\top} K^{-\top}$. Equating these two expressions for R_i we get $K^\top B_i^{-\top} K^{-\top} = K^{-1} B_i K$, from which it follows that

$$(KK^\top)B_i^{-\top} = B_i(KK^\top) \tag{14}$$

Given sufficiently many views and corresponding matrices B_i equation 14 may be used to solve for the entries of the matrix $KK^\top$. In particular, denoting $KK^\top$ by C and writing

$$C = KK^\top = \begin{pmatrix} a & b & c \\ b & d & e \\ c & e & f \end{pmatrix}$$

the equation (14) gives rise to a set of nine linear equations in the six independent entries of C. It may be seen that multiplying C by a constant factor does not have any effect on the equation (14). Consequently, C can only be solved up to a constant factor. It turns out that because of redundancy, the nine equations derived from (14) for a single known transformation B_i are not sufficient to solve for C. However, if two or more such B_i are known, then we may solve for C. In particular, for each view and corresponding B_i for $i = 1, \ldots, N-1$ we have nine equations in the entries of C. This overconstrained system of equations may be written in the form $X\mathbf{a} = 0$, where X is a matrix of dimension $9(N-1) \times 6$ and the vector $\mathbf{a}$ contains the independent entries of C. The least-squares solution $\mathbf{a}$ is the eigenvector corresponding to the least eigenvalue of $X^\top X$. This is easily found using the Jacobi method for finding the eigenvalues of a symmetric matrix ([15]). Note that the views are numbered starting at 0, so we need three views to provide two independent transforms B_i, and hence to solve for C.

Once $C = KK^\top$ is found it is an easy matter to solve for K using the Choleski factorization ([1, 15]). A solution for K is only possible when C is positive-definite. This is guaranteed for noise-free data, since by construction, C possesses such a factorization. If we insist that the diagonal entries or K are positive, then the Choleski factorization $C = KK^\top$ is unique.

In cases where the input data is defective, or the plane at infinity is not accurately known it is possible that the matrix C turns out not to be positive-definite, and so the calibration matrix can not be found. In practice however, the algorithm works extremely well, provided the plane at infinity is accurately placed and there are no gross inaccuracies (mistaken matched points) in the data.

It may be remarked that the matrix C has a geometric interpretation. It is the dual of the image of the absolute conic. The condition that $C = BCB^\mathsf{T}$ is related to the fact that C is invariant under translation and rotation of the camera.

8.1 Euclidean reconstruction from Affine Constraints

If certain collateral data is given that allows the affine structure of the scene to be determined, then this algorithm can be used to determine the Euclidean structure. For instance, if three independent pairs of parallel lines are known, then these can be used to determine where the true plane at infinity lies in a projective reconstruction. In particular, the points of intersection of the parallel lines must all lie on the plane at infinity. Given three pairs of lines, and hence three points on the plane at infinity the plane at infinity is determined. This determines the affine structure of the scene. The above algorithm then may be used to determine the Euclidean reconstruction of the scene.

Another affine constraint that may be used is a known ratio of distances of points on a line. For instance, suppose collinear points O, A and B are given and the ratio of distances $OA/OB = a/b$ is known. The line OAB in a projective reconstruction may be parametrized such that O, A and B have parameter values 0, a and b. The point with parameter ∞ on this line must lie on the plane at infinity.

Another method using Euclidean constraints to get the Euclidean reconstruction of a scene is reported by Boufama [2]. On the other hand, Sparr ([18]) gives a method of computing affine structure given a single view, and Koenderink and van Doorn [11] give a method for computing affine structure from pairs of orthographic views. Quan [16] gives a method of affine construction from two views given affine constraints.

9 Quasi-affine Reconstruction

We are interested, however, in finding the plane at infinity without any extra given information. The first step will be to get an approximation to the plane at infinity. This will be done by considering the *cheirality* of the images, in other words, by taking into account the fact that the points must lie in front of the cameras that view them.

The subject of cheirality of cameras was considered in detail in [6]. It was shown in that paper that if $(\{M_i\}, \{\mathbf{x}_j\})$ is a projective reconstruction of a set of image correspondences derived from a real scene, then there exist constants

η_j and ϵ_i equal to ± 1, such that $\epsilon_i \eta_j M_i \mathbf{x}_j = (u_j^i, v_j^i, w_j^i)^\top$ where each $w_j^i > 0$. It should be noted that the equality sign here means exact equality, and not equality up to a constant factor. Given the reconstruction $(\{M_i\}, \{\mathbf{x}_j\})$ we may replace M_i by $\epsilon_i M_i$ and $\mathbf{x}_j$ by $\eta_j \mathbf{x}_j$ to obtain a reconstruction such that $M_i \mathbf{x}_j = (u_j^i, v_j^i, w_j^i)^\top$ and each $w_j^i > 0$. Suppose that this has been done. Now ([6]) there exists a matrix $H = \begin{pmatrix} \beta I & 0 \\ \alpha \mathbf{v}^\top & \alpha \end{pmatrix}$ with $\alpha, \beta = \pm 1$ such that $H \mathbf{x}_j = (x_j', y_j', z_j', s_j')^\top$ with $s_j' > 0$ for all j, and such that $M_i H^{-1} = (A_i' \mid -A_i' \mathbf{t}_i)$ with $\det A_i' > 0$ for all i.

The conditions satisfied by the matrix H transform into inequalities. In particular, $s_j' > 0$ means that

$$\alpha(\mathbf{v}^\top 1)\mathbf{x}_j > 0 \tag{15}$$

for each point $\mathbf{x}_j$. The condition $\det A_i' < 0$ also gives rise to a linear inequality as follows. Writing $M_i = (A_i \mid -A_i \mathbf{t}_i)$ then $M_i H^{-1} = (A_i' \mid -A_i' \mathbf{t}_i')$ where $A_i' = \beta A_i (I + \mathbf{t}_i \mathbf{v}^\top)$. Then

$$\det A_i' = \beta \det A_i \det(I + \mathbf{t}_i \mathbf{v}^\top) = \beta(1 + \mathbf{t}_i^\top \mathbf{v}) \det A_i \ .$$

Since A_i and $\mathbf{t}_i$ are known this gives a linear inequality

$$\beta(1 + \mathbf{t}_i^\top \mathbf{v}) \det A_i > 0 \tag{16}$$

in the entries of $\mathbf{v}$. These set of inequalities (15) and (16) constraining the placement of the plane at infinity are called the *cheiral inequalities*.

Naturally, we propose to solve the cheiral inequalities using linear programming (LP). The four cases corresponding to the choices of α and β must be considered. In order to obtain a single solution it is necessary to define an appropriate goal function to optimize. We choose to maximize the margin by which the given inequalities are satisfied, since this should correspond informally to a placement of the plane at infinity at a maximum distance from the points and the cameras. For this to make sense, the homogeneous coordinate expression for $\mathbf{x}_j = (x_j, y_j, z_j, s_j)^\top$ should first be normalized so that $\|\mathbf{x}_j\| = 1$. Now, we have a set of inequalities of the form $\mathbf{f}_i^\top \mathbf{v} \geq g_i$, where $\mathbf{f}_i$ is simply the vector of coefficients of the i-th equation. We add an extra variable δ to obtain equations of the form $\mathbf{f}_i^\top \mathbf{v} - \delta \geq g_i$. The LP problem is to maximize δ subject to the given inequalities. If $\delta > 0$ in the optimum solution, then the original inequalities have a solution, and this is the solution that we accept to obtain $\mathbf{v}$. Once $\mathbf{v}$ has been found by solving the LP problem, the projective reconstruction is transformed by the corresponding matrix H. The new reconstruction may be termed a *quasi-affine* reconstruction.

By solving this cheiral inequalities, we find a candidate value for $\mathbf{v}$. By the method of Section 8 we can now compute the corresponding value of K. This estimate may then be refined using the method described in Section 7. There is one flaw in this scheme, namely that it may not be possible to find K corresponding to the estimated $\mathbf{v}$, because the matrix C, which should equal $KK^\top$, is not positive definite. In this case, it is necessary to select a different $\mathbf{v}$. This may be done by carrying out a random search over the convex region of 3-space defined by the cheirality inequalities. In fact, a reasonable approach is to find several candidate vectors **v** and iterate from each of them, finally selecting the best solution. This is what I have done in practice.

10 Algorithm Outline

Since the details of the outline have been obscured by the necessary mathematical analysis, the complete algorithm for Euclidean reconstruction will now be given. To understand the details of the steps of the algorithm, the reader must refer to the relevant section of the previous text.

1. Compute a projective reconstruction of the scene (Section 6)
   (a) Compute the essential matrix Q for a pair of images and use this to parametrize the first two cameras, and reconstruct the points
   (b) Use LM iteration to refine this initial projective reconstruction.
   (c) Parametrize the other cameras by the DLT method. Compute new point locations as appropriate.
   (d) Refine the complete projective reconstruction using LM iteration.
2. Compute a quasi-affine reconstruction of the scene (Section 9)
   (a) Formulate the cheiral inequalities for the projective reconstruction
   (b) Use LP to solve the inequalities to find a vector **v**.
   (c) Use the transformation matrix $H = \begin{pmatrix} I & 0 \\ \mathbf{v}^\top & 1 \end{pmatrix}$ to transform the projective reconstruction to a quasi-affine reconstruction.
3. Search for a quasi-affine reconstruction from which the calibration matrix K may be computed (Section 9)
   (a) For a randomly selected set of vectors **v** contained within the region determined by the cheiral inequalities solve the equations $CB_i^{-\top} = B_i C$ as described in Section 8 until we find a **v** such that the solution C is positive-definite.
   (b) Determine K by Choleski factorization of $C = KK^\top$.
4. Carry out LM iteration using the method of Section 7 to find a Euclidean reconstruction.
5. Using the values of K, R_i and $\mathbf{x}_j$ that come out of the previous step, do a complete LM iteration to find the optimal solution minimizing the image-coordinate error, using the method described in Section 5.

Various comments are in order here. First of all, some of the steps in this algorithm may not be necessary. Step 1(b) of the algorithm may not be needed, but it is easy to include and ensures an accurate starting point for the computation of the other camera parameters. The second step (determination of a specific quasi-affine reconstruction) may not be necessary either, since the third step does a search for a modified quasi-affine reconstruction. However, it is included, since it provides a point of reference for the subsequent search. The vector **v** found in the third step of the algorithm should be small, so that the modified quasi-affine reconstruction is close to the original one. In fact, as mentioned previously it is possible to use the cheiral inequalities to give bounds on the individual entries in the vector **v**. Finally, it has been found that the last step of the algorithm, the final iteration is scarcely necessary, and does not make a very large difference to the solution. It commonly decreases the value of the image coordinate error by no more that about 10%, at least when there are many views. In addition, this last step is relatively costly in terms of computation time.

11 Experimental Evaluation

This algorithm has been evaluated on both real and synthetic data.

11.1 Solution with Three Cameras

Since three cameras are the minimum number needed for Euclidean reconstruction the algorithm was tested on synthetic data with three views. The algorithm was found to converge without difficulty for noise-free data, and for data with added gaussian noise of 0.1 and 0.5 pixels in an image of size approximately 700×600 pixels. The degradation becomes progressively worse for greater degrees of noise, however the ratio k_u/k_v remains relatively stable. These results are shown in Table 1. The first line gives the correct values for the camera parameters. Subsequent lines show greater degrees of noise. The final column marked Δ gives the residual RMS pixel error, that is, the difference between the measured image coordinates and the ones derived from the reconstruction. This error should be of magnitude comparable with the noise level.

Noise	p_u	p_v	k_v	$skew$	k_u/k_v	Δ
–	3.0000e+02	3.5000e+02	2.5000e+03	2.0000e+01	9.0000e-01	–
0.0	3.0008e+02	3.5003e+02	2.4999e+03	2.0013e+01	8.9999e-01	0.0
0.1	2.7604e+02	3.3369e+02	2.5590e+03	1.7532e+01	8.9947e-01	0.09
0.5	1.2937e+02	2.3553e+02	2.9044e+03	3.2273e+00	8.9715e-01	0.50
1.0	-2.5284e+02	-1.1118e+01	3.5934e+03	4.6454e+01	8.7611e-01	5.67
2.0	2.3709e+02	2.7905e+02	2.3448e+03	6.6483e+01	8.7752e-01	5.22

Table 1. Reconstruction from Three Views

11.2 Solution with Large Numbers of Views

The algorithm was then carried out on synthetic data with 15 views of 50 points. The 50 points were randomly scattered in a sphere of radius 1 unit. The cameras were given random orientations and were placed at varying distances from the centre of the sphere at a mean distance from the centre of 2.5 units with a standard deviation of 0.25 units. They were placed in such a way that the principal rays of the cameras passed through randomly selected points on a sphere of radius 0.1 units. The calibration matrix was given a known value. In order to assess the quality of the Euclidean reconstruction the positions of the reconstructed points were compared with the known locations of the 3D points. Since the reconstructed points and the original points are not known in the same coordinate frame, it is necessary to align the two sets of points first. Then the RMS error was computed and used as a measure of quality of the reconstruction. The algorithm of Horn ([10]) was used to compute a rotation, translation and scaling that bring the reconstructed points into closest-possible alignment with the original point locations.

Noise	p_u	p_v	k_v	skew	k_u/k_v	Δ_1	Δ_2	Δ_3
–	5.00e+02	4.00e+02	1.0000e+03	-5.0000e+01	9.0000e-01	0.0	0.0	0.0
0.0	5.00e+02	4.00e+02	9.9999e+02	-5.0000e+01	9.0000e-01	9.805e-08	0.0	0.0
0.5	4.99e+02	3.98e+02	9.9959e+02	-4.9857e+01	9.0045e-01	8.359e-04	0.95	0.88
1.0	4.99e+02	3.97e+02	9.9911e+02	-4.9722e+01	9.0091e-01	1.678e-03	1.91	1.76
2.0	4.98e+02	3.95e+02	9.9792e+02	-4.9472e+01	9.0185e-01	3.386e-03	3.82	3.52
4.0	4.97e+02	3.90e+02	9.9463e+02	-4.9062e+01	9.0376e-01	6.911e-03	7.64	7.04
8.0	4.93e+02	3.81e+02	9.8455e+02	-4.8618e+01	9.0768e-01	1.454e-02	15.25	14.00
16.0	4.84e+02	3.67e+02	9.5125e+02	-4.9325e+01	9.1536e-01	3.314e-02	30.10	27.05

Table 2. Reconstruction from 15 Views

The results are shown in Table 2. The first line gives the correct values of the camera parameters and subsequent lines show the computed values with added noise. The last three columns have the following meaning.

Δ_1 The error in reconstruction, namely the distance between the actual and the reconstructed point locations.

Δ_2 The residual pixel error after step 4 of the algorithm in Section 10.

Δ_3 The residual pixel error after step 5 of the algorithm. This shows only a 10% reduction compared with Δ_2.

As can be seen from the Table 2, the results of the reconstruction are extremely good and immune to noise, both as regards the extracted camera calibration parameters and the quality of the point reconstruction. Even for gaussian noise as high as 16 pixels standard deviation in an image of size approximately 600 × 600 (far greater levels of noise than will be encountered in practice) the camera parameters are reasonably accurate, and the reconstruction is accurate to within 0.033 units, or 3.3 centimetres in a sphere of radius 1 metre. Note that the three error estimates show extraordinary linearity in terms of the added noise.

11.3   Solution with Real Data

The algorithm was evaluated on a set of image coordinate correspondences kindly supplied by Boubakeur Boufama and Roger Mohr. The object in question was a wooden house, for which 9 views were used and a total of 73 points were tracked, not all points being visible in all views. This is the same image set as used in the paper [14]. The image coordinates were integer numbers ranging between 0 and 500. Figure 1 shows one of the views of the house. The algorithm converged very successfully on this data. The measured residual RMS pixel error was found to be 0.6 pixels per point, which is about as good as can be expected, since the image correspondences were not supplied with sub-pixel accuracy. Not having any ground truth information, I was unable to compare the reconstruction against the correct points. The right side of Figure 1 shows a reconstructed view of the set of 73 points looking directly down the edge of the house. Clearly visible is the corner of the house, showing a right-angled corner. This indicates the success of the Euclidean reconstruction, since angles are a Euclidean attribute of the scene.

There is, however, one reason to suspect the accuracy of the reconstruction. In cases where all the camera rotations are about a common axis (as occurs when the camera is stationary and the image rotates), it appears that the problem is not well posed, for the scene may be expanded in the direction of the rotation axis at will. This is possibly the case in this present case, since the the computed camera parameters showed non-square pixels, which seems to be unlikely.

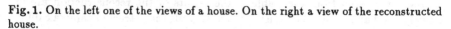

Fig. 1. On the left one of the views of a house. On the right a view of the reconstructed house.

References

1. K.E. Atkinson. *An Introduction to Numerical Analysis, 2nd Edition*. John Wiley and Sons, New York, 1989.

2. B. Boufama, R. Mohr, and F. Veillon. Euclidean constraints for uncalibrated reconstruction. *Technical Report, LIFIA - IRIMAG*, 1993.

3. O. D. Faugeras. What can be seen in three dimensions with an uncalibrated stereo rig? In *Computer Vision - ECCV '92 ,LNCS-Series Vol. 588, Springer-Verlag*, pages 563 – 578, 1992.

4. O. D. Faugeras, Q.-T Luong, and S. J. Maybank. Camera self-calibration: Theory and experiments. In *Computer Vision - ECCV '92 ,LNCS-Series Vol. 588, Springer-Verlag*, pages 321 – 334, 1992.

5. R. Hartley, R. Gupta, and T. Chang. Stereo from uncalibrated cameras. In *Proc. IEEE Conf. on Computer Vision and Pattern Recognition*, pages 761–764, 1992.

6. R. I. Hartley. Cheirality invariants. In *Proc. DARPA Image Understanding Workshop*, pages 745 – 753, 1993.

7. Richard Hartley and Rajiv Gupta. Computing matched-epipolar projections. In *Proc. IEEE Conf. on Computer Vision and Pattern Recognition*, pages 549 – 555, 1993.

8. B. K. P. Horn. Relative orientation. *International Journal of Computer Vision*, 4:59 – 78, 1990.

9. B. K. P. Horn. Relative orientation revisited. *Journal of the Optical Society of America, A*, Vol. 8, No. 10:1630 – 1638, 1991.

10. Berthold K. P. Horn. Closed-form solution of absolute orientation using unit quaternions. *Journal of the Optical Society of America, A*, Vol. 4:629 – 642, 1987.

11. Jan J. Koenderink and Andrea J. van Doorn. Affine structure from motion. *Journal of the Optical Society of America, A*, 1992.

12. Q.-T Luong. *Matrice Fondamentale et Calibration visuelle sur l'environnement*. PhD thesis, Universite de Paris-Sud, Centre D'Orsay, 1992.

13. S. J. Maybank and O. D. Faugeras. A theory of self-calibration of a moving camera. *International Journal of Computer Vision*, 8:2:123 – 151, 1992.

14. R. Mohr, F. Veillon, and L. Quan. Relative 3d reconstruction using multiple uncalibrated images. In *Proc. IEEE Conf. on Computer Vision and Pattern Recognition*, pages 543 – 548, 1993.

15. William H. Press, Brian P. Flannery, Saul A. Teukolsky, and William T. Vetterling. *Numerical Recipes in C: The Art of Scientific Computing*. Cambridge University Press, 1988.

16. Long Quan. Affine stereo calibration for relative affine shape reconstruction. In *Proc. BMVC*, pages 659–668, 1993.

17. C. C. Slama, editor. *Manual of Photogrammetry*. American Society of Photogrammetry, Falls Church, VA, fourth edition, 1980.

18. Gunnar Sparr. Depth computations from polyhedral images. In *Computer Vision - ECCV '92 ,LNCS-Series Vol. 588, Springer-Verlag*, pages 378–386, 1992.

19. I.E. Sutherland. Three dimensional data input by tablet. *Proceedings of IEEE*, Vol. 62, No. 4:453–461, April 1974.

Accurate Projective Reconstruction *

Roger Mohr, Boubakeur Boufama, Pascal Brand

LIFIA–INRIA,
46 avenue Félix Viallet,
F-38031 Grenoble Cedex,
e-mail : last-name@imag.fr

Abstract. It is possible to recover the three-dimensional structure of
a scene using images taken with uncalibrated cameras and pixel correspondences. But such a reconstruction can only be computed up to a
projective transformation of the 3D space. Therefore, constraints have
to be added to the reconstructed data in order to get the reconstruction in the euclidean space. Such constraints arise from knowledge of the
scene: location of points, geometrical constraints on lines, etc. We first
discuss here the type of constraints that have to be added then we show
how they can be fed into a general framework. Experiments prove that
the accuracy needed for industrial applications is reachable when measurements in the image have subpixel accuracy. Therefore, we show how
a real camera can be mapped into an accurate projective camera and
how accurate point detection improve the reconstruction results.

1 Introduction

One of the principal goals of research in computer vision is to enable machines
to perceive the three-dimensional nature of the environment. Unfortunately in
many cases, the only information we dispose about the scene is two-dimension
images. It is very well known that recovering depth from a single image is not
possible. But if we use more than one image the problem becomes feasible.
Usually the process requires the calibration of the cameras and the matching
of the features in the different images. This approach suffers from two major
drawbacks: firstly the calibration process is very sensitive to errors and difficult
to obtain; secondly, in many applications it is not possible to calibrate on-line,
for example, if the camera is involved in visual tasks.

An alternative approach is to use points in the scene as a reference frame
without knowing their absolute coordinates nor the camera parameters. This
has been investigated by several researchers these past few years using projective geometry [13] or affine shape [21]. Koenderink and van Doorn [9] and Lee
and Huang[10] developed two similar methods for shape recovering under orthography hypothesis.

---

* The reasearch described in this paper has been partially supported by Esprit Bra
project Viva

Recently, Faugeras [5] developed a reconstruction method using standard tools of projective geometry. He demonstrates that it is possible to reconstruct three-dimensional scenes only from point matches, but such reconstruction is defined up to a collineation, i.e. a projective transformation. He first determines the projection matrices up to a collineation. To do so, he chooses 5 reference points and assigns them the standard projective coordinates basis. This is equivalent to have 5 image points and space points matches, and provides 10 unknowns among 11. Thus in each projection matrix remains only 1 unknown parameter. The author supposes that the epipoles have been computed. This computation is directly done from point matches. Since the epipoles are intrinsically related to the projection matrix, each projection matrix is entirely determined up to a collineation. Once each projection matrix is known, the reconstruction becomes the straightforward resolution of a linear set of equations.

Simultaneously and independently other groups converged to the same kind of approach. Hartley et al. [8] reconstruct a solution determined up to a projective transformation of 3D space, that is to say 15 unknowns. Then they use 8 ground reference points, each providing 2 equations, to solve the ambiguity and to obtain both the location of points in 3D space and the camera parameters. The method is linear and non-iterative.

The approach developed in our group [13] was primarily inspired by Tomasi and Kanade's works [22] who solve the similar problem in the affine case, i.e., dealing with orthographic projection. They simultaneously filter out noise and solve the system using SVD for least-square approximation. Unfortunately, this approach does not extend to the projective case. Therefore we developed a parameter estimation approach to this 3D reconstruction problem with several views (images). It allows to put in the same framework the resolution of the previous problem and the integration of euclidean constraints on the world to be reconstructed. This differs substantially from Faugeras and Hartley approaches which mainly rely on the estimation of the fundamental matrix. It is much more linked to photogrammetrist work [20], where least square approximation is used to find accurate and robust solutions in reconstruction.

Section 2 describes our proposed method for reconstruction, Section 3 shows how a priori geometric constraints can be used in order to get a unique solution, and how the least square approach deals naturally with such constraints. Then, the problem of accuracy in reconstruction is addressed, two error sources have to be corrected: the mathematical model of perspective projection and the error in localisation in the images. Section 5 explains how to get a projectively correct image and section 6 presents how to get accurate localisation for corners. Finally, experiments are presented and discussed.

2 The Reconstruction Method

This section considers the problem of computing the location of points in three dimensional space given perspective views (at least two) taken with uncalibrated cameras. Our solution has been influenced by the way photogrammetrists simultaneously calibrate a camera and reconstruct the scene, using carefully located beacons [1].

2.1 The basic equations

We consider v images of a scene ($v \geq 2$) composed of p points. For simplicity, it is assumed that all points have been matched in all the images, thus providing $p \times v$ image points. In fact, this assumption is not necessary: a point has only to appear in at least 2 images.

$\{P_i, i = 1, \ldots, p\}$ are the unknown 3-D points projected in each image.

For each image j, the point P_i, represented by a column vector of its homogeneous coordinates $(x_i, y_i, z_i, t_i)^T$, is projected on the point p_{ij}, represented by a column vector of its three homogeneous coordinates $(u_{ij}, v_{ij}, w_{ij})^T$ or its usual non homogeneous coordinates $(U_{ij}, V_{ij})^T$. Let M_j be the 3×4 projection matrix of the jth image.

We have for homogeneous coordinates:

$$\rho_{ij} p_{ij} = M_j P_i, \quad i = 1, \ldots, p, \quad j = 1, \ldots, v \tag{1}$$

where ρ_{ij} is an unknown scaling factor.

Equation 1 is usually written in the following way, hiding the scaling factor, using the non homogeneous coordinates of the image points:

$$
\begin{cases}
U_{ij} = \dfrac{m_{11}^{(j)} x_i + m_{12}^{(j)} y_i + m_{13}^{(j)} z_i + m_{14}^{(j)} t_i}{m_{31}^{(j)} x_i + m_{32}^{(j)} y_i + m_{33}^{(j)} z_i + m_{34}^{(j)} t_i} \\[4mm]
V_{ij} = \dfrac{m_{21}^{(j)} x_i + m_{22}^{(j)} y_i + m_{23}^{(j)} z_i + m_{24}^{(j)} t_i}{m_{31}^{(j)} x_i + m_{32}^{(j)} y_i + m_{33}^{(j)} z_i + m_{34}^{(j)} t_i}
\end{cases}
\tag{2}
$$

These equations express simply the collinearity of the space points and their corresponding projection points.

Since we have p points and v images, this leads to $2 \times p \times v$ equations. The unknowns are $11 \times v$ for the M_j which are defined up to a scaling factor, plus $3 \times p$ for the space points. So if v and p are large enough we have a redundant set of equations.

In general configuration, the solution of this system is unique [5]. But the solution of system (1) can only be defined up to a collineation. As a matter of fact, if M_j and P_i are a solution, so are $M_j W^{-1}$ and $W P_i$ where W is a collineation of the 3-D space, i.e. a 4×4 invertible matrix.

As a consequence of this result, a basis for any 3-D collineation can be arbitrarly chosen in the 3-D space. For the projective space $I\!\!P^3$, 5 algebraically free points (i.e. no four of them being coplanar) form a basis.

2.2   Direct non linear reconstruction

From the above, the problem can be formulated as a conditional parameter estimate problem. In the general case we have to estimate parameters (the matrices M_j and the 3-D coordinates of points P_i) having noisy measurements (the image coordinates). We assume that the measurements are obtained with a mean value equal to the observed one, and with a covariance matrix C.

Let us call Q the vector of all parameters, and q_k one of its elements, U the vector of all the measurements U_{ij} and V_{ij}, and let u_l be one of its elements.

If the relation between the measures u_l and parameters q_k is linear, i.e. $U = AQ$, then the maximum likelyhood estimation of the parameters is the vector Q which minimizes the Mahalanobis distance, i.e. the least square criterion

$$\chi^2 = (U - AQ)^t C^{-1} (U - AQ) \tag{3}$$

In the non linear case, linearization may be obtained by taking the first order Taylor expansion of the non linear function linking Q with each u_l.

Noise has several sources, but the major error source are the location of points in the images. This source of noise is highly uncorrelated, unlike distorsion noise for example. So our major error source can be considered as uncorrelated noise. As the covariance matrix of the noise due to other sources was less important and very hard to estimate, it was not taken into account.

As a consequence our covariance matrix is a diagonal matrix, with values equal to the variances σ_{ij}. Therefore, in our case, equation (3) leads to the minimization of this simple sum:

$$\chi^2 = \sum_{ij} \left(\frac{U_{ij} - \frac{m_{11}^{(j)} x_i + m_{12}^{(j)} y_i + m_{13}^{(j)} z_i + m_{14}^{(j)} t_i}{m_{31}^{(j)} x_i + m_{32}^{(j)} y_i + m_{33}^{(j)} z_i + m_{34}^{(j)} t_i}}{\sigma_{ij}} \right)^2 + \sum_{ij} \left(\frac{V_{ij} - \frac{m_{21}^{(j)} x_i + m_{22}^{(j)} y_i + m_{23}^{(j)} z_i + m_{24}^{(j)} t_i}{m_{31}^{(j)} x_i + m_{32}^{(j)} y_i + m_{33}^{(j)} z_i + m_{34}^{(j)} t_i}}{\sigma_{ij}} \right)^2$$

2.3   Results

Five views of a wood house, covering about a $\pi/2$ rotation of the camera have been used. Figure 1 is one of the original images of the house. A total of 73 points have been tracked, some of them vanishing and reappearing from view to view. Five points on the house have been measured and chosen as a basis. They are denoted by an x on Figure 2. Confidence regions (ellipsoids) of the reconstructed points have been, for simplicity, represented by their best bounding parallelepiped. They have been computed with all σ_{ij} equal to 1.0, and correspond to a 68.3% confidence limit. The difference between the reconstructed point coordinates and the measured ones (with a ruler) was less than $1.5mm$

However, in many cases, the need of located reference points is a drawback, and the next section describes how this can be avoided by use of geometrical constraints.

Fig. 1. A scene view with its corresponding contours and points to be reconstructed

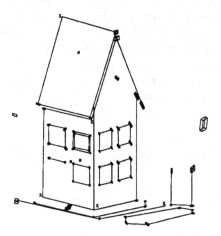

Fig. 2. The reconstructed scene with confidence ellipsoids

3 The Euclidean Constraints

The previous section showed how to reconstruct a three-dimensional scene using five known points as a reference frame. But if no point is known, the only kind of 3-D reconstruction that can be obtained is projective, i.e., the solution has no metric information and is defined up to a collineation.

Let us assume that the reconstruction is done up to a projective transformation W. We address here the problem of recovering the euclidean solution without knowing any 3-D point, i.e., finding the transformation W which brings the solution to an euclidean world. Since W is a 4×4 homogenous matrix, and therefore has 15 degrees of freedom, so at least 15 euclidean constraints are needed to define W. This is done by using geometrical knowledge about the scene and translating them into constraints, for instance setting position of points as we already did in the previous section.

How geometric information can be inserted is first discussed on a general geometrical basis. The goal is to highlight the geometrical aspects of the problem. The case of our practical example is then explained in the second subsection.

3.1 Geometrical move towards an Euclidean solution

We know that an affine transformation fixes three of the 15 degrees of freedom we are looking for. An euclidean transformation has only six. So six constraints on the affine transformation have to be added if we want to have our transformation being defined up to a rigid transformation. This can be done gradually.

Projective to affine. The set of affine transformations is the subset of projective transformations which leaves the plane at infinity Π_∞ invariant. The affine space is defined from the projective space by choosing Π_∞. This plane has to be defined in the projective space by at least three points which are not collinear. The most common way to get such points is to consider lines which are known to be parallel and therefore intersect at infinity.

An alternative to this case is to consider the basic affine invariant: the ratio of three colinear points A, B, C. It should be noticed that this ratio is related to the cross ratio of the four points A, B, C, D where D is the point a infinity on the line $[A, B]$, as

$$\frac{AB}{AC} \times \frac{DC}{DB} = \frac{AB}{AC} \times \frac{\infty}{\infty} = \frac{AB}{AC}$$

If we know the projections of these points in the images, we are therefore able to derive from the value of this ratio the location of the projections of D and therefore to reconstruct its position in the projective space.

Such a case happens for instance when we know that A is the middle of BC. The previous ratio is then -1, and D is the harmonic conjugate of A with respect of B and C.

Stating that Π_∞ should have equation $t = 0$ leads to three independent linear equations which link the last line of the matrix W.

Affine to euclidean. We consider here the extended euclidean space, i.e., the space invariant under similarity transformations: rotation, translation, and uniform scaling. Let us now consider that the plane Π_∞ has been defined and that a change in coordinates has set its equation to $t = 0$. This space is deduced from the affine space by setting the position of the absolute conic Ω. The absolute conic is located in Π_∞ [12] [19] and defined by the equations:

$$\begin{cases} x^2 + y^2 + z^2 = 0 \\ t = 0 \end{cases} \tag{4}$$

where the previous equations are expressed in an "extended" euclidean reference frame, i.e., an orthogonal reference frame with similar unit length on each axis.

Points on this conic have only complex coordinates. From direct computation it is straightforward to check that Ω is invariant by uniform scaling, translation and rotation.

The easiest way to determine such conic is to reconstruct known circles in the 3D space. Each such circle cuts Π_∞ in two points which belong to Ω [19]. From three such circles the reconstruction of Ω is then possible. Let its equation be:

$$a_1 x^2 + a_2 y^2 + a_3 z^2 + 2a_4 xy + 2a_5 xz + 2a_6 yz = 0$$

a change in coordinates has to be made in order to bring it in the form of equation (4). This is done by considering that the equation of the conic is associated to the quadratic form Q defined by

$$0 = (x, y, z) \begin{pmatrix} a_1 & a_4 & a_5 \\ a_4 & a_2 & a_6 \\ a_5 & a_6 & a_3 \end{pmatrix} \begin{pmatrix} x \\ y \\ z \end{pmatrix} = X^T Q X$$

As the matrix Q is symmetric, there exists an orthogonal matrix P such that

$$Q = P^T \begin{pmatrix} \lambda_1 & 0 & 0 \\ 0 & \lambda_2 & 0 \\ 0 & 0 & \lambda_3 \end{pmatrix} P$$

So by setting $X' = PX$, we have:

$$X^T Q X = (X')^T \begin{pmatrix} \lambda_1 & 0 & 0 \\ 0 & \lambda_2 & 0 \\ 0 & 0 & \lambda_3 \end{pmatrix} X'$$

Finally with one more step of scaling along the axes, we get equation (4).

The basic extended euclidean invariant is the value α of the angle formed by two lines. This invariant can also be used for the computation of Ω, as such knowledge introduces a constraint on its location. Let A and B be the intersections of the two lines with Π_∞. Let I and J be the intersections of the plane defined by these two lines and Ω. Laguerre's formula states that:

$$\alpha = \frac{1}{2i} \log(\{A, B; I, J\})$$

We can write $I = A + tB, J = A + t'B$. With this notation $\{A, B; I, J\} = \frac{t}{t'} = e^{2i\alpha}$. If we express that both points lie on Ω we get the equations

$$t^2 B^T Q B + 2t A^T Q B + A^T Q A = 0$$
$$e^{4i\alpha} t^2 B^T Q B + 2e^{2i\alpha} t A^T Q B + A^T Q A = 0$$

from which a polynomial constraint on Q is easily derived.

Final setting. At this stage, angles are defined. Seven degrees of freedom still remain: the scaling factor, the translational and the rotational parts. For many problems such a final setting can be omitted and arbitrary parameters may be chosen. For instance the translation parameters are fixed by choosing one arbitrary point for origin. If the translational part has to be defined, absolute positions of features have to be provided, for instance the position of a point.

If scaling has to be defined, a length information has to be added. Let us assume that A and B are known as having a distance d. If the rotational and translational parts can be arbitrarily chosen, A can be set as the origin, AB as the direction of the x axis, and using d the unit can be set on this axis. One additional point has then to be used for defining the Axy plane. As orthogonality is already defined, the y is then defined and this sets the final rotation.

3.2 An application

The constraints of a real problem do not exactly fit the previous steps. Understanding these steps helps to avoid underconstrained systems.

We consider here as an example the previous reconstruction. All the constraints were a mixture of affine and euclidean ones.

To get a unique euclidean solution we fixed a reference frame in the scene where our constraints are expressed. This is not a restriction in our opinion as in almost all the scenes we can find such a reference frame: In an indoor or outdoor scene the floor is present and can be used as the horizontal plane XOY. Also two vertical planes which are perpendicular to each other can be found (building walls, room walls, etc...), we can use them as the XOZ and YOZ planes respectively.

So in the following we must keep in mind that we have a reference frame, but no coordinates are supposed known.

The following constraints were used:

- fixing a reference horizontal plane.
- point alignment with the axes.
- distance between points.

Example of contraints Our method has been tested on several examples. We will give details in this paragraph its application to the reconstruction of an object, "the house" (see Figure 1).

As it was already noticed, a priori information can be extracted from an image like the vertical lines [17]. One can easily find by observing Figure 1 the existence of some natural knowledge.

As for Section 2, we used the 73 points tracked over the image sequence and we solved the same non linear system but without giving the euclidean coordinates to the five points. The matrix W is estimated using the following constraints:

- The floor is used as the horizontal plane for our euclidean reference frame.
- The two walls of the house are considered as the plane (XOZ) and (YOZ).

– Up to now, the 3 planes of our reference frame are fixed. The axes are obtained from the intersection of theses planes and if a pair of points forms a line parallel to one of the 3 axes we will obtain an alignment constraint.
– Metric information must be introduced to get a correct solution. We used distances between pairs of points aligned with one of the axis. This translates into a second-degree equation.

This problem can be formulated as a conditional estimate of parameters (here the matrix W), therefore we used the same method as in Section 2 for solving this system, i.e, Levenberg-Marquardt method [16].

4 Solving the System

The reconstruction problem is specified by the set of equations (1) and by the set of equations derived by the euclidean constraints presented in the previous section. Solving directly this highly non-linear system often leads to divergent computations. This section explains how we solved all our examples, on real or simulated data and discusses accuracy of the results. The computation is done in three steps, first a computation of a projective solution, secondly computation of a first estimate of the euclidean solution and then the final estimation.

4.1 Finding a projective solution

At this stage we solve only the system (1). As the projective coordinates of the spatial points are defined up to scaling factor, we added the constraint

$$x_i^2 + y_i^2 + z_i^2 + t_i^2 = 1 \tag{5}$$

Experimentally, equation (5) is crucial in order to guarantee convergence of the system. Similarly a scaling constraint has to be added on the projection matrices. Usually the following constraint used is: $\sum_{i=1}^{i=3} m_{3i}^2 = 1$.
As this condition was not crucial for convergence, we prefered to take $m_{34} = 1$.
Finally equations (1) were linearized leading to minimization of the square of

$$U_{ij} \times (m_{31}^{(j)} x_i + m_{32}^{(j)} y_i + m_{33}^{(j)} z_i + t_i) - (m_{11}^{(j)} x_i + m_{12}^{(j)} y_i + m_{13}^{(j)} z_i + m_{14}^{(j)} t_i) \tag{6}$$

and

$$V_{ij} \times (m_{31}^{(j)} x_i + m_{32}^{(j)} y_i + m_{33}^{(j)} z_i + t_i) - (m_{21}^{(j)} x_i + m_{22}^{(j)} y_i + m_{23}^{(j)} z_i + m_{24}^{(j)} t_i) \tag{7}$$

together with

$$x_i^2 + y_i^2 + z_i^2 + t_i^2 - 1 \tag{8}$$

So as to fit with Levenberg-Marquardt formulation, the problem is written as minimizing over

$$(x_i,\ y_i,\ z_i,\ t_i,\ m_{11}^{(j)}, \ldots m_{33}^{(j)}) \text{ for } i = 1, \ldots, v, \ j = 1, \ldots, p;$$

$$\sum_{k=1}^{2 \times p \times v + p} (\frac{f_k(x_{ij}, y_{ij}; x_i, y_i, z_i, t_i, m_{11}^{(j)}, \ldots m_{34}^{(j)})}{\sigma_k})^2 \qquad (9)$$

where σ_k is the variance of the kth measure, and $f_k(\cdot)$ are the functions (6), (7) or (8).

Such a linearization does not lead to the correct estimation, but as it will be plugged in a final optimization step, we just keep it as an approximation. On the other hand it leads to faster convergence.

This method involves also an initialization of all the parameters. From our experiments, it came out that the initial data for the 5 reference point should be the coordinates

$$(0,0,0,1)^T, (1,0,0,1)^T, (0,1,0,1)^T, (0,0,1,1)^T \text{ and } (1,1,1,1)^T$$

and that they correspond roughly to a configuration of similar position in the space (see the first case in Fig. 3) , but with a strong wrong relative position of a point like $P4$ in the case b the system diverges.

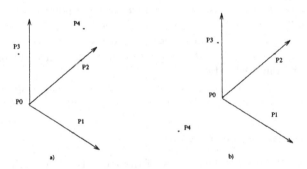

Fig. 3. Five reference points. a) case of convergence, b) case of divergence.

Initialisation of the projection matrices and the other points proved to be less important, a key point was to put enough high value in the first elements of the last column (see for a real camera where these componant comes from). Practically convergence was obtained after five to ten iterations. Unfortunately no mathematical proof or warranties of convergence can be provided.

4.2 Estimation of the euclidean solution

At this stage a projective solution is computed. The final projective mapping will be the computation of the matrix W which satisfies the best added euclidean constraints as they are described in Section 3. As W is defined up to a scaling factor, we added here the constraint $\sum_{i,j}(W_{ij})^2 = 1$.

Similarly, the problem can be written as minimizing over:

$$\sum_{k=1}^{n}\left(\frac{f_k(W_{11},\ldots W_{44})}{\sigma_k}\right)^2 \tag{10}$$

where $f_k(\cdot)$ are the previously mentioned constraints.

4.3 Final estimation

The two previous steps provide a solution close to the optimal estimate. Therefore this solution is fed into the general system where the equations provide from both steps. Variance has to be adapted to errors in our measures. Therefore a low threshold was chosen for exact constraints and the estimated variance was put on measures. Here we were not able to get an exact estimation of this noise measure and we set the variance to 1.

4.4 Experimental results

Two experiments are presented here:

- real data: the images were the ones used for the 5 points method described in Section 2. To estimate the matrix W, 4 points laying on each plane and 4 pairs of points parallel to each axis are used giving rise to 48 equations. On a qualitative basis, the result is similar to one of Section 2. Accuracy will be studied for simulated data.
- simulated data: we simulated a scene similar to the real scene. Four images were simulated with 60 points and the same kind of constraints were used.

4.5 Accuracy in reconstruction

This subsection discusses the accuracy of the reconstruction of simulated data, then it provides a comparison of this accuracy to the one obtained using 5 known points as in Section 2. We will not detail the accuracy obtained on real data because we had not the exact 3-D coordinates of points in that case.

Table (1) gives for 10 points, the 3-D coordinates of the simulated scene, the ones computed by our method using constraints and the errors. Noise on pixel was generated as uniform noise within ± 1 pixels.

In order to study the stability of the method, noise is added to our data (2-D coordinates), then 3-D coordinates are computed with both the method of Section 2 and the method using constraints. Figure 4 displays the mean errors on 3D positions when perturbing the images. Of course both are perfect with no noise, up to tiny numerical round-off errors. As it could be guessed from the beginning, redundant euclidean constraints provide a better accuracy in the reconstruction. Particularly, it has to be noticed that the method with five points is very sensitive to the location of these five points in the image.

With larger noise amplitude, results degrade quickly [14]. If accuracy in 3-D position is needed, subpixel measurements are the only issue.

3-D coordinates			computed coordinates			errors		
X	Y	Z	X_c	Y_c	Z_c	$X - X_c$	$Y - Y_c$	$Z - Z_c$
0.000	0.000	0.500	0.000	0.030	0.478	0.000	0.030	0.022
12.000	0.000	0.500	12.041	0.059	0.504	0.041	0.059	0.004
0.000	18.000	0.500	0.000	18.030	0.478	0.000	0.030	0.022
0.000	0.000	14.500	0.000	0.025	14.458	0.000	0.025	0.042
6.000	18.000	22.500	5.946	17.982	22.431	0.054	0.018	0.069
0.000	18.000	14.500	0.000	18.025	14.458	0.000	0.025	0.042
6.000	0.000	22.500	5.946	-0.018	22.431	0.054	0.018	0.069
12.000	0.000	14.500	12.000	0.025	14.458	0.000	0.025	0.042
13.500	-1.500	0.500	13.489	-1.526	0.523	0.011	0.026	0.023
-1.500	-1.500	0.500	-1.511	-1.526	0.523	0.011	0.026	0.023

Table 1. example of reconstructed 3D coordinates, and the errors

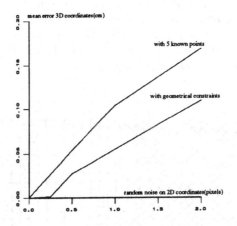

Fig. 4. Since the noise is important the method using constraints is more suitable

5 Camera Distortion Correction

This section is concerned with the problem of correcting different distortions of the imaging system. If reseachers often focus on radial optical distortion [23], it should be noticed that many other sources of distortion exist in a real system [2]: alignment default in the lens system, electronic noise,... Some of them are unstable, for instance heat-up of a camera causes a change in its parameters. To find a parametric model for all these sources seems to be impossible, therefore this section explains how stable distortion can be corrected in order to bring the system back to a projective transformation.

Two assumptions are made here: the unstable noise is a second order noise with regard to the other sources of distortions, and the projection is a continuous deformation of the true perspective projection. Experiments show that the first assumption is satisfied on real systems. The second one is also satisfied with sufficient accuracy, even if we were not able to evaluate it with enough precision.

5.1 Principle of the algorithm

The perfect pin-hole model is a projective mapping from $I\!P^3$ into $I\!P^2$. Hence, 3D lines of the scene are mapped into 2D lines on the image. However, this is not the case for a real camera.

Our algorithm transforms pixel by pixel a real image (image with distortions) into a corrected one and is based on the following theorem [19]

Theorem 1. each collineation is a self–dual transformation, which transforms points into points and lines into lines.

The correction has to bring image of lines back to straight lines. To do this, we will observe an image of a calibration plane (see figure 5a) which contains a set of straight lines. Intersections of lines form crosses, we detect the sub-pixel location of these intersection points. With these points, we can build the grid which is shown on figure 5b. Each line of this grid should be a straight line if the hypothesis of the pin-hole model was true.

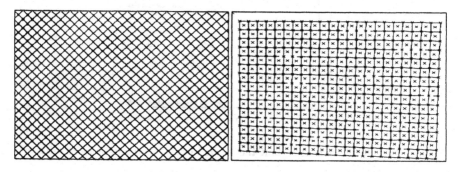

Fig. 5. a) The calibration plane. b) The grid associated with the calibration plane

The first step consists of transforming the grid cross by cross in order to obtain a grid with straight lines. So, we will map the high–left cross to the coordinates $(0,0)$, the cross on its right in $(0,1)$, the cross down in $(1,0)$ ... This new coordinate frame is called **virtual coordinate frame** and does't contain distortion because the 3D lines are projected into 2D lines.

Hence, we have defined a point correction for each of the intersection point of the grid. This transformation aligns the crosses, and replaces them at new positions. These new positions arise from a perfect projective transformation.

This transformation is then extended for all the pixels of the image. The transformation T for an image point p is defined by the bi-linear interpolation of the four intersection points around p (distortions are supposed locally negligible).

Therefore, the points which are expressed in the virtual coordinate frame satisfy the pin-hole model hypothesis. As this virtual coordinate frame is far from the initial one, we will reproject all the points from the virtual coordinate frame to the one, which is close to the initial coordinate frame. This transformation is defined by an homography $M : \mathbb{P}^2 \to \mathbb{P}^2$. To build M, we use 4 points as a basis. We suppose that these 4 points have no distortion :

In practice, these 4 points are chosen close to the image border in order to reduce the influence of the errors due to the extraction of the intersection points.

The reprojection of the points allows:

1. a better visualization of the results.
2. a comparaison of the distortions of 2 different cameras because the virtual coordinate frame depends on the position of the calibration frame in the image. But the final coordinate frame depends only on the chosen basis.

The complete algorithm used to remove the distortion is illustrated in Figure 6. An example of the obtained distortions is showed in Figure 7.

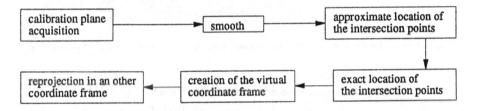

Fig. 6. Algorithm to remove the distortions

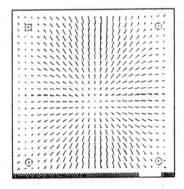

Fig. 7. An example of the obtained distortion. Each cross shows the location of a point before the distortion correction. Each line shows the direction of the correction, scaled by a factor of 40. The four encircled points form the basis for the collineation

6 Accurate Detection in the Image

Inaccuracy in localization of image features is the second source of errors in our process. Therefore, we developed a corner detector which is a model-based method. Similar methods have appeared the last few years [4], [18], [15]. Such methods make use of a model for a corner and are driven by a first coarse approximation of the location.

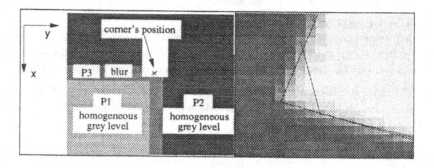

Fig. 8. Corner model and a zoom on a corner (first approximation and final estimation)

The corner model we use is an adaptation of R. Deriche's model [4]. It consists of 3 regions (Fig.8): P_1 and P_2 have two homogeneous grey levels, whereas the third region P_3 is a Gaussian blur of the 2 first regions. In the model, the corner is at position (x'_0, y'_0). The pixel intensity (x, y) can be written as :

$$I_m(x,y) = \begin{cases} A \text{ if } (x,y) \in P_1 \\ B \text{ if } (x,y) \in P_2 \\ \int_{-\infty}^{+\infty} \int_{-\infty}^{+\infty} g(\alpha)g(\beta)I'(x-\alpha, y-\beta)\, d\alpha\, d\beta & \text{if } (x,y) \in P_3 \end{cases}$$

where $I'(x,y)$ is equal to A if $x \geq x'_0$ and $y \leq y'_0$, and $I'(x,y) = B$ otherwise. $g(\alpha)$ is the Gaussian function

$$g(\alpha) = \frac{1}{\sqrt{\pi \sigma^2}} \exp^{-\alpha^2/\sigma^2}$$

The variance σ was fixed to 0.5.

Our goal is to find the best transformation which minimizes the criterion

$$\sum_{x,y} (I_c(x,y) - I_m(x',y'))^2$$

where

- $I_c(x,y)$ is the pixel intensity at point (x,y) in the image.
- (x',y') is defined by a rotation, a skew and a translation of the point (x,y).

The unknowns are the parameters of the rotation, the skew and the translation, and the two homogeneous grey levels A and B. The used optimization algorithm is the Levenberg–Marquardt algorithm [16].

From the parameters of the transformation, the corner's position in the image is estimated (see Figure 8).

7 Experiments

It is well known that fundamental matrix and 3-D reconstruction are very sensitive to pixel noise [11]. Our experiments show an analysis of reconstruction and fundamental matrix accuracy depending on image errors.

The fundamental matrix is computed from the matched points [6], and the reconstruction is done according to Section 2.

Both real and simulated images are used in our analysis, the first ones show the difficulties of such analysis and the latter give quantitative results.

7.1 Real data

All our experiments were conducted with a PULNIX TM-6EX camera with a $12.5mm$ focal length and FG150 Imaging technology grab board. As the accuracy is the goal of these tests, we used a scene which is based on our standard calibration pattern (Fig. 9). Each image is the combination of 3 calibration patterns (to get volume we moved the calibration pattern with high accuracy).

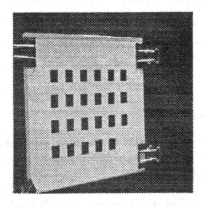

Fig. 9. Our calibration pattern

Fundamental matrix analysis One way to measure the accuracy of the fundamental matrix is to compute the mean distance between points and theirs corresponding epipolar lines. This mean distance is a euclidean distance expressed in pixels and is used as a quality value; it will be called *mean error*.

The black square corners of our calibration pattern are extracted by our corner detector according to section 6.

- Corners accuracy: the fundamental matrix is first computed by ignoring the subpixel accuracy of our corner detector, then it is computed by taking into account this subpixel accuracy. The result gives for the first fundamental matrix 0.357 pixel as mean error and 0.100 pixel for the second one. From these results it is clear that subpixel precision of the image points increases the quality of the epipolar geometry.
- Distortions: with subpixel precision of the corners and in the same way, we computed the fundamental matrix before and after distortions correction. the mean errors were 0.100 and 0.106. The difference between the two errors is negligible (6/1000 pixel), we will discuss this at the end of this section.

reconstruction analysis The accuracy of the reconstruction is summarized in table 2. As in the previous case, correcting distortions did not give a significant improvement for the reconstruction compared with what subpixel corner localization provides.

different reconstructions	mean errors on X (mm)	mean errors on Y (mm)	mean errors on Z (mm)
without subpixel accuracy	0.11810	0.15366	0.35979
with subpixel accuracy	0.10663	0.09556	0.08809
with subpixel accuracy and corrected distortions	0.10124	0.09254	0.09247

Table 2. mean errors on the 3D coordinates of the reconstructed points

7.2 Simulated data

The experiment setup were similar to the ones with real data (the 3D points coordinates of the calibration pattern, the distance between the camera and the 3D points and the simulated camera).

Image locations of points were perturbed with a uniform noise, which varies from ± 0.20 pixel to ± 1 pixel. Furthermore, we added radial distortions obtained from the following formulaes:

$$\begin{cases} \delta_x(x,y) = k.(x - x_0).r^2 \\ \delta_y(x,y) = k.(y - y_0).r^2 \end{cases}$$

where

- (x_0, y_0) is the center of the radial distortion, which has been chosen as the center of the image.

- Two k values have been used, such that the distortion at the image borders (for instance image point $(x_0, 0)$) is either 4 pixels or 8 pixels.
- r is the distance between the point (x, y) and the image center.

Table 3 presents the results of our tests.

pixel noise	distortion	mean observed distortion	3D mean error (mm)	3D max error (mm)	mean error(pixel) for epipolar geometry
0.00	0		0.00002	0.00008	0.000182
	4	0.319744	0.16641	0.32726	0.041599
	8	0.852651	0.51074	1.08101	0.110439
0.20	0		0.14829	0.35080	0.128447
	4	0.426275	0.27030	0.56102	0.144560
	8	0.852551	0.46742	0.91912	0.183152
0.30	0		0.22257	0.52503	0.192601
	4	0.426251	0.31624	0.67532	0.204567
	8	0.852503	0.49762	1.01165	0.235238
0.40	0		0.29696	0.69860	0.256721
	4	0.426228	0.37036	0.80235	0.267011
	8	0.852457	0.53499	1.11001	0.290246
0.50	0		0.37148	0.87142	0.320843
	4	0.426206	0.43010	0.94421	0.330938
	8	0.852412	0.57826	1.21427	0.349814
1.00	0		0.74624	1.72599	0.641193
	4	0.426106	0.76461	1.78190	0.677313
	8	0.852213	0.85372	1.90528	0.686698

Table 3. Results of simulated analysis. The data volume is 162mm x 126mm x 60mm

7.3 Discussions

At a first glance, it seems strange that distortion has a less influence than accuracy in feature detection. This is due in fact to several reasons:

- optical distortion might be large, but its equivalence for a projective distortion is far less larger. Furthermore, most of the points are located in the central part of the image where distortion is less important.
- error due to optical distortion is highly correlative with regard to the feature localization errors. This point should be explored more precisely.

For many industrial applications, reconstruction accuracy should be at least 1/1000 of the explored volume size. At this level, accuracy in the feature detection has to reach already the subpixel, but lens distortion can be neglected. If the 1/10000 of accuracy is wished, then distortion has to be integrated.

8   Conclusion

This paper shows how reconstruction can be done from multiple uncalibrated cameras using the parameter estimation approach. Such an approach allows for instance to work with a camera with automatic focus and aperture, without knowing the position from where each view is taken and without knowing the internal camera parameters. However reconstruction is only done up to a projective transformation of the 3D space. Therefore, euclidean information have to be added. The minimal set of information is the position of five fiducial points. The parameter estimation framework allows to add euclidean constraints to the projection equations from where we get a solution in the euclidean space.

The exact values for the fiducial points do not have to be known, this approach allows a relative reconstruction with respect to this reference frame. Resolution of such a non linear optimization process was possible in all our experiments on real and simulated data and convergence was very fast. This convergence was probably due to the large redundancy of the equations.

Results are excellent on a qualitative basis. However, to reach high accuracy reconstruction, subpixel precision has to be reached as it is proven by the experiments on simulated data. This is not really new and is in accordance with what is done by photogrammetrists [3]. In our experiments, even with $12.5mm$ focal length, the projective equivalence of optical distortions was small (less than 0.5 pixel). Correcting these distortions when the localization errors are important is therefore useless. On the other hand, subpixel accuracy in image features localization was more crucial. The major reason is the uncorrelated nature of the feature noise compared with distortions which introduce systematic correlated noise.

Another direction remains to be explored: the outliers problem in the data. Tools exist for this kind of problem and come from what is called "robust estimation" (see for instance [7]); this direction will be explored in the near future.

References

1. H.A. Beyer. Accurate calibration of CCD cameras. In *Proceedings of the Conference on Computer Vision and Pattern Recognition, Urbana-Champaign, Illinois, USA*, pages 96–101, 1992.
2. H.A. Beyer. *Geometric and Radiometric Analysis of a CCD-Camera Based Photogrammetric Close-Range System.* PhD thesis, ETH-Zurich, 1992.
3. D.C. Brown. Close-range camera calibration. *Photogrammetric Engineering*, 37(8):855–866, 1971.
4. R. Deriche and T. Blaszka. Recovering and characterizing image features using an efficient model based approach. In *Proceedings of the Conference on Computer Vision and Pattern Recognition, New York, USA*, pages 530–535, June 1993.
5. O. Faugeras. What can be seen in three dimensions with an uncalibrated stereo rig? In G. Sandini, editor, *Proceedings of the 2nd European Conference on Computer Vision, Santa Margherita Ligure, Italy*, pages 563–578. Springer-Verlag, May 1992.

6. O.D. Faugeras, Q.T. Luong, and S.J. Maybank. Camera Self-Calibration: Theory and Experiments. In G. Sandini, editor, *Proceedings of the 2nd European Conference on Computer Vision, Santa Margherita Ligure, Italy*, pages 321–334. Springer-Verlag, May 1992.

7. W. Förstner. Reliability analysis of parameter estimation in linear models with applications to mensuration problems in computer vision. *Computer Vision, Graphics and Image Processing*, 40:273–310, 1987.

8. R. Hartley, R. Gupta, and T. Chang. Stereo from uncalibrated cameras. In *Proceedings of the Conference on Computer Vision and Pattern Recognition, Urbana-Champaign, Illinois, USA*, pages 761–764, 1992.

9. J.J. Koenderink and A. J. van Doorn. Affine structure from motion. Technical report, Utrecht University, Utrecht, The Netherlands, October 1989.

10. C.H. Lee and T. Huang. Finding point correspondences and determining motion of a rigid object from two weak perspective views. *Computer Vision, Graphics and Image Processing*, 52:309–327, 1990.

11. Q.T. Luong. *Matrice Fondamentale et Autocalibration en Vision par Ordinateur*. Thèse de doctorat, Université de Paris-Sud, Orsay, France, December 1992.

12. S.J. Maybank and O.D. Faugeras. A theory of self calibration of a moving camera. *International Journal of Computer Vision*, 8(2):123–151, 1992.

13. R. Mohr, L. Morin, and E. Grosso. Relative positioning with uncalibrated cameras. In J.L Mundy and A. Zisserman, editors, *Geometric Invariance in Computer Vision*, pages 440–460. MIT Press, 1992.

14. R. Mohr, L. Quan, F. Veillon, and B. Boufama. Relative 3D reconstruction using multiples uncalibrated images. Technical Report RT 84-I-IMAG LIFIA 12, LIFIA–IRIMAG, 1992.

15. C.M. Orange and F.C.A Groen. Model based corner detection. In *Proceedings of the Conference on Computer Vision and Pattern Recognition, New York, USA*, pages 690–691, June 1993.

16. W.H. Press, B.P. Flannery, S.A. Teukolsky, and W.T. Vetterling W.T. *Numerical Recipes in C*. Cambridge University Press, 19°8.

17. L. Quan and R. Mohr. Determining perspective structures using hierarchial Hough transform. *Pattern Recognition Letters*, 9(4):279–286, 1989.

18. K. Rohr. Recognizing corners by fitting parametric models. *International Journal of Computer Vision*, 9(3):213–230, December 1992.

19. J.G. Semple and G.T. Kneebone. *Algebraic Projective Geometry*. Oxford Science Publication, 1952.

20. C.C. Slama, editor. *Manual of Photogrammetry, fourth edition*. American Society of Photogrammetry and Remote Sensing, Falls Church, Virginia, USA, 1980.

21. G. Sparr. Projective invariants for affine shapes of point configurations. In *Proceeding of the DARPA–ESPRIT workshop on Applications of Invariants in Computer Vision, Reykjavik, Iceland*, pages 151–170, March 1991.

22. C. Tomasi and T. Kanade. Factoring image sequences into shape and motion. In *Proceedings of IEEE Workshop on Visual Motion, Princeton, New Jersey*, pages 21–28, Los Alamitos, California, USA, October 1991. IEEE Computer Society Press.

23. R.Y. Tsai. A versatile camera calibration technique for high-accuracy 3D machine vision metrology using off-the-shelf TV cameras and lenses. IEEE *Journal of Robotics and Automation*, 3(4):323–344, 1987.

Applications of Motion Field of Curves

Théo Papadopoulo and Olivier Faugeras

INRIA Sophia-Antipolis,
2004 Route des Lucioles,
B.P. 93, 06902 SOPHIA-ANTIPOLIS, FRANCE

1 Introduction

In [FP93], we have seen that a rigidity assumption allows us, theoretically, to recover the 3D structure and motion of a 3D curve from a monocular sequence of images. Moreover, it is shown that this same framework permits one to disambiguate stereo matches for curves. The data needed in order to achieve these tasks are derivatives defined on the so-called spatio-temporal surface. In order to implement these ideas, we focussed on three main directions :

- Simplify the existing equations.
- Find methods to compute the needed derivatives.
- Implement some simpler cases, namely the case of planar 3D curves.

After the introduction of notations, we examine briefly why the equations for the general case can be simplified and how to relate the 3D motion of planar curves to the first order derivatives in space and time on the spatio-temporal surface. Then, we describe how it is possible to verify the computed motion when using real images and how to use this same method to disambiguate curve matches with a stereo rig for which only the internal parameters are known. In the final section, we discuss our implementation for the planar curve case and results on both synthetic and real images. As well, results of the derivative computation needed for the general monocular and stereo cases are presented.

2 Notations and Basic Results

The goal of this section is to introduce some notations relative to the problem of recovering the 3D motion from 2D motion fields. We will also recall some basic results that are described in details in [FP93] and explain without proof why one of the basic results of this paper can be simplified.

2.1 The Camera Model

We assume that the camera obeys the pinhole model as shown in Fig. 1. The model composes of a retina plane $\mathcal{R}$ and of a focal center point O. The retina $\mathcal{R}$ is parallel to the plane (O, X, Y) and is at distance f of O where f is the focal distance. By applying an adequate scaling on the coordinates (X, Y, Z), it is always possible to suppose that $f = 1$. The unit focal length (normalized to 1) is therefore assumed in the the discussion to follow.

The frame (O, X, Y, Z) being naturally attached to the camera model, all equations involving 3D parameters will be written in this frame.

Given a 3D point $\mathbf{M} = (X, Y, Z)$ and its 2D perspective projection $\mathbf{m} = (x, y, 1)$ on the $\mathcal{R}$ plane, their relationship is characterized b the following equation :

$$\mathbf{M} = Z\mathbf{m} \qquad (1)$$

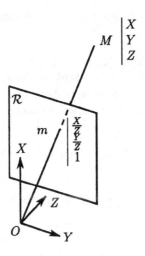

Fig. 1. The pinhole model of a camera

This equation is fundamental in that all the constraints we will present here are direct consequences of it. The concept of temporal variance can be incorporated with the introduction of a time factor τ.

2.2 Definitions

We now assume that we observe in a sequence of images a family (c_τ) of curves, where τ denotes time, which we assume to be the perspective projection in the retina of a 3D curve (C) that moves in space. If we consider the three-dimensional space (x, y, τ), this family of curves sweeps in that space a surface (Σ) defined as the set of points $((c_\tau), \tau)$. Figure 2 illustrates an example of one such spatio-temporal surface generated by a circle rotating around one of its diameters in front of the camera.

At a given time instant τ, let s be the arclength of (c_τ) and S the arclength of (C). We further suppose that S is not a function of time (i.e. the motion

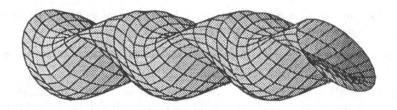

Fig. 2. The spatio-temporal surface generated by a circle rotating and translating in front of the camera

is isometric). Now, for a point $\mathbf{m}$ on (c_τ), it is possible to define two different motion fieds :

- The *apparent motion field* $\mathbf{v}_m^a$ (*a* for *apparent*) of $\mathbf{m}(s, \tau)$ is the partial derivative with respect to time when s is kept constant, $\frac{\partial \mathbf{m}}{\partial \tau} = \mathbf{m}_\tau$.
- The *real motion field* $\mathbf{v}_m^r$ (*r* for *real*) is the partial derivative of $\mathbf{m}(s, \tau)$ with respect to time when S is kept constant, or its total time derivative $\dot{\mathbf{m}}$. This field is the projection of the 3D velocity field in the retina.

Moreover, introducing the Frenet frame $(\mathbf{t}, \mathbf{n})$, where $\mathbf{n}$ is the unit normal vector to (c_τ) at $\mathbf{m}$, we have

$$\mathbf{v}_m^a = \alpha \mathbf{t} + \beta \mathbf{n}$$
$$\mathbf{v}_m^r = w \mathbf{t} + \beta \mathbf{n}$$

where α is the tangential apparent motion field, w is the tangential real motion field and β is the normal motion field. Note that β has a nice geometric interpretation as shown in Fig. 3. We consider the normal $\mathbf{n}$ at point m of curve (c_τ). At time $\tau + d\tau$, the curve $c_{\tau+d\tau}$ is intersected by the line defined by m and $\mathbf{n}$ at a point p represented by $\mathbf{m} + \beta \mathbf{n} d\tau$.

With these notations, under the weak assumption of *isometric* motion, we reach the following conclusions from the study of the spatio-temporal surface :

1. The normal motion field β can be recovered from the normal to the spatio-temporal surface,
2. the tangential apparent motion field can be recovered from the normal motion field,
3. the tangential real motion field *cannot* be recovered from the spatio-temporal surface.

Therefore, the full real motion field is not computable from the observation of the image of a moving curve under the isometric assumption. This can be considered as a new statement of the so-called *aperture* problem. In order to solve it we *must* add more constraints, for example that the 3D motion is rigid.

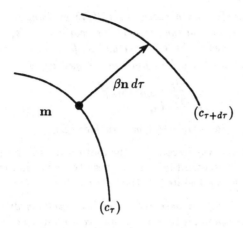

Fig. 3. A geometric interpretation of β

2.3 The Case of a Rigid 3D Curve

Assuming now that the curve (C) is moving rigidly. Let $(\Omega, \mathbf{V})$ be its kinematic screw at the optical center O of the camera. We assume also that the camera has been normalized by calibration to unit focal length. Finally, recall that the velocity $\dot{\mathbf{M}}$ of any point $\mathbf{M}$ attached to the rigid body is given by

$$\mathbf{V}_M = \dot{\mathbf{M}} = \mathbf{V} + \Omega \times \mathbf{M} \tag{2}$$

where the vector $\mathbf{V}_M$ is the three-dimensional velocity of point M.

Taking the total derivative of (1) with respect to time, we get :

$$V_{M_z}\mathbf{m} + Z(w\mathbf{t} + \beta\mathbf{n}) = \mathbf{V}_M$$

Projecting this vector equation onto $\mathbf{t}$ and $\mathbf{n}$ yields two scalar equations :

$$Z(w + \Omega \cdot \mathbf{b}) = -\mathbf{U_n} \cdot \mathbf{V} \tag{3}$$

$$Z(\beta - \Omega \cdot \mathbf{a}) = \mathbf{U_t} \cdot \mathbf{V} \tag{4}$$

where $\mathbf{U_t}$ denotes $\mathbf{m} \times \mathbf{t}$ and $\mathbf{U_n}$ denotes $\mathbf{m} \times \mathbf{n}$ and $\mathbf{a}$ and $\mathbf{b}$ are given by :

$$\mathbf{a} = \mathbf{m} \times \mathbf{U_t}$$

$$\mathbf{b} = \mathbf{m} \times \mathbf{U_n}$$

These equations are fundamental (especially (4)) in the sense that they express the relationship between the unknown 3D motion of a point and the real motion field of its image.

Let's now recall some previous result that is given in [FP93].

Theorem 1. *At each point of an observed curve (c_τ) evolving during time, it is possible to write two polynomial equations in the coordinates Ω, $\mathbf{V}$, $\dot{\Omega}$ and $\dot{\mathbf{V}}$ (The kinematic screw attached to the 3D curve and its first time derivative). The coefficients of these equations are polynomials in the quantities*

$$\begin{matrix} \beta & \frac{\partial \beta}{\partial s} & \frac{\partial^2 \beta}{\partial s^2} & \partial_{\mathbf{n}_\beta}\beta & \partial_{\mathbf{n}_\beta}\frac{\partial \beta}{\partial s} \\ \kappa & \frac{\partial \kappa}{\partial s} & \partial_{\mathbf{n}_\beta}\kappa \end{matrix}$$

that can be measured from the spatio-temporal surface (Σ).

These equations lead to a way to compute the motion and the structure of the 3D curve. In fact, it can be shown that one of these two equation is redundant and the previous result can be restated as the new result :

Theorem 2. *At each point of an observed curve (c_τ) evolving during time, it is possible to write one polynomial equation in the coordinates Ω, $\mathbf{V}$, $\dot{\Omega}$ and $\dot{\mathbf{V}}$ (The kinematic screw attached to the 3D curve and its first time derivative). The coefficients of this equation are polynomials in the quantities*

$$\begin{matrix} \beta & \frac{\partial \beta}{\partial s} & \partial_{\mathbf{n}_\beta}\beta \\ \kappa \end{matrix}$$

that can be measured from the spatio-temporal surface (Σ).

The nice thing with this new theorem is that we get rid of all third order derivatives with only first and second order derivatives being left. Therefore we are only interested in the above-mentionned derivatives and we will show later that it is possible to compute them quite precisely.

3   The Motion of 3D Planar Rigid Curves

We study here a special case of the motion of rigid curves sketched in the previous section : the case of a 3D rigid curve that is planar. By making this hypothesis, it is possible to write an equation similar to those obtained in the general case but :

- in which $\dot{\Omega}$ and $\dot{\mathbf{V}}$ are no longer involved, thus leading to a system of equations with less unknowns.
- of total degree 2 (instead of 4).
- in which only the first order derivatives of Σ will appear.

The first two characteristics show that the systems we obtain is much simpler (less unknowns with lower degrees), thus the number of possible solutions is smaller. The second characteristic means that not only the equation are simpler but also they are more stable with respect to the measurement noise. We thus may hope that the solutions of the system are also more stable. These two reasons have appeared sufficently attractive to motivate us to implement this case before going to the general case.

Basically, all these simplifications are possible because of the introduction of new unknowns that correspond to the normal $\mathbf{N} = [a, b, c]^T$ to the curve plane.

3.1 The Equation in the Planar Case

Let $M = [X, Y, Z]^T$ be a point on the 3D planar curve. This point belongs to the plane of the curve. If we suppose that the image of the curve is not degenarated into a segment, then the optical center of the camera is not on the curve plane. The point M thus verifies the following equation :

$$N \cdot M + 1 = aX + bY + cZ + 1 = 0 \tag{5}$$

Combining (5) with the perspective equation (1), we obtain :

$$ZN \cdot m + 1 = 0$$

or :

$$Z = \frac{-1}{N \cdot m} \tag{6}$$

Equation (6) is fundamental because it connects the plane structure of the curve Z to the measures in the image x, y. Now remember (4) :

$$Z(\beta - \Omega \cdot a) = U_t \cdot V$$

Replacing Z by its value given by (6) in (4), we obtain :

$$-\frac{\beta - \Omega \cdot a}{N \cdot m} = U_t \cdot V \tag{7}$$

Equation (6) is essential : it allows one to replace the quantity Z that varies along the observed curve by 3 quantities a, b, c that are constant along this same curve. We thus obtain the following theorem :

Theorem 3. *At each point of (c_τ) considered as the projection of a 3D planar curve, it is possible to write a polynomial equation in the unknowns Ω, V, N.*

$$\beta - \Omega \cdot a + (U_t \cdot V)(N \cdot m) = 0 \tag{8}$$

This equation is not homogeneous in V but we can see that if (V, N) is a solution then $(\lambda V, \frac{1}{\lambda} N)$ is also a solution for every $\lambda \neq 0$. This property shows that, as in the general case, only the direction of V can be recovered. The equation is of degree 2 in (V, N), of degree 1 in Ω and of total degree 2.

In the following we will call this equation the planar equation.

Expressing this equation at 8 points, we obtain a system in (Ω, V, N) of degree 2 with 9 unknowns. A direct application of Bezout's theorem shows that such a system has $2^8 = 256$ complex solutions.

It is then possible to reformulate the conjecture we have made in the previous section for this particular case :

Conjecture 4. The kinematic screw $(\Omega, \mathbf{V})$ and the normal $\mathbf{N}$ to the plane of a 3D rigid planar curve can, in general, be estimated from the observation of the spatio-temporal surface generated by its image on the retina by solving a system of polynomial equations. The quantity Z can be estimated at each point up to a scale factor by using (6).

Of course, as in the general case, this conjecture is wrong in some special cases such as straight lines but also, as we will see later, conics. See [Ber89] for other examples of ambiguity. Practically, for non ambiguous curves, this conjecture has always been proved to be true.

3.2 Ambiguousness of the Solutions

We are interested here in describing the structure of the solutions. The question is : is it possible generically to find a relation between two solutions (here this means that the result we look for does not depend on the actual values of the estimated parameters). One way to do this is to search for a transformation on $(\Omega, \mathbf{V}, \mathbf{N})$ that leaves the equation unchanged.

Let us thus look at the coefficients of (8) in variables x, y, t, β. We obtain :

$$
\begin{aligned}
&\text{coefficient in } \beta: && 1 \\
&\text{coefficient in } t_x: && \Omega_x + c\mathbf{V}_y && (9) \\
&\text{coefficient in } t_y: && \Omega_y - c\mathbf{V}_x && (10) \\
&\text{coefficient in } xt_x: && a\mathbf{V}_y - \Omega_z && (11) \\
&\text{coefficient in } yt_y: && -\Omega_z - b\mathbf{V}_x && (12) \\
&\text{coefficient in } xt_y: && c\mathbf{V}_z - a\mathbf{V}_x && (13) \\
&\text{coefficient in } yt_x: && b\mathbf{V}_y - c\mathbf{V}_z && (14) \\
&\text{coefficient in } x(xt_y - yt_x): && \Omega_y + a\mathbf{V}_z && (15) \\
&\text{coefficient in } y(xt_y - yt_x): && b\mathbf{V}_z - \Omega_x && (16)
\end{aligned}
$$

These different terms represent the way the information relative to $(\Omega, \mathbf{V}, \mathbf{N})$ is coded in (8) and this is independent of the point at which the equation is written. In some way, every quantity that cannot be computed from these terms or that remains ambiguous will exhibit the same behaviour when computed from (8). We use this property to prove that there is a companion solution to each solution of the system.

It is possible to eliminate the components of Ω between (9),(10), equations (11),(12) and (13),(14). We thus obtain the following expressions :

$$
b\mathbf{V}_z + c\mathbf{V}_y
$$
$$
c\mathbf{V}_x + a\mathbf{V}_z
$$
$$
a\mathbf{V}_y + b\mathbf{V}_x
$$

$$c\mathbf{V}_z - a\mathbf{V}_x$$
$$c\mathbf{V}_z - b\mathbf{V}_y$$

Note that it is possible to swap $\mathbf{V}$ and $\mathbf{N}$ in these expressions without changing their values. Let us look if it is possible to find a value of Ω that verifies the equations. By equating the new values with the old ones, we obtain :

$$\Omega_x' + b\mathbf{V}_z = \Omega_x + c\mathbf{V}_y$$
$$\Omega_y' + c\mathbf{V}_x = \Omega_y + a\mathbf{V}_z$$
$$\Omega_z' + a\mathbf{V}_y = \Omega_z + b\mathbf{V}_x$$

Solving this system in Ω', we see that we must take $\Omega' = \Omega + \mathbf{V} \wedge \mathbf{N}$.

We thus obtain the following theorem :

Theorem 5. *If $(\Omega, \mathbf{V}, \mathbf{N})$ is a solution of the system obtained for a planar curve then $(\Omega + \mathbf{V} \wedge \mathbf{N}, \mathbf{N}, \mathbf{V})$ is also a solution of this same system.*

This theorem is the specialization to planar curves of a well-known theorem on planar points [LH84, May92]. This is not surprising since a planar curve is nothing more than a set of planar points. What is more surprising however is that it can be shown that there is no new ambiguity introduced by the fact we only use normal flow information. Moreover, expressions (9–16) can also be used to show that there is at least one and at most 3 solutions (counting only once the two related solutions) which is a much better bound than that computed from Bezout's theorem.

To conclude this section, let us briefly present some results concerning a special case of 3D planar curves : conics and algebraic planar curves.

3.3 The Case of Conics and Algebraic Curves

When the observed curve is, at each time instant, a conic, on can prove that the 3D curve associated to it is also a conic. It is thus possible to apply our theory for planar curves to this more specific case. Moreover there is a standard mathematical technique, called elimination, that can be used here to write directly all the equations that can be written along the conic. This will give a finite set of algebraic equations instead of an (theoretically) infinite set of equations at each point of the conic. Elimination is a technique of suppressing a variable between two polynomials that vanish simultaneously. Here one polynomial is (8) and the other is the equation of the conic. Both equations depend on the retinal coordinates x and y. Thus eliminating one of these variables (for example y) between these two polynomials, we obtain a new polynomial in one variable (x) that must vanish everywhere. Thus all the coefficients of this polynomial (considered as a polynomial in x) must be zero. These coefficients are new polynomials in Ω, $\mathbf{V}$ and $\mathbf{N}$. These new polynomials relate globally the observed conic to the motion of the 3D conic. Doing this one obtains a system of 5 equations with 8 unknowns. This proves definitively that the observation of a conic without making any other hypothesis is insufficient for recovering the 3D motion. Actually it is possible to give an arbitrary value to $\mathbf{V}$ (or equivalently $\mathbf{N}$) to get a linear system with 5 equations and 6 unknowns $(\mathbf{\Omega}, \mathbf{N})$ (respectively $(\mathbf{\Omega}, \mathbf{V})$) which generically gives always a unique solution. Thus the observation of a conic gives rise to a triple infinity of different 3D motions (and thus also 3D structures). Moreover, there is no way to obtain some new constraint (by, for example, deriving once again the obtained equations) without introducing other parameters or assuming something on either the motion or on the conic.

Note that the scheme that was sketched here is valid for any given algebraic curve. Then for a generic algebraic curve of degree n, we obtain $\frac{n(n+3)}{2}$ equations. It is interesting to note that this number is exactly the number of 2D points necessary to define the curve uniquely. This result shows us that for any 3D generic rigid planar curve whose projection is an algebraic curve of degree higher than 3, there will be a finite set of solutions.

4 How to Use $(\mathbf{\Omega}, \mathbf{V})$

The main goal of this section is to show what can be done once $(\mathbf{\Omega}, \mathbf{V})$ has been computed : one obvious thing to do is to recover the 3D structure of the curve but it is also possible to compute quantities that are independent of the frame in which $(\mathbf{\Omega}, \mathbf{V})$ has been computed. This is most interesting to help verifying quantitatively the quality of the results when dealing with real images as well as for combining information coming from many different cameras.

4.1 Reconstruction of the Curve

From previous formulas, once the motion is computed, it is possible to reconstruct the 3D curve up to a scale factor by two different means :

- Using (5) which relates Z to the plane parameters $\mathbf{N}$. Here we are using explicitly the planar hypothesis.
- Using the general (4) that is true for all 3D rigid curve. It relates Z to the kinematic screw $(\mathbf{\Omega}, \mathbf{V})$. Since we do not use the planar hypothesis, the reconstructions computed this way are more unstable than the previous ones.

4.2 Motion Invariants

The goal of this section is twofold :

- Show how it is possible to verify quantitatively the quality of the results. Usually when experimenting with real images, it is possible to know precisely the 3D motion in some frame that cannot be related easily to the camera frame. Thus the easiest way to achieve this goal is to compare quantities depending on $(\mathbf{\Omega}, \mathbf{V})$ that are invariant to this Euclidean change of frame.

– Expanding on this idea, if a scene is observed by a stereo rig for which only the internal parameters are known, it is possible to disambiguate curve matches as soon as the candidate curves are undergoing motions different enough. This has to be compared with the method for calibrated stereo rigs that has been sketched in [FP93].

To achieve this goal, let's recall two basic properties of the kinematic screw.

– The component Ω is independant of the point at which the kinematic screw is expressed whereas $\mathbf{V}$ depends on it.
– The quantity $\Omega \cdot \mathbf{V}$ is also independent of the point at which the kinematic screw is expressed even though $\mathbf{V}$ is not. It expresses the values of the translationnal velocity along the instantaneous rotation axe.

But, since we don't know the frame in which the 3D motion is measured and since $\mathbf{V}$ is known only up to a scale factor, we cannot directly rely on these quantities. However, the norm of Ω as well as the angle between Ω and $\mathbf{V}$ are invariant to any change of frame and can thus be used as the searched quantitative measure for veryfing the quality of the results using real images.

Moreover, for the planar case, it is possible to use $\mathbf{N}$ to derive two more invariants : $\Omega \cdot \mathbf{N}$ and $\mathbf{V} \cdot \mathbf{N}$.

Using a stereo rig with known internal parameters, it is also possible to use these quantities to disambiguate stereo matches for curves with different underlying motions. Suppose you have computed the kinematic screws $(\Omega_1, \mathbf{V}_1)$ and $(\Omega_2, \mathbf{V}_2)$ respectively for a curve (C_1) in camera 1 and for a curve (C_2) in camera 2. If the quantities, $\|\Omega_1\|$ and $\|\Omega_2\|$ or $(\widehat{\Omega_1, \mathbf{V}_1})$ and $(\widehat{\Omega_2, \mathbf{V}_2})$ disagree then the curve match is wrong. If they agree, however, it is possible to match the reconstructions R_1 and R_2 to verify the matching hypothesis and to improve the quality of the recovered 3D structure since the two structures R_1 and R_2 are related by a similitude in that case.

5 Implementation

We describe here the implementation of the theory described in the previous section and show the results we have obtained on both synthetic and real images.

In all these experiments the first stage is to adapt the camera model we have hypothesized to derive the valid equations for the real camera. This is explained in the next section.

5.1 Normalized Coordinates and Image Coordinates

In the previous sections, we have assumed that a Euclidean structure is defined on the retinal plane $\mathcal{R}$. This structure is inherited from the 3D Euclidean structure. This hypothesis allows us to write scalar and cross products that are necessary to obtain the equations. In fact, if one considers the normal flow, it immediately leads to the notion of angle, which is closely tied to scalar product.

However, when working with images, people are used to, for convinience, to work in a frame in which the coordinates of a pixel correspond to the indices of that pixel in the image considered as a two dimensionnal array of pixels. These coordinates are called *image coordinates*. Working with these coordinates has two consequences :

- First, the usual scalar product does not define in this frame an Euclidean structure compatible with that of the observed 3D space.
- Secondly, the origin of these frames are usually in the top left corner of the image whereas in our theoretical study that origin is at the orthogonal projection (in 3D space) of the optical center onto the retina $\mathcal{R}$.

The consequence of these is that, before doing anything else, it is necessary to map the Euclidean structure of the 3D space onto the retina $\mathcal{R}$. This is equivalent of being able to define a special scalar product on the retina that is comptatible with that of 3D space. One way of doing this is to transform the image coordinates to obtain some *normalized coordinates* with which the standard scalar product behaves the right way.

Relations between image and normalized coordinates have been extensively studied under the framework of camera calibration. We will utilize the commonly used camera calibration model as defined in [Tos87] :

$$x = h_1 u + h_2 v + h_3 \qquad (17)$$
$$y = h_4 v + h_5 \qquad (18)$$

where x,y denote the normalized coordinates of a point and u,v denote image coordinates of this same point. $(h_1, h_2, h_3, h_4, h_5)$ are the internal parameters of the camera. The change of coordinates defined by (17) and (18) must be applied before any motion computation.

Note that we have assumed here that the transformation between normalized and image coordinates is time independent. We have assumed as well that the period of time between two consecutive images is constant and known precisely.

5.2 Solving the Polynomial System

We have seen that, in order to find the 3D motion of the planar curve, we need to solve an over-constrained polynomial system. It is crucial for both finding real solutions and dealing with noise in the measures, to have a numerical stable method that allows us to work with over-constrained polynomial systems (that is more equations than unknowns). Generally speaking this kind of systems has no solutions but we know that our systems are in that very special case where (in the absence of noise) there is at least one solution (the actual motion of the 3D curve).

Moreover, experience that are not described here have convinced us that, in practise, the number of solutions is quite small and that there is a good chance to find the good one considering any reasonable initial estimate. Since we are unable (neither theoretically nor practically) to count the number of real solutions of the system, we are not actually able to find all of them. Instead we will focus on a method that allows us to compute a solution given any random starting point. Some other experiments not described here allow us to believe that tracking this solution through time bring always us back to the searched for solution or to its companion as described in Theorem 5.

One obvious choice to solve this problem is to use least-squares. However, since our equations are non-linear this introduces many fictious solutions (depending on the degrees of the equations in the unknowns and on the number of these unknowns). Therefore we decided to modify the multi-dimensional Newton method to adapt it to our requirements. In this method, the hypothesis of having exactly the same number of equations as the number of unknowns is used only to inverse the jacobian of the system (thus we need a square jacobian matrix, which means that there must be as many unknowns as equations). Since this inversion is only needed to solve a linear system, we may apply least-square methods directly on this linear system that as exactly the same number of equations and the same number of unknowns as the initial system. Since this system is linear we know that least squares will not introduce spurious solutions and this seems much better than directly applying least squares on the original system.

We tested this method on a system of equations chosen among the equations of a linear family of circles and it gave good results even when we added noise onto the equations. It showed good properties of convergence and stability.

5.3 Motion of Planar Curves

Many tests have shown that it is difficult to estimate with a good accurate spatio-temporal parameters. Temporal derivatives are especially difficult to obtain : this phenomenon seems to come from sampling problems in time. Whereas spatial sampling of an image may be known and constant (it is fixed by the physical parameters of the camera), time sampling of the spatio-temporal surface Σ around a point P depends on the speed of that point. In other words, around a point P that has a small normal flow, Σ is better sampled than around a point where the normal flow is important. The importance of this fact on temporal derivatives is illustrated in Fig. 3 : as the curves (c_τ) and $(c_{\tau+d\tau})$ move further apart, the sampling of surface Σ in the direction of n_β deteriorates. Temporal derivatives can be obtained very easily by considering the curve drawn on Σ that lies in the plane defined by the point m at which we want to compute the spatio-temporal parameters, and being spanned by the vectors n the normal vector to the observed curve at m and by τ the unit vector on the time axis.

Therefore, the accuracy of the temporal derivatives depends upon how well this curve is sampled. This is the reason why we have implemented first the case of planar curves since it involves only first order derivatives whereas second order derivatives are needed to solve the general case.

In the remaining of this paper, we will suppose that the points of the curve that we are observing have been linked together into pixel chains. Moreover, we will use two image sequences (of about 30 to 40 images each). The first one (see Fig. 4) is a synthetic sequence of a planar 3D quartic on which intensity images we added up to 20% of noise on intensities. The second one (see Fig. 5) is a real sequence. In all these images the 3D curve rotates around a vertical axis and translates in the same direction.

Here is the general scheme of the implementation :

- Building the spatio-temporal surface.
- Estimating the spatio-temporal parameters at every point of the curve at one time instant.
- Normalising the parameters and finally solving of the polynomial system.

Each of these stages will be described in the next paragraphs.

5.4   Building the Spatio-Temporal Surface

In order to speed up computation times, we must gather the points of the spatio-temporal surface in a data structure that will allow us to compute easily the neighbours of a given point on the surface. To do this, we will take the ouput of the linker and map its result in a doubly linked list of points. In order to recover on some errors of the edge detector we link points that are not contiguous with some threshold. During this work a curvilinear abscissa is computed for each point by choosing an arbitrary origin and by addind the elementary distances between points along the edge. A second phase consists in linking the data structure obtained for the curve (c_τ) (observed at time τ) to that of the curve $(c_{\tau+d\tau})$ (observed at time $\tau+d\tau$). To do this at each point $\mathbf{m}_\tau$ of the curve (c_τ), we associate one of the points of $(c_{\tau+d\tau})$ that is at minimal distance from $\mathbf{m}_\tau$ (because of discretization there might be several such points but they are all in a same neighborhood. We are chosing one of these arbitrarily). The algorithm attempts to use the continuity of the curves to avoid walking through to many points of either (c_τ) or $(c_{\tau+d\tau})$. This time linking is done simultaneously in the two directions : from (c_τ) to $(c_{\tau+d\tau})$ and from $(c_{\tau+d\tau})$ to (c_τ). This give us a two-way link in time.

5.5   Estimating Spatio-Temporal Parameters

The estimation of the spatio-temporal parameters is just sketched here. Because of the discrepancy between space and time sampling rates we will compute independently spatial and temporal parameters. First we compute the local orientation at each point : to do so, we construct the two signals $x(s)$ and $y(s)$ and fit

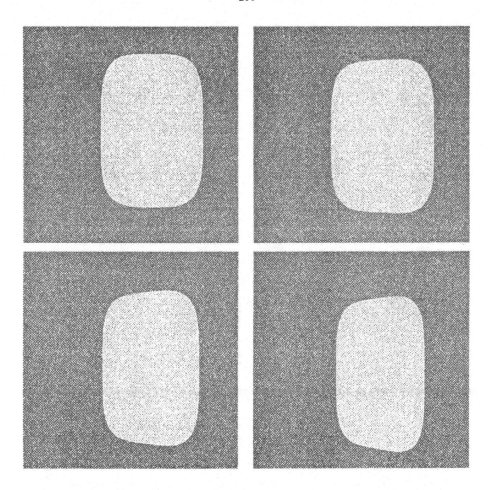

Fig. 4. From right to left and top to bottom : the images of the synthetic sequence at instants 0,10,20 and 30. A Gaussian noise of signal/noise ratio of 20% has been added on intensities.

locally models to them. Deriving these models gives the local derivatives $x'(s)$ and $y'(s)$ that describe the local tangent to the curve which is closely related to the orientation represented here by the angle $\theta(s)$ between the normal and the horizontal. Then, we eventually smooth this result.

The left part of Fig. 6 shows the angle estimates along the curve. The maximal error between the theoric curve and the measures is 0.011 radians.

We then compute the value of the β parameter at each point. To reach this goal, we use the method described at the begining of this section. At each point **m**, which orientation is given by **n**, we build the curve that is defined as the intersection of the spatio-temporal surface Σ with the plane Π defined by **m**, **n** and τ the time axis. This curve can be represented in the plane $(\tau,)$ where

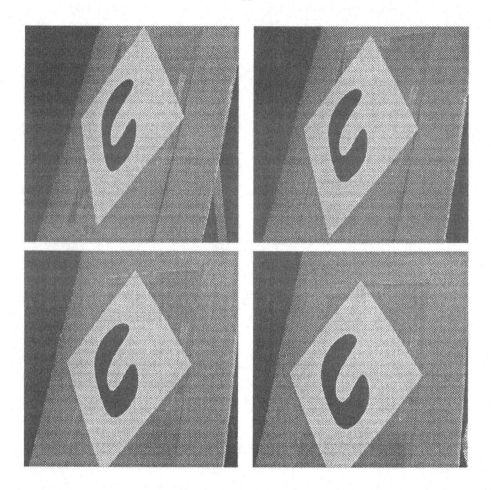

Fig. 5. From right to left and top to bottom : the images of the second real sequence at instants 1,10,20 and 30.

d is the distance in the direction of **n** between a point of plane Π and **m** (this distance is also the distance of this point to the tangent to (c_τ) at **m** if we represent (c_τ) and $(c_{\tau+d\tau})$ in the same plane). We thus obtain a curve that is approximated by a truncated Chebyshev polynomial (to reduce the effects of noise). The derivative of this polynomial at time τ is then computed and is nothing other than β. Again, we smooth the curve $\beta(s)$ in order to reduce the noise on the measured β. This is justified by the assumption that the surface Σ is smooth enough to compute derivatives. The function $\beta(s)$ is then continuous.

The right part of Fig. 6 shows the β estimates along the curve at one time instant for the synthetic image sequence. The maximal error between the theoric curve and the measures is 0.017152 pixels by image (the image number here is the time coordinate).

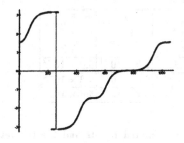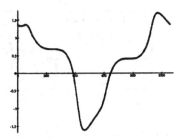

Fig. 6. Estimated angle (left) and β (right) along the curve. The X-axis is curvilinear abscissa. The crosses represent measures whereas plain curves represent theoretical values of the angle.

5.6 Parameters Normalisation of System Resolution

At this point, we have for each point of the curve (c_τ) all the spatio-temporal parameters we need. For each of these, we compute their normalized values. Then we build the polynomial system made from the plane equation expressed at each of these points. This system has 8 unknowns and as many equations as there are points on the edge. In order to take into account the ambiguity on $(\mathbf{V}, \mathbf{N})$ that was described in Theorem 3 we will arbitrarily normalize the first component of $\mathbf{N}$ to 1 (this choice is of course a bad choice as soon as this component approaches 0). The system we obtain has then only 7 unknowns and is solved using the method described earlier in this section.

For the synthetic sequence, using the theoretical values of the parameters we have proved that there are only two solutions to the motion problem. Namely the true solution and its companion solution as described in Theorem 5. In what follows we will always consider errors between the true solution and the corresponding solution.

In Table 1, we have tabulated the accuracy of the computed solution for all the components of $(\Omega, \mathbf{V}, \mathbf{N})$ as a function of the number of images of the synthetic sequence (around image 14) used to compute the spatio-temporal parameters. Note that (and this will be true for all results showed here) that for $\mathbf{V}$ and $\mathbf{N}$ only the angle between the theoretical and estimated values are shown since these values are only defined up to a scale factor. The time needed to do all the computations (including parameter estimation and resolution of the system which has 1112 equations) is about 32 seconds when 5 images are used and about 36 seconds when all 29 images are used. These times have been obtained on a Sun Sparc 2.

Figure 7 show the reconstructions and the values of Z along the curve for the good solution.

Number of images considered	$\| \Omega - \Omega_{\text{theor}} \|$ in °/image	$\widehat{\Omega, \Omega_{\text{theor}}}$ in °	$\widehat{V, V_{\text{theor}}}$ in °	$\widehat{N, N_{\text{theor}}}$ in °
5	1.6×10^{-1}	4.1×10^{-1}	1.2	1.2
13	2.4×10^{-2}	1.1	1.0×10^{-1}	6.0×10^{-2}
20	1.4×10^{-2}	6.4×10^{-1}	6.4×10^{-1}	6.2×10^{-2}
29	1.1×10^{-2}	5.4×10^{-1}	5.1×10^{-1}	5.6×10^{-2}

Table 1. Errors in norm and angle between the estimated results and the theoretical ones as a function of the number of images used to compute the spatio-temporal parameters.

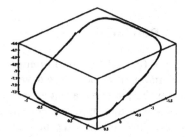
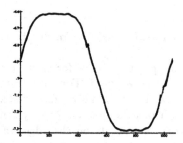

Fig. 7. 3D reconstructions for the good solution (left) and the estimates for Z along the curve (right). The plain curve is the reconstruction based on (5) whereas the crosses represent the reconstruction based on (4).

A nice experimental consequence resulting from the comparison of the planar and general reconstruction is that it seems possible to distinguish automatically the good solution from the bad one : the good solution is always associated to the reconstructions between which the errors is the smallest. The exact explanation of this phenomena is still unclear.

Verifying quantatively the results obtained with the real sequences is a difficult task : as described in Sect. 4 the best way to do it is to look at the angular speed. With the measured data of Fig. 8 the measured angular speed is $-1.055°/image$ where it should be $-1°/image$.

Figure 8 shows the angle and beta estimates along the curve. Figure 9 shows normal flow along the curve. Figure 10 shows the reconstructions obtained from the good and the bad solutions.

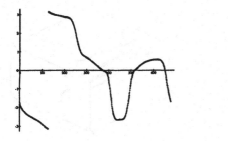 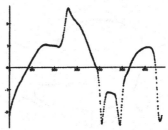

Fig. 8. Estimated angle (left) and β (right) along the curve. The X-axis is curvilinear abscissa. The crosses represent measures whereas plain curves represent theoretical values of the angle.

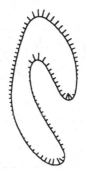

Fig. 9. Normal flow along the curve. The flow has been scaled 4 times for readability.

5.7 Higher Order Derivatives

We conclude this chapter by showing some figures giving the parameters κ, $\frac{\partial \beta}{\partial s}$ and $\partial_{\mathbf{n}_\beta}\beta$ along the curve for the synthetic image sequence. These measures seem good enough to allow a practical implementation of the stereo disambiguation described in [FP93] as well as that of the general 3D rigid curve case based on Theorem 2.

Figures 12 and 13 show the parameters κ, $\frac{\partial \beta}{\partial s}$ and $\partial_{\mathbf{n}_\beta}\beta$ along the observed curve. There are still some problems around curvature extrema. In fact, the origin of these problems is now well understood and will be corrected.

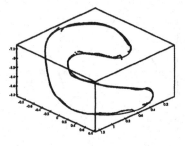 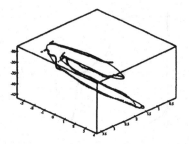

Fig. 10. 3D reconstructions for the good solution (left) and the bad solution (right). The plain curve is the reconstruction based on (5) whereas the crosses represent the reconstruction based on (4).

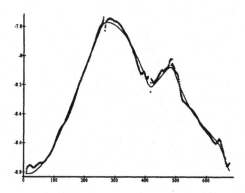

Fig. 11. Estimates for Z along the curve. The plain curve represent the values obtained using (5) whereas the crosses represent the values based on (4).

References

[Ber89] Fredrik Bergholm. Motion from Flow along Contours: A Note on Robustness and Ambiguous Cases. *The International Journal of Computer Vision*, 2(4):395–415, April 1989.

[FP93] Olivier D. Faugeras and Théo Papadopoulo. A theory of the motion fields of curves. *The International Journal of Computer Vision*, 10(2):125–156, 1993.

[LH84] H.C. Longuet-Higgins. The visual ambiguity of a moving plane. *Proceedings of the Royal Society London, B*, 223:165–175, 1984.

[May92] S.J. Maybank. *Theory of reconstruction From Image Motion*. Springer-Verlag, 1992.

[Tos87] G. Toscani. *Système de Calibration optique et perception du mouvement en vision artificielle*. PhD thesis, Paris-Orsay, 1987.

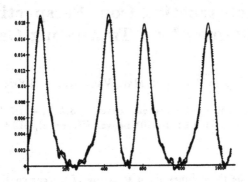

Fig. 12. Measured κ along the curve. Crosses represent measures whereas the plain curve represent the theoretical values.

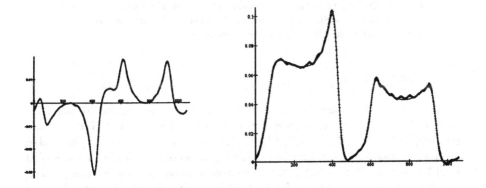

Fig. 13. Estimated $\frac{\partial \beta}{\partial s}$ (left) and $\partial_{\mathbf{n}_\beta}\beta$ (right) along the curve. Crosses represent measures whereas the plain curve represent the theoretical values.

Affine Reconstruction from Perspective Image Pairs Obtained by a Translating Camera *

Theo Moons, Luc Van Gool, Marc Van Diest, and Eric Pauwels

Katholieke Universiteit Leuven, E.S.A.T. – MI2
Kard. Mercierlaan 94, B-3001 Leuven (Heverlee), BELGIUM

Abstract. The three-dimensional structure of a scene consisting of at least five points whose images are identified in two perspective views taken from different positions with a relative object-camera translation in between, can be reconstructed up to a 3D affine transformation. Hence, a more detailed reconstruction is possible using less information when compared to the results reported on arbitrary stereo views with uncalibrated, perspective cameras. The forementioned result is then further specialised towards single views of objects containing parallel structures and translations in camera coordinate planes. In the former case four points suffice for affine reconstruction, whereas the latter case allows the direct use of relatively simple stereo coordinates.

1 Introduction

During the past few years, important new insights have been gained in the information that can be extracted from multiple views taken with uncalibrated cameras (e.g. [KV1, F1, M1, MVQ1, S1, H2]. Structure can often only be extracted up to some non-Euclidean transformation. As an example, viewing a scene of at least 7 points (or even 8 points for a linear computation) from two perspective, uncalibrated cameras with arbitrary relative positions and with known point correspondences allows reconstruction of the point cloud up to an arbitrary 3D projective transformation. On the other hand, efforts to fully calibrate cameras keep on being presented ([FLM1, H1, WS1] to give just a few recent examples). Such work usually is aimed at achieving a complete Euclidean reconstruction, which is needed for quite a number of applications. Whereas complete calibration is a painstaking operation, the practicality of using as many as 7 (or 8) point correspondences from completely different perspective views can be questioned also.

This paper deals with structure that can be extracted from a pair of *perspective* views taken with a translating camera (or alternatively, with a static camera taking two views of translating objects). Translations are a particularly

---

* Theo Moons and Eric Pauwels are supported by a Post-Doctoral Research grant from the Belgian National Fund for Scientific Research (N.F.W.O). The support by Esprit Basic Research Action 6448 'VIVA' and the co-financing by the Flemish government are gratefully acknowledged.

important type of motion since they represent the most efficient paths between points in the absence of obstacles. Hence, robots and mobile platforms often perform this type of motion. As will be shown in Sect. 3, affine reconstruction on the basis of five points can be achieved. This puts the precision of reconstruction and the complexity to be handled at the same level as the results for arbitrary, *orthographic* stereo pairs [KV1]. In a sense this result is complementary to that case, since no 3D information can be gathered from a translating camera taking a series of orthographic images. Under perspective viewing conditions, affine invariants of the scene can be obtained when the given image is combined with a fixed reference view [S1]. Using the same camera, Euclidean reconstruction is possible from three or more perspective views [H2]. This approach needs a rather good initial approximation of the scene, and an affine one was found satisfactory. This is exactly the kind of reconstruction provided by the methods to be expounded here. In the subsequent sections the analysis is further specialized towards situations where the translation is fixed with respect to the object structure (as with objects having parallel parts, cfr. Sect. 4) or where the translation is special with respect to the camera coordinate frame (e.g. translation in a horizontal image coordinate plane, cfr. Sect. 5).

A considerable fraction of the work presented follows an intermediate route between complete calibration and completely unconstrained camera configurations. There obviously can be no doubt about the usefulness of absorbing camera parameters into the group describing the changes at the image level induced by projection. Typically however, keeping a parameter unspecified means enlarging the transformation group to be handled and therefore adversely affecting the complexity of the reconstruction as well as the degree of uncertainty left open (e.g. reconstruction up to a 3D affine rather than a 3D Euclidean transformation). Since the optimal compromise normally will depend on the application, it is worthwhile to investigate intermediate cases requiring partial calibration. The paper is a modest contribution towards that end. The point of departure for Sect. 5 is a piece of earlier work [Vea3, Mea1], where it was observed that a stereo pair of images obtained by perspective projection on parallel and aligned image planes, is governed by a 6-, 11- or 12-dimensional group depending on the available amount of information about the configuration parameters. These groups are representations of respectively the Euclidean motion group, the 3D unimodular group and the (positive) 3D affine group. Here it is shown that the same groups remain appropriate whenever the second image plane is a 2D translation of the first one. In some cases it can even be shown that the group of 3D similarities is the optimal choise.

2   The Camera Model

Throughout the discussion, the *pinhole camera* model will be adhered to. Moreover, the intrinsic camera parameters will be assumed to be controlled to some extent. The image plane coordinate axes are supposed to be orthogonal to one another, and also to the optical axis of the camera. Furthermore, we assume that the position of the optical center is known and that the pixels are square. Some results will be preserved when relaxing one or several of these constraints though. For instance, knowledge of the position of the optical center is not needed in case the camera translates parallel to the image plane. Anyway, most of these assumptions usually are made tacitly, except perhaps for the pixel's aspect ratio. This, however, is quite easy to measure experimentally and to be compensated for through modified sampling or computationally via the application of the appropriate scale factors.

A pair of images of the scene may be obtained by taking one image with two different cameras (the usual 'stereo' set-up) or by taking two images with one camera from different camera positions. From a mathematical point of view there is no real difference between these two situations. From a practical perspective however, keeping the focal length the same for two views — an assumption that will be made repeatedly — is much easier if both views are taken with the same camera. To avoid confusion: whatever the actual number of cameras used, reference will be made to the *first image* and the *second image*, and to the *image pair* to indicate a pair of images taken under the conditions described. Quantities related to the first image in the pair will be denoted with subscript 1, and a subscript 2 will refer to the second image. Coordinates of scene points will always refer to a camera-centred reference frame coupled to the camera position and orientation used to take the first image. The first image of a scene point with scene coordinates (X, Y, Z) then has coordinates (x_1, y_1) given by

$$x_1 = f_1 \frac{X}{Z} \quad \text{and} \quad y_1 = f_1 \frac{Y}{Z} , \tag{1}$$

where f_1 denotes the focal length of the first camera. A second image of the scene is obtained by translating the camera over a vector (u, v, w). If the camera is not rotated with respect to the first camera position, then the second image of the scene point (X, Y, Z) has coordinates (x_2, y_2) given by

$$x_2 = f_2 \frac{X - u}{Z - w} \quad \text{and} \quad y_2 = f_2 \frac{Y - v}{Z - w} , \tag{2}$$

where f_2 is the focal length of the second camera. For the sake of clarity, we will assume that the focal lengths before and after the translation are equal; i.e. $f_1 = f_2 = f$. This restriction can quite easily be removed, as discussed in Sect. 7. A discussion of the general case (i.e. $f_1 \neq f_2$) can be found in [Mea2].

3 3D Affine Reconstruction from Translating Cameras

Suppose a number of scene points are observed with a perspective camera that translates relatively to the points. Two views are taken, one before and one after the relative translation. The direction of the translation is arbitrary. The question now is whether the simplicity of the motion lowers the complexity of the 3D reconstruction of the scene when compared with the general perspective stereo case [F1, MVQ1]. In the case of arbitrary relative motions of cameras and objects two views of at least 6 points and the knowledge of their correspondences is necessary to arrive at projective reconstruction. As will be shown in this section, the analysis under translation can be simplified substantially: *using only 5 point correspondences, and affine rather than projective reconstruction can be achieved.*

Suppose 5 point correspondences are given between two images of the same scene, one taken before the translation, the other one after. In the image taken before the translation, we will refer to these points as P_1, P_2, P_3, P_4, P_5; and in the image after the translation, the corresponding points after are denoted by P_1', P_2', P_3', P_4', P_5', respectively. Moreover, the distinction between the views will systematically be made by indicating values after translation with primes. The original scene points of which these points are the images, will be called $\tilde{P}_1$, $\tilde{P}_2$, $\tilde{P}_3$, $\tilde{P}_4$, $\tilde{P}_5$. Much of what follows capitalizes on the *a priori* knowledge that, for the translation case, three-dimensional orientations are known to be preserved. To exploit this fact, the two images of the five points are superimposed, thus yielding one image containing both the points P_i as well as the P_I' ($i = 1, \ldots, 5$).

Before proceeding, some additional notational issues will be settled. The image coordinates of a point P_i will be specified as (x_i, y_i), and those of P_i' are written as (x_i', y_i'). In the sequel, the straight line connecting the points P_i and P_j will be denoted by $< P_i, P_j >$. The epipole for the direction of a line $< P_i, P_j >$ will be denoted by E_{ij}. The epipole of the translational direction will be referred at as E_T. These epipoles are found as the intersection of lines from the two views. As an example, E_T is found as the intersection of $< P_1, P_1' >$ and $< P_2, P_2' >$ (cfr. Fig. 1). The cross ratio $C(P_i, P_j, P_k, P_l)$ of four points is defined as

$$C(P_i, P_j, P_k, P_l) = \frac{(x_i - x_k)\,(x_j - x_l)}{(x_i - x_j)\,(x_k - x_l)} \ .$$

We start off by considering three points P_1, P_2, P_3 and their corresponding points under translation P_1', P_2', P_3'. These two point triples define two triangles and the directions of their sides have collinear epipoles on a line at infinity. This line together with the point triples fixes a projective frame in the plane of either triangle. Since we also know that the epipolar line should be moved to infinity, this frame can be made an affine frame by doing so. The points P_1, P_2, P_3 (resp. P_1', P_2', P_3') are the images of a plane in the scene formed by the points $\tilde{P}_1$, $\tilde{P}_2$, $\tilde{P}_3$. We will call this plane the *base plane*. Note that the three points $\tilde{P}_1$, $\tilde{P}_2$, $\tilde{P}_3$ define an affine reference frame for the base plane (with $\tilde{P}_1$ taken as the origin). Now consider an additional point P_4 and its corresponding point P_4' in the images. If the corresponding scene point does not belong to the base plane, then the four points $\tilde{P}_1$, $\tilde{P}_2$, $\tilde{P}_3$ and $\tilde{P}_4$ define an affine reference frame for the scene.

Now if the images P_5 and P_5' of a fifth scene point $\tilde{P}_5$ are identified, its 3D position with respect to the affine frame $\tilde{P}_1$, $\tilde{P}_2$, $\tilde{P}_3$, $\tilde{P}_4$ can be reconstructed. The idea is to construct (the images of) the line through $\tilde{P}_5$ that is parallel to $< \tilde{P}_1, \tilde{P}_4 >$. The intersection $\tilde{I}$ of this line with the base plane yields the first two affine coordinates. In the image these coordinates are given by the coordinates of I with respect to the (affine) frame P_1, P_2, P_3; or equivalently, the coordinates of I' with respect to the (affine) frame P_1', P_2', P_3'. How this intersection can be found is explained in the next paragraph. The third (affine) coordinate of the scene point $\tilde{P}_5$ is obtained as follows: construct (the image of) the intersection $\tilde{T}$ of the plane parallel to the base plane and containing $\tilde{P}_4$ with the line through $\tilde{P}_5$ that is parallel to $< \tilde{P}_1, \tilde{P}_4 >$. In practice, if we denote the epipole of the line $< P_1, I >$ by E_{1I}, then T is the intersection of the line $< P_5, E_{14} >$ with the line $< P_4, E_{1I} >$ in the first image. A similar construction yields the corresponding image point T' in the second image. The cross ratio $C(I, T, P_5, E_{14}) = C(I', T', P_5', E_{14}))$ gives the third affine coordinate.

It remains to be shown how the image I of the intersection $\tilde{I}$ of a line $\tilde{L}$ with the base plane is found. To that end, consider in the scene the plane defined by this line $\tilde{L}$ and the centre of the lens of the first camera (position). Let $\tilde{M}$ be the intersection line of this plane with the base plane. The image M of this intersection line $\tilde{M}$ in the first image coincides with the projection L of the line $\tilde{L}$ in the first image. Since $\tilde{M}$ lies in the base plane, it intersects the sides of the triangle $\tilde{P}_1, \tilde{P}_2, \tilde{P}_3$. For instance, let $\tilde{A}$ and $\tilde{B}$ be the intersection of $\tilde{M}$ with $< \tilde{P}_1, \tilde{P}_2 >$ and $< \tilde{P}_2, \tilde{P}_3 >$ respectively. Their images A and B are found as the intersection of the line M (which coincides with L) with $< P_1, P_2 >$ and $< P_2, P_3 >$ respectively. The image A' of $\tilde{A}$ after the translation is now found as the intersection of the lines $< P_1', P_2' >$ and $< A, E_T >$. Similarly, B' is found as the intersection of $< P_2', P_3' >$ and $< B, E_T >$. Consequently, $M' = < A', B' >$. Of course, other pairs of lines such as $< \tilde{P}_1, \tilde{P}_2 >$ and $< \tilde{P}_1, \tilde{P}_3 >$, or $< \tilde{P}_1, \tilde{P}_3 >$ and $< \tilde{P}_2, \tilde{P}_3 >$, could have been used as well. By construction, the point $\tilde{I}$ lies on the line $\tilde{L}$ as well as on the line $\tilde{M}$. Hence, its projection I' on the second image is the intersection of L' and M'. Its image I obtained by the first camera then is found as the intersection of the line $< I', E_T >$ with $M = L$. Figure 1 illustrates this procedure.

Figure 2 shows a pair of views of a basket, one before and one after the basket translated. For the reconstruction of the scene, a number of points were indicated manually, using a mouse. No special efforts were made to obtain high precision (e.g. points were *not* extracted as the intersections of fitted lines or using sophisticated corner detectors). These points were then connetced by straight lines. Two orthographic views of the reconstructed scene are shown in Fig. 3. Notice the good planarity of the reconstructed plane in the right view.

4 Objects with Parallel Structures

A special case arises when an object comprises some parallel structures, e.g. parallel space curves. Taking a *single view* of such an object is akin to the situations previously discussed. Only, in this case the translation between the parallel structures is fixed with respect to the structures themselves. This knowledge – that one always observes the same translation with respect to the structure from whatever viewpoint the image is taken – leads to a further simplification. Indeed, in this case, four points on a single, repeated structure together with the corresponding four points on a parallel version is all it takes for 3D affine

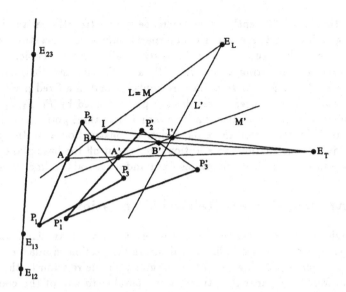

Fig. 1. *Due to the translational motion, a simple construction based on the auxiliary points A and B yields the intersection I of a line L with the plane formed by the points P_1, P_2, P_3.*

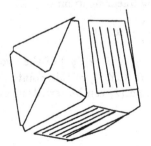

Fig. 2. Pair of views of a translating basket, taken with a static camera.

Fig. 3. Two orthographic views of the reconstructed basket.

reconstruction. Put differently, three reference points (together with their corresponding points on the parallel counterpart) suffice to allow the 3D affine reconstruction of the structure in as far as its parallel copy is visible.

We start by considering two points, P_1 and P_2 say, and their translated counterparts P_1' and P_2'. These points are coplanar and in a fixed position with respect to the object. Hence, we can let the plane defined by P_1, P_2, P_1' assume the role of the base plane. Notice that two rather than three points are needed to arrive at its definition. From there on, a similar construction as in the previous section allows reconstruction: an additional point out off the base plane fixes an affine frame in which a fourth point has fixed and measurable affine coordinates.

5 Restricted, Camera-Related Translation

In the previous section it was shown that translations which are fixed relative to the scene structure allow a simplified analysis. In this section, similar conclusions will be drawn for translations with a particularly simple relation to the camera coordinate frame. In particular, translations parallel to one of the coordinate planes will be considered. As in Sect. 3, but unlike the approach of Sect. 4, two different views of the same scene will be taken. The special types of translations to be discussed, e.g. in a horizontal plane for a horizontally mounted camera, are of particular practical importance, since they naturally arise during navigation tasks.

5.1 Camera Model and Reconstruction

As discussed in Sect. 2, the pair of images of a scene point (X, Y, Z) is given by the four image coordinates x_1, y_1, x_2 and y_2. However, these four numbers are not independent. Indeed, by the way in which the images are formed, it follows that the centres of the lenses and the two image projections of a particular scene point are coplanar. Expressing this fact algebraically, we obtain the Longuet-Higgins relation for the image pair:

$$uf(y_1 - y_2) - vf(x_1 - x_2) + w(x_1 y_2 - x_2 y_1) = 0 . \tag{3}$$

Dividing this relation by the factor $\Delta := x_1 y_2 - x_2 y_1$, we see that the numbers x_1/Δ, y_1/Δ, x_2/Δ and y_2/Δ satisfy the following linear relation:

$$uf \left(\frac{y_1}{\Delta} - \frac{y_2}{\Delta} \right) - vf \left(\frac{x_1}{\Delta} - \frac{x_2}{\Delta} \right) + w = 0 .$$

Conversely, given the image coordinates (x_1, y_1) and (x_2, y_2) of the two images of a given scene point, the scene coordinates (X, Y, Z) of this point can be computed. Indeed, the projection equations (1) and (2) can be rewritten as:

$$\begin{cases} fX & - x_1 Z = 0 , \\ fY - y_1 Z = 0 , \\ fX & - x_2 Z = fu - x_2 w , \\ fY - y_2 Z = fv - y_2 w . \end{cases} \tag{4}$$

By Cramer's rule, the first and the third equation can be solved for X and Z:

$$X = \frac{x_1(fu - x_2 w)}{f(x_1 - x_2)} \quad \text{and} \quad Z = \frac{fu - x_2 w}{x_1 - x_2}, \tag{5}$$

and similarly, the second and the fourth equation yield:

$$Y = \frac{y_1(fv - y_2 w)}{f(y_1 - y_2)} \quad \text{and} \quad Z = \frac{fv - y_2 w)}{y_1 - y_2}. \tag{6}$$

At first glance, the two solutions for Z differ. However, using the Longuet-Higgins relation (3), it is an easy exercise to show that these expressions are actually the same. Moreover, using the same relation (3), these solutions can be rewritten as rational expressions in x_1, y_1, x_2 and y_2 with common denominator Δ. Explicitly,

$$\frac{fu - x_2 w}{f(x_1 - x_2)} = \frac{(fu - x_2 w)\Delta}{f(x_1 - x_2)\Delta} = \frac{fux_1 y_2 - fux_2 y_1 - x_2 w \Delta}{f(x_1 - x_2)\Delta}$$

$$= \frac{fu(x_1 - x_2)y_2 - fux_2(y_1 - y_2) - x_2 w \Delta}{f(x_1 - x_2)\Delta}$$

$$= \frac{fu(x_1 - x_2)y_2 - x_2[fv(x_1 - x_2) + w\Delta] - x_2 w \Delta}{f(x_1 - x_2)\Delta}$$

$$= \frac{f(x_1 - x_2)[uy_2 - vx_2]}{f(x_1 - x_2)\Delta} = \frac{uy_2 - vx_2}{\Delta},$$

and similarly,

$$\frac{fv - y_2 w}{fy_1 - fy_2} = \frac{uy_2 - vx_2}{\Delta}.$$

Hence,

$$X = \frac{x_1(uy_2 - vx_2)}{\Delta}, \quad Y = \frac{y_1(uy_2 - vx_2)}{\Delta} \quad \text{and} \quad Z = \frac{f(uy_2 - vx_2)}{\Delta}. \tag{7}$$

In particular, (X, Y, Z) is a multiple of the triple (x_1, y_1, f), the scalar factor being $(uy_2 - vx_2)/\Delta$. If the configuration parameters f, f, u, v and w are accurately known, then these formulae permit a Euclidean reconstruction of the scene. For recognition purposes, image retrievable invariants under 3D Euclidean motions of the scene are simply found by substituting the above expressions for X, Y and Z in the invariants of Euclidean 3-space. For instance, the simplest Euclidean 2-point invariant is $[X - \tilde{X}]^2 + [Y - \tilde{Y}]^2 + [Z - \tilde{Z}]^2$; and the corresponding invariant for the image pairs of these points is

$$\left[\frac{x_1(uy_2 - vx_2)}{\Delta} - \frac{\tilde{x}_1(u\tilde{y}_2 - v\tilde{x}_2)}{\tilde{\Delta}}\right]^2 + \left[\frac{y_1(uy_2 - vx_2)}{\Delta} - \frac{\tilde{y}_1(u\tilde{y}_2 - v\tilde{x}_2)}{\tilde{\Delta}}\right]^2$$

$$+ \left[\frac{f(uy_2 - vx_2)}{\Delta} - \frac{f(u\tilde{y}_2 - v\tilde{x}_2)}{\tilde{\Delta}}\right]^2.$$

Clearly, the relevant transformation group in this case is the 3D Euclidean motion group $M(3)$, which is a 6-dimensional.

In general however, the configuration parameters are not known (part of the calibration problem). Reconstruction formulae and invariants for the image pairs involving one or more of these parameters are completely useless then. In order to find reconstructions and invariants which are independent of some configuration parameters, these configuration parameters have to be absorbed in the group up to which reconstruction is possible and under which invariants can be extracted from the image pair. Usually, this implies that a larger group has to be accepted. For instance, whereas the above analysis with all configuration parameters known allowed working with the 3D Euclidean motion group, the lack of knowledge of one or several parameters will typically preclude Euclidean reconstruction and the use of Euclidean invariants. Much of what is to follow therefore is about the smallest group that emerges when "absorbing" different sets of parameters. To this end, one first has to investigate what kind of transformations a Euclidean motion of the scene induces on the image coordinates. Since the reconstruction equations (7) are nonlinear, the transformation formulae of x_1, y_1, x_2 and y_2 will also be nonlinear, and finding the relevant transformation group becomes a difficult problem. From a theoretical point of view, however, we know that the appropriate group is a Lie subgroup of the 3D affine group (see Sect. 3). So the non-linearity just observed is due to the non-linearity of the action of $Af(3)$ on the images. However, if one of the translation components u or v is zero, then the configuration parameters and the image pair coordinates in (7) can be separated, and moreover, by a suitable change of image coordinates, (7) becomes linear. Let us consider this in more detail.

5.2   Linear Formulations for Camera Restricted Translations

The Camera Translates Parallel to the XZ-plane.

If the camera moves parallel to the XZ-plane, then $v = 0$. The formulae (7) become

$$X = u\,\frac{x_1 y_2}{\Delta} \quad , \quad Y = u\,\frac{y_1 y_2}{\Delta} \quad \text{and} \quad Z = uf\,\frac{y_2}{\Delta} \ ;$$

or equivalently,

$$\begin{pmatrix} X \\ Y \\ Z \end{pmatrix} = \begin{pmatrix} u & 0 & 0 \\ 0 & u & 0 \\ 0 & 0 & uf \end{pmatrix} \begin{pmatrix} x_1 y_2/\Delta \\ y_1 y_2/\Delta \\ y_2/\Delta \end{pmatrix} . \tag{8}$$

A Euclidean motion of the scene is described by the transformation formulae $\mathbf{X}' = R\mathbf{X} + T$, where $\mathbf{X} = (X, Y, Z)^t$, R is a 3D rotation matrix, T a translation vector, and with primes denoting coordinates of the scene points after the motion. The image of the scene changes accordingly. More precisely, if a pair of images of the scene is obtained after the motion by translating the camera over the vector $(u', 0, w')$ and with focal length f', then the triple $\mathbf{r} = (y_2/\Delta)\,(x_1, y_1, 1)^t$ changes as follows:

$$\mathbf{r}' = U'^{-1}\,\mathbf{X}' = U'^{-1}\,[R\,\mathbf{X} + T] = U'^{-1}\,[R\,U\,\mathbf{r} + T]$$

where

$$U = \begin{pmatrix} u & 0 & 0 \\ 0 & u & 0 \\ 0 & 0 & uf \end{pmatrix} \quad \text{and} \quad U' = \begin{pmatrix} u' & 0 & 0 \\ 0 & u' & 0 \\ 0 & 0 & u'f' \end{pmatrix} .$$

Clearly, a Euclidean motion of the scene induces an affine transformation of the r-coordinates. Hence, every affine invariant of the r-coordinates will be an invariant under the 3D Euclidean motions of the objects in the scene, and yet is retrievable from the image pair. However, it is important to investigate whether the above transformations form a *proper subgroup* of the affine transformations. The importance is two-fold: a smaller group allows one to distinguish more space curves on the basis of their image pairs (i.e. to arrive at more precise reconstructions); and moreover, smaller groups admit less complex invariants. In matrix notation, the relevant set of transformations is:

$$\left\{ \begin{pmatrix} U'^{-1}RU & U'^{-1}T \\ 0 & 1 \end{pmatrix} \mid R \in SO(3),\ T \in \mathbb{R}^3 \text{ and with } U' \text{ and } U \text{ as above} \right\} .$$

(9)

This set of matrices is not closed under matrix multiplication, and hence certainly is not a subgroup in its own right. So we first have to identify the smallest matrix group G containing all these transformations. Obviously, G must be a subgroup of the affine group

$$Af(3) = \left\{ \begin{pmatrix} A & b \\ 0 & 1 \end{pmatrix} \mid A \in GL(3) \text{ and } b \in \mathbb{R}^3 \right\} .$$

So, what is G?

The answer to this question is not unique in the sense that depending on the knowledge about the camera configuration and its variability, different transformation groups may occur. Table 1 shows the appropiate transformation groups corresponding to the different possibilities for u, u', f and f'. $Af(3)$ stands for the 3D affine transformation group, $EAf(3)$ represents the group of 3D equiaffine transformations (affine transformations preserving volumes, i.e. having unity as the value of their determinant), $Sim(3)$ for the group of 3D similarities, and $M(3)$ represent the 3D Euclidean motions. Note that other parameters than u, u', f, f' do not appear in the formulae of the generating set of matrices, and thus have not to be taken into account for the analysis. This does not mean that they play no role and can be chosen completely free. On the contrary, they are connected with the parameters u, u', f and f' by the Longuet-Higgins relation (3). But that they do not appear in the above formulae is because we used this relationship to eliminate the dependencies between the different parameters.

It should be noted that the table does not give a rigorous overview, in the sense that some further cases can be distinguished, where subgroups of $Af(3)$ are relevant. For instance, for all $Af(3)$ entries imposing the additional constraint $uu' > 0$ singles out $Af^+(3)$ as the smallest subgroup. This means that no reflections are included. A similar remark holds for the $Sim(3)$ entries. It is also clear that $u = u'$ implies that this constraint is satisfied. However, from a practical point of view, there is no real point in making these distinctions, since the same

Table 1. For translations in the XZ-plane, the above classification identifies the smallest transformation group to be dealt with under relative Euclidean motions of the scene.

$\begin{array}{c}\text{u}\\ \text{u'}\end{array}$		both known		one known one unknown	both unknown	
f_1 f_1'		=	≠		=	≠
both known	=	M(3)	Sim(3)	Sim(3)	M(3)	Sim(3)
	≠					
one known one un- known		Af⁺(3)		Af(3)	Af(3)	
both un- known	=	EAf(3)		Af(3)	EAf(3)	Af(3)
	≠	Af⁺(3)			Af⁺(3)	Af(3)

invariants have to be used and the same qualitative levels of reconstruction can be obtained. This might seem contradictory to the claim made at the outset, i.e. the hope of finding simpler invariants by searching proper subgroups. This simplification only results from a lowering of the group dimension, however, and $Af(3)$ and $Af^+(3)$ are both 12-dimensional. A mathematical formulation of the above results and a proof thereof is to be found in [Mea2].

Note that cases where $Af(3)$ is the relevant group do not allow to distinguish structures and affinely modified copies, e.g. skewed versions. This certainly is already one price to pay for not knowing certain parameters. Similar remarks hold for all the entries other than $M(3)$.

Camera Translations Parallel to the Other Coordinate Planes.

A similar analysis yields the same results in the case of a camera translation parallel to the YZ-plane (i.e. $u = 0$). A special situation occurs when the pair of images is obtained by a translation of the camera along its optical axis. In that case $u = v = 0$ and (7) becomes degenerate. Indeed, if $u = v = 0$, then the numerator $uy_2 - vx_2$ is zero as well as the denominator

$$\Delta = x_1 y_2 - x_2 y_1 = f^2 \frac{X(Y-v)-(X-u)Y}{Z(Z-w)} = f^2 \frac{-vX+uY}{Z(Z-w)}.$$

Also in the case of a translation parallel to the image plane (i.e. $w = 0$, (7) does not yield a linear relationship as in the previous situations. However, in these cases the original solution (5) and (6) to the system (4) can be used. Indeed, recall that

$$X = \frac{x_1(fu - x_2 w)}{f(x_1 - x_2)} \quad, \quad Y = \frac{y_1(fv - y_2 w)}{f(y_1 - y_2)} \quad \text{and} \quad Z = \frac{fu - x_2 w}{x_1 - x_2} = \frac{fv - y_2 w}{y_1 - y_2} \; .$$

In both the situations $u = v = 0$ and $w = 0$, this again yields a linear relationship between the scene coordinates (X, Y, Z) of a scene point and a triple defined by the image coordinates (x_1, y_1) and (x_2, y_2) of the corresponding image pair. A similar analysis as in the previous section shows that the results of Table 1 remain valid. For further details, we refer to [Mea2].

6 Semi-Differential Invariants for Translated, Perspective Image Pairs

6.1 Invariants for the Equiaffine and Affine Groups

Thus far, several types of translated, perspective projection pairs were considered. The underlying idea was to observe the scene using two translated camera positions, and to extract geometrical information from this image pair, irrespective of some unknown 3D rotation and translation of the scene with respect to the image pair. This information may take the form of a reconstruction, or one might content oneself with sufficient information to recognize objects. The latter problem calls for the extraction of *invariant features*, that are measurable from the image pairs and remain unchanged when the pose of the objects in the scene has undergone a relative Euclidean motion in 3D. In this section, such invariant features are derived. Since there are several relevant groups, this discussion risks to be quite extensive. However, it seems most useful to restrict it to the least straightforward cases, $EAf(3)$ and $Af(3)$, the unimodular (i.e. equiaffine) and affine transformation groups.

It is well known that the basic invariants for the unimodular group are determinants of 3×3-matrices whose columns are differences of the affine coordinates of two points. For the case of general translations, these coordinates can be obtained following the reconstruction procedure outlined in Sect. 3. However, for the special translation types discussed in Sect. 5 the r coordinates can be used. They can be extracted from the image pair on a pointwise basis, i.e. for each point separately without reference to any other point. Denoting as r the reconstructed coordinates for the general case as well as these directly extracted coordinates for special camera related translations, and combining this information for four points r_1, r_2, r_3 and r_4, yields as invariant for the unimodular group $EAf(3)$ the determinant $|r_2 - r_1 \; r_3 - r_1 \; r_4 - r_1|$.

For the affine group $Af(3)$, the basic invariants are quotients of two such determinants. For instance, if r_0, r_1, r_2, r_3 and r_4 are the r-coordinates corresponding to the image pair of five scene points, then the quotient

$$\frac{|r_2 - r_1 \; r_3 - r_1 \; r_4 - r_1|}{|r_2 - r_1 \; r_3 - r_1 \; r_5 - r_1|}$$

is an invariant.

Determinants of the above form can be rewritten as follows:

$$|r_2 - r_1 \ r_3 - r_1 \ r_4 - r_1| = \begin{vmatrix} r_1 & r_2 - r_1 & r_3 - r_1 & r_4 - r_1 \\ 1 & 0 & 0 & 0 \end{vmatrix} = \begin{vmatrix} r_1 & r_2 & r_3 & r_4 \\ 1 & 1 & 1 & 1 \end{vmatrix}$$

and this observation is now used to simplify the expressions a bit further for the special translation cases.

6.2 Stereo Coordinates

We first consider translations parallel to the XZ plane. In Sect. 5 the following r-coordinates were shown to transform linearly:

$$\begin{pmatrix} r \\ 1 \end{pmatrix} = \frac{1}{\Delta} \begin{pmatrix} x_1 y_2 \\ y_1 y_2 \\ y_2 \\ x_1 y_2 - x_2 y_1 \end{pmatrix} .$$

Since the invariants are determinants and taking linear combinations of their rows and columns doesn't change their value, a more elegant definition of special coordinates is obtained as follows. By subtracting the first row from the last one, and then interchanging the last two rows, we get $|r_2 - r_1 \ r_3 - r_1 \ r_4 - r_1| = |s_1 \ s_2 \ s_3 \ s_4|$ where the s_i are column vectors of the form $s = \frac{1}{\Delta}(x_1 y_2, y_1 y_2, x_2 y_1, y_2)^t$. The *stereo coordinates* of the point are then defined as the 4-tuple

$$s = \frac{1}{x_1 y_2 - x_2 y_1} \begin{pmatrix} x_1 y_2 \\ y_1 y_2 \\ x_2 y_1 \\ y_2 \end{pmatrix} .$$

Note that these stereo coordinates can directly be calculated from a given pair of images. Using these stereo coordinates has two main advantages:

1. as the r-coordinates, there is a linear relationship between the stereo coordinates and the scene coordinates, namely

$$s = VX \quad \text{with} \quad V = \frac{1}{u} \begin{pmatrix} 1 & 0 & 0 & 0 \\ 0 & 1 & 0 & 0 \\ 1 & 0 & 0 & -u \\ 0 & 0 & \frac{1}{f} & 0 \end{pmatrix} \quad \text{and} \quad X = \begin{pmatrix} X \\ Y \\ Z \\ 1 \end{pmatrix} .$$

2. a Euclidean motion $X' = RX + T$ of the scene induces a linear transformation of the stereo coordinates:

$$s' = V'EV^{-1}s \quad \text{with} \quad E = \begin{pmatrix} R & T \\ 0 & 1 \end{pmatrix} \text{ and with } V \text{ and } V' \text{ as above.}$$

This proves again that determinants of 4×4-matrices whose columns are the stereo coordinates of four image pair points are the basic (relative) invariants of the stereo coordinates.

A similar analysis can be carried out for the other translation types. The results are summarized in Table 6.2.

It is useful to note that if $w = 0$, then the Longuet-Higgins relation simplifies to $y_1 = y_2$, and the stereo coordinates can be rewritten as

$$s = \frac{1}{x_1 - x_2} \begin{pmatrix} x_1 \\ y \\ x_2 \\ 1 \end{pmatrix} .$$

Table 2. Table of stereo coordinates s and transformation matrices V relating them linearly to the three-dimensional point coordinates X (i.e. $s = VX$).

direction of translation	stereo coordinates s	linear transformation V
XZ	$\dfrac{1}{x_1 y_2 - x_2 y_1} \begin{pmatrix} x_1 y_2 \\ y_1 y_2 \\ x_2 y_1 \\ y_2 \end{pmatrix}$	$\dfrac{1}{u} \begin{pmatrix} 1 & 0 & 0 & 0 \\ 0 & 1 & 0 & 0 \\ 1 & 0 & 0 & -u \\ 0 & 0 & \frac{1}{f} & 0 \end{pmatrix}$
YZ	$\dfrac{1}{x_1 y_2 - x_2 y_1} \begin{pmatrix} x_1 x_2 \\ x_1 y_2 \\ x_2 y_1 \\ x_2 \end{pmatrix}$	$\dfrac{1}{v} \begin{pmatrix} 1 & 0 & 0 & 0 \\ 0 & 1 & 0 & -v \\ 0 & 1 & 0 & 0 \\ 0 & 0 & \frac{1}{f} & 0 \end{pmatrix}$
Z	$\dfrac{1}{x_1 - x_2} \begin{pmatrix} x_1 x_2 \\ y_1 x_2 \\ x_2 \\ x_1 \end{pmatrix}$	$-\dfrac{1}{w} \begin{pmatrix} f & 0 & 0 & 0 \\ 0 & f & 0 & 0 \\ 0 & 0 & 1 & 0 \\ 0 & 0 & 1 & -w \end{pmatrix}$
XY $\setminus$ Y	$\dfrac{1}{x_1 - x_2} \begin{pmatrix} x_1 \\ y_1 \\ x_2 \\ 1 \end{pmatrix}$	$-\dfrac{1}{u} \begin{pmatrix} 1 & 0 & 0 & 0 \\ 0 & 1 & 0 & 0 \\ 0 & 0 & 1 & -u \\ 0 & 0 & \frac{1}{f} & 0 \end{pmatrix}$
XY $\setminus$ X	$\dfrac{1}{y_1 - y_2} \begin{pmatrix} y_1 \\ x_1 \\ y_2 \\ 1 \end{pmatrix}$	$-\dfrac{1}{v} \begin{pmatrix} 1 & 0 & 0 & 0 \\ 0 & 1 & 0 & 0 \\ 0 & 0 & 1 & -v \\ 0 & 0 & \frac{1}{f} & 0 \end{pmatrix}$

6.3 Semi-Differential Invariants

As explained in Sect. 6.1 the different translation cases admit invariants under $EAf(3)$ and $Af(3)$ that are of an identical form. For the specificiaton of the invariants, one therefore doesn't need to know *a priori* which case is under scrutiny. One can adapt swiftly to the different cases by choosing the corresponding types of stereo coordinates, or for the general translation case by simply taking $\binom{\mathbf{r}}{1}$. It follows that invariants published earlier for the case of translations along the X-axis [Mea1, Vea3] can be generalized in their use without further notice. A few examples are in place here to make the paper sufficiently self-contained. In particular, examples of *semi-differential invariants* are given, the use of which further helps reducing the number of points needed. The idea behind such invariants is that, instead of building invariants from point coordinates only, one might introduce low order derivatives of the coordinates to lower the number of points and yet stay clear of the numerical problems associated with differential invariants. A theoretical underpinning for the semi-differential framework can be found in [Vea2, Vea1].

Before giving some examples of semi-differential invariants, some further notational issues are discussed. In the previous sections, several types of stereo coordinates were introduced. Whatever their precise definition, these are all (4×1) vectors. Here we specialize towards the case where we want to describe space curves, $\mathbf{X}(t)$, on the basis of the corresponding stereo coordinates $\mathbf{s}(t)$. The parameter t is arbitrary. Expressions like $\mathbf{s}^{(i)}$ stand for $\left(\frac{d^i s_1}{dt^i}, \frac{d^i s_2}{dt^i}, \frac{d^i s_3}{dt^i}, \frac{d^i s_4}{dt^i} \right)^T$ with s_1, s_2, s_3, s_4 the components of the vector $\mathbf{s}$. . Whereas $\mathbf{s}$ will represent an arbitrary contour point, subscripts as in $\mathbf{s}_j$ indicate a fixed reference point. Reference points are assumed to lie in a fixed position with respect to the space curve, and possibly but not necessarily on the curve.

First, it is illustrated how the use of semi-differential invariants for the affine group helps in reducing the number of points required. If correspondence search would not be a problem, five points would normally be used, yielding three independent invariants of the type

$$\frac{|\mathbf{s}\ \mathbf{s}_1\ \mathbf{s}_2\ \mathbf{s}_3|}{|\mathbf{s}_1\ \mathbf{s}_2\ \mathbf{s}_3\ \mathbf{s}_4|} .$$

As the search for five corresponding points might be quite a difficult problem to solve in practice, one might consider using first order derivatives in the points. This clearly is possible for points lying on curves, but also to vertices can be assigned directional vectors of the different edges joining there, with the additional advantages of potentially using more than one at the same point. For the moment we assume only a single directional vector is assigned to each point (i.e. a single first order derivative). Combining three points and their first order derivatives, invariants are e.g.

$$\frac{|\mathbf{s}^{(1)}\ \mathbf{s}_1\ \mathbf{s}_1^{(1)}\ \mathbf{s}_2|}{|\mathbf{s}\ \mathbf{s}^{(1)}\ \mathbf{s}_1\ \mathbf{s}_1^{(1)}|}$$

and

$$\int \text{abs} \left(\frac{|\mathbf{s}\ \mathbf{s}^{(1)}\ \mathbf{s}_1\ \mathbf{s}_1^{(1)}|}{|\mathbf{s}\ \mathbf{s}_1\ \mathbf{s}_1^{(1)}\ \mathbf{s}_2|} \right) dt.$$

Again three independent invariants can be derived from these data. Assuming that several directions are available at the points (the points are line junctions), the availability of two directions at the points (indicated by subscripts) allows the use of the following invariant:

$$\frac{\left|\mathbf{s}\ \mathbf{s}^{(1)_1}\ \mathbf{s}^{(1)_2}\ \mathbf{s}_1^{(1)_1}\right|\left|\mathbf{s}\ \mathbf{s}_1\ \mathbf{s}^{(1)_1}\ \mathbf{s}_1^{(1)_2}\right|}{\left|\mathbf{s}\ \mathbf{s}^{(1)_1}\ \mathbf{s}_1^{(1)_1}\ \mathbf{s}_1^{(1)_2}\right|\left|\mathbf{s}\ \mathbf{s}_1\ \mathbf{s}^{(1)_1}\ \mathbf{s}^{(1)_2}\right|}$$

using only two points and first order derivatives. Relative invariants for the affine case are absolute invariants for the unimodular one. Hence,

$$\int \text{abs}\left(\left|\mathbf{s}\ \mathbf{s}^{(1)}\ \mathbf{s}_1\ \mathbf{s}_2\right|\right) dt$$

is an invariant parameter for the unimodular transformations.

Although invariants with only coordinates of four points such as

$$\left|\mathbf{s}\ \mathbf{s}_1\ \mathbf{s}_2\ \mathbf{s}_3\right|$$

can be constructed for the unimodular case, no complete description, i.e. a description specifying a shape up to a unimodular transformation, can be generated this way. But, if the unimodular case is relevant, the inclusion of such invariant is not only useful to single out cases which are affine but not unimodular, moreover they may help in selecting an additional reference point. If one would for instance decide to work with point coordinates only, still a fifth point will be needed, since four points yield only a single unimodular invariant. However, this invariant can be invoked to support the selection of an additional reference point, once three reference points have been found.

Another interesting use of such invariant is as a check for rigidity, e.g. in distinguishing physical from occluding contours. Taking four fixed points on a surface, the above invariant must not change when calculated from stereo view pairs allowing the use of $EAf(3)$ and taken from different positions. If, however, one of the points is found as a point on an occluding contour, then the "invariant" is bound to change.

As an example, consider Fig. 4, which shows two stereo pairs taken with cameras displaced along their X-axis and with a fixed distance between them. The conditions for the use of $EAf(3)$ are satisfied. Using the appropriate stereo coordinates (the $XY \setminus Y$ entry in Table 6.2) the invariant

$$\left|\mathbf{s}_1\ \mathbf{s}_2\ \mathbf{s}_3\ \mathbf{s}_4\right|$$

can be calculated for each quadruple of points. If the same points are used for the two stereo pairs, then this invariant should have the same value, otherwise it will probably change. This was tested by selecting a number of points on the cup's surface, identified by the numbers shown in Fig. 5. As suggested, the invariant was used to distinguish points on the occluding contour from points fixed to the surface. Table 6.3 shows the values of the invariant extracted from the two stereo pairs for the same point quadruples. As can be seen, if one of the points actually is a point on the occluding contour, then the variation in the invariant is much larger (about an order of magnitude in the examples of the table). To get an intuitive grasp, it is useful to note that comparing these inviarants essentially is comparing the distance of one of the points point to the plane defined by the other three reference points. Most of the labelled points in Fig. 5 are "fixed" surface points. However, points 3 and 24 are on the apparent contour. These points are extracted as the intersection of the grid lines on the plane behind the cup, with the cup's apparent contour.

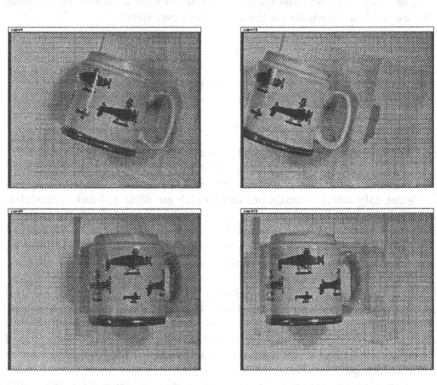

Fig. 4. Two stereo pairs of a cup, taken from different viewing directions.

7   Conclusions and Future Work

It was shown that translated image pairs allow simpler yet more precise reconstruction of three-dimensional scenes. In particular, 3D affine reconstruction is possible for a set of five points visible in both views. This result could then be further simplified towards situations with restricted translations.

A first example is given by objects with parallel structures. In that case all what is required are four sets of corresponding points. obtained from a single view. Parallel structures are related by a translation which is fixed with respect to the object. On the other hand, analysis can be simplified greatly when considering

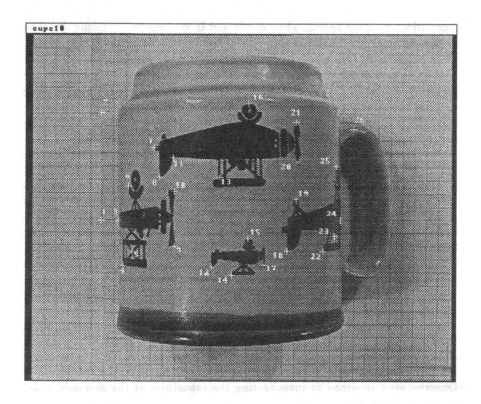

Fig. 5. Cup with identification tags for the selected points.

Table 3. Values of the "invariant" for two different choices of 3 reference points. From left to right: four points used; invariant (a) computed from the first position of the stereo rig; invariant (b) computed from the second position of the stereo rig; and, absolute value of the difference. Note, when one of the four points arises from an apparent contour (points 3 and 24) values vary substantially more than for fixed points.

points used	I_4 (a)	I_4 (b)	diff.
12, 11, 18, 26	−909.5	−921.8	12.3
12, 11, 18, 25	−252.2	−254.3	2.1
12, 11, 18, 24	−679.2	−1251.7	572.6
12, 11, 18, 23	−342.8	−325.1	17.7
12, 11, 18, 22	−227.8	−209.4	18.4
12, 11, 18, 3	−1003.6	−298.2	705.4
12, 11, 18. 10	−36.2	−14.8	21.4
12, 11, 18, 13	111.8	106.6	5.2
12, 11, 18, 14	−16.3	17.8	34.2

points used	I_4 (a)	I_4 (b)	diff.
19, 16, 9, 26	1878.5	2001.0	122.5
19, 16, 9, 25	645.2	700.2	55.0
19, 16, 9, 24	1113.3	2146.2	1032.9
19, 16, 9, 23	529.5	571.9	42.4
19, 16, 9, 22	286.0	291.7	5.7
19, 16, 9, 3	1400.7	317.6	1083.1
19, 16, 9, 10	62.3	24.7	37.7
19, 16, 9, 13	−83.8	−58.8	25.0
19, 16, 9, 14	197.3	240.9	43.6

translations that are special when considered in the coordinate frame attached to the cameras. For translations in any of the coordinate planes, point coordinates can be used independently in the form of stereo coordinates.

This latter part of the work also takes a different angle compared to much of the literature in that no *explicit* attempt to a 3D reconstruction of any kind is made in order to extract invariants. All operations are purely image based. So, there is no 3D reconstruction step, followed by a further step to somehow characterize the reconstructed geometric object.

Ongoing work encompasses a further relaxation of the camera model. The conditions imposed in the paper are to some extent overly constrained. It is e.g. possible to compensate for differences in focal lengths by the use of a scale factor that can be extracted from a number of point correspondences. How many of such correspondences are needed depends on the case, but it sometimes is as low as two, as e.g. for translations in the XZ or YZ planes. Moreover, no additional correspondences are needed, i.e. those used for reconstruction suffice. Thus, the discussion for general translations can be generalized towards cameras with different focal lengths, whereas for some special translation cases in Table 1 $EAf(3)$ rather than $Af(3)$ comes within grasp distance by compensating for the difference in focal lengths (i.e. changing the $f \neq f'$ for the $f = f'$ option).

Similarly, pixel aspect ratios may differ from 1:1. There never is a problem when the same aspect ratio has to be used for both stereo images, although the dimension of the relevant group might increase. Having to deal with $Af(3)$ is the worse that may happen. Some cases allow different aspect ratios for the two views.

Ongoing work is aimed at investigating the robustness of the methods under such generalized conditions.

References

[F1]   O. Faugeras, What can be seen in three dimensions with an uncalibrated stereo rig, *Proc. 2nd European Conf. Computer Vision*, pp.563-578, 1992.

[FLM1] O. Faugeras, Q. Luong, and S. Maybank, Camera self-calibration: theory and experiments, *Proc. 2nd European Conf. Computer Vision*, pp.321-334, 1992.

[H1]   C. Harris, Geometry from visual motion, in: Blake and Yuille (eds.), *Active Vision*, pp.263-284, MIT Press, 1992.

[H2]   R. Hartley, Euclidean reconstruction from uncalibrated views, in: J. Mundy and A. Zisserman, Applications of Invariance for Computer Vision II, *Proceedings of the Second ESPRIT – ARPA / NSF Workshop on Invariance*, Ponta Delgada, Azores, 9 - 14 October 1993, pp. 187-202.

[KV1]   J.J. Koenderink and A.J. van Doorn, Affine structure from motion, *J. Opt. Soc. Am. A*, Vol. 8 (1991), pp. 377–385.

[M1]   S. Maybank, Ambiguity in reconstruction from image correspondences, in: Goos, Hartmanis, and Faugeras (eds.), *Lecture Notes in Computer Science*, pp.177-186, Springer-Verlag, Berlin / Heidelberg / New York / Tokyo, 1990.

[MVQ1] R. Mohr, F. Veillon, and L. Quan, Relative 3D reconstruction using multiple uncalibrated images, *Proc. Conf. Computer Vision and Pattern Recognition*, pp.543-548, 1993.

[Mea1]   T. Moons, E.J. Pauwels, L.J. Van Gool, M.H. Brill and E.B. Barrett, Recognizing 3D curves from a stereo pair of images : a semi-differential approach, in: O Ying-Lie, A. Toet, H.J.A.M. Heijmans, D.H. Foster, and P. Meer (eds.), *SHAPE IN PICTURE – Mathematical description of shape in greylevel images*, Springer Verlag, Berlin / Heidelberg / New York / Tokyo, 1994, pp. 433–442.

[Mea2]   T. Moons, L. Van Gool, M. Van Diest, and E. Pauwels, *Affine structure from perspective image pairs under relative translations between object and camera*, Technical Report KUL/ESAT/MI2/9306, Katholieke Universiteit Leuven, 1993.

[Mea3]   T. Moons, L. Van Gool, M. Van Diest, and E. Pauwels, Affine reconstruction from perspective image pairs, in: J. Mundy and A. Zisserman, Applications of Invariance for Computer Vision II, *Proceedings of the Second ESPRIT – ARPA / NSF Workshop on Invariance*, Ponta Delgada, Azores, 9 - 14 October 1993, pp. 249-266.

[M1]   J. Mundy, Repeated structures: image correspondence constraints and ambiguity of 3D reconstruction, in: J. Mundy and A. Zisserman, Applications of Invariance for Computer Vision II, *Proceedings of the Second ESPRIT – ARPA / NSF Workshop on Invariance*, Ponta Delgada, Azores, 9 - 14 October 1993, pp. 51-64.

[Rea1]   C. Rothwell, D. Forsyth, A. Zisserman, and J. Mundy, Extracting projective structure from single perspective views of 3D point sets, *Proc. Int. Conf. Computer Vision*, pp.573-582, 1993.

[SW1]   A.A. Sagle, and R.E. Walde, *Introduction to Lie Groups and Lie Algebras*, Pure and Applied Mathematics, Vol. 51, Academic Press, New York, 1973.

[S1]   A. Shashua, On geometric and algebraic aspects of 3D affine and projective structures from perspective 2D views, in: J. Mundy and A. Zisserman, Applications of Invariance for Computer Vision II, *Proceedings of the Second ESPRIT – ARPA / NSF Workshop on Invariance*, Ponta Delgada, Azores, 9 - 14 October 1993, pp. 87-112.

[Vea1]   L. Van Gool, P. Kempenaers, and A. Oosterlinck, Recognition and semi-differential invariants, *IEEE Conf. on Computer Vision and Pattern Recognition*, pp.454-460, 1991.

[Vea2]   L. Van Gool, T. Moons, E. Pauwels, and A. Oosterlinck, Semi-differential invariants, Chapter 8, pp. 157–192, in: J.L. Mundy and A. Zisserman (eds.), *Geometric Invariance in Computer Vision*, MIT Press, Cambridge, Massachusetts, 1992.

[Vea3]   L.J. Van Gool, M.H. Brill, E.B. Barrett, T. Moons, and E.J. Pauwels, Semi-differential invariants for nonplanar curves, Chapter 15, pp. 293–309, in: J.L. Mundy and A. Zisserman (eds.), *Geometric Invariance in Computer Vision*, MIT Press, Cambridge, Massachusetts, 1992.

[WS1]   G.-Q. Wei and Song De Ma, A complete two-plane camera calibration method and experimental comparisons, *Proc. 4th Int. Conf. Computer Vision*, pp.439-446, 1993.

Using Invariance and Quasi-Invariance for the Segmentation and Recovery of Curved Objects[1]

Mourad Zerroug and Ramakant Nevatia

Institute for Robotics and Intelligent Systems, University of Southern California, Los Angeles, CA 90089-0273

Abstract. There has been much interest recently in using invariant theory in computer vision. Most work has concentrated on recognition of 3-D objects from 2-D images using algebraic or differential invariants. In this work, we address the usage of a class of projective invariants and quasi-invariants for the segmentation and 3-D recovery of generalized cylinders from a monocular image. We derive important projective invariants of straight homogeneous generalized cylinders and describe an implemented system for their segmentation and recovery from a monocular intensity image. We then derive quasi-invariant properties of circular planar right generalized cylinders and describe another implemented system for recovering their 3-D shape from 2-D contours. This work shows that the problem of shape description and scene segmentation from a monocular image can be solved for a large class of objects in our environment. Examples of results of both systems are also given.

1 Introduction

There has been increasing interest recently in using invariance theory in computer vision. Most work has focused on deriving invariant properties that can be used for recognition. What distinguishes this line of approach from traditional ones is the fact that, in order to hypothesize objects, it is no longer necessary to compute transformations (projection from 3-D to 2-D, for example), a difficult and costly process.

Several classes of invariant properties have been derived and suggested as characteristic signatures that do not change with changes in viewpoint. Two major types of such invariants have been used: algebraic invariants and differential invariants. The former are functions of algebraic entities such as point sets, lines and conics [9,23,24,31] and the latter functions of (local) differential entities such as curvature and higher order derivatives [6,32]. Such properties usually require careful selection of image points and curves over which functions are computed. The computed invariants can be used as indexing keys in large data bases of models. Most of the derived invariant properties relate (local) features such as points or curves and are limited to plane to plane transformations; i.e. address planar objects (see [9,37] for a discussion on curved surfaces).

---

1. This research was supported by the Advanced Research Projects Agency of the Department of Defense and was monitored by the Air Force Office of Scientific Research under Contract No. F49620-90-C-0078. The United States Government is authorized to reproduce and distribute reprints for governmental purposes notwithstanding any copyright notation hereon.

In this paper, we address the usage of invariant properties for 3-D scene segmentation and shape recovery from a monocular image. That is, given a single image of a 3-D scene containing objects with unknown identities and which are not necessarily planar, detect the objects and recover their 3-D shape using information from the 2-D image only. The purpose of such descriptions could be, among others, to recognize scene objects based on higher level 3-D descriptions. This problem of *generic shape detection, recovery and recognition* is perhaps one of the most basic in the field of computer vision.

We believe that achieving object level descriptions is crucial for object recognition in complex scenes. Such descriptions are far less ambiguous than those at the point or curve level. For this, among the key problems that need to be addressed are the segmentation and the 3-D shape recovery problems from a monocular image.

Our approach to scene segmentation and recovery is based on deriving and using projective properties of generalized cylinders (GCs). GCs do capture a large number of objects in our environment. Furthermore, besides providing stable and rich descriptions, they are robust to noise and even to substantial occlusion [33,34]. A major difficulty in dealing with curved objects is that their image contours are not viewpoint invariant; i.e. they can project from different 3-D contours on the same surface for different viewpoints. This is the case for *limbs* (also called *contour generators*) which are those contours giving the outline at the curved regions of the object. In more precise terms, they are the loci of surface points where the viewing line is tangential to the surface. Thus, it is at best very difficult to find rigorous properties of projected contours of curved objects.

The class of projective properties we discuss in this paper are those that provide rich shape information and that can be used to both segment the scene into separate objects and recover the 3-D shape of each of them. Scene segmentation and shape recovery thus become viewpoint invariant processes. There has been much interest to derive projective invariant properties of GCs [16,20,26,28,29,30,33,34,35,36]. However, little work has been done on automatic segmentation of GCs from a real intensity image.

We discuss the problem of recovery of two sub-classes of GCs from a monocular image: straight homogeneous generalized cylinders (SHGCs) and Circular planar right generalized cylinders (Circular PRGCs). SHGCs capture objects obtained by scaling a planar cross-section curve along a straight axis. Examples include bottles, tools and other industrial objects. Circular PRGCs are obtained by scaling a circular cross-section along a curved, planar, axis. Examples include animal shapes such as horns and limbs. These two primitives together generate a large number of objects we see daily (tea pots, lamps, etc.). Thus, by addressing recovery of these two classes of primitives, we are also addressing recovery of compound objects that consist of their arrangements.

For this, we find relevant two classes of properties: *geometric* projective properties and *structural* properties. Geometric projective properties include shape regularities such as symmetries between object contours whereas structural properties capture interactions, such as occlusion and joints, between objects (and their features). Two classes of geometric projective properties are of interest: invariant properties and *quasi-invariant* properties. Invariant properties are properties that hold independently of the viewing parameters[2]. Thus, when they exist, they provide necessary constraints for detecting relevant objects in an image. However, projective invariants may not exist for all classes of curved objects. In their absence, it is desirable to use well-behaved properties that can also be used to rigorously detect and recover objects in an image. The term "quasi-invariant" has been introduced by [4,5] to refer to properties that may vary but do so within a small range of values over a large fraction of the space of viewing transformations. Algebraic formulation of quasi-invariants is not as clear as that of invariants despite an attempt to characterize them as precisely [5]. Hence, we will use statistical analysis of such properties to study their behavior.

Structural properties establish relationships between objects and between features of objects. For example, a joint between two parts can be observed in the image either through the intersection curve of the parts surfaces or through occlusion junctions. Thus, such properties not only allow to infer feature interactions, but may provide "explanations" as to the absence of expected geometric properties in the image (for example occlusion may prevent observation of geometric regularities).

We have derived and used geometric projective properties of SHGCs and Circular PRGCs to develop two sub-systems of a larger system for segmentation and recovery of composite objects. In this paper, we concentrate the discussion on the properties and the methods used in those two sub-systems. We organize the discussion as follows. In Sect. 2, we discuss the problem of scene segmentation and shape description (figure-ground) and the 3-D recovery in the context of SHGCs. We derive useful projective invariant properties of SHGCs and discuss an implemented approach for their detection and 3-D shape recovery from a monocular real intensity image with noise, shadows, markings and occlusion. A fundamental aspect of that approach is the usage of invariant properties of SHGCs to generate strong constraints for hypothesizing objects, grouping partial descriptions into global ones, verifying consistency and inferring missing information. In Sect. 3, we describe the 3-D shape recovery of Circular PRGCs from monocular contours. We derive new quasi-invariant properties of Circular PRGCs, invariant properties of their subclasses and propose a method, based on the derived quasi-invariants, to recover 3-D object centered descriptions from 2-D contours. Resulting descriptions of both methods have direct applications to recognition. We conclude this paper in Sect. 4.

2 Segmentation and Recovery of SHGCs from a Real Intensity Image

We start by giving the properties of SHGCs then give an overview of the method for their detection. Subsequent sections discuss some of the steps of the method.

---

2. except perhaps on a set of measure zero in the parameter space; *i.e. almost everywhere.*

2.1 Properties of SHGCs

First, we give relevant definitions.

Definition 1: An SHGC (straight homogeneous generalized cylinder) is the surface obtained by sweeping a planar *cross-section curve* C along a straight axis A while scaling it by a function r.

Let $C(t) = (u(t), v(t))$ be a parametrization of C, $r(s)$ the scaling function and α the angle between the cross-section plane and the SHGC axis (s-direction), then the surface of the SHGC can be parameterized as follows (using the formulation of [27]; see Fig. 2.1):

$$S(t, s) = (\, u(t)\, r(s)\, \sin\alpha,\ v(t)\, r(s),\ s + u(t)\, r(s)\, \cos\alpha\,) \tag{2.1}$$

When $\alpha = \pi / 2$, we obtain a *right* SHGC (RSHGC). When $r(s)$ is linear, we obtain an LSHGC. Curves of constant t are called *meridians* and curves of constant s are called *cross-sections* (also *parallels*).

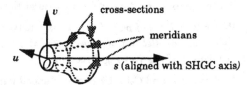

Figure 2.1   SHGC representation and terminology

Definition 2: Two planar unit speed curves $C_1(w_1)$ and $C_2(w_2)$ are said to be *parallel symmetric* [28] if there exists a continuous and monotonically increasing function f, such that $\underline{T}_1(w_1) = \underline{T}_2(w_2)$ and $w_2 = f(w_1)$. Where $\underline{T}_i(w_i)$ is the unit tangent vector of $C_i(w_i)$. That is corresponding points have parallel tangent vectors.

The correspondence is said to be linear if f is a linear function. In this case the two curves are similar up to scale and translation. The axis is the locus of midpoints of lines of symmetry (correspondence lines). Figure 2.2. gives an example.

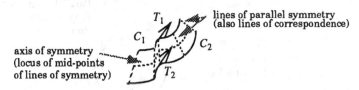

Figure 2.2   Example of parallel symmetry

Now we state the invariant properties of SHGCs. We start by those that have been derived in previous work [20,27,28] then give the new properties. Proofs of the previous properties will be omitted but the new ones are proved in the appendix. Figure 2.3 illustrates the properties.

Property P1: Cross-section curves of an SHGC are mutually parallel symmetric with a *linear* correspondence. This property holds in 3-D and in the 2-D projection.

The proof can be found in theorem 4 and its corollary in [28].

Property P2: Contour generators (limbs) of an LSHGC are straight (they are meridians). This property holds also for the 2-D projection of limbs which are projections of those meridians. Therefore, in 2-D, the tangent line and any correspondence line at each limb point are colinear.

The proof can be found in Sect. 4 of [27].

Property P3: In 3-D, tangents to the surface in the direction of the meridians at points on the same cross-section, when not parallel, intersect at a common point on the axis of the SHGC [27]. In 2-D, tangents to the projections of limbs intersect on the projection of the axis at a common point [20,28].

The properties we add are given below. Their proofs are given in the appendix. Equivalent ones have been independently derived by [26].

Property P4: We give this property in the form of a theorem and its corollary.

Theorem P4: *Lines of correspondence* between any pair of cross-section curves are either *parallel* to the axis or intersect on the axis at the *same point*.

Corollary P4: In 2-D, *lines of parallel symmetry* between any pair of *projected* cross-sections are either *parallel* to the *projection* of the axis or intersect on it at a *common point*, regardless of the viewing direction.

Property P5: Let $C_1(u)$ and $C_2(v)$ be two unit speed parallel symmetric curves with a linear correspondence $f(u) = au + b$. Then for all u and u' the vectors $\underline{V}_1 = C_1(u') - C_1(u)$ and $\underline{V}_2 = C_2(au' + b) - C_2(au + b)$ are *parallel* and $|\underline{V}_2| / |\underline{V}_1| = a$ (i.e. the ratio of their lengths is *constant* and equal to the *scaling* of the correspondence).

The usage of these properties will be discussed throughout the description of the method in the next sections.

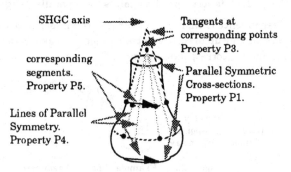

Figure 2.3   Invariant properties of SHGCs

2.2 Overview of the Segmentation Method

The study of SHGCs and their properties or their usage has been addressed by many researchers [10,12,20,22,26,27,28,33,34] but little can be found on their automatic detection in real image contours. The closest method to ours is [26] which differs in the way SHGC properties are used (also restricted to surfaces of revolution and LSH-GCs) and which does not handle occlusion.

There are many difficulties in dealing with real intensity images as the contours they produce are usually noisy and broken and may include surface markings and shadows. Scene occlusion introduces additional difficulties as it may prevent visibility of important object boundaries. Figure 2.4 gives an example of a real image and its extracted contours. These difficulties make contour segmentation methods based

Figure 2.4   A real intensity image and its extracted edges

on contour following and junction analysis (such as [1]) impractical. Our method of segmentation and description (figure-ground separation) consists of using the properties of SHGCs as strong constraints in a three-level perceptual grouping approach. The three levels are the *curve level*, the *parallel symmetry level* and the *SHGC patch level*.

The curve level is intended to form global contours by grouping co-curvilinear contour fragments. The parallel symmetry level is intended to hypothesize SHGC cross-sections by detecting linear parallel symmetries. The SHGC patch level is intended to form SHGC object descriptions whenever there is evidence of their presence in the image.

The method assumes orthographic projection with a general viewing direction. In this discussion, we will omit many details of the method as they are available in [33,34]. Also, for lack of space, we will not discuss the curve level and briefly summarize the parallel symmetry level in Sect. 2.3. In Sect. 2.4, we discuss the SHGC patch level. In Sect. 2.5, we will show results on 3-D shape recovery from the resulting segmented descriptions.

2.3 Hypothesizing Cross-Sections (Level 2)

It is useful to find cross-sections of SHGCs in an image because they allow to locate the rest of the object [33,34]. We assume that the cross-sections of scene SHGCs are visible in the image. From property P1, we know that such cross-sections produce linear parallel symmetries in the image. The method to detect cross-sections thus consists of a hypothesize-verify process of several steps which starts from the detection of local parallel symmetry correspondences and ends with cross-section hypotheses. Detection of local parallel symmetries uses a quadratic B-spline representation of the curves [25] and may produce sparse (due to boundary discontinuities) and noisy correspondences. The symmetry grouping step generates grouping hypotheses between symmetries (thus forming global symmetries) and consequently groups the boundaries involved in the symmetries. The verification and completion steps filter out non-linear symmetries and fill in missing boundaries of selected ones. The constraints used for the grouping and verification steps are derived from property P5. More details on each of those steps can be found in [33,34].

Examples of this level are given in Fig. 2.5 which shows, in the top row, input contours resulting from the curve level and, in the bottom row, the detected and completed cross-sections using the above process.

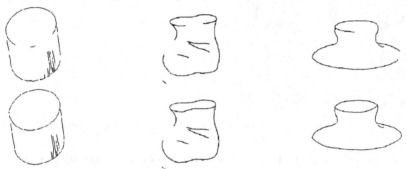

Figure 2.5   Results of the parallel symmetry level on some examples.

2.4 Detecting SHGC Descriptions (Level 3)

To detect SHGC objects, we also have to detect their surfaces in the image whenever there exists evidence of their presence. Here too we have to define what the projective properties of such surfaces are and how we can use them to hypothesize presence of relevant objects. Since object contours can have discontinuities in the image due to errors in edge localization, low contrast and occlusion, the detection of SHGCs must proceed by first *detecting* local surface patches that are likely to correspond to visible portions of SHGCs. The obtained patches can then be *grouped* whenever there is evidence that they belong to the same object. Obtained global SHGC hypotheses may then be *completed* and *verified* for geometric and structural consistency. The constraints to use in those steps can be derived from the projective invariant properties of SHGCs. The steps are described below. To make the discussion rigorous, we first give the definition of a local SHGC patch.

Definition 3: A *local SHGC patch* is given by a hypothesized closed cross-section and a pair of corresponding limb curves (*limb patches*) satisfying the projective properties P2 or P4; i.e. the limb patches are either straight (for a local LSHGC) or have the property that lines of symmetry between any pair of projected cross-sections intersect on a straight line (projection of the axis).

Figure 2.6 shows sample local SHGC patches.

    1) Detection of Local SHGC Patches

For each hypothesized cross-section, pairs of curves can be checked whether they satisfy the definition of a local SHGC patch. For this, correspondences between each

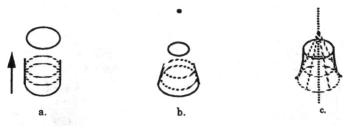

Figure 2.6   Sample local SHGC patches. a. cylindrical. b. conical . c. non-linear

pair of curves are detected (if any). The correspondence finding method is based on the method of [28] which consists of ruling the area between two curves by finding the scale of the (hypothesized) cross-section which makes the cross-sections tangential to the limbs. This yields a set of recovered cross-sections (Fig. 2.8). Pairs of curves that admit such correspondences (henceforth called *limb patches*[3]) are hypothesized to form local SHGC patches if:

- both limb patches are straight, in which case if they are parallel they form a *cylindrical patch* with the limb patches giving the projection of the direction of the axis; Fig. 2.6.a (corollary P4) else they form a *conical patch* whose apex is a point of the projection of the axis (Fig. 2.6.b) (also corollary P4). An LSHGC patch is thus hypothesized (property P2).

- the limb patches are not both straight; then between each pair of recovered cross-sections, the intersection point of lines of symmetry is determined (Fig. 2.6.c). A local SHGC patch is hypothesized if the locus of such points is a straight line (using fitting criteria; Fig. 2.7). This line is a local estimate of the projection of the axis (corollary P4). We call this patch a *non-linear* SHGC patch.

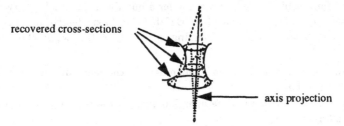

recovered cross-sections

axis projection

Figure 2.7   Using corollary P4 to find the projection of the axis

This process of detecting curves that satisfy the projective invariant properties of SHGCs may not result in only the right hypotheses (corresponding to real scene objects). For example, not all straight lines in the image correspond LSHGCs. Figure 2.8 shows some of the local SHGC patches detected by our system from the contours of Fig. 2.4. In the figure, the "right" hypotheses (corresponding to the real objects we perceive) are shown separately from some of the "wrong" ones, although at this stage

---

3. we will use the term limb patches although in some cases the bounding contours of an SHGC may not be limb projections but meridian projections.

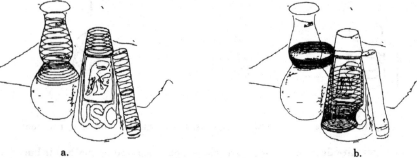

a.   b.

Figure 2.8   Examples of hypothesized local SHGC patches detected from the contours of
Fig. 2.4. a. the right hypotheses. b. examples of wrong hypotheses.

the system cannot differentiate between them. The total number of hypothesized local SHGC patches is 94, only 4 of them (those of Fig. 2.8.a) belong to real objects.

   2) Grouping of Local SHGC Patches

Boundary discontinuities cause surface description discontinuities. Thus, among the
detected local SHGC patches, some may be part of the same object whose image contours have been broken. It is necessary to group such patches so as to form complete
object descriptions. Expressing the compatibility of local SHGC patches belonging to
the same object is central to the grouping (segmentation) process. We seek compatibility constraints that are independent of the viewing direction and that produce relevant grouping hypotheses. By a simple examination of Corollary P4, we can derive
a set of geometric compatibility constraints between local SHGC patches that project
from the same SHGC in the scene. As seen in step 1, each local SHGC patch is given
with a local description of the projection of the axis: a direction for a cylindrical
patch, a point for a conical patch and a line for a non-linear patch. Thus, two local
SHGC patches project from the same SHGC if their local axis descriptions are "similar". The similarity relationships, depending on the type of the two patches are giv-
en below:

   • *non-linear* and *non-linear*: the axes must be colinear (up to some error;
     Figure 2.9.c and d)
   • *non-linear* and *conical*: the cone apex must lie on the axis (up to some error;
     Figure 2.9.a)
   • *non-linear* and *cylindrical*: the direction of the cylinder must be parallel to the
     axis
   • *conical* and *conical*: the limbs must be colinear (same apex as in Figure 2.9.b)
     otherwise a line is generated between the apexes[4]
   • *cylindrical* and *cylindrical*: the limbs must be colinear (for the same LSHGC)
     otherwise the directions must be parallel
   • *conical* and *cylindrical*: a line from the apex in the direction of the cylinder is
     generated

---

4. the line could be the projection the global SHGC axis; it will be later used in the
verification stage.

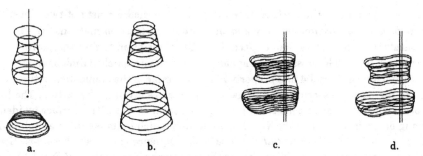

Figure 2.9   Examples of geometrically compatible local SHGC patches.

In addition to geometric compatibility constraints, structural compatibility constraints are also used to generate grouping hypotheses of local SHGC patches. Structural compatibility constraints take into account the fact that limb boundaries are not necessarily continuous in the image due to real image imperfections or self-occlusion. A detailed discussion of the different structural arrangements of limb patches and hypothesis selection criteria are given in [33,34].

3)   Verification of SHGC Hypotheses

Object hypotheses made on the basis of geometric projective invariants may not always correspond to meaningful scene objects. There are two reasons why this is so. First, the projective invariants are necessary properties of the projections of SHGCs but not sufficient ones to firmly conclude their presence in the scene (the examples of Fig. 2.8.b demonstrate this). Second, error thresholds are used to make object hypotheses so as to account for noise, quantization, etc. This inevitably results in making more than the relevant hypotheses. Thus, it is necessary to verify hypotheses on the basis of additional criteria which should filter out the wrong ones. The verification consists of both a geometric test and a structural one.

Geometric consistency is intended to filter out globally inconsistent (yet locally consistent) groupings and uses the rules mentioned in the discussion of the grouping step. In the case of a non-linear global patch, the global axis is computed by applying corollary P4 to the cross-sections of all the aggregated patches; it is then compared to the axes of the grouped local patches.

Structural consistency is intended to filter out non closed patches. The surfaces of a scene object project onto closed (or occluded) image surfaces. Closure tests consist of verifying required junction properties at both ends of each hypothesized SHGC. Junction measures are used in order to account for real image imperfections (more details are given in [33,34]).

However, closure may not be directly obtained due to occlusion or false negatives in the curve level grouping. For example, in Fig. 2.4, the occluded vase (left most object) has a substantial portion of its lower right limb occluded by the cone, which is itself occluded by the right most object. In [23], projective invariants of 3-D point sets have been used to recover projective structure and infer non-visible vertices in the image of a polyhedron. Here, we demonstrate that projective invariants of SHGCs (curved objects) can be used to complete partial descriptions and infer invisible (occluded) portions of the surface. Our completion method consists of two steps: the *axis-based cross-section recovery* and the *limb reconstruction* methods. The former consists of using the available (partial) SHGC description to find the position and scaling of the SHGC cross-section at each point of the unmatched limb boundary. For this, it uses corollary P4 and property P1. An example of the application of the method to the partial descriptions of Figs. 2.9.a and c are given in Fig. 2.10.a. The limb reconstruction method consists of finding the actual extent of the surface by identifying on each previously recovered cross-section which of its points is a limb point. For this, it finds the *tangential envelope* of the sequence of recovered cross-sections. This reconstruction method, applied to the recovered cross-sections of Fig. 2.10.a are shown in Fig. 2.10.b. Details of the two steps for completion of descriptions can be found in [33,34].

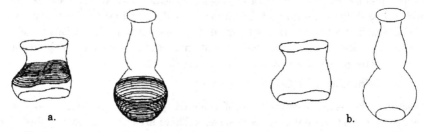

a.   b.

Figure 2.10   Cross-section recovery and limb reconstruction for previous SHGCs.

Selected objects are those which are both geometrically and structurally consistent (closed). Results of the whole process on the contours of Figs. 2.4 and 2.5 are given in Fig. 2.11.The figure shows the global descriptions in terms of recovered (and completed) cross-sections, limbs and axes. Additional examples of the results of the method on another intensity image are shown in Fig. 2.12. Figure 2.12.a shows the intensity and edge images (there are more markings in this example than the previ-

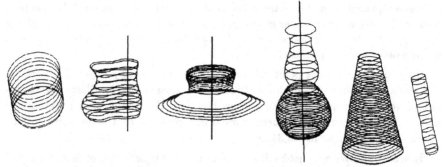

Figure 2.11   Results obtained in level 3.on previous input contours. The last example is
                from the image in Fig. 2.4..

ous ones). Figure 2.12.b shows the detected (and grouped) local SHGC patches (only the verified hypotheses are shown). Figure 2.12.c shows the completed descriptions of the segmented objects. More results are available in [33].

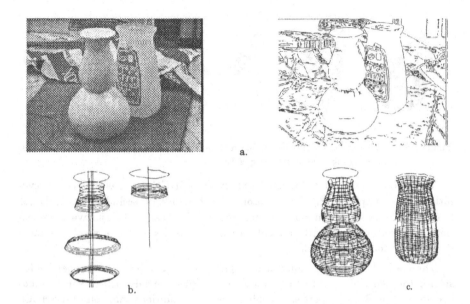

Figure 2.12   Additional example of results obtained by our method.

2.5 Recovery of 3-D Shape

Recovering 3-D shape of SHGCs has been addressed by many researchers [10,26,28]. Ulupinar and Nevatia [28] have proposed a method that recovers 3-D shape of SHGCs using contour information only. It produces a viewer-centered description in terms of surface normals. In [33,34], we show how our 2-D descriptions and the viewer-centered description of [28] can be used to recover 3-D object-centered descriptions consisting of the 3-D cross-section curve, the 3-D axis and the 3-D scaling function which provide information about the whole object independent of the particular viewpoint. Results of that recovery method on the descriptions of Figs. 2.11 and 2.12 are shown in Fig. 2.13. The figure shows the recovered primitives for different 3-D poses.

2.6 Discussion

This method has been fully implemented and tested on several images with satisfactory results. It uses a number of parameters (thresholds) in the hypothesize-verify steps. For all tested images (more than 10) the same parameter values have been used. However, robustness of the system to changes in those parameters has been tested by changing their values up to 50% of their default ones. Those changes have only affected the number of hypotheses (more hypotheses for looser thresholds) but not the final results. This is due to the fact that the method uses strong constraints derived from the projective invariants of SHGCs and that it does not commit to strong decisions based on local evidence only, but also uses global evidence of regularity as well.

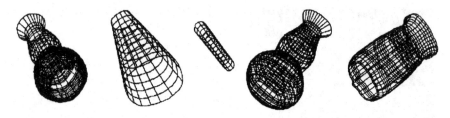

Figure 2.13   Recovered 3-D descriptions of previous SHGC scenes shown for different poses.
a. from Fig. 2.11. b. from Fig. 2.12.

The method is not limited to particular types of SHGCs such as surfaces of revolution (the examples of Figs. 2.11, second object, and 2.12, occluded object, do not have circular cross-sections). It also handles complex cases with concave cross-sections and cross-sections with tangent discontinuities. Examples of results on such cases can be found in [33,34].

The method shows the importance of global projective invariant properties for solving the segmentation problem and obtaining rich scene descriptions from a monocular image. Such properties provide necessary conditions that relevant SHGCs must satisfy. However, the method is limited to single SHGC objects whose projections satisfy the expected projective regularities, most notably visibility of the cross-sections. In the case of composite objects made up of several parts additional difficulties arise. Most of those difficulties relate to the non-visibility of geometric projective regularities due to complex interactions among connected primitives. In this case, a more thorough analysis of structural properties than has been done in this method is necessary. This is the focus of our current research.

3   Recovery of Circular PRGCs from Monocular Contours

In this section, we discuss geometric projective properties and recovery of Circular PRGCs from monocular contours. The primitives studied in the past have either a straight axis such as SHGCs [10,20,26,28,33,34] and their special case of surfaces of revolution [16] or a curved axis but with constant cross-section such as planar right constant generalized cylinders (PRCGCs [30]; which include objects like tori). Projective properties and recovery of objects with both a curved axis *and* a non-constant cross-section have not been addressed by other researchers. Although past work has addressed ribbon descriptions of complex curved objects [7,17,21], it has not actually related ribbon descriptions to 3-D descriptions of those objects. Thus, the obtained descriptions can be different for different viewpoints or occlusion patterns.

This work addresses Circular PRGCs which are characterized by a planar curved axis and a non-constant, circular, cross-section. Figure 3.1 shows some examples. Special cases of Circular PRGCs include surfaces of revolution (SORs; straight axis) and Circular PRCGCs (constant cross-section). The mathematical formulation of the projection of the contours of Circular PRGCs is far more complex than that of straight axis or constant cross-section primitives. The non-constancy of the cross-section and the curvature of the axis affect the contours in very complex ways. We were unable to find global *invariant* properties of general Circular PRGCs (except for

Figure 3.1   Sample Circular PRGCs.

special cases), and we believe that none exist. In fact, global projective invariants may not always exist for arbitrarily complex shapes. In their absence, we wish to investigate properties that are still well-behaved and that provide useful constraints for recovering shape information from an image. Binford and colleagues [4,5] have introduced *quasi-invariance* to refer to a class of properties which, unlike invariant properties, have measures that vary but do so in a relatively small range of values over a large fraction of the space of viewing transformations. Despite a recent attempt to characterize quasi-invariants as rigorously as invariants [5], quasi-invariants are still best analyzed statistically [4,8].

The type of quasi-invariant properties we are interested in are those which give a rigorous relationship between 2-D image and 3-D shape descriptions. Thus, such properties allow to have descriptions that do not vary (much) with changes in viewpoint. We have found such quasi-invariant properties for general Circular PRGCs and which turn out to be invariant for their special cases. Those properties have also been exploited to derive a method for recovering 3-D shape of Circular PRGCs from their monocular contours. The method assumes that the projection geometry is orthographic with a general viewing direction.

The discussion in this section starts by giving a brief mathematical analysis of the projection of Circular PRGCs in Sect. 3.1. In Sect. 3.2, we derive projective invariant properties of special cases of Circular PRGCs and in Sect. 3.3 we derive quasi-invariant properties of general Circular PRGCs. In Sect. 3.4, we discuss the usage of the derived quasi-invariants to recover estimates of 3-D shapes from monocular contours of Circular PRGCs. Since this work has already been described in [35,36], we will omit certain details of the mathematical formulation.

3.1 Projections of Circular PRGCs

In this section, we give useful mathematical preliminaries that characterize the limb equations and projections of Circular PRGCs. We first give a more precise definition of such objects.

Definition 4: A Circular PRGC is the surface obtained by scaling a circular cross-section C along a non-necessarily straight planar axis curve A while (orthogonally) scaling it by a function r.

Letting the cross-section radius be ρ, the arclength parameterization of the axis $A(s)$ and the scaling function $r(s)$, the surface of a Circular PRGC can be parameterized as follows:

$$P(s, \theta) = A(s) + \rho r(s)(\cos\theta\vec{n} + \sin\theta\vec{b}) \tag{3.1}$$

where $\hat{n}$ and $\vec{b}$ are respectively the normal and binormal to the axis curve and θ denotes angular position on the cross-section. Figure 3.2 illustrates this parameterization.

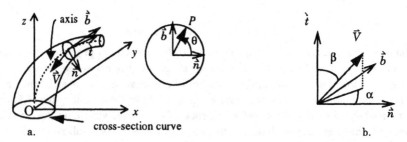

Figure 3.2   Circular PRGC parameterization and viewing geometry

Derivation of the limb equation of generalized cylinders has been addressed by Ponce and Chelberg in [18]. For Circular PRGCs, the derivation is discussed in [35,36]. Here, we report the limb equations of general Circular PRGCs, and their special cases of Circular PRCGCs (constant cross-section) and SORs (straight axis). The limb equation of a general Circular PRGC is given by:

$$[1 - \kappa(s)\, \rho r(s)\, \cos\theta]\; \cos(\theta - \alpha(s)) = \rho\; \dot{r}(s)\; \cot\beta(s) \tag{3.2}$$

where $\kappa(s)$ is the curvature of the axis, $\dot{r}(s)$ the derivative of $r(s)$ and $(\alpha(s), \beta(s))$ the angular coordinates of the unit viewing vector $\vec{V}$ in the Frenet-Serret frame attached to the axis curve $A(s)$ (Fig. 3.2.b). There are usually two solutions of the limb equation 3.2 for each value of s along the axis. For SORs the limb equation becomes

$$\cos(\theta - \alpha(s)) = \rho\dot{r}(s)\cot\beta(s) \tag{3.3}$$

and for Circular PRCGCs

$$\cos(\theta - \alpha(s)) = 0 \tag{3.4}$$

The orthographic projection of a point with coordinates $(t, n, b)^t$ in the Frenet-Serret frame on a plane orthogonal to the viewing direction $\vec{V}$ is given by (dropping the argument s)

$$p = (-\sin\beta\; t + \cos\beta\cos\alpha\; n + \cos\beta\sin\alpha\; b,\, -\sin\alpha\; n + \cos\alpha\; b)^t \tag{3.5}$$

where the coordinates are expressed in a 2-D "moving" frame whose first vector is the projection of the vector tangent to the axis and whose second vector is orthogonal to the first following the right hand rule. The origin of this frame is the projection of the axis point $A(s)$. A point $P(s, \theta)$ on the surface of a Circular PRGC thus projects as (without loss of generality fixing $\rho = 1$)

$$p = r \begin{pmatrix} \cos\beta\cos(\theta - \alpha) \\ \sin(\theta - \alpha) \end{pmatrix} \tag{3.6}$$

The segment connecting the projection of such limb points will be called a *co-cross-section segment*, as its joins points projecting from the same cross-section. The midpoint of a co-cross-section segment will be called a *2-D axis point*. The locus of the 2-D axis points so defined will be called the *2-D axis*. In the following two sections, we will derive some projective properties of the contours of Circular PRGCs. Those properties characterize image points that project from the same cross-section of the 3-D description. This has also been the focus of previous work [16,20,26,28,29,30,33,34]. The properties give the relationship between the co-cross-section segments and the 2-D axis defined above. We start by giving projective invariants of the two special cases of a Circular PRGC: Circular PRCGCs and SORs.

3.2 Invariant Properties of Special Circular PRGCs

The proofs of the properties are given in the appendix.. As previously mentioned, all properties assume orthographic projection.

Property P6: in the projection of a Circular PRCGC (constant cross-section) the 2-D axis and the projection of the 3-D axis *coincide* regardless of the viewing direction. Furthermore each 2-D axis point is the projection of the corresponding 3-D axis point (Fig. 3.3.a).

Property P7: in the projection of a Circular PRCGC, co-cross-section segments and the tangents to the 2-D axis at the corresponding 2-D axis points are *orthogonal* regardless of the viewing direction (Fig. 3.3.a).

Property P8: in the projection of a SOR, the 2-D axis and the projection of the 3-D axis *coincide* regardless of the viewing direction (Fig. 3.3.b; the 2-D axis points are *not* necessarily projections of the corresponding 3-D axis points).

Property P9: in the projection of a SOR, co-cross-section segments are *orthogonal* to the 2-D axis regardless of the viewing direction.

The last two properties are related to the bilateral symmetry of SORs derived by Nalwa [16]. The above properties can be interpreted as saying that the projections of the 3-D descriptions of Circular PRCGCs and SORs are ribbons with cross-section segments orthogonal to the ribbon axis (so-called Brooks' ribbons with right angle [19], henceforth *right ribbons*).

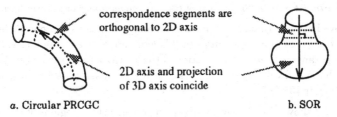

correspondence segments are
orthogonal to 2D axis

2D axis and projection
of 3D axis coincide

a. Circular PRCGC   b. SOR

Figure 3.3   Invariant properties of special Circular PRGCS

3.3 Quasi-Invariant Properties of General Circular PRGCs

In the general case, it can easily be shown that the above properties are not projective invariants. However, we show that there exist quasi-invariant properties. First, let us rewrite the limb equation 3.2 in the following form

$$(1 - e\cos\theta)\cos(\theta - \alpha) = \dot{r}\cot\beta \qquad (3.7)$$

where $e = \kappa r = r / R$ (R being the radius of curvature of the axis). e measures the relative thickness of the shape and $\dot{r}$ measures how 'fast' the sweep is. Equation 3.7 indicates that the image contours of a Circular PRGC are affected by:

- $(e, \dot{r})$, which are shape parameters and
- (α, β) which are viewing parameters

To show that a property is quasi-invariant (as defined in the introduction of Sect. 3) with respect to some parametric transforms, we have to show that its measure remains within a small range over most the parameter space of those transforms. It is difficult to algebraically formulate this statement for complex properties such as the ones we give. However, the range of values of the property can be numerically analyzed as a function of the parameter values. For this, we have to first define our parameter space of observation.

The parameter space is a 4-dimensional space $(\alpha, \beta, e, \dot{r})$. It is sufficient to constrain $\alpha \in [0, \pi]$ and $\beta \in (0, \pi)$ due to the symmetric nature of equation 3.7. The shape parameters are also constrained. We have $|e| < 1$ (the cross-section radius r is smaller than the radius of curvature, R, of the axis), otherwise the surface self-intersects. By manipulating equation 3.7, it can be shown that $|\dot{r}| \leq 2|\tan\beta|$. This implies that $|\dot{r}|$ has to be small enough if the surface has to admit limb points for a large range of views. For example, for $\beta = 15^\circ$, the cross-section has limbs if $|\dot{r}| < 0.53$. Curved axis objects we see in our environment appear not to have high values for both $|e|$ and $|\dot{r}|$ (otherwise the thickness ratio would rapidly increase, which would cause self-intersection). Now we state the quasi-invariant properties then give an analysis to demonstrate that they have the desired behavior.

Property P10: in an orthographic projection of a Circular PRGC, co-cross-section segments and tangents to the 2-D axis at the corresponding 2-D axis points are *almost orthogonal over most the parameter space of observation.*

Property P11: in an orthographic projection of a Circular PRGCs, tangents to the 2-D axis and the projection of the tangents to the 3-D axis at the corresponding points are *almost parallel over most of the parameter space of observation.*

To prove both properties, we give a brief analysis of the behavior of the angle, γ, between co-cross-section segments and 2-D axis tangents and the angle, ϕ, between the 2-D axis tangents and the projection of the 3-D axis tangents as functions of the previous shape and viewing parameters. The method used to derive both angle functions is given in [35,36].

Figure 3.4 shows the plots of the sizes (in percent) of the regions of the parameter space ($\alpha \in [0, \pi]$, $\beta \in (0, \pi)$, $e \leq 0.5$ and $\dot{r} < 0.5$) for which the angle γ is within different angular values of 90° (measure or orthogonality) and the angle ϕ within different angular values of 0° (measure of parallelism). The first graph shows that γ is within 5° of 90° over 84.30% of the 4-D parameter space (excluding the subspaces $e = 0$ and $\dot{r} = 0$) and within 10° of 90° over 92.63% of the space. The second graph shows that ϕ is within 3° of 0° over 94.48% and within 5° over 96.90% of the space.

Figure 3.5.a shows the plot of the values of γ as a function of the viewing angles (α, β) for $(e, \dot{r}) = (0.2, 0.2)$ and the corresponding half-viewing sphere displaying

334

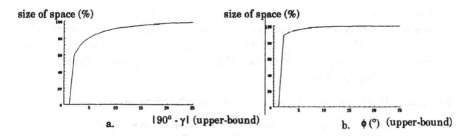

size of space (%)   size of space (%)

a. $|90° - \gamma|$ (upper-bound)   b. ϕ (°) (upper-bound)

Figure 3.4   Plots of the relative sizes of the regions of the parameter space for different ranges of the image angles.

where γ is within 5° of 90°; vertical circles correspond to constant β values with a 5° step. Figure 3.5.b shows a similar plot for the values of ϕ as a function of (α, β) for the same values of $(e, \dot{r})$ and the display of the half-viewing showing where ϕ is within 3° of 0°.

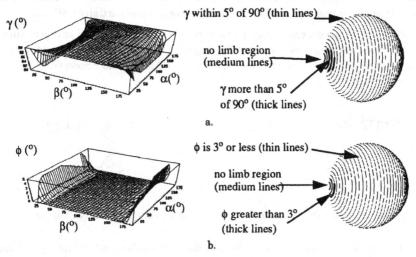

γ (°)

γ within 5° of 90° (thin lines)

no limb region (medium lines)

γ more than 5° of 90° (thick lines)

a.

ϕ (°)

ϕ is 3° or less (thin lines)

no limb region (medium lines)

ϕ greater than 3° (thick lines)

b.

Figure 3.5   Plots of the values of γ (a.) and ϕ (b.) and display of the half-viewing sphere for $(e, \dot{r}) = (0.2, 0.2)$

The above plots show that the angles γ and ϕ not only vary slowly when the viewing angles and shape parameters change but remain within relatively small bounds over a large fraction the parameter space. They also show that the properties gradually degrade (larger angular values) as both e and $\dot{r}$ take high values. The plots of Fig. 3.5 show that the space regions where the angles remain within small bounds are connected and that the bounds tend to increase only close to regions of the space where limbs do not exist; i.e. for specific viewing directions that are close to being in the direction of the tangent to the axis *and* in the axis plane (unlikely viewing directions).

The previous two properties are quasi-invariant with respect to the 4-D parameter space. Thus they are both orthographic quasi-invariant and shape parameters quasi-invariant. They can be interpreted as saying that a right ribbon gives a "good approximation" of the projection of the 3-D description of a general Circular PRGC *over most viewing directions.*

3.4 Using the Quasi-Invariants to Recover 3-D Shape

Previous work on the usage of quasi-invariants [4,5], or view variation [8], has addressed applications to recognition of 3-D objects from 2-D images. Here, we show that the quasi-invariant properties P10 and P11 can be used to recover 3-D shape from monocular contours. The recovery method consists of first detecting right ribbons from given 2-D contours. From the argument given above, the resulting descriptions are close to the projection of the 3-D descriptions of a Circular PRGC. Then, the 3-D object centered description consisting of the 3-D axis, the 3-D cross-section and the 3-D scaling function is recovered. The method assumes that contours are given in a labeled form (i.e. limbs and cross-sections) and that no markings exist. Furthermore, it assumes that both end cross-sections are at least partially visible.

We will omit the description of the right ribbon detection method as it is available in [36]. Here, we only give some results. Figure 3.6 shows the right ribbon descriptions obtained for both objects of Fig. 3.1. The figure shows the ribbon cross-sections and ribbon axes.

Figure 3.6   Resulting right ribbon descriptions for the Circular PRGCs of Fig. 3.1.

The 3-D recovery method uses the 2-D description obtained by the right ribbon detection method to estimate the axis plane orientation and recover the surface cross-sections and the 3-D axis points. Based on property P10, it uses the 2-D correspondences as approximates of the projection of co-cross-section segments and based on property P11 is uses the tangents to the 2-D axis as approximates of the projection of the tangents to the 3-D axis. The different steps of the method are described in detail in [35,36]. Figure 3.7 shows the recovered 3-D primitives shown from different viewing directions. Since the 2-D descriptions are close to the projection of the 3-D descriptions over most viewing directions, the resulting 3-D descriptions are also close to the actual ones over most viewing directions.

3.5 Discussion

The properties we have derived give a rigorous relationship between known 2-D shape descriptions (ribbons) and the projection of complex shape primitives (Circular PRGCs). Their analysis shows that the former give good approximates of the pro-

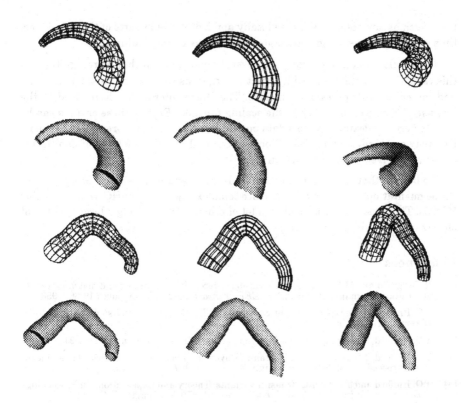

Figure 3.7   Results of 3D shape recovery for the previous two Circular PRGCs.

jection of the latter over most viewing directions and that the approximates tend to be poor only close to degenerate viewing directions (or shapes). An analysis of the noise sensitivity of this relationship indicates that it is robust to noise. It has been successfully applied in a recently developed method for automatic segmentation and 3-D recovery of circular PRGCs from a real intensity image.

The usage of quasi-invariants, and similar properties, is receiving more interest in the research community. In the absence of more precise invariant properties, they prove a promising tool for estimating descriptions of complex 3-D objects from a monocular image.

4   Conclusion

Projective invariant and quasi-invariant properties of volumetric shapes are key to rigorously solving the scene segmentation and shape recovery problems from monocular images. The type of properties we have presented relate computable 2-D descriptions to (the projection of) 3-D descriptions of generic shapes such as generalized cylinders. An important characteristic of the properties is that while they are of a global nature, capturing stable and rich properties of higher level features such as surfaces, they can be locally applied to visible parts of those features, thus handling occlusion and other sources of image discontinuities.

The results of both methods have several applications including recognition. In this case, the 3-D shapes provide object descriptions that can be used for indexing and matching with preexisting models. The shape information is reduced to the cross-section curve, the axis and the scaling function. Each of these entities can be used to derive indexing keys to a data base of object models so represented. Comparison between recovered and model objects could also be on the basis of qualitative measures derived from our descriptions.

We believe that there is much to do in deriving and using similar properties for the segmentation and description of more complex objects than SHGCs and Circular PRGCs. This type of approach offers a lot of promise for handling a large number of objects in our environment.

References

[1]   R. Bergevin and M.D. Levine, "Generic object recognition: Building and matching coarse descriptions from line drawings," in *IEEE Transactions PAMI*, 15, pages 19-36, 1993.

[2]   T.O. Binford, "Visual perception by computer," *IEEE Conference on Systems and Controls*, December 1971, Miami.

[3]   T.O. Binford, "Inferring surfaces from images," *Artificial Intelligence*, 17:205-245, 1981.

[4]   T.O. Binford, T.S. Levitt and W.B. Mann, "Bayesian inference in model-based machine vision," Proceedings of *AAAI Uncertainty Workshop*, 1987.

[5]   T.O. Binford and T.S. Levitt, "Quasi-invariants: Theory and Exploitation", in Proceedings of the *Image Understanding Workshop*, pages 819-829, Washington D.C., 1993.

[6]   M.H. Brill, E.B. Barrett and P.M. Payton, "Projective invariants for curves in two and three dimensions", in *Geometric Invariance in Computer Vision*, J.L. Mundy and A. Zisserman editors, MIT Press, pages 193-214, 1992.

[7]   R.A. Brooks, "Model-based three dimensional interpretation of two dimensional images," *IEEE Transactions PAMI*, 5(2):140-150, 1983.

[8]   J.B. Burns, R.S. Weiss and E.M. Riseman, "View Variation of Point-Set and Line Segment Features", *IEEE Transactions PAMI*, 15, pages 51-68, 1993.

[9]   D.A. Forsyth, J.L. Mundy, A.P. Zisserman, C. Coelho, A. Heller and C.A. Rothwell, "Invariant Descriptors for 3-D Object Recognition and Pose," *IEEE Transactions PAMI*, 10:971-991, 1991.

[10] A. Gross and T. Boult, "Recovery of generalized cylinders from a single intensity view," In *Proceedings of the Image Understanding Workshop*, pages 557-564, Pennsylvania, 1990.

[11] J.J. Koenderink, *"Solid Shape,"* M.I.T. Press, Cambridge, MA, 1990.

[12] J. Liu, J. Mundy, D. Forsyth, A. Zisserman and C. Rothwell, "Efficient recognition of rotationally symmetric surfaces and straight homogeneous generalized cylinders," In *Proceedings of IEEE CVPR*, pages 123-128, 1993.

[13] A.K. Mackworth, "Interpreting pictures of polyhedral scenes," *Artificial Intelligence*, 4:121-137, 1973.

[14] R.S. Millman and G.D. Parker, *"Elements of differential geometry,"* Prentice Hall. 1977.

[15] R. Mohan and R. Nevatia, "Perceptual organization for scene segmentation", *IEEE Transactions PAMI*. 1992.

[16] V. Nalwa, "Line drawing interpretation: Bilateral symmetry," *IEEE Transactions PAMI*, 11:1117-1120, 1989.

[17] R. Nevatia and T.O. Binford, "Description and recognition of complex curved objects," *Artificial Intelligence*, 8(1):77-98, 1977.

338

[18] J. Ponce and D. Chelberg, "Finding the limbs and cusps of generalized cylinders," *International Journal of Computer Vision*, 1:195-210, 1987.

[19] J. Ponce, "Ribbons, Symmetries and Skewed Symmetries," In *Proceedings of the Image Understanding Workshop*, pages 1074-1079, Massachusetts, 1988.

[20] J. Ponce, D Chelberg and W.B. Mann, "Invariant properties of straight homogeneous generalized cylinders and their contours," *IEEE Transactions PAMI*, 11(9):951-966, 1989.

[21] K. Rao and R. Nevatia, "Description of complex objects from incomplete and imperfect data," In *Proceedings of the Image Understanding Workshop*, pages 399-414, Palo Alto, California, May 1989.

[22] M. Richetin, M. Dhome, J.T. Lapestre and G. Rives, "Inverse Perspective Transform Using Zero-Curvature Contours Points: Applications to the Localization of Some Generalized Cylinders from a Single View," *IEEE Transactions PAMI*, 13(2):185-192, 1991.

[23] C.A. Rothwell, D.A. Forsyth, A. Zisserman and J.L Mundy, "Extracting projective structure from single perspective views of 3D point sets", in the proceedings of the *ICCV*, pages 573-582, Berlin, Germany. 1993.

[24] C.A. Rothwell, A. Zisserman, D.A. Forsyth and J.L. Mundy, "Fast recognition using algebraic invariants", in *Geometric Invariance in Computer Vision*, J.L. Mundy and A. Zisserman editors, MIT Press, pages 398-407, 1992.

[25] P. Saint-Marc and G. Medioni, "B-spline contour representation and symmetry detection," In *First ECCV*, pages 604-606, Antibes, France, April 1990.

[26] H. Sato and T.O. Binford, "Finding and recovering SHGC objects in an edge image," *Computer Vision Graphics and Image Processing*, 57(3), pages 346-356, 1993.

[27] S.A. Shafer and T. Kanade, "The theory of straight homogeneous generalized cylinders," Technical Report CS-083-105, Carnegie Mellon University, 1983.

[28] F. Ulupinar and R. Nevatia, "Shape from contours: SHGCs," In *Proceedings of ICCV*, pages 582-582, Osaka, Japan, 1990.

[29] F. Ulupinar and R. Nevatia, "Perception of 3-D surfaces from 2-D contours," *IEEE Transactions PAMI*, pages 3-18, 15, 1993.

[30] F. Ulupinar and R. Nevatia, "Recovering Shape from Contour for Constant Cross Section Generalized Cylinders," In *Proceedings of IEEE CVPR*, pages 674-676. Maui, Hawaii. 1991.

[31] I. Weiss, "Projective invariants of shapes," in *Proceedings of IEEE CVPR*, pages 291-297, 1988.

[32] I. Weiss, "Noise resistant invariants of curves," in *Geometric Invariance in Computer Vision*, J.L. Mundy and A. Zisserman editors, MIT Press, pages 135-156, 1992

[33] M. Zerroug and R. Nevatia, "Volumetric descriptions from a single intensity image", in *International Journal of Computer Vision*. (to appear).

[34] M. Zerroug and R. Nevatia, "Segmentation and Recovery of SHGCs from a Real Intensity Image," In *Proceedings of the 3rd ECCV, Stockholm 1994 (to appear)*. Also in *Proceedings of the Image Understanding Workshop*, pages 905-916, Washington DC, 1993.

[35] M. Zerroug and R. Nevatia, "Quasi-invariant properties and 3D shape recovery of non-straight, non-constant generalized cylinders", In *Proceedings of IEEE CVPR*, pages 96-103, New York, 1993.

[36] M. Zerroug and R. Nevatia, "Quasi-invariant properties and 3D shape recovery of non-straight, non-constant generalized cylinders", In *Proceedings of Proceedings of the Image Understanding Workshop*, pages 725-735, Washington DC, 1993.

[37] A. Zisserman, D.A. Forsyth, J.L. Mundy and C.A. Rothwell, "Recognizing general curved objects efficiently," in *Geometric Invariance in Computer Vision*, J.L. Mundy and A. Zisserman editors, MIT Press, pages 228-251, 1992.

Appendix: Proofs

Proof of Theorem P4:

Let $P_1 = S(t, s_1)$ and $P_2 = S(t, s_2)$ be two corresponding points on two different cross-sections. The line L joining these points can be parameterized as follows:

$$u = [u(t) \sin\alpha \, (r(s_1) - r(s_2))] \, m + u(t) \sin\alpha \, r(s_1) \tag{A.1}$$

$$v = [v(t) \, (r(s_1) - r(s_2))] \, m + v(t) \, r(s_1) \tag{A.2}$$

$$s = [s_1 - s_2 + u(t) \cos\alpha \, (r(s_1) - r(s_2))] \, m + s_1 + u(t) \cos\alpha \, r(s_1) \tag{A.3}$$

Case 1. $r(s_1) \neq r(s_2)$. The intersection point, M, of L with the SHGC axis (s-axis) is given by setting $u = v = 0$ which implies $m = -r(s_1) / (r(s_1) - r(s_2))$ and M has coordinates $(0, 0, (s_2 \, r(s_1) - s_1 \, r(s_2))) / (r(s_1) - r(s_2)))^t$ which are independent of t (no matter what pair of corresponding points on the cross-sections).

Case2. $r(s_1) = r(s_2)$. In this case the direction of L is given by the vector $(0, 0, s_1 - s_2)^t$ which is independent of t and parallel to the SHGC axis ☐.

Proof of Corollary P4:

An algebraic proof is not necessary as it is similar to the previous one, except that the expression of lines of correspondence is in the image plane. Instead, we give the following argument: if the correspondence lines are parallel to the axis, then they are also parallel in the image (orthographic projection), otherwise the intersection property holds also true in the image since intersecting lines in 3D project onto intersecting lines in the 2D image (general viewpoint) ☐.

Proof of Property P5:

$$C_1(u') - C_1(u) = \int_u^{u'} T_1(s)ds = \int_u^{u'} T_2(as + b)ds = \frac{1}{a}\int_v^{v'} T_2(t)dt = \frac{1}{a}(C_2(v') - C_2(v))$$

☐.

Proof of Property P6:

Using equation 3.6 the cross-section segment is given by

$$r \begin{pmatrix} \cos\beta \, (\cos(\theta_2 - \alpha) - \cos(\theta_1 - \alpha)) \\ \sin(\theta_2 - \alpha) - \sin(\theta_1 - \alpha) \end{pmatrix} \tag{A.4}$$

and its mid-point (2-D axis point) by

$$\frac{r}{2} \begin{pmatrix} \cos\beta \, (\cos(\theta_2 - \alpha) + \cos(\theta_1 - \alpha)) \\ \sin(\theta_2 - \alpha) + \sin(\theta_1 - \alpha) \end{pmatrix} \tag{A.5}$$

But from equation 3.4, at limb points of a circular PRCGC, we have

$$\cos(\theta_1 - \alpha) = \cos(\theta_2 - \alpha) = 0, \text{ and thus, } \sin(\theta_1 - \alpha) = -\sin(\theta_2 - \alpha) = \pm 1 \tag{A.6}$$

for each s along the axis. Therefore, from equation A.5, the 2-D axis point is given by $(0, 0)^t$, the origin of the local 2-D frame which, as mentioned in section 3.1, is the projection of the axis point $A(s)$ no matter what the viewing direction (given locally by α and β) is ❑.

Proof of Property P7:

Reporting the results of the previous proof in equation A.4, we obtain the expression of the cross-section segment

$$r (0, \pm 2)^t \tag{A.7}$$

The 2-D axis shown to be the projection of the 3-D axis, its tangent vector is the projection of the 3-D tangent vector $\vec{t}$. This latter, from the projection equation 3.5, is given by

$$(-\sin\beta, 0)^t \tag{A.8}$$

which is orthogonal the previous cross-section segment ❑.

Proof of Property P8:

From equation 3.3, since the right hand side is a function of s only, we have

$$\cos(\theta_1 - \alpha) = \cos(\theta_2 - \alpha) \text{ and thus } \sin(\theta_1 - \alpha) + \sin(\theta_2 - \alpha) = 0 \tag{A.9}$$

Reporting this in equation A.5, the 2-D axis point is given by

$$(r / 2) (\cos\beta [\cos (\theta_2 - \alpha) + \cos (\theta_1 - \alpha)], 0)^t \tag{A.10}$$

which is always a point on the u-axis of the local 2-D frame; i.e. the direction of the projection of the tangent to the 3-D axis. Note that unlike property P6, this point does *not* coincide with the projection of the 3-D axis point $A(s)$. However, since the 3-D axis is straight, its projection is also straight and it is determined by the origin of the local 2-D frame (projection of $A(s)$) and the projection of the 3-D tangent; *i.e.* the u-axis ❑.

Proof of Property P9:

From the previous proof and equation A.4, the cross-section segment is given by

$$r (0, \sin (\theta_2 - \alpha) - \sin (\theta_1 - \alpha))^t \tag{A.11}$$

which is parallel to the v-axis of the local 2-D frame. But also from the previous proof the 2-D axis is the u-axis, orthogonal to the v-axis ❑.

Representations of 3D Objects that Incorporate Surface Markings

David Forsyth[1] and Charlie Rothwell[2]

[1] Department of Computer Science, University of Iowa, Iowa City, Iowa.
[2] Oxford University Robotics Research Group, Parks Rd, Oxford.

Abstract. In many cases, the geometric representation that a recognition system could recover is insufficient to identify objects. When object geometry is simple, it is not particularly distinctive; however, a rich representation can be obtained by mapping the surface markings of the object onto the geometry recovered. If edges are mapped, a representation that is relatively insensitive to the details of lighting can be recovered. Mapping grey levels or color values leads to a highly realistic graphical representation, which can be used for rendering. The idea is demonstrated using extruded surfaces, which consist of a section of a general cone cut by two planes. Such surfaces possess a simple geometry, yet are widespread in the real world. The geometry of an extruded surface is simple, and can easily be recovered from a single uncalibrated image. We show examples based on images of real scenes. **Keywords:** Object recognition, representation, surface markings, invariants.

1 Introduction

Efficient object recognition programs require distinctive object representations; in many applications, such as surveillance, video processing and image databases, only a single image is available. Much work has been done on recovering object geometry from single, uncalibrated images. This paper shows how surface patterns and markings can be recovered and associated with the geometry recovered, and demonstrates a representation, that captures both shape and pattern, for a large class of surfaces covering many man-made objects.

1.1 Recognition Using Indexing

In typical modern systems, recognition proceeds by:

- **Feature extraction:** Edges are extracted and the resulting geometric primitives are grouped into likely object groups (for example, a group of five lines, of two conics, or of a single "M-curve" in [11]).
- **Indexing and hypothesis merging:** Feature groups are used to compute geometric primitives that index the object in a model base (for example, the projective invariants of a pair of conics in [11]). Normally, one object leads to several groups of features indexing the appropriate model, so the resulting hypotheses must be merged using consistency criteria to obtain a single recognition hypothesis.

- **Verification:** Hypothesized objects are back-projected into the image; the results are used to obtain further information that may confirm the hypothesis.

Systems of this sort have been demonstrated for plane objects in a number of papers [3, 11, 4, 7, 13, 16]. Typically, object models consist of a system of invariant values and are therefore relatively sparse, meaning that hypothesis verification is required to confirm a model match. However, no searching of the model base is required because the hypothesised object's identity is determined by the invariant descriptors measured. These systems are attractive because, in the ideal case, an object description is computed from the image and identifies the object, without requiring that a model base be searched. As a result, systems with relatively large model bases can be constructed[3].

1.2 Recognising Curved Surfaces

The indexing systems described assume either that the model base contains only plane or polyhedral objects, or that depth data is available. Recognising curved surfaces in single images presents a particularly difficult problem, as the change in appearance of a curved surface as it is imaged from different viewing positions is not easily analysed. Throughout the paper, we assume an idealised pinhole camera. These cameras possess a *focal point* and an *image plane*. For each point in space, there is a line through that point and the focal point; the point in space appears in the image as the intersection of this line with the image plane. An orthographic view occurs when the pinhole is "at infinity".

If the focal point is fixed and the image plane is moved, the resulting distortion of the image is a collineation. In what follows, it is assumed that neither the position of the image plane with respect to the focal point nor the size and aspect ratio of the pixels on the camera plane is known, so that the image presented to the algorithm is within some arbitrary collineation of the "correct" image. In this model, the image plane makes no contribution to the geometry, and its position in space is ignored.

The *outline* of a surface is a plane curve in the image, which itself is the projection of a space curve, known as a *contour generator*[4]. The contour generator is given by those points on the surface where the surface turns away from the image plane; formally, the ray through the focal point to the surface is tangent to the surface. As a result, at an outline point, if the relevant surface patch is visible, nearby pixels in the image will see vastly different points on the surface, and so outline points usually have sharp changes in image brightness associated with them. Figure 1 illustrates these concepts.

It is generally accepted that the problem of recovering surface geometry from an outline alone is intractable if the surface is constrained only to be smooth, or

---

[3] Current systems using this approach have model-bases containing of the order of thirty objects.

[4] There are a number of widely used terms for both curves, and no standard terminology has yet emerged.

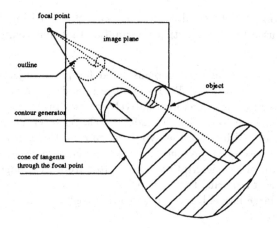

Fig. 1. The outline and contour generator of a curved object, viewed from a perspective camera.

piecewise smooth, as in this case significant changes can be made to the surface geometry without affecting the outline from a given viewpoint. As a result, an important part of the problem involves constructing as large a class of surfaces as possible that can either be directly recognised or usefully constrained from their outline alone. There have been advances in a number of special cases:[5, 8, 2] describe a systems for recognising rotationally symmetric surfaces from outlines, [1, 8, 10, 14, 15] treat straight homogenous generalised cylinders and [6] describes recognising algebraic surfaces from outlines. All these systems emphasize surface geometry in recognition.

Other systems, such as those of [12, 9] emphasize cues such as color and surface lightness over geometry. These cues are particularly effective in dealing with objects whose geometry is ill-defined or hard to describe (such as shirts or jerseys). Such cues cannot, however, be completely divorced from shape, as by themselves they are not particularly distinctive. Difficulties with these cues include perspective effects making it difficult to frame colour features in a truly shape independent fashion (foreshortening can have substantial effects on a colour histogram) and the profound sensitivity of colour and grey-level to illumination.

2 Recovering Extruded Surfaces

An *extruded surface* is a surface formed by a section cut from a general cone by two planes (see figure 2) in such a way that the section of surface does not include the vertex of the cone. This is the projective generalisation of the a surface formed by a system of parallel lines, with plane ends (such a surface can be extruded from a nozzle). Surfaces with this geometry have been the subject of a number of investigations (see, for example, [10, 14, 15], whose more general theories cover these surfaces as special cases), as they are extremely common, either in themselves or as components of more complex objects - examples include most tin cans, boxes, books, and many plastic bottles.

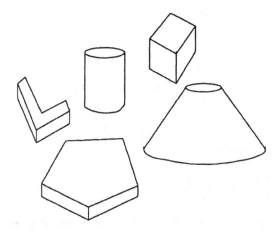

Fig. 2. A range of examples of extruded surfaces; note that for most examples, the vertex is at infinity.

The outline of an extruded surface consists of a system of line segments (possibly empty for some views), the projection of one plane section, and the (possibly occluded) projection of the other plane section; in particular, for all focal points outside a simple "forbidden zone", which lies between the top and bottom sectioning planes and to the object's side of their line of intersection, one or the other plane section is completely visible, and there are usually at least two line segments in the outline.

The projective geometry of an extruded surface can be completely reconstructed in a single image (given the focal point is generic), because it is so simple. Consider one of the plane sections, taken with the line on that plane where the two sectioning planes intersect; call the plane chosen the *defining plane* and the configuration of plane section and line a *defining plane section* or D.P.S. The complete projective geometry of the surface can be represented by a defining plane sections, as it is possible can choose a projective transformation of space that fixes the D.P.S., and transforms the vertex to any given point off the defining plane section and the other sectioning plane, which must pass through the line in the D.P.S., to any given plane not the defining plane nor containing the vertex. As a result, the surface can be reconstructed by taking a D.P.S, choosing a second sectioning plane through the line on the D.P.S. arbitrarily, and choosing an arbitrary vertex in space[5]. The section of surface that

---

[5] Of course, the second plane must not be a second copy of the defining plane, and the vertex may not lie on either plane.

lies between the planes and does not include the vertex is the reconstruction.

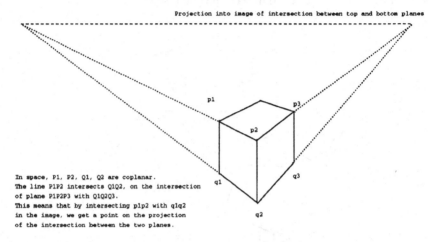

Fig. 3. Determining the projection into the image of the line of intersection of the two sectioning planes.

As at least one plane section is visible in most images, it is possible to recover the surface's projective geometry the projection of the line of intersection between the planes in space can be recovered in the image. This can be done, if the projection of the vertex is known, using the following approach (which is illustrated in figure 3):

- Mark three points, p_1, p_2 and p_3 on one plane section. These correspond to the three coplanar points P_1, P_2 and P_3 in space.
- Construct the corresponding points on the other plane section (for objects with a convex cross-section, self-occlusion is not, in fact, a problem here; see below). Call these points p'_1, p'_2, p'_3, and the corresponding coplanar points in space P'_1, P'_2, P'_3.
- Intersect the image lines p_1p_2, $p'_1p'_2$ to form q_{12} and the lines p_2p_3, $p'_2p'_3$ to form q_{23}. Since P_i, P'_i, P_j, P'_j must be coplanar (the lines $P_iP'_i$ and $P_jP'_j$ are rulings of the surface, and hence pass through the vertex), the intersections in the image are projections of actual intersections in space of the lines P_1P_2, $P'_1P'_2$, etc.
- Since P_1P_2 lies on the top plane, and $P'_1P'_2$ lies on the bottom plane, their intersection must lie on the intersection between the two planes. Thus, the projected line of intersection must pass through q_{12} and through q_{23}.

The aspect of this construction most likely to provide problems for early vision is the identification of corresponding points, which is complicated by self-occlusion. This problem is relatively easy to deal with if the cross-section of the cone is convex[6]. For such cross-sections, which are well represented in applications, reasoning from a plane cross-section of the object is sufficient. It is apparent that only three possible cases of self-occlusion are significant:

1. one sectioning plane is occluded, and one is visible;
2. both sectioning planes are visible;
3. both are occluded.

Figure 4 shows how each case can occur. In case 3, it is possible to recover the projective geometry of the object only partially; as this case is "unusual" (from the position of the focal point), we concentrate on the other two cases.

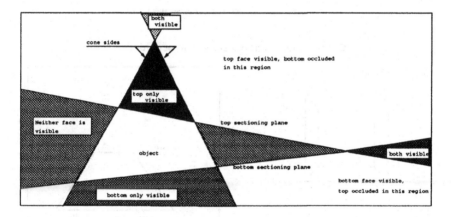

Fig. 4. The possible cases of occlusion of both top and bottom section curves depend on the position of the focal point with respect to the cone, and with respect to the top and bottom sectioning planes; this figure shows the possible cases, for an object viewed in section. Reasoning from a section is sufficient if the cross-section is convex.

For a convex object, top-bottom correspondences are also easily obtained. Consider a general plane through the vertex and through the focal point; such a plane (which appears in the image as a line), and cuts the top and bottom sections in a number of points, some or all of which are visible in the image as points along a line. The cases are as follows:

– **One section visible:** if (say) the bottom section is occluded, all but one of the points of intersection between the given plane and the bottom section are occluded (figure 5). Hence, the number of visible intersections is odd, and points appear in a cyclic permutation of the order (u_1, u_2, v_2) (where u

---

[6] For neatness' sake, we use a definition of convexity compatible with projective transformations; define a region to be convex if its intersection with any line is connected. This definition is broader than the usual definition, but the property is preserved under projective transformations.

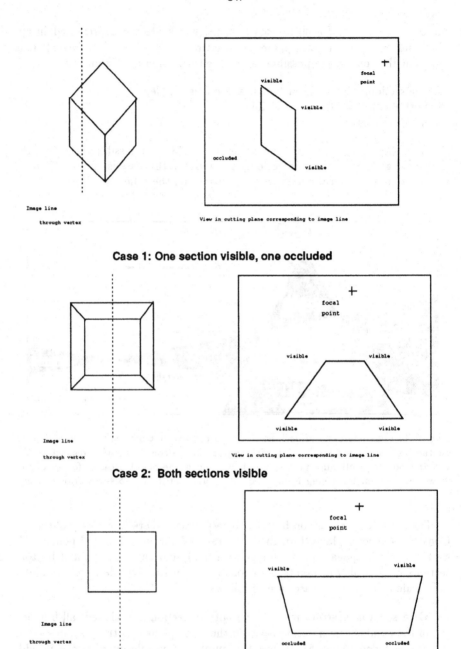

Case 1: One section visible, one occluded

Case 2: Both sections visible

Case 3: Both sections occluded

Fig. 5. The effects of occlusion on determining top-bottom correspondences, for a convex cross section and the three cases given in the text.

and v are either top or bottom respectively, and u_i and v_i correspond) along the image line.

- **Both sections visible:** if neither section is occluded, all points of intersection will be visible and there will be an even number of intersections between the outline and the image line, which appear in a cyclic permutation of the order (u_1, u_2, v_2, v_1) along the image line.

- **Both sections occluded:** if both sections are occluded, one point of intersection will be visible for both top and bottom sectioning plane, and there will be two intersections between the outline and the image line, which clearly appear in a cyclic permutation of the order (u_1, v_1) along the image line.

2.1 Obtaining Surface Markings for Extruded Surfaces

To transfer surface markings from the image to the representation of the surface, it is convenient to break up the cross-section in the image into a polygonal approximation (the polygons can be arbitrarily small), and then note that this leads to a representation of the surface as a system of plane quadrilaterals. Finally, the positions of the vertices in the image to which the 3D vertices project, are known. This determines the projective transformation from the image quadrilateral to the surface quadrilateral (four points and their images determine a projective transformation), and this transformation applied to pattern points maps them onto the surface representation (figure 6). Clearly, if this texture mapping process works for grey-level surface markings, it will work for color surface markings as well. A number of color sequences exist, although production expense dictates that the examples given show results only for the grey level case.

3 Experimental Results and Discussion

This scheme has been implemented for images of real scenes. We use a simple manual process to mark outline points in images; in particular, the operator marks the two lines that determine a vertex, points on the top curve, and corresponding points on the bottom curve. This manual interface was used to allow a quick implementation to demonstrate the recovery process; we do not believe that it is essential. The representations extracted are 3D geometrical objects with associated surface markings, and therefore lend themselves well to display as a movie. Figure 7 shows typical images from which models are extracted; figures 8 and 9 show frames from movies of tumbling objects. Note that the texture on the object is stable as the object tumbles, indicating that the surface markings are being correctly extracted and placed; note further that, if the operator chooses a projective frame in which, for example, the soda cans have a circular cross section and roughly the right aspect ratio, the models are impressively realistic. Figure 10 shows two views of a simple 3D world constructed using a tool that places extruded models in space with respect to one another.

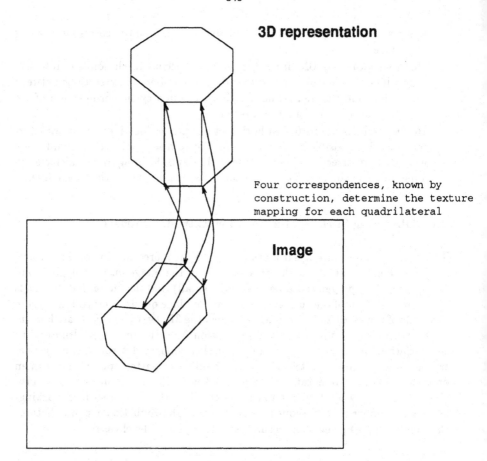

3D representation

Four correspondences, known by
construction, determine the texture
mapping for each quadrilateral

Image

Fig. 6. Patterns and surface markings are transferred to the representation of the extruded surface, using the fact that four known correspondences determine a plane to plane projection. These correspondences are determined by construction.

3.1 Recovering Surface Markings in General

Ideally, a representation of a surface would contain information both about shape and about surface pattern features; in general, edges in surface pattern are likely to be more effective recognition cues due to their relative insensitivity to illumination, but for some applications such cues as pattern colour and lightness may be appropriate. The surface marking information should be provided as a pattern on a representation of the surface (i.e. referred to its position on the surface in some canonical frame[7]), so that foreshortening effects and the like can

---

[7] A canonical representation of the object's markings is one that is independent of the camera geometry. For instance, a canonical representation of a ruled surface such as a drinks can would be the unwrapped planar surface (modulo starting point), bounded by a rectangle.

Fig. 7. Four typical images, from which models were recovered.

be discounted. If the geometry of an object can be recovered from an image, then it is generally also possible to recover a representation that incorporates surface markings.

Typically, processes that recover geometry from outline information alone in an uncalibrated camera can only recover the projective geometry of an object. This means that an object is associated with a large equivalence class of possible recovered representations, each within a projective transformation of the original object geometry. The property required, that the surface markings be in the "right place" on the surface, is more properly referred to as *covariance*. Covariance in recovering surface markings would mean that, for any two projectively equivalent representations of an object recovered from two images of that object, the projective equivalence extends to the surface markings as well.

It is possible to produce algorithms with this property, given that one allows for occlusion of surface markings. The natural approach, is to compute a camera matrix that takes the inferred object geometry to the image outline; this matrix will be a three by four matrix (homogenous coordinates), whose kernel represents the focal point of the camera, in the model frame. The preimage of an image point in this matrix will be a line in space, passing through the focal point; the intersection, closest to the focal point, between this ray and the object must then be marked with the grey-level or colour in the camera. Thus, transferring surface markings from the image to the representation involves an intersection process, akin to ray-tracing. Because the points obtained by this process are defined by

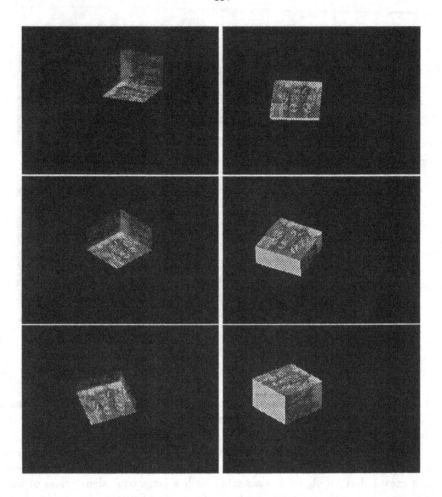

Fig. 8. Six frames from a motion sequence, showing a box for soda cans tumbling.

intersections, the construction is covariant.

The most significant ambiguities that will operate here will be the effects of illumination and self-occlusion. The traditional solution to illumination problems is to use edges, and it is clear that edge maps can be transferred to geometric representations as well as grey-levels. Self-occlusion represents a more interesting problem in determining feature properties.

3.2 Recognition Using Surface Markings

This form of representation can be used to support a hierarchical recognition system, that uses both shape and surface marking information to represent and recognise objects. As the geometry of objects of this form is so simple (as we have seen, it is completely determined by a plane curve and a line), objects can easily

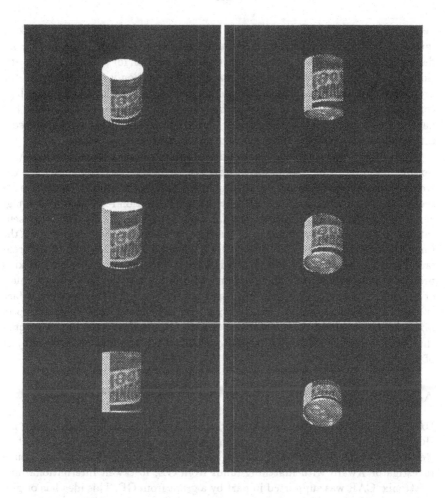

Fig. 9. Six frames from a motion sequence, showing a soda can tumbling backwards.

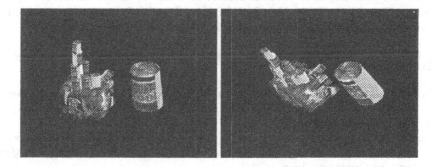

Fig. 10. Two views of a three dimensional world created and rendered using the representations described in the text.

be indexed using a geometrical description. At that point, the surface marking information, which is in a canonical frame, can be used to generate further indexing information for the surfaces using the methods of, for example, Nayar and Bolle [9]. A judicious use of surface marking information is likely to break the projective ambiguity implicit in the geometrical reconstruction - for example, a container for cans of grape soda and a matchbox are projectively equivalent, but have different markings on their faces. Figure 11 shows the canonical representations of face texture for three views of three different object faces.

Geometric representations of extruded surfaces can, therefore, be effectively texture mapped using image data. However, grey-level texture maps are extremely sensitive to illumination details, making them potentially ineffective for recognition. It is possible to texturemap the representation recovered with image edges to overcome this difficulty, and figures 12 to 14 show canonical representations of face edges for a range of surfaces. In general, these views look the same for different views of the same faces and different for views of different faces, and so should allow effective indexing. In fact, constructing an indexing process that works reliably for a large number of faces is not fully solved; much of the difficulty appears to stem from spatial quantisation noise, as when a face is strongly foreshortened, an image pixel may correspond to a large clump of pixels in the canonical representation. Constructing robust indexing techniques that use the surface marking information in these representations is the subject of active research.

Acknowledgements

DAF was upported in part by the National Science Foundation under award no. IRI-9209729, in part by a grant from United States Air Force Office of Scientific Research AFOSR-91-0361, and in part by a National Science Foundation Young Investigator Award with matching funds from GE, Rockwell International and Tektronix. CAR was supported in part by a grant from GE. This idea has origins in both authors' collaborative work with Joe Mundy and Andrew Zisserman. DAF was encouraged to consider surface markings by a discussion with Shree Nayar. Thanks to David Mumford for helpful and informative conversations. Rodney André built the tool for modeling worlds of extruded surfaces.

References

1. Binford, T.O., Levitt, T.S., and Mann, W.B., "Bayesian inference in model-based machine vision," in Kanal, L.N., Levitt, T.S., and Lemmer, J.F., *Uncertainty in AI 3*, Elsevier, 1989.
2. Dhome, M., LaPreste, J.T, Rives, G., and Richetin, M. "Spatial localisation of modelled objects in monocular perspective vision," *Proc. First European Conference on Computer Vision*, 1990.
3. Forsyth, D.A., Mundy, J.L., Zisserman, A.P., Coelho, C., Heller, A. and Rothwell, C.A. "Invariant Descriptors for 3-D Object Recognition and Pose," *PAMI-13*, No. 10, p.971-991, October 1991.

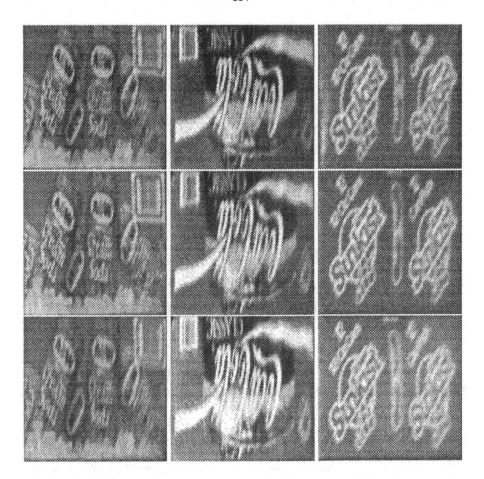

Fig. 11. Canonical representations of face markings for three views of three different object faces; note that different views of the same face look the same, and views of different faces look different.

4. Forsyth, D.A., Mundy, J.L., Zisserman, A.P. and Rothwell, C.A. "Applications of invariant theory in vision," In Kapur, D. and Donald, B.R., (eds) *Proceedings Workshop on Integration of Symbolic and Numerical Methods, Saratoga N.Y.*, Academic Press, 1992.

5. Forsyth, D.A., Mundy, J.L., Zisserman, A.P. and Rothwell, C.A. "Recognising Curved Surfaces from their Outlines," Proceedings ECCV2, p.639-648, 1992.

6. Forsyth, D.A., "Recognizing Algebraic Surfaces from their Outlines," *Accepted for Publication, International J. of Computer Vision*, 1993.

7. Lamdan, Y., Schwartz, J.T. and Wolfson, H.J. "Object Recognition by Affine Invariant Matching," Proceedings CVPR88, p.335-344, 1988.

8. Liu J., Mundy J.L., Forsyth D.A., Zisserman A. and Rothwell C.A., "Efficient Recognition of Rotationally Symmetric Surfaces and Straight Homogeneous Generalized Cylinders", *CVPR*, 1993.

Fig. 12. Canonical representations of face edges for three views of of a box in which soda cans are sold. Each column shows three different faces from a single view; different columns correspond to different views. These representations should be compared with those of figures 13 and 14; note that different views of the same face look the same, and views of different faces look different. This information is much richer than the geometry of the object, which is rather simple.

9. Nayar, S.K. and Bolle, R. "Reflectance Ratio: A Photometric Invariant for Object Recognition," *Proc ICCV-4*, Berlin, 1993.

10. Ponce, J. "Invariant properties of straight homogenous generalised cylinders," *IEEE Trans. Patt. Anal. Mach. Intelligence*, **11**, 9, 951-965, 1989.

11. Rothwell, C.A., Zisserman, A., Forsyth, D.A. and Mundy, J.L. "Planar Object Recognition using Projective Shape Representation," to appear, IJCV 1994.

12. Swain, M.J. and Ballard, D.H., "Color Indexing," *International Journal of Computer Vision*, **7**, 1, 11-32, 1991.

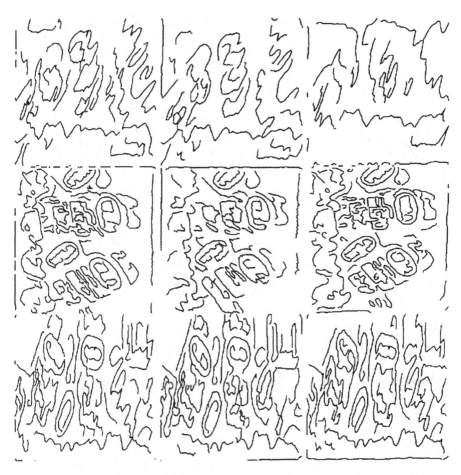

Fig. 13. Canonical representations of face edges for three views of of a box in which soda cans are sold. Each column shows three different faces from a single view; different columns correspond to different views. These representations should be compared with those of figures 12 and 14; note that different views of the same face look the same, and views of different faces look different.

13. Taubin, G. and Cooper, D.B. "Recognition and Positioning of 3D Piecewise Algebraic," Proceeding DARPA Image Understanding Workshop, p.508-514, September 1990.
14. Ulupinar, F, and Nevatia, R. "Shape from Contour using SHGCs," *Proc. ICCV*, Osaka, 1990.
15. Ulupinar, F, and Nevatia, R. "Recovering shape from contour for constant cross-section generalisd cylinders," *Proc. CVPR*, Mauii, 1991.
16. Weiss, I. "Projective Invariants of Shapes," Proceedings DARPA Image Understanding Workshop, p.1125-1134, April 1988.

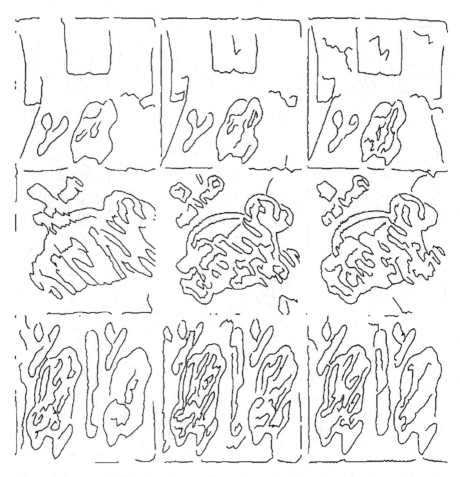

Fig. 14. Canonical representations of face edges for three views of of a box in which soda cans are sold. Each column shows three different faces from a single view; different columns correspond to different views. These representations should be compared with those of figures 12 and 13; note that different views of the same face look the same, and views of different faces look different.

Model-based invariant functions and their use for recognition

Daphna Weinshall*

Institute of Computer Science
The Hebrew University of Jerusalem
91904 Jerusalem, Israel
email: daphna@cs.huji.ac.il.

Abstract. Using three dimensional invariant representations, we address the problem of changes in appearance that result from a change in camera orientation (or change of viewpoint). This approach is based on a Euclidean invariant representation of three dimensional objects, where the metric information is kept using the Gramian of 4 basis points and the affine coordinates of the remaining points, or using the generalized inverse Gramian of all the object points. We describe functions which operate on two dimensional images of three dimensional objects, and which are invariant under changes of viewpoint. These functions can be used to improve and extend various existing recognition approaches, including alignment, linear combination, and indexing. The invariant representation can be computed with a linear algorithm from a sequence of images.

1 Introduction

One of the fundamental problems in the recognition of three dimensional objects in two dimensional images is the change in object appearance due solely to the imaging process. In this work we address the problem of changes in appearance that result from a change in camera orientation (or change of viewpoint). This paper summarizes the work described in [17], and refers to related work described in [18, 19, 9].

Efficient object representation is a key to a successful application of pattern recognition methods. Invariance under a group of transformations is a desired component of any efficient representation. In vision, such a transformation is naturally given by the possible transformations of the observer, e.g., $3D$ rotations and translations, or discrete symmetries like a left-right reflection. Whereas such transformations change the appearance of the object, they should not affect its intrinsic representation. It is therefore desirable to represent objects by explicit invariants under such transformations, which yet depend on the particular object.

Koenderink & van-Doorn [6] (see also [17]) described a hierarchy of representations produced by the particular selection of the group of $3D$ transformations:

---

* This paper describes research done at IBM T.J. Watson Res. Ctr., Hawthorne, NY.

Complete: The complete representation of the scene includes the $3D$ coordinates of each point, possibly as a depth map, and the pose of the camera relative to the object. This representation is typically sought in reconstruction algorithms in computer vision.

Euclidean invariant: A description of the $3D$ shape of objects which is invariant to the action of the group of similarity transformations in $3D$, which includes rotations, translations, and isotropic scaling.

Affine invariant: A description of the $3D$ shape of objects which is invariant to the action of the group of linear transformations in $3D$ and translations. The group of affine transformations includes the group of similarity transformations.

A *complete* representation describes uniquely the object and its orientation relative to the camera. It includes the largest amount of information, and therefore not surprisingly it is the most difficult to compute. On the other hand, both *invariant* representations do not require the computation of camera pose, and therefore they are expected to be easier to compute robustly. Moreover, since they provide a single description for a particular object in different scenes, they can be used to integrate information across time. Therefore when the pose information is not needed, which is typically the case in recognition tasks, the use of invariant representations promises significant computational advantages.

An *affine* representation is not unique: objects which are related by a linear transformation have the same affine representation. Affine representations were initially used for recognition, in geometric hashing [8] and linear combination [16]. Geometric hashing uses an affine representation to obtain an efficient indexing scheme from images to memory. The linear combination scheme uses an affine representation to describe novel images as a linear combination of stored "canonical" images. The cost of using an affine representation is more false positive matches, since affine representations are not unique. Affine $3D$ shape can be computed from a sequence of $2D$ images with a linear algorithm [12, 17], and therefore can be used by reconstruction algorithms which compute $3D$ structure from $2D$ images.

Unlike *affine* shape, a *Euclidean* representation is unique for every general $3D$ object. Given an affine representation, the computation of a Euclidean representation requires additional steps. We have shown in [17] that this computation can be linear. This guarantees that a solution can always be obtained, and that the algorithm converges as long as the noise in the images has 0 mean. Moreover, the algorithm proposed in [19] to compute this representation is incremental, which implies that an estimate for the shape can be obtained from a few images, and improved with additional data.

Most Structure From Motion algorithms attempt to compute the *complete* representation of the scene, namely, structure in the form of a depth map and pose, using a sequence of $2D$ images. SFM algorithms differ in their assumption on the projection from $3D$ to $2D$ (perspective vs. orthographic), in the input used (optical flow vs. motion disparities), and the amount of information used (2 or more images, 4 or more points). Thus, for example, the algorithms described in [15, 13] assume weak perspective (orthographic projection and scale) and use many frames to increase their robustness, whereas the algorithms described in [3, 11] use perspective projection.

In [17] we described a hierarchical representation of the type discussed above, where object points were represented by their affine coordinates in some affine coordinate system, and the Euclidean metric information was represented by the Gramian matrix of the basis points. In [19] we described an efficient algorithm to linearly compute this representation, and compared it to other algorithms using simulated data and a few sequences of images. In [9] we used the Euclidean invariant with a recognition scheme which uses a few images to compute an index into a database of models. In [18] we used the Euclidean invariant to compute a metric, a closed-form expression, which gives the distance between three dimensional objects and two dimensional images.

The rest of this paper is organized as follows: In Section 2 we define model-based invariant functions, identify and characterize a few invariant functions, and discuss the advantages of using such invariant functions for the representation of three dimensional objects and surfaces. In Section 3 we discuss the application of these invariant functions to model-based recognition; we discuss their use with alignment [5], linear combination [16], and indexing [7]. In Section 4 we describe a linear algorithm for the computation of the model-based invariant functions from image streams, showing results with real and simulated data.

2   Model Based Invariants

In the following, we first define invariant functions and model-based invariant functions (Section 2.1). We describe two model-based invariant functions (Section 2.2) which can be learned from examples (images) with a linear computation, and which are also easy to evaluate in real-time. In Section 2.3 we discuss the computation of these model-based invariant functions. Finally, we discuss the use of these invariant functions for the representation of $3D$ shape of objects composed of points (Section 2.4).

2.1   Definitions:

Let $\mathcal{G}$ denote a group of transformations acting on a space $\mathcal{M}$ such that an element $g \in \mathcal{G}$ is a transformation $g : \mathcal{M} \to \mathcal{M}$. A (scalar) **invariant** with respect to these transformations, $I(x)$, is a function $I : \mathcal{M} \to \mathbf{R}$ whose values do not change under the action of all the elements of $\mathcal{G}$, i.e., $I(g(x)) = I(x) \forall g \in \mathcal{G}$. For such an invariant function to be of any use it should have a nontrivial dependence on the parameters of the object that we want to characterize. In this paper we will be interested in $3D$ transformations, namely, $\mathcal{M} = \mathcal{R}^3$.

Let an object be a set of n points in $\mathcal{R}^3$, to be denoted $\omega = \{P_i\}_{i=1}^n$, $\omega \in \Omega$. The image of the object is a set of n 2D points $\{p_i\}_{i=1}^n$ (disregarding occlusion), produced by a $3D$ transformation $g \in \mathcal{G}$ of the object, and followed by a projection π which is a $3D$ to $2D$ mapping:

$$p_i = \pi(g(P_i)) \qquad p_i \in \mathcal{R}^2, \ \pi : \mathcal{R}^3 \to \mathcal{R}^2, \ g \in \mathcal{G}, \ P_i \in \mathcal{R}^3$$

A (projective) view-invariant function[2] $f : \pi(g(\omega)) \to \mathbf{R}$ with respect to group $\mathcal{G}$ is a real function on the viewed set of points $\{p_i\}$, which has the property that it is invariant to the action of the group $\mathcal{G}$. More precisely, it is the projection of an invariant function $I(x)$ on the $3D$ points $\{P_i\}_{i=1}^{n}$. f is a universal invariant function if there is no restriction on the domain Ω, the set of possible objects (namely, $\Omega = \mathcal{R}^{3n}$). f is model-based invariant if its domain of objects is a single general $3D$ object, namely, $\Omega = \{\omega\}$, $\omega \in \mathcal{R}^{3n}$. The parameters of the invariant function depend on the choice of object (thus it is model-based).

For $3D$ objects that move in $3D$ space rigidly and unconstrained, or when the camera is moving, the group of rigid transformations $\mathcal{G}$ is the Euclidean group of rotations and translations, and the projection mapping π is the perspective projection. Often weak perspective is assumed, in which case $\mathcal{G}$ includes the similarity transformations (rotations, translations, and isotropic scaling), and π is the orthographic projection. This approximation is valid when the relative distances between points in the object are much smaller than their distances to the camera. In this paper we assume weak perspective.

For both the orthographic and perspective projections, Burns et al. [1] (as well as Clemens & Jacobs [2] and Moses & Ullman [10]) have shown that universal invariants do not exist. Not surprisingly, therefore, most of the research in this area of projective invariance has concentrated on the identification of computable invariances in some special cases. In fact, most of the published results address planar collections of points or curves (e.g., [4]). More generally, Moses & Ullman [10] studied the existence of general-view invariants for specific classes of objects, such as bilaterally symmetric objects.

In this paper we are mostly interested in $3D$ rigid transformations, namely, $\mathcal{G}$ is the $3D$ similarity group (the similarity is used since weak perspective is assumed). Functions which are invariant under $\mathcal{G}$ will be called similarity invariants. We will also consider the group of $3D$ affine transformations, which include $3D$ linear transformations and translations. Functions which are invariant under the $3D$ affine group will be called affine invariants. Since the linear group includes the similarity group, affine invariants are also similarity invariants. Note, however, that affine invariants are less powerful since they cannot distinguish objects that are related by a linear transformation.

Let $\mathcal{G}$ be the similarity group (rigid transformations and scale), and let f be a model-based invariant function for $\Omega = \{\omega\}$. It is possible that for another object ω', $f(\pi(\omega)) = f(\pi(g'(\omega')))$ for some transformation g'. Such false identifications are called accidental matches. If, however, $f(\pi(\omega)) = f(\pi(g'(\omega')))$ for all $g' \in G$, these false identifications are called non-accidental matches. It follows

---

[2] We will only use the adjective "projective" when context is not sufficient to clarify the exact meaning.

from the definition that affine invariants lead to non-accidental matches, whereas similarity invariants do not.

2.2 Model based invariant functions:

Similarity invariant: Consider an object ω composed of 4 non-coplanar $3D$ points. (If all points are coplanar, there exist a few other projective invariants, e.g. the affine invariant discussed in [8]). Let $\{P_i\}_{i=0}^{3}$ denote the $3D$ coordinates of the 4 points in some (unknown) initial frame of reference. Assume $P_0 = (0,0,0)$ without loss of generality, and let $\{p_i\}_{i=1}^{3}$ denote the $3D$ vectors corresponding to the 3 remaining points. Let B denote the inverse of the Gramian of the points, namely:

$$B = \begin{pmatrix} p_1^T p_1 & p_1^T p_2 & p_1^T p_3 \\ p_1^T p_2 & p_2^T p_2 & p_2^T p_3 \\ p_1^T p_3 & p_2^T p_3 & p_3^T p_3 \end{pmatrix}^{-1} \tag{1}$$

The matrix B is invariant to rigid transformations, i.e., $3D$ rotations and translations of the 4 points. Moreover, B is a 3×3 symmetric matrix which includes all the relative $3D$ information on the points. B can be generalized to any number of points as discussed in Section 2.4.

Given the image coordinates of the 4 points (x_0, y_0), (x_1, y_1), (x_2, y_2), (x_3, y_3), assume without loss of generality $x_0 = 0$, $y_0 = 0$. (Otherwise, replace any x_i in the following expressions by $x_i - x_0$, and y_i by $y_i - y_0$.) Let $\mathbf{x} = (x_1, x_2, x_3)$ and $\mathbf{y} = (y_1, y_2, y_3)$.

Definition 1. Given 4 non-coplanar $3D$ points, let

$$f_B(\mathbf{x}, \mathbf{y}) = \frac{|\mathbf{x}^T B \mathbf{y}| + |\mathbf{x}^T B \mathbf{x} - \mathbf{y}^T B \mathbf{y}|}{|\mathbf{x}| \|B\| |\mathbf{y}|} \tag{2}$$

Proposition 2. f_B *is a similarity model-based projective invariant function, which allows accidental matches only. Moreover, the elements of its parameters, the matrix B, can be computed from (at least) 3 images by solving a linear system of equations. (B is computed up to a scaling factor, but the scaling of B does not change f_B.)*

Proof. Let $\mathcal{G}$ be the $3D$ similarity group (rigid transformations and scale). By fixing the origin in the first point, we account for the translation and can ignore it in further discussion. Let $\{p_i = (X_i, Y_i, Z_i)\}_{i=1}^{3}$ denote the $3D$ coordinates of the 3 remaining points in some fixed frame of reference. Any image is the orthographic projection of the object rotated from this absolute frame by a rotation matrix $R = \{r_{i,j}\}_{i,j=1}^{3}$ and scaled by s.

First note that:

$$\begin{pmatrix} X_1 & Y_1 & Z_1 \\ X_2 & Y_2 & Z_2 \\ X_3 & Y_3 & Z_3 \end{pmatrix} \begin{pmatrix} sr_{11} \\ sr_{12} \\ sr_{13} \end{pmatrix} = \begin{pmatrix} x_1 \\ x_2 \\ x_3 \end{pmatrix}, \quad \begin{pmatrix} X_1 & Y_1 & Z_1 \\ X_2 & Y_2 & Z_2 \\ X_3 & Y_3 & Z_3 \end{pmatrix} \begin{pmatrix} sr_{21} \\ sr_{22} \\ sr_{23} \end{pmatrix} = \begin{pmatrix} y_1 \\ y_2 \\ y_3 \end{pmatrix}.$$

Using the notations

$$A = \begin{pmatrix} X_1 & Y_1 & Z_1 \\ X_2 & Y_2 & Z_2 \\ X_3 & Y_3 & Z_3 \end{pmatrix}, \quad \mathbf{r}_1 = \begin{pmatrix} r_{11} \\ r_{12} \\ r_{13} \end{pmatrix}, \quad \text{and} \quad \mathbf{r}_2 = \begin{pmatrix} r_{21} \\ r_{22} \\ r_{23} \end{pmatrix} \tag{3}$$

we can rewrite the above equations as follows:

$$\mathbf{r}_1 = \frac{1}{s} A^{-1} \mathbf{x}, \qquad \mathbf{r}_2 = \frac{1}{s} A^{-1} \mathbf{y}. \tag{4}$$

From the orthonormality of the columns of the rotation matrix $\mathbf{r}_1, \mathbf{r}_2$ we have:

$$\mathbf{x}^T (AA^T)^{-1} \mathbf{y} = 0, \qquad \mathbf{x}^T (AA^T)^{-1} \mathbf{x} - \mathbf{y}^T (AA^T)^{-1} \mathbf{y} = 0. \tag{5}$$

We denote $B = (AA^T)^{-1}$, and rewrite B as follows:

$$B^{-1} = \begin{pmatrix} X_1 & Y_1 & Z_1 \\ X_2 & Y_2 & Z_2 \\ X_3 & Y_3 & Z_3 \end{pmatrix} \begin{pmatrix} X_1 & X_2 & X_3 \\ Y_1 & Y_2 & Y_3 \\ Z_1 & Z_2 & Z_3 \end{pmatrix} = \begin{pmatrix} \mathbf{p}_1^T \mathbf{p}_1 & \mathbf{p}_1^T \mathbf{p}_2 & \mathbf{p}_1^T \mathbf{p}_3 \\ \mathbf{p}_1^T \mathbf{p}_2 & \mathbf{p}_2^T \mathbf{p}_2 & \mathbf{p}_2^T \mathbf{p}_3 \\ \mathbf{p}_1^T \mathbf{p}_3 & \mathbf{p}_2^T \mathbf{p}_3 & \mathbf{p}_3^T \mathbf{p}_3 \end{pmatrix} \tag{6}$$

B is therefore the inverse Gramian of the points. It follows from Eq. (5) that:

$$\mathbf{x}^T B \mathbf{y} = 0, \quad \text{and} \quad \mathbf{x}^T B \mathbf{x} - \mathbf{y}^T B \mathbf{y} = 0. \tag{7}$$

Every element of B^{-1}, of the type $\mathbf{p}_i^T \mathbf{p}_j$, is determined by the length of the $3D$ vectors $\mathbf{p}_i$ and the angles between them. These are all geometrical properties of the 4 points which are invariant to rigid transformations. Thus the inverse-Gramian matrix B is invariant to $3D$ similarity transformations.

Another way to see the invariance of B is the following: We could have started the derivation from any initial $3D$ configuration of the 4 points, rotated from the original configuration by matrix R'. Let A' denote another initial configuration, where $A' = A \cdot R'$. It follows that $B'^{-1} = A' \cdot A'^T = A \cdot R' \cdot R'^T A^T = A \cdot A^T = B^{-1}$. Thus B is invariant of the particular viewpoint, or the orientation of the initial coordinate system. The invariance of B makes it possible to compute it from a few images, and to use it in a structure from motion algorithm.

The equations defining B in (5) correspond to 2 orthonormality constraints on the columns of the rotation matrix R. For $\mathbf{r}_3 = (r_{31}, r_{32}, r_{33})^T$, the constraints $\mathbf{r}_3^2 = 1$, $\mathbf{r}_3^T \mathbf{r}_2 = 0$, and $\mathbf{r}_3^T \mathbf{r}_1 = 0$ cannot be verified from a single $2D$ image. This makes accidental matches possible, where the invariant function defined in Def. 1 returns 0 for isolated views of different objects. It can be readily shown, however, that non-accidental matches are not possible.

From Eq. (7) it follows that f_B, defined in Eq. (2), is projective invariant with respect to the similarity group. f_B returns 0 for all the views of a single object, and possibly for accidental views of other objects. f_B is normalized, which guarantees that its value does not depend on the distance from the camera to the object (or the scale factor). (Note that f_B requires knowledge of the aspect-ratio of the camera.)

The discussion of the linear computation of B is postponed to Section 2.3.

□

The model-based invariant function f_B can be extended from 4 to n points: the extended matrix $\tilde{B}$ is a symmetric $n \times n$ matrix of rank 3, as will become clear from its construction in Section 2.4. Thus $\tilde{B}$ cannot be computed directly from images. It is therefore useful to represent additional points in a way more suitable for direct computation from images. For this purpose we define the following affine model-based invariant function for each additional point. This affine invariant has been used before for representation and recognition [8, 6, 12].

Affine invariant: Consider an object composed of (at least) 5 $3D$ points, and assume w.l.g. that the first 4 points are not coplanar. Let $\{P_i\}_{i=0}^4$ denote the $3D$ coordinates of the 5 points in some (unknown) initial frame of reference. Assume $P_0 = (0,0,0)$ without loss of generality, and let $\{\mathbf{p}_i\}_{i=1}^4$ denote the $3D$ vectors corresponding to the 4 remaining points. Let $\mathbf{b} = (b_1, b_2, b_3)$ denote the affine coordinates (as defined and used in [6, 8]) of $\mathbf{p}_4$, in the basis $\{\mathbf{p}_1, \mathbf{p}_2, \mathbf{p}_3\}$, namely:

$$\mathbf{p}_4 = b_1\mathbf{p}_1 + b_2\mathbf{p}_2 + b_3\mathbf{p}_3 \tag{8}$$

$\mathbf{b}$ is a $3D$ affine invariant of the 5 points, and it does NOT contain the relative $3D$ information on the 5 points.

Given the image coordinates of the 5 points $(x_0, y_0), (x_1, y_1), (x_2, y_2), (x_3, y_3)$, (x_4, y_4), assume without loss of generality that $x_0 = 0, y_0 = 0$, namely, the origin is defined to be at point 0. (Otherwise, replace any x_i in the following expressions by $x_i - x_0$, and y_i by $y_i - y_0$.)

Definition 3. Given 5 non-coplanar $3D$ points, let

$$f_{\mathbf{b}}(\mathbf{x}, \mathbf{y}) = \frac{|x_4 - \sum_{i=1}^3 b_i x_i|}{|\mathbf{x}||\mathbf{b}|} + \frac{|y_4 - \sum_{i=1}^3 b_i y_i|}{|\mathbf{y}||\mathbf{b}|}. \tag{9}$$

Proposition 4. $f_{\mathbf{b}}$ *is an affine model-based projective invariant function for the 5 points. Moreover, the elements of its parameters, the vector $\mathbf{b}$, can be computed from (at least) 2 images (or one image and the perpendicular optical flow) by solving a linear system of equations.*

Proof. From the definition of $\mathbf{b}$, it follows that in any image:

$$x_4 = \sum_{i=1}^3 b_i x_i, \quad \text{and} \quad y_4 = \sum_{i=1}^3 b_i y_i. \tag{10}$$

Being themselves linear, the relations in Eq. (10) are invariant to the actions of the $3D$ affine group. It follows that $f_{\mathbf{b}}$ is an affine projective invariant function.

This function returns 0 for non-accidental views of a family of related objects. The function is normalized, which guarantees that its value does not depend on the distance from the camera to the object (or the scale factor). (Note that the projective invariant f_b does not require knowledge of the aspect-ratio of the camera.)   □

The vector b does not contain $3D$ information on the 5 points (such as depth). Moreover, all the views of any object, which is obtained by a linear transformation of the original 5 points, lead to a robust (non-accidental) identification. Thus, for example, the 5 corners of boxes and parallelograms of all sizes are recognized by the same affine model-based invariant function. It follows that the linear function only indexes into a family of objects related by affine transformation.

2.3   The computation of model-based invariant functions:

An efficient algorithm to compute the similarity and affine invariant functions, as well as results with real images and comparisons to other algorithms, are described in [19].

The similarity invariant: The equations in (7), which are linear in B, can be used to compute B directly from images by solving an overdetermined linear system of equations. This computation requires correspondence and the use of at least 3 images. Since the equations in (7) are homogeneous, B is only determined up to a scaling factor. Moreover, since B is also positive definite, all the diagonal elements of B must be strictly positive. Thus, without loss of generality, we fix $B_{33} = 1$.

From (7) it also follows that each image gives two linear equations in the elements of B. There are 5 remaining unknown elements in B, thus we need 5 equations, or at least 3 views, to compute B. This is the theoretically minimal information required for structure from motion [14]. Note, however, that 3 views give us 6 equations, enough to compute B and to verify that the 3 views of the 4 points indeed come from a rigid object and a rigid transformation. Thus we extend the minimal structure from motion theorem to the following:

Extended minimal structure from motion theorem: *Assuming weak perspective projection, 3 views of 4 points give enough equations to compute the structure of the points and to verify that they are moving rigidly.*

The affine invariant: From (10) it follows that each image gives 2 linear equations in the elements of b. There are 3 unknown elements in b, thus we need 3 equations, or at least 2 views, to compute b.

Note that 2 views give us 4 equations, 1 too many. Indeed, it can be readily shown that it is sufficient to use one view and the perpendicular component of the $2D$ motion field at each point. This result has also been shown by Shashua in [12]. It is useful when the aperture problem constrains the computation of the $2D$ motion field, and for the generalization of this analysis to continuous optical flow.

More specifically, if the perpendicular optical flow vector at point (x_i, y_i) is $(x'_i - x_i, y'_i - y_i)$ for some (x'_i, y'_i), let m_i denote the slope of the line perpendicular to $(x'_i - x_i, y'_i - y_i)$, then $\mathbf{b}$ can be computed from the 2 equations in (10) and the following equation:

$$y'_4 + m_4 x'_4 = \sum_{i=1}^{3} b_i (y'_i + m_i x'_i).$$

2.4 Invariant representation of three dimensional shape:

Let an object be a set of n features, whose coordinates in $\mathcal{R}^3$ are the vectors $\{\mathbf{p}_i\}_{i=1}^{n}$.

The affine coordinates defined in Def. 3 can be used to represent the affine structure of the object, in an affine coordinate system whose basis is the vectors $\{\mathbf{p}_1, \mathbf{p}_2, \mathbf{p}_3\}$. The metric (Euclidean) information on the basis points is represented by their Gramian matrix B, defined in (1). This hierarchical representation contains the complete metric information on all the points in the object [17, 6]. We will discuss below the transformation between bases, and the transformation of this representation to an orthonormal coordinate system.

Alternatively, it is possible to represent the Euclidean invariant structure of the object by the set of metric representations of subsets of 4 points, thus capturing only local properties of the object. This can be implemented by storing up to $O(n^4)$ 3×3 matrices. This method was used for object recognition in [9].

It is also possible to represent the Euclidean invariant structure of the object with a $(n-1) \times (n-1)$ symmetric matrix $\tilde{B}$, the extension of the inverse Gramian B to n points. For 4 points, matrix B was defined above, using the 3×3 coordinates matrix A defined in (3), as $B = (AA^T)^{-1} = (A^{-1})^T A^{-1}$. For n points and a $(n-1) \times 3$ coordinate matrix $\tilde{A}$, we define[3] $\tilde{B} = (\tilde{A}^+)^T \tilde{A}^+$. Applying similar considerations, it can be readily shown that the invariant equations in (7) hold for $\tilde{B}$ as well. This representation was used for the computation of a distance between two dimensional images and three dimensional objects in [18].

Change of basis: Let B denote the 3×3 Gramian matrix of the four original basis points, and let $\mathbf{b}^s$ denote the affine coordinates of point P_s in the original basis. Let D denote the Gramian matrix of another basis P_0, P_l, P_m, P_n, and let $\mathbf{d}^s$ denote the affine coordinates of point P_s in the new basis. Let $S = (\mathbf{b}^l \quad \mathbf{b}^m \quad \mathbf{b}^n)^T$ denote the 3×3 matrix whose rows are the affine coordinates of the new basis points in the original basis. It can be readily shown that:

---

[3] $\tilde{A}^+$ denotes the pseudo-inverse of $\tilde{A}$.

$$\mathbf{D} = (\mathbf{S}^{-1})^T \mathbf{B} \mathbf{S}^{-1}$$
$$\mathbf{d}^s = (\mathbf{S}^{-1})^T \mathbf{b}^s$$

Change to orthonormal basis, or depth: It may be necessary to represent points or surfaces by their coordinates in a Cartesian coordinate system (i.e., a coordinate system with orthonormal axes). This may be useful when differential properties of surfaces, such as the Gaussian curvature, are required. We therefore define an invariant Cartesian coordinate system $Q = \{\mathbf{X}, \mathbf{Y}, \mathbf{Z}\}$ with orthonormal axes. Let $\mathcal{P}$ denote the affine coordinate system defined in Def. 3, whose basis is the vectors $\{\mathbf{p}_1, \mathbf{p}_2, \mathbf{p}_3\}$. We obtain Q by orthonormalizing the basis of $\mathcal{P}$, in a similar way to Gram-Schmidt: we choose $\mathbf{X}$ to parallel $\mathbf{p}_1$, $\mathbf{Y} \in span\{\mathbf{p}_1, \mathbf{p}_2\}$ is perpendicular to $\mathbf{X}$, and $\mathbf{Z}$ is perpendicular to the $\mathbf{X} - \mathbf{Y}$ plane.

Let $\mathbf{q}_l$ denote the coordinates of point P_l in system Q. Let Q denote the upper triangular 3×3 matrix whose columns are $\mathbf{q}_1, \mathbf{q}_2, \mathbf{q}_3$, the coordinates of the basis points. It follows from the definition in Eq. (8) that $\mathbf{q}_l = Q\mathbf{b}^l$, $\forall l$. Since any rigid transformation of the coordinate system does not change the values of $\{\mathbf{q}_l\}_{l=1}^n$, $\{Q\mathbf{b}^l\}_{l=1}^n$ is a similarity-invariant representation of the object, which is equivalent to a depth map.

It follows from Eq. (6) that $B^{-1} = Q^T Q$. Q, which is the root of B^{-1}, can be easily computed using a decomposition known as **Choleski** factorization. Since B is positive definite, the computation of Q from B is straightforward and very fast. Thus the following lemma immediately follows:

Lemma 5. *Given a 3D point whose coordinates in the affine system $\mathcal{P}$ are $\mathbf{b} = (b_1, b_2, b_3)$, its coordinates in the Cartesian system Q are $(X, Y, Z) = Q\mathbf{b}$, where $B^{-1} = Q^T Q$.*

The transformation to the new orthonormal coordinate system requires a non-linear step, taking the root (or Cholesky decomposition) of the original Gramian B^{-1}. Although this root is simple to compute, it only exists for positive-definite matrices. When the inverse Gramian B is computed from noisy data, it may not turn out to be positive definite, and the root may not exist.

Computation of the generalized inverse Gramian: Since the $(n-1) \times (n-1)$ matrix $\tilde{B}$ is of rank 3, it cannot be computed directly from images. It can, however, be obtained from the hierarchical affine and similarity invariant representation, since, if we let S denote the matrix whose l-th row is $\mathbf{b}^l$:

$$\tilde{B} = (S^+)^T B S^+$$

3 Invariant Model-based Recognition

A model-based invariant function can be viewed as a recognition operator that operates on a single image. This operator can distinguish images of a particular object from images of all other objects (ignoring accidental matches). We now discuss how the model-based invariant functions can be used to simplify, improve and extend various existing and new recognition schemes.

In Section 3.1 we discuss their use with computationally-intense recognition strategies, alignment and linear combination. In Section 3.2 we discuss their use with a memory-intense indexing strategy, summarizing the work described in [9].

3.1 Alignment and linear combination:

Alignment without transformation: The alignment method for recognition [5] can be summarized as follows:

1. match 3 points in the image to the model;
2. compute the transformation between the model and the image;
3. verify recognition by matching additional model points using the computed transformation.

The model-based invariants can be used to implement alignment without computing the transformation, and with the same time complexity. The modified scheme can be described as follows (modified steps are marked with *):

1. match 3 points in the image to the model;
2. *compute from the appropriate B the image coordinates of the 4th basis point and verify its existence;
3. *verify recognition by matching additional model points using their affine coordinates.

Like the original alignment scheme, this scheme involves one non-linear step, the prediction of the location of the 4th basis point from the locations of the matched 3 basis points. The worst-case time complexity of this algorithm is $O(M \cdot m^3 \cdot n^3)$, for M models, n image points and m model points.

The model-based invariants may be used more effectively for verification, rather than prediction. In this case, the recognition scheme does not involve any calculation other than the computation of the value of quadratic and linear invariant functions, and comparing them to 0. The following linear alignment scheme has higher time complexity, but may be more robust and easier to implement:

1. match 4 points in the image to the model;
2. verify the match with the quadratic invariant f_B;
3. verify recognition by matching additional model points using their affine coordinates.

The worst-case time complexity of this scheme is $O(M \cdot m^4 \cdot n^4)$ for M models, n image points and m model points.

Rigid linear combination: Recently, Ullman & Basri [16] have shown that each view of an object, composed of 5 points or more, can be described as a linear combination of 1.5 views of the object. They proposed a linear recognition scheme, in which the algorithm attempts to describe a new image as a linear combination of the stored set of representative views of one of the stored objects. This scheme cannot distinguish objects whose space of affine transformations are identical, e.g., boxes and parallelograms of all sizes, without computing the transformation from the model to the image. Moreover, since we cannot expect a perfect matching using noisy data, it is possible that the best affine match to an image is not the best rigid match.

In the previous section we showed how the quadratic invariant matrix B can be used to describe the space of rigid transformations (including uniform scaling) of an object composed of 4 points as a linear subspace of dimension 5 in $\mathcal{R}^6$. This can be extended to n points using $\tilde{B}$ discussed in Section 2.4. We can use B for a subset of 4 points on the object (or $\tilde{B}$ for all the points on the object[4]) to extend the linear combination scheme to a rigid linear combination scheme. In this geometrical scheme, 3 "canonical" views are stored for each object, and the recognition algorithm attempts to describe a new image as a linear combination of the stored canonical views of one of the stored objects.

3.2 Recognition (indexing) from a few frames:

Both model acquisition and recognition require correspondence between image ($2D$) features and model ($3D$) features. The second correspondence task is by far harder, since local searches, which are usually sufficient to match successive frames in an image sequence, are not usually sufficient for image to model matching. Correspondence can be aided by assigning labels to features, such as curvature based labels on curves [20]. However, the available labels are limited, and the labels for $3D$ features and $2D$ features may not be the same. Correspondence between unlabeled $3D$ points and $2D$ points is difficult, since all combinations have to be examined. These combinations can be limited in schemes such as alignment [5], but nevertheless all models have to be matched and verified with any subset of image points.

To avoid the problem of model to image correspondence, we used indexing [8]. Most existing indexing schemes are used with $2D$ objects. The indexing of $3D$ objects, using $3D$ models, was discussed in [7, 8]. Any such scheme for indexing $3D$ model points requires filling $2D$ planes in $4D$ index spaces [2]. Typically, high dimensionality and sparsity of the index table is required for suitable performance of indexing schemes, thus filling $2D$ planes is not a viable solution. Moreover, these schemes only test for the existence of an affine transformation between model and image, allowing non-rigid interpretations. An indexing system that requires filling $3D$ planes in $4D$ **Euclidean** index spaces was outlined in [17].

---

[4] In this case the linear combination is still done in $\mathcal{R}^6$, since the rank of $\tilde{B}$ is 3.

In [9] we presented a scheme in which models were acquired and recognized from a sequence of $2D$ images. At least three views of four feature points were required. Feature correspondence was required between the $2D$ images in a sequence. Such correspondence is needed by all schemes that use $2D$ views to acquire models of $3D$ objects. In our case, the motion system provides the correspondence. Recognition was performed by indexing. As the need for correspondence between the model features and the input sequence was eliminated, the two sequences were obtained at different times, from different scenarios, and from different motions.

Since we are dealing here with general $3D$ objects, and since there are no projective invariant functions for such objects, we relaxed the constraint that recognition is done from a single image. Instead, we used a few images to build unique invariant indices for each object. Thus we solved an active recognition problem. For indices we used the Gramian matrix B described above. One may argue that if we already use a few images, we might as well recover the complete $3D$ structure. The reason is that the structural invariants we used were both simple to compute robustly *and* could be used directly as indices.

This indexing scheme for recognition makes model to image correspondence unnecessary. On the other hand, the use of a few images to compute the index makes image to image correspondence necessary. However, as argued above, this second kind of correspondence, which is usually called feature tracking, is significantly easier when given an image sequence with small motion between successive frames.

4 Invariant Model Acquisition

Invariant representations make it possible to integrate information across different frames in a natural way. This integration offers robustness and stability in building the $3D$ description of objects from multiple images. In Section 4.1 we use this property to outline a new structure from motion algorithm. In Section 4.2 we show results with simulated and real data. A more complete and efficient algorithm is described in [19], with additional results and a quantitative comparison to other algorithms.

4.1 Linear structure from motion algorithm given correspondence

In Section 2.3 we showed that the inverse Gramian matrix B can be computed from as few as three images of four points with a linear algorithm. We have also shown how to obtain the depth map representation from B and the affine coordinates. We now use these results to describe a linear structure from motion algorithm for n points from $m \geq 3$ views. This algorithm assumes weak perspective, of which orthographic projection is a special case, and it requires correspondence.

The proposed algorithm differs from other SFM algorithms in that it does not compute structure in the usual sense, and it does not compute the transformation between the images. Thus it is a shape from motion algorithm without depth and without transformation. Instead, the algorithm computes an invariant $3D$ representation of the object. Depth can be optionally computed from this representation by computing the square root of a 3×3 matrix.

The algorithm:

Initialization: Select the origin P_0 and subtract its coordinates from the image measurements of all the other points. Select three independent basis points.

Affine: For all but the basis points, compute their affine representation $\mathbf{b}$ by solving the overdetermined linear system defined in Eq. (10).

Rigid: For the three basis points, compute their inverse Gramian B by solving the overdetermined linear system defined in Eq. (7).

Verify with principal component analysis that the homogeneous linear system has a solution, namely, that the basis points move rigidly.

This algorithm is completely linear. In order to compare its results to other algorithms which compute depth, we add the following step:

Depth (optional): Compute Q, the triangular root of B^{-1}, and multiply the affine vector $\mathbf{b}$ at each point by Q.

This step is non-linear and may not always have a solution when B is computed from noisy images.

We now describe in detail the computation of the inverse Gramian B, the second step of the algorithm:

The computation of B: First, we rewrite Eq. (7) as 2 linear equations in the elements of B. B is a 3×3 symmetric matrix and therefore has 6 unknown elements. Since the equations in (7) are homogeneous, we can only compute B up to a scaling factor, and therefore we arbitrarily set $B_{33} = 1$. (This can be done since B is positive definite, and therefore B_{33} is always positive.) We define a 5-dimensional vector $\mathbf{h} = \begin{pmatrix} B_{11} & B_{12} & B_{13} & B_{22} & B_{23} \end{pmatrix}^T$, where $\mathbf{h}$ includes the remaining unknown elements of matrix B. We can now rewrite (7) as follows:

$$\mathbf{u}_1^l \mathbf{h} = v_1^l, \qquad\qquad \mathbf{u}_2^l \mathbf{h} = v_2^l \qquad (11)$$

where

$$\mathbf{u}_1^l = \begin{pmatrix} x_i y_i \\ x_i y_j + x_j y_i \\ x_i y_k + x_k y_i \\ x_j y_j \\ x_j y_k + x_k y_j \end{pmatrix}^T, \qquad \mathbf{u}_2^l = \begin{pmatrix} x_i x_i - y_i y_i \\ 2(x_i x_j - y_i y_j) \\ 2(x_i x_k - y_i y_k) \\ x_j x_j - y_j y_j \\ 2(x_j x_k - y_j y_k) \end{pmatrix}^T$$

and

$$v_1^l = -(x_k y_k), \qquad\qquad v_2^l = -(x_k x_k - y_k y_k)$$

i, j, k are the indices of the basis points, and l is the image index.

Each image l, $1 \leq l \leq m$, provides 2 linear constraints on $\mathbf{h}$. We define a constraint matrix U of dimensions $(2m) \times 5$, whose rows $(2l - 1)$ and $2l$ are $\mathbf{u}_1^l$ and $\mathbf{u}_2^l$ of Eq. (11) respectively. We denote the solution of the linear system $\mathbf{v}$, a $2m$-dimensional vector whose elements $(2l - 1)$ and $2l$ are v_1^l and v_2^l of Eq. (11) respectively. Given $m \geq 3$ frames, $\mathbf{h}$ can be computed by solving the following overdetermined linear system of equations:

$$U\mathbf{h} = \mathbf{v}$$

We obtain the minimal least square solution of this system by using the pseudo-inverse:

$$\mathbf{h} = (U^T U)^{-1} \cdot U^T \mathbf{v} \tag{12}$$

The solution of $\mathbf{h}$ above is described in terms of a 5×5 matrix multiplied by a 5-dimensional vector. It can be readily seen that both the inverse of the matrix, $U^T U$, and the vector, $U^T \mathbf{v}$, are additive in the number of images (number of rows in U and $\mathbf{v}$), and therefore this algorithm can be implemented in an incremental way as follows:

- $U^T U$ and $U^T \mathbf{v}$ are computed from three images or more and stored.
- $\mathbf{h}$ is computed from Eq. (12).
- When additional data is obtained, $U^T U$ and $U^T \mathbf{v}$ are computed from the new data, and their new values are added to their stored estimates.
- $\mathbf{h}$ is computed from Eq. (12).

Note that if the basis points move rigidly, the five columns of matrix U and vector $\mathbf{v}$ are linearly dependent. An indication that the points do not move rigidly, or that the weak perspective approximation is not appropriate, can be obtained from an analysis showing that the vectors are independent.

4.2 Experiments with simulated and real data:

The discussion of model-based invariants and structure from motion above assumes weak perspective. The analysis and conclusions are therefore only approximately correct for real images, which are produced by perspective projection, and which are noisy. The simulations in Section 4.2 were designed to test the effects of perspective projection and noise on the SFM algorithm and the model-based invariant functions. In Section 4.2 we present results with a real matched sequence of images.

Simulated perspective projection and noise In the following simulations we generated a test object of four points, for which we computed the invariant matrix B. For the computation we used 20 simulated random views of the test object, with noise added to the image, and with either real or weak perspective projection. B was then used to define the model-based invariant function f_B

(defined in Eq. (1)) specific to the test object. We evaluated f_B on $10,000$ new random views of the test object. We also evaluated f_B on views of different objects.

We varied the distance from the camera to the object, which affected the relative size of the object in the image and the amount of perspective distortions. We present comparative plots of the value of f_B as a function of the varying distance between the camera and the object, using two different test objects:

- The first test object (graphs I in Fig. 1) was composed of four points selected randomly in $[0, 1]^3$. We compared it to two other types of objects: in type 1 the objects were composed of four points selected randomly in $[0, 1]^3$; in type 2 the object was composed of four non-coplanar corners of the unity cube.
- The second test object (graphs II in Fig. 1) was composed of four non-coplanar corners of the unity cube. We compared it to two slightly different types of objects: type 1 as above; in type 2 the object was composed of four non-coplanar corners of a box with edges of length 1,2,3.

We repeated the simulation 1000 times (each time generating a new random object), and for each set of objects we repeated the simulation 10 times (for 10 randomly generated views).

Each graph in Fig. 1 shows three plots of the value of f_B, where B represents one of the two test objects. The three plots were generated by applying f_B to the test object and to two other types of objects (as discussed above). For each test object, three conditions are shown: (a) weak perspective, (b) full perspective, (c) full perspective and Gaussian noise. In condition (c), we added 1% Gaussian noise to the data. The noise was added to the image $x-$ and $y-$ coordinates, and its mean value amounted to 1% of the actual radius of the $3D$ object. (Thus, in images obtained at 10 units away from the camera, this noise was equivalent to 10% Gaussian noise in the image plane.) The value of f_B was computed using simulated images at randomly selected viewpoints, and was averaged over 10,000 repetitions. The error bars at each data point indicate half the standard deviation of the distribution of the value of f_B.

In all the graphs, for both test objects and under all conditions, the average value of the invariant operator, when applied to the test object, was always lower than its average value when applied to different objects of all the types tested. This was true even with high perspective distortions (when the distance to the camera was smaller than the size of the object), as can be seen in Fig. 1(b). Thus the invariant operator can be used to distinguish the test object from most views of other objects at any distance, using a fixed threshold of 0.3. Moreover, a comparison of plots (a) and (b) shows that the dominant source of error was the variation in the appearance of objects, some of which appear similar to the test object at some viewpoints, rather than the distortion due to perspective projection.

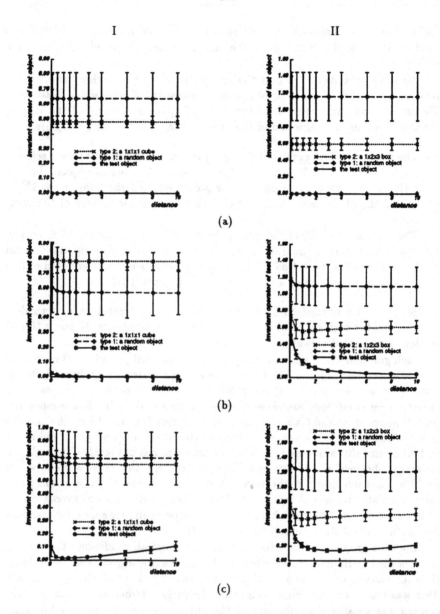

Fig. 1. The invariant operator of a test object, applied to images of the same object and two other types of objects (see text): I- The test object was generated randomly, II- the test object was a cube. (a) The images were produced with weak perspective projection at different distances from the camera, (b) full perspective, (c) perspective projection and Gaussian noise.

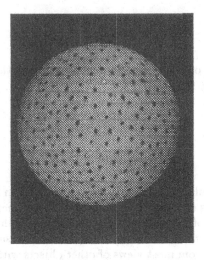

Fig. 2. One frame from the ping-pong sequence.

Experiments with real data We used a sequence of 226 images of a ping-pong ball with black marks on it, rotating 450 degrees in front of the camera. The sequence was provided by Carlo Tomasi, who also provided the coordinates of the tracked marks. One image of the sequence is shown in Fig. 2. The object was relatively far from the camera, and therefore the weak perspective assumption is appropriate for this sequence.

Four points were selected to serve as basis points. The invariant matrix B was computed for the four points using half the frames in which all the basis points had appeared. The affine coordinates vectors b, for each of the remaining points, were also computed using the same frames. B and b were used to compute the model-based invariant functions: f_B from Eq. (2) and f_b from Eq. (9). These functions were then evaluated on all the frames in which the relevant points appeared. As expected, they returned small values, distributed around 0 with a small variance. The average result and standard deviation were:

$$f_B = 0.0264 \pm 0.0157$$
$$f_b = 0.0194 \pm 0.0217$$

Typically, the model-based invariant functions returned higher values when applied to the wrong points (higher by an order of magnitude or 2 orders of magnitude). As expected from the simulations above, the results varied around 1, with a large variance. One example of a wrong correspondence between the image and the model, where the model-based invariants strongly suggested rejection of the model, was the following:

$$f_B = 1.7073 \pm 0.1209$$
$$f_{\mathbf{b}} = 0.8034 \pm 0.2888$$

Another example of a wrong correspondence, where the rejection was somewhat weaker, was the following:

$$f_B = 0.1708 \pm 0.0417$$
$$f_{\mathbf{b}} = 0.8015 \pm 0.2644$$

Discussion The results of the simulations, discussed in Section 4.2, show robustness to the effects of perspective distortions. Even when the depth variations between points were of the same order of magnitude as the depth of the points, the model-based invariant in Eq. (2) could be used to successfully distinguish the "correct" object from most views of other objects with a fixed threshold.

5 Summary

In the introduction we argued that invariant properties of objects should be sought for constructing useful object representations. Since universal invariants do not exist, we studied the existence of model base invariants, providing examples of similarity and affine invariant functions. Both could be computed from a few images with a linear computation, and verified given a single image.

We discussed how model based invariant functions can be used for recognition with alignment, linear rigid combination, and indexing. In the last case we discussed a novel approach where a few images were used to compute an invariant index into a database of models. The use of a few images made it possible to use a sparse table (and therefore this approach may be useful for relatively large databases), and the use of Euclidean invariants made the recognition more robust.

References

1. J.B. Burns, R. Weiss, and E. Riseman. View variation of point-set and line segment features. In *Proceedings Image Understanding Workshop*, pages 650–659, April 1990.
2. D. T. Clemens and D. W. Jacobs. Space and time bounds on indexing 3-D models from 2-D images. *IEEE Transactions on Pattern Analysis and Machine Intelligence*, 13(10):1007–1017, 1991.
3. O. Faugeras. What can be seen in three dimensions with an uncalibrated stereo rig? In *Proceedings of the 2nd European Conference on Computer Vision*, pages 563–578, Santa Margherita Ligure, Italy, 1992. Springer-Verlag.

4. D. Forsyth, J. L. Mundy, A. Zisserman, C. Coelho, A. Heller, and C. Rothwell. Invariant descriptors for 3-D object recognition and pose. *IEEE Transactions on Pattern Analysis and Machine Intelligence*, 13:971–991, 1991.

5. D. P. Huttenlocher and S. Ullman. Object recognition using alignment. In *Proceedings of the 1st International Conference on Computer Vision*, pages 102–111, London, England, June 1987. IEEE, Washington, DC.

6. J. J. Koenderink and A. J. van Doorn. Affine structure from motion. *Journal of the Optical Society of America*, 8(2):377–385, 1991.

7. Y. Lamdan, J. T. Schwartz, and H. Wolfson. Object recognition by affine invariant matching. In *Proceedings IEEE Conf. on Computer Vision and Pattern Recognition*, pages 335–344, Ann Arbor, MI, 1988.

8. Y. Lamdan and H. Wolfson. Geometric hashing: a general and efficient recognition scheme. In *Proceedings of the 2nd International Conference on Computer Vision*, pages 238–251, Tarpon Springs, FL, 1988. IEEE, Washington, DC.

9. R. Mohan, D. Weinshall, and R. R. Sarukkai. 3D object recognition by indexing structural invariants from multiple views. In *Proceedings of the 4th International Conference on Computer Vision*, pages 264–268, Berlin, Germany, 1993. IEEE, Washington, DC.

10. Y. Moses and S. Ullman. Limitations of non model-based schemes. A.I. Memo No. 1301, Artificial Intelligence Laboratory, Mass. Inst. of Tech., 1991.

11. H. S. Sawhney, J. Oliensis, and A. R. Hanson. Description and reconstruction from image trajectories of rotational motion. In *Proceedings of the 3rd International Conference on Computer Vision*, pages 494–498, Osaka, Japan, 1990. IEEE, Washington, DC.

12. A. Shashua. Projective depth: a geometric invariant for 3D reconstruction from two perspective/orthographic views and for visual recognition. In *Proceedings of the 4th International Conference on Computer Vision*, pages 583–590, Berlin, Germany, 1993. IEEE, Washington, DC.

13. C. Tomasi and T. Kanade. Shape and motion from image streams under orthography: a factorization method. *International Journal of Computer Vision*, 9(2):137–154, 1992.

14. S. Ullman. Computational studies in the interpretation of structure and motion: summary and extension. In J. Beck, B. Hope, and A. Rosenfeld, editors, *Human and Machine Vision*. Academic Press, New York, 1983.

15. S. Ullman. Maximizing rigidity: the incremental recovery of 3D structure from rigid and rubbery motion. *Perception*, 13:255–274, 1984.

16. S. Ullman and R. Basri. Recognition by linear combinations of models. *IEEE Transactions on Pattern Analysis and Machine Intelligence*, 13:992–1006, 1991.

17. D. Weinshall. Model-based invariants for 3D vision. *International Journal of Computer Vision*, 10(1):27–42, 1993.

18. D. Weinshall and R. Basri. Distance metric between 3d models and 2d images for recognition and classification. In *Proceedings IEEE Conf. on Computer Vision and Pattern Recognition*, New-York City, NY, 1993. IEEE, Washington, DC.

19. D. Weinshall and C. Tomasi. Linear and incremental acquisition of invariant shape models from image sequences. In *Proceedings of the 4th International Conference on Computer Vision*, pages 675–682, Berlin, Germany, 1993. IEEE, Washington, DC.

20. A. P. Witkin. Scale-space filtering. In *Proceedings IJCAI*, pages 1019–1022, 1983.

Recognition

Integration of Multiple Feature Groups and Multiple Views Into A 3D Object Recognition System *

Jianchang Mao[1] — Anil K. Jain[1] — Patrick J. Flynn[2]

[1] Department of Computer Science, Michigan State University, East Lansing, MI 48824

[2] School of Electrical Engineering and Computer Science, Washington State University, Pullman, WA 99164

Abstract. This paper proposes two approaches for utilizing multiple-feature group and multiple-view information to reduce the number of hypotheses passed to the verification stage in an invariant feature indexing (IFI)-based object recognition system [8]. The first approach is based on a majority voting scheme that tallies the number of consistent votes cast by prototype hypotheses for particular object models. The second approach examines the consistency of estimated object pose from multiple scene-triples from one or more views. Monte Carlo experiments employing several hundred synthetic range images of objects in a large CAD-based 3D object database [7] show that a significant number of hypotheses can be eliminated by using these approaches. The proposed approaches have also been tested on real range images of several objects. A salient feature of our system and experiment design compared to most existing 3D object recognition systems is our use of a large object data base and a large number of test images.

1 Introduction

Model-based object recognition has been a popular and exciting research topic for many years [13]. A number of systems for 2D or 3D object recognition have been developed. Typical examples are 3DPO [1], SCERPO [16], ACRONYM [2], the Evidence-Based System [14], BONSAI [6], the Vision Algorithm Compiler [12], 3D-POLY [3], the CAGD-Based Vision system [10], INGEN [19], OPTICA [4], RAF [9], and the system of Stein and Medioni [18], *etc.* These systems differ in one or several aspects which generally describe a 2D or 3D object recognition system including sensor type, model dimensionality, model source, representation strategies and recognition control strategies.

* This research was supported by NSF grants CDA-8806599 (to MSU), CDA-9121675 and IRI-9209212 (to WSU), and by the WSU Research Grant-In-Aid Program. ©1994 IEEE. Reprinted, with permission, from *Proceedings of 2nd IEEE CAD-Based Vision Workshop*, Champion, PA, February 1994, pp. 184-191.

Most existing object recognition systems have been tested only on a few objects (a small model database, typically containing tens of objects). In situations where object models can be built off-line, *geometric hashing* or indexing techniques (e.g., Lamdan and Wolfson [15], Stein and Medioni [18], and Flynn and Jain [8]) can be used to simplify the problems caused by large databases. In these techniques, hypotheses of object identity are stored in one or several tables which can be indexed by invariant features. The purpose of introducing invariant feature indexing of interpretation tables is to quickly reject a significant number of incorrect hypotheses before verification stage, which is usually computationally demanding.

Flynn and Jain [8] have developed a 3D object recognition system using invariant feature indexing (IFI) of interpretation tables. A limitation of this system is the use of only two invariant indices in the retrieval of hypotheses from the tables. This can often produce a large number of candidate hypotheses, each of which must be verified by a computationally demanding verification procedure. These interpretation tables are very sparse; hence, they are inefficiently utilized. Increasing the table dimensionality may reduce the number of prototype hypotheses in some table entries, but also increase the degree of sparseness. The sparseness problem has recently been improved to a certain degree by exploiting finite rotational symmetry for certain 3D models [5]. However, the number of hypotheses to be verified is still very large, especially when we use a large object database. While parallel implementation of the verification procedure can yield dramatic improvements in speed [17], we would also like to improve the procedure by reducing the number of hypotheses generated.

In this paper, we propose two approaches for reducing the number of hypotheses retrieved from IFI. The proposed approaches make efficient use of *multiple-triple* and *multiple-view* information. As a result, a significant number of hypotheses can be eliminated without affecting the recognition accuracy. This is demonstrated by Monte Carlo experiments involving 500 single-view synthetic range images and 195 pairs of synthetic range images (with known inter-frame rotations) using a large database of 107 objects. The new system equipped with the proposed approaches is also tested and compared with the original system [8] using several real objects sensed by a Technical Arts 100X range scanner.

The rest of the paper is organized as follows. Section 2 briefly describes the 3D object recognition system using invariant feature indexing [8]. A case study is provided in Section 3 to explore why a large number of hypotheses need to be verified in the original system, which motivated us to seek new approaches. Section 4 presents our two new approaches to incorporate multiple triple information, and the Monte Carlo experiments on evaluating the efficiency of the two approaches. Extensions of these two approaches to utilize the multiple view information and the Monte Carlo experiments are discussed in Section 5. Section 6 provides results on recognizing several real objects using our recognition system. Finally, Section 7 presents conclusions and discusses future work.

2   3D Object Recognition System Using IFI

In this section, we briefly describe the IFI 3D object recognition system developed by Flynn and Jain. For details, see [8]. In this system, model objects and scene objects are decomposed into a set of primitive entities (quadric surfaces are currently used). An invariant feature is defined as either an angle or a distance (depending on surface types) between a pair of primitive entities which can be extracted reliably from both the model and the segmented scene range image. Quantized feature values are used as indices to interpretation tables whose entries are so-called *proto-hypotheses*. A proto-hypothesis $\mathcal{PH}$ is defined as an ordered pair: $\mathcal{PH} = \langle \text{ID}, (M_{\text{ID},i_1}, M_{\text{ID},i_2}, M_{\text{ID},i_3}) \rangle$, where ID identifies the model associated with the proto-hypothesis, and $M_{\text{ID},x}$ are model entries. The set $(M_{\text{ID},i_1}, M_{\text{ID},i_2}, M_{\text{ID},i_3})$ is called an *entity group*. An *interpretation table* T_{f_1,f_2} defined for a pair of invariant feature types f_1, f_2 is a two-dimensional array $T_{f_1,f_2} = \{T_{ij}, i = 1, \cdots, N_{f_1}, j = 1, \cdots, N_{f_2}\}$, where each T_{ij} is a list (possibly empty) of proto-hypotheses, and N_{f_1} and N_{f_2} are the number of quantization levels of f_1 and f_2, respectively. For three types of surfaces (plane, cylinder, and sphere), there are 10 such interpretation tables.

The interpretation tables are built off-line by examining all visible and *usable* triples of entities in 320 views for each model in the object database, calculating the three invariant features relating the three pairs of entities in the triple, and inserting proto-hypotheses into the appropriate tables at locations determined by two of those invariant features. A triple is said to be usable, if, when bound to a triple of compatible scene entities, it can uniquely determine the pose for the model. Once the interpretation tables are constructed, object recognition can be performed in an efficient way (recognition by "table look-up"). First, a scene (range image) is segmented into surface patches of the same types as in the models. A method proposed by Hoffman and Jain [11] and subsequently modified by Flynn and Jain [6] is adopted. Then, all usable triples of these scene entities are considered, each leading to three invariant features. Two of these three features are used as indices to one of the ten tables to retrieve a list of proto-hypotheses. This list of proto-hypotheses is then used to construct a list of hypotheses each of which is an interpretation $\mathcal{H}$,

$$\mathcal{H} = \langle \text{ID}, \{(S_{i_1}, M_{\text{ID},i_1}), (S_{i_2}, M_{\text{ID},i_2}), (S_{i_3}, M_{\text{ID},i_3})\}\rangle,$$

binding the scene entities making up the triple $\{S_{i_1}, S_{i_2}, S_{i_3}\}$ and the model entities in the retrieved proto-hypotheses. These hypotheses are tested by a number of predicates based on geometric constraints originally developed in BONSAI [6]. The surviving hypotheses undergo a pose estimation procedure, and are verified and ranked. Object pose can be estimated very efficiently from the binding between a model triple and a scene triple. The system finally provides the highest ranking hypotheses. This recognition procedure in shown in Figure 1(a).

384

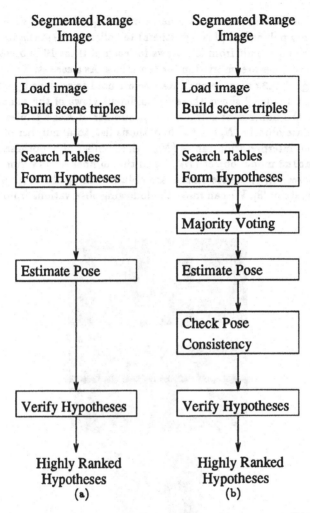

Fig. 1. Block diagrams of two recognition systems. (a): system 1. (b): system 2.

3 Retrieval of Large Numbers of Hypotheses

There are a few problems associated with the object recognition system described above, especially when a large object database is used. For instance, the proto-hypotheses are nonuniformly distributed in the tables. Consequently, the tables are very sparse, and some entries in the tables have long lists of proto-hypotheses [8]. For many scene triples, a large number of proto-hypotheses will be retrieved from the table. This situation, which occurs very frequently when (for example) the database contains many polyhedral objects with similar substructures, places a heavy burden on the verification procedure which is computationally expensive.

385

We have performed some experiments on a large database with 107 object models (mainly polyhedral plus few others) to collect some statistics. Ten interpretation tables are built from 320 views for each of these 107 object models. A total of 71,811 triples are inserted in the ten tables. As a case study, five synthetic views of the grnblk3 object in our database are used to retrieve hypotheses from the ten tables. Figure 2 shows these five different views of the grnblk3 object. Table 1 lists the number of surfaces (N_s), number of scene triples (N_t), number of candidate objects (N_c) in the hypothesis list, total number of hypotheses retrieved from interpretation tables (N_{tb}), the number of hypotheses associated with the grnblk3 model object (N_{hg}), and the number of surviving hypotheses with valid poses (N_{pv}). These results are obtained using the original 3D object recognition system [8]. We can make the following observations from Table 1: (i)

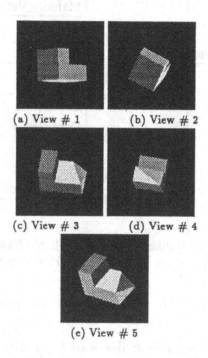

(a) View # 1   (b) View # 2

(c) View # 3   (d) View # 4

(e) View # 5

Fig. 2. Five different views (surface label images) of the grnblk3 object.

The number of candidate models retrieved from the interpretation tables (after forming the hypotheses which are tested by a number of predicates) is relatively small compared to the total number of models in the database (less than 10%). This means that most of the models can be ruled out by using a single surface triple. (ii) A large number of hypotheses are retrieved from the interpretation tables, especially for views 3 and 5 which have more visible surfaces and hence more triples than others. (iii) Among the hypotheses retrieved from the interpretation tables, only a small portion is generated by the correct candidate model. (iv) Most of the hypotheses retrieved from the interpretation tables do not have valid pose transformations. However, after deleting the hypotheses with invalid pose, the number of surviving hypotheses is still large. These observations are generally true for most object models in the data base. The efficiency of our proposed approaches in reducing the number of hypotheses will further support these observations.

Intuitively, if the scene contains many surfaces, then it provides more information about the object, so we should be generating fewer hypotheses. However, observations (ii) and (iii) above indicate that the original 3D object recognition system does not take advantage of multiple triples. This is the main reason why so many hypotheses are retrieved from the interpretation tables. Observations (ii) and (iii) motivate us to utilize the multiple-triple (surface) information, which results in two new approaches to reduce the number of hypotheses passed to the verification procedure.

View No.	1	2	3	4	5
N_s	3	4	6	5	6
N_t	1	4	20	10	20
N_c	5	8	10	9	10
N_{tb}	168	971	2367	740	2415
N_{hg}	12	70	246	35	248
N_{pv}	64	275	631	204	720

Table 1. Statistics for the five views of the grnblk3 object.

4 Multiple-Triple Information

In this section, we propose two approaches to make efficient use of multiple triple information.

4.1 Majority Voting for Model Candidates

The main idea is based on the fact that multiple triples from the same scene object should support the same model candidates. If we accumulate votes of candidate models by hypotheses, the model candidate(s) with higher votes should be considered as correct model candidate(s) with higher confidence.

Let $\mathcal{PH}_i$ be the proto-hypothesis list retrieved from the interpretation tables by the ith scene triple, $i = 1, 2, \cdots, N_t$. Define an indicator function $I(\text{ID}, \mathcal{PH})$ as

$$I(\text{ID}, \mathcal{PH}) = \begin{cases} 1, & \text{if ID} \in \mathcal{PH}, \\ 0, & \text{otherwise,} \end{cases}$$

where ID is the model identifier and ID $\in \mathcal{PH}$ is true if one or more of the proto-hypotheses in $\mathcal{PH}$ involves model ID. Then, the number of votes that model ID receives, $V(\text{ID})$, is

$$V(\text{ID}) = \sum_{i=1}^{N_t} I(\text{ID}, \mathcal{PH}_i).$$

The most likely candidate model ID* has the largest number of votes, ID* = arg max$_{\text{ID}} V(\text{ID})$.

Table 2 lists the number of hypotheses (retrieved from the tables) associated with all the candidate models (N_h) and the model candidate(s) that has(have) the highest votes (N_{mv}), respectively. The corresponding reduction rate R is also provided, which is calculated using $R = \frac{N_h - N_{hv}}{N_h}$. In views 1 and 2, no reduction is achieved, because views 1 and 2 of grnblk3 have only a small number of triples (1 triple for view 1 and 4 triples for view 2). On the other hand, a significant number (>89%) of hypotheses retrieved from the interpretation tables is eliminated for views 3, 4 and 5.

View No.	1	2	3	4	5
N_h	168	971	2367	740	2415
N_{mv}	168	971	246	35	248
R (%)	0	0	89.6	95.3	89.7

Table 2. The number of hypotheses associated with the model candidate(s) that has(have) highest votes for the five views of the grnblk3 object.

4.2 Pose Consistency Test for Hypothesis Lists

The consistency of estimated poses from multiple triples can be used as another constraint to further prune the hypothesis list. Multiple triples drawn from the same scene object should yield similar pose estimates, when bound to the same object model. Suppose a set of N_p hypotheses, $\{\mathcal{H}_1, \mathcal{H}_2, \cdots, \mathcal{H}_{N_p}\}$, survive the pose estimation stage. Each hypothesis, $\mathcal{H}_k$, is associated with a pose estimate, P_k, which consists of a rigid rotation matrix, $R_k = [r_{ij}^k]_{3\times 3}$, and a translation vector, $T_k = [t_1^k, t_2^k, t_3^k]^T$. Let $d(R_k, R_l)$ and $d(T_k, T_l)$ be the Euclidean distances between two pose estimates, $\{R_k, T_k\}$ and $\{R_l, T_l\}$. Two pose estimates P_k and P_l are said to be consistent if $d(R_k, R_l) < t_r$ and $d(T_k, T_l) < t_t$, where t_r is a threshold which controls the degree of consistency for rotation and t_t for translation which can be measured in distance units (inches in our current system). In our experiments, $t_r = 0.1$, $t_t = 0.1$ inch for the synthetic range images and single-view real range images. We define a consistency relation Θ between two hypotheses, $\mathcal{H}_1$ and $\mathcal{H}_2$. We say $\mathcal{H}_1 \Theta \mathcal{H}_2$, if $\mathcal{H}_1$ and $\mathcal{H}_2$ have (i) consistent pose estimates, and (ii) the same hypothesized model ($ID_1 = ID_2$). We define the indicator function $I(\mathcal{H}_k \Theta \mathcal{H}_l)$ which takes value 1, if $\mathcal{H}_k \Theta \mathcal{H}_l$ and 0, otherwise. For each hypothesis in the set, we compute a quantity, V_p,

$$V_p(\mathcal{H}_k) = \sum_{l=1}^{N_p} I(\mathcal{H}_k \Theta \mathcal{H}_l), \quad k = 1, 2, \cdots, N_p.$$

The hypothesis $\mathcal{H}_k$ is eliminated if $V_p(\mathcal{H}_k) < t_c$. The threshold t_c is determined as $t_c = \lfloor (N_t + 2)/3 \rfloor$, where N_t is the number of scene triples.

The sequence of procedures for running the recognition system (system 2) equipped with the proposed two procedures is shown in Figure 1(b).

Table 3 shows the number of hypotheses before (but after pose estimation, N_{pv}) and after (together with majority voting, N_{pc}) pruning using the consistency of pose estimation for the five views of the grnblk3 object. The reduction rate, $R = (N_{pv} - N_{pc})/N_{pv}$, and the number of candidate models (N_c) sharing these surviving hypotheses for the each view are also provided. While the num-

View No.	1	2	3	4	5
N_{pv}	64	275	631	204	720
N_{pc}	64	42	12	7	12
R (%)	0	84.7	98.1	96.6	98.3
N_c	5	4	1	1	1

Table 3. Reduction rates (pruning by pose consistency) for the five views of the grnblk3 object.

ber of surviving hypotheses after pruning is very small, the correct hypotheses (with the highest matching scores produced by the verification procedure) are still retained.

4.3 Monte Carlo Experiments

To evaluate the overall performance of these methods, we performed some Monte Carlo experiments on a large number of test images. Five randomly chosen views for each of the 100 (out of 107) objects in our database were generated from CAD models. All the 500 synthetic range images are segmented using the method in [11, 6]. After all the 107 object models are loaded into the recognition systems, ten interpretation tables are constructed.

Table 4 shows some statistics which are collected after each of the procedures in Figure 1 for both the systems. The reduction rates, R, is provided in the last column in Table 4. The value of R is computed using $R = \frac{N_{pv}^1 - N_{pc}^2}{N_{pv}^1}$. The last row in Table 4 shows the overall expected values for the above statistics weighted by the normalized frequency (freq/500). The new system rejects 2.6% of 500 images because no hypothesis survives the pose consistency test procedure. All others are correctly recognized.

Scene			System 1		System 2 (single view)			
N_s	N_t	freq	N_{tb}^1	N_{pv}^1	N_{mv}^2	N_{pv}^2	N_{pc}^2	$R\%$
3	1	129	1072	411	1063	411	411	0.0
4	4	93	2664	732	1881	496	134	81.7
5	10	76	6233	1514	2195	550	139	90.8
6	20	91	8512	1927	3582	946	479	75.1
7	35	47	15486	2987	1881	548	294	90.1
8	56	35	26915	5336	5885	1482	744	86.1
9	84	17	39549	6962	3607	1119	794	88.6
10	120	5	72265	13015	17846	4027	1829	85.9
11	165	6	39480	7999	4507	1493	1003	87.5
13	286	1	119713	28244	15132	4044	2401	91.5
Expected values			9389	1997	2584	714	381	62.3

Table 4. Some statistics for two recognition systems from Monte Carlo experiments.

It can be seen from Table 4 that the new system significantly reduces the number of hypotheses passed to the verification procedure over the original system. For scenes which contain more than one triple (about 74% of cases in our experiments), the average reduction rate is very high (75%-92%). The overall expected rate drops to about 60% due to 129 scene objects with a single triple (about 26% of cases) on which the two proposed methods have no effect. The overall expected number of hypotheses passed to the verification procedure in the new system is 381, which is much smaller than the number (1997) in the original system.

The third column in Table 4 provides a histogram of the number of triples in the scene. We notice that the probability of a scene which contains only one triple is quite high. Due to the very limited information provided by the scene object with one triple, the proposed two approaches in this section are not able to improve the recognition speed. In the next section, we will incorporate the multiple view information in our system.

5   Multiple View Information

The two approaches in the previous section can be easily extended to incorporate multiple view information.

5.1 Majority Voting by Multiple Triples from Multiple Views

The main idea is based on the fact that triples drawn from different views of the same object should support the same correct object model(s).

Suppose that n_v views of the scene object are available. Let $\mathcal{PH}_i^j$ be the proto-hypothesis list retrieved from the interpretation tables by the ith triple of the jth view, $i = 1, 2, \cdots, t_j, j = 1, 2, \cdots, n_v$. Then, the number of votes $V(\text{ID})$ for model ID is

$$V(\text{ID}) = \sum_{j=1}^{n_v} \sum_{i=1}^{t_j} I(\text{ID} \in \mathcal{PH}_i^j).$$

The most likely candidate model ID^* is the model with the highest vote, $\text{ID}^* = \text{argmax}_{\text{ID}} V(\text{ID})$.

Note that this method does not require knowledge of the view angle. In the situation where we can control the position of the range scanner, or the object being sensed is on a turnable stand whose rotation angle can be recorded, the geometric relationships between different views can be utilized to further prune the hypotheses. In the next section, we will derive an object pose constraint between different views.

5.2 Consistency of Pose Estimates for Multiple Views

Suppose a set of N_p^v hypotheses, $\{\mathcal{H}_1^v, \mathcal{H}_2^v, \cdots, \mathcal{H}_{N_p^v}^v\}$, survive after the pose estimation stage for view v, $v = 1, 2, \cdots, n_v$. Each hypothesis, $\mathcal{H}_k^v$, is associated with a pose estimate, P_k^v, which consists of a rigid rotation matrix, $R_k^v = [r_{k,ij}^v]_{3\times3}$, and a translation vector, $T_k^v = [t_{k,1}^v, t_{k,2}^v, t_{k,3}^v]^T$.

The consistency of two pose estimates for two triples from the same view was defined in Section 4.2. Now consider two hypotheses, $\mathcal{H}_{k_1}^{v_1}$ and $\mathcal{H}_{k_2}^{v_2}$ from two different views ($v_1 \neq v_2$). Suppose the relative rotation transition between two views (v_1 and v_2) is known, whose X-Y-Z Euler angles are denoted by θ_x, θ_y and θ_z. We assume no translation occurs between the two views. Then, if the pose, $P_{k_1}^{v_1}$, of view v_1 is correctly estimated, the pose of view v_2, $P_{k_2}^{v_2}$, can be estimated from $P_{k_1}^{v_1}$ and $\{\theta_x, \theta_y, \theta_z\}$, denoted by $\hat{P}_{k_2}^{v_2} = \{\hat{R}_{k_2}^{v_2}, \hat{T}_{k_2}^{v_2}\}$, using $\hat{R}_{k_2}^{v_2} = R_{\theta_z} R_{\theta_y} R_{\theta_x} R_{k_1}^{v_1}$, and $\hat{T}_{k_2}^{v_2} = R_{\theta_z} R_{\theta_y} R_{\theta_x} T_{k_1}^{v_1}$, where R_{θ_x}, R_{θ_y}, and R_{θ_z} are the standard matrices for rotation about x, y, and z axes, respectively. We define the errors between two pose estimates as before (Euclidean distances). Then, two pose estimates, $P_{k_1}^{v_1}$ and $P_{k_2}^{v_2}$, are said to be *consistent* if the errors between the inferred pose and estimated pose $d(\hat{R}_{k_2}^{v_2}, R_{k_2}^{v_2}) < t_r$ and $d(\hat{T}_{k_2}^{v_2}, T_{k_2}^{v_2}) < t_t$. In our experiments, $t_r = 0.1$, $t_t = 0.1$ inch for multiple-view synthetic range images, and $t_r = 0.1, t_t = 0.5$ inches for the multiple-view real range images. We relax the threshold t_t for multiple-view real range images because it is difficult to control the translation between two views to be zero using our Technical Arts 100X Scanner. Similarly, we define that two hypotheses are *consistent*, i.e., $\mathcal{H}_{k_1}^{v_1} \Theta_{v_1 v_2} \mathcal{H}_{k_2}^{v_2}$, if they have (i) the same hypothesized model candidate ($\text{ID}_{k_1}^{v_1} = \text{ID}_{k_2}^{v_2}$), and (ii) consistent pose estimates.

For each hypothesis, $\mathcal{H}_k^v$, we compute a quantity, $V_p(\mathcal{H}_k^v)$,

$$V_p(\mathcal{H}_k^v) = \sum_{u=1}^{n_v} \sum_{l=1}^{N_p^*} I(\mathcal{H}_k^v \Theta_{vu} \mathcal{H}_l^u),$$

$k = 1, 2, \cdots, N_p^v$, $v = 1, 2, \cdots, n_v$, where $\Theta_{vu} = \Theta$ when $v = u$. The hypothesis $\mathcal{H}_k^v$ can be eliminated if $V_p(\mathcal{H}_k^v) < t_c$. The threshold t_c is determined as $t_c = \sum_{v=1}^{n_v} \lfloor (N_t^v + 2)/3 \rfloor$, where N_t^v is the number of scene triples in view v.

5.3 Monte Carlo Experiments

Five pairs of views with known rotation transition from one view to the other are generated from the CAD model for each of the 39 objects which have less than 11 surfaces per object. So, there are a total of 195 pairs of test images. In our experiments, we use only two views because we find that two views are sufficient to eliminate most of the hypotheses. Again, 107 object models are loaded into the recognition systems. Table 5 shows the result obtained from the Monte Carlo experiments. For simplicity, these statistics in Table 5 are computed

Scene			System 1		System 2 (2 views)			
N_s	N_t	freq	N_{tb}^1	N_{pv}^1	N_{mv}^2	N_{pv}^2	N_{pc}^2	$R\%$
3	1	201	941	339	772	282	2	99.3
4	4	151	3633	1102	2202	637	71	93.5
5	10	25	4469	1378	1460	419	166	88.0
6	20	11	8315	1795	1350	442	223	87.5
7	35	1	35695	6315	3158	1031	482	92.4
Expected values			2504	757	1390	434	47	95.7

Table 5. Some statistics for two recognition systems from Monte Carlo experiments using multiple views.

and organized (grouped) with respect to the number of scene surfaces. About 5% of the 390 test images are rejected by system 2 with multiple views because no consistent hypothesis survives after the pose consistency test procedure. The other 95% of the 390 test images are all correctly recognized. As we can see from Table 5, system 2 with multiple views significantly reduces the number of hypotheses passed to the verification stage, compared to system 1 and system 2 with a single view (see Table 4), even for those views containing only one triple (3 surface patches). The overall reduction rate reaches 95.7%. The expected number of hypotheses passed to the verification procedure in system 2 which incorporates multiple view information is 47, which is much smaller than 757 in system 1. In our current implementation of the recognition systems, verifying

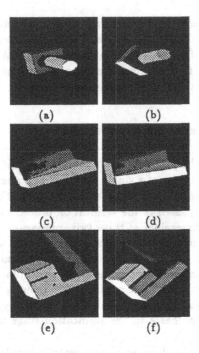

Fig. 3. Segmentation and classification of the range images in Figure 4. Surface patches are labeled with different colors.

one hypothesis takes about one second of CPU time on a Sun Sparc 2 station. The significant reduction in the number of hypotheses passed to the verification procedure makes the system more practical.

6   Experiments on Real Data

Figure 3 shows the surface segmentation and classification results of two views of each of three real objects (column1, block1 and block2) obtained from the Technical Arts 100X range scanner. The relative Euler angles between the views on the left column and the views on the right column in Figure 3 are denoted as θ_x, θ_y and θ_z. The setup of the Technical Arts 100X Range Scanner restricts the value of θ_x and θ_y to be zero. The value of θ_z can be obtained from the turnable table. In Figure 3, $\theta_z = 30°$ for the objects column1 and block2, and $\theta_z = 10°$ for block1. Note that the front surface of the object in Figure 3(f) is split into two patches due to the missing depth data.

Table 6 shows results obtained from the recognition experiments using system 1, system 2 with single view and system 2 with multiple views on the range images in Figure 3. All the three objects are correctly recognized. ¿From Table 6, we can see that the new system (system 2) is very efficient in eliminating a significant number of incorrect hypotheses, even though the sensed objects contain missing data and the object surfaces are noisy and even over-segmented (see Figure 3(f)). Similar to the Monte Carlo experiments, we find that two nonaccidental views of an object are generally sufficient to pass a very small number of hypotheses to the verification stage without affecting the recognition accuracy for our object database containing 107 objects.

7   Conclusions and Extension

We have shown that the proposed two methods (majority voting for candidate models from multiple triples of a single view and hypothesis pruning using consistency of pose estimates for a single view) are very effective in reducing the number of hypotheses passed to the verification procedure, when the scene contains many surfaces. Extensions of these two approaches to multiple views were shown to further reduce the number of hypotheses, even when each of the views contains only a single triple. The new 3D object recognition system equipped with these two approaches is much more efficient and practical than the original system. For our object database containing 107 essentially polyhedral objects, we have found that two nonaccidental views are generally sufficient to pass only a small number of hypotheses to the verification stage without degrading the recognition accuracy.

More work needs to be done with the interpretation tables. We suspect that scene triples or model triples do not have sufficient discriminatory power to build the interpretation tables alone; higher level primitives (such as groups of multiple triples) should be considered to form indices to the interpretation tables. Of course, doing this will involve more features. Therefore, an important problem is the design of a good coding scheme to encode many high-level features in one or two indices because we want to keep the interpretation tables of low dimensionality for efficiency reasons. The Gray code as used in [18] might be a candidate to adopt.

References

1. R. C. Bolles and P. Horaud. 3DPO: A three-dimensional part orientation system. *Intl. J. Rob. Res.*, 5(3):3–26, 1986.
2. R. A. Brooks. Model-based three-dimensional interpretations of two-dimensional images. *IEEE Trans. Pattern Anal. Machine Intell.*, PAMI-5(2):140–150, 1983.
3. C. Chen and A. Kak. A robot vision system for recognizing 3-d objects in low-order polynomial time. *IEEE Trans. Systems, Man, and Cybernetics*, 19(6):1535–1563, 1989.
4. S. J. Dickinson, A. P. Pentland, and A. Rosenfeld. From volumes to views: An approach to 3-d object recognition. In *Proc. IEEE Workshop on Directions in Automated CAD-Based Vision*, pages 85–96, Maui, Hawaii, 1991.
5. P. J. Flynn. Saliencies and symmetries: Toward 3D object recognition from large model databases. In *Proc. 1992 IEEE Computer Society Conference on Computer Vision and Pattern Recognition*, pages 322–327, Champaign, Illinois, June 1992.

Object		column1		block1		block2	
View No.		1	2	1	2	1	2
N_s		5	5	5	5	5	7
N_t		10	10	10	10	10	35
Recognition	N_{tb}	3245	3279	1826	1717	906	7678
System 1	N_{pv}	1173	1176	592	543	267	1740
Recognition	N_{tb}	3245	3279	1826	1717	906	7678
System 2	N_{mv}	161	161	979	950	413	3143
(1 view)	N_{pv}	86	86	239	229	71	466
	N_{pc}	52	52	134	128	29	234
Recognition	N_{tb}	3245	3279	1826	1717	906	7678
System 2	N_{mv}	161	161	979	950	413	3143
(2 views)	N_{pv}	86	86	239	229	71	466
	N_{pc}	19	16	6	4	2	40

Table 6. Some results collected from the recognition experiments using system 1, system 2 with single view and system 2 with multiple views on the range images in Figure 4 of the three real objects.

6. P. J. Flynn and A. K. Jain. BONSAI: 3-D object recognition using constrained search. *IEEE Trans. Pattern Anal. Machine Intell.*, 13(10):1066–1075, October 1991.

7. P. J. Flynn and A. K. Jain. CAD-based computer vision: From CAD models to relational graphs. *IEEE Trans. Pattern Anal. Machine Intell.*, 13(2):114–132, February 1991.

8. P. J. Flynn and A. K. Jain. 3D object recognition using invariant feature indexing of interpretation tables. *CVGIP: Image Understanding*, 55(2):119–129, March 1992.

9. W. E. L. Grimson and T. Lozano-Péres. Localizing overlapping parts by searching the interpretation tree. *IEEE Trans. Pattern Anal. Machine Intell.*, PAMI-9(4):469–482, July 1987.

10. C. Hansen and T. Henderson. CAGD-based computer vision. *IEEE Trans. Pattern Anal. Machine Intell.*, PAMI-11(11):1181–1193, November 1989.

11. R. L. Hoffman and A. K. Jain. Segmentation and Classification of Range Images. *IEEE Trans. Pattern Anal. Machine Intell.*, PAMI-9(5):608–620, 1987.

12. K. Ikeuchi and T. Kanade. Automatic generation of object recognition programs. *Proc. IEEE*, 76(8):1016–1035, 1988.

13. A. K. Jain and P. J. Flynn (eds.). *Three-Dimensional Object Recognition Systems*. New York: Elsevier, 1993.

14. A. K. Jain and R. Hoffman. Evidence-based recognition of 3-d objects. *IEEE Trans. Pattern Anal. Machine Intell.*, PAMI-10:783–802, 1988.

15. Y. Lamdan and H. Wolfson. Geometric hashing: A general and efficient model-based recognition scheme. In *Proc. Second IEEE International Conference on Computer Vision*, pages 238–249, Tarpon Springs, 1988.

16. D. Lowe. *Perceptual Organization and Visual Recognition*. Kluwer, Boston, 1985.

17. J. Moody, P. J. Flynn, and D. L. Cohn. Parallel hypothesis verification. *Pattern Recognition*, 1994 (to appear).

18. F. Stein and G. Medioni. Structural indexing: Efficient three-dimensional object recognition. *IEEE Trans. Pattern Anal. Machine Intell.*, 14(2):125–145, February 1992.
19. A. Vayda and A. Kak. A robot vision system for recognition of generic shaped objects. *CVGIP: Image Understanding*, 54(1):1–46, July 1991.

Hierarchical Object Description Using Invariants

Charles A. Rothwell

GE CRD, Room 5C39, Building K-1, PO Box 8, Schenectady, NY 12309. USA.
rothwell@sol.crd.ge.com

Abstract. Invariant indexing functions have recently been shown to be effective for producing efficient recognition algorithms. However, the most useful shape descriptors for recognition are *local* or *semi-local* rather than *global*. In this paper we introduce an approach that ties together local invariant descriptions into larger object descriptions. The method works well for planar objects and has been used within two different recognition systems.

1 Introduction

1.1 Using Invariant Indexes for Recognition

The task of recognising objects from unknown viewpoints is speeded up significantly when indexing functions are used. Even though it is clear that a three phase paradigm using *selection, indexing* and *correspondence* [11] is necessary for recognition, the indexing phase has until recently been almost entirely ignored. In practice, the emphasis of the recognition procedure has been placed on producing reliable correspondence algorithms (a review is given in [11]). Generally, such algorithms commute indexing to a linear search through the model base producing an inefficient process due to attempts to match every model to the scene.

Since the application of geometric invariants to computer vision it has become clear how the indexing problem may be overcome. Invariants provide shape descriptions that are unchanged by viewpoint, and measures of an invariant can be used to index into model space and hypothesise the presence of an object in a scene. A review of some of the earlier application of invariants in vision is given in [21], other works where invariants have been computed for a variety of different data types are [1, 4, 6, 14, 18, 19, 22, 25, 27, 29, 31]. Although indexes can be computed in situations where invariants cannot [12], in general, invariants provide the most efficient route to their creation.

We emphasise that invariants and indexes are not exactly the same objects. Frequently, the invariant description for a set of world features is a list of numbers that can be used directly to form a multi-dimensional index. This is true for plane algebraic invariants. However, invariant descriptors are sometimes *signatures* computed from a *canonical frame* which cannot be used as an index to a model base, but must be mapped to a numeric value using a chosen transform prior to indexing. Examples of this case are the plane curve signatures in [7, 23, 29], and 3D signatures for objects containing planes of bilateral symmetry [25].

1.2 Tying Together Local Shape Cues

Certain criteria qualify the utility of a shape descriptor; some of these criteria are listed in [3, 17]. Subsequent to an evaluation of a working recognition system one realises that tolerance to occlusion is necessary. Without this we cannot hope for any measure of reliability under a spectrum of viewing conditions. Independence from occlusion can be achieved when *local* or *semi-local*, rather than *global*, descriptors are used. In our context, we define local measures to be observable at a single point, and semi-local to be measured at a number of proximal points covering a small proportion of an object boundary. However, in the sequel there is little need to distinguish between these two cases; both will be described as *local*.

In practice many of the invariants reported in the literature are local. However, some by nature are global and so are not relevant to the discussion in the paper[1]. Predominant examples of these are: moment based methods [1, 27]; iso-perimetric measures [26]; and global fitting of algebraic curves [13, 28].

Tolerance to occlusion can be achieved only if there are a large number of shape cues spread around the boundary of an object (this prevents the pathological case of a single descriptor being occluded). This is *redundancy* and from any normal viewpoint one would observe a number of descriptors (generally more than one). The problem encountered in using a local measure for recognition is that although it may hypothesise the presence of an object in a scene, such a hypothesis frequently yields only a poor estimate of the object pose (this is shown later in figure 9d). Furthermore, local descriptions tend to yield very sparse representations of objects that do not provide a sufficiently rich description of the geometry of an object for many tasks.

In this paper we present a framework that enables local invariant feature groups to be tied together into global structures. Ultimately these provide complete object descriptions useful for recognition. The process of merging local object hypotheses together is known as *hypothesis extension* [25], and can be compared to the *clique formation* process of Bolles and Cain [2]. Extension actually provides a complete hierarchical object description similar to that introduced by Ettinger [5].

The rest of this paper is organised as follows: section 2 briefly describes the architecture of the index based recognition system used to test the hypothesis extension algorithms; section 3 provides specific examples of the algorithms applied to real data; and 4 suggests some ways in which the current methods can be extended to other object classes.

---

[1] However, ingenious segmentation techniques can often yield a local invariant using a description normally reserved for global use.

2 The Invariant Indexing Paradigm

This paper relates to a planar object recognition system, called LEWIS, described in detail in [25]. LEWIS has the framework shown in figure 1:

1. **Edge Detection:** edgel chains are extracted from greyscale images using a Canny edge detector [10]. Single edgel dropouts between chains are patched up to overcome minor segmentation failures.
2. **Feature Extraction:** points, lines and conics are extracted from the edgel chains and grouped according to criteria given in [8, 15, 25] to form algebraic feature groups. Portions of curve between curve bitangents are also extracted (called $\mathcal{M}$ curves) and used for the recognition of more general plane curve structures.
3. **Invariant Formation:** invariant descriptions are measured for the feature groups.
4. **Indexing:** indexes are computed from the measured invariants, these are used to index models in a multi-dimensional index space. Each time an index finds a match a hypothesis is created for the indexed object.
5. **Hypothesis Merging:** individual hypotheses from the same object are combined to create a single hypothesis corresponding to larger model and image feature groups. This step is *hypothesis extension* and provides the detail of this paper.
6. **Verification:** The recognition hypotheses are verified by back-projection, though in practice, any of a number of other verification methods could be used.

3 Combining Local Cues

Extending local feature groups enables more reliable recognition through hierarchical object description. Essentially, the rôle of extension is to combine local feature configurations into groups that are used to drive a higher level of recognition. The combination of the features is achieved through the exploitation of invariance between the configurations, the invariants formed between the configurations are called *joint invariants*.

Extension can be understood better when one realises that it occurs at many stages throughout the recognition process; the lowest level occurs during segmentation and grouping. Initially the input to a recognition system is a set of edgel points. First, segmentation exploits the property of collinearity (which is invariant under projection) to group edgels into lines; the value of an invariant for collinearity is boolean (either a set of points is collinear, or is not, at least up to an error threshold). Other invariants are also used for segmentation: the preservation of conic sections; incidence and tangency. After segmentation the tokens used for recognition become lines, conics, etc., instead of the original edgels. These features are then grouped into higher order configurations (such as groups of five lines) using invariants that take real number values[2]. Hypothesis

---

[2] In practice we may measure invariants that take complex values.

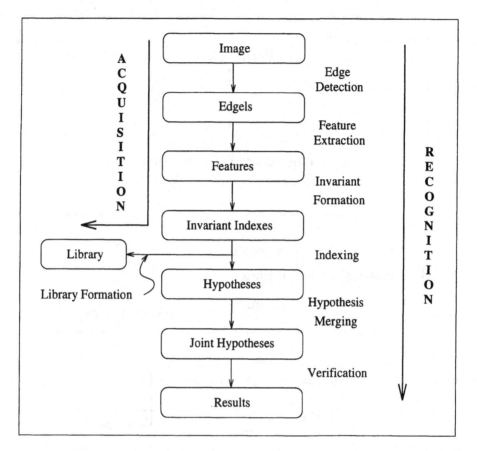

Fig. 1. *LEWIS is implemented as a pipeline. The details are given in the text.*

extension takes this one stage further by combining groups of algebraic features, or different $\mathcal{M}$ curves, into more complex groups. The whole of this process is shown in figure 2.

The rest of this section describes more detail how hypothesis extension is achieved for algebraic invariants and $\mathcal{M}$ curves.

3.1 Plane Algebraic Invariants

Planar objects containing algebraic features are described by the following invariant feature groups:

- I_1: a pair of points and a pair of lines (one invariant value).
- I_2: a pair of conics (two invariant values).
- I_3: a conic and a pair of lines (one invariant value).
- I_4: five lines (two invariant values).

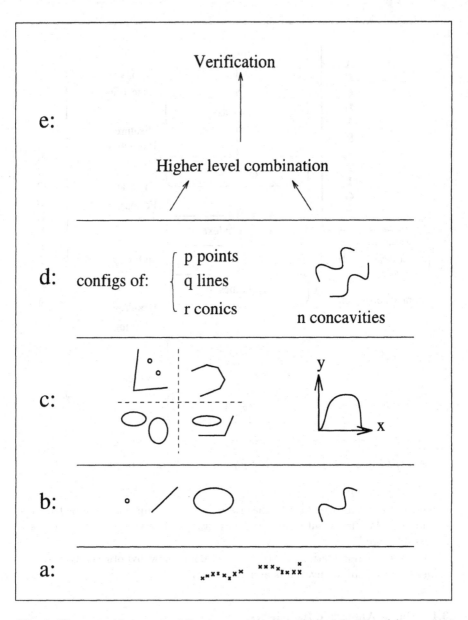

Fig. 2. *The recognition process follows a number of levels in a hierarchy: (a) connected edgel chains are extracted from the image; (b) edgels are grouped together using invariants such as collinearity, etc., to form points, lines, conics and M curves; (c) these are then grouped using specific invariant values to give local invariant hypotheses; (d) higher order invariants are formed between the initial feature groups to give larger feature configurations; (e) after a (possibly zero) number of other levels the model image correspondence is evaluated by verification.*

Of course one could take any suitable combination of points, lines and conics with a sufficient number of degrees of freedom and derive other invariant feature groups, but these are the ones we have used for recognition.

Normally recognition proceeds by finding feature groups from any of the above four classes, computing their invariants and using these to index into a model library. Resulting hypotheses are verified by determining other model to image feature correspondences. However, due to redundancy we frequently find more than one feature group in a scene that hypothesises a single object. These individual hypotheses should be combined prior to recognition to give a richer object description. Note that drawing a conclusion that multiple hypotheses for a single model in a scene correspond to the presence of a single object could be false due to multiple object instances in the scene. As a result of this, extension should not exploit a voting scheme such as that used by Lamdan, *et al.* [14].

Two individual hypotheses can be combined if structures between the groups exist that are preserved by projection. In LEWIS, the actual property exploited is the consistency of topology between the invariant feature groups; for this to be achieved the groups must be *overlapping* (cf. the overlapping and non-overlapping sub-part strategy in [5]). For example, consider three feature groups in a scene that index the same model and create hypotheses H_i, $i \in \{a, b, c\}$ (see figure 3). In this case H_a corresponds to an invariant of type I_2, and H_b and H_c to type I_3. H_a and H_b are compatible as the correspondence of model to image features is unique and is given by $\{C_1 : c_1, C_2 : c_2, L_1 : l_1, L_2 : l_2\}$. However, H_b and H_c are incompatible as the two correspondences $\{L_1 : l_1, L_2 : l_2\}$ and $\{L_5 : l_1, L_1 : l_2\}$ cannot be satisfied simultaneously.

Examples of this form of extension are demonstrated in figure 4 where multiple hypotheses are used to recognise the highlighted objects. The process can be repeated between the higher order invariant groups and other individual hypotheses. In this way we can form extended hypotheses containing any number of individual hypotheses; examples of three hypotheses being combined are given in figures 5 and 6.

The short-coming of this method of extension occurs when the feature groups are not overlapping, should this happens the topologies of the different feature groups become independent and so there is no possibility of a contradiction occurring. This is overcome though a further use of projective invariants that usually provides a much stronger test of the compatibility of the hypotheses than achieved through topology. In practice, not only are algebraic invariants measured within single feature groups, but following indexing, other algebraic invariants are computed between pairs of groups.

This more general form of extension is demonstrated in figure 7. Feature groups **a** and **b** in a scene are found through indexing to correspond to model groups **A** and **B** (from the same model). Note that the correspondence is not just **a** : **A** and **b** : **B**, but is a_i : A_i and b_i : B_i, $i \in \{1, \ldots, 5\}$ (indexing provides a correspondence between the individual features as well as between the groups). If **a** and **b** come from the same object in the scene rather than from different instances of the same model, there are other tests of geometric

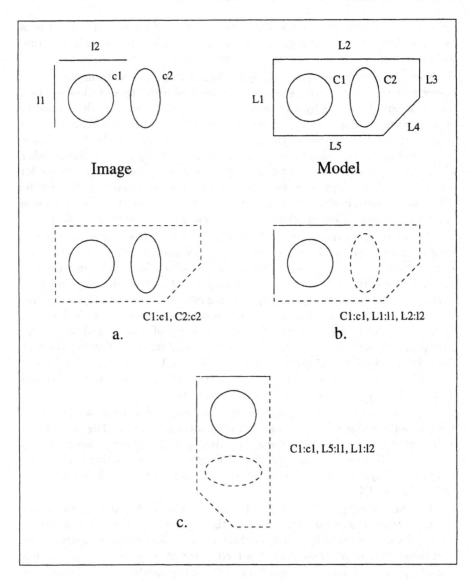

Fig. 3. *A single view of an object yields two lines (l_1 and l_2) and two conics (c_1 and c_2). The two different hypotheses in (a) and (b) are consistent as in both cases the correspondence $C_1 : c_1$ is made and all the other correspondences are independent. However, hypotheses (b) and (c) are not consistent with each other as there is the contradictions $\{L_1 : l_1, L_2 : l_2\} \wedge \{L_5 : l_1, L_1 : l_2\}$.*

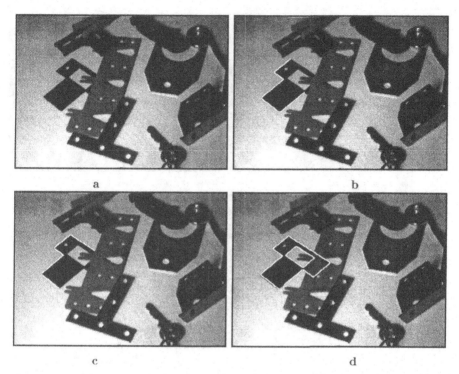

Fig. 4. *The lock striker plate to the left of the scene is recognised using two different visible five line feature groups. These are highlighted in (b) and (c), and could each be used independently to recognise the object. However, a much better understanding of the scene is gained when the two hypotheses are combined prior to verification (d).*

consistency that can be applied. For example any projective invariant for the features $\{a_1, a_2, a_3, a_4, b_1\}$ should match (modulo noise) that on the model for $\{A_1, A_2, A_3, A_4, B_1\}$.

In practice, the consistency of two individual hypotheses is tested by computing invariants between any of the combinations of the features in **a** and **b**, and comparing them to invariants computed for **A** and **B** (the model invariant values can be precomputed and stored in a look-up table). Note that one can form only twelve independent projective invariants from a set of ten points (using the counting argument of [6]), and so the comparisons should be over such an independent set[3].

---

[3] There are situations in which no more independent projective invariants can be measured between a pair of configurations than have already been used for indexing. Suppose we have a set of six points formed into two overlapping five point configurations. For each set of five points measure two projective invariants (the maximum possible) and index to give model hypotheses; thus a total of four independent invariants have been used for indexing. Now, compute invariants for the joint configuration of the six points; using the counting argument of [6] we can measure four independent invariants. However, these must be functionally dependent on the four invariants used for indexing, and so nothing can be gained in using these for extension. As a result, the only constraint useful for extension is topology.

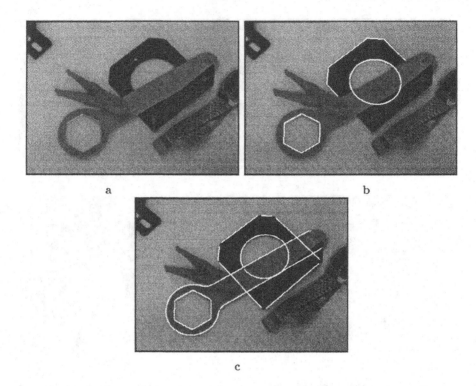

a   b

c

Fig. 5. *Two objects are recognised using the features in (b) which form three individual hypotheses for each object. After extension, single hypotheses are created for each object that are verified in (c).*

Fig. 6. *In the example of figure 4, three different objects can be recognised using extended hypotheses containing different numbers of individual hypotheses. From left to right the objects are recognised using: two hypotheses; a single hypothesis; and three combined hypotheses.*

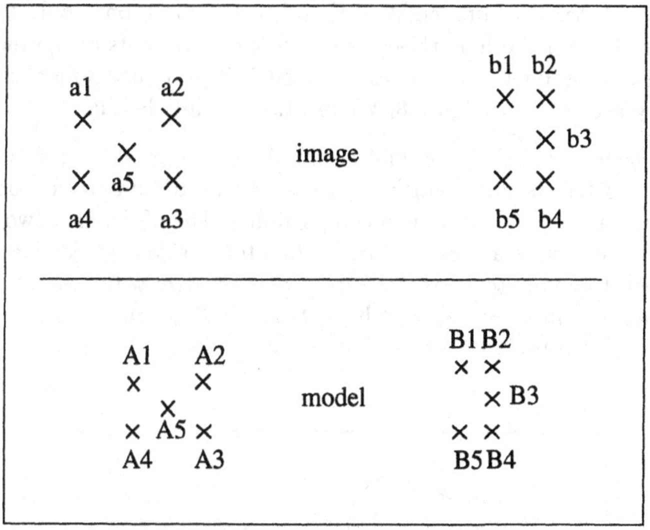

Fig. 7. *Two feature groups index the same model and form image to model correspondences* **a** : **A** *and* **b** : **B**. *We test for compatibility between the groups* **a** *and* **b** *by checking for consistency of algebraic invariants with the model groups* **A** *and* **B**. *Details are in the text.*

This procedure suggests a general strategy for testing the compatibility of a pair of image hypotheses derived from algebraic features within a single model. The method relies simply on the exchange of features from one feature group to the other, and then comparison of the newly computed invariants with those for the same configuration on the model. In practice the features need not be algebraic but may include any of the differential structures in [7, 29].

3.2   Smooth Plane Curves

Smooth plane curves are recognised using a canonical frame construction that relies on the measurement of *bitangency* and *cast tangency* points; four such points are measured for each canonical frame [23]. The bitangency points bound segments of curve ($\mathcal{M}$ curves) that are recognised using the invariant indexing paradigm (a more complete description of the process is given in [25]). Two examples of $\mathcal{M}$ curves are given in figure 9b.

The four measured points for each $\mathcal{M}$ curve are preserved by projection (distinguished), and it is through these that we see how to extend hypotheses for $\mathcal{M}$ curves. The approach builds directly on that for algebraic features: for a pair of hypotheses (yielding eight distinguished points), one could take sets of five points between the hypotheses and compare invariants computed for these points with those on the hypothesised model. The actual points used to test consistency are shown in figure 8. We use these points because:

1. For efficiency reasons it is undesirable to compute all of the independent invariants for the distinguished points. We need compute enough only to provide a confident estimate of compatibility. Therefore, only two configurations of five points are used which yield a total of four projective invariants.
2. We wish to compute measures that are symmetric with respect to the distinguished points, and so a fifth point for each concavity is computed and used as shown in figure 8.

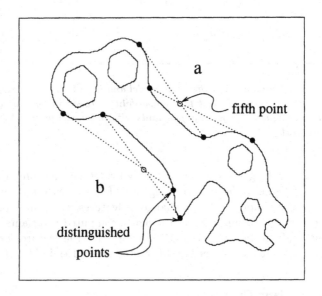

Fig. 8. *For a pair of interest curves there are 8 distinguished points which could be used to form* $2 \times 8 - 8 = 8$ *different five point invariants. Rather than computing so many, which is inefficient, we compute invariants between the four distinguished points of each concavity, and the central point of the other. This yields four invariants, and does so using a symmetric construction. These invariants are sufficient to hypothesise compatibility.*

The correctness of the extended hypothesis is tested by comparing the four measured image invariants with the matching ones on the model. The cost function used to test consistency exploits of the fact that the expected errors in the measured invariants are roughly proportional to their values [6, 25]:

$$e = \sum_{i=1}^{4} \left| \frac{M_i - m_i}{M_i} \right|,$$

and the extended hypothesis is accepted if e lies below a threshold. Figures 9 and 10 show examples of hypothesis extension for $\mathcal{M}$ curves. Note in figure 9d how the benefit of combining hypotheses rather than using individual hypotheses is realised as can be observed by the better model registration in 9c.

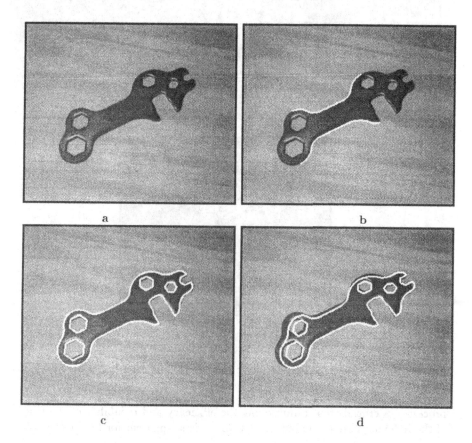

Fig. 9. *(a) shows an unoccluded view of a spanner. The indexing scheme correctly locates the $\mathcal{M}$ curves in (b). These are used to form an extended hypothesis for the model which is verified using backprojection in (c) and provides very good registration of the object. If, as in (d), only the lower $\mathcal{M}$ curve is used for recognition the registration is good in the region of the curve, but extrapolates poorly over the rest of the object. Subsequently we have gained a geometrically worse understanding of the scene in (d) compared to (c).*

4 Discussion

The above approaches work well for the recognition of plane algebraic objects and those containing smooth plane curves. In fact, the hypothesis extension

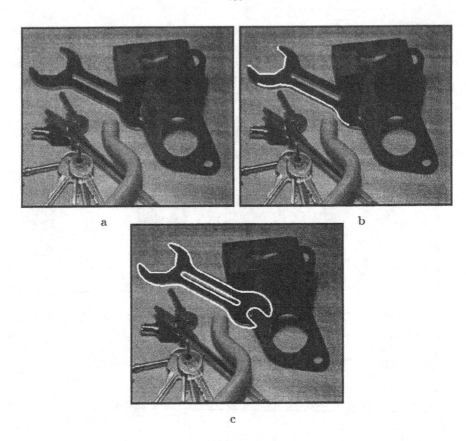

Fig. 10. *Two M curves are found on the spanner (b) and combined before hypothesis verification (c).*

process is a crucial step in improving the efficiency and reliability of the whole of the indexing paradigm used in LEWIS. This is apparent for two reasons:

- We can assume a much higher confidence in a verification score when multiple feature groups have hypothesised the presence of an object in a scene.
- The increased number of model to image correspondences provided through extension immediately leads to better model registration and scene understanding.

The following sections highlight how results about hypothesis extension can be applied to a variety of other object classes and so improve the capabilities of current invariant indexing based recognition systems.

4.1 Extensions to other Classes of Objects

Invariants for three dimensional objects are now becoming familiar in the literature. Two example classes of objects are considered below for which extension can be applied.

Objects possessing Rotational Symmetry

Invariant indexing functions can be measured for objects that are projectively equivalent to solids of revolution [16]. The computation of the indexes relies on the detection of lines of bitangency and inflection in the image of the occluding boundary of the object. However, producing the correspondence between different sides of the object appears at first to be a hard task. This can be overcome using the following strategy and exploiting the fact that the images of the two sides of the outline are projectively equivalent through a harmonic homology of the plane (see figure 11):

1. Search the image for $\mathcal{M}$ curves. For each curve found, hypothesise the presence of an object of revolution.

2. Determine whether any pair of $\mathcal{M}$ curves are projectively equivalent using the canonical frame construction; this can be achieved using the method employed to solve jigsaw puzzles given in [23]. This is the hypothesis extension stage.

3. Match tangents and other features that allow the invariants required for recognition to be measured.

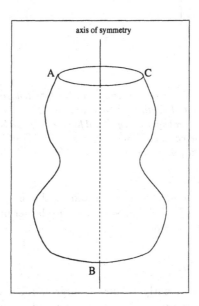

Fig. 11. *In the image of a solid of revolution, the two sides (curves AB and BC) are projectively equivalent [16].*

Polyhedral Objects

Invariants can be computed for objects that are based on polyhedra, or for objects with a plane of bilateral symmetry [24]. However, grouping the features required to form the invariants is a hard task. One way to overcome this is to use the *affine invariant* construction of Wayner [30] to highlight small local features that might come from a polyhedral structure and then these can be grouped together into actual polyhedra. The invariants in [30] can be use to detect trihedral vertices of various types. Figure 12 shows how feature groups can be extracted from these simple vertices through extension.

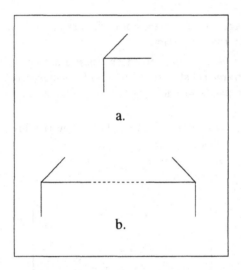

Fig. 12. *Trihedral vertices of a specific shape can be detected using the affine invariants in [30]. These can be used to hypothesise the initial presence of a polyhedral object, or an object with a plane of bilateral symmetry. Local hypotheses can be extended by combining pairs of vertices that have collinear line segments. When a sufficient number of vertices have been grouped the full projective invariants of [24] can be measured.*

Extension may also find a rôle in combining the simple polyhedra that are recognised in [24], each of which has six sides, into larger polyhedral objects that are more familiar in the world.

4.2 Quasi-Invariants

Projective invariants frequently require a large number of features to be extracted efficiently from a scene. The grouping problem that results from these relatively large feature groups can be eased if a number of invariants to a simpler imaging deformation are measured first (affine invariants could be used for example), or through the use of quasi-invariant [9] (informally, quasi-invariants are measures that remain approximately invariant over a specific range of viewpoints). These are beneficial as their formation requires a smaller number of features.

First, hypotheses are created through indexing on the weaker affine or quasi-invariants (the indexing error bounds on these invariants are larger as they have to account for errors in the imaging model). Then, pairs of proximal groups can be combined using extension to form larger groups that posses projective invariants. Subsequently, any number of the reduced groups can be combined. This is exactly the same strategy used above for the construction of projective polyhedral invariants from local trihedral vertices.

4.3 Parameterised Objects

Hypothesis extension has till now been applied only to rigid objects. Parameterised objects can be handled easily if they satisfy certain well defined constraints. Rigid objects require the invariants used in extension to take a single value (modulo noise); parameterised objects will generally have the invariants taking a range of values, and so long as any joint invariant falls within the range it may be hypothesised that a certain parameterised object class is present. This approach will be most effective when the joint invariants change monotonically with respect to the parameterisation (for example, for a pair of scissors any joint invariant measured between the handles should change monotonically with respect to the angle of opening). This approach is analogous to the way that Grimson treats parameterisations in [11].

One interesting case of a parameterisation has been noted by Moons, *et al.* [20], where the joint invariant takes a single value. Consider the task of recognising objects containing pairs of coplanar (but non-rigidly orientated) triangles under affine distortions. On finding any triangle in a scene we may hypothesise the presence of such an object. When two triangles have been located a joint invariant of the ratio of the triangle areas can be measured. This takes a unique value independent of the relative positions of the triangles and allows a further level indexing to be substantiated.

4.4 Combining Invariants From Different Classes

The examples given in this paper allow the extension of hypotheses within the following three classes: algebraic; $\mathcal{M}$ curves; and (semi)-differential measures. From the way that the $\mathcal{M}$ curves were reduced to an algebraic configuration for the computation of the joint invariants we see that, in practice, hypotheses can be formed between different classes. In fact, it is likely that the only way to recover a useful quantity of geometric data from a scene will be by combining cues in this manner.

Acknowledgements

The author would like to express thanks for discussions with David Forsyth, Joe Mundy, Andrew Zisserman and Mike Brady. The support of General Electric is also acknowledged, as well as that of ESPRIT and the NSF.

References

1. Åström, K. "Affine Invariants of Planar Sets," *TR*, Department of Mathematics, Lund Institute of Technology, Sweden, 1993.
2. Bolles, R. and Cain, R. "Recognising and Locating Partially Visible Objects: The Local-Feature-Focus Method," *IJRR*, Vol. 1, No. 3, p.57-82, 1982.
3. Brady, M. "Criteria for Representation of Shape," in *Human and Machine Vision*, Beck, Hope and Rosenfeld editors, Academic Press, 1983.
4. Carlsson, S. "Projectively Invariant Decomposition of Planar Shapes," in [21], p.267-273, 1992.
5. Ettinger, G.J. "Large Hierarchical Object Recognition Using Libraries of Parameterized Model Sub-Parts," Proceedings CVPR88, p.32-41, 1988.
6. Forsyth, D.A., Mundy, J.L., Zisserman, A.P., Coelho, C., Heller, A. and Rothwell, C.A. "Invariant Descriptors for 3-D Object Recognition and Pose," *IEEE Trans. PAMI*, Vol. 13, No. 10, p.971-991, October 1991.
7. Barrett, E.B., Payton, P.M. and Brill, M.H. "Contributions to the Theory of Projective Invariants for Curves in Two and Three Dimensions," Proceedings 1st DARPA-ESPRIT Workshop on Invariance, p.387-425, March 1991.
8. Binford, T.O. "Inferring Surfaces from Images," *Artificial Intelligence*, Vol. 17, p.205-244, 1981.
9. Binford, T.O. and Levitt, T.S. "Quasi-Invariants: Theory and Explanation," Proceeding Darpa IUW, p.819-829, 1993.
10. Canny J.F. "A Computational Approach to Edge Detection," *IEEE Trans. PAMI*, Vol. 8, No. 6, p.679-698, 1986.
11. Grimson, W.E.L. *Object Recognition by Computer, The Role of Geometric Constraints*, MIT Press, 1990.
12. Jacobs, D.W. "Space Efficient 3D Model Indexing," Proceedings CVPR92, p.439-444, 1992.
13. Keren, D., Subrahmonia, J. and Cooper, D.B. "Robust Object Recognition Based on Implicit Algebraic Curves and Surfaces," Proceedings CVPR92, p.791-794, 1992.
14. Lamdan, Y., Schwartz, J.T. and Wolfson, H.J. "Object Recognition by Affine Invariant Matching," Proceedings CVPR88, p.335-344, 1988.
15. Lowe, D.G. *Perceptual Organization and Visual Recognition*, Kluwer Academic Publishers, 1985.
16. Liu, J., Mundy, J.L., Forsyth, D.A., Zisserman, A. and Rothwell, C.A. "Efficient Recognition of Rotationally Symmetric Surfaces and Straight Homogeneous Generalized Cylinders," Proceedings CVPR93, p.123-128, 1993.
17. Marr, D. *Vision*, Freeman, 1982.
18. Maybank, S.J. "The Projective Geometry of Ambiguous Surfaces," *Proc. R. Soc. Lond.*, Series A, Vol. 332, p.1-47, 1990.
19. Mohr, R. and Morin, L. "Relative Positioning from Geometric Invariants," Proceedings CVPR91, p.139-144, 1991.

20. Moons, T., Pauwels, E., Van Gool, L. and Oosterlinck, A. "Viewpoint Invariant Characterization of Objects Composed of Different Rigid Parts: a Mathematical Framework," in *Geometry and Topology of Submanifolds*, Vol. 5., Verstraelen, P. and Dillen, F. editors, World Scientific, 1993.

21. Mundy, J.L. and Zisserman, A.P. *Geometric Invariance in Computer Vision*, MIT Press, 1992.

22. Nielsen, L. "Automated Guidance of Vehicles using Vision and Projective Invariant Marking," *Automatica*, Vol. 24, p.135-148, 1988.

23. Rothwell, C.A., Zisserman, A., Forsyth, D.A. and Mundy, J.L. "Canonical Frames for Planar Object Recognition," Proceedings ECCV2, p.757-772, 1992.

24. Rothwell, C.A., Forsyth, D.A., Zisserman, A. and Mundy, J.L. "Extracting Projective Information from Single Views of 3D Point Sets," Proceedings ICCV4, p.573-582, 1993.

25. Rothwell, C.A. *Object Recognition through Invariant Indexing*, To appear OUP, 1994.

26. Sinclair, D.A. and Blake, A. "Isoperimetric Normalisation of Planar Curves," *TR*, Department of Engineering Science, Oxford University, Oxford, 1993.

27. Taubin, G. and Cooper, D.B. "Object Recognition Based on Moment (or Algebraic) Invariants," *IBM TR-RC17387*, IBM T.J. Watson Research Centre, P.O. Box 704, Yorktown Heights, NY 10598, 1991.

28. Taubin, G. "An Improved Algorithm for Algebraic Curve and Surface Fitting," Proceedings ICCV4, p.658-665, 1993.

29. Van Gool, L. Kempenaers, P. and Oosterlinck, A. "Recognition and Semi-Differential Invariants," Proceedings CVPR91, p.454-460, 1991.

30. Wayner, P.C. "Efficiently Using Invariant Theory for Model-Based Matching," Proceedings CVPR91, p.473-478, 1991.

31. Weiss, I. "Projective Invariants of Shapes," Proceedings DARPA Image Understanding Workshop, p.1125-1134, April 1988.

Generalizing Invariants for 3-D to 2-D Matching

David W. Jacobs[1]

NEC Research Institute, 4 Independence Way, Princeton, NJ 08540

Abstract. Invariant representations of images have proven useful in performing a variety of vision tasks. However, there are no general invariant functions when one considers a single 2-D image of a 3-D scene. One possible response to the lack of true invariants is to attempt to generalize the notion of an invariant by finding the most economical characterization possible of the set of all 2-D images that a group of 3-D features may produce. A true invariant exists when, for each model, we can represent all its images at a single point in some representational space. When this is not possible, it is still very useful to find the simplest and lowest-dimensional representation of each model's images.

We show how this can be done for a variety of different types of model features, and types of projection models. Of particular interest, we show how to represent the set of images that a group of 3-D points produces by two lines (1-D subspaces), one in each of two orthogonal, high-dimensional spaces, where a single image group corresponds to one point in each space. We demonstrate the value of our results by applying them to a variety of vision problems. In particular, we describe a space-efficient indexing system that performs 3-D to 2-D matching by table lookup. We also show how to find a least squares solution to the structure-from-motion problem using point features that have associated orientations, such as corners. We show how to determine when a restricted class of models may give rise to an invariant function, and construct a model-based invariant for pairs of planar algebraic curves that are not coplanar.

1 Introduction

Invariant descriptions of images have proven useful in object recognition and motion understanding. An invariant function of some image features means that the function will remain constant over the set of images produced by any possible object, even as the object is viewed from different positions. Such a function is valuable because it removes the effects of viewpoint from image analysis. There is a long history of considering invariant descriptions in image understanding (see [8] for a review). More recently, invariants have been used extensively in computer vision to interpret either a single image of a 2-D planar object[9, 22, 23, 39, 12, 35, 25, 7, 37, 26] or 3-D information about 3-D objects[31, 19].

However, it is well-known that no general invariants exist when one considers 2-D image points produced by an arbitrary set of 3-D scene points. This was shown in the computer vision literature simultaneously by [4] and [5]. It was

416

independently shown by [24], who demonstrate further restrictions to general case invariants, as does [17]. These results are easily extended to apply to other types of features.

There are several approaches that one can take, given the lack of general invariants for interpreting 3-D scenes from a single 2-D image. For example, one can consider situations in which 3-D information about the scene is available, either from a motion sequence or from a range sensor [31, 20, 11, 19]. Or one can consider invariants that arise when the class of models or images are restricted. For example, [24], and [27] consider invariants produced by symmetric objects. [27] also considers points that form the vertices of certain types of polyhedra.

In this paper, we continue to consider the general case, in which a model may be any possible configuration of 3-D features, and an image may be any view of that model. Since invariants do not exist in this domain, we must proceed by trying to find an appropriate generalization of the notion of an invariant.

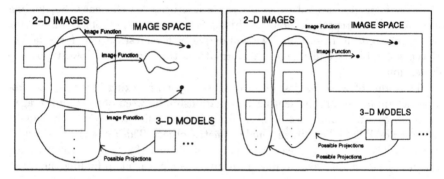

Fig. 1. On the left, we illustrate the idea of image space. An image function maps images to points in some space. The image function maps the set of images that a particular model can produce to a set of points in image space. Implicitly, the image function maps models to surfaces in image space. On the right, we illustrate that an invariant image function is one in which all images of a model map to the same point in image space.

To do this, we can think of any image function as mapping each image to a point in an *image space*, which is just an alternate representation of the images, illustrated in figure 1. Then we can think of the image function as mapping each object to a region of image space, which is the union of all the points in image space that are mapped to by images of the object. This view of image functions is developed in [3, 6], and implicit in other work as well. A function is invariant, then, when each object is mapped to a single point in image space. This means that the value of the function is fixed for each object, even as the viewpoint changes. When an invariant function does not exist, there is no non-trivial function that, for every object, maps all of the object's images to a single point. In this case, it is natural to ask what is the most compact possible representation of an object's images? What function maps objects to the smallest regions of some image space?

This is a natural generalization of invariants when we consider using them to recognize objects through indexing (or geometric hashing). With indexing, we place pointers to each object in a lookup table. We then compute an index into the lookup table from the image, and at that point in the table, we expect to find pointers to all objects that could have produced this image. The lookup table can be formed by discretizing image space. A function from images to image space gives us our lookup index. At each point in image space, we place pointers to all objects that can produce an image that is mapped to that point in image space. An invariant function allows us to make a single entry in the lookup table for each object we wish to recognize. When this is not possible, if we can determine the lowest-dimensional representation of models in image space, we have also found the most space-efficient way of representing a model in a lookup table, using multiple entries. Alternately, [3], who also considers image space representations of objects, discusses an approach to indexing that does not discretize image space; but in this approach also the dimensionality of the objects represented in image space is crucial for efficiency. So, finding low-dimensional representations of objects is central to the problem of efficient object recognition. In section 3 we will derive such representations for a variety of types of objects and image transformations that are of the lowest possible dimension.

The value of these results, however, goes beyond indexing. Image space provides a simple way of representing the relationship between objects and images. Each image corresponds to a point in image space, while each object corresponds to some possibly higher-dimensional geometric object. This allows us to consider vision problems as simple, easily visualized problems of geometry. Determining which objects might have produced an image is equivalent to finding the set of geometric objects that contain a point in image space. Structure from motion becomes the problem of finding which possible geometric objects might include a set of points. In section 4 we will provide examples of this type of reasoning and also of how we may use our results to construct invariants when we consider only a restricted class of possible objects.

2 Definitions and a Projection Model

We assume that a real object may be described, at least partially, using a collection of local 3-D geometric features. We use the word "model" to refer to such a collection of features. By a "model group", we will mean a particular ordered subset of model features. Thus a model may give rise to many, possibly overlapping model groups. We will also use the words "scene" and "scene group" to refer to collections of 3-D features. The word "scene" will be synonymous to "model", but will stress the fact that in the structure from motion problem features do not come from a particular known object, but from an arbitrary scene. We refer to points in a model group with the variables: $p_1, p_2, ...p_n$. By "general" model groups we mean that any configuration of 3-D features is a possible model group.

This is in contrast to a "restricted" class of model groups, such as model groups with features that are coplanar.

We also assume that we can identify some corresponding local features in the image. We call an ordered collection of these features an "image group". We refer to points in an image group as: $q_1, q_2, ...q_n$.

In addition to perspective, and scaled orthographic projection, we use the following novel model of projection. First, we assume that the object is imaged from an arbitrary viewpoint using scaled orthographic projection. Next, we allow an arbitrary 2-D affine transform to be applied to the resulting image. Applying an arbitrary affine transform to an image is equivalent to viewing that image from an arbitrary position, assuming that this projection also is a scaled orthographic projection. Therefore, our projection model encompasses all images that a model might produce, as well as all images that a photograph of the model might produce. We show in [17] that this projection model is equivalent to linear projection models used by [34, 20, 23], so we will call it a *linear projection*.

Throughout this paper, we assume that all features are visible from all viewpoints. Work on aspect graphs deals with the complementary problem of describing which sets of features in a solid object are visible from a single viewpoint. Some recent work on aspect graphs can be found in [13], [21], and [2].

3 Minimal Representations of an Object's Images

To begin with the simplest type of feature, we consider model and image groups consisting of at least five ordered point features. We show that the set of images produced by any 3-D model group, under a linear transformation, can be described by the cross product of two lines in two orthogonal spaces, as shown in figure 2. If the model group is actually planar, it will be described by a point in each of these spaces. For the case of general 3-D models groups this is the simplest and lowest dimensional representation possible. This shows that the problem of matching a 3-D model group and an error-free 2-D image group is essentially the problem of matching a point and a line in a high dimensional space. This will demonstrate that in our approach, we generalize invariants by finding an image space that represents each set of images produced by a model in the simplest possible way. In this case, we are able to acheive a greater simplification by mapping image points into two, separate image spaces.

To acheive this result, we represent images as follows. As an image consists of 2-D point features, we use the first three points to define an affine basis. That is, we let

$$o = q_1, \qquad\qquad u = q_2 - q_1, \qquad\qquad v = q_3 - q_1$$

and consider o the origin of the coordinate system, with u and v as its axes. Then we may fully describe the locations of the remaining points using affine coordinates derived with respect to this basis. That is, we describe q_i with the parameters (α_i, β_i), where:

$$q_i = o + \alpha_i u + \beta_i v .$$

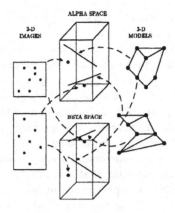

Fig. 2. We show how to decompose image space into two orthogonal parts. Each image corresponds to a point in each of these subspaces. Each model corresponds to a line in each subspace.

It is important to what follows that the affine coordinates of a point are left unchanged by any affine transform. This is well known from affine geometry, and this fact is used in [22]'s recognition system. A derivation may be found there, in [17], or in elementary geometry texts.

An image is fully described by the parameters: $(\mathbf{o}, \mathbf{u}, \mathbf{v}, (\alpha_4, \beta_4), ...(\alpha_n, \beta_n))$. Due to the model of projection we use, we may ignore the first three of these parameters, since they can take on any values independent of the values of the other variables. To see this, we note that, except in degenerate cases, there exists an affine transform that will map any three image points to any other three image points. Therefore, under a linear projection model, if a model group can produce the image, $(\mathbf{o}, \mathbf{u}, \mathbf{v}, (\alpha_4, \beta_4), ...(\alpha_n, \beta_n))$, it can also produce the image $(\mathbf{o}', \mathbf{u}', \mathbf{v}', (\alpha_4, \beta_4), ...(\alpha_n, \beta_n))$ for any choice of $(\mathbf{o}', \mathbf{u}', \mathbf{v}')$, by combining the affine transform that maps $(\mathbf{o}, \mathbf{u}, \mathbf{v})$ to $(\mathbf{o}', \mathbf{u}', \mathbf{v}')$ with the affine transform that was part of the projection that produced the original image.

The remaining image parameters form what we will call an *affine space*. An image with n ordered points is mapped to a point in a $2(n-3)$-dimensional affine space by finding the affine coordinates of the image points, using the first three as a basis. We divide the affine space into two orthogonal subspaces, an α-*space*, and a β-*space*. The α-*space* is the set of α coordinates of the image's affine coordinates, and the β-space is similarly defined. The affine space is then equal to the cross product of the α-*space* and the β-*space*, and each image corresponds to a point in each of these two spaces. The previous paragraph states that the images that a model group can produce are fully described by the locus of points these images map to in affine space.

We now show that for any model group, these images map to the cross product of lines in α-*space* and β-*space*. First note that our model of projection consists of parallel projection of 3-D features into 2-D, followed by planar rotation, translation, scaling and an affine transformation. All the operations but the parallel projection can be combined into a single affine transformation, that leaves the affine coordinates of the points unchanged. So to find the parts of affine space corresponding to images of a particular model group, we only need to consider the sets of affine coordinates that a model group may produce in an image as the viewing direction varies.

We now assume the model group consists of at least five points. Call the plane determined by the first three model points, the *model plane*. If we project the fourth model point, p_4, perpendicularly into the model plane, we call this point p'_4. Since p'_4 is in the plane of the first three model points, we can discuss its affine coordinates with respect to these three model points. We call these affine coordinates (a_4, b_4). Similarly, for the j'th model point, p_j, we define p'_j and (a_j, b_j) (see figure 3). Without loss of generality, assume the model plane is $z = 0$. So z_4 is the height of p_4 above this plane, and z_j is the height of p_j above the model plane. We define $r_j = \frac{z_j}{z_4}$.

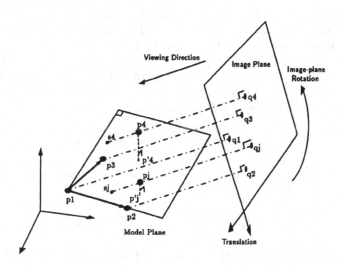

Fig. 3. The image points q_1, q_2, q_3, q_4, and q_j are the projections of the model points p_1, p_2, p_3, p_4, and p_j, before the affine transform portion of the projection is applied. The values of the image points depend on the pose of the model group relative to the image plane. In the viewing direction shown, s_4 and p_4 project to the same image point. p'_4 is in the model plane, directly below p_4. Note that q_4 has the same affine coordinates as s_4.

We now show that for any affine coordinates (α_4, β_4), there is a viewpoint in which the projection of p_4 has those affine coordinates. We then express the affine coordinates of the remaining projected model points as a function of (α_4, β_4). Some point, s_4, in the model plane has affine coordinates (α_4, β_4). If we form a line including s_4 and p_4, this line describes a viewing direction from which p_4 and s_4 project to the same image point, q_4. Since s_4 is coplanar with the first three model points, it has the same affine coordinates when viewed from any direction, since affine coordinates of planar points are not changed by any affine transformation, and viewing a planar object from an arbitrary viewpoint is equivalent to applying an affine transform. So q_4 has affine coordinates (α_4, β_4), in this viewpoint.

A line parallel to the viewing direction will also pass through p_j, and intersect the model plane at a point we call s_j. The affine coordinates of q_j, the image of p_j, are the same as the affine coordinates of s_j in the model plane. Since the line connecting p_j to s_j is parallel to the line connecting p_4 to s_4, the triangle $p_j p'_j s_j$ will be similar to the triangle $p_4 p'_4 s_4$, and scaled by a factor of r_j. In particular, this means that: $(s_4 - p'_4) = r_j(s_j - p'_j)$, and therefore:

$$(\alpha_j, \beta_j) = (a_j, b_j) + \frac{((\alpha_4, \beta_4) - (a_4, b_4))}{r_j} \ . \tag{1}$$

This equation describes all image parameters that these five points may produce. For any image, this equation will hold. And for any values described by the equation, there is a corresponding image that the model group may produce. a_4, b_4, a_j, b_j, r_j are constants that depend on the geometric structure of the model group, but not on the viewpoint. Therefore, the set of equations that we get as j varies are linear, and describe a 2-D plane in a high-dimensional, affine space.

Taking the α component of these equations:

$$\alpha_j = a_j + \frac{(\alpha_4 - a_4)}{r_j} \qquad 5 \le j \le n \ ,$$

we have equations that describe a line in α-space. We may derive a similar set of equations in β-space:

$$\beta_j = b_j + \frac{(\beta_4 - b_4)}{r_j} \qquad 5 \le j \le n \ .$$

These equations are independent. That is, for any set of α coordinates that a model group may produce in an image, it may still produce any feasible set of β coordinates.

There are also degenerate cases. If some of the model points are coplanar, than some of the r_j are zero, and the lines are vertical in those dimensions. If all the model points are coplanar, the affine coordinates of the projected model points are invariant, and each model group is represented by a point in affine space. If the first three model points are collinear, then the lines are undefined.

Notice that for any line in α-space, there is some model group whose images are described by that line. It is not true that there is a model group corresponding to any pair of lines in α-space and β-space because the parameters r_j are the same in the equations for the two lines. This means that the two lines are constrained to have the same directional vector, but they are not further constrained.

This result shows how we may represent models geometrically in an image space. We use affine space as an image space, defining a function from images to this image space. This also defines a function from model groups to planes in image space. In this case, we can further simplify our representation by splitting affine space in two. The problem of comparing models and images is reduced essentially to the simple geometric problem of comparing points and lines.

We note that this representation is optimal in terms of space, if we desire an error-free representation. By error-free, we mean that a point in image space is included in a model group's representation if all images that map to that point in image space could have been produced by that model. [6] shows that if we represent a model group's images in a single image space, and use scaled orthographic projection, we must use a surface that is at least 2-D. This result also holds for a linear transformation, so our representation using planes in affine space is optimal if a single image space is used. And it is not possible to represent a 2-D surface as the cross-product of any countable number of countable sets. This means that no combination of 0-D sets of points in orthogonal spaces can represent a model group's images; we must use at least two 1-D surfaces in two image subspaces. And by representing images using two lines, we have found the simplest pair of 1-D surfaces possible.

For the case of general model groups of points undergoing a linear transformation, we have found the closest thing possible to an invariant. We may look for similar results when we consider either different types of features, or different viewing transformations.

Perhaps the simplest way to generalize from simple point features is with *oriented* points. By orientation, we mean that one or more 3-D vectors are associated with some or all of the 3-D points, where only the directions and not the magnitudes of the vectors are known. For example, if we use the vertices of a polyhedra as our model, the directions of the lines that form the vertices associate three direction vectors with each point. To handle these features, we extend affine space to provide an affine invariant representation of oriented point features. In this paper we describe results when a model group consists of three points with three orientation vectors. [18] contains a general treatment for three or more points and any number of orientation vectors. We continue to use three image points to define an affine basis, and describe the points' orientation vectors using this basis. We describe each orientation vector by its *affine slope*. The affine slope of a vector at the origin is just $\frac{\alpha}{\beta}$, where (α, β) is any point in the direction of the vector. It is easily seen from the properties of affine transformations that the affine slope of a vector is well defined and is invariant under affine transformations. This representation of vectors is equivalent to an affine invariant representation derived by [35]. The affine slope of the three orientations in the image form a 3-D image space that we call *affine slope space*. As before, the problem of determining a model group's representation in this image space becomes one of determining the set of affine invariant values it may produce when viewed from all directions. We may again ignore the actual position of the first three image points, except in using them to determine the affine invariant values of the orientation vectors.

We can then show that the sets of affine slopes produced by any model are described by the equation:

$$- xz + (1 - c_3)yz + c_1 z + c_3 xy - (c_1 - c_2)x - c_2 y = 0 \ . \tag{2}$$

Here x, y and z are the affine slopes of the three image vectors. c_1, c_2 and c_3 are constant for any 3-D model group, and characterize the model group's shape. Given any model group, we may derive c_1, c_2, and c_3, and an equation describing all the images that the model may produce. And for any values of c_1, c_2, and c_3 we may derive the structure of the corresponding model group. Again, this equation does not hold for some degenerate cases involving planarity, which we may handle separately.

Fig. 4. An hyperboloid of one sheet.

Equation 2 describes a hyperboloid of one sheet, for general values of c_1, c_2, and c_3 (see figure 4). So we have once again shown that, with the appropriate choice of an image space, we can represent model groups using a class of simple geometric shapes. We are again able to demonstrate that this is the simplest representation possible (see [17, 18]). We can show first of all that any error-free representation of oriented points must map model groups to surfaces that are at least two-dimensional. We then go on to show that these surfaces cannot all be linear; a quadratic surface is the simplest one that can describe all model groups. Finally, we show that we cannot represent the images of oriented points with lower dimensional surfaces using two image spaces. This contrasts sharply with the case of simple point features, in which we could achieve significantly greater simplification by using two image spaces. For groups of oriented point features, the simplest representation possible is found with affine slope space, in which we map each model group to a hyperboloid. A similar result holds when a model group contains more than three oriented points. This has significant implications for indexing, since it requires far more space to discretely represent one 2-D surface than to represent two 1-D surfaces. This shows that in an important way, indexing oriented points is more complex than indexing simple points.

So far, we have considered only local geometric features. There has been considerable work on finding invariants of planar algebraic curves, and it is interesting to consider what happens with such curves in the 3-D case. A curve can contain much more information about the scene than can a single local feature, although curves may be more sensitive to occlusion, and their algebraic description may be sensitive to noise.

We consider the case of two closed planar curves described implicitly by polynomials, that are not mutually coplanar, where at least one curve is cubic, or of higher degree. We also assume that we can determine the center of mass of each curve. This is useful because the center of mass of a planar curve is fixed relative to the rest of the curve. That is, if we transform a curve with an affine transformation, the center of mass undergoes the same affine transformation.

This type of model group is of interest since real objects often contain several planar curved faces. Our results extend easily to the combination of one or more planar curves, and one or more sets of planar points. We continue to suppose a linear projection model.

Without loss of generality, we may apply any 3-D affine transformation to the model curves without changing the set of images they produce. Under a linear transformation, any 3-D affine transformation of the model results in a 2-D affine transformation of the image. We will choose a 3-D affine transformation that will put our two curves into a canonical form.

We call the plane of the first curve, which is at least cubic, P_1, and the plane of the second curve P_2. We may first of all rotate and translate the curves so that P_1 is described by the equation $z = 0$. We then describe this curve with the equation

$$f(x, y) = \sum_{i=0}^{n} \sum_{j=0}^{n-i} c_{ij} x^i y^j = 0 . \tag{3}$$

We use this curve to define an affine reference frame in the x-y plane, just as we previously used three points to define a reference frame. We apply a 3-D affine transformation, $A' + t'$, to the curves as a preprocessing step, where A' is a 3×3 matrix, and t' is a 3-D translation vector. We choose this transformation so that the first curve remains in the $z = 0$ plane. Let the inverse of that transformation be $A + t$. So a point, p', in the x-y plane is part of the transformed curve if and only if the point p is mapped to p' by $A' + t'$, and the point p satisfies equation 3. So the transformed curve contains all points (x', y') such that

$$x = a_{11} x' + a_{12} y' + t_x ,$$
$$y = a_{21} x' + a_{22} y' + t_y ,$$

and (x, y) satisfies equation 3, where a_{ij} is the value in the i'th row and j'th column of A, and where $t = (t_x, t_y, t_z)$.

We can choose $a_{11}, a_{12}, a_{21}, a_{22}, t_x, t_y$ to put the curve into a canonical form. For example, we can translate the curve so that it's center of mass is at the origin. It is then known from classical mathematics that we may choose $a_{11}, a_{12}, a_{21}, a_{22}$ so that $c'_{30} = c'_{03} = 1$ and $c'_{12} = c'_{21} = 0$, except when the cubic coefficients have a degenerate relationship, in which case other canonical forms are available[10].

Since the first curve lies in the $z = 0$ plane, we have not yet specified any part of the affine transformation that applies to the z values of space. That is, we have not specified the third column of A. (The condition that $A' + t'$ leaves the first curve in the $z = 0$ plane implies that $a_{13}, a_{23}, t_z = 0$). This leaves us sufficient flexibility to choose an affine transformation that will place the center of mass of the second curve at the point $(0, 0, 1)$ (as long as the center of mass point is not in P_1).

So we have transformed the two curves into a canonical form. As we have noted above, a linear 3-D to 2-D transformation is equivalent to a parallel projection of 3-D space, in any direction, onto any plane, followed by a 2-D affine transformation of that plane. So we now consider our projection model as a parallel projection of P_2 onto P_1, followed by a 2-D affine transformation of P_1. However, a 2-D affine transformation of P_1 takes the first curve out of canonical form, and we can undo this transformation by retransforming the image to place the first plane back in canonical form. So to determine the different images the two curves may produce we only need to consider the images that they produce when the first curve is in canonical form. This means that we need only consider the images produced by a parallel projection of P_2 onto P_1. This is essentially the same approach that we took in the case of point features.

We may describe the second curve, after the two curves are placed in canonical form, with two equations:

$$g(x, y) = \sum_{i=0}^{n} \sum_{j=0}^{n-i} b_{ij} x^i y^j = 0 \; ; \tag{4}$$

$$Ax + By + z + C = 0 \; ;$$

where the second is the equation for P_2. That is, we represent the curve as the intersection of a 2-D algebraic surface and a plane.

After the second curve is projected orthographically onto P_1, its center of mass may appear anywhere in that plane, because a line connecting any point in the plane with the center of mass of the second curve defines a legal viewing direction. The location of the center of mass will fully determine the direction of projection, and the location in P_1 of the rest of the curve. We will call the projected location of the center of mass: (x_m, y_m). Now suppose that the point (x_0, y_0, z_0) is on the second curve. It will project to the point:

$$(x, y) = (x_0 + z_0 x_m, y_0 + z_0 y_m) \; ,$$

because the triangle: $(x_m, y_m, 0) \, (0, 0, 1) \, (0, 0, 0)$ is similar to the triangle: $(x, y, 0)$ $(x_0, y_0, z_0) \, (x_0, y_0, 0)$, and scaled by a factor of z_0.

Since: $z_0 = -(C + Ax_0 + By_0)$, we have:

$$(x, y) = (x_0 - (C + Ax_0 + By_0)x_m, y_0 - (C + Ax_0 + By_0)y_m) \; .$$

To avoid messy algebra, we may write this as:

$$(x, y) = M(x_0, y_0) \; ,$$

where M is an affine transform. In fact, M just represents the projection of P_2 onto P_1. Then:

$$(x_0, y_0) = M^{-1}(x, y) ,$$

where M^{-1} is the inverse of M. We will use M_1^{-1} to denote the part of this inverse transform that produces the x value when applied to a point. Similarly, M_2^{-1} produces a y value. We know that M is invertible, except for the degenerate case where projection is parallel to P_2 and the second curve appears as a line in the image, because M expresses a projection from one plane to another.

So (x, y) will belong to the projection of the second curve into the first plane when $M^{-1}(x, y)$ satisfies equation 4. This condition is described by the equation:

$$g'(x, y) = \sum_{i=0}^{n} \sum_{j=0}^{n-i} b_{ij} (M_1^{-1}(x, y))^i (M_2^{-1}(x, y))^j = 0 . \qquad (5)$$

This is a polynomial in the unknowns: x and y. The coefficients of the polynomial are functions of the constants, b_{ij}, A, B and C that describe the pair of 3-D curves, and of x_m, y_m, which depend on the viewing direction. To use equation 5, we could rewrite it as a series of equations that express the coefficients of the image polynomial as a function of the model description, and of the image polynomial's center of mass. These equations would be analagous to equations 1, but much more complicated. We could in principle use these equations to define a new image space, as well. Consider the image space formed by x_m, y_m and a set of polynomial coefficients of the same number that g' has. A point in this space represents a 2-D algebraic curve, by denoting its coefficients and center of mass.[1] Given a 3-D structure, equation 5 describes a 2-D surface in this space. We can see that this is a 2-D surface because x_m and y_m can take on any values, while their values determine the coefficients of the polynomial in equation 5, and hence a single point in the image space. So every pair of model curves defines a surface in this image space. Given a pair of image curves, after we transform the image so that the first curve is in canonical form, the coefficients and center of mass of the second curve define a point in this image space.

In addition to the information given in equation 5, the first planar curve will contain some affine invariants. Except for these invariants, however, equation 5 expresses all available information about the set of images that the two planar curves can produce.

The case of planar curves shows that we can continue to push our interpretation of matching in image space to more and more complex objects. As we do so, however, we may find that the surfaces in image space that represent a model group become more complicated.

A second way in which we can extend our approach to matching is by considering different kinds of image-producing transformations. It is particularly interesting to consider perspective and projective transformations, which model

---

[1] Note that this space is redundant. The polynomial coefficients will determine its center of mass.

camera projection more accurately than do orthographic or linear transformations. In [17] we show that for point features, when either a perspective or projective transformation is used, a model group must be represented by a 3-D surface in image space, if we wish to avoid errors. This is interesting, because [6] shows that only a 2-D surface was needed in the orthographic or linear cases. This demonstrates that in some sense, recognition using perspective projection is inherently more difficult than is recognition using orthographic projection. It is also not difficult to derive equations that describe this 3-D surface in a projectively-invariant image space.

We also consider articulated objects under scaled orthographic projection in [17]. For example, a scissors, if considered perfectly flat, is a planar articulated object, with a rotational degree of freedom. We show how to represent the images of such an object using a 1-D curve in image space, and show that at least a 1-D curve is needed. Similarly, we need at least a 3-D surface in any image space to represent a 3-D object with a single rotational degree of freedom undergoing a scaled orthographic projection. And if we add independent rotational degrees of freedom to the object, we can add the same number of dimensions to the lower bound on the dimensionality of the surface in image space that represents such models. These results again demonstrate that we can extend our approach to handle a very wide range of types of objects, while also showing that as the problem becomes more complicated, our representations in image space may also become inherently more complex.

4 Applications of these Results

We may use a representation of a model group's images in image space to solve a wide variety of vision problems. In this section we will survey some of these applications. Most directly, we may use the representations that we have developed to perform indexing. We can build a lookup table by just discretizing image space. We may also use our results to determine structure from motion. In this case, a motion sequence can be represented by a set of points in image space that we can use to estimate a geometric structure equivalent to the scene structure. We may also use our results to help understand when a restricted library of objects will give rise to an invariant function, and to construct model-based invariants.

First, we have implemented an indexing system for groups of model points undergoing a linear transformation. This system takes a large set of model groups at compile time and stores them in a discrete lookup table. At run time, an image group is matched to all compatible model groups through table lookup. In the previous section, we have shown that in this case, the set of images that a model group may produce is fully represented by a line in α-space along with a parallel line in β-space. To represent model groups in a lookup table, we divide α- and β-space into discrete cells so that we can finitely represent these continuous regions. We do this in a straight-forward way, dividing each dimension of each space into discrete units, so that the entire spaces are tesselated into rectanguloids. To fill this lookup table, we simply compute the appropriate lines for all model groups of interest using equation 1. We may then determine which cells in the discrete α- and β-space intersect these lines, and place a pointer in those cells to the appropriate model group. At run time, to account for error we compute ranges of affine coordinates consistent with an image group, allowing for a bounded amount of error in the location of the image points. We then look up all cells in α space that intersect the range of α values consistent with the image. This guarantees that we find all model groups that might produce an image with the same α values as the current image group. We similarly find all model groups consistent with the image's β values and intersect the results. This gives us all model groups that might have produced the image group.

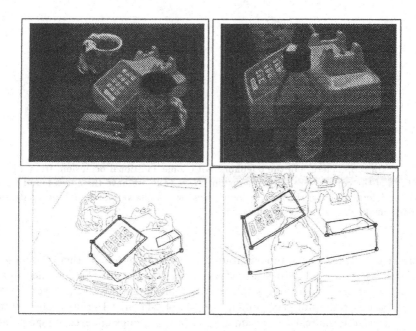

Fig. 5. On the top are two scenes containing a phone. Underneath each scene is a hypothetical projection of the model based on hand-grouped image points. Both are correct. In the hypotheses, edges are shown as dotted lines, projected line segments appear as lines, circles represent the image corners in the match, and squares show the location of the projected model corners.

We have tested this indexing system in isolation, and as part of a complete recognition system that uses a grouping algorithm to find image groups of points likely to come from a single object. The grouping system also forms model groups likely to show up as image groups. Figure 5 shows two scenes on which we tested the indexing system using feature points that we automatically located, then grouped by hand. Overall, we indexed with twelve image groups. All were

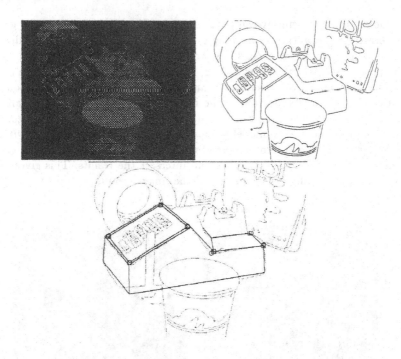

Fig. 6. On top, a picture of the telephone with some additional occlusion, from a series of tests of the complete recognition system. Next to it, we have the edges found in the image. Below, we show the correct hypothesis, which the system found automatically, for the image shown in the previous figure.

correctly matched to the model group that actually produced them. Because it allowed for error, and used a discretized space, the system also matched image groups to some model groups that did not produce them. When we indexed using groups containing six points, one out of 244 model groups, on average, were incorrectly matched to an image group. For groups of seven image points, there were about one in 3,465 false matches. When we tested the indexing system along with the grouping system, recognition was possible with very little search. Figure 6 shows an example. We searched among image groups, and the model groups they matched, for a hypothesis that would allow us to match lines from the phone to edges in the image. In this example, the 80'th hypothesis considered led to correct recognition. This constrasts sharply with the large amounts of search that 3-D recognition systems must typically perform.

We have given only a cursory description of our system and experimental results here, however. A much more complete description, along with more extensive experiments, can be found in [17]. In addition, a good deal of related work on object recognition using indexing can be found in: [36, 28, 19, 14, 3, 31, 32, 22, 23, 6].

We next consider an example of how we may apply our results to the problem of determining structure from motion. There have been a number of recent approaches to finding the affine structure of point features using a linear transformation model. [33] and [34] show how to find the affine structure of a scene group that provides a least squares fit to a sequence of image groups. [33] shows in detail how to efficiently determine the affine structure of the scene group that best explains the image groups, how to determine the image transformations, and how to use this to find a Euclidean structure and corresponding orthographic projections. [20] and [29] consider the problem of finding the affine structure of a scene of 3-D points from two images of the points. [11] and [30] also consider the problem of determining projective structure using images taken with perspective projection.

All of this work applies only to simple point features, however. We may use our results for oriented points to determine how to extend this work to somewhat more complex features. We consider a model with three points and three orientation vectors. We know that for any hyperboloid of the following form:

$$-xz + (1 - c_3)yz + c_1z + c_3xy - (c_1 - c_2)x - c_2y = 0 \ ,$$

there is a model whose images are described by this hyperboloid, where x, y, z are the affine slopes of the three image vectors, and c_1, c_2, c_3 are parameters of the scene, which may take on any values. Determining the affine structure of the scene is equivalent to finding the values of c_1, c_2, c_3. If we do not know these values, we do not know the set of images that the scene can produce and so we can not know the scene's affine structure.

Every image of the scene gives us a set of values for x, y, and z, while c_1, c_2, and c_3 remain to be determined. This gives us one linear equation in three variables. We need three independent equations to solve for these variables, and hence we need at least three views of the object to find its affine structure. Given two views of the scene, there will still be an infinite number of different hyperboloids that might produce those two images, but that would each go on to produce a different set of images. This result is easily extended to four or more oriented points.

This result shows us how to solve for the affine structure of an object of oriented points by just solving a set of linear equations, provided that we have three views of the object. But the need for three views is a non-trivial limitation. [20] suggested that affine structure is an intermediate representation that we can compute using less information than is required to determine rigid structure, which we can compute from three views. However, we see that this is not always true.

If we have more than three images of the points, we can readily find a least squares solution to the affine structure. In this case, we have more than three linear equations in three unknowns, so we could just find a least squares solution to these equations, estimating the coefficients that describe the hyperboloid corresponding to the unknown scene. However, it might be more accurate to use each image as a point in affine slope space, and fit these points to a hyperboloid by minimizing the distance from the points to the hyperboloid.

We can also use our results to determine when a restricted set of model groups might give rise to an invariant function. An especially interesting special case is that of model groups containing five points and undergoing a linear transformation. This is the smallest group that can produce invariants, because in general any four model points can appear as any four image points. Most systems based on invariants have used the smallest possible model groups, in order to limit the number of possible model groups they must consider (this is true of [22], [12] and [35], for example). We know that there is no function that is invariant over the class of all model groups with five points, so we ask whether some subset of these model groups could give rise to an invariant function. A set of model groups of five points will each produce a pair of lines in 2-D α-space and β-space. Furthermore, recall that these two lines will have the same slope, which means that two different models will produce lines that are either parallel in both spaces, or that intersect in both spaces. Therefore, an invariant function for groups of five points is possible only when all lines produced by all models are parallel. For example, if one model produces lines not parallel to the others, it will have an image in common with each of them, implying that the invariant function must be constant over all images produced by all models. The lines produced by all models will be parallel only when r_5, (see equation 1), is the same for all models, that is, when the ratio of the height above the model plane of the fourth point to the height of the fifth point is always the same. In fact, the class of all planar model groups is a special case of this condition.

Finally, we mention that our results for planar curves may be used to construct a model-based invariant. [38] has defined a model-based invariant as an image function that is constant for all images of one particular model group, and has demonstrated a model-based invariant for point features. As we noted, equation 5 allows us to derive a series of equations that express the coefficients of the image polynomial as a function of the model description, and of the image polynomial's center of mass. By plugging into these equations the actual coefficients that we find for an image polynomial, and the image curve's center of mass, we get a series of equations that is satisfied if and only if the image curves could be a projection of the model curves. As it stands, however, these model-based invariants are probably not useful, since the coefficients of a polynomial are a very unstable description of an image curve.

5 Conclusions

The main goal of this paper has been to demonstrate the power of an approach to matching which begins by analytically characterizing the set of all images that any model can produce. This approach provides us with some of the advantages offered by invariant representations, in the general 3-D to 2-D case in which true invariants do not exist. We have presented characterizations of the images that simple and oriented points and algebraic curves can produce when viewed with a linear transformation. In the first two cases, this gives us a simple way of conceptualizing the matching problem. We have shown that the problem of matching groups of 2-D image points to groups of 3-D model points is equivalent to the problem of matching pairs of lines to pairs of points in a high-dimensional space. We have shown that this becomes a problem of matching single points to single hyperbolic surfaces when we consider oriented point features. These characterizations are optimal. We have also produced a more complex analytic description of the images of planar curves, and described lower bounds to representing model groups undergoing other transformations.

We feel that this geometric formulation of the matching problem has considerable intuitive appeal. To make this appeal more concrete, we have shown how these results may be applied to a variety of different matching problems. Most directly, finding the best characterization of a model's images is fundamental to the problem of indexing using table lookup. We have shown that our representation of the images of point models as a pair of lines can lead to a simple, space efficient approach to indexing. We have also shown that our conception of matching readily leads to new results in structure from motion. We have also indicated how a geometric representation of an object's images can be used to understand when restricted classes of objects may produce invariants, also describing a model-based invariant for non-coplanar pairs of planar curves.

Within the framework addressed in this paper, many interesting questions remain open, particularly concerning different models of projection, and different types of features. In the case of scaled orthographic projection, we know that model groups of simple point features require a 2-D surface when represented in a single index space, but we do not know whether these surfaces can be decomposed into pairs of 1-D surfaces, or whether it is possible to represent these surfaces linearly. In the case of perspective projection, we know that a 3-D surface is needed in a single image space, but again, we do not know the best way to characterize this surface, or whether we can decompose it. The same is true of the more general, projective generalization of perspective projection.

We also would like to understand how to characterize the images produced by more complex models. There are many ways to extend from the type of models that we have considered. First, orientation is the first derivative of a curve; it would be useful to understand the behavior of higher order derivatives, such as the curvature at a point. It does not appear that our treatment of oriented points extends in a straight-forward way to allow us to understand the images of points with associated curvature. We would also like to characterize the images produced by 3-D algebraic curves. And our results on non-coplanar pairs of planar curves could be improved with the use of a more robust description of these curves. And, of course, in all these cases, we would like to find an analytic treatment of error, and also of partial occlusion. We hope, though, in this paper to have demonstrated some of the value of answering these questions.

Acknowledgements

This research was performed in part at the MIT Artificial Intelligence laboratory. Support for this research was provided in part by the University Research Initiative under Office of Naval Research contract N00014-86-K-0685, and in part by the Advanced Research Projects Agency under Army contract DACA76–85–C–0010 and under Office of Naval Research contract N00014–85–K–0124. Further support for this research was provided by the NEC Research Institute.

The author gratefully acknowledges the many suggestions of Todd Cass, David Clemens, and Eric Grimson, and the assistance with illustrations provided by David Clemens and Liz Edlind.

References

1. Basri, R. and Ullman, S., 1988, "The Alignment of Objects with Smooth Surfaces," *Second International Conference on Computer Vision*, pp. 482–488.
2. Bowyer, K. and C. Dyer, 1990, "Aspect Graphs: An Introduction and Survey of Recent Results," *International Journal of Imaging Systems and Technology*, 2:315-328.
3. Breuel, T., 1993, "The 3D Indexing Problem," IDIAP Memo 93-08.
4. Burns, J., R. Weiss, and E. Riseman, 1990, "View Variation of Point Set and Line Segment Features," *DARPA IU Workshop*:650-659.
5. Clemens, D. and D. Jacobs, 1990, "Model-Group Indexing for Recognition," *DARPA IU Workshop*:604-613.
6. Clemens, D. and Jacobs, D., 1991, "Space and Time Bounds on Model Indexing," *IEEE Transactions on Patern Analysis and Machine Intelligence*, 13(10):1007-1018.
7. Costa, M., R.M. Haralick, and L.G. Shapiro, 1990, "Optimal Affine-Invariant Point Matching," *Proceedings 6th Israel Conference on AI*, pp. 35–61.
8. Cutting, J., 1986, *Perception with an Eye for Motion*, MIT Press, Cambridge.
9. Cyganski, D. and J.A. Orr, 1985, "Applications of Tensor Theory to Object Recognition and Orientation Determination," *IEEE Transactions on Patern Analysis and Machine Intelligence*, 7(6):662-673.
10. Elliott, E., 1913, *Algebra of Quantics* Oxford University Press, Second Edition.
11. Faugeras, O., 1992, "What can be Seen in Three Dimensions with an Uncalibrated Stereo Rig?" *Second European Conference on Computer Vision*:563-578.
12. Forsyth, D., J.L. Mundy, A. Zisserman, C. Coelho, A. Heller, and C. Rothwell, 1991, "Invariant Descriptors for 3-D Object Recognition and Pose", *IEEE Transactions on Patern Analysis and Machine Intelligence*, 13(10):971–991.
13. Gigus, Z., J. Canny, and R. Seidel, 1991, "Efficiently Computing and Representing Aspect Graphs of Polyhedral Objects," *IEEE Transactions on Patern Analysis and Machine Intelligence*, 13(6):542-551.
14. Jacobs, D., 1989, "Grouping for Recognition," MIT AI Memo 1177.
15. Jacobs, D., 1991, "Optimal Matching of Planar Models in 3D Scenes," *IEEE Conference Computer Vision and Pattern Recognition*, pp. 269–274.
16. Jacobs, D., 1992, "Space Efficient 3D Model Indexing," *Conf. on Comp. Vis. and Pat. Rec.*, pp. 439–444.
17. Jacobs, D., 1992, "Recognizing 3-D Objects Using 2-D Images," MIT AI TR–1416.
18. Jacobs, D., 1993, "2-D Images of 3-D Oriented Points." *IEEE Conference on Computer Vision and Pattern Recognition*, pp. 226-232.
19. Keren, D. J. Subrahmonia, G. Taubin, D. Cooper, 1992, "Bounded and Unbounded Implicit Polynomial Curves and Surfaces, Mahalanobis Distances, and Geometric Invariants, for Robust Object Recognition," *DARPA IU Workshop*, pp. 769–777.

20. Koenderink, J. and van Doorn, A., 1991, "Affine Structure from Motion," *Journal of the Optical Society of America*, **8**(2):377-385.
21. Kriegman, D. and J. Ponce, 1990, *International Journal of Computer Vision*, **5**(2):119–136.
22. Lamdan, Y., J.T. Schwartz and H.J. Wolfson, 1990, "Affine Invariant Model-Based Object Recognition," *IEEE Transactions Robotics and Automation*, **6**:578–589.
23. Lamdan, Y. & H.J. Wolfson, 1988, "Geometric Hashing: A General and Efficient Model-Based Recognition Scheme," *Second International Conference Computer Vision*, pp. 238–249.
24. Moses, Y. and Ullman, S. 1992, "Limitations of Non Model-Based Recognition Schemes," *Second European Conference on Computer Vision*:820-828.
25. Rigoutsos, I. & R. Hummel,, 1991, "Robust Similarity Invariant Matching in the Presence of Noise," *Eighth Israeli Conference on Artificial Intelligence and Computer Vision*, Tel Aviv.
26. Rothwell C., A. Zisserman, J. Mundy, and D. Forsyth, 1992, "Efficient Model Library Access by Projectively Invariant Indexing Functions," *IEEE Conference on Computer Vision and Pattern Recognition*, pp. 109-114.
27. Rothwell, C. A., Forsyth, D. A., Zisserman, A., Mundy, J. L, 1993, "Extracting projective structure from single perspective view of 3D point sets," *Proc. of 4th Int. Conf. on Computer Vision*, 573–582.
28. Schwartz, J. and M. Sharir, 1987, "Identification of Partially Obscured Objects in Two and Three Dimensions by Matching Noisy Characteristic Curves," *The International Journal of Robotics Research*, **6**(2):29-44.
29. Shashua, A., 1991, "Correspondence and Affine Shape from Two Orthographic Views: Motion and Recognition," MIT AI Memo 1327.
30. Shashua, A., 1993, "On Geometric and Algebraic Aspects of 3D Affine and Projective Structures from Perspective 2D Views," MIT AI Memo 1405.
31. Stein, F. and G. Medioni, 1992, "Structural Indexing: Efficient 3-D Object Recognition," *IEEE Transactions on Patern Analysis and Machine Intelligence*, **14**(2):125-145.
32. Thompson, D. & J.L. Mundy, 1987, "Three-Dimensional Model Matching From an Unconstrained Viewpoint", *Proceedings IEEE Conference Rob. Aut.*, pp. 208-220.
33. Tomasi, C. and T. Kanade, 1992, "Shape and Motion from Image Streams Under Orthography: a Factorization Method," *International Journal of Computer Vision*, pp.137-154.
34. Ullman, S. and Basri, R., 1991, "Recognition by Linear Combinations of Models," *IEEE Transactions on Patern Analysis and Machine Intelligence*, **13**(10):992-1007.
35. Van Gool, L., P. Kempenaers & A. Oosterlinck, 1991, "Recognition and Semi-Differential Invariants," *IEEE Conference Computer Vision and Pattern Recognition*, pp. 454–460.
36. Wallace, A., 1987, "Matching Segmented Scenes to Models Using Pairwise Relationships Between Features," *Image and Vision Computing*, **5**(2):114-120.
37. Wayner, P.C., 1991, "Efficiently Using Invariant Theory for Model-based Matching," *IEEE Conference Computer Vision and Pattern Recognition*:473-478.
38. Weinshall, D., 1991, "Model Based Invariants for Linear Model Acquisition and Recognition," IBM Research Report RC-17705 (#77262).
39. Weiss, I., 1988, "Projective Invariants of Shape," *DARPA IU Workshop*, pp. 1125–1134.

Recognition by Combinations of Model Views: Alignment and Invariance

Ronen Basri

The Weizmann Institute of Science, Rehovot 76100, Israel

Abstract. A scheme for recognition of 3D objects from single 2D images is introduced. An object is modeled in this scheme by a small set of its views with the correspondence between the views. Novel views of the object are obtained by linearly combining the model views. The scheme accurately handles rigid objects under weak-perspective projection, and it is extended to handle rigid objects with smooth bounding surfaces and articulated objects. Unlike in other schemes, explicit 3D representations of the objects are not used. The presented scheme can be used both under an alignment framework and as a means for deriving object-specific invariant functions for indexing. Under an alignment framework, given a model and an image, the coefficients of the linear combination that aligns the model with the image need to be recovered. A small number of points in the image and their corresponding points in the model can be used for this purpose, or a search can be conducted in the space of possible coefficients. Alternatively, the scheme can be used to derive functions that are invariant to viewpoint changes of a specific object. A number of such functions are derived in this paper.

1 Introduction

Visual object recognition is a process of identifying 3D objects from their 2D projections. Recognition is difficult partly because objects may look different from different viewing positions. Two common approaches to overcome this difficulty are alignment and invariance. *Alignment* attempts to overcome view variations by bringing the object model and the image into a common coordinate frame. The *invariance* approach generates functions that eliminate from the image any view dependent elements. This paper proposes a scheme for recognition that can be used both in an alignment framework and as a means for deriving invariant functions for specific objects.

Alignment is a process in which object models are compared to the incoming image in a two-step procedure. First, the position and orientation (*pose*) of the observed object is hypothesized. Then, the object's appearance from this pose is compared with the actual image [BU93, CA87, FH86, FB81, HU90, Lo85, Ul89]. Existing systems often assume that a stored set of 3D models of the objects is given. These models can be acquired (in a preceding learning phase) by applying shape recovery algorithms to images of the objects or by using non-visual sensors. Recently, a few systems have been proposed that represent objects by sets of their 2D images [AP87, Va87, TM87]. These systems usually take the naive approach, in which all the available images of the objects are stored. This approach suffers from two shortcomings. First, it requires relatively large storage, and second, it does not enable the recognition of objects from their novel views.

The *invariance* approach to recognition uses a stored function that when applied to any image of a certain object returns the same value. This value is then used to index into the appropriate representation of the recognized object. Most existing invariant systems apply to planar objects [We88, LSW87, FMZCHR91] or to other restricted classes of objects (e.g., [RFZM93]). In these cases the invariant functions (or their parameters) can be constructed from single images of the objects. This, however, is not possible when recognition of 3D objects from single 2D images is attempted. Recent studies indicate that in this case there exist no general-case invariant functions [BWR91, CJ91, MU92]. As a result, indexing algorithms that use the so called *model-based invariants* [We93] were proposed. These invariants can be learned from several images of the object.

The ability to learn object representations from images is important for building fully-autonomous vision systems. Recognition in these systems is composed of two phases. The first phase is an off-line *learning* phase in which (familiar) images of objects are used to generate object models (e.g., by reconstructing their 3D shape or by deriving the appropriate parameters in the corresponding invariant functions). The second phase is the on-line *recognition* phase in which the stored models are compared with the incoming (novel) image. The scheme below is unique since it explicitly specifies the relation between familiar and novel images of objects. It can therefore be used to construct an alignment system in which objects are represented by (small subsets of) their familiar images, or to learn object invariances from these images. The method applies to rigid (polyhedral) objects under weak-perspective projection (that is, orthographic projection followed by an arbitrary uniform scaling), and is extended to handle rigid objects with smooth bounding surfaces and articulated objects.

The rest of the paper is divided into two parts. In Section 2 the scheme for recognition by combinations of model views is outlined. Section 3 discusses the use of this scheme under an alignment framework and as a means for deriving invariant functions. More details can be found in [Ba93, UB91, WB93].

2   Recognition by Combinations of Model Views

The scheme for recognizing 3D objects is based on the following observation. If a view is represented by vectors that contain the position of feature points in the image, then in many cases the novel views of objects can be expressed by linearly combining small numbers of the objects' views. In the scheme below recognition is a problem of determining whether an incoming image can or cannot be obtained by a linear combination of a given model images. We refer to this scheme as the linear combinations (LC) scheme. Below we show (Section 2.1) that images of rigid (polygonal) 3D objects obtained under weak-perspective projection can be expressed by linear combinations of as low as two views of the object. Extensions to rigid objects with smooth bounding surfaces and to articulated objects are briefly mentioned in Section 2.2. A detailed description of the scheme can be found in [Ba93, UB91].

2.1 Rigid Objects

We begin with the following definitions. Given an image I containing n feature points, $\mathbf{p}_1 = (x_1, y_1), ..., \mathbf{p}_n = (x_n, y_n)$, a *view* V_I is a pair of vectors $\mathbf{x}, \mathbf{y} \in \mathcal{R}^n$, where $\mathbf{x} = (x_1, ..., x_n)^T$ and $\mathbf{y} = (y_1, ..., y_n)^T$ contain the location of the feature points, $\mathbf{p}_1, ..., \mathbf{p}_n$, in the image. A *model* is a set of views $\{V_1, ..., V_k\}$. The location vectors in these views are ordered in correspondence, namely, the first point in V_1 is the projection of the same physical point on the object as the first point in V_2, and so forth. The objects we consider undergo rigid transformations, namely, rotations and translations in space. We assume that the images are obtained by weak-perspective projection, namely, orthographic projection followed by a uniform scaling.

Below we show that the novel views of a rigid object can be expressed as linear combinations of a small number of its views. The proof proceeds in the following way. First, we show (Theorem 1) that the set of views of a rigid object is contained in a four-dimensional linear space. Any four linearly independent vectors from this space therefore can be used to span the space. Consequently, we show (Theorem 2) that two views suffice to represent the space. Any other view of the object can be expressed as (two) linear combinations of the two basis views. Finally, we show (Theorem 3) that not every point in this 4D space necessarily corresponds to a legal view of the object. The coefficients satisfy two quadratic constraints. These constraints depend on the transformation relating the two model views. A third view can be used to derive the constraints.

Theorem 1. *The views of a rigid object are contained in a four-dimensional linear space.*

Proof. Consider an object O that contains n feature points $\mathbf{P}_1 = (X_1, Y_1, Z_1), ..., \mathbf{P}_n = (X_n, Y_n, Z_n)$. Let I be an image of O obtained by a rotation R, translation $\mathbf{t}$, and scaling s, followed by an orthographic projection, Π. Let $\mathbf{p}_1 = (x_1, y_1), ..., \mathbf{p}_n = (x_n, y_n)$ be the projected location in I of the points $\mathbf{P}_1, ..., \mathbf{P}_n$ respectively. For every $1 \le i \le n$

$$\mathbf{p}_i = s\Pi(R\mathbf{P}_i + \mathbf{t}) \tag{1}$$

more explicitly, these equations can be written as

$$\begin{aligned} x_i &= s(r_{11}X_i + r_{12}Y_i + r_{13}Z_i + t_x) \\ y_i &= s(r_{21}X_i + r_{22}Y_i + r_{23}Z_i + t_y) \end{aligned} \tag{2}$$

where $\{r_{ij}\}$ are the components of the rotation matrix, and t_x, t_y are the horizontal and the vertical components of the translation vector. (Under weak-perspective projection the depth component of the translation vector, t_z, affects only the value of s.) Since these equations hold for every $1 \le i \le n$, we can rewrite them in a vector notation. Denote $\mathbf{X} = (X_1, ..., X_n)^T$, $\mathbf{Y} = (Y_1, ..., Y_n)^T$,

$\mathbf{Z} = (Z_1, ..., Z_n)^T$, $\mathbf{1} = (1, ..., 1)^T$, $\mathbf{x} = (x_1, ..., x_n)^T$, and $\mathbf{y} = (y_1, ..., y_n)^T$, we obtain that

$$\mathbf{x} = a_1\mathbf{X} + a_2\mathbf{Y} + a_3\mathbf{Z} + a_4\mathbf{1}$$
$$\mathbf{y} = b_1\mathbf{X} + b_2\mathbf{Y} + b_3\mathbf{Z} + b_4\mathbf{1} \tag{3}$$

where

$$\begin{array}{ll}
a_1 = sr_{11} & b_1 = sr_{21} \\
a_2 = sr_{12} & b_2 = sr_{22} \\
a_3 = sr_{13} & b_3 = sr_{23} \\
a_4 = st_x & b_4 = st_y
\end{array} \tag{4}$$

The vectors $\mathbf{x}$ and $\mathbf{y}$ can therefore be expressed as linear combinations of four vectors, $\mathbf{X}$, $\mathbf{Y}$, $\mathbf{Z}$, and $\mathbf{1}$. Notice that changing the view would result merely in a change in the coefficients. We can therefore conclude that

$$\mathbf{x}, \mathbf{y} \in span\{\mathbf{X}, \mathbf{Y}, \mathbf{Z}, \mathbf{1}\} \tag{5}$$

for any view of O. Note that if translation is omitted the views space is reduced to a three-dimensional one. $\square$

Theorem 2. *The views space of a rigid object O can be constructed from two views of O.*

Proof. Theorem 1 above establishes that the space of views of a rigid object is four-dimensional. Any four linearly independent vectors in this space can be used to span the space. The constant vector, $\mathbf{1}$, belongs to this space. Therefore, only three more vectors remain to be found. An image supplies two vectors. Two images supply four, which is already more than enough to span the space (assuming the two images are related by some rotation in depth, otherwise they are linearly dependent). Let $V_1 = \{\mathbf{x}_1, \mathbf{y}_1\}$ and $V_2 = \{\mathbf{x}_2, \mathbf{y}_2\}$ be two views of O, a novel view $V' = \{\mathbf{x}', \mathbf{y}'\}$ of O can be expressed as two linear combinations of the four vectors $\mathbf{x}_1$, $\mathbf{y}_1$, $\mathbf{x}_2$, and $\mathbf{1}$. The remaining vector, $\mathbf{y}_2$, already depends on the other four vectors. (See also [KV91, Po90].) $\square$

Up to this point we have shown that the views space of a rigid object is contained in a four-dimensional linear space. Theorem 3 below establishes that not every point in this space corresponds to a legal view of the object. The coefficients of the linear combination satisfy two quadratic constraints.

Theorem 3. *The coefficients satisfy two quadratic constraints, which can be derived from three images.*

Proof. Consider the coefficients $a_1, ..., a_4$, $b_1, ..., b_4$ from Theorem 1. Since R is a rotation matrix, its row vectors are orthonormal, and therefore the coefficients satisfy the following quadratic constraints

$$a_1^2 + a_2^2 + a_3^2 = b_1^2 + b_2^2 + b_3^2$$
$$a_1b_1 + a_2b_2 + a_3b_3 = 0 \tag{6}$$

Choosing a different basis to represent the object (as we did in Theorem 2) will change the constraints. The constraints depend on the transformation that separates the model views. Given an object $O = \{\mathbf{X}, \mathbf{Y}, \mathbf{Z}\}$, let $V_1 = \{\mathbf{x}_1, \mathbf{y}_1\}$ and $V_2 = \{\mathbf{x}_2, \mathbf{y}_2\}$ be two model views of O such that $\mathbf{x}_1 = \mathbf{X}$, $\mathbf{y}_1 = \mathbf{Y}$, and V_2 is obtained by a rotation U, translation $\mathbf{t}'$, and scaling s'. According to Theorem 2, a novel view $V' = \{x', y'\}$ of O can be expressed as

$$\mathbf{x}' = \alpha_1 \mathbf{x}_1 + \alpha_2 \mathbf{y}_1 + \alpha_3 \mathbf{x}_2 + \alpha_4 \mathbf{1}$$
$$\mathbf{y}' = \beta_1 \mathbf{x}_1 + \beta_2 \mathbf{y}_1 + \beta_3 \mathbf{x}_2 + \beta_4 \mathbf{1} \tag{7}$$

for some $\alpha_1, ..., \alpha_4$, $\beta_1, ..., \beta_4$. Substituting the value of $\mathbf{x}_2$

$$\mathbf{x}_2 = s'(u_{11}\mathbf{X} + u_{12}\mathbf{Y} + u_{13}\mathbf{Z} + t'_x)$$
$$\mathbf{y}_2 = s'(u_{21}\mathbf{X} + u_{22}\mathbf{Y} + u_{23}\mathbf{Z} + t'_y) \tag{8}$$

into Eq. 7, we obtain

$$\mathbf{x}' = (\alpha_1 + \alpha_3 s' u_{11})\mathbf{X} + (\alpha_2 + \alpha_3 s' u_{12})\mathbf{Y} + (\alpha_3 s' u_{13})\mathbf{Z} + (\alpha_4 + \alpha_3 s' t'_x)\mathbf{1}$$
$$\mathbf{y}' = (\beta_1 + \beta_3 s' u_{11})\mathbf{X} + (\beta_2 + \beta_3 s' u_{12})\mathbf{Y} + (\beta_3 s' u_{13})\mathbf{Z} + (\beta_4 + \beta_3 s' t'_x)\mathbf{1} \tag{9}$$

which contains the explicit values of the coefficients $a_1, ..., a_4$, $b_1, ..., b_4$ from Eq. 6. Substituting these values into Eq. 6, we obtain the following constraints on $\alpha_1, ..., \alpha_4$, $\beta_1, ..., \beta_4$:

$$\alpha_1^2 + \alpha_2^2 + \alpha_3^2 - \beta_1^2 - \beta_2^2 - \beta_3^2 = 2(\beta_1\beta_3 - \alpha_1\alpha_3)u_{11} + 2(\beta_2\beta_3 - \alpha_2\alpha_3)u_{12}$$
$$\alpha_1\beta_1 + \alpha_2\beta_2 + \alpha_3\beta_3 + (\alpha_1\beta_3 + \alpha_3\beta_1)u_{11} + (\alpha_2\beta_3 + \alpha_3\beta_2)u_{12} = 0 \tag{10}$$

where u_{11} and u_{12} are the two upper left components of U. To derive the constraints, the values of u_{11} and u_{12} should be recovered. A third view can be used for this purpose. When a third view of the object is given, the constraints supply two linear equations in u_{11} and u_{12}, and, therefore, in general, the values of u_{11} and u_{12} can be recovered from the two constraints. This proof suggests a simple, essentially linear structure from motion algorithm that resembles the method used in [HL89, KV91, TK91, Ul79], but the details will not be discussed further here. □

The scheme therefore is the following. An object is modeled by a set of views, with the correspondence between the views, together with the two constraints. Novel views of the object are generated by linearly combining the model views. Applying the quadratic constraints to the coefficients guarantees that the novel views in fact represent a rigid transformation of the object. In recognition applications, the obtained views are compared with the actual image, and if a satisfactory match is achieved the object's identity is determined. Figure 1 shows the application of the linear combination scheme to an artificially made object.

Although two views are sufficient to represent an object, in order to reduce noise and occlusion one may seek to use additional views to improve the accuracy of the model. The problem then is the following. Given l view vectors $\mathbf{v}_1, ..., \mathbf{v}_l$, recover the nearest four-dimensional hyperplane to these vectors. The obtained

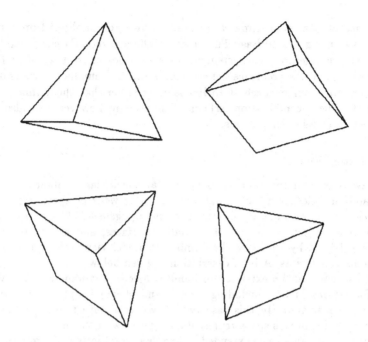

Fig. 1. Generating views of a pyramid. Top: two model pictures of a pyramid. Bottom: two of their linear combinations.

hyperplane is the linear sub-space that best explains the view vectors. The nearest hyperplane can be found by applying principal components techniques. A detailed algorithm can be found in [UB91] (see also [TK91]).

For transparent objects, a single model is sufficient to predict their appearance from all possible viewpoints. For opaque objects, due to self occlusion, a number of models is required to represent the objects from all aspects. These models are not necessarily independent. For example, in the case of a convex object as few as four images are sufficient to represent the object from all possible viewpoints. A pair of images, one from the "front" and another one from the "back" contains a single appearance of each object point. Two such pairs contain two appearances of all object points, which is what is required to obtain a complete representation of all object points. For concave objects additional views may be required.

Note that positive values of the coefficients ("convex combinations") correspond to interpolation between the model views, while extrapolation is obtained by assigning one or more of the coefficients with negative values. This distinction between intermediate views and other views is important, since if two views of the object come from the same aspect (namely, include the same parts of the object), then intermediate views are likely to also come from that aspect, while in other views other aspects of the objects may be observed.

A method that approximates the space of views of an object from a number of its views using Radial Basis Functions [PG90] was recently suggested [PE90]. Similar to our method, the system represents an object by a set of its familiar views with the correspondence between the views. The number of views used for this approximation, between 10 to 100, is much larger than the number required under the linear combinations scheme. The system, however, can also handle perspective views of the objects.

2.2 Extensions

We have shown in the previous section that the linear combinations scheme accurately handles rigid (polygonal) objects under weak-perspective projection. The scheme can also handle objects that undergo general affine transformation in 3D, rigid objects with smooth bounding surfaces, and articulated objects. This is achieved by changing the number of model views, or by changing the functional constraints. A brief description is given below.

The scheme can be extended to handle objects that undergo general affine transformations in 3D (including stretch and shear) simply by ignoring the quadratic constraints. In this case two views are required to span the space, and every point in this space represents a legal view of the object.

The scheme can also be extended to handle rigid objects with smooth bounding surfaces. The problem with such an object is that its contours appear in different locations on the object at different views. Using three rather than two views (the space of views for such objects is six- rather than four-dimensional), the curvature of the points along the contour is (implicitly) taken into account, providing a better prediction of the contour position following rotation. For details see [BU93, UB91].

Finally, articulated objects can also be modeled by our scheme. An articulated object is a collection of links connected by joints. Each link is a rigid component. It can move independently of the other links when only its joints constrain its motion. The space of views of an articulated object with l links is at most $(4 \times l)$-dimensional. The joints contribute additional constraints, some of which may be linear, and they reduce the rank of the space, others are nonlinear, in which case they are treated in the same way the quadratic constraints are treated in the rigid case. For example, an object with two rigid links connected by a rotational joint can be modeled by a six-dimensional linear space [Ba93]. Three views can be used in these cases to span the space. Articulated objects with different numbers of links or with different types of joints require different number of views. Advance knowledge of the number of links and the type of joints, however, is not required. When sufficiently many views are presented, the correct rank of the views space can be recovered using principal components analysis.

Figure 2 shows the application of the scheme to several objects with smooth bounding surfaces and to articulated objects. The figure shows views of the objects generated by combining several model views and the matching of these views to actual contour images of the objects.

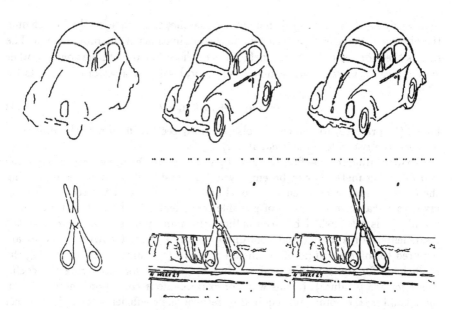

Fig. 2. Generating views of a VW car and a pair of scissors. Top: matching the model to a picture of the VW car. A linear combination of model images (left), an actual edge image (middle), and the two images overlayed (right). Bottom: matching a model to a picture a scissors. A linear combinations of model images (left), an actual edge image (middle), and the two images overlayed (right). The prediction images and the actual ones align almost perfectly.

3 Applying the LC Scheme

In the previous section we have introduced an image representation for object recognition. An object is modeled in this scheme by a small set of its images with the correspondence between the images. Novel images of the object are expressed by linear combinations of the model images. In addition, the coefficients of these linear combinations may follow certain functional constraints.

In this section we discuss how this representation can be used in a recognition system. The task assigned to the recognition system is to determine, given an incoming image, whether the image belongs to the space of views of a particular model. We discuss two principal methods to reach such a decision. The first (Section 3.1) involves alignment of the model to the image by explicitly recovering the coefficients of the linear combination, and the second (Section 3.2) involves the derivation and application of object invariances.

3.1 Recovering the Alignment Coefficients

The alignment approach to object recognition identifies objects by first recovering the transformation that aligns the model with the incoming image, and then verifying that the transformed model matches the image. In the LC scheme, the observed image is expressed by linear combinations of the model views. The task is therefore to recover the coefficients of these linear combinations. In other words, given a view $\mathbf{v}'$ and a model $\{\mathbf{v}_1, ..., \mathbf{v}_k\}$ we seek a set of coefficients for which

$$\mathbf{v}' = a_1\mathbf{v}_1 + ... + a_k\mathbf{v}_k \tag{11}$$

holds. (In practice, to overcome noise, we may seek to minimize the difference between the two sides of this equation.)

To determine the coefficients that align a model to the image either one of the two following methods can be employed. The first method involves recovering the correspondence between the model and the image, and the second method involves a search in the space of possible coefficients. In the first method correspondence is established between sufficiently many points so as to recover the coefficients. For a model that contains k views, at least k correspondences are required to solve a system of $2k$ linear equations (k equations for recovering the coefficients for the x-values, and another k equations for recovering the coefficients for the y-values). In this way, for example, four correspondences between model and image points are required to recover the coefficients for a rigid object by solving a linear system. If in addition we consider the quadratic constraints this number is reduced to three. This resembles the three-point alignment suggested by Huttenlocher and Ullman [HU90, Ul89]. Applications of this method usually try to match triplets of model points to all combinations of triplets of image points to guarantee recognition.

An alternative approach to determining the coefficients involves a search in the space of possible coefficients. This method does not require the correspondence between the model and the image. The idea is the following. Using global properties of the observed object, such as axes of elongation, an initial guess for the values of the coefficients can be made. This initial guess can be then improved by an iterative process. At every step in this process a new set of coefficients is generated. The model is transformed using these coefficients, and the result is compared to the actual image. If the two match, the observed object is recognized, otherwise the process is repeated until it converges. Minimization techniques such as gradient descent may be employed to reduce the complexity of the search. Such techniques, however, involve the risk of converging into a local minimum, which occasionally may be significantly worse than the desired solution.

3.2 Object invariances

One difficulty with the alignment approach arises when it is expected to recognize a large variety of objects. A naive implementation of alignment algorithms will then involve the comparison of the image against each of the models stored in memory. This exhaustive search can be avoided if invariant properties of the observed object can be extracted. Unfortunately, it has been shown recently that single 2D projections of 3D objects contain no general-case invariants [BWR91,

CJ91, MU92]. These findings prompted a search for new techniques for indexing. These techniques involve the application of the so called *model-based invariant functions* [We93].

A model-based invariant is a function $f(M; \mathbf{v})$ that returns some constant value (say zero) if and only if $\mathbf{v}$ is a view of M. (We refer to such functions as *object-specific* since they identify the images of a single object. Note that these functions are not general-case view invariant.) Model-based invariants are used for indexing in the following manner. Given an image $\mathbf{v}$ we use f to find which of the stored models in the library could have generated $\mathbf{v}$. For example, Jacobs [Ja92] showed that the set of affine images of an object can be represented as straight lines in some hyperspace. (Images are points in this hyperspace.) Under this representation $f(M, \mathbf{v}) = 0$ if and only if the line corresponding to the model M passes through the point corresponding to the image $\mathbf{v}$. Using this formulation, a lookup table containing a discrete representation of the hyperspace is constructed, and given an image $\mathbf{v}$, indexing is obtained by locating those lines that pass through the table entry corresponding to $\mathbf{v}$.

Below we construct several examples for object-specific invariant functions. We begin by building a function that takes into account the enveloping linear space spanned by the model views. Later, we construct functions that are equivalent to imposing the quadratic constraints. We conclude by combining the linear function with the quadratic ones. The use of these functions for indexing is not addressed here. Note that the application of these functions does not require the explicit recovery of the alignment coefficients. However, it assumes that the correspondence between the model and the image points is given. This assumption can be overcome by applying the functions over all possible subsets of image points.

Note that according to our definition if $\mathbf{v}$ is not an instance of M then $f(M, \mathbf{v})$ may return any non-zero value. While this property is sufficient in the error-free case, a more robust definition is required in the presence of errors. In this case it is desired that the functions would change monotonically with increasing amounts of noise. The natural choice for such functions would be metrics that are related to the distance between the given image and the space of views of the object. The definition of such metrics is our concern in the discussion below.

Linear invariants. In the LC scheme a view is treated as a point in $\mathcal{R}^n$. A view is an instance of an object if it belongs to the space of views spanned by the object's model. In particular, such a view must be contained in the linear space spanned by the model views. A possible definition for an object-specific invariant function is the distance between the incoming view and the linear space of view spanned by the object model. This function returns zero if and only if the given view is an affine view of the object. We can derive this function by projecting the incoming view to the views space of the object.

Let $\mathbf{v}_1, ..., \mathbf{v}_k$ be the model views. ($\mathbf{v}_i$ may contain either the x- or the y-coordinates of the object's points in a certain model view.) Denote $M = [\mathbf{v}_1, ..., \mathbf{v}_k]$, M is a $k \times n$ matrix. Theorem 4 below defines an operator, L. L

obtains a view vector $\mathbf{v}'$ and returns the difference vector between $\mathbf{v}'$ and the linear space spanned by the model views, $\mathbf{v}_1, ..., \mathbf{v}_k$.

Theorem 4. *Let*

$$L = I - MM^+$$

where I is the identity matrix, and $M^+ = (M^T M)^{-1} M^T$ denotes the pseudo inverse of M. Then $L\mathbf{v}' = 0$ if and only if $\mathbf{v}'$ is a linear combination of $\mathbf{v}_1, ..., \mathbf{v}_k$.

Proof. $L\mathbf{v}' = 0$ if and only if $\mathbf{v}' = MM^+\mathbf{v}'$. MM^+ is a projection operator; it projects the vector $\mathbf{v}'$ onto the column space of M. Therefore, the equality holds if and only if $\mathbf{v}'$ belongs to the column space of M, in which case it can be expressed by a linear combination of $\mathbf{v}_1, ..., \mathbf{v}_k$. The matrix L is therefore invariant for all views of the object; it maps all its views to zero. □

We can therefore construct a linear distance function as follows

$$l(\mathbf{x}, \mathbf{y}) = \| L\mathbf{x} \|^2 + \| L\mathbf{y} \|^2 \tag{12}$$

where $\mathbf{x} = (x_1, ..., x_n)$ and $\mathbf{y} = (y_1, ..., y_n)$ contain the image coordinates of the feature points.

Note that L only considers the linear envelop of the views space of the object. It does not verify any of the quadratic constraints. This means that the operator L would return zero also for a stretched images of the object (as it would for any image obtained by applying a general affine transformation to the object). Functions that verify the quadratic constraints are presented later in this section.

The operator L can be made associative. The idea is the following. Suppose L is a linear operator that maps all model views to the same single vector, that is, $\mathbf{u} = L\mathbf{v}_1 = ... = L\mathbf{v}_k$. Since L is linear it maps combinations of the model to the same vector (up to a scale factor). Let $\mathbf{v}'$ be a novel view of the object, $\mathbf{v}' = \sum_{i=1}^{n} a_i \mathbf{v}_i$, then

$$L\mathbf{v}' = L \sum_{i=1}^{n} a_i \mathbf{v}_i = \sum_{i=1}^{n} a_i L\mathbf{v}_i = (\sum_{i=1}^{n} a_i)\mathbf{u} \tag{13}$$

$\mathbf{u}$ serves as a name for the model, and it can be either zero (in which case we obtain an operator that is identical to the operator in Theorem 4 above) or it can be a familiar view of the object (e.g., $\mathbf{v}_1$).

A constructive definition of the associative operator is given below. Let $\{\mathbf{v}_1, ..., \mathbf{v}_n\}$ be a basis for $\mathcal{R}^n$ such that the first k vectors are composed of the model views. Denote

$$V = [\mathbf{v}_1, ..., \mathbf{v}_k, \mathbf{v}_{k+1}, ..., \mathbf{v}_n]$$
$$U = [\mathbf{u}\ , ..., \mathbf{u}\ , \mathbf{v}_{k+1}, ..., \mathbf{v}_n]$$

(We filled the matrix U with the vectors $\mathbf{v}_{k+1}, ..., \mathbf{v}_n$ so that the operator L would preserve the magnitude of noise if such is added to the novel view. These vectors can in principle be replaced by any vectors that are linearly independent of **u**.) We require that

$$LV = U \qquad (14)$$

Therefore

$$L = UV^{-1} \qquad (15)$$

(Notice that since V is a basis for $\mathcal{R}^n$ its inverse exists.) We have implemented the associative version of the recognition operator and applied it to the pyramid from Figure 1. The results are given in Figure 3. It can be seen that when this operator is applied to a novel view of the pyramid it returns a familiar view of the pyramid, and when it is applied to some other object it returns an unknown view.

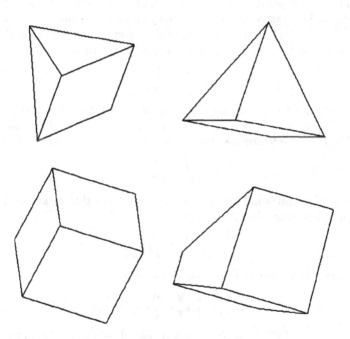

Fig. 3. Top: applying an associative "pyramidal" operator to a pyramid (left) returns a model view of the pyramid (right, compare with Figure 1 top left). Bottom: applying the same operator to a cube (left) returns an unfamiliar image (right).

Quadratic invariants. As has already been mentioned, the functions developed above identify all the images that can be expressed by linear combinations of the model views. Therefore, in the case of a rigid object, these functions would confuse images obtained by applying a general affine transformation (including stretch and shear) to the object with rigid images of the object. In order to verify that the given image is indeed a rigid image of the object the coefficients of the corresponding linear combination must satisfy the two quadratic constraints (Eq. 6 and 10). In this section we develop functions that reflect these quadratic constraints. The construction of the functions is borrowed from [We93].

To develop the desired functions, we need to substitute the coefficients in the quadratic constraints with variables that depend on the image only. We do that in the following way. Consider a 3D object O with n feature points $\mathbf{p}_1 = (X_1, Y_1, Z_1), ..., \mathbf{p}_n = (X_n, Y_n, Z_n)$. Denote

$$P = \begin{pmatrix} X_1 & Y_1 & Z_1 \\ & \vdots & \\ X_n & Y_n & Z_n \end{pmatrix}$$

a matrix of object point positions. Let I be an image of O obtained by applying a scaled rotation matrix R to O. Denote by $\mathbf{r}_1, \mathbf{r}_2, \mathbf{r}_3$ the three row vectors of R. Denote $\mathbf{q}_1 = (x_1, y_1), ..., \mathbf{q}_n = (x_n, y_n)$ the corresponding positions of $P_1, ..., P_n$ in I, and denote $\mathbf{x} = (x_1, ..., x_n)$ and $\mathbf{y} = (y_1, ..., y_n)$ then

$$\begin{aligned} \mathbf{x} &= P\mathbf{r}_1 \\ \mathbf{y} &= P\mathbf{r}_2 \end{aligned} \tag{16}$$

(Translation can be ignored by assuming that both the object and the image points are translated such that their centroid lies on the origin, see [WB93].) Assuming P is overdetermined we can write

$$\begin{aligned} \mathbf{r}_1 &= P^+\mathbf{x} \\ \mathbf{r}_2 &= P^+\mathbf{y} \end{aligned} \tag{17}$$

The quadratic constraints are equivalent to requiring that $\mathbf{r}_1$ and $\mathbf{r}_2$ be orthogonal and equal-norm, that is

$$\begin{aligned} \mathbf{r}_1^T \cdot \mathbf{r}_2 &= 0 \\ \mathbf{r}_1^T \cdot \mathbf{r}_1 &= \mathbf{r}_2^T \cdot \mathbf{r}_2 \end{aligned} \tag{18}$$

Substituting for $\mathbf{r}_1$ and $\mathbf{r}_2$ using Eq. 17 we obtain

$$\begin{aligned} (P^+\mathbf{x})^T \cdot P^+\mathbf{y} &= 0 \\ (P^+\mathbf{x})^T \cdot P^+\mathbf{x} &= (P^+\mathbf{y})^T \cdot P^+\mathbf{y} \end{aligned} \tag{19}$$

Denote $B = (P^+)^T P^+$ (B is $n \times n$ positive semi-definite), we obtain the identities

$$\begin{aligned} \mathbf{x}^T B\mathbf{y} &= 0 \\ \mathbf{x}^T B\mathbf{x} &= \mathbf{y}^T B\mathbf{y} \end{aligned} \tag{20}$$

from which we can derive two invariant functions

$$\begin{aligned} q_1(\mathbf{x}, \mathbf{y}) &= \mathbf{x}^T B\mathbf{y} \\ q_2(\mathbf{x}, \mathbf{y}) &= \mathbf{x}^T B\mathbf{x} - \mathbf{y}^T B\mathbf{y} \end{aligned} \tag{21}$$

Note that in our definition B is dependent upon the 3D coordinates of the object points. A constructive algorithm to derive B from a set of images is given in [We93].

Combining the linear and the quadratic constraints. Till now we have developed invariant functions that eliminate either the linear or the quadratic effects of viewing position. In this section we attempt to combine these functions into a single function.

Given a matrix of n object point positions P and an image I with corresponding location vectors $\mathbf{x}$ and $\mathbf{y}$, a natural definition to the function we seek is the following. Consider the rigid view of P that is nearest to I, the sum of distances between the points in this nearest view and their corresponding points in I defines a distance function that is optimal in image-space. (For a discussion of possible criteria for optimality see [WB93].) Formally, the distance function $n(\mathbf{x}, \mathbf{y})$ is given by

$$n(\mathbf{x}, \mathbf{y}) = \min_{\mathbf{r}_1, \mathbf{r}_2 \in \mathcal{R}^3} \|\mathbf{x} - P\mathbf{r}_1\|^2 + \|\mathbf{y} - P\mathbf{r}_2\|^2$$
$$\text{s.t. } \mathbf{r}_1^T \cdot \mathbf{r}_2 = 0, \quad \mathbf{r}_1^T \cdot \mathbf{r}_1 = \mathbf{r}_2^T \cdot \mathbf{r}_2 \tag{22}$$

Unfortunately, a closed form solution for $n(\mathbf{x}, \mathbf{y})$ is not yet known. However, using the linear and the quadratic invariants we can bound $n(\mathbf{x}, \mathbf{y})$ from both above and below. Let $l(\mathbf{x}, \mathbf{y})$ be the linear invariant (Eq. 12), and denote

$$q(\mathbf{x}, \mathbf{y}) = \frac{1}{2}\left(\mathbf{x}^T B \mathbf{x} + \mathbf{y}^T B \mathbf{y} - 2\sqrt{\mathbf{x}^T B \mathbf{x} \cdot \mathbf{y}^T B \mathbf{y} - (\mathbf{x}^T B \mathbf{y})^2}\right) \tag{23}$$

Note that $q(\mathbf{x}, \mathbf{y})$ combines the two quadratic invariants (Eq. 21). It measures the amount of "affine deformations" applied to the object in the image (see [WB93]). The following theorem hold.

Theorem 5.

$$l(\mathbf{x}, \mathbf{y}) + \lambda_1 q(\mathbf{x}, \mathbf{y}) \leq n(\mathbf{x}, \mathbf{y}) \leq l(\mathbf{x}, \mathbf{y}) + \lambda_3 q(\mathbf{x}, \mathbf{y})$$

where $\lambda_1 \leq \lambda_2 \leq \lambda_3$ are the eigenvalues of $P^T P$.

(A proof is given in [WB93].)

4 Summary

A scheme for recognition of 3D objects from single 2D images was presented. An object is modeled in this scheme by a small set of its views with the correspondence between the views. Novel views of the object are obtained by linearly combining the model views. The scheme accurately handles rigid objects under weak-perspective projection, and it is extended to handle rigid objects with smooth bounding surfaces and articulated objects. Unlike in other schemes, explicit 3D representations of the objects are not used.

The presented scheme can be used both under an alignment framework and as a means for deriving object-specific invariant functions for recognition. Under an alignment framework, given a model and an image, the coefficients of the linear combination that aligns the model with the image need to be recovered.

A small number of points in the image and their corresponding points in the model can be used for this purpose, or a search can be conducted in the space of possible coefficients.

Alternatively, the scheme can be used to derive functions that are invariant to viewpoint changes of a specific object. A number of linear and quadratic functions are derived in this paper, and a single function that combines together all of them was presented. Unfortunately, a closed-form solution to this function is not yet known. Instead, lower and upper bounds to this function were derived.

Acknowledgments. I wish to thank Shimon Ullman and Daphna Weinshall for their role in developing the results presented in this paper and David Jacobs for his comments to earlier drafts of this paper. A partial version of this paper was reported in C. H. Chen, L. F. Pau and P. S. P. Wang (Eds.), *Handbook of Pattern Recognition and Computer Vision*, World Scientific Publishing Company, Singapore.

References

[AP87]   Y. S. Abu-Mostafa and D. Pslatis: Optical neural computing, *Scientific American* **256** (1987) 66–73.

[BU93]   R. Basri and S. Ullman: The alignment of objects with smooth surfaces. *Computer Vision, Graphics, and Image Processing: Image Understanding*, **57(3)**, (1993) pp 331–345.

[Ba93]   Basri, R.: Viewer-centered representations in object recognition: a computational approach. In C. H. Chen, L. F. Pau and P. S. P. Wang (Eds.), *Handbook of Pattern Recognition and Computer Vision*, World Scientific Publishing Company, Singapore (to appear).

[BWR91] Burns, J., Weiss, R., and Riseman, E.: The non-existence of general-case view-invariants, *Geometric Invariance in Computer Vision*, edited by J. Mundy and A. Zisserman, MIT Press, Cambridge (1992).

[CA87]   Chien, C. H. and Aggarwal, J. K.: Shape recognition from single silhouette. *Proc. of 1st Int. Conf. on Computer Vision, London* (1987) 481–490.

[CJ91]   Clemens, D. and Jacobs, D.: Space and time bounds on model indexing, *IEEE Transactions on Pattern Analysis and Machine Intelligence*, **13(10)** (1991) 1007–1018.

[FH86]   Faugeras, O. D. and Hebert, M.: The representation, recognition and location of 3D objects. *Int. J. Robotics Research* **5(3)** (1986) 27–52.

[FB81]   Fischler, M. A. and Bolles, R. C.: Random sample consensus: a paradigm for model fitting with application to image analysis and automated cartography. *Com. of the A.C.M.* **24(6)** (1981) 381–395.

[FMZCHR91] Forsyth, D., Mundy, J. L., Zisserman, A., Coelho, C., Heller, A., and Rothwell, C.: Invariant descriptors for 3-D object recognition and pose. *IEEE Transactions on Pattern Analysis and Machine Intelligence*, **13** (1991) 971–991.

[HL89]   Huang, T. S. and Lee, C. H.: Motion and structure from orthographic projections. *IEEE Trans. on Pattern Analysis and Machine Intelligence* **11(5)** (1989) 536–540.

[HU90]   Huttenlocher, D. P., and Ullman, S.: Recognizing solid objects by alignment with an image, *Int. J. Computer Vision* **5(2)** (1990) 195–212.

[Ja92]   Jacobs, D.: Space efficient 3D model indexing, *IEEE Conference on Computer Vision and Pattern Recognition*, (1992) 439–444.

[KV91]   Koenderink, J. and van Doorn, A.: Affine structure from motion, *Journal of the Optical Society of America*, **8(2)** (1991) 377–385.

[LSW87] Lamdan, Y., Schwartz, J. T., and Wolfson, H.: On recognition of 3-D objects from 2-D images. *Courant Inst. of Math. Sci., Rob. TR 122* (1987).

[Lo85]   Lowe, D. G.: Three-dimensional object recognition from single two-dimensional images. *Courant Inst. of Math. Sci., Rob. TR 202* (1985).

[MU92]   Moses, Y. and Ullman, S.: Limitations of non model-based recognition schemes, *Second European Conference on Computer Vision* (1992) 820–828.

[Po90]   Poggio, T.: 3D object recognition: on a result by Basri and Ullman, *TR 9005-03, IRST, Povo, Italy* (1990).

[PE90]   Poggio, T. and Edelman, S.: A network that learns to recognize three-dimensional objects, *Nature* **343** (1990) 263–266.

[PG90]   Poggio, T. and Girosi, F.: Regularization algorithms for learning that are equivalent to multilayer networks, *Science* **247** (1990) 978–982.

[RFZM93] Rothwell, C. A., Forsyth, D. A., Zisserman, A., Mundy, J. L.: Extracting projective structure from single perspective view of 3D point sets. *Proc. of 4th Int. Conf. on Computer Vision*, Berlin, Germany (1993) 573–582.

[TM87]   Thompson, D. W. and Mundy, J. L.: Three dimensional model matching from an unconstrained viewpoint. *Proc. of IEEE Int. Conf. on robotics and Automation* (1987) 208–220.

[TK91]   Tomasi, C. and Kanade, T.: Factoring image sequences into shape and motion, *IEEE Workshop on Visual motion*, Princeton, NJ (1991) 21–29.

[Ul79]   Ullman, S.: The interpretation of visual motion. *M.I.T. Press*, Cambridge, MA (1979).

[Ul89]   Ullman, S.: Aligning pictorial descriptions: an approach to object recognition. *Cognition* **32(3)** (1989) 193–254.

[UB91]   Ullman, S. and Basri, R.: Recognition by linear combinations of models. *IEEE Trans. on Pattern Analysis and Machine Intelligence* **13(10)** (1991) 992–1006.

[Va87]   P. Van Hove: Model based silhouette recognition, *Proc. of the IEEE Computer Society Workshop on Computer Vision* (1987).

[We88]   Weiss, I.: Projective invariants of shape, *DARPA Image Unerstanding Workshop* (1988) 1125–1134.

[We93]   Weinshall, D.: Model-based invariants for 3D vision. *International Journal on Computer Vision* (1993).

[WB93]   Weinshall, D. and Basri, R.: Distance Metric between 3D Models and 2D Images for Recognition and Classification *Proc. of IEEE conf. on Computer Vision and Pattern Recognition* (1993) 220–225.

Statistics

Classification Based on the Cross Ratio

Stephen J. Maybank

GEC Marconi Hirst Research Centre, Elstree Way, Borehamwood, Hertfordshire,
WD6 1RX, UK

Abstract. The performance of the cross ratio in model based vision is
quantified for a decision rule which is computationally expensive, but
which makes good use of the available information. The probabilities
of rejection, false alarm and misclassification are calculated, correct to
leading order in the noise level. The probability of false alarm is closely
related to the complete elliptic integral of the third kind. An expression
is obtained for the probability density function of the cross ratio of four
points with independent identical Gaussian distributions.

A general framework is sketched to show how the methods of calculation
employed here for the cross ratio can in principle be extended to more
complicated scalar invariants or to vectors of invariants.

1 Introduction

One of the main tasks in model based vision is to recognise an object from a
small number of projected images. A geometric approach to object recognition
can be used when the image resolution is high enough and the object is near
enough to allow the detection of detailed structure or shape within the images.
In typical object recognition systems, for example as described in [10], standard
techniques from low level vision are used to identify feature points, lines or
curves in the images. If more than one image of the object is available then
the features are matched from one image to another; two features match if they
are the projections of the same feature in space. Geometrical properties of the
object are then calculated either from the features in a single image or from the
matching pairs of features. The object is recognised by comparing the calculated
geometry with the geometry predicted by any one of a set of models held in a
data base. The object is assigned to the class described by the model which best
accounts for the observed geometry.

The appearance of an image depends both on the object and on the position
and orientation (pose) of the object relative to the camera. In many previous
approaches to model based vision it is necessary to estimate the pose of the
object before comparing the object geometry, as deduced from the image or
images, with a model. The resulting algorithms are computationally expensive,
especially if the number of models is high. They are also error prone, because
the estimates of pose from image measurements are notoriously unstable.

Invariants provide a way of decoupling recognition from pose estimation.
Invariants are geometrical properties of objects that are unchanged under projection to an image. It is possible to measure the value of an invariant in a single

image and use it as a key into the data base of models. The models record the value of the invariant for each class of object. The resulting recognition algorithms are fast, even when the number of models is high. The papers collected in [9] constitute a review of the applications of invariants to computer vision, as at 1992.

The simplest, most fundamental invariant is the cross ratio of four collinear points. It is computed as a simple algebraic function of the coordinates of the four points. The cross ratio is unchanged under projection, thus it can be estimated from a single image. A simplified, mathematical version of a recognition system based on the cross ratio is described in [5]. The data base of models is a list of the values of the cross ratio. Each value corresponds to a different class of objects. The system is given the coordinates of four collinear points, as measured in an image. The cross ratio of the four points is calculated and compared with the model cross ratios. If a model cross ratio is close to the calculated cross ratio then the image is accepted as a projection of an object in the class described by the model cross ratio.

The advantage of using a simplified recognition system is that it is possible to calculate the performance of the system. Reasonable assumptions are made about the distributions of the image points both in the presence of an object O_σ and when the image is generated by random noise. The probabilities of rejection, false alarm and misclassification are then calculated. This program has been carried out in [5], [6], [7]. The results depend in part on the rule for deciding if a given image is a projection of an object O_σ.

The decision rule used in [5], [6], [7] is computationally simple, but it does not make the best possible use of the available information. In this paper a second decision rule is analysed. The rule is computationally more expensive, but it does make good use of the available information. It is found that the probability, F_σ, of a false alarm is significantly reduced and that the probability, $p_\sigma(\varsigma)$, of misclassification is changed slightly.

The background necessary for this paper includes the basic geometric properties of the cross ratio, as described in [11], and elementary probability theory, for which [12] is a good introduction. A discussion of the use of the cross ratio in model based vision can be found in the introductory chapter of [9]. The general framework for model based vision employed below is closely related to the hypothesis testing paradigm in statistics, as described in [3]. A closely related paradigm is described in [4].

Section 2 sets the scene by describing the cross ratio, stating the two decision rules and stating the probabilistic hypotheses underlying the calculations of F_σ and $p_\sigma(\varsigma)$. A new method for obtaining the probability density function of the cross ratio of four points with independent, identical, Gaussian distributions is described in Sect. 3. The calculation of F_σ is carried out in Sect. 4, and the calculation of $p_\sigma(\varsigma)$ is carried out in Sect. 5. Section 6 describes a framework in which the calculations can in principal be extended to more complicated invariants or to sets of invariants. Some concluding remarks are made in Sect. 7.

2   Model Based Vision

The analysis of the effectiveness of the cross ratio in model based vision is carried out using the simplified recognition system sketched in Sect. 1. Background information about the cross ratio is given in Sect. 2.1. Two rules for deciding when a measured cross ratio is close to a model cross ratio are stated in Sect. 2.2. The first of the two rules is analysed in the succeeding sections. The second rule is analysed in [5], [6], [7]. The measures used to quantify system performance are stated in Sect. 2.3, together with the probabilistic hypotheses concerning the distributions of the feature points.

2.1   Cross Ratio

Each set of four collinear image points defines a vector $\boldsymbol{\theta} = (\theta_1, \theta_2, \theta_3, \theta_4)$ in the measurement space $\mathbb{R}^4$. The component θ_i of $\boldsymbol{\theta}$ is the coordinate of the ith point in the quadruple of points. The cross ratio $X(\boldsymbol{\theta})$ of the four points is defined by

$$X(\boldsymbol{\theta}) = \left(\frac{\theta_1 - \theta_3}{\theta_2 - \theta_3}\right)\left(\frac{\theta_2 - \theta_4}{\theta_1 - \theta_4}\right). \tag{1}$$

The cross ratio is the simplest and most fundamental projective invariant. It is unchanged under all bilinear transformations $\theta \mapsto (a\theta + b)/(c\theta + d)$, where a, b, c, d are constants chosen such that $ad - bc \neq 0$. The projection π from a line in space to a line in the image is a special case of a bilinear transformation, thus the cross ratio is preserved under projection to the image,

$$X(\theta_1, \theta_2, \theta_3, \theta_4) = X(\pi(\theta_1), \pi(\theta_2), \pi(\theta_3), \pi(\theta_4)).$$

The value of the cross ratio, as given by (1), depends on the order in which the points θ_i are taken. If the θ_i are permuted then up to six different values of the cross ratio are obtained. The six values are

$$\sigma \qquad \sigma^{-1} \qquad 1 - \sigma$$
$$(1 - \sigma)^{-1} \qquad \sigma(\sigma - 1)^{-1} \qquad \sigma^{-1}(\sigma - 1). \tag{2}$$

A permutation of the θ_i can always be found such that the resulting cross ratio is in the range $[2, \infty]$.

2.2   Two Decision Rules

Let I be the image containing four collinear points. Let θ_i for $1 \leq i \leq 4$ be the measured coordinates of the points and let σ be a cross ratio stored in the data base of models. Let M_σ be the closure of the set of points in the measurement space $\mathbb{R}^4$ that have a cross ratio σ. It follows from (1) that a point $\mathbf{x} = (x_1, x_2, x_3, x_4)$ of $\mathbb{R}^4$ is in M_σ if and only if

$$(x_2 - x_3)(x_1 - x_4)\sigma = (x_1 - x_3)(x_2 - x_4). \tag{3}$$

It is apparent from (3) that M_σ is a quadric hypersurface. Let $\mathbf{x}$ be a general point of $\mathbb{R}^4$. Let $d : \mathbb{R}^4 \to \mathbb{R}$ be the function defined such that $d(\mathbf{x})$ is the minimum distance from $\mathbf{x}$ to M_σ. To avoid possible ambiguities in the notation the quadric M_σ is included as an argument, $d(\mathbf{x}, M_\sigma)$. Let n be the standard deviation of the error in measuring the position of a point in the image. The rule for deciding if I is a projection of an object O_σ is

$$\text{If } d(\boldsymbol{\theta}, M_\sigma) \leq nt \qquad \text{accept } I \text{ as a projection of } O_\sigma. \qquad (4)$$

The variable t in (4) is a threshold. It can be varied to adapt the performance of the decision rule to different applications. The rule is not exclusive, in that I may be accepted as the projection of several objects O_{σ_i} with different cross ratios σ_i. The rule (4) is a natural one; it assumes there is a high probability that the unperturbed measurement lies within a ball of radius nt centred at $\boldsymbol{\theta}$.

The rule (4) has the disadvantage that it is computationally expensive. A simpler decision rule is

$$\text{If } |X(\boldsymbol{\theta}) - \sigma| \leq nt \left\| \frac{\partial X}{\partial \boldsymbol{\theta}} \right\| \qquad \text{accept } I \text{ as a projection of } O_\sigma. \qquad (5)$$

The term $\|\partial X/\partial\boldsymbol{\theta}\|$ on the right-hand side of (5) is large if small perturbations in $\boldsymbol{\theta}$ cause large perturbations in the cross ratio $X(\boldsymbol{\theta})$. It is then more likely that the quadruple of image points is compatible with the model cross ratio σ to within the limits set by the measurement errors. The rule takes this behaviour into account, in that it is more likely that $\boldsymbol{\theta}$ is accepted as a projection of O_σ. The rule (5) is analysed in detail in [5], [6], [7].

An example is given which suggests that in practice (5) is likely to perform less well than (4). Let $|\theta_1 - \theta_4| = \eta > 0$, and let σ be a fixed cross ratio in the data base of models not equal to 0, 1 or ∞. Then it follows that

$$\left\| \frac{\partial X}{\partial \boldsymbol{\theta}} \right\| = O\left(\eta^{-2}\right) \qquad \text{and} \qquad |X(\boldsymbol{\theta}) - \sigma| = O(\eta^{-1}). \qquad (6)$$

It follows from (6) that the rule (5) accepts the image I as a projection of O_σ if $\eta < Ant$ where A depends on θ_2, θ_3, θ_4. However, the rule (4) may reject $\boldsymbol{\theta}$ as a projection of O_σ because $\boldsymbol{\theta}$ need not be close to M_σ. For example, let $\phi = (1, 2, 3, 1)$ and let $\mathbf{r}$ be a small perturbation of ϕ. Then it follows that

$$X(\phi + \mathbf{r}) = -\frac{2}{r_1 - r_4} + O(1)$$

thus $X(\phi + \mathbf{r}) \neq \sigma$ for all $\mathbf{r}$ such that $\|\mathbf{r}\|$ is sufficiently small. Points near to ϕ are accepted by (5); however if n is small then it is very unlikely that such points are perturbations of vectors in M_σ.

2.3 Quantification of System Performance

The performance of the recognition system is quantified using the probability of rejection, R, the probability of false alarm, F_σ, and the probability of misclassification, $p_\sigma(\varsigma)$. The values of R, F_σ, $p_\sigma(\varsigma)$ depend on the probability density functions describing the distributions of the image points. For the purposes of calculation it is assumed that

i) The measurements θ_i are subject to unknown random perturbations with independent, identical, zero mean Gaussian distributions with standard deviation n.

ii) In the absence of any object the image points have independent, identical zero mean Gaussian distributions (iid Gaussian), with standard deviation λ.

iii) In the presence of an object O_σ and prior to a measurement, the projection θ of O_σ has the distribution obtained from (ii) by imposing the condition that the cross ratio of the four image points is σ.

The quantity λ in (ii) is an estimate of the half width of the image.

Let C be the class of images generated by the random variables with iid Gaussian distributions, and let C_σ be the class of images obtained by projection from an object O_σ. Then R, F_σ and $p_\sigma(\varsigma)$ are defined by

$$R = \text{Prob}(\text{Assign } I \text{ to } C \mid I \text{ in } C_\sigma)$$
$$F_\sigma = \text{Prob}(\text{Assign } I \text{ to } C_\sigma \mid I \text{ in } C)$$
$$p_\sigma(\varsigma) = \text{Prob}(\text{Assign } I \text{ to } C_\varsigma \mid I \text{ in } C_\sigma). \tag{7}$$

Expressions for F_σ and $p_\sigma(\varsigma)$ are obtained below, correct to leading order in $\epsilon = n/\lambda$. The expression for R obtained in [5] still applies to the new decision rule. To leading order R is given by $R = 2(1 - \Phi(t))$ where Φ is the cumulative distribution function for the Gaussian distribution.

3 Probability Density Function for the Cross Ratio

The probability density function $\tau \mapsto p(\tau)$ for the cross ratio of four collinear points with iid Gaussian distributions is obtained. The method given below is shorter than the method described in [5] and the final expression, (28), is simpler. Certain formulae obtained in this section are used in Sect. 4, in the estimation of F_σ. During in the calculation it is assumed that $\tau(\theta) \geq 2$. There is little loss of generality in making this assumption because the components of θ can always be permuted such that the resulting cross ratio is in the range $[2, \infty]$.

3.1 Cumulative Density Function for the Cross Ratio

Let the measurement vector θ be distributed as described in Sect. 2.3, (ii). Let U be the orthogonal matrix defined by

$$U = \frac{1}{2} \begin{pmatrix} 1 & -1 & -1 & 1 \\ -1 & -1 & 1 & 1 \\ -1 & 1 & -1 & 1 \\ 1 & 1 & 1 & 1 \end{pmatrix} \tag{8}$$

and let ψ be the vector of random variables defined by $\psi = U\theta$. The components ψ_i of ψ are iid Gaussian random variables with standard deviation λ. It follows from (1) and the definition of U that the cross ratio $X(\theta)$ is given in terms of ψ by

$$X(\theta(\psi)) \equiv Y(\psi) = \frac{\psi_2^2 - \psi_1^2}{\psi_2^2 - \psi_3^2}. \tag{9}$$

The right-hand side of (9) is independent of ψ_4, thus the probability density function $p(\tau)$ for the cross ratio can be found using the space $\mathbb{R}^3$ spanned by ψ_1, ψ_2, ψ_3. Let $\mathbf{x} = (x_1, x_2, x_3)$ be a general point of $\mathbb{R}^3$, and let N_σ be the quadric in $\mathbb{R}^3$ defined by

$$\sigma(x_2^2 - x_3^2) - (x_2^2 - x_1^2) = 0. \tag{10}$$

It is apparent from (10) that N_σ is a cone with a vertex at the origin.

The probability density function $p(\tau)$ satisfies

$$\int_{-\infty}^{\sigma} p(\xi)\,d\xi = \frac{1}{(2\pi\lambda^2)^{3/2}} \int_{Y(\mathbf{x})\leq\sigma} \exp\left(-\frac{1}{2\lambda^2}\|\mathbf{x}\|^2\right)\,d\mathbf{x}. \tag{11}$$

The equation (11) is obtained by integrating the joint Gaussian density for ψ_1, ψ_2, ψ_3 over the points $\mathbf{x}$ of $\mathbb{R}^3$ for which $Y(\mathbf{x}) \leq \sigma$. The left-hand side is the cumulative distribution function for the cross ratio. The right-hand side of (11) is reduced to an integral over the unit sphere. The reduction is possible because $Y(\mathbf{x})$ is independent of $\|\mathbf{x}\|$ provided $\mathbf{x} \neq 0$. Let dS be the uniform measure for surface area on the unit sphere, let $r = \|\mathbf{x}\|$ and let $\hat{\mathbf{x}}$ be defined for $\mathbf{x} \neq 0$ by $\hat{\mathbf{x}} = \mathbf{x}/\|\mathbf{x}\|$. It follows from (11) that

$$\int_{-\infty}^{\sigma} p(\xi)\,d\xi = \frac{1}{(2\pi\lambda^2)^{3/2}} \int_{Y(\hat{\mathbf{x}})\leq\sigma} \int_0^\infty \exp\left(-\frac{r^2}{2\lambda^2}\right) r^2\,dr\,dS$$

$$= \frac{1}{4\pi} \int_{Y(\hat{\mathbf{x}})\leq\sigma} dS. \tag{12}$$

3.2 Probability Density Function for the Cross Ratio

An expression for $p(\tau)$ as a one dimensional integral is obtained from (12). The first step is to describe the curve $Y(\hat{\mathbf{x}}) = \sigma$. It follows from the definition (9) of Y and the condition $\|\hat{\mathbf{x}}\| = 1$ that the curve $Y(\hat{\mathbf{x}}) = \sigma$ in $\mathbb{R}^3$ is obtained as the intersection of the following two surfaces,

$$\sigma(\hat{x}_2^2 - \hat{x}_3^2) - \hat{x}_2^2 + \hat{x}_1^2 = 0$$
$$\hat{x}_1^2 + \hat{x}_2^2 + \hat{x}_3^2 = 1. \tag{13}$$

The variable $\hat{x}_3$ is eliminated from (13) to yield

$$(\sigma + 1)\hat{x}_1^2 + (2\sigma - 1)\hat{x}_2^2 = \sigma. \tag{14}$$

Let a, b be defined by

$$a = \sqrt{\frac{\sigma}{\sigma + 1}} \qquad b = \sqrt{\frac{\sigma}{2\sigma - 1}}. \tag{15}$$

It follows from (14) and (15) that an angle ϕ can be defined such that

$$\hat{x}_1 = a\cos(\phi) \qquad\qquad \hat{x}_2 = b\sin(\phi). \tag{16}$$

It follows from (13) and (16) that

$$\hat{x}_3 = \pm\sqrt{1 - a^2\cos^2(\phi) - b^2\sin^2(\phi)}. \tag{17}$$

The curve $Y(\hat{\mathbf{x}}) = \sigma$ has two real components, corresponding to the two choices of sign for the square root on the right-hand side of (17). Each component is parameterised by ϕ in the range $[0, 2\pi)$. To simplify the calculations, the positive sign is chosen on the right-hand side of (17). Let c^+ be the corresponding component of the curve $Y(\hat{\mathbf{x}}) = \sigma$. A general point $\hat{\mathbf{x}}(\phi)$ of c^+ is given by

$$\hat{\mathbf{x}}(\phi) = \left(a\cos(\phi), b\sin(\phi), \sqrt{1 - a^2\cos^2(\phi) - b^2\sin^2(\phi)} \right). \tag{18}$$

The point $\hat{\mathbf{x}}(\phi)$ is a function both of ϕ and the cross ratio σ. Let the vectors $\mathbf{e}_\phi$, $\mathbf{e}_\sigma$ be defined by $\mathbf{e}_\phi = \partial\hat{\mathbf{x}}/\partial\phi$, $\mathbf{e}_\sigma = \partial\hat{\mathbf{x}}/\partial\sigma$. It follows from (18) that

$$\begin{aligned}
\mathbf{e}_\phi &= (-a\sin(\phi), b\cos(\phi), \hat{x}_3^{-1}(a^2 - b^2)\cos(\phi)\sin(\phi)) \\
\mathbf{e}_\sigma &= (\dot{a}\cos(\phi), \dot{b}\sin(\phi), -\hat{x}_3^{-1}(a\dot{a}\cos^2(\phi) + b\dot{b}\sin^2(\phi)))
\end{aligned} \tag{19}$$

where $\dot{a} = \partial a/\partial\sigma$, $\dot{b} = \partial b/\partial\sigma$. The vector $\mathbf{e}_\phi$ is tangent to c^+.

The variables ϕ, σ together parameterise a region of the the unit sphere, as described by (18). It follows from (12) and the formula for the change of variables in an integral that

$$\int_{-\infty}^{\sigma} p(\xi)\, d\xi = \frac{1}{2\pi} \int_{-\infty}^{\sigma} \int_0^{2\pi} \left\| \frac{\partial\mathbf{x}}{\partial\phi} \times \frac{\partial\mathbf{x}}{\partial\xi} \right\| d\phi\, d\xi. \tag{20}$$

A factor two is introduced on the right-hand side of (20) to compensate for the choice of a single sign for $\hat{x}_3$ in (18). On differentiating (20) with respect to σ it follows that

$$p(\sigma) = \frac{1}{2\pi} \int_0^{2\pi} \|\mathbf{e}_\phi \times \mathbf{e}_\sigma\|\, d\phi. \tag{21}$$

The expressions (19) for $\mathbf{e}_\phi$ and $\mathbf{e}_\sigma$ yield after a short calculation the following expression for $\|\mathbf{e}_\phi \times \mathbf{e}_\sigma\|$,

$$\|\mathbf{e}_\phi \times \mathbf{e}_\sigma\| = |\hat{x}_3|^{-1}|a\dot{b}\sin^2(\phi) + \dot{a}b\cos^2(\phi)|. \tag{22}$$

It follows from (17), (21) and (22) that

$$p(\sigma) = \frac{2}{\pi} \int_0^{\pi/2} \frac{|a\dot{b}\sin^2(\phi) + \dot{a}b\cos^2(\phi)|}{(1 - a^2\cos^2(\phi) - b^2\sin^2(\phi))^{1/2}}\, d\phi. \tag{23}$$

A factor of four is introduced on the right-hand side of (23) to compensate for the reduction in the range of ϕ from $[0, 2\pi)$ to $[0, \pi/2)$. It follows from (15) that $a^{-2} + b^{-2} = 3$, thus $\dot{b} = -a^{-3}b^3\dot{a}$. The elimination of $\dot{b}$ from (23) yields

$$p(\sigma) = \frac{2|\dot{a}b|}{\pi a^2} \int_0^{\pi/2} \frac{|a^2 \cos^2(\phi) - b^2 \sin^2(\phi)|}{(1 - a^2 \cos^2(\phi) - b^2 \sin^2(\phi))^{1/2}} \, d\phi. \tag{24}$$

3.3 Reduction to a Standard Form

The expression (24) for p is rewritten in terms of elliptic integrals of the first and second kinds. Let $I(\zeta, \alpha, \beta)$ be the integral defined by

$$I(\zeta, \alpha, \beta) = \int_0^\zeta \frac{\alpha^2 \cos^2(\phi) - \beta^2 \sin^2(\phi)}{(1 - \alpha^2 \cos^2(\phi) - \beta^2 \sin^2(\phi))^{1/2}} \, d\phi. \tag{25}$$

Let ξ be defined by $\xi = \tan^{-1}(a/b)$. The function $a^2 \cos^2(\phi) - b^2 \sin^2(\phi)$ in the numerator of (24) is monotonic decreasing for $0 \leq \phi \leq \pi/2$. It has a zero at $\phi = \xi$. Thus it follows from (24) and (25) that

$$p(\sigma) = 2\pi^{-1}|\dot{a}a^{-2}b| \left[2I(\xi, a, b) - I\left(\frac{\pi}{2}, a, b\right) \right]. \tag{26}$$

The elliptic integrals F, E of the first and second kinds are defined in [1] by

$$F(\zeta|m) = \int_0^\zeta (1 - m \sin^2(\theta))^{-1/2} \, d\theta$$

$$E(\zeta|m) = \int_0^\zeta (1 - m \sin^2(\theta))^{1/2} \, d\theta.$$

Let h be defined by

$$h = -\frac{a^2 - b^2}{1 - a^2} = -\frac{\sigma(\sigma - 2)}{2\sigma - 1}.$$

A short calculation shows that

$$I(\xi, a, b) = \frac{a^2 b^2 (F(\xi|h) - 3(1 - a^2)E(\xi|h))}{(1 - a^2)^{1/2}.(a^2 - b^2)} \tag{27}$$

The final expression for p, obtained from (26) and (27), is

$$p(\sigma) = \frac{2F(\xi|h) - F(\frac{\pi}{2}|h) - 3(\sigma + 1)^{-1}(2E(\xi|h) - E(\frac{\pi}{2}|h))}{\pi(2\sigma - 1)^{1/2}(\sigma - 2)}. \tag{28}$$

An alternative and more complicated expression for p is obtained in [5]. The two expressions define identical functions of σ. This fact is confirmed by numerical calculations with Mathematica [13]. There is at present no direct proof that the two expressions are equivalent.

The probability density function for the cross ratio of four points with independent, identical uniform distributions is obtained in [2]. The resulting graph is similar in shape to $p(\sigma)$, but the formulae defining it are simpler.

4 The Probability of a False Alarm

The probability F_σ of a false alarm is estimated for the decision rule (4). The estimate is correct to leading order in the small quantity $\epsilon = n/\lambda$, where n, λ are as defined in Sect. 2.3. An integral expression which approximates F_σ is obtained in Sect. 4.1. It is rewritten as an elliptic integral of the third kind in Sect. 4.2. Finally, in Sect. 4.3 a comparison is made between F_σ and the probability of false alarm calculated in [5] for the rule (5). It is assumed throughout that $\sigma \geq 2$.

4.1 An Integral Expression for F_σ

It is recalled from Sect. 3.1 that N_σ is the quadric in $\mathbb{R}^3$ defined by (10). It follows from (4) and the assumption $\sigma \geq 2$ that $F_\sigma/6$ is the probability that a random point $\mathbf{x}$ of $\mathbb{R}^3$ with a Gaussian distribution lies within a distance nt of the quadric N_σ. The factor $1/6$ appears for the following reason. Before applying the decision rule the coordinates of $\boldsymbol{\theta}$ are permuted to give a cross ratio in the range $[2, \infty]$. There are in general exactly six different cross ratios that can be obtained by permuting the coordinates of $\boldsymbol{\theta}$. The six cross ratio values are listed in (2). Exactly one of these values is in the range $[2, \infty]$. The contributions to F_σ associated with the different values are all equal. Thus, the assumption $\sigma \geq 2$ entails a reduction in the probability of a false alarm from F_σ to $F_\sigma/6$.

A general point of N_σ is given by

$$(\rho, \phi) \mapsto \mathbf{x}(\rho, \phi) \equiv \left(\rho a \cos(\phi), \rho b \sin(\phi), \rho\sqrt{1 - a^2 \cos^2(\phi) - b^2 \sin^2(\phi)} \right)$$

where $\rho = \|\mathbf{x}\|$. The variables ρ, ϕ are coordinates for N_σ in the region $x_3 \geq 0$. The area of a small element of N_σ at (ρ, ϕ) is

$$\left\| \frac{\partial \mathbf{x}}{\partial \phi} \times \frac{\partial \mathbf{x}}{\partial \rho} \right\| d\phi\, d\rho = \|\mathbf{e}_\phi \times \mathbf{e}_\rho\| \rho\, d\phi\, d\rho \tag{29}$$

where $\mathbf{e}_\phi$ is defined by the first equation of (19) and $\mathbf{e}_\rho$ is defined by

$$\mathbf{e}_\rho = \frac{\partial \mathbf{x}}{\partial \rho} = \left(a \cos(\phi), b \sin(\phi), \sqrt{1 - a^2 \cos^2(\phi) - b^2 \sin^2(\phi)} \right).$$

The element of area (29) is associated with an element of the volume of points within a distance nt of N_σ. The volume element is

$$2nt\|\mathbf{e}_\phi \times \mathbf{e}_\rho\| \rho\, d\phi\, d\rho + O(n^2). \tag{30}$$

It follows on integrating the volume element (30) over N_σ, weighted by the Gaussian density,

$$\frac{1}{(2\pi\lambda^2)^{3/2}} \exp\left(-\frac{1}{2\lambda^2} \|\mathbf{x}\|^2 \right)$$

that

$$\frac{1}{6}F_\sigma = \frac{4nt}{(2\pi\lambda^2)^{3/2}} \int_0^\infty \int_0^{2\pi} \exp\left(-\frac{\rho^2}{2\lambda^2}\right) \|e_\phi \times e_\rho\| \rho \, d\phi \, d\rho + O(\epsilon^2). \qquad (31)$$

A factor of two is included on the right-hand side of (31) to compensate for the restriction of the integral to the region $x_3 \geq 0$. On setting $u = \lambda^{-1}\rho$ in (31) it follows from (31) that

$$F_\sigma = \frac{6\sqrt{2}\epsilon t}{\pi^{3/2}} \int_0^\infty \int_0^{2\pi} \exp\left(-\frac{1}{2}u^2\right) \|e_\phi \times e_\rho\| u \, d\phi \, du + O(\epsilon^2). \qquad (32)$$

The vector e_ρ has unit norm, and e_ϕ is orthogonal to e_ρ. Thus it follows from (19) and (32) that

$$F_\sigma = \frac{6\sqrt{2}\,\epsilon t}{\pi^{3/2}} \int_0^\infty \int_0^{2\pi} \exp\left(-\frac{1}{2}u^2\right) \|e_\phi\| u \, d\phi \, du + O(\epsilon^2)$$

$$= \frac{6\sqrt{2}\,\epsilon t}{\pi^{3/2}} \int_0^{2\pi} \|e_\phi\| \, d\phi + O(\epsilon^2)$$

$$= \frac{24\sqrt{2}\,\epsilon t}{\pi^{3/2}} \int_0^{\pi/2} \left(\frac{a^2\sin^2(\phi) + b^2\cos^2(\phi) - a^2 b^2}{1 - a^2\cos^2(\phi) - b^2\sin^2(\phi)}\right)^{1/2} d\phi + O(\epsilon^2). \qquad (33)$$

A factor of four is included on the right-hand side of the last equation of (33) because the range of ϕ is reduced from $[0, 2\pi)$ to $[0, \pi/2)$.

Let l, m be defined by

$$l = \frac{a^2 b^2}{a^2 - b^2} = \frac{\sigma}{\sigma - 2}$$

$$m = \frac{2 - 3a^2 b^2}{a^2 - b^2} = \frac{\sigma^2 + 2\sigma - 2}{\sigma(\sigma - 2)}. \qquad (34)$$

The above expressions for l and m in terms of σ are obtained from (15). It follows from (33), (34) and the equation $a^2 + b^2 = 3a^2 b^2$ that

$$F_\sigma = \frac{24\sqrt{2}\,\epsilon t}{\pi^{3/2}} \int_0^{\pi/2} \sqrt{\frac{l - \cos(2\phi)}{m - \cos(2\phi)}} \, d\phi + O(\epsilon^2). \qquad (35)$$

4.2 Reduction to a Standard Form

The leading order term in the expression (35) for F_σ is expressed in terms of the complete elliptic integral of the third kind, $\Pi(n\backslash\alpha)$. The integral $\Pi(n\backslash\alpha)$ is defined in [1] by

$$\Pi(n\backslash\alpha) = \int_0^{\pi/2} \frac{d\theta}{(1 - n\sin^2(\theta))(1 - \sin^2(\alpha)\sin^2(\theta))^{1/2}}. \qquad (36)$$

The expression (36) for $\Pi(n\backslash\alpha)$ is transformed by the substitution $t = \tan(\theta)$ to yield

$$\Pi(n\backslash\alpha) = \int_0^\infty \frac{(1+t^2)^{1/2}\, dt}{(1+(1-n)t^2)(1+\cos^2(\alpha)t^2)^{1/2}}. \tag{37}$$

Let I be the integral defined by

$$I = \int_0^{\pi/2} \sqrt{\frac{1-\cos(2\phi)}{m-\cos(2\phi)}}\, d\phi. \tag{38}$$

A change of variables is applied to I to bring it to a form similar to the right-hand side of (37). Let y, p, β be defined by

$$y = \left(\frac{l+1}{l-1}\right)^{1/2} \tan(\phi)$$

$$1-p = \frac{l-1}{l+1} = \frac{1}{\sigma-1}$$

$$\cos^2(\beta) = \left(\frac{m+1}{m-1}\right)\left(\frac{l-1}{l+1}\right) = \frac{\sigma+1}{2\sigma-1}. \tag{39}$$

The change of variables $\phi \mapsto y(\phi)$ is applied to (38) to yield

$$I = \frac{l-1}{(m-1)^{1/2}(l+1)^{1/2}} \int_0^\infty \frac{(1+y^2)^{1/2}\, dy}{(1+(1-p)y^2)(1+\cos^2(\beta)y^2)^{1/2}}. \tag{40}$$

A comparison of (37) and (40) shows that

$$I = \frac{(l-1)\Pi(p\backslash\beta)}{(m-1)^{1/2}(l+1)^{1/2}}. \tag{41}$$

It follows from (35), (39) and (41) that

$$F_\sigma =$$

$$\frac{24\sqrt{2\sigma}\, \epsilon t}{\pi^{3/2}(2\sigma-1)^{1/2}(\sigma-1)^{1/2}} \Pi\left(\frac{\sigma-2}{\sigma-1}\Big\backslash \cos^{-1}\left(\sqrt{\frac{\sigma+1}{2\sigma-1}}\right)\right) + O(\epsilon^2). \tag{42}$$

The complete elliptic integral of the third kind $\Pi(p\backslash\beta)$ is reduced to an expression involving the elliptic integrals F, E of the first and second kinds [1]. The exact formula for the reduction depends on an inequality involving $\sin^2(\beta)$ and p. The inequality is

$$\sin^2(\beta) < p < 1. \tag{43}$$

It holds under the assumption $\sigma > 2$. The inequality (43) ensures that the reduction of $\Pi(p\backslash\beta)$ falls within the so-called circular case, as described in [1], 17.7.9. In detail, let $\tilde{\epsilon}$, δ_2 be defined by

$$\tilde{\epsilon} = \sin^{-1}\left(\frac{\sqrt{1-p}}{\cos(\beta)}\right)$$

$$\delta_2 = \frac{\sqrt{p}}{\sqrt{(1-p)(p-\sin^2(\beta))}}.$$

The symbol $\tilde{\epsilon}$ replaces the ϵ employed in [1], to avoid confusion with $\epsilon = n/\lambda$, as defined in Sect. 2.3. It is stated in [1] that

$$\Pi(p\backslash\beta) = F\left(\frac{\pi}{2}\Big|\sin^2(\beta)\right) + \frac{\pi}{2}\delta_2(1 - \Lambda_0(\tilde{\epsilon}\backslash\beta))$$

where Λ_0 is Heuman's Lambda function, defined by

$$\frac{\pi}{2}\Lambda_0(\tilde{\epsilon}\backslash\beta) = F\left(\frac{\pi}{2}\Big|\sin^2(\beta)\right) E(\tilde{\epsilon}|\cos^2(\beta))$$
$$- \left[F\left(\frac{\pi}{2}\Big|\sin^2(\beta)\right) - E\left(\frac{\pi}{2}\Big|\sin^2(\beta)\right)\right] F(\tilde{\epsilon}|\cos^2(\beta)).$$

4.3 Comparison of Probabilities of a False Alarm

Let F'_σ be the probability of a false alarm for the rule (5). The following expression for F'_σ is obtained in [5],

$$F'_\sigma = \epsilon t\left(J(\sigma) + \sqrt{\frac{72}{\pi}}\right) + O(\epsilon^2\ln(\epsilon^{-1})). \tag{44}$$

The function $J(\sigma)$ is defined in the interval $\sigma \geq 2$ by

$$\left(\frac{\pi^3}{1152\sigma}\right)^{1/2} J(\sigma) =$$

$$\int_0^{\pi/2} \frac{((\sigma+1)\cos^2(\theta) + (\sigma-1)(2\sigma-1)\sin^2(\theta))^{1/2}}{((\sigma+1)\cos^2(\theta) + (2\sigma-1)\sin^2(\theta))(\cos^2(\theta) + (\sigma-1)\sin^2(\theta))^{1/2}} d\theta.$$

The term $\epsilon t J(\sigma)$ on the right-hand side of (44) arises from random quadruples of image points with cross ratios close to the model cross ratio σ. The term $\epsilon t\sqrt{72/\pi}$ arises from random quadruples in which two of the points are close together.

Numerical calculations with Mathematica suggest strongly that the leading order term on the right-hand side of (42) is equal to $\epsilon t J(\sigma)$, and that in consequence

$$F_\sigma = F'_\sigma - \epsilon t\sqrt{\frac{72}{\pi}}$$

to leading order. The new decision rule (4) removes to leading order the contribution to the probability of false alarm arising from measurement vectors θ in which one or more of the components are close together. A graph of $F_\sigma/(\epsilon t)$ as a function of σ is shown in Figure 1.

The graph suggests that $F_\sigma/(\epsilon t)$ is monotonic increasing in the range $(2, \infty)$. The minimum value is $F_2/(\epsilon t) = \sqrt{192/\pi}$ and the least upper bound is

$$\lim_{\sigma\to\infty} (\epsilon t)^{-1}F_\sigma = \sqrt{288/\pi}.$$

It follows that $F_\sigma/(\epsilon t)$ varies by about 10% in the range $(2, \infty)$.

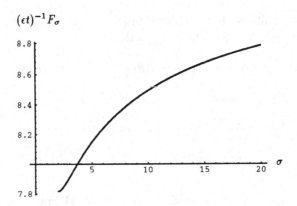

Fig.1. Graph of $F_\sigma/(\epsilon t)$

5 The Probability of Misclassification

The probability of misclassification, $p_\sigma(\varsigma)$, is the probability that the rule (4) accepts an image I as a projection of an object O_ς when I is truly the projection of an object O_σ. The formal definition is given in (7). An expression correct to leading order in $\epsilon = n/\lambda$ is obtained for $p_\sigma(\varsigma)$. The expression is similar to the leading order term of the probability of misclassification for the rule (5), as obtained in [6]. An exact integral expression for $p_\sigma(\varsigma)$ is obtained in Sect. 5.1. It is then approximated in Sect. 5.2. It is assumed throughout this section that $\sigma, \tau \geq 2$.

5.1 An Integral Expression for $p_\sigma(\varsigma)$

Let H be the function of θ, τ defined by

$$H(\theta, \tau) = ((1 + \tau^{-1})\cos^2(\theta) + (2 - \tau^{-1})\sin^2(\theta))^{1/2}.$$

The variable θ should not be confused with the measurement vector $\boldsymbol{\theta}$ or the individual measurements θ_i. The vector $\boldsymbol{\psi}$ is defined by $\boldsymbol{\psi} = U\boldsymbol{\theta}$, as in Sect. 3.1, where U is the orthogonal matrix (8). The space $\mathbb{R}^3$ with coordinates ψ_1, ψ_2, ψ_3 is reparameterised as in [5] by

$$(\psi_1, \psi_2, \psi_3) \mapsto (\psi_1, \psi_2, \tau) \mapsto (r, \theta, \tau) \mapsto (y, \theta, \tau). \qquad (45)$$

The coordinate τ is the cross ratio, as defined by the right-hand side of (9). The inverses of the three coordinate transformations (45) are given in order by

$$(\psi_1, \psi_2, \tau) \mapsto \left(\psi_1, \psi_2, \sqrt{\tau^{-1}\psi_1^2 + (1 - \tau^{-1})\psi_2^2}\right) = (\psi_1, \psi_2, \psi_3)$$

$$(r, \theta, \tau) \mapsto (r\cos(\theta), r\sin(\theta), \tau) = (\psi_1, \psi_2, \tau)$$
$$(y, \theta, \tau) \mapsto (\lambda H(\theta, \tau)^{-1} y, \theta, \tau) = (r, \theta, \tau). \qquad (46)$$

The second equation of (46) defines r, θ and the third equation of (46) defines y.

It is shown in [5] that the joint Gaussian probability density function for ψ_1, ψ_2, ψ_3 induces the density $q(y, \theta, \tau)$ defined by

$$q(y, \theta, \tau) = \frac{|\cos(2\theta)| y^2 \exp\left(-\frac{1}{2} y^2\right)}{(2\pi\tau)^{3/2} H(\theta, \tau)^3 (\cos^2(\theta) + (\tau - 1)\sin^2(\theta))^{1/2}} \qquad (\tau \geq 1).$$

It is assumed in Sect. 2.3, (iii) that in the presence of an object O_σ the four image points have the distribution obtained by imposing the condition that the cross ratio of the four image points is σ. The probability density function $q_\sigma(y, \theta)$ for y, θ given that the four image points have a cross ratio σ is thus defined by $q_\sigma(y, \theta) = c_\sigma q(y, \theta, \sigma)$ where c_σ is a normalising constant defined by

$$c_\sigma^{-1} = \int_0^{2\pi} \int_0^\infty q(y, \theta, \sigma)\, dy\, d\theta$$
$$= \frac{1}{\pi\sigma^{3/2}} \int_0^{\pi/2} \frac{|\cos(2\theta)|\, d\theta}{H(\theta, \sigma)^3 (\cos^2(\theta) + (\sigma - 1)\sin^2(\theta))^{1/2}}. \qquad (47)$$

Let N_ς be the quadric defined by (10), with ς in place of σ. A measurement vector $\theta = \theta(\psi)$ is accepted by the rule (4) as a projection of an object O_ς if and only if $d(\psi, N_\varsigma) \leq nt$. The function $d(\psi, N_\varsigma)$ is homogeneous in $\|\psi\|$, thus $\theta(\psi)$ is accepted if and only if

$$\|\psi\| d(\hat{\psi}, N_\varsigma) \leq nt \qquad (48)$$

where $\hat{\psi} = \psi / \|\psi\|$. A short calculation yields

$$\|\psi\| = \sqrt{\psi_1^2 + \psi_2^2 + \psi_3^2} = rH(\theta, \tau).$$

Thus $\theta(\psi)$ is accepted if and only if $rH(\theta, \tau)d(\hat{\psi}, N_\varsigma) \leq nt$, or equivalently $y \leq \epsilon t d(\hat{\psi}, N_\varsigma)^{-1}$. Let Λ be the function of θ defined by

$$\Lambda(\theta) = t d(\hat{\psi}, N_\varsigma)^{-1}. \qquad (49)$$

The probability of misclassification is obtained by integrating $q_\sigma(y, \theta)$ over the region of N_σ in which the rule (4) accepts $\theta(\psi)$ as the projection of an object O_σ,

$$p_\sigma(\varsigma) = \int_0^{2\pi} \int_0^{\epsilon\Lambda} q_\sigma(y, \theta)\, dy\, d\theta. \qquad (50)$$

In deriving (50) it is assumed that the image points have a cross ratio of exactly σ. In practice the perturbations in the measurements cause ψ to lie near to but not on N_σ. This effect is negligible because it causes a perturbation of magnitude $O(\epsilon p_\sigma(\varsigma))$ in the value of $p_\sigma(\varsigma)$.

5.2   Reduction to a Standard Form

The leading order contribution to $p_\sigma(\varsigma)$ arises from the integration of $q_\sigma(y, \theta)$ over the region of N_σ near to $N_\sigma \cap N_\varsigma$. The curve $N_\sigma \cap N_\varsigma$ splits into four lines, namely $\psi_1 = \pm\psi_2 = \pm\psi_3$. In view of the symmetry between ψ_1, ψ_2, ψ_3 it is sufficient to consider just one of the four lines, for example the line k defined by $\psi_1 = \psi_2 = \psi_3$. The scaling behaviour (48) of the function $d(\psi, N_\varsigma)$ allows a reduction from N_σ, N_ς to the curves f_σ, f_ς defined by $f_\sigma = N_\sigma \cap S^2$, $f_\varsigma = N_\varsigma \cap S^2$, where S^2 is the unit sphere centred at the origin.

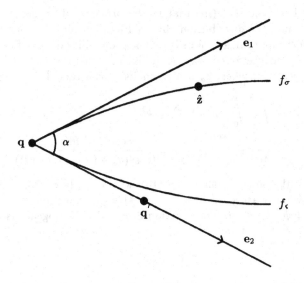

Fig.2. The curves f_σ and f_ς

Let $\mathbf{q}$ be the point $(1/\sqrt{3}, 1/\sqrt{3}, 1/\sqrt{3})$ at which k intersects S^2. Let S^2 be parameterised in the neighbourhood of $\mathbf{q}$ by r, θ such that a point $\hat{\mathbf{x}}$ of S^2 is given by

$$\hat{\mathbf{x}} = (r\cos(\theta), r\sin(\theta), \sqrt{1 - r^2}).$$

The unit sphere is also parameterised in the neighbourhood of $\mathbf{q}$ by σ, θ. Let $\mathbf{e}_1$, $\mathbf{e}_2$ be the tangent vectors to f_σ, f_ς respectively at $\mathbf{q}$,

$$\mathbf{e}_1 = \left.\frac{\partial\hat{\mathbf{x}}(\sigma, \theta)}{\partial\theta}\right|_{\mathbf{q}} \qquad \mathbf{e}_2 = \left.\frac{\partial\hat{\mathbf{x}}(\varsigma, \theta)}{\partial\theta}\right|_{\mathbf{q}}$$

and let $\eta = \theta - \pi/4$. The variable η parameterises f_σ and f_ς in a neighbourhood of $\mathbf{q}$. The point $\mathbf{q}$ corresponds to $\eta = 0$ (or equivalently $\theta = \pi/4$) on both curves. Let α be the acute angle between $\mathbf{e}_1$ and $\mathbf{e}_2$, as shown in Figure 2.

The function Λ defined by (49) is approximated as follows. There exists a bounded function $B(\sigma, \eta)$ such that

$$\Lambda(\eta) = \frac{t}{\sin(\alpha)|\eta|\|e_1\|} + \frac{tB(\sigma, \eta)}{\sin(\alpha)}. \tag{51}$$

To prove (51), let $\hat{z}$ be a general point of f_σ. Let q' be the closest point of the line $q + \lambda e_2$ to $\hat{z}$ and let $u = \|\hat{z} - q'\|$. Let β be the angle between the lines $\langle q, q' \rangle$ and $\langle q, \hat{z} \rangle$. Then it follows that

$$u = \|\hat{z} - q\| \sin(\beta).$$

A Taylor series expansion yields

$$\hat{z} = q + \eta e_1 + O(\eta^2)$$
$$\beta = \alpha + O(\eta^2)$$

thus

$$u = |\eta|\|e_1\|(1 + O(\eta)) \sin(\alpha). \tag{52}$$

It follows from (49) and (52) that

$$\begin{aligned}\Lambda(\hat{z}) &= t\|\hat{z} - q'\|^{-1}\\ &= tu^{-1}\\ &= \frac{t}{\sin(\alpha)|\eta|\,\|e_1\|} + \frac{tB(\sigma, \eta)}{\sin(\alpha)}\end{aligned}$$

where $B(\sigma, \eta)$ is a bounded function.

It is shown in [6] that the probability of misclassification for the rule (5) is given by an integral similar to the right-hand side of (50). The limit $\epsilon\Lambda$ is replaced by a limit ϵL where L is defined by

$$L(\varsigma, \eta) = \frac{2t\sigma^2(a_1 + a_2)}{|\sigma - \varsigma|\,|\sin(2\eta)|}$$

where

$$a_1 = \sqrt{\frac{3}{2}}(1 - \sigma^{-1} + \sigma^{-2})^{1/2}$$
$$a_2 = O(\sin(2\eta)).$$

The functions Λ, L have a singularity in η of the same type at q. It follows that Theorem 4 of [6] can be adapted, with Λ in place of L, to yield

$$p_\sigma(\varsigma) = \frac{2c_\sigma}{3\sqrt{3}\pi\sigma^2}\left(\frac{2\epsilon t}{\sin(\alpha)\|e_1\|}\right)^2 + O\left(\left(\frac{2\epsilon t}{\sin(\alpha)\|e_1\|}\right)^{8/3}\frac{\sigma^{1/2}}{\ln(\sigma)}\right). \tag{53}$$

where c_σ is given by (47).

It remains to find expressions for $\sin(\alpha)$ and e_1. The vector $\hat{z}$ in f_σ and the angle α are given by

$$\hat{z} = \left(r\cos(\theta), r\sin(\theta), \sqrt{1-r^2}\right)$$

$$\|e_1 \times e_2\| = \|e_1\|\,\|e_2\|\sin(\alpha). \tag{54}$$

The fact that $\hat{z}$ is in f_σ leads to the following equation constraining r and θ,

$$\sigma = \frac{r^2(\sin^2(\theta) - \cos^2(\theta))}{r^2\sin^2(\theta) - 1 + r^2}.$$

Thus r is given by

$$r^2 = \frac{\sigma}{\cos(2\theta) + \sigma(1 + \sin^2(\theta))}. \tag{55}$$

Equation (55) is differentiated with respect to θ to yield

$$2r\frac{\partial r}{\partial \theta} = -\frac{\sin(2\theta)\sigma(\sigma - 2)}{(\cos(2\theta) + \sigma(1 + \sin^2(\theta)))^2}. \tag{56}$$

Equation (56) gives the variation of r with θ on f_σ. It follows from (55) and (56) that

$$r(\mathbf{q}) = \sqrt{\frac{2}{3}}$$

$$2\sqrt{\frac{2}{3}}\frac{\partial r}{\partial \theta}\bigg|_{\mathbf{q}} = \frac{4}{9}\left(\frac{2-\sigma}{\sigma}\right).$$

It follows that

$$e_1(\mathbf{q}) = \left(\frac{\partial}{\partial \theta}\left(r\cos(\theta), r\sin(\theta), \sqrt{1-r^2}\right)\right)\bigg|_{\mathbf{q}}$$

$$= \left(-r\sin(\theta) + \frac{\partial r}{\partial \theta}\cos(\theta), r\cos(\theta) + \frac{\partial r}{\partial \theta}\sin(\theta), -\frac{r}{\sqrt{1-r^2}}\frac{\partial r}{\partial \theta}\right)\bigg|_{\mathbf{q}}$$

$$= \frac{1}{\sqrt{3}}(-1, 1, 0) + \frac{2-\sigma}{3\sqrt{3}\sigma}(1, 1, -2)$$

hence

$$\|e_1\| = \frac{2\sqrt{2}}{3\sigma}(1 - \sigma + \sigma^2)^{1/2}$$

$$\|e_2\| = \frac{2\sqrt{2}}{3\varsigma}(1 - \varsigma + \varsigma^2)^{1/2}$$

$$e_1 \times e_2 = \frac{4}{3\sqrt{3}}\left(\frac{1}{\sigma} - \frac{1}{\varsigma}\right)\mathbf{q}. \tag{57}$$

It follows from (54) and (57) that

$$\sin(\alpha) = \frac{\|\mathbf{e}_1 \times \mathbf{e}_2\|}{\|\mathbf{e}_1\| \|\mathbf{e}_2\|}$$

$$= \frac{4|\sigma - \varsigma|}{3\sqrt{3}\|\mathbf{e}_1\| \|\mathbf{e}_2\|\sigma\varsigma} \tag{58}$$

It follows from (53) and (58) that to leading order

$$p_\sigma(\varsigma) = \frac{2c_\sigma}{3\sqrt{3}\pi\sigma^2} \left(\frac{2\epsilon t}{\sin(\alpha)\|\mathbf{e}_1\|} \right)^2 + O\left(\frac{\sigma^{35/6}}{\log(\sigma)} \left(\frac{\epsilon}{|\sigma - \varsigma|} \right)^{8/3} \right)$$

$$= \frac{3\sqrt{3}\,\epsilon^2 t^2 c_\sigma \|\mathbf{e}_1\|^2 \sigma^2}{2\pi(\sigma - \varsigma)^2} + O\left(\frac{\sigma^{35/6}}{\log(\sigma)} \left(\frac{\epsilon}{|\sigma - \varsigma|} \right)^{8/3} \right)$$

$$= \frac{4\epsilon^2 t^2 c_\sigma (1 - \varsigma + \varsigma^2)}{\sqrt{3}\pi(\sigma - \varsigma)^2} + O\left(\frac{\sigma^{35/6}}{\log(\sigma)} \left(\frac{\epsilon}{|\sigma - \varsigma|} \right)^{8/3} \right). \tag{59}$$

The leading order term (59) of $p_\sigma(\varsigma)$ is similar to the leading order term of the probability of misclassification obtained in [6], namely

$$\frac{4\epsilon^2 t^2 c_\sigma (1 - \sigma + \sigma^2)}{\sqrt{3}\pi(\sigma - \varsigma)^2}$$

for the decision rule (5). The density of models and the maximum number of models are estimated in [6] for the rule (5). It is conjectured that the density of models and the maximum number of models for (4) are similar to those obtained for (5).

6 General Method

The calculations in Sect. 4 and Sect. 5 leading to estimates of F_σ and $p_\sigma(\varsigma)$ rely in part on certain general properties of the cross ratio which are likely to hold for other invariants. The general form of the calculation is as follows. There is a measurement space $\mathbb{R}^n$ which carries a probability density function q derived from a probability density function defined on the space of images. The invariants take values in a second space $\mathbb{R}^m$. There is a function $\pi : \mathbb{R}^n \rightarrow \mathbb{R}^m$ defined such that $\pi(\mathbf{x})$ is the vector of invariants calculated from the measurements $\mathbf{x}$. In the case of the cross ratio, $n = 4, m = 1$ and π is the cross ratio function. In some cases π is not defined on the whole of $\mathbb{R}^n$. For example the cross ratio function $\mathbb{R}^4 \rightarrow \mathbb{R}$ is not defined at those points of $\mathbb{R}^4$ for which the cross ratio is infinite.

Let $\mathbf{y}$ be a general point of $\mathbb{R}^m$ and let $M_\mathbf{y}$ be the closure of $\pi^{-1}(\mathbf{y})$. The decision rule defines a neighbourhood $V_\mathbf{y}$ of $M_\mathbf{y}$ such that a measurement $\mathbf{x}$ is accepted as the projection of an object $O_\mathbf{y}$ if and only if $\mathbf{x}$ is contained in $V_\mathbf{y}$. The probability of false alarm is then the integral of q over $V_\mathbf{y}$. In the case of the decision rule (4), V_σ consists of all points of $\mathbb{R}^4$ within a distance nt of the quadric M_σ defined by (3).

Let $W_{\mathbf{y},\mathbf{z}}$ be the set of points contained in $M_{\mathbf{y}}$ such that the decision rule accepts each point $\mathbf{x}$ of $W_{\mathbf{y},\mathbf{z}}$ as the projection of an object $O_{\mathbf{z}}$, where $\mathbf{z} \neq \mathbf{y}$. Let $q_{\mathbf{y}}$ be the conditional density induced on $M_{\mathbf{y}}$ by q. If $q_{\mathbf{y}}$ is an appropriate density to describe the distribution of images obtained when viewing objects with invariant values $\mathbf{y}$ then the probability of misclassification, $p_{\mathbf{y}}(\mathbf{z})$, is the integral of $q_{\mathbf{y}}$ over $W_{\mathbf{y},\mathbf{z}}$. Under reasonable hypotheses concerning the invariants and the density q the set $W_{\mathbf{y},\mathbf{z}}$ is confined to a neighbourhood of $M_{\mathbf{y}} \cap M_{\mathbf{z}}$. The probability $p_{\mathbf{y}}(\mathbf{z})$ can then be estimated by examining the behaviour of q in the neighbourhood of $M_{\mathbf{y}} \cap M_{\mathbf{z}}$.

7 Conclusion

The performance of a model based object recognition system has been analysed in detail, for a decision rule close to the optimal one. Expressions have been obtained for the probability F_σ of a false alarm and the probability $p_\sigma(\varsigma)$ of misclassification. The expressions are compared with the analogous expressions obtained in [5], [6], [7] for a similar recognition system in which the decision rule is suboptimal, but computationally less expensive. It is found that the false alarm rate is reduced significantly by using the near optimal decision rule, but that in contrast there is only a small change in the leading order term of $p_\sigma(\varsigma)$. The results suggest that a careful formulation of the decision rule is important when it is necessary to reduce the probability of a false alarm. The details of the decision rule are less important when it is only necessary to reduce the probability of misclassification.

The results of this paper support the importance of the definition in [5],[6] of invariants which are non-degenerate for model based vision. To reiterate the definition, a scalar invariant is non-degenerate for model based vision if the probabilities R, F_σ, $p_\sigma(\varsigma)$ are given to leading order, for reasonable probability distributions on the data and for reasonable decision rules, by expressions of the form

$$R = 2(1 - \Phi(t))$$
$$F_\sigma = \epsilon r_F t$$
$$p_\varsigma(\sigma) = \left(\frac{e_\sigma \epsilon t}{\sigma - \varsigma} \right)^2$$

where r_F is a slowly varying function of σ, Φ is the cumulative distribution function for the Gaussian distribution and $\epsilon = n/\lambda$ is the ratio of the standard deviation in the measurement errors to the half width of the image. The function e_σ depends only on the cross ratio σ.

Acknowledgement: This work is funded by the ESPRIT Project BRA 6448 (VIVA).

References

1. Abramovitz, M., Stegun, I.A. (eds.): *Handbook of Mathematical Functions with Formulas, Graphs, and Mathematical Tables.* Dover: New York, USA (1965)
2. Åström, K., Morin, L.: Random cross ratios. Rapport Technique RT88 IMAG-14 LIFIA, LIFIA, Institut Imag, Grenoble, France (1992)
3. Cramér, H.: *Mathematical Methods of Statistics.* Princeton Mathematical Series vol 9. Princeton: Princeton University Press. (1945, eighteenth printing 1991)
4. Devijver, P.A., Kittler, J.: *Pattern Recognition: a statistical approach.* Prentice Hall: London, UK (1982)
5. Maybank, S.J.: Probabilistic analysis of the application of the cross ratio to model based vision. Submitted for publication (1994)
6. Maybank, S.J.: Probabilistic analysis of the application of the cross ratio to model based vision: misclassification. International Journal of Computer Vision (to appear)
7. Maybank, S.J., Beardsley, P.A.: Applications of invariants to model based vision. Journal of Applied Statistics (to appear)
8. Maybank, S.J., Beardsley, P.A.: Experimental investigation of the probability of misclassification. In preparation (1994)
9. Mundy, J.L., Zisserman, A. (eds): *Geometric Invariance in Computer Vision.* MIT Press: Cambridge, Massachusetts, USA (1992)
10. Rothwell, C.A.: Recognition using projective invariants. PhD thesis, Dept. Engineering Science, University of Oxford, UK (1993)
11. Semple, J.G., Kneebone, G.T.: *Algebraic Projective Geometry.* Oxford University Press: Oxford (1952, reprinted 1979)
12. Whittle, P.: *Probability.* Library of University Mathematics, Penguin Books Ltd., Harmondsworth, Middlesex, UK (1970)
13. Wolfram, S.: *Mathematica: a system for doing mathematics by computer.* Addison Wesley: Redwood City CA, USA (1991, 2nd edition)

Correspondence of Coplanar Features Through P²-Invariant Representations

Peter Meer[1], Sudhir Ramakrishna[1] and Reiner Lenz[2]

[1] Department of Electrical and Computer Engineering, Rutgers University,
P.O. Box 909, Piscataway, NJ 08855-0909, USA.
[2] Image Processing Laboratory, Department of Electrical Engineering,
Linköping University, S-58183 Linköping, Sweden.

Abstract. An algorithm for establishing the correspondence between two projectively transformed sets of coplanar points (or lines) is proposed and its performance analyzed. Five-tuples of features are represented by projective/permutation (p^2) invariants which are insensitive to the order of the features in the computation. Matched five-tuples yield feature correspondence hypotheses accumulated in a contingency table. The final correspondence is extracted from the table by a greedy algorithm. Positional uncertainties of up to five pixels and the presence of outliers are tolerated.

1 Introduction

Establishing the correspondence between features in two image frames (or finding the instance of a model) is an important prerequisite for the execution of many computer vision tasks. The two sets of features involved in a correspondence problem will be referred to as the *reference set* and the *transformed set*. A projective transformation is assumed to map features from the reference to the transformed set. The presence of noise introduces uncertainty and for convenience all the uncertainty is allocated to the features in the transformed set. This assumption bears no relevance to the proposed method and it is true in object recognition where the reference set contains the models.

Many different techniques for establishing feature correspondence were proposed. Most of them make use of metrical properties, i.e., the correspondence is obtained from proximity relations ([17], [18]). When the two feature sets are projectively related metrical properties are no longer preserved and different methods must be employed. In this paper we are interested in the class of *indexing methods* in which invariant representations for both feature sets are computed. These methods were developed for viewpoint invariant object recognition. In geometric hashing [7] a randomly chosen noncollinear triplet of points serves as the two-dimensional affine basis for computing the affine invariant coordinates of all the remaining points.

The amount of computation is drastically reduced if invariant representations are computed for subsets of features and the entire feature set is described as an ensemble of these representations. The reference and transformed sets are then put into correspondence by matching the invariant representations of the subsets. Projective invariants are most often used as representation. For a complete reference on the use of projective invariants in computer vision see [15]. We are interested here in algebraic invariants, an algebraic function in the parameters of a configuration containing a few features. The first object recognition system using projective invariants employed the two invariants defined by two coplanar ellipses to index objects from a model library [4]. Other invariants, computed for different types of configurations (line segments, conics, etc.) were used by Wayner [19] and Rothwell *et al.* [16]. The topological relations among the features in the model were employed to generate the list of invariants representing the same object. Recognition was based on graphs [19] or hashing techniques [16].

Invariant representation of a configuration of k features is a mapping from the high-dimensional space spanned by the independent parameters of the configuration to the low-dimensional space of its invariants. For example, five points in a plane have ten degrees of freedom but yield only two invariants since the eight degrees of freedom of the planar projective transformation group must be eliminated first. The mapping is from a ten-dimensional space to a two-dimensional one, and different point sets can have very similar invariants. Thus, when designing an algorithm using invariant representations for the selection of corresponding subsets of features (i.e., to index a data base) the existence of matching errors must be taken into account.

Most projective invariants are permutation-sensitive. That is, the value of a projective invariant depends on the order in which the features were considered in its computation. A different ordering of the set, i.e., associating indices with the features in a different way, can yield a different value for the projective invariant. In the current object recognition systems an invariant has to be stored for every possible ordering of the feature subset from which it is computed.

In this paper we introduce the concept of *projective and permutation* (p^2) invariant which is not sensitive to the order of the features in the computation of a projective invariant. In Section 2 the p^2-invariants of four collinear and five coplanar points are derived. In Section 3 the p^2-invariants are used in a new feature correspondence (indexing) algorithm. The performance of the correspondence algorithm is analyzed in Section 4. The advantages and limitations of the invariance based correspondence techniques are discussed in Section 5.

2 Projective and Permutation Invariants

Let $I[\cdot]$ be an absolute scalar projective invariant computed from k features from the reference set, $r_1, \ldots, r_k$. After the transformation $T(\cdot)$ from the projective group is applied to the reference set, the k features become $T(r_1), \ldots, T(r_k)$ in the transformed set. The invariant then satisfies

$$I[r_1, \ldots, r_k] = I[T(r_1), \ldots, T(r_k)] ,\qquad (1)$$

and thus provides a transformation independent representation for the subset of k features. The invariants currently used in computer vision, however, are feature order sensitive, i.e., their values depend on the order in which the features r_i or $T(r_i)$ are considered. To match a given reference k-tuple of features with a k-tuple from the transformed set using an order sensitive invariant representation, invariants must be computed for all the $k!$ permutations of the transformed k-tuple.

Interchanging the indices of the k features is equivalent to a permutation group acting on the k-tuple. The permutation group has its own permutation invariants, expressions whose values are unchanged by the reordering of the elements. Let $\pi\{r_1, \ldots, r_k\}$ describe a permutation. An invariant will be called *projective and permutation* (p^2) invariant when it satisfies the condition

$$I[r_1, \ldots, r_k] = I[\pi\{r_1, \ldots, r_k\}] = I[\pi\{T(r_1), \ldots, T(r_k)\}] . \tag{2}$$

A p^2-invariant discards not only the influence of the feature transformation $T(\cdot)$ on the k-tuple, but also the influence of the order in which the k features were chosen. Thus, the k features can be represented by the ensemble of independent p^2-invariants computed for an arbitrary ordering of them. A $k!$ speedup is achieved in the matching between the reference and transformed sets using p^2-invariant representations relative to the case of projective invariant representations.

2.1 P^2-Invariant of Four Collinear Points

The p^2-invariants are obtained exploiting the properties of the fundamental projective invariant, the cross-ratio. In one dimension the cross-ratio of four collinear points A_i, $i = 1 \ldots 4$; with homogeneous coordinates $(x_i, 1)$, is defined as

$$\lambda = \langle A_1 A_2 A_3 A_4 \rangle = \frac{(A_1 A_3)(A_2 A_4)}{(A_3 A_2)(A_4 A_1)} = \frac{\begin{vmatrix} x_1 & x_3 \\ 1 & 1 \end{vmatrix} \begin{vmatrix} x_2 & x_4 \\ 1 & 1 \end{vmatrix}}{\begin{vmatrix} x_3 & x_2 \\ 1 & 1 \end{vmatrix} \begin{vmatrix} x_4 & x_1 \\ 1 & 1 \end{vmatrix}} , \tag{3}$$

where $(A_i A_j)$ is the oriented length of the segment delineated by the points A_i and A_j.

The four points can be considered in $4! = 24$ different orderings which yield only six different cross-ratio values:

$$\lambda_1 = \lambda, \quad \lambda_2 = \frac{1}{\lambda}, \quad \lambda_3 = \frac{\lambda - 1}{\lambda}, \quad \lambda_4 = \frac{\lambda}{\lambda - 1}, \quad \lambda_5 = \frac{1}{1 - \lambda}, \quad \lambda_6 = 1 - \lambda . \tag{4}$$

The order sensitivity of the cross-ratio is the effect of the permutation group S_4 acting on the four points. The six λ_i expressions define a six-dimensional vector Λ. A mapping Φ from S_4 into the set of nonsingular $n \times n$ matrices that satisfies

$$\Phi(\pi_{k_1} \pi_{k_2}) = \Phi(\pi_{k_1})\Phi(\pi_{k_2}) \tag{5}$$

for all permutations $\pi_{k_1}, \pi_{k_2} \in S_4$, is called an n-dimensional representation of S_4. The mappings of the cross-ratio under permutations of the indices of the four points satisfy the above definition.

The subspace **U** of **V** is an *invariant subspace* if for all the elements $u \in$ **U** and all the $\pi \in S_4$ we have $\Phi(\pi)u \in$ **U**. An invariant subspace is *irreducible* if it contains no proper invariant subspaces. The irreducible subspaces contain vectors which are invariant under the mapping Φ of the permutation group S_4. Projection of Λ on the irreducible subspaces provides the sought p^2-invariants.

To obtain useful p^2-invariants for the configuration of four collinear points a representation of S_4, based on the pairwise products $\lambda_i \lambda_j$ must be used [9]. Only 18 of the 21 products $\lambda_i \lambda_j$, $i \geq j$; $i, j = 1 \ldots 6$, are meaningful (the remaining three are equal to 1). It can be shown using standard tools from representation theory (e.g., [5]; Sections 2.1-2.3) that the spanned 18 dimensional vector space representation of S_4 have six one-dimensional and six two-dimensional irreducible subspaces. The p^2-invariants of interest are

$$J_1[\lambda] = \frac{\lambda^6 - 3\lambda^5 + 3\lambda^4 - \lambda^3 + 3\lambda^2 - 3\lambda + 1}{\lambda^2 (\lambda - 1)^2}, \qquad J_3[\lambda] = 3$$

$$J_2[\lambda] = \frac{2\lambda^6 - 6\lambda^5 + 9\lambda^4 - 8\lambda^3 + 9\lambda^2 - 6\lambda + 2}{\lambda^2 (\lambda - 1)^2}, \quad J_4[\lambda] = -3 . \qquad (6)$$

All p^2-invariants derived from products of λ_i-s are linear combinations of the four invariants (6). For example,

$$J_{11}[\lambda] = \frac{(\lambda^2 - \lambda + 1)^3}{\lambda^2 (\lambda - 1)^2} = J_1[\lambda] + J_3[\lambda] . \qquad (7)$$

The p^2-invariant $J_{11}[\lambda]$ is often mentioned in the mathematical literature (e.g. [6], p.317; [1], p.127), and was used in computer vision by Maybank [11] to investigate nonplanar conics. Since the number of possible cross-ratio expressions is small (4), p^2-invariants can also be defined as symmetric functions of the six λ_i-s. These functions, e.g., the sum of squares or the sum of pairwise products, can be expressed as linear combinations of $J_1[\lambda] \ldots J_4[\lambda]$ [9].

The nontrivial p^2-invariants $J_1[\lambda]$ and $J_2[\lambda]$ are unbounded functions. Their ratio

$$J[\lambda] = \frac{J_2[\lambda]}{J_1[\lambda]} , \qquad (8)$$

however, is bounded between 2 and 2.8 (Figure 1). The p^2-invariant $J[\lambda]$ will be used to build the indexing function of the correspondence algorithm.

2.2 P²-Invariant of Five Coplanar Points

In two dimensions a configuration of five points A_i, $i = 1 \ldots 5$; defines two independent cross-ratios. Without loss of generality we can assume that all the points have the homogeneous coordinates $(x_i, y_i, 1)$. The points must be in arbitrary

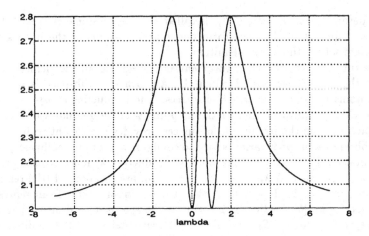

Fig. 1. The J[λ] function.

positions, i.e., no three collinear. A convenient definition for the cross-ratio in two dimensions is

$$\mu = \langle A_1 A_2 A_3 A_4 A_5 \rangle = \frac{(\Delta A_1 A_2 A_4)(\Delta A_1 A_3 A_5)}{(\Delta A_1 A_3 A_4)(\Delta A_1 A_2 A_5)} = \frac{\begin{vmatrix} x_1 & x_2 & x_4 \\ y_1 & y_2 & y_4 \\ 1 & 1 & 1 \end{vmatrix} \begin{vmatrix} x_1 & x_3 & x_5 \\ y_1 & y_3 & y_5 \\ 1 & 1 & 1 \end{vmatrix}}{\begin{vmatrix} x_1 & x_3 & x_4 \\ y_1 & y_3 & y_4 \\ 1 & 1 & 1 \end{vmatrix} \begin{vmatrix} x_1 & x_2 & x_5 \\ y_1 & y_2 & y_5 \\ 1 & 1 & 1 \end{vmatrix}}$$

(9)

where $(\Delta A_i A_j A_k)$ is the oriented area of the triangle defined by the points A_i, A_j and A_k. Note that one point (A_1 in this case) is shared by all four triangles.

The expression of the second independent cross-ratio of the five collinear points configuration can be derived from (9) by interchanging the two indices 1 and 2. Thus the cross-ratio associated with the point A_2 is:

$$\nu = \langle A_2 A_1 A_3 A_4 A_5 \rangle = \frac{(\Delta A_2 A_1 A_4)(\Delta A_2 A_3 A_5)}{(\Delta A_2 A_3 A_4)(\Delta A_2 A_1 A_5)} .$$

(10)

The usual definition of the cross-ratio (10) would involve cyclically increasing all the indices by one, i.e., the ordering $\langle A_2 A_3 A_4 A_5 A_1 \rangle$ would be used. These two definitions are related and our choice leads to simpler p²-invariant expressions.

The common point of all four triangles in (9) can be regarded as the center of perspective through which we can project any two of the remaining points on the line defined by the other two. The value of the two-dimensional cross-ratio of the five coplanar points is defined by the one-dimensional cross-ratio computed on the line. There are 5! = 120 different orderings of the five coplanar points.

Changing the order of points in the computation of the cross-ratio is equivalent to the action of the permutation group S_5 on the configuration. Exploiting the above mentioned property, the mapping of the two-dimensional cross-ratios by S_5 can be decomposed into five distinct classes, each corresponding to one of the points being used as the center of perspective. Within a class the p^2-invariant found in Section 2.1 assures insensitivity to the ordering of the other four points. For each class the argument of the J[λ] function can be computed from μ and ν [9]. Changing the center of perspective (i.e., relabeling the five points) only permutes the p^2-invariants associated with the classes.

The following procedure yields the five-dimensional p^2-invariant vector for the five coplanar points configuration:

1. Arbitrarily label the five points.
2. Compute the cross-ratios (9) and (10).
3. Using the p^2-invariant (8) compute

$$J^{(1)} = J\left[\mu\right] \quad J^{(2)} = J\left[\nu\right] \quad J^{(3)} = J\left[\tfrac{\mu}{\nu}\right]$$

$$J^{(4)} = J\left[\tfrac{\nu-1}{\mu-1}\right] \qquad J^{(5)} = J\left[\tfrac{\mu(\nu-1)}{\nu(\mu-1)}\right] . \tag{11}$$

Note that the five points are uniquely associated with the five components.
4. Sort (11) in ascending order. The vector having as components the sorted values, $\mathbf{J} = (J^{[1]}, J^{[2]}, J^{[3]}, J^{[4]}, J^{[5]})^t$, is the p^2-invariant of the configuration. Only two of the five components are independent.

The vector $\mathbf{J}$ will be used as indexing function when determining the correspondence between the reference and the transformed set of points.

3 Feature Correspondence Algorithm

The algorithm will be described for the case of establishing the correspondence between two sets of points, however, the point/line duality in the projective plane makes it applicable for sets of coplanar lines as well. Several issues must be solved when designing a reliable correspondence algorithm.

— Eliminate the degenerate configurations from the computation of indexing functions, i.e., the configurations containing three or more quasi-collinear points. Degenerate configurations yield numerically unstable indexing functions with increased probability of matching errors (Section 3.1).
— Account for the effect of positional uncertainty of the points in the transformed set. The value of the indexing function $\mathbf{J}$ changes with the noise in a configuration dependent way. We associate with each vector $\mathbf{J}$ a region in the five-dimensional space within which a match is validated (Section 3.2).
— Minimize the effect of matching errors on the overall performance of the correspondence algorithm. Any invariant representation is a projection into a lower dimensional space and therefore matching errors are unavoidable.

We use the convex hull constraint to reduce the number of false matches (Section 3.3) and distribute the errors across the entire point set (Section 3.4).

- Minimize the computational complexity. This condition is satisfied by using the p^2-invariant as indexing functions. A five-tuple of points is represented by the five-dimensional vector **J** instead of $2 * 5! = 240$, not all distinct, invariant values.

3.1 Collinearity Verification

The points in a five-tuple must be in a general position with no three of them collinear. Should three points be quasi-collinear, the area of the defined triangle is close to zero and the expression of the cross-ratio (9) becomes numerically unstable. Let A_1, A_2 and A_3 be three points. The value of the determinant of the three points' coordinates is not a reliable indicator of collinearity. Instead, following [10] we define the moment matrix M_{123} of the vectors $a_i = (x_i, y_i, 1)^t$, $i = 1, 2, 3$;

$$M_{123} = \sum_{i=1}^{3} a_i a_i^t \qquad (12)$$

where the superscript t stands for transpose. The value of the smallest eigenvalue of M_{123} measures the collinearity of the three points. The closer they are to the same line, the closer to zero is the value of this positive eigenvalue. The correspondence algorithm will not include three points into a five-tuple if their smallest eigenvalue is less than 0.001. The collinearity verification procedure is applied to both the reference and transformed sets. While collinearity is a projective invariant property, quasi-collinearity which involves metric relations, is not. Given the probabilistic nature of the correspondence algorithm, an invariant representation of the reference set with a few five-tuples missing, however, suffices.

3.2 Positional Uncertainty

The noise corrupting the transformed set modifies the coordinate of a point A_i from $(x_i, y_i, 1)$ to $(X_i, Y_i, 1)$,

$$X_i = x_i + \epsilon_{x_i}, \qquad Y_i = y_i + \epsilon_{y_i}, \qquad (13)$$

where ϵ_{x_i} and ϵ_{y_i} are zero-mean random variables with a range significantly smaller than x_i and y_i respectively.

The function $J[\lambda]$ is strictly monotonic on the six intervals $(-\infty, -1)$, $(-1, 0)$, $(0, 0.5)$, $(0.5, 1)$, $(1, 2)$, $(2, \infty)$ (Figure 1). These intervals correspond to the six distinct cases of the one-dimensional cross-ratio (4). The boundaries $\lambda = -\infty, 0, 1, \infty$ are reached when two of the four points coincide; the boundaries $\lambda = -1, 0.5, 2$, when the four points form a harmonic range. Given a *labeled* configuration of five points, it is assumed that the order of the four collinear points in any equivalent one-dimensional configuration remains unchanged by the noise. Thus, the effect of the noise on the components of **J** is confined to the interval in which the value computed for the uncorrupted configuration lies. In the case in which the perturbation of λ exceeds an interval boundary (a change of order appears), most of $J[\lambda]$ values were already obtained for λ-s within the interval. The function $J[\lambda]$ being p^2-invariant, one representation suffices.

The expressions (9, 10) are nonlinear in the random variables ϵ_{x_i} and ϵ_{y_i} and the influence of noise on the two-dimensional cross-ratios μ and ν is difficult to investigate analytically. Maybank [12] gave a thorough theoretical analysis of the behavior of one-dimensional cross-ratio under perturbation of the point coordinates. Morin [14] obtained similar results which were then extrapolated for the two-dimensional case. Since we assume that the noise changes the value of a monotonic function (one interval of $J[\lambda]$), only the range of values of μ and ν are required for a given noise level. The analysis is further simplified if the effect of the noise on the areas of the four triangles (9) is considered separately.

The signed area of a triangle defined by the corrupted points is (neglecting the second order error terms)

$$(\Delta A_1 A_2 A_3)_{noise} = \begin{vmatrix} X_1 & X_2 & X_3 \\ Y_1 & Y_2 & Y_3 \\ 1 & 1 & 1 \end{vmatrix} \approx (\Delta A_1 A_2 A_3) + \qquad (14)$$

$$+\epsilon_{x_1}(y_2-y_3)+\epsilon_{y_1}(x_3-x_2)+\epsilon_{x_2}(y_3-y_1)+\epsilon_{y_2}(x_1-x_3)+\epsilon_{x_3}(y_1-y_2)+\epsilon_{y_3}(x_2-x_1).$$

Let $\epsilon = \max_i\{|\,\epsilon_{x_i}\,|, |\,\epsilon_{y_i}\,|\}$. Then the error is bounded by the quantity

$$E_{123} = \epsilon[|\,x_1-x_2\,| + |\,x_2-x_3\,| + |\,x_3-x_1\,| + |\,y_1-y_2\,| + |\,y_2-y_3\,| + |\,y_3-y_1\,|].$$
$$(15)$$

The minimum and maximum of the area are obtained by adding and subtracting E_{123} from $(\Delta A_1 A_2 A_3)$. Which operation yields which bound depends on the sign of $(\Delta A_1 A_2 A_3)$. The bounds on μ and ν can now be computed using the bounds on the areas of the four triangles. These bounds are looser than the ones taking into account that the triangles share points, but they suffice for our purpose.

Let $(\mu_{min}, \mu, \mu_{max})$ and $(\nu_{min}, \nu, \nu_{max})$ be the values of the two independent cross-ratios for a *labeled* configuration of five coplanar points assumed to be corrupted at a noise level ϵ. The minimum and maximum values of the other three arguments required for the p^2-invariant vector **J** can be derived from that of μ and ν (11). The ranges of all five arguments are then intersected with the intervals in which the uncorrupted values lie. For example, if $\mu = 0.3$, the range (μ_{min}, μ_{max}) is intersected with $(0, 0.5)$. The bounds on the components of **J** are obtained by substituting the results of these intersections into the function $J[\lambda]$.

The reference set contains n uncorrupted points. To account for the noise corrupting the transformed set, a positional uncertainty ϵ is assumed *for the reference set*. Since projective transformations do not preserve metric properties, ϵ cannot be directly equated with a distance in the transformed set. For all the $\binom{n}{5}$ possible five-tuples of points in the reference set, the three vectors $\mathbf{J}_{min}$,

J and **J**$_{max}$ determine configuration dependent regions in the five-dimensional space. Whenever a **J** vector from the transformed set falls within such a region, the reference and transformed five-tuples are candidates for a match. The vectors should match component-wise, i.e.,

$$J_{min}^{[i],ref} < J^{[i],trans} < J_{max}^{[i],ref} \quad i = 1 \ldots 5. \tag{16}$$

The points in the five-tuples and the components of the vectors are uniquely associated. Since $J^{[i],ref}$ represents the point labeled j in the reference set five-tuple, and $J^{[i],trans}$ represents the point labeled k in the transformed set five-tuple, their correspondence is established.

Table 1. An example of the influence of ϵ on the range of the components of **J**.

	$J^{[1]}$	$J^{[2]}$	$J^{[3]}$	$J^{[4]}$	$J^{[5]}$
$\epsilon = 0$	2.132	2.295	2.469	2.675	2.776
$\epsilon = 0.04$	2.158	2.334	2.537	2.694	2.800
	2.109	2.261	2.401	2.654	2.704
$\epsilon = 0.2$	2.289	2.532	2.752	2.762	2.800
	2.040	2.158	2.162	2.570	2.256
$\epsilon = 1$	2.459	2.800	2.800	2.800	2.800
	2.000	2.053	2.000	2.241	2.000

In Table 1 an example is shown how the ranges of the components of **J** change with the increase of ϵ. Several ranges may overlap, as for $\epsilon = 0.2$, but (16) must be satisfied for each component separately. Whenever more than one **J**^{trans} vector is satisfying (16), the pair yielding the smallest L_2 distance in the five-dimensional space is the validated match. Experiments using the L_∞ norm gave significantly worse performance for the correspondence algorithm. Large values of ϵ open the ranges to the widest possible extent (2, 2.8), and a match will always be found ($\epsilon = 1$). The role of ϵ as the parameter controlling the matching of five-tuples from the reference and transformed sets becomes important when outliers are present (i.e., points without a correspondent), or when the probabilistic sampling of the transformed set covers only a small ensemble of the possible five-tuples.

3.3 Convex Hull Constraints

The example in Table 1 shows that the $J^{[i]}$ values are very sensitive to positional uncertainty due to the sensitivity of the cross-ratio to perturbations, as reported by others as well ([14], [11]). In practical situations, a projective transformation preserves the convex hull. This provides us with three constraints which can be applied to filter out a significant number of incorrect five-tuple matches. The following constraints must be satisfied by the points in a matched reference and transformed five-tuple pair :

1. The number of points on the convex hull must be the same.
2. Corresponding points must both lie on or inside the convex hull.
3. For points lying on the convex hull, neighbourhood relations must be preserved.

Similar constraints were used by Morin [14] to construct two P^2-type invariants for a five-tuple of points. Since a matched pair of five-tuples already provides the correspondence between the points, the convex hull constraints can be employed more efficiently.

The power of these constraints is illustrated by the examples in Figure 2. The convex hull of five points can contain three, four or five points.

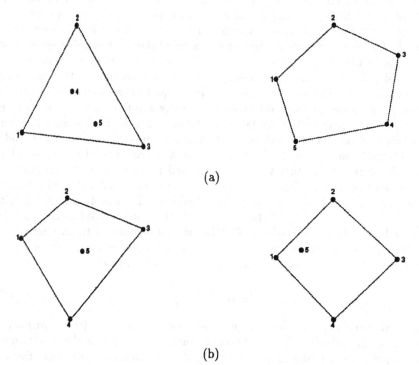

(a)

(b)

Fig. 2. Examples of the convex hull constraints. The left configuration is the reference five-tuple, the right configuration is the transformed five-tuple.

Whenever the number of points belonging to it differs (Figure 2a), the matched five-tuples are discarded. The number of points constraint is satisfied in Figure 2b. Assume for the moment that the reference point labeled R1 was put in correspondence with the point T5 in the transformed five-tuple. This correspondence obviously violates the second constraint and the five- tuple pair is discarded. In another situation, the following correspondences can be found : (1, 1), (2, 3), (3, 2), (4, 4), (5, 5). The neighbors on the convex hull of the point R2 are R1 and R3, while it's correspondent T3 has the neighbors T2 and T4. The neighbors are not in correspondence, violating the third constraint, and the five-tuple pair is discarded. Note that this constraint cannot be used if the convex hull contains only three points.

A matched five-tuple pair satisfying all the three convex hull constraints is not necessarily the correct one. However, the probabilities of yielding correct point correspondences is significantly increased as will be shown in Section 4.

3.4 Tolerated Mismatch

Matching errors are unavoidable with invariant indexing functions since several configurations can have very similar representations. The five points have ten degrees of freedom (their x and y coordinates), but are associated with only two independent invariants (μ and ν). Matching of a reference and a transformed five-tuple yields five point pairs in correspondence. Let the probability of an incorrectly detected point correspondence be P_{error}. Note that, after a match zero to five erroneous correspondences can be obtained. Extensive simulations have shown that P_{error} remains the same for all the points in a five-tuple.

To simplify the analysis, we assume that the two sets contain the same number of points, n, and that all the points have an equal chance to pass the matching criterion. Every established correspondence casts a vote in a *contingency table*. The contingency table has the labels of the reference set as row addresses and the labels of the transformed set as column addresses. Thus a reference and a transformed point pair uniquely defines a cell. A reference point casts a vote into the cell addressed together with its correspondent point from the transformed set, with probability $1 - P_{error}$. The same point will cast, under the uniform sampling assumption, a vote into a given cell which is incorrectly addressed, with probability $P_{error}/(n-1)$. To be able to detect the correct point correspondence after all the votings, the latter probability should not exceed the former.

The above condition gives the tolerated probability of error in pairing a point from the reference set with a point from the transformed set:

$$P_{error} < 1 - \frac{1}{n}. \tag{17}$$

The correspondence algorithm requires at least six points in (unknown) correspondence in both sets. Thus (17) predicts that P_{error} can exceed 0.8, with most of the point pairs erroneously voting into the contingency table while the two sets are still put into correct correspondence. In Section 4 it is shown that this is indeed the case.

3.5 The Correspondence Algorithm

The sequence of computations is summarized below. The input into the algorithm is two sets of points having a subset in projective correspondence, and the tolerable positional uncertainty for the reference set, ϵ.

1. P^2-*Invariant Representations.*
   1.1. Arbitrarily label the points in both sets.
   1.2. For all possible five-tuples in the reference set:
      1.2.1. Verify collinearity for all three-tuples of points. If quasi-collinear, discard the five-tuple.
      1.2.2. Compute the cross-ratios μ, ν.
      1.2.3. Compute the p^2-invariant vector J^{ref}.
      1.2.4. Define the region in the five-dimensional space within which a match is accepted for positional uncertainty ϵ.
   1.3. For N randomly chosen five-tuples from the transformed set:
      1.3.1. Verify collinearity for all three-tuples of points. If quasi-collinear, discard the five-tuple.
      1.3.2. Compute the cross-ratios μ, ν.
      1.3.3. Compute the p^2-invariant vector J^{trans}.
2. *Building the Contingency Table.*
   2.1. Find the ensemble of five-tuple pairs satisfying the p^2-invariant matching criterion.
   2.2. Verify the the convex hull constraints. Discard non-obeying five-tuple pairs.
   2.3. From the remaining matched five-tuples, select the nearest pair.
   2.4. Cast a vote in the contingency table for every point correspondence established.
3. *Recovering the Correspondence Between the Two Sets.*
   3.1 Identify in the contingency table the cell with the highest number of votes. It indicates the most probable point correspondence.
   3.2 Remove from the table the column and the row of the cell found at 3.1.
   3.3 Return to 3.1. if the contingency table is not empty.

Once a point correspondence is correctly identified none of the two points can be paired with any other. Removing from the table the row and the column of the cell which carries the correspondence, compensates for the artifacts of nonuniform sampling. When a point is more frequently present in the matched five-tuples, it will cast more correct *and* incorrect votes. Therefore, among all the cells that a given reference point addresses in the contingency table, the one carrying the correct correspondence may not have the largest value. This, however, should not necessarily lead to an error at the output of our greedy algorithm. As long as the cells with (incorrectly) large values are removed from the table before the decision involving the given reference point is taken, they do not influence the outcome. The analysis of the contingency table obeys the Optimality Principle in dynamic programming: at every stage of the analysis the decision is optimal given the decisions at the previous steps.

4 Experimental Results

Extensive simulations were performed to study the properties of the p^2-invariant indexing function and the performance of the correspondence algorithm.

4.1 Generation of the Synthetic Data

Both the reference and the transformed sets contained the same number of points. Point sets of up to fifteen points were used, with none to three points having no correspondent in the transformed set (outliers). The projective camera model had a camera constant 50. To maximize the effect of projective transformations on the *reference set*, the reference scene plane was placed in a plane perpendicular to the optical axis Oz at distance 300. Their coordinates were randomly chosen between $(-127, -127)$ and $(128, 128)$ and projected into the image plane. The optical axis pierced the reference scene and image planes at $(0, 0)$. The image was then rescaled independently along the x and y coordinates to extend over a 256×256 pixel array, and the point coordinates were quantized to the closest pixel center.

To obtain the *transformed set*, the reference scene plane was rotated around the three axis in a random order. The closeness of the image plane put limitations on the range of allowed rotations. The angles of rotation were uniformly distributed within the maximum range of rotations around Ox and Oy axes (between $-57°$ and $57°$), and full rotations around the optical axis. The transformed scene plane was then projected into the image plane and rescaled to a 256×256 array.

Positional uncertainty was introduced by independently perturbing, in the image plane, the x and y coordinates of the points with uniformly distributed random variables in the range $(-u, u)$. The values of u up to five pixels were investigated. After the perturbation, the point coordinates were quantized to the closest pixel center. It is important to recognize that when results for the noiseless case ($u = 0$) are shown, the two point sets are already quantized, i.e., the point coordinates are integers as they would be in real images. Thus a positional uncertainty is always present. The point sets were unconstrained, no conditions on minimum distance between points or alignment among them were set [14].

4.2 Analysis of an Experiment

The data from a ten point, no outliers correspondence experiment is given in Figure 3. The reference and transformed sets are very different, and methods using proximity measures, e.g., [17], [18], would have difficulty to recover the correspondence. The positional uncertainty of the transformed set was $u = 3$. The correspondence algorithm was run with $\epsilon = 0.4$, and $N = 200$ five-tuples were randomly chosen from the transformed set. The reference set was represented by all the 252 possible **J** vectors.

Without using the convex hull constraints, the number of correctly matched five-tuples was 11 while 189 were erroneously paired. Note that all the five-tuples chosen from the transformed set were matched. For this case, probability of an incorrect vote into the contingency table was $P_{error} = 0.878$ which satisfies (17). Nevertheless, five of the extracted correspondences (Figure 3e) are incorrect. The uniform sampling assumption behind the analysis in Section 3.4 may be strongly violated for the small number of points used in a correspondence algorithm.

When the convex hull constraints were used, the total number of correctly matched five-tuples increased to 25, while the number of incorrectly matched five-tuples decreased to 154. Thus, the constraint successfully filtered out a significant number of erroneous matches. The probability of an incorrect vote into the contingency table decreased to 0.815. All the point correspondences are correctly recovered now (Figure 3f). While the convex hull constraints reduce the probability of an incorrect correspondence, we must conclude that the power of the p^2-invariant indexing function (rejection of mismatches) is extremely low. Since the components of the p^2-invariant vector are strictly monotonic functions (within the allowed interval of their argument), it results that the indexing power of the two-dimensional cross-ratio is also unsatisfactory. The same conclusion was obtained in other studies as well ([12], [14]).

The success of the proposed correspondence algorithm is in large part due to the use of the contingency table as was discussed in Section 3.4. The example was selected to illustrate the performance of the algorithm close to its breakdown. The use of a smaller ϵ value in order to have stricter matching conditions may not help. The number of correct matches can decrease faster than that of the incorrect ones. For example, when convexity is not used, for $\epsilon = 0.04$ there are only 5 correctly matched five-tuple pairs, while the number of mismatches is 42. Taking into account the convex hull constraints reduces the influence of ϵ, but it may also lead to an insufficient number of votes into the contingency table.

4.3   Performance Statistics

To obtain statistically significant performance measures for the correspondence algorithm, the results of many trials were analyzed for several experimental conditions. The mapping between the five-tuples and a p^2-invariant vector is many-to-one and a given J^{ref} will match several J^{trans}-s. The correct J^{trans} vector is usually not the closest to its corresponding J^{ref} and using tighter matching bounds is not helpful.

In Figure 4, the distribution of the distances between matched J^{ref} and J^{trans} vectors is shown, for 500 trials, $u = 3$, and ten points, no outliers. To analyze the distribution of matched J vectors, the convex hull constraints were not taken into account in matching.

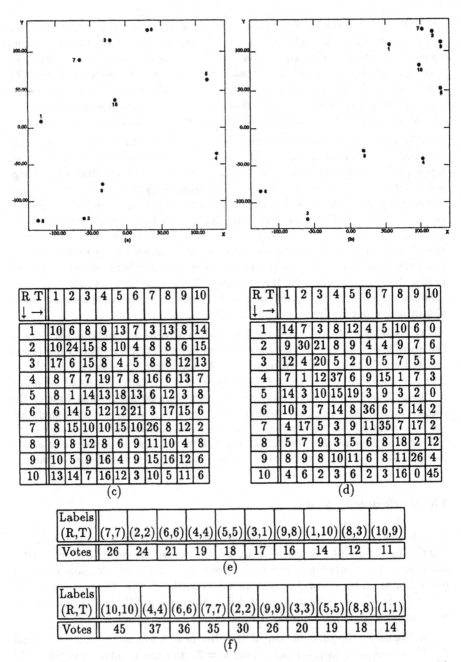

Table (c):

R T ↓→	1	2	3	4	5	6	7	8	9	10
1	10	6	8	9	13	7	3	13	8	14
2	10	24	15	8	10	4	8	8	6	15
3	17	6	15	8	4	5	8	8	12	13
4	8	7	7	19	7	8	16	6	13	7
5	8	1	14	13	18	13	6	12	3	8
6	6	14	5	12	12	21	3	17	15	6
7	8	15	10	10	15	10	26	8	12	2
8	9	8	12	8	6	9	11	10	4	8
9	10	5	9	16	4	9	15	16	12	6
10	13	14	7	16	12	3	10	5	11	6

(c)

Table (d):

R T ↓→	1	2	3	4	5	6	7	8	9	10
1	14	7	3	8	12	4	5	10	6	0
2	9	30	21	8	9	4	4	9	7	6
3	12	4	20	5	2	0	5	7	5	5
4	7	1	12	37	6	9	15	1	7	3
5	14	3	10	15	19	3	9	3	2	0
6	10	3	7	14	8	36	6	5	14	2
7	4	17	5	3	9	11	35	7	17	2
8	5	7	9	3	5	6	8	18	2	12
9	8	9	8	10	11	6	8	11	26	4
10	4	6	2	3	6	2	3	16	0	45

(d)

Table (e):

Labels (R,T)	(7,7)	(2,2)	(6,6)	(4,4)	(5,5)	(3,1)	(9,8)	(1,10)	(8,3)	(10,9)
Votes	26	24	21	19	18	17	16	14	12	11

(e)

Table (f):

Labels (R,T)	(10,10)	(4,4)	(6,6)	(7,7)	(2,2)	(9,9)	(3,3)	(5,5)	(8,8)	(1,1)
Votes	45	37	36	35	30	26	20	19	18	14

(f)

Fig. 3. An example of the correspondence algorithm. a) The reference set. b) The transformed set. Corresponding points have the same label. c) The contingency table, built without the convex hull constraints; (d) with the convex hull constraints. (e)Correspondences extracted from (c). (f)Correspondences extracted from (d).

The left graph is for $\epsilon = 0.4$, the right graph for $\epsilon = 0.02$. For a given distance, the number of mismatches is much higher than that of correctly matched 5-tuple pairs (all five point correspondences correct). Reducing ϵ, i.e., using a stricter matching criterion, shifts the two curves downward and further decreases the number of correct matches. For $\epsilon = 0.4$, 85.6% of the five-tuples were mismatched, and for $\epsilon = 0.02$, 92.9 %. For $\epsilon = 0.02$ the algorithm was no longer able to recover the correct correspondence in a statistically significant way.

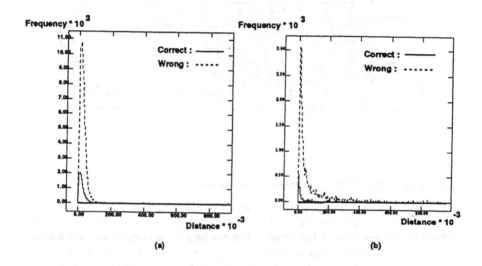

(a)   (b)

Fig. 4. The distribution of distances between matched $\mathbf{J}^{ref}$ and $\mathbf{J}^{trans}$ vectors for 10 points, no outliers, $u = 3$. (a) $\epsilon = 0.4$ and (b) $\epsilon = 0.02$.

To study the correlation between positional uncertainty and the presence of outliers in the transformed set, 100 trials were performed with 15 points and none to three outliers. In each trial, N = 2000 transformed set five-tuples were used. Positional uncertainties of $u = 0, 2, 4$ pixels were introduced in the transformed set. The probabilities of having *at most* $k = 0, 2, \ldots, 12$ errors out of the 15 correspondences are given in Table 2. Note that there are always at least two errors once a mistake was made when analyzing the contingency table.

The algorithm recovers most of the correspondences for practical positional uncertainties It does that in spite of most of the votes cast in the table being incorrect. As expected, the performance deteriorates with the increase in the number of outliers. The randomly chosen reference sets were not preselected to exclude degenerate configurations, e.g, points very close to each other. The only spatial condition to be satisfied is the collinearity verification described in Section 3.1, set to be a very mild test. Thus the probabilities in Table 2 reflect the performance over *all* possible reference sets.

Table 2. The probability of having *at most k* errors for various positional uncertainties and number of outliers in a 15 points correspondence experiment.

#outliers	u	0	2	3	4	5	6	7	8	9	10	11	12
3	4.0	0.04	0.16	0.2	0.3	0.36	0.47	0.53	0.61	0.68	0.83	0.94	1
	2.0	0.37	0.64	0.72	0.79	0.85	0.89	0.9	0.94	0.96	0.99	0.99	0.99
	0.0	0.76	0.88	0.93	0.97	0.97	0.98	0.98	0.99	0.99	1	1	1
2	4.0	0.15	0.32	0.39	0.56	0.65	0.68	0.79	0.88	0.95	0.98	0.99	0.99
	2.0	0.61	0.88	0.9	0.94	0.95	0.97	0.98	0.99	1	1	1	1
	0.0	0.89	0.98	0.98	0.99	0.99	1	1	1	1	1	1	1
1	4.0	0.37	0.58	0.66	0.75	0.84	0.89	0.92	0.97	0.98	0.99	0.99	0.99
	2.0	0.88	0.98	0.98	0.99	1	1	1	1	1	1	1	1
	0.0	0.99	1	1	1	1	1	1	1	1	1	1	1
0	4.0	0.71	0.91	0.93	0.94	0.94	0.95	0.99	1	1	1	1	1
	2.0	0.96	1	1	1	1	1	1	1	1	1	1	1
	0.0	1	1	1	1	1	1	1	1	1	1	1	1

4.4 Correspondence Between Two Images

The algorithm was also tested on real data. Images of a scene consisting of three (almost) planar objects, a ruler and two polygonal shapes, were used. Two different arrangements of the object (Figures 5a and 6a) provided the reference image in the two trials. The camera was then rotated and translated, and a new image of the scene was taken. The transformed images are shown in Figures 5b and 6b, respectively. While the natural choice for such scenes would be line features, we restricted ourselves to salient points.

The fifteen points used in the correspondence algorithm were extracted manually from the images by fitting a cursor. (The last four points defined are on the inner rectangle). No special care was taken about the positional accuracy, and errors up to several pixels can be present. Corresponding points have the same label in both images. All the correspondences were correctly recovered as can be seen from the tables. It may be noted that no information about grouping of points on the same object was taken into account. Such topological constraints can allow processing of larger point sets.

5 Discussion

The condition that the features are uniquely associated with the components of the p^2-invariant vector can be relaxed. For example, the functions $J[\mu]$ and $J[\nu]$ already suffice to represent five coplanar points. In this case, however, every point from the reference five-tuple must vote for every point in the matched transformed five-tuple. To obtain reliable performance, P_{error} is now bounded

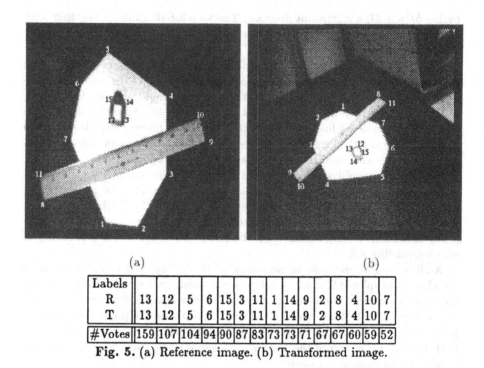

(a)   (b)

Labels															
R	13	12	5	6	15	3	11	1	14	9	2	8	4	10	7
T	13	12	5	6	15	3	11	1	14	9	2	8	4	10	7
#Votes	159	107	104	94	90	87	83	73	73	71	67	67	60	59	52

Fig. 5. (a) Reference image. (b) Transformed image.

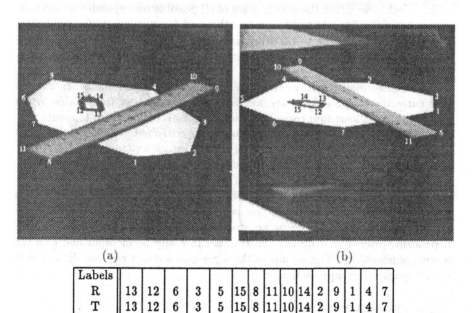

(a)   (b)

Labels															
R	13	12	6	3	5	15	8	11	10	14	2	9	1	4	7
T	13	12	6	3	5	15	8	11	10	14	2	9	1	4	7
#Votes	143	126	115	103	103	90	89	89	85	82	72	71	64	62	56

Fig. 6. (a) Reference image.(b) Transformed image.

by $1 - 5/(n + 4)$, a significant decrease. The vote-for-all strategy, together with a numerically unstable p^2-invariant cannot be used in practical correspondence algorithms [13].

The proposed correspondence algorithm is a "blind" technique which does not use any information beyond the point coordinates. Since the invariant representations are many-to-one mappings, the performance depends on the number of features shared by the reference and transformed sets. Similar behavior was reported for geometric hashing ([2], [3], [8]). Unrelated reference and transformed five-tuples are matched since two subsets of coplanar features can appear as projectively equivalent, even though they are not in correspondence.

The high probability of mismatched five-tuples, the sensitivity of invariant representations to positional uncertainty and outliers cannot be avoided. This negative result was obtained in other studies as well ([12], [14]). Nevertheless, when the matching errors are distributed over the entire point set in a contingency table, the correspondences can be recovered in spite of a probability of errors exceeding 0.8.

Additional improvement in performance is obtained when an ensemble of matched five-tuples is filtered by independent constraints derived from the data. One such constraint based on the convex hull was successfully used, as can be seen in Section 4.3. When the sets contain line features, the projective invariant property of incidence can be employed: corresponding lines must intersect in both images. Grouping of the features belonging to the same object is also an important topological constraint.

In object recognition the search space of all possible correspondences must be reduced to a feasible size to backproject the model onto the data for validation. The described algorithm provides a one-to-one mapping between the reference and the transformed sets, and therefore minimizes the number of required backprojections.

The transformation between the two features sets can be found when at least four correct correspondences are available. As can be seen from Table 2, the probability of at least four correct correspondences is high enough to assure that the transformation between the two sets can be recovered. The backprojections of available correspondences can also be used to attach a robust confidence measure to each pair, and thus select the reliable ones for postprocessing.

We have described a new algorithm to put two projectively related feature sets into correspondence. The very high probability of mismatch between invariant representations of five-tuples is partially compensated by building an accumulator in which the errors are distributed over the entire feature set. Independent, projective invariant constraints can easily be incorporated into the matching procedure. The output of the algorithm spans a reduced dimensional search space for backprojection.

Acknowledgement

Peter Meer and Sudhir Ramakrishna gratefully acknowledge the support of the National Science Foundation under the grant IRI-9210861.

References

1. Berger, M. : *Geometry I*, Springer, Berlin, 1987.
2. Grimson, W. E. L., Huttenlocher, D. P. : On the sensitivity of geometric hashing, *Proceedings of the Third International Conference on Computer Vision*, Osaka, Japan (December 1990) 334–338.
3. Grimson, W. E. L., Huttenlocher, D. P., Jacobs, D. W. : A study of affine matching with bounded sensor error, *Computer Vision-ECCV '92*, G. Sandini (Ed.), Springer, Berlin (1992) 292–306 .
4. Forsyth, D., Mundy, J. L., Zisserman, A., Coelho, C., Heller, A. : Invariant descriptors for 3-D object recognition and pose, *IEEE Trans. Pattern Anal. Mach. Intell.*, **13** (1991) 971–991.
5. Fulton, W., Harris, J. : *Representation Theory*, Graduate Texts in Mathematics (Vol. 129), Springer, Heidelberg, 1991.
6. Hartshorne, R. : *Algebraic Geometry*, Springer, New York, Corrected third printing, 1983.
7. Lamdan, Y., Schwartz, J. T., Wolfson, H. J. : Affine invariant model-based object recognition, *IEEE Trans. Robot. Autom.*, **6** (1990) 578–589.
8. Lamdan, Y., Wolfson, H. J. : On the error analysis of 'Geometric Hashing', *Proceedings of the 1991 IEEE Computer Society Conference on Computer Vision and Pattern Recognition*, Lahaina, Maui, Hawaii (June 1991) 22–27.
9. Lenz, R., Meer, P. : Projection and permutation invariant object recognition, *Proceedings of the 8th Scandinavian Conference on Image Analysis* (May 1993) 389–396. Accepted for publication, *Pattern Recognition*.
10. Kanatani, K. : Computational projective geometry, *CVGIP: Image Understanding*, **54** (1991) 333–348.
11. Maybank, S. J. : The projection of two non-coplanar conics, 105–119 in [15].
12. Maybank, S. J. : Classification based on the cross ratio, *Applications of Invariance in Computer Vision II. Proceedings of the Second European-US Workshop on Invariance*, Ponta Delgada, Azores (October 1993) 113–132 (in this volume).
13. Meer, P., Weiss, I. : Point/line correspondence under 2D projective transformation, *Proceedings of the 11th International Conference on Pattern Recognition: Computer Vision and Applications*, The Hague, The Netherlands (September 1992) 399–402.
14. Morin, L. : Quelques contributions des invariants projectifs a la vision par ordinateur. PdD Thesis, Institut National Polytechnique de Grenoble, January 1993.
15. Mundy, J. L., Zisserman, A., editors : *Geometric Invariance in Machine Vision*, MIT Press, Cambridge, Mass, 1992.
16. Rothwell, C. A., Zisserman, A., Mundy, J. L., Forsyth, D. A. : Efficient model library access by projective invariant indexing functions, *Proceedings of the 1992 IEEE Computer Society Conference on Computer Vision and Pattern Recognition*, Champaign, Illinois (June 1992) 109–114.
17. Shapiro, L. S., Brady, J. M. : Feature-based correspondence: an eigenvector approach, *Image and Vision Computing*, **10** (1992) 283–288.
18. Scott, G. L., Longuet-Higgins, H. C. : An algorithm for associating the features of two images, *Proc. R. Soc. Lond. B*, **244** (1991) 21–26.
19. Wayner, P. C. : Efficiently using invariant theory for model-based matching, *Proceedings of the 1991 IEEE Computer Society Conference on Computer Vision and Pattern Recognition*, Lahaina, Maui, Hawaii (June 1991) 473–478.

Integrating Algebraic Curves and Surfaces, Algebraic Invariants and Bayesian Methods for 2D and 3D Object Recognition *

Daniel Keren, Jayashree Subrahmonia and David B. Cooper

Laboratory for Engineering Man/Machine Systems,
Division of Engineering, Brown University, Providence, RI 02912, USA

Abstract. This paper presents a new *low-computational-cost* approach to *minimum probability of error recognition of freeform objects* in 3D range data or in 2D curve data in the image plane. Objects are represented by implicit polynomials (i.e., 3D algebraic surfaces or 2D algebraic curves) of degrees greater than 2, and are recognized by computing and matching vectors of their algebraic invariants (which are functions of their coefficients that are invariant to translations, rotations, and general linear transformations). Such polynomials of 4th degree can represent objects considerably more complicated than superquadrics and realize object recognition at significantly lower computational cost. This paper presents the Bayesian (i.e., minimum probability of error) recognizers for these models and their invariants, which requires the use of asymptotic methods little used in computer vision previously, and presents a new approach to discovering suitable invariants. Our sytem results in practical recognizers that are robust to noise, considerable partial occlusion, arbitrary sensor viewpoint,and other a priori unknown perturbations of the data sets.

1 Introduction

The simplest general object-recognition problem of interest is that a model is stored in the database for each of L objects. Then, given a set of noisy data points from either the entire object or from a portion of the object, the system has to reliably recognize the object. The minimum probability of error recognizer is to determine which of the L stored models fits the sensed data the best, i.e., minimizes the mean squared distance from the data points to a model which is the stored shape. *Note, if the object shapes and the data noise model are known, it is impossible to improve recognition accuracy over that of this recognizer. Recognizers based on invariants of a small number of feature points will function with lower probability of correct recognition. If the shape and noise representation that we use is not exactly correct, then the appropriate minimum probability of error*

---

* This work was partially supported by NSF Grant #IRI-8715774, NSF-DARPA Grant #IRI-8905436, USAF Grant #F49620-93-1-0501ARPA, and NSF Grant #IRI-9224963

recognizer may be somewhat different. There are two computational drawbacks with this approach, however. First, if there are N data points, order of NL computations must be made for computing the mean squared distance from the N data points to the L objects. This can be considerable if L is large. Second, since the position and orientation of the object being sensed will be different than the model stored in the database, the model has to be rotated and translated for checking its match to the sensed data; more generally, if the object is a planar curve representing an object silhouette and perhaps interior markings which are curves, the model must be affine transformed for checking its match with the sensed data. This involves a huge amount of computation. *This paper presents an approach to object recognition that avoids both drawbacks.*

A number of representations have been used in the past for modeling 2D curves and 3D surfaces. Among them are feature vectors; splines [27]; Fourier series [5]; moments [10, 21, 24]; parametric curves [16]; curvature invariants [26, 1]; reaction diffusion equation transformation [19]; stochastic transformations [9]; quadratic patches such as patches of spheres, cylinders, cones and planes [2]; and high degree implicit polynomial functions [6, 21]. In this paper, the data sets are modeled by algebraic curves and surfaces, i.e., as *zero sets* of implicit polynomials (these are points where the polynomials have value 0). A stored model for the object then is simply the set of coefficients for the polynomial. For example, $0 = (x-x_0)^2+(y-y_0)^2+(z-z_0)^2-R^2 = x^2+y^2+z^2-2x_0x-2y_0y-2z_0z+(x_0^2+y_0^2+z_0^2-R^2)$ is the second degree implicit polynomial representation of a sphere of radius R centered at the point (x_0, y_0, z_0) in 3D space. These are global 3D models, unlike explicit polynomials where z is given as an explicit function of x and y as in a depth map. Most of the early work on implicit polynomial curves and surfaces was limited to quadrics. [4, 3, 18, 15, 2, 17] . Implicit polynomials of degree greater than 2, on the other hand, have great modeling power for complicated objects and can be fit to data very well. In [21], Taubin has presented a very well organized and understandable introduction to these polynomials and some of their properties, and developed very effective approaches to low computational cost algorithms for fitting these polynomials. Hence we can now use these high degree implicit polynomials for representing complicated objects. In addition, we [13] and others [25] have developed a technique for fitting polynomials with bounded zero sets, which results in more stable descriptions of objects.

For the implicit polynomial models, checking the fit of a stored surface or curve to data can be done *approximately* by fitting an implicit polynomial to the data, and then comparing the resulting polynomial coefficients with the L coefficient vectors (one for each object) stored in the database. We show this to be the case in section 4. The required computation to check the matching of each of the L stored models to the data then is the amount of computation required to fit one implicit polynomial to the data set. This is $\frac{1}{L}$ of that required for directly checking how well the L boundary models fit the data set. Unfortunately, the situation is not quite so simple. The first problem is that since the object to be recognized might be in a different position than the object in the database, the coefficients for the best fitting polynomial to the data will be different than the coefficients for the same object in the database. Our solution to this problem is to use a vector of algebraic invariants for the recognizer. An algebraic invariant is a function of the implicit polynomial coefficients that is invariant to rotations and translations for 3D surfaces and is invariant to translations and general linear transformations for 2D curves. Thus, stored in the database for each of the L polynomials is a vector having components each of which is the value of an algebraic invariant. The recognizer compares the vector of algebraic invariant values for the polynomial fitted to the data with the stored vectors of invariants. The additional computation for computing the invariants is negligible compared to the computation for fitting a polynomial to the data.

The known invariants in the mathematical literature [8] are affine invariants (i.e., quantities that are invariant under translations, rotations and stretchings along the x, y and z axes) that are functions of only the leading form (the leading form is the part of the polynomial that contains terms of the highest degree. For example, $a_{20}x^2 + a_{11}xy + a_{02}y^2$ is the leading form of the second degree implicit polynomial $f(x, y) = a_{20}x^2 + a_{11}xy + a_{02}y^2 + a_{10}x + a_{01}y + a_{00}$, in 2D). We assume that a primary reason for restricting consideration to the leading form of a polynomial was because the leading form does not change under translations and hence the problem of finding invariants is easier and the theory more elegant. This was extended in [22, 23] where new large classes of affine and Euclidean invariants of all the coefficients in a polynomial were introduced. In [12], a symbolic computation method is presented for finding Euclidean and affine invariants that are functions of all the coefficients. These are the invariants used in the recognition approach presented in this paper.

The second problem that had to be solved is that small changes in a data set often result in large changes in the coefficients of the best fitted polynomial, and, hence, large changes in the algebraic invariants. Consider the following example to illustrate the problem. A data set, the zero set of the best fitting third degree

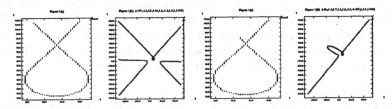

Fig. 1. Illustration of the fact that small changes in the data set result in large changes in the zero-set

polynomial, is shown in Figure 1(a). In Figure 1(c), a slight variation of the data set is shown, specifically, missing a few points at one end of the curve. The third degree polynomial fits to the data sets are shown in Figures 1(b) and 1(d). (Note that the scales in Figures 1(b) and 1(d) are different than the ones in Figures 1(a) and 1(c). The scales in Figures 1(b) and 1(d) are chosen to be bigger in order to give a feeling for how the polynomials look globally. The data points in Figures 1(b) and 1(d) are in the center of the figures.) Note how well the polynomials fit the data sets. As seen in the figures, on the one hand, the two curves are essentially identical over the region occupied by the data, but on the other hand, the curves go off to infinity, and are the same only over a negligible portion of their extents. The two curves differ greatly almost everywhere, and the coefficients of the two polynomials, which are global descriptors of the polynomial, differ greatly. The reason for this variability is that the data used in fitting the polynomials is insufficient to uniquely determine the coefficients. Since the curve coefficients differ greatly, we cannot compare the curves over the local region of interest based on their coefficients *or the invariants*, which are functions of these coefficients. Our solution to this problem is to treat recognition as Bayesian statistical recognition in the presence of noisy data. Object recognition then involves computing the probability of a data set given that it is a noisy measurement of the zero set of a polynomial having coefficient vector α. This is usually a complicated function of α. However, there is a simple form for the asymptotic behavior, as the number of data points becomes large, of this function, and this approximation is used in this paper to realize low computational cost algorithms for a variety of important object recognition and information extraction problems.

2 The Proposed Method for Finding Invariants: Mathematical Foundation

In order to find simple and explicit invariants of polynomials, the tool of symbolic computation was utilized. We have used the *Mathematica* package [28], running on a SPARC working station. Recently, symbolic computation is finding more applications to vision [14, 11].

The suggested method for finding invariants is simple: assume that the invariants are low-degree homogeneous polynomials in the coefficients. This is a reasonable assumption, as we know that the known invariants can be represented in such a manner. The degree of the homogeneous polynomials is called the *rank* of the invariant. Now, try to solve for the coefficients of this homogeneous polynomial. A more detailed explanation follows.

Formally, let a polynomial be denoted by $f(x, y) = \sum_{0 \leq i+j \leq n}^{n} a_{ij} x^i y^j$. Let x and y be subjected to some kind of transformation $(u, v)^t = T(x, y)^t$, where T is determined by a certain number of parameters t_{ij} (six in the case of an affine transformation, three for Euclidean, and one for rotation). Then, $f(x, y)$ transforms into a polynomial $g(u, v)$, where g's coefficients, b_{ij}, are functions of the a_{ij}'s and t_{ij}'s. From here on, it will be more convenient to look at the coefficients a_{ij} and b_{ij} as being indexed by a single variable. So let us revise the notations as follows: $f(x, y)$ is determined by the coefficients $\{a_i\}_{i=1}^{i=N}$, and $g(u, v)$ by the coefficients $\{b_i\}_{i=1}^{i=N}$, where each b_i is a function of the a_i's and the t_{ij}'s, and $N = \frac{1}{2}(d+1)(d+2)$, where d is the degree of $f(x, y)$.

Now, a particular algebraic structure for the invariant I is assumed – a homogeneous polynomial (or *form*) Ψ in the a_i's, say of second degree, so $I = \sum_{0 \le i < j \le N} \Psi_{ij} a_i a_j$, which has to be equal to $\sum_{0 \le i < j \le N} \Psi_{ij} b_i b_j$. Let us consider a simple kind of transformation T, e.g. rotation by an angle θ. In that case, each b_i is a function of the a_i's and θ; more specifically, it is a polynomial in the a_i's and in $\cos(\theta)$ and $\sin(\theta)$. For instance, if $d = 2$, than the polynomial $a_{20}x^2 + a_{11}xy + a_{02}y^2 + a_{10}x + a_{01}y + a_{00}$ is transformed into the polynomial $b_{20}x^2 + b_{11}xy + b_{02}y^2 + b_{10}x + b_{01}y + b_{00}$, where

$$b_{20} = a_{20} \cos^2(\theta) + a_{11} \sin(\theta) \cos(\theta)$$

$$b_{11} = a_{11}(\cos^2(\theta) - \sin^2(\theta)) + 2a_{02} \cos(\theta) \sin(\theta) - 2a_{20} \cos(\theta) \sin(\theta)$$

etc.

Let us denote the relation between the a_i's and θ and the b_i's by Φ. Formally,

$$\Phi : \mathcal{R} \times \mathcal{R}^N \to \mathcal{R}^N$$

Here $\Phi(\theta, a) = b$, where as before θ is the rotation angle, a the vector of coefficients of the polynomial $f(x, y)$, and b the vector of coefficients of $g(u, v)$, where $(u, v)^t$ is the rotation of the (x, y) coordinate system by θ.

The following simple property of Φ is needed in the sequel: $\Phi(\theta_1 + \theta_2, a) = \Phi(\theta_1, \Phi(\theta_2, a))$. This is obvious, as rotation by $\theta_1 + \theta_2$ is equivalent to rotation by θ_1 followed by a rotation by θ_2.

As noted before, we are looking for an invariant $I = \sum_{0 \le i < j \le N} \Psi_{ij} a_i a_j$. Thus, the following has to hold for every coefficient vector a and every angle θ:

$$\Psi(\{a_i\}) = \sum_{0 \le i < j \le N} \Psi_{ij} a_i a_j = \sum_{0 \le i < j \le N} \Psi_{ij} b_i b_j = \Psi(\{b_i\})$$

Theorem 1. *For the above to hold – e.g., for the form Ψ to define an invariant – it is necessary and sufficient that for every a,*

$$(\frac{\partial}{\partial \theta} \Psi[\Phi(\theta, a)])_{\theta=0} = 0 \tag{1}$$

Proof: [12].

Since the partial derivative of $\Psi[\Phi(\theta, a)]$ by θ is equal to zero everywhere, it does not depend on θ; hence, Ψ defines an invariant.

The case for more general transformations is similar; let T_α be any family of transformations, indexed by a real parameter α, satisfying $T_{\alpha_1 + \alpha_2} = T_{\alpha_1} \circ T_{\alpha_2}$; then the same proof extends to show that if $(\frac{\partial}{\partial \alpha} \Psi[\Phi(\alpha, a)])_{\alpha=0} = 0$ (using the same notation as for rotation), then Ψ defines an invariant.

Now, this property is satisfied by translation; but affine transformations include also stretching at the x and y directions, and these do not satisfy

$T_{\alpha_1+\alpha_2} = T_{\alpha_1} \circ T_{\alpha_2}$, but $T_{\alpha_1\alpha_2} = T_{\alpha_1} \circ T_{\alpha_2}$. In order to overcome this, let us define stretching by a factor of $1 + \alpha$ by T_α; then, the following holds –

$$T_{\alpha_1+\alpha_2+\alpha1\alpha2} = T_{\alpha_1} \circ T_{\alpha_2}$$

Now, we have for every α_0

$$(\frac{\partial}{\partial\alpha}\Psi[\Phi(\alpha,a)])_{\alpha=\alpha_0} = \lim_{\alpha\to 0} \frac{\Psi[\Phi(\alpha_0 + \alpha + \alpha\alpha_0, a)] - \Psi[\Phi(\alpha_0, a)]}{\alpha + \alpha\alpha_0}$$

$$= \lim_{\alpha\to 0} \frac{\Psi[\Phi(\alpha, \Phi(\alpha_0, a))] - \Psi[\Phi(\alpha_0, a)]}{\alpha + \alpha\alpha_0}$$

Denoting $\Phi(\alpha_0, a)$ by a_0, the above reduces to

$$\lim_{\alpha\to 0} \frac{\Psi[\Phi(\alpha, a_0)] - \Psi[a_0]}{\alpha + \alpha\alpha_0}$$

Which is equal to

$$\frac{1}{1 + \alpha_0} \lim_{\alpha\to 0} \frac{\Psi[\Phi(\alpha, a_0)] - \Psi[a_0]}{\alpha}$$

But this is simply

$$\frac{1}{1 + \alpha_0}(\frac{\partial}{\partial\alpha}\Psi[\Phi(\alpha, a_0)])_{\alpha=0}$$

Hence, in this case also, for Ψ to define an invariant it is enough that $(\frac{\partial}{\partial\alpha}\Psi[\Phi(\alpha,a)])_{\alpha=0} = 0$ for every a.

These derivatives are special cases of *Lie derivatives*, but are simple enough to be derived in a straight-forward manner without relying on the general theory. For a short introduction to Lie derivatives and their applications to invariant theory, see [7].

Since the group of affine transformations is generated by rotations, translations and stretchings in the x and y axis, it is enough to test that Ψ is invariant under each of these type of transformations to prove that it is an affine invariant. Thus, the technique described here, which handles only very simple transformations, really covers general linear transformations. All this generalizes easily to invariants of 3D polynomials; in 3D, we assume that objects undergo Euclidean transformations, which are generated by rotations and translations on the x, y, and z axis. Hence, to test if I is an invariant, it is enough to test that it doesn't change under rotations around the three axis or translations along them. This is done in exactly the same way as for the 2D case.

3   Reducing the Invariant Problem to a Linear System

Next, the theorem of the previous section is used to find invariants of polynomials. All the invariants we shall find are homogeneous polynomials (or forms) in the coefficients of the polynomials – either all the coefficients or only those of the leading form.

The algorithm for finding the invariants follows:

1) Write down the expression whose invariants are sought (in this work, either polynomials or forms were selected).

2) Replace the variables in that expression by new variables, which are a transformed version of the old ones. Use only the first approximation for the transformation. This results in a polynomial whose coefficients are polynomials in the original variables and the transformation parameters. This is repeated, as noted before, for all the generators of the transformation group in question.

3) After deciding on some shape for the invariant (say, a form in the coefficients – the method adopted in this work) expand the invariant in the original coefficients, and also in the coefficients which are combinations of the original coefficients and the transformation parameters. Call these I_1 and I_2.

4) Take the expression $I_1 - I_2$. It is a polynomial in the original coefficients and the transformation parameters. Of course, it has to be zero. Take as many partial derivatives of this expression as necessary to get rid of the original coefficients and the transformation parameters; equate all these derivatives to zero. This results in a linear system in the coefficients which determine the invariants (a word of caution here: these are *not* the coefficients of the original polynomial, but the coefficients of the invariant, which is a polynomial in the original coefficients). Solve this system, and you have the invariants (of course, there may be no solutions; this will indicate that there are no invariants of the type you decided to look for).

One should note that the invariants are not necessarily independent. We currently know of no method which produces algebraic invariants that are guaranteed to be independent. After the invariants are found, symbolic computation can be used to discover dependencies among them. However, this is not guaranteed to work, especially if there are many invariants and their shape is complicated.

Dependency in the invariants can cause a bias in the recognition process, for the following reason. Suppose I_1, I_2, I_3 are invariants and $P(I_1, I_2, I_3) = 0$ for some polynomial P. Then, if one uses I_1 and I_2 for recognition, I_3 should be omitted, as it brings no new information. The recognition system developed at LEMS [20] can overcome this to some extent, as it computes a covariance matrix for the invariants and uses it as a weight measure when comparing invariants of two different objects. The question is how effective the covariance matrix is for detecting high-order dependencies between the invariants; this has to be studied further, but is outside the scope of this limited work which is confined to finding the invariants.

In [12], the ideas presented here are extended to deal with affine invariants.

It is interesting to observe that the process described here is bound to find *all* invariants of the type it assumes. This is in contrast to other methods, such as the symbolic method [8], which does not allow any control on the complexity of the resulting invariants. (Note that the "symbolic method" referred to here dates back to the previous century, and has nothing to do with the tool of symbolic computation used in this work).

Lack of space prevents us from listing the invariants we have found using these methods. Interested readers can contact the first author at dk@lems.brown.edu. The most complicated case we have tackled so far involved finding invariants of rank 4 of a fourth-degree polynomial in x, y, z. It was necessary to solve about 5,000 linear equations, and 7 invariants were found. Running time was about 5 hours. This invariants were used for recognizing 3D objects.

4 Asymptotic Parameter Distributions, Mahalanobis Distances, And Bayesian Recognition

This section addresses the problem of variability in the polynomial coefficients with small changes in the data set by formulating it within a probabilistic framework. If the polynomial coefficients vary considerably, so will the invariants that are functions of these coefficients, thus giving unreliable results for recognition based on coefficients or invariants. Thus, the first problem is to get the covariance matrix for the polynomial coefficients, or, more generally, an aposteriori distribution for the coefficients given the data set. This provides an understanding of the extent to which the data constrains the coefficients of the best fitting polynomial. The second problem is to derive minimum probability of error recognizers based on the polynomial coefficients or the invariants for comparing two polynomial zero sets over the region where the data exists.

The input data here is a sequence of range data points, $Z^N = \{Z_1, Z_2, \ldots, Z_N\}$, with $Z_i = (x_i, y_i, z_i)^t$.

Let α denote the vector of coefficients of the polynomial $f(x, y, z)$ that describes the given object. We assume that the range data points $Z_1, Z_2, \ldots, Z_N$ are statistically independent, with Z_i having probability density function (pdf)

$$p(Z_i \mid \alpha) = \frac{1}{\sqrt{2\pi\sigma^2}} \exp\left[-\frac{1}{2\sigma^2} \frac{f^2(Z_i)}{\| \nabla f(Z_i) \|^2}\right] \tag{2}$$

The assumption is that Z_i is a noisy Gaussian measurement of the object boundary in the direction perpendicular to the boundary at its closest point. This model is introduced and discussed in [2, 20].

Thus, the joint probability of the data points is

$$p(Z^N \mid \alpha) = \frac{1}{(2\pi\sigma^2)^{\frac{N}{2}}} \exp\left[-\frac{1}{2\sigma^2} \sum_{i=1}^{N} \frac{f^2(Z_i)}{\| \nabla f(Z_i) \|^2}\right] \tag{3}$$

The maximum likelihood estimate $\hat{\alpha}_N$ of α given the data points is the value of α that maximizes (3).

A very useful tool for solving the problems of object recognition and parameter estimation is an asymptotic approximation to the joint likelihood function, (3), which can be shown to have a Gaussian shape in α [2], i.e.,

$$p(\mathbf{Z}^N \mid \alpha) \approx [p(\mathbf{Z}^N \mid \hat{\alpha}_N)] \exp\{-\frac{1}{2}(\alpha - \hat{\alpha}_N)^t \Psi_N (\alpha - \hat{\alpha}_N)\} \qquad (4)$$

where Ψ_N is the second derivative matrix having i,jth component $-\frac{\partial^2}{\partial\alpha_i\partial\alpha_j}\ln p(\mathbf{Z}^N \mid \alpha) \mid_{\alpha=\hat{\alpha}_N}$. Hence, all the useful information about α is summarized in the quadratic form in the exponent of equation (4). If Ψ_N is not singular, then it is the inverse covariance matrix of $\hat{\alpha}_N$. We refer to the matrix Ψ_N as the *Information* matrix in the remainder of the paper.

The aposteriori distribution of α given the data, i.e., $p(\alpha \mid \mathbf{Z}^N)$, is propotional to $p(\mathbf{Z}^N \mid \alpha)p(\alpha)$. This can be written using the asymptotic approximation as

$$constant \times p(\mathbf{Z}^N \mid \hat{\alpha}_N) \exp\left[-\frac{1}{2}(\alpha - \hat{\alpha}_N)^t \Psi_N (\alpha - \hat{\alpha}_N)\right] p(\alpha) \qquad (5)$$

where $p(\alpha)$ is a prior distribution for α. When there is none or little prior information about α, $p(\alpha)$ is taken to be uniform or Gaussian. Then (5) is Gaussian.

This distribution addresses the first problem because it tells us about the uncertainity in the polynomial coefficients given the data points. The Information matrix Ψ_N defines an ellipsoid around $\hat{\alpha}_N$ in the d-dimensional coefficient space. The axes of this ellipsoid are the directions of the eigenvectors of the Information matrix, and the lengths of the axes are equal to the square roots of the eigenvalues. The volume of this ellipsoid gives a measure of the uncertainity in the parameter estimates. If the volume is large, the coefficients are not reliable. If the coefficients are not reliable, neither will be the invariants that are functions of these coefficients. Then, instead of using the existing measurements to recognize the object, the system can collect more data in order to improve the parameter estimates (i.e., reduce the uncertainity volume). Details of how to collect more data in order to reduce the uncertainity volume as quickly as possible are given in [20].

4.1 Mahalanobis Distance as a Comparison Measure for Polynomial Zero Sets

The scenario that we consider here is one where we have a set of objects labeled $l = 1, 2, \ldots, L$ in the database, and each is represented by a polynomial of degree n in x,y and z. Let α_l be the parameter vector for object l. The optimum recognition rule is: 'choose l for which $p_l(\mathbf{Z}^N \mid \alpha_l)$ is maximum'. This requires considerable computation because the data is used L times to compute $p_l(\mathbf{Z}^N \mid \alpha_l)$ for $l = 1, 2, \ldots, L$. However, replacing α by α_l in the asymptotic approximation, (4), we see that since $p(\mathbf{Z}^N \mid \hat{\alpha}_N)$ is independent of l, an approximately equivalent recognition is : choose l for which (6) is minimum

$$(\alpha_l - \hat{\alpha}_N)^t \Psi_N (\alpha_l - \hat{\alpha}_N) \tag{6}$$

The advantage in using (6) is that the data is involved just once (not L times) to compute the Information matrix. Note that (6) is a Mahalanobis distance measure. The coefficient vector of the best fitting polynomial to the data is compared with the coefficient vector of each of the stored polynomials. To reiterate, the justification for using this distance measure is its equivalence to checking how well the data set $Z_1, Z_2, \ldots, Z_N$ is fit by the polynomial having coefficient vector α_l.

4.2   Mahalanobis distance between two sets of Invariants

This section deals with using explicit invariants for minimum probability of error object recognition. Let $\mathbf{G} = (g_1(\alpha), g_2(\alpha), \ldots, g_k(\alpha))^t$ be a set of k invariants ($k < d$), where each invariant $g_i(\alpha)$ is a polynomial function (or a ratio of polynomial functions) in the set of coefficients α. Consider the simplest case for recognition, where the database consists of a set of L objects labeled $l = 1, 2, \ldots, L$. All objects are modeled by polynomials of the same degree and each object is characterized by one point α_l in coefficient space. Let $\mathbf{G}_l$ denote the set of invariants for object l. Then, if the object to be recognized is a transformed version of one of the database objects, the minimum probability of error recognition rule is - 'Choose l for which $p(\mathbf{Z} \mid \mathbf{G}_l)$ is maximum'.

Thus, the next problem is to compute the likelihood of the data given $\mathbf{G}$. One approach is to reparameterize the polynomial in terms of $\mathbf{G}$, and use the analysis outlined in Appendix 2 of [20] for computing $p(\mathbf{Z} \mid \mathbf{G})$. The problem with reparameterizing the polynomial in terms of $\mathbf{G}$ however, is that the number of invariants is smaller than the number of parameters and hence there is not a 1-1 correspondance between α and $\mathbf{G}$. This is because the maximum of number of invariants is (number of parameters) - (number of degrees of freedom of the transformation), and, in many cases, it may not be possible to find all of them. Hence, in order to get a 1-1 correspondance between α and $\mathbf{G}$, we append to the $\mathbf{G}$ vector a vector of additional parameters $\mathbf{H}$ such that there is a 1-1 correspondance between α and the augmented vector, $\Lambda^t = (\mathbf{G}^t, \mathbf{H}^t)$. We refer to the $\mathbf{H}$ parameters as nuisance parameters. The question is : how to pick these nuisance parameters? Any set of $\mathbf{H}$ parameters that gives a 1-1 correspondance between α and Λ can be used.

Under the assumption that

$$\exp\left\{ -\frac{1}{2}(\alpha - \hat{\alpha}_N)^t \Psi_N (\alpha - \hat{\alpha}_N) \right\} \tag{7}$$

is concentrated about $\hat{\alpha}$, we assume that $\mathbf{G} - \hat{\mathbf{G}}_N$ is well approximated by

$$D\mathbf{G}(\alpha - \hat{\alpha}_N) \tag{8}$$

where DG is the Jacobian matrix $\left[\frac{\partial g_1(\alpha)}{\partial \alpha} \frac{\partial g_2(\alpha)}{\partial \alpha} \ldots \frac{\partial g_k(\alpha)}{\partial \alpha}\right]^t$ evaluated at $\hat{\alpha}_N$, and $\hat{G}_N$ is the vector $[g_1(\hat{\alpha}_N), g_2(\hat{\alpha}_N), \ldots, g_k(\hat{\alpha}_N)]^t$.

In order to get a 1:1 mapping between α and G, we can use any matrix B such that

$$\binom{G - \hat{G}_N}{H} = \begin{bmatrix} DG \\ B \end{bmatrix} (\alpha - \hat{\alpha}_N)$$

is a nonsingular transformation to get a new set of variables for representing α. Denote $\begin{bmatrix} DG \\ B \end{bmatrix}$ by C. Hence, $\alpha - \hat{\alpha}_N = C^{-1} \binom{G - \hat{G}_N}{H}$ is a 1:1 onto linear transformation, and

$$\begin{aligned} &\exp\left[-\tfrac{1}{2}(\alpha - \hat{\alpha}_N)^t \Psi_N(\alpha - \hat{\alpha}_N)\right] = \\ &\exp\left[-\tfrac{1}{2}\left((G - \hat{G}_N)^t \ H^t\right)^t C^{-t} \Psi_N C^{-1} \left((G - \hat{G}_N)^t \ H^t\right)\right] \end{aligned} \tag{9}$$

For N large, (9) as a function of $\binom{G}{H}$ is highly concentrated about the point $\binom{\hat{G}_N}{0}$. We assume some uniform distribution, $p(H)$ for H, and integrate out H to get

$$\begin{aligned} &\int_{-\infty}^{\infty} \exp\left[-\tfrac{1}{2}\left((G - \hat{G}_N)^t \ H^t\right)^t C^{-t}\Psi_N C^{-1}\left((G - \hat{G}_N)^t \ H^t\right)\right] p(H)dH = \\ &constant \times \exp\left[-\tfrac{1}{2}(G - \hat{G}_N)^t \Psi_N^G (G - \hat{G}_N)\right] \end{aligned} \tag{10}$$

Thus, $p(Z \mid G)$ is also a gaussian shape for N large. For the simplest scenario of recognition, the optimum recognition rule is – 'Choose l for which $p(Z \mid G_l)$ is maximum.' From (10), this is equivalent to – 'Choose l for which the Mahalanobis distance, $(G_l - \hat{G}_N)^t \Psi_N^G (G_l - \hat{G}_N)$, is minimum.' This is because, for the simplest case, all the database objects are modeled by polynomials of the same degree and, hence, the only part of (10) that is a function of l is $\exp\{-\tfrac{1}{2}(G_l - \hat{G}_N)^t \Psi_N^G (G_l - \hat{G}_N)\}$.

The next problem is that of computing Ψ_N^G. Lack of space does not allow us to give the details here; they are presented in [20].

In summary, object recognition using invariants is done as follows.

1. Fit the best polynomial to the data set using Taubin's approach of fitting unconstrained polynomials [21] or our approach of fitting bounded polynomials [13].
2. Compute the invariants $\hat{G}_N$ which are functions of the coefficients of the polynomial.
3. Compute the Information matrix Ψ_N^G using the method outlined above.
4. Compute the Mahalanobis distance, $(G_l - \hat{G}_N)^t \Psi_N^G (G_l - \hat{G}_N)$ to each object in the database and pick the l for which it is a minimum.

5 Experimental Results

The experiments in this section illustrate the use of the Mahalanobis distance in the space of invariants for recognizing objects that are rotated and translated versions of one of the objects in the database. The simplest case of recognition is assumed where each object class in the database is a single object, i.e., a single instance.

The first set of examples for 2D shapes. All the data sets in this experiment are handwritten characters that are well fit by fourth degree polynomials in x, y. The objects in the database are the handwritten characters, 'a', 'q', 'g' and 'w', shown in Figures 2.1 - 2.4. Three invariants for a fourth degree polynomial in x,y obtained using our approach are

$g_1 = 3a_{13}^2 - 8a_{04}a_{22} + 2a_{13}a_{31} + 3a_{31}^2 - 32a_{40}a_{04} - 8a_{22}a_{40}$,

$g_2 = 3a_{04}^2 + 2a_{04}a_{22} + a_{13}a_{31} + 2a_{04}a_{40} + 2a_{22}a_{40} + 3a_{40}^2$,

$g_3 = a_{22}^2 - 3a_{13}a_{31} + 12a_{04}a_{40}$,

Since scaling the coefficients should not change the invariants, there are only two functionally independent invariants. One set of two invariants is $\frac{g_1}{g_3}$ and $\frac{g_2}{g_3}$. Thus, for object recognition in this case, the Mahalanobis distance between the ratios of $g's$ is used. The values of the two invariants for the polynomial fits to the characters in the database are :

char 'a' : (1.99, 5.58), char 'q' : (0.102, 1.217), char 'g' : (0.207, 1.219)
char 'w' : (0.196, 0.314)

Data sets for the objects to be recognized are shown in Figures 3.1 - 3.4. These are rotated, translated and noisy versions of the objects in the database. The following table shows the value of the two invariants for the polynomial fit to these data sets, and the values of the Mahalanobis distances to the handwritten characters 'a', 'q', 'g' and 'w' in the database. The Mahalanobis distances shown are the true distances divided by the number of data points. This is because the true Mahalanobis distance is a linearly increasing function of the number of data points, and hence all the distances for a given data set are scaled by the same number.

	char 'a' (rotated) (1.8,3.89)	char 'q' (rotated) (0.124,1.13)	char 'g' (rotated) (0.185,1.22)	char 'w' (rotated) (0.146,0.03)
INVARIANTS				
char 'a'	0.387	14.81	10.89	08.41
char 'q'	09.88	0.471	09.61	12.96
char 'g'	12.88	0.12	0.366	14.66
char 'w'	12.11	13.35	15.23	0.634

As seen from the results, the Mahalanobis distance is indeed small for the right object, and a factor of 20 smaller than that for the next closest object. Thus, the Mahalanobis distance in the space of invariants is a useful tool for comparing two data sets where one is a transformed version of the other.

The next set of experiments illustrate the performance of the recognizer for 3D objects. The objects in this experiment are keyboard mice. Figure 4.1 shows the four mice used in this experiment. Figures 4.2 - 4.5 are the data sets and the polynomial fits for the mice in standard position. (The polynomial fits were obtained using the approach of fitting bounded polynomials). The data sets were obtained using the Brown and Sharpe Microval Manual coordinate measuring machine. All the data sets are well fit by fourth degree polynomials in x, y, z. These are the four objects in the database.

Figures 5.1 - 5.4 are the data sets and polynomial fits for the rotated and translated versions of the mice in the database. Using our approach, 7 invariants for a fourth degree polynomial in x, y, z are found [12]. The goal in this experiment is to recognize the mice in Figures 5.1 - 5.4 using the Mahalanobis distance measure and compare the results with that using the Euclidean distance.

Tables 1 and 2 show the Mahalanobis and the Euclidean distances, respectively, between the vector of invariants for the polynomial fits to the rotated mice and the vectors of invariants for the four mice in the database. The Mahalanobis distances in these tables are the true distances divided by the number of data points.

TABLE 1 (Mahalanobis distances) :

	Mouse1 (rotated)	Mouse2 (rotated)	Mouse3 (rotated)	Mouse4 (rotated)
Mouse1	0.456	09.89	12.79	14.51
Mouse2	12.63	0.314	13.87	11.99
Mouse3	16.22	10.17	0.403	13.39
Mouse4	08.91	10.61	12.33	0.5041

TABLE 2 (Euclidean distances) :

	Mouse1 (rotated)	Mouse2 (rotated)	Mouse3 (rotated)	Mouse4 (rotated)
Mouse1	1.000	2.535	9.614	2.741
Mouse2	1.822	1.000	1.125	1.547
Mouse3	13.51	2.322	1.000	7.568
Mouse4	1.446	1.327	24.35	1.000

Thus, the Mahalanobis distance measure is reliable measure for discriminating the right object from the rest. Also, the Mahalanobis distance has much better discriminatory power than the Euclidean distance.

The last set of experiments illustrate the use of the Mahalanobis distance for recognizing occluded 2D objects that are rotated and translated versions of one of the objects in the database. Figure 6.1 shows the data set for the occluded object to be recognized. Figure 6.1 is a portion of a 'w'. The objects in the database are modeled by fourth degree polynomials in x, y. We fit a fourth degree polynomial to the occluded object in order to compare its invariants with those for the unoccluded database objects. Figure 6.2 is the fourth degree polynomial fit to the data set in 6.1. The invariants for the polynomial fit to this data set are (0.23, 0.29); and the Mahalanobis distances (in the space of invariants) to the letters 'a', 'q', 'g' and 'w' in the database (shown in Figure 2) are :

char 'a' : 1.19, char 'q' : 1.23, char 'g' : 9.67, char 'w' : 0.644

The distance to 'w' is minimum. However, the distance is small to 'a' and 'q'. This is because, the data set in 6.1 also fits the model for 'a' and 'q' as shown in 6.3 and 6.4. These distances would probably be larger if strictly Euclidean invariants were used; in these experiments, one of the three invariants, g_3, is affine. An affine transformation can transform Figure 6.1 to make it fit the 'a' and the 'q' fairly well. The distance to 'g' is large because the data set doesn't fit the model for 'g'. The experiment illustrates that even under a large amount of occlusion, the recognizer comes up with the best possible results.

The next set of experiments illustrate the use of the Mahalanobis distance in the space of invariants for recognizing occluded 3D objects. Figure 7 shows the partial data (with the polynomial fit superimposed) for the mouse in Figure 4.2. The partial data in this experiment is what a stereo sensor would see when looking at the mouse from a point near the bottom left corner. The Mahalanobis and Euclidean distances between the vector of invariants for the polynomial fit to the occluded object and the stored vectors of invariants are :

Mahalanobis distance:

Mouse1: 0.604   Mouse2: 11.23   Mouse3: 12.03   Mouse4: 0.842

Euclidean distance:

Mouse1: 1.000   Mouse2: 183.9   Mouse3: 1.619   Mouse4: .9012

The Mahalanobis distance to Mouse1 is the smallest. However, the Mahalanobis distance to Mouse4 is almost the same as that to Mouse1. This is because the occluded data does not contain the curved front part of Mouse1 and since that is the part that really distinguishes Mouse1 from Mouse4, it is hard to distinguish between them based on the partial data. The distances to Mouse2 and Mouse3 are big compared to those to Mouse1 and Mouse4. The Euclidean distance does not give good recognition results with partial data. In fact, the Euclidean distance from the occluded object to Mouse4 is smaller than that to Mouse1.

The experiment on recognizing the occluded objects illustrates the fact that the Mahalanobis distance (in the space invariants) can be used effectively to recognize a subobject of a more complicated object stored in the database, even if the subobject can be modeled by a polynomial of much smaller degree compared to the complicated object.

The recognition involves a single computation and hence, we refer to the recognition as *Single Computation Substructure Recognition*.

All the experiments were run on a SPARC 2. The polynomial fitting takes 1-2 seconds for fitting a fourth degree polynomial in x, y to about 200 points. We are currently experimenting with different ways speeding this up by 4 to 5 orders of magnitude. The computation of the uncertainty matrix takes 1-2 seconds for a fourth degree polynomial in x, y because there are explicit expressions for the elements of the matrix. Other following computations incur negligible time. Thus the recognizers introduced in this thesis are reliable and incur low computational cost.

6   Conclusions

Minimum probability of error recognizers are given in this paper for objects modelled by 2D curves in images or 3D surfaces in range data. The data may be very noisy with signifcant portions missing due to occlusion. It is assumed that the object data has been segmented from the rest. (The segmentation problem is treated in work in progress.) The simplest recognition case is treated: which of L specific objects stored in a data-base is that sensed in the data.

A number of approximations are made in arriving at the recognizers presented in this paper. Discussion and justification for these are given in [20].

Also in [20] it is shown that the approach extends easily to the recognition of to which of L classes the sensed object belongs.

This approach also extends to the recognition of complex objects by invariantly partitioning them into parts, representing each part by a vector of invariants, and recognizing the object by recognizing its vectors of invariants.

References

1. P.J. Besl and R.C Jain. Three-Dimensional Object Recognition. *Computer Surveys*, 17(1), March 1985.
2. R.M. Bolle and D.B. Cooper. On Optimally Combining Pieces of Information, With Applications to Estimating 3D Complex-object Position From Range Data. *IEEE Transactions on Pattern Analysis and Machine Intelligence*, 8(5):619–638, September 1986.
3. B. Cernuschi-Frias. *Orientation and location parameter estimation of quadric surfaces in 3D from a sequence of images*. PhD thesis, Brown University, May 1984.
4. D.B. Cooper and N. Yalabik. On the computational cost of approximating and recognizing noise-perturbed straight lines and quadratic arcs in the plane. *IEEE Transactions on Computers*, 25(10):1020–1032, October 1976.
5. R.O Duda and P.E. Hart. *Pattern Classification and Scene Analysis*. John Wiley and Sons, 1973.
6. D. Forsyth, J.L. Mundy, A. Zisserman, and C.M. Brown. Projectively Invariant Representation Using Implicit Algebraic Curves. In *Proceedings, First European Conference on Computer Vision*, 1990.
7. D. Forsyth, J.L. Mundy, A. Zisserman, C. Coelho, A. Heller, and C. Rothwell. Invariant descriptors for 3d object recognition and pose. *IEEE Trans. on Pattern Analysis and Machine Intelligence*, 13:971–992, October 1991.
8. J.H Grace and A. Young. *The Algebra of Invariants*. Cambridge University Press, 1903.
9. U. Grenander and D. M. Keenan. Towards Automated Image Understanding. *Applied Statistics*, 16:207–221, 1989.
10. Ming-Kuei Hu. Visual Pattern Recognition by Moment Invariants. *IRE Transactions on Information Theory*, 8:179–187, 1962.
11. C. Jerian and R. Jain. Polynomial methods for structure from motion. *IEEE Trans. on Pattern Analysis and Machine Intelligence*, 12:1150–1167, December 1990.
12. D. Keren. Some New Invariants in Computer Vision. 1992. Accepted for publication in *IEEE Transactions on Pattern Analysis and Machine Intelligence*.
13. D. Keren, D. B. Cooper, and J. Subrahmonia. Describing Complicated Objects by Implicit Polynomials. *IEEE Transactions on Pattern Analysis and Machine Intelligence*, 16:38–54, January 1994.
14. D.J. Kriegman and J. Ponce. On Recognizing and Positioning Curved 3D Objects from Image Contours. *IEEE Trans. on Pattern Analysis and Machine Intelligence*, 12:1127–1138, December 1990.
15. O.D.Faugeras, M.Hebert, and E.Pauchon. Segmentation of range data into planar and quadratic patches. In *Proceedings, IEEE Conference on Computer Vision and Pattern Recognition*, pages 8–13, Washington DC, June 1983.
16. J. Ponce and D.J. Kriegman. On Recognizing and Positioning Curved 3D Objects From Image Contours. In *Proceedings, IEEE Workshop on Interpretation of 3D Scenes*, November 1989.
17. V. Pratt. Direct least squares fitting of algebraic surfaces. *Computer Graphics*, 21:145–152, July 1987.
18. P.D Sampson. Fitting conic sections to very scattered data: an iterative improvement of the bookstein algorithm. *Computer Vision, Graphics, and Image Processing*, 18:97–108, 1982.

508

19. Kaleem Siddiqi and Benjamin B. Kimia. Parts of visual form: Computational aspects. *IEEE Trans. on Pattern Analysis and Machine Intelligence*, To Appear, 1994.

20. J. Subrahmonia, D. B. Cooper, and D. Keren. Practical Reliable Bayesian Recognition of 2D and 3D Objects Using Implicit Polynomials and Algebraic Invariants. Technical Report LEMS-107, Brown University, May 1992. Under review for publication in the *IEEE Transactions on Pattern Analysis and Machine Intelligence*.

21. G. Taubin. Estimation of Planar Curves, Surfaces and Nonplanar Space Curves Defined by Implicit Equations, with Applications to Edge and Range Image Segmentation. *IEEE Transactions on Pattern Analysis and Machine Intelligence*, 13:1115–1138, November 1991.

22. G. Taubin. *Recognition and Positioning of Rigid Objects Using Algebraic and Moment Invariants*. Technical Report LEMS-80, Brown University, May 1991.

23. G. Taubin and D. B. Cooper. 3D Object Recognition and Positioning with Algebraic Invariants and Covariants. pages 147–182, July 1990. A chapter in *Symbolic and Numerical Computations-Towards Integration*, pages 147–182, B. R. Donald, D. Kapur and J. Mundy editors, Academic Press, 1992.

24. G. Taubin and D. B Cooper. 2D and 3D Object Recognition and Positioning System Based on Moment Invariants. In *Proceedings of the DARPA-ESPIRIT Workshop on Geometric Invariants*, *Rikjavik, Iceland*, pages 235–258, May 1991. Also in book *Geometric Invariance in Machine Vision*, pages 375–397, J. Mundy and A. Zisserman editors, MIT Press, 1992.

25. G. Taubin, F. Cukierman, S. Sullivan, J. Ponce, and D. J. Kriegman. Parameterized Families of Polynomials for Bounded Algebraic Curve and Surface Fitting. *IEEE Trans. on Pattern Analysis and Machine Intelligence*, 16:287–304, March 1994.

26. B.C. Vemuri, A. Mitiche, and J.K. Aggarwal. Curvature-based representations of objects from range data. *Image and vision computing*, 4(2):107–114, May 1986.

27. J. Y. Wang and F. S. Cohen. 3D Object Recognition and Shape Estimation from Image Contours using B-splines, Shape Invariant Matching, and Neural Networks. *IEEE Transactions on Pattern Analysis and Machine Intelligence*, 16(1):13–23, January 1994.

28. S. Wolfram. *Mathematica, a System for Doing Mathematics by Computer*. Addison-Wesley, 1988.

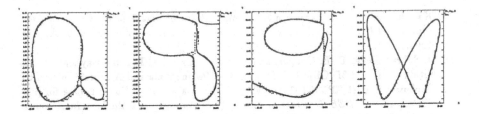

Fig. 2. Data sets and polynomial fits to the handprinted characters in the database

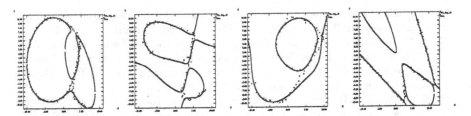

Fig. 3. Data sets and polynomial fits to rotated and translated versions of the hand-printed characters in the database

Fig. 4. Data sets and polynomials fits for the mice in standard position

510

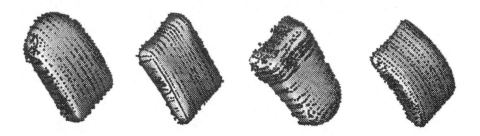

Fig. 5. Data sets and polynomial fits for rotated and translated versions of the mice in the database

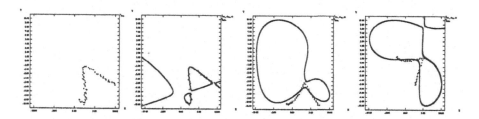

Fig. 6. Recognition of handprinted characters based on only partial data due to occlusion or poor segmentation

Fig. 7. Data set and polynomial fit to partial data from mouse1

Springer-Verlag
and the Environment

We at Springer-Verlag firmly believe that an international science publisher has a special obligation to the environment, and our corporate policies consistently reflect this conviction.

We also expect our business partners – paper mills, printers, packaging manufacturers, etc. – to commit themselves to using environmentally friendly materials and production processes.

The paper in this book is made from low- or no-chlorine pulp and is acid free, in conformance with international standards for paper permanency.

Lecture Notes in Computer Science

For information about Vols. 1–751
please contact your bookseller or Springer-Verlag

Vol. 752: T. W. Finin, C. K. Nicholas, Y. Yesha (Eds.), Information and Knowledge Management. Proceedings, 1992. VII, 142 pages. 1993.

Vol. 753: L. J. Bass, J. Gornostaev, C. Unger (Eds.), Human-Computer Interaction. Proceedings, 1993. X, 388 pages. 1993.

Vol. 754: H. D. Pfeiffer, T. E. Nagle (Eds.), Conceptual Structures: Theory and Implementation. Proceedings, 1992. IX, 327 pages. 1993. (Subseries LNAI).

Vol. 755: B. Möller, H. Partsch, S. Schuman (Eds.), Formal Program Development. Proceedings. VII, 371 pages. 1993.

Vol. 756: J. Pieprzyk, B. Sadeghiyan, Design of Hashing Algorithms. XV, 194 pages. 1993.

Vol. 757: U. Banerjee, D. Gelernter, A. Nicolau, D. Padua (Eds.), Languages and Compilers for Parallel Computing. Proceedings, 1992. X, 576 pages. 1993.

Vol. 758: M. Teillaud, Towards Dynamic Randomized Algorithms in Computational Geometry. IX, 157 pages. 1993.

Vol. 759: N. R. Adam, B. K. Bhargava (Eds.), Advanced Database Systems. XV, 451 pages. 1993.

Vol. 760: S. Ceri, K. Tanaka, S. Tsur (Eds.), Deductive and Object-Oriented Databases. Proceedings, 1993. XII, 488 pages. 1993.

Vol. 761: R. K. Shyamasundar (Ed.), Foundations of Software Technology and Theoretical Computer Science. Proceedings, 1993. XIV, 456 pages. 1993.

Vol. 762: K. W. Ng, P. Raghavan, N. V. Balasubramanian, F. Y. L. Chin (Eds.), Algorithms and Computation. Proceedings, 1993. XIII, 542 pages. 1993.

Vol. 763: F. Pichler, R. Moreno Díaz (Eds.), Computer Aided Systems Theory – EUROCAST '93. Proceedings, 1993. IX, 451 pages. 1994.

Vol. 764: G. Wagner, Vivid Logic. XII, 148 pages. 1994. (Subseries LNAI).

Vol. 765: T. Helleseth (Ed.), Advances in Cryptology – EUROCRYPT '93. Proceedings, 1993. X, 467 pages. 1994.

Vol. 766: P. R. Van Loocke, The Dynamics of Concepts. XI, 340 pages. 1994. (Subseries LNAI).

Vol. 767: M. Gogolla, An Extended Entity-Relationship Model. X, 136 pages. 1994.

Vol. 768: U. Banerjee, D. Gelernter, A. Nicolau, D. Padua (Eds.), Languages and Compilers for Parallel Computing. Proceedings, 1993. XI, 655 pages. 1994.

Vol. 769: J. L. Nazareth, The Newton-Cauchy Framework. XII, 101 pages. 1994.

Vol. 770: P. Haddawy (Representing Plans Under Uncertainty. X, 129 pages. 1994. (Subseries LNAI).

Vol. 771: G. Tomas, C. W. Ueberhuber, Visualization of Scientific Parallel Programs. XI, 310 pages. 1994.

Vol. 772: B. C. Warboys (Ed.),Software Process Technology. Proceedings, 1994. IX, 275 pages. 1994.

Vol. 773: D. R. Stinson (Ed.), Advances in Cryptology – CRYPTO '93. Proceedings, 1993. X, 492 pages. 1994.

Vol. 774: M. Banâtre, P. A. Lee (Eds.), Hardware and Software Architectures for Fault Tolerance. XIII, 311 pages. 1994.

Vol. 775: P. Enjalbert, E. W. Mayr, K. W. Wagner (Eds.), STACS 94. Proceedings, 1994. XIV, 782 pages. 1994.

Vol. 776: H. J. Schneider, H. Ehrig (Eds.), Graph Transformations in Computer Science. Proceedings, 1993. VIII, 395 pages. 1994.

Vol. 777: K. von Luck, H. Marburger (Eds.), Management and Processing of Complex Data Structures. Proceedings, 1994. VII, 220 pages. 1994.

Vol. 778: M. Bonuccelli, P. Crescenzi, R. Petreschi (Eds.), Algorithms and Complexity. Proceedings, 1994. VIII, 222 pages. 1994.

Vol. 779: M. Jarke, J. Bubenko, K. Jeffery (Eds.), Advances in Database Technology — EDBT '94. Proceedings, 1994. XII, 406 pages. 1994.

Vol. 780: J. J. Joyce, C.-J. H. Seger (Eds.), Higher Order Logic Theorem Proving and Its Applications. Proceedings, 1993. X, 518 pages. 1994.

Vol. 781: G. Cohen, S. Litsyn, A. Lobstein, G. Zémor (Eds.), Algebraic Coding. Proceedings, 1993. XII, 326 pages. 1994.

Vol. 782: J. Gutknecht (Ed.), Programming Languages and System Architectures. Proceedings, 1994. X, 344 pages. 1994.

Vol. 783: C. G. Günther (Ed.), Mobile Communications. Proceedings, 1994. XVI, 564 pages. 1994.

Vol. 784: F. Bergadano, L. De Raedt (Eds.), Machine Learning: ECML-94. Proceedings, 1994. XI, 439 pages. 1994. (Subseries LNAI).

Vol. 785: H. Ehrig, F. Orejas (Eds.), Recent Trends in Data Type Specification. Proceedings, 1992. VIII, 350 pages. 1994.

Vol. 786: P. A. Fritzson (Ed.), Compiler Construction. Proceedings, 1994. XI, 451 pages. 1994.

Vol. 787: S. Tison (Ed.), Trees in Algebra and Programming – CAAP '94. Proceedings, 1994. X, 351 pages. 1994.

Vol. 788: D. Sannella (Ed.), Programming Languages and Systems – ESOP '94. Proceedings, 1994. VIII, 516 pages. 1994.

Vol. 789: M. Hagiya, J. C. Mitchell (Eds.), Theoretical Aspects of Computer Software. Proceedings, 1994. XI, 887 pages. 1994.

Vol. 790: J. van Leeuwen (Ed.), Graph-Theoretic Concepts in Computer Science. Proceedings, 1993. IX, 431 pages. 1994.

Vol. 791: R. Guerraoui, O. Nierstrasz, M. Riveill (Eds.), Object-Based Distributed Programming. Proceedings, 1993. VII, 262 pages. 1994.

Vol. 792: N. D. Jones, M. Hagiya, M. Sato (Eds.), Logic, Language and Computation. XII, 269 pages. 1994.

Vol. 793: T. A. Gulliver, N. P. Secord (Eds.), Information Theory and Applications. Proceedings, 1993. XI, 394 pages. 1994.

Vol. 794: G. Haring, G. Kotsis (Eds.), Computer Performance Evaluation. Proceedings, 1994. X, 464 pages. 1994.

Vol. 795: W. A. Hunt, Jr., FM8501: A Verified Microprocessor. XIII, 333 pages. 1994.

Vol. 796: W. Gentzsch, U. Harms (Eds.), High-Performance Computing and Networking. Proceedings, 1994, Vol. I. XXI, 453 pages. 1994.

Vol. 797: W. Gentzsch, U. Harms (Eds.), High-Performance Computing and Networking. Proceedings, 1994, Vol. II. XXII, 519 pages. 1994.

Vol. 798: R. Dyckhoff (Ed.), Extensions of Logic Programming. Proceedings, 1993. VIII, 362 pages. 1994.

Vol. 799: M. P. Singh, Multiagent Systems. XXIII, 168 pages. 1994. (Subseries LNAI).

Vol. 800: J.-O. Eklundh (Ed.), Computer Vision – ECCV '94. Proceedings 1994, Vol. I. XVIII, 603 pages. 1994.

Vol. 801: J.-O. Eklundh (Ed.), Computer Vision – ECCV '94. Proceedings 1994, Vol. II. XV, 485 pages. 1994.

Vol. 802: S. Brookes, M. Main, A. Melton, M. Mislove, D. Schmidt (Eds.), Mathematical Foundations of Programming Semantics. Proceedings, 1993. IX, 647 pages. 1994.

Vol. 803: J. W. de Bakker, W.-P. de Roever, G. Rozenberg (Eds.), A Decade of Concurrency. Proceedings, 1993. VII, 683 pages. 1994.

Vol. 804: D. Hernández, Qualitative Representation of Spatial Knowledge. IX, 202 pages. 1994. (Subseries LNAI).

Vol. 805: M. Cosnard, A. Ferreira, J. Peters (Eds.), Parallel and Distributed Computing. Proceedings, 1994. X, 280 pages. 1994.

Vol. 806: H. Barendregt, T. Nipkow (Eds.), Types for Proofs and Programs. VIII, 383 pages. 1994.

Vol. 807: M. Crochemore, D. Gusfield (Eds.), Combinatorial Pattern Matching. Proceedings, 1994. VIII, 326 pages. 1994.

Vol. 808: M. Masuch, L. Pólos (Eds.), Knowledge Representation and Reasoning Under Uncertainty. VII, 237 pages. 1994. (Subseries LNAI).

Vol. 809: R. Anderson (Ed.), Fast Software Encryption. Proceedings, 1993. IX, 223 pages. 1994.

Vol. 810: G. Lakemeyer, B. Nebel (Eds.), Foundations of Knowledge Representation and Reasoning. VIII, 355 pages. 1994. (Subseries LNAI).

Vol. 811: G. Wijers, S. Brinkkemper, T. Wasserman (Eds.), Advanced Information Systems Engineering. Proceedings, 1994. XI, 420 pages. 1994.

Vol. 812: J. Karhumäki, H. Maurer, G. Rozenberg (Eds.), Results and Trends in Theoretical Computer Science. Proceedings, 1994. X, 445 pages. 1994.

Vol. 813: A. Nerode, Yu. N. Matiyasevich (Eds.), Logical Foundations of Computer Science. Proceedings, 1994. IX, 392 pages. 1994.

Vol. 814: A. Bundy (Ed.), Automated Deduction—CADE-12. Proceedings, 1994. XVI, 848 pages. 1994. (Subseries LNAI).

Vol. 815: R. Valette (Ed.), Application and Theory of Petri Nets 1994. Proceedings. IX, 587 pages. 1994.

Vol. 816: J. Heering, K. Meinke, B. Möller, T. Nipkow (Eds.), Higher-Order Algebra, Logic, and Term Rewriting. Proceedings, 1993. VII, 344 pages. 1994.

Vol. 817: C. Halatsis, D. Maritsas, G. Philokyprou, S. Theodoridis (Eds.), PARLE '94. Parallel Architectures and Languages Europe. Proceedings, 1994. XV, 837 pages. 1994.

Vol. 818: D. L. Dill (Ed.), Computer Aided Verification. Proceedings, 1994. IX, 480 pages. 1994.

Vol. 819: W. Litwin, T. Risch (Eds.), Applications of Databases. Proceedings, 1994. XII, 471 pages. 1994.

Vol. 820: S. Abiteboul, E. Shamir (Eds.), Automata, Languages and Programming. Proceedings, 1994. XIII, 644 pages. 1994.

Vol. 821: M. Tokoro, R. Pareschi (Eds.), Object-Oriented Programming. Proceedings, 1994. XI, 535 pages. 1994.

Vol. 822: F. Pfenning (Ed.), Logic Programming and Automated Reasoning. Proceedings, 1994. X, 345 pages. 1994. (Subseries LNAI).

Vol. 823: R. A. Elmasri, V. Kouramajian, B. Thalheim (Eds.), Entity-Relationship Approach — ER '93. Proceedings, 1993. X, 531 pages. 1994.

Vol. 824: E. M. Schmidt, S. Skyum (Eds.), Algorithm Theory - SWAT '94. Proceedings. IX, 383 pages. 1994.

Vol. 825: J. L. Mundy, A. Zisserman, D. Forsyth (Eds.), Applications of Invariance in Computer Vision. Proceedings, 1993. IX, 510 pages. 1994.

Vol. 826: D. S. Bowers (Ed.), Directions in Databases. Proceedings, 1994. X, 234 pages. 1994.

Vol. 827: D. M. Gabbay, H. J. Ohlbach (Eds.), Temporal Logic. Proceedings, 1994. XI, 546 pages. 1994. (Subseries LNAI).

Vol. 828: L. C. Paulson, Isabelle. XVII, 321 pages. 1994.

Vol. 829: A. Chmora, S. B. Wicker (Eds.), Error Control, Cryptology, and Speech Compression. Proceedings, 1993. VIII, 121 pages. 1994.

Vol. 831: V. Bouchitté, M. Morvan (Eds.), Orders, Algorithms, and Applications. Proceedings, 1994. IX, 204 pages. 1994.